The New World Secretarial Handbook
COMPACT DESK EDITION

CONTRIBUTORS:

Jeanette L. Bely, Ph.D., Assistant Professor, Division of Office Management and Secretarial Studies, Department of Accountancy, the Bernard M. Baruch School of Business and Public Administration, The City College of the City University of New York.

Elizabeth M. Clarke, B.A., Executive Secretary to the Senior Vice President, Traffic and Sales, Pan American Airways.

Mary E. Connelly, M.Ed., Professor of Business Education and Secretarial Studies, Boston University.

Gerald Crowningshield, M.S., Professor of Accounting, Rider College, Trenton, New Jersey.

Harry Katz, J.S.D., Counsel to New York City Finance Administration; Associate Professor, Graduate School of Business Administration, Pace College, New York, New York.

A. E. Klein, Ph.D., Associate Professor, Supervisor of the Division of Office Management and Secretarial Studies, Department of Accountancy, the Bernard M. Baruch School of Business and Public Administration, The City College of the City University of New York.

John I. McCollum, Ph.D., Professor and Chairman, Department of English, University of Miami, Coral Gables, Florida.

Adele F. Schrag, Ph.D., Associate Professor and Chairman, Department of Business Education, Temple University, Philadelphia, Pennsylvania.

Elizabeth T. Van Derveer Tonne, Ed.D., formerly Professor of Business Education, Montclair State College, Upper Montclair, New Jersey.

Marion Wood, M.Ed., Educational Consultant, Office Products Division, International Business Machines Corporation.

The New World Secretarial Handbook

COMPACT DESK EDITION

SUPERVISORY EDITOR:

A. E. KLEIN, Ph.D.

*The Bernard M. Baruch School of Business and Public Administration,
The City College of the City University of New York*

Published by William Collins-World Publishing Co., Inc.
2080 West 117th Street, Cleveland, Ohio 44111

Published simultaneously in Canada by
Nelson, Foster & Scott Ltd.

Material from *Essentials of Grammar and Style,* by
John I. McCollum, ©1966, is reproduced by permission
'of the author.

Library of Congress catalog card number: 74-5542
ISBN 0-529-05089-7

Printed in the United States of America

Dear Reader:

You hold in your hands what is probably the most comprehensive handbook for secretaries ever published. Within its covers you can find answers to practically all of the questions that arise in the secretary's daily activities. This handbook may also be profitably consulted by the busy executive, for it contains a wealth of useful information that will contribute to his efficiency, especially in that phase of his work involving the secretary.

Today, the secretary's position is a challenge, demanding knowledge, a sense of responsibility, initiative, administrative ability, and office skills. As the executive's right-hand "man," the secretary must display these qualities and exercise these skills, so as to lighten her employer's heavy work load and keep the wheels of the office rolling smoothly. To make this task easier, we have searched far and wide for a group of authors with the right background. We chose ten authorities, who have drawn on a lifetime of business experience and study to give you the benefit of their wisdom.

Whether you are a new or an experienced secretary, you will find THE NEW WORLD SECRETARIAL HANDBOOK the most useful reference book in your office. Especially valuable will be the Grammar and Usage section, probably the largest ever included in a secretary's handbook; and the Appendix, a reference work in itself, which includes a guide to the spelling and division of the 33,000 most common words.

As you reach for THE NEW WORLD SECRETARIAL HANDBOOK for daily help, you will come to view it more and more as your indispensable office "bible." May it serve you well.

Sincerely,

A. E. Klein
Supervisory Editor

Contents

PART ONE

The Role of the Professional Secretary

Chapter 1

The Secretary's Position in the Business Community

ELIZABETH M. CLARKE

THE SECRETARY'S JOB goes back to the scribes of antiquity. The Romans gave a name to the holder of the job—*secretarius*, "keeper of secrets." Large-scale manufacturing of the first practical typewriter, about a hundred years ago, and the tragedy of two world wars brought women into the secretarial field and formed the prototype of today's secretary. It was not until well into the second half of the twentieth century that the secretary was defined in terms of her job as it now exists. This definition appears in the application for membership in the National Secretaries Association (International), as follows:

> A secretary shall be defined as an assistant to an executive, possessing a mastery of office skills and ability to assume responsibility, without direct supervision, who displays initiative, exercises judgment, and makes decisions within the scope of her authority.

History has not recorded how the scribe of ancient times fared or how Cicero liked his secretary's filing system. Although as early as 1714, Queen Anne of England granted a patent on a "writing machine," it was not until 1866 that the first practical typewriter was developed. Christopher Latham Sholes was the inventor, assisted by Samuel W. Soulé and Carlos Glidden. In September 1873 the first commercial typewriter, the Remington No. 1, was produced. Similarly, various methods of shorthand had existed through the ages, but it was not until 1837 that Pitman was introduced in England and not until 1893 that Gregg shorthand was introduced in the United States. Our first clue to management expectations in regard to female secretaries came with the entry of the "typewriters" (as the girls were called) to the business world. Management expected them to fall apart!

"Women are too delicate," they cried. "for such strenuous work!" There are definite indications that management considered the work beyond a woman's mental capacity as well! However, it was soon discovered that women took to clerical work quite well, and by the end of World War I women were firmly established in the business world. Like all workers, women suffered through the depression years following 1929, but World War II gave them fresh impetus to use their abilities, as critical shortages of available employees developed from the absence of men in service and the increased demands of a wartime economy.

The unprecedented growth of the postwar economy, combined with the low birth rate of the 1930s, caused an acute shortage of qualified secretarial help in the 1950s. The tendency toward early marriage, the quickened interest in science, with its demand for higher education, and the increased financial ability of parents to give their children a college education contributed to the shortage. The situation was further aggravated by the poor quality of the new entrants into the secretarial field. Not only were they not qualified secretaries; they typed poorly, their spelling and grammar left much to be desired, and their general attitude was that management should be grateful for whatever service they rendered. At that point management should have put down its collective foot, but the title "secretary" had become a matter of prestige to both the manager and the employee. By granting a man a "secretary," management made him feel important, but at the same time it often obtained the services of a mediocre employee.

Fortunately for the good secretary and for the young woman who now aspires to a secretarial career, the situation has changed since then. Management is beginning to recognize the great contribution a good secretary can make to her company. More importantly, perhaps, management also is beginning to realize the harm and havoc that can be created by an incompetent one. Management magazines regularly publish articles on how to utilize the service and skill of secretaries, develop their initiative, or recognize their capabilities. In 1962 the American Management Association held its first seminar for executive secretaries, thus recognizing the importance of the executive secretary to management. The National Secretaries Association has moved steadily toward its goal of professional status for secretaries. The Certified Professional Secretary certificate is granted only to those who pass all sections of a rigorous two-day examination.

Why should a woman become a secretary? The first and foremost reason is that the secretarial field is one in which women not only are accepted but actually dominate. Of all the secretaries employed in 80 metropolitan areas, more than 99 percent are women. Secondly, in number the secretarial job is the largest single category of office occupations. Significantly, the next largest category is that of the general stenographer.

The relative ease with which she may enter the field is an important reason for a woman's becoming a secretary. A high-school education, a knowledge of shorthand and typing, a willingness to learn, and good common sense are usually sufficient to qualify for a stenographic position and receive on-the-job training leading to a secretarial position. A woman desiring to be a nurse or teacher, on the other hand, must receive several years of training and be properly certificated before she can begin earning.

Then, too, the secretarial field offers a diversity of interests. A nurse must work within the medical profession, and a teacher in education, but the secretarial field holds no such limitations. A secretary may work with artists or demolition experts, captains of industry or the unfortunate (social work), outer-space experts or oceanographers, youngsters or oldsters, the genius or the mentally retarded. Doctors, lawyers, chemists, engineers, salesmen, buyers, writers, stockbrokers, statisticians, and even the overseers of those two certainties of life, death and taxes, need secretaries. The field of the secretary is almost limitless. No matter what the sphere of her interest, her secretarial skills can provide an entry.

Closely allied to the diversity of interests is the opportunity the secretarial position gives a woman to pursue other career objectives. A woman who aspires to be a lawyer can gain valuable experience as a secretary in the legal field; one interested in the medical profession could profit by working as a secretary in the administrative office of a hospital or in a doctor's office. A secretarial position in an art gallery would be most helpful to an artist. A housewife could exchange secretarial service at a university for college financial aid for her children. A copywriter may enter the advertising field through the secretarial door. And a woman who wants to climb the ladder to the rank of executive secretary, a key position in today's corporate management, must come up through the ranks.

It is to be hoped that one of the prime results of the women's liberation movement will be the opening of more jobs for women in areas heretofore dominated by men. However, it would be difficult to name an occupation that provides greater opportunity for anyone—male or female—to train for and move into a chosen profession than that of secretary.

In addition to a relatively attractive salary, there are fringe benefits that a secretary may enjoy. Typists and stenographers generally work in pools, that is, large, open offices with row upon row of typists or stenographers doing the same type of work day in and day out. The secretary may share an office with her boss or with one or two other secretaries, or she may have her own office. Often her office is more attractive than the general office, perhaps having a rug on the floor, a window, drapes, or even fresh flowers. Furthermore, her work is always varied, never routine. True, there are certain things she does daily, but the content of her work changes frequently each day.

The secretarial field, then, is appealing for a variety of reasons: it is accessible; it is remunerative; it's diversified; it offers pleasant surroundings and the opportunity for advancement. As a secretary, you enjoy a prestigious position among your co-workers, the confidence of your employer and the stimulation of contributing actively to the exciting world of business.

What can management rightfully expect in return? What are the responsibilities of the manager? What are your responsibilities as his secretary? Where and how can your particular abilities and interests flourish?

Bringing together the right manager and the right secretary can be a very complex procedure. It will be helpful to you in setting your goals to examine first the general expectations of management and then some of the requirements for secretaries in specific fields.

THE COMPETENT SECRETARY

A secretary plans. Her plans must be long-range and short-range, just as a corporation's must. Her short-range planning enables her to do each day those things that must be done daily. For example, she establishes a routine of getting her employer's desk ready for him each day, of handling his mail at a specified time each morning and afternoon, of advising him of telephone calls in a standard way, and of handling her dictation and transcription.

Planning does not lead to inflexibility but allows her to take in stride any interruption. An emergency may delay her schedule but does not wreck it. When the emergency is behind her, she automatically goes back into her routine at the point at which it was interrupted.

Her long-range planning includes keeping her social calendar free at times of the year when she knows the work load will be exceptionally heavy or arranging to accomplish special projects when the work load will be light.

Her time is a valuable and perishable commodity. She performs all her duties as quickly as she can, so that she is prepared to handle the unexpected. She develops a sense of the relative urgency of activities, so that she can quickly, almost instinctively, distinguish the important from the trivial. A long-distance telephone call does not distract her from the necessity to transcribe an urgent letter. An unexpected visitor is not allowed to waste her time. She knows how to start him on his way courteously and firmly. She recognizes "telephonitis" as a disease to which she can succumb and inoculates herself against it by evaluating the length of business calls and not continuing them even one second longer than is absolutely essential. She limits personal calls to the minimum, even (or, perhaps, especially) those from people within the company.

A secretary has a command of and a respect for the English language, both in writing and in speaking. Her dictionary, thesaurus, and grammar book are always close at hand for immediate checking of spelling, usage, and construction. Her letters, whether she composes them or transcribes them from her employer's dictation, favorably represent her company, her employer, and herself. A recipient of her letter must never get the impression that any one of the three is less than top-notch. Most executives have a good speaking command of the language; this asset is often one of the reasons why he reaches a top management position. But he may not consider the fine points of grammar, spelling, and punctuation, nor is there any reason why he should. These details are definitely the responsibility of his secretary. An employer with an excellent command of English presents a double challenge to his secretary. Her transcribed letters must be absolutely perfect, and the letters she composes for him must match his in composition, tone, and clarity. Along with her command of English, a secretary knows intimately all the terms used in her business.

Alertness to the mistakes of others—not so that she can pounce on them, but so that the mistakes may be corrected—is characteristic of the competent secretary. Especially if work is done under pressure, people have a tendency not to check a figure, proofread a page, or make certain that a statement conforms to policy. The secretary must check and double-check to avoid errors that, more than simply being embarrassing, might affect important decisions adversely.

Dag Hammarskjöld, for example, always insisted that United Nations secretaries work in shifts during a crisis, so that someone would be alert to catch errors that conceivably could have worldwide repercussions. It was the responsibility of the secretaries to make certain that the weary men who were trying to solve a problem did not worsen it or cause another by an ill-chosen word or unfortunate phrase.

The good secretary knows that she, too, can make mistakes and does all that she possibly can to avoid them. No matter how excellent her typing skill, for example, she asks someone to proofread with her any important document, just in case she has made a typographical error.

While dispensing helpful information freely, the secretary never imparts confidential information. Her employer relies on her loyalty not to betray him deliberately and on her intelligence not to betray him inadvertently. The grapevine in any large company can transmit more inaccurate information more rapidly than any machine yet invented. The secretary must be constantly on guard against feeding the rumor mill, and even if asked point-blank about a confidential matter, she must remain noncommittal. Much better that people think that she is dumb than know that she is stupid!

On the other hand, she always passes on to her employer any significant information that she picks up from the grapevine. The information may not be correct, may even be inconsequential, but it may give him an opportunity to pinpoint a potential source of trouble.

A secretary should constantly differentiate between her own requests to others and those of her employer. In the first instance she has no authority, and in the second, a great deal. "I'd like that report by 4 P.M." and "Mr. Brown needs that report by 4 P.M." are entirely different statements, and the tactful secretary does not confuse the two. The details needed for the report may be difficult to obtain on short notice. Getting the report to her by 4 P.M. may entail great effort and expense. If she says she would like it by 4 P.M., the person preparing the report can explain. If Mr. Brown needs it by 4 P.M., the effort and expense may be inconsequential in comparison to the importance of his having it by 4 P.M. Even with suggestions she follows the same rule. A natural human tendency is to do what the "boss" wants. A suggested course of action is far more likely to be implemented if put forward as his idea instead of hers, particularly if it involves difficulty.

Honesty is her policy, not only in this area but in all her dealings with others. She may tell white lies to protect her employer from bother, fib to make the path run more smoothly, but in anything involving principle, she sticks to the truth.

The secretary's filing system gets the same careful attention given her other duties. She knows that, to take future action, her employer must have an accurate record of what has happened in the past. For those files that she handles herself—highly confidential matters or her employer's personal correspondence, for example—she sets up the system best suited to her needs. If her company has a central files department, she works closely with the file clerk assigned to her files. She knows that the file clerk can be her worst enemy or her best friend.

The worst enemy is the stereotype of file clerks. "You never gave it to me." "I can't find it." "It's all mixed up with that other file you gave me." "It's not filed yet. I haven't had time to get to it." Why do these excuses represent the stereotype of the file clerk? Because most people downgrade filing. "Anyone can do it. It takes no intelligence, no training, and it is a dull, boring job."

The wise secretary makes a friend of the file clerk by recognizing that none of this is true. Filing requires intelligence, an intimate knowledge of the subject matter, and an organized method of recording. It is a historical recording of events that have occurred in a given aspect of a company's development. The secretary should make a team effort. She should carefully mark all material to indicate whether there has been any previous correspondence on the subject. If the previous reference could not be easily identified by the file clerk, she makes a notation indicating the subject with which it should be filed. If a subject is especially important or unusually complicated, she discusses it with the file clerk to make certain that the file clerk understands the subject matter well enough to set up the file intelligently. A sense of history on the part of the secretary and the file clerk will enable them to build up a file coherently, so that a person reading it will be able to determine the sequence of events and the actions taken. When the secretary makes a friend of the file clerk, the employer gets the file he is looking for—not an excuse.

The secretary has a sense of responsibility toward her work and her company. She demonstrates this responsibility daily by arriving promptly and by carefully following through on any tasks assigned to her, whether or not her employer is there. She realizes that at times it may be even more important for her to be at her desk when her employer is out than when he is there. Take, for example, a situation in which the executive and his secretary are the only ones who know all aspects of a given situation. While he is away, something that vitally affects that matter happens (and, as every experienced secretary knows, it usually happens at 9 o'clock in the morning!). The secretary realizes that it is her responsibility to be there and to get in touch with her employer, if possible, so that he can decide his course of action and so that she can notify all concerned for their appropriate action. Her employer does not have to supervise her. He has absolute confidence in her dependability.

The skilled secretary knows that, without the executive to set the over-all objectives of the firm or of the department and to plan for action to attain these objectives, her job would not exist. Nevertheless, she takes quiet pride in the realization that she is indispensable to him in the execution of his work.

She likes and respects her employer, and he likes and respects her. This mutual feeling is essential to good teamwork, but she knows that any adjustment of personalities is up to her. She adjusts her temperament to balance—not necessarily match—his. For example, if her employer is a rather formal person, her warm, friendly greeting to a visitor may put the visitor at ease and establish a cordial atmosphere. If her employer has disorganized work methods, she does her best to keep at least her own desk organized. To quote one executive, "Her stability balances my instability." On the other hand, if he is an organized person, she keeps in step with him.

Above all, the secretary keeps her personal problems to herself and does not inflict her moods on her employer. One executive said of a former secretary, "As soon as I'd walk into the office in the morning, I'd know she'd had a fight with her boyfriend. Halfway through the morning, I'd be. all in knots because of her unpleasant attitude." He fired her!

On the other hand, the secretary cannot expect her boss to be clairvoyant when some aspect of her personal life affects her work performance. One executive whose secretary had been ill said when she returned to work, "Now, I know you've been ill, but when I get involved in my work, I will forget it completely, so if you are tired or not feeling well, please tell me." Another secretary, faced with a serious operation, said nothing until her deteriorating work performance brought criticism. When the executive learned the reason for her poor performance, he was as solicitous as any member of her family. The criticism could have been avoided had she discussed her problem.

No job is without its dull routines as well as its stimulating aspects. No employer is without faults. There may be times when you consider your employer unreasonable. You may be asked to do chores that you consider demeaning or outside your province. How you respond to these situations depends upon how intrusive they are, how much you value your job and your relationship with your employer. You have a choice: you can resign; you can ignore the problem; or you can discuss your objections with your employer. Serving coffee and watering the plants, for example, may not be your idea of the duties of a secretary. But if you like your job in most respects, if your employer is generally appreciative of your efforts and considerate of your personal needs (like those dentist appointments during working hours, or that early departure on summer weekends), you may be inclined to regard these services as reciprocal acts of friendship rather than unwarranted duties. Should you find it necessary to discuss your objections with your employer, do so reasonably and only after you have assured yourself that you are performing your legitimate duties fully and efficiently. Be sure, too, that the duties you object to in no way contribute to the overall objectives of your department or company or to your own personal goals. Most important, bear in mind that you are working for your employer, not your employer for you.

THE EXECUTIVE SECRETARY

The executive secretary is more than a secretary to an executive. In terms of her responsibility, her knowledge of the company's business, her judgment and experience, she is an executive herself. She may indeed employ a secretary or, in a large corporation, a whole staff. She may often be required to make decisions which affect an important segment of the company's operation. In some cases, an executive secretary may be expected to take charge of his business when her executive is absent for any length of time.

Undoubtedly, she is well recompensed for this demanding position, not just financially but personally as well. But these benefits are earned. Having attained the highest level of secretarial authority, her responsibilities are such that she must make the greatest possible effort to check procedures and avoid errors. Planning, discretion, knowledge, accuracy, efficiency, dependability are no mere words to the executive secretary. They are the by-laws of her job. Her long-range planning, for example, includes keeping her social calendar free at times of the year when she knows the work load will be exceptionally heavy, or arranging to accomplish special projects when the work load will be light.

The executive secretary has top skills and keeps them serviceable. Article after article and book after book state emphatically that when a secretary reaches the executive-secretary level, her skills become unimportant. Less used? Perhaps. Unimportant? Definitely not. She does use her technical skills less than a stenographer, for example, but she must look constantly for opportunities to exercise them.

One secretary, who accompanied her employer to a meeting in Austria, requested an IBM Executive typewriter. She got it, but the machine "spoke" German. "Z" is as common in German as "y" is in English. The "z" was where the "y" is on an American typewriter, and the "y" was where the "z" is. This did not seem to present any insurmountable problem. After all, she had only to remember the difference. Unfortunately her fingers still "spoke" English! A "hunt-and-peck" typist might have coped well with the situation, but the secretary's skill was so developed that the movement of her fingers was a reflex action.

At the same meeting she was asked suddenly to take down in shorthand a statement being read by a man with a foreign accent. The man was reading, his diction was unfamiliar to her, and he had an accent. Yet she got every word. Why? Because even though she rarely took dictation, she had kept up her shorthand speed by other means. Unusual? No. Any executive secretary can attest to the fact that the infrequency of use in no way lessens the importance of good skills.

The confidence of her executive's staff is built slowly and carefully. These are the people to whom he has given the responsibility of carrying out the objectives of the company or of his department. The executive secretary's duty is to screen demands on her executive's time, not to drop an iron curtain between him and his staff.

Decisions must be made promptly, action taken swiftly. Anything that slows that action is detrimental to the overall operation of the company.

When a member of the staff has to see the boss, it may be because he faces some decision beyond the scope of his particular authority. It may seem a simple matter to tell the executive that the subordinate has to see him, but what if the secretary has six or seven calls from different subordinates? Who sees him first, who next, who not at all? It is up to the secretary to win the confidence of each member of the staff so that he will be absolutely honest with her as to the urgency of any particular request. Each has to know that if he says, "I must have five minutes before noon," he will have it if it is humanly possible, and that if he says, "Tomorrow will be fine," he will see the executive tomorrow without any further follow-up on his part. In such circumstances, maximum use is made of everyone's time. The secretary can work out an orderly plan with the executive to conserve his time. The subordinate can attend to other projects without wasting time in calling back or attempting to waylay the executive in the hall. In this cooperative atmosphere, everyone realizes that the short-term advantage would not be worth the risk of losing the secretary's confidence.

She must always keep in mind that she represents the executive and that, while the staff is subordinate to him, it is not subordinate to her. She will find that as the subordinates' confidence in her grows, they will ask her advice or want her opinion on how the boss would like something done. The secretary has a responsibility to give accurate advice within her scope and to confine her opinions to those which truly represent her executive's feelings. If she gives her own advice or opinion, she runs the risk of misrepresenting her executive and misleading the subordinate.

She cannot play favorites. The executive must view his operation as a whole, and he depends upon his secretary to reflect this accurately in her dealings with his subordinates. It is important that each staff member be made to feel that he is an integral part of the team and that he is making his contribution to the company. He wants the boss to have a good opinion of him, and, perhaps even without consciously recognizing it, he may interpret the secretary's reaction to him as a reflection of the boss's opinion. The secretary must remember that a personality trait which she may find unattractive may be exactly the trait that makes the subordinate effective in his particular function. Thus, the subordinate who insists upon "dotting every 'i' and crossing every 't'" may be far more effective in controlling his costs than the easy-going, affable subordinate who has difficulty in keeping even his own expense account within proper bounds. The boss may have a higher opinion of the former than of the latter, and if the secretary should favor the affable over the precise subordinate, she would be doing an injustice to both men and to her executive. She might dampen the enthusiasm of the one and give the other a false sense of confidence, thus misrepresenting her executive and impeding the company's objectives.

As you can see, the attainment of an executive secretarial position requires more than experience and training. A high degree of intelligence, interest and dedication are the prime requisites for anyone aspiring to be an executive secretary.

THE LEGAL SECRETARY

Accuracy and speed are important qualifications for any secretarial position. For the legal secretary, they are vital.

Many legal forms must be prepared without erasures in conformance to exacting standards. The terminology is precise. As many law actions have to follow an initial action in exact sequence, timing is essential.

The legal secretary must have a good general education and an intimate knowledge of legal terms, their meanings and their spellings. One law firm's personnel director stated emphatically that no one could be considered for a secretarial position in her firm without at least two years experience as a legal stenographer.

The legal secretary's job is not easy but it is one of the most lucrative in the secretarial field. Moreover, the fringe benefits are generally excellent and the vacation periods usually generous.

THE MEDICAL SECRETARY

Secretarial work in medicine may be divided into two categories.

Insurance companies, research foundations, publishers of medical textbooks, hospital administrators, city public-health departments, and drug companies, for example, require secretaries with a good medical vocabulary and training in medical shorthand.

A doctor, dentist, or health clinic, on the other hand, would need a secretary with a highly developed talent for dealing with people who are ill.

In a small office the secretary may have to know how to perform certain medical tasks, what benefits are allowed under various medical plans, how to take a patient's medical history or handle the doctor's billings and other clerical duties peculiar to a doctor's office.

In medicine, as in law, the secretary must be discreet. No comments or questions regarding a patient's condition or ailments should be made in the presence of other persons.

For the person with specialized training in medicine, the opportunities are many in both secretarial work and as a medical technician.

THE EDUCATIONAL SECRETARY

As the need for education grows, so do the opportunities for secretaries in educational institutions from the grade school to the graduate level. It is an attractive field. In many institutions the secretary enjoys all the benefits of the teaching staff; in others, particularly in the colleges, her fringe benefits may include free tuition, sometimes even for her children.

The duties of the secretary vary from institution to institution and often depend on its size. In a small school the secretary may have to handle student records, classroom assignments, grade transcripts, and personnel records and may even consult with teachers, parents, and students concerning school policy and procedures. In larger institutions the secretary may be assigned just one of these duties or may be one of the staff of a department responsible for one special function.

The minimum education required varies, too, from one institution to another. In some a high-school education may be sufficient, whereas others require a college degree.

A word of advice from a college administrator to the educational secretary is, "Don't talk down to the students."

THE SECRETARY IN ADVERTISING, TV, JOURNALISM

"Glamour" is the term associated with these fields. The secretarial requirements vary little from other businesses', but, generally, management can demand and get college graduates. Competition is keen, because the secretarial position provides an entry to other careers.

Those who aspire to careers as copywriters or researchers or who wish to enter fashion, marketing, or merchandising, for example, may have difficulty in finding positions without experience. They can and frequently do gain this experience via the secretarial route.

THE TECHNICAL SECRETARY

Advances in automation, engineering, and other scientific fields have created the need for secretaries with a knowledge of technical terms. Secretaries already in these fields say that their work is much the same as in other jobs, but that a knowledge and understanding of the technical terms is essential to effective performance. For the secretary with a scientific background, these fields provide an interesting and stimulating opportunity.

THE SECRETARY IN THE PERFORMING ARTS

"Egomaniacs, including me, need special talents in their secretaries," said a theatrical agent. Above all, the secretary in the performing arts needs the ability to deal effectively with the artistic temperament.

The star of the show expects the secretary to know him, to cater to him, even to be impressed by him, but not so impressed that she swoons when he walks in the door! She must maintain a delicate balance between showing that she appreciates his talents and being sufficiently poised to take care of his needs. While a secretary to an individual can concentrate on his particular characteristics, the secretary in the theatrical agency must study the likes, dislikes, habits, idiosyncrasies, strengths, and weaknesses of each client of her agency. She must cajole, reassure, flatter, advise, and commiserate but never demonstrate any artistic temperament of her own. Any one of them can upstage her!

The rewards, however, are sweet. The secretary knows prominent artists well, perhaps even on a first-name basis; she may receive tickets to plays, concerts, ballets, and musicals; she has the satisfaction of knowing that her services contribute to the world of art; and perhaps, via the secretarial position, she may progress to that of theatrical agent or to other activities in the theatrical world.

THE SECRETARY IN TRAVEL

Excitement and adventure are the fruits of secretarial work in the travel industry. Airlines, steamship companies, railroads, bus companies, hotels, and travel agencies often offer free or reduced rates in transportation, hotel accommodations, and tours to their employees. A New York secretary can weekend in Miami. The secretary in San Francisco can spend her vacation in Hawaii. The secretary who works for an international company may buy her sweaters in London, her handbags in Buenos Aires, and her perfume in Paris. She can ski in Austria in December and in Chile in July. Hong Kong and Sydney can be as familiar to her as Des Moines and Chicago.

However, she does not get all this just for the asking. She must have a sincere liking for and a desire to help people. She must know geography well, be able to read timetables, plan itineraries, make reservations, check all documentation, and perhaps speak a foreign language. In short, she must know how to do everything and anything that will contribute to the comfort and enjoyment of her company's customers. Above all, she must be accurate. A vacation trip's pleasure can be marred or a business opportunity lost by her mistake.

Each year the volume of travel exceeds the previous year's by a considerable margin. A young woman with the right characteristics will find a bright future in the travel industry.

THE SECRETARY OVERSEAS

Mention "overseas," and the words "glamour," "adventure," and "excitement" come to mind. Secretarial work overseas has all these allures, provided a secretary is adaptable and has an open mind.

Opportunities in the developed countries are limited. United States government positions are usually filled by persons with service seniority, and private corporations usually can obtain the services of competent, bilingual nationals of the countries in which their offices are located. It is the underdeveloped countries that offer a woman the opportunity to contribute to international understanding and aid a country in its economic development while enjoying a stimulating experience and enriching her own life.

Experience at home is a necessity. Living abroad requires so many adjustments that a secretary must be well versed in her profession before she leaves the country. Familiarity with office procedures at home will ease the transition to a foreign country. Additionally, her experience may be needed to train personnel native to that country.

Respect for and understanding of the people with whom she works and humility regarding her own talents and abilities are important requisites for the secretary in another country. In most of the emerging nations education has been a luxury enjoyed by only a small minority. On the other hand, her co-workers may be better educated than she, speak several languages, and have many admirable qualities, different though they may be from hers. Perhaps their contact with her will be their first intimate acquaintance with an American. Her attitude toward them may determine their general feelings toward the United States. She must take care to represent her country faithfully and to be as diplomatic in her dealings with her co-workers as the American ambassador is with the prime minister.

Customs vary greatly, and the secretary must be careful not to get off on the wrong foot. Europeans, for example, are more formal in their business relationships than are Americans, and Brazilians would not think of starting a business meeting without having a cup of coffee. The tactful American secretary will be alert to these differences and conform as much as possible to local custom.

Living conditions will be different from her standards. The electric power may fail frequently, the water may not always flow freely from the tap, and heat may be supplied by a fireplace. She may have a maid, but the nearest automatic laundry may be 3,000 miles away!

An assignment abroad widens the secretary's horizons, gives her an intimate knowledge of the country in which she works, broadens her knowledge of the world, and provides her with an opportunity for travel and adventure. For her part, she must adjust gracefully to different customs and living conditions and represent her company and her country well.

THE PART-TIME OR TEMPORARY SECRETARY

Flexibility is the characteristic most needed in temporary work. The temporary secretary's geographical location changes with every assignment, the type of business of the firm is different, the nature of her work varies, and the length of time she spends on any given job has considerable range.

Temporary employment can be sought through employment agencies, particularly those specializing in the field, or from individual firms. The woman returning to business after several years' lapse may approach the firm for which she previously worked full time. If she has a good record, she will find the firm receptive to employing her on a temporary basis. Many firms employ temporary secretaries on a "permanent" basis; that is, the secretary works for that firm in any capacity assigned to her, to substitute for those who are ill or on vacation or to help in a special project. She is paid for the time that she actually works, rather than on the salary basis of full-time employees, but she may receive some of the fringe benefits granted to permanent employees.

Temporary work can be exciting or dull, interesting or dreary, varied or routine. For a woman with family responsibilities, it offers the opportunity to work at times convenient to her and to decline assignments if necessary. On the other hand, there is considerable insecurity. Work may not be available when she needs it, the pay scale is usually lower than that of a permanent secretary, and there are usually no fringe benefits, such as hospitalization or pension.

There is great need for part-time workers among doctors, ministers, lawyers, small businesses, and, in some instances, large corporations. Often the individual or the firm needs only a few hours of work per week and is willing to have the work done at times convenient to the secretary. Part-time work has the further advantage of enabling the woman to keep up her skills in the event that she decides one day to return to full time work.

PRESENT TRENDS AND SIGNS FOR THE FUTURE

All signs are "go" for the immediate and long-range future of the secretary. Our economy is expected to continue to grow, providing more jobs. It has been estimated that 200,000 more secretaries and stenographers will be needed each year. By 1975 it is expected that women will comprise 35 percent of a total labor force of 93 million in the United States.

The average work span of the individual woman is steadily increasing. Women used to retire from the labor force when they married. Today about half the working women are married, and this trend shows every sign of continuing. Not only are women continuing to work after marriage, but older women are returning to the labor market. The young woman who intends to leave secretarial work when she marries will do well to establish a good reputation; she may be back. She should keep up with developments in the secretarial field and maintain her skills.

Automation, rather than being a threat to a secretary, will be an asset. Just as the typewriter provided entry to the business world for women and the copying machines eased the typing burden, so automation will give the secretary the opportunity to use her brain instead of brawn, and it will relieve her of much of the drudgery of present-day secretarial work.

Nevertheless, if automation is not competition, it is a challenge—a challenge to a woman to keep her knowledge ahead of the machine's. A machine cannot do anything until it receives instructions from a human being, whereas a secretary can be a self-starter. That means education, through both formal schooling and self-development.

Just as it is rarely possible for a man without a college education to rise in management today, so it will be for the woman. A college degree will be mandatory for top secretarial jobs. Businessmen do not ask for a secretary with a college degree just because it is fashionable or because the field is overcrowded and they can pick and choose at will. On the contrary, good secretaries are hard to find. A college education gives a woman knowledge that she might never gain otherwise, knowledge that enables her to make decisions that the executive with a high-school-educated secretary might have to make himself. It gives her training in thinking things through, in obtaining information from outside sources (researching for an assignment), and in getting material (term papers) prepared on schedule, and it gives her poise and self-confidence.

If a woman has to enter the business world with just a high-school education, she may be able to achieve her degree by taking night courses. There are subtle advantages in evening courses which compensate for the disadvantage of part-time study. Class members are usually more mature than day students, the discussions may be more stimulating, and, because she is working during the day, the secretary may find immediate application for the knowledge gained in the classroom or may be able to assimilate that knowledge more readily.

Whether or not she has a college education, the woman who plans a career as a secretary should work toward the Certified Professional Secretary certificate of the National Secretaries Association (International). Seven years' experience as a secretary or a combination of post-high-school education and secretarial experience totaling seven years are necessary to qualify for the examination. Only a thorough knowledge of each section will enable a secretary to pass a 12-hour examination which includes business law, business administration, secretarial accounting, secretarial skills, human relations, and secretarial procedures.

As soon as she has two years of secretarial experience, the secretary will want to join the National Secretaries Association. In addition to the CPS program, individual chapters have seminars, workshops, and study groups on subjects in or related to the secretarial field. In cooperation with universities, colleges, and other educational institutions, the Association sponsors educational courses. The secretary will find membership in NSA richly rewarding, not only for the benefits that she will derive from it but also from the contribution she can make through the Association to the attainment of its goal. NSA has also sponsored The Future Secretaries Association, for the student who intends to enter the secretarial field upon completion of her studies.

The good secretary will never stop learning, no matter how old she is or how high up the ladder she may climb. She will take advantage of every opportunity to learn, in her company's training programs, in night school, or in special seminars or workshops, and she will read, read, read.

The woman who consistently turns in a fine performance and who constantly seeks self-improvement will derive great satisfaction from her work, and management will appreciate and reward her professionalism.

PART TWO

Fundamental Procedures
and Techniques

Chapter 2

The Secretary's Day

THE SECRETARY'S DAY actually starts before she leaves the office the previous day. She has spent her last fifteen or twenty minutes checking her memo pad and calendar, entering notes for the next day, checking her follow-up file, sorting her work into folders and files, clearing her desk so that the maintenance people can clean, brushing the mechanism of her typewriter and closing it up. When she arrives at her desk in the morning, all systems are go.

The secretary arrives promptly. If nine o'clock is starting time, she is at her desk ready to work at nine o'clock. She is not hanging up her coat or visiting the ladies' room.

The duties of a secretary are as varied as are jobs and employers. But in any situation it is safe to assume that the secretary is responsible for handling the mail, making calls and answering the telephone, taking and transcribing dictation, following up orders and work in progress, and organizing her work. More often than not, the secretary must keep track of her employer's appointments and maintain a filing system—all in addition to the specifics of her job.

How does she keep so much in mind? The answer is that she doesn't. She writes it down. The experienced secretary may have her work so well organized that certain routines are gone through automatically each day. But she has also learned how unreliable a filing place is one's head. She has a memo pad and pencil at hand at all times. Every request, every assignment, every message is noted. Nothing is left to memory or chance.

The secretary's work procedure depends upon the nature of the job and the size of the company. Some offices have established routines; some employers will specify the methods they prefer; sometimes a departing secretary will train an incoming one. But how you carry out your assignments, how you organize your work is up to you. And whatever means you employ, your basic tools will be a memo pad, a calendar, an appointment book and a telephone-address book.

MEMO BOOK AND CALENDAR

Your memo pad may be a section of the notebook you use for dictation, a separate pad or part of your calendar. In any case, it is a good idea to have a desk calendar with space for daily notations so that you can transfer your memos to the calendar under the proper dates. Some desk calendars also have a section for addresses and telephone numbers in the back.

List everything you have to do. As each job is done, cross it off. If an assignement requires a follow-up at a future time, make a note of it under the date indicated.

THE APPOINTMENT BOOK

The appointment book is one of the most important records in the office. There are various methods of recording and following up appointments, but essential to each is the appointment book.

In some offices the book is kept on the executive's desk. In this case the secretary maintains duplicate appointment memoranda, so that both she and the executive will know how each day is to be spent.

In other offices the executive assigns the appointment book to the secretary and refers all appointment making to her. To examine the book he must either remove it temporarily from her desk or read it as he stands at her desk; otherwise, he checks a list of appointments that his secretary prepares for him daily.

Before making appointments the secretary must familiarize herself with the office procedure. Such matters as availability of executives; length of lunch hour; daily arrival and departure time; weekend arrival and departure hours; and average schedules and length of conferences affect the making of appointments.

The appointment should be entered under the day and hour agreed upon by the person requesting the appointment and the secretary. The entry includes the name of the person concerned, some notation of the topic to be discussed, and any other pertinent information. The secretary uses these notes to prepare herself to assist in the conference by producing needed documents or being ready to help in other ways. Days ahead of time she may use the pad to remind her employer that appointments are coming up, so that he may be prepared. On the day of the appointment she follows

Appointments	Thursday, January 16

9:00 _Mail_

9:30 _Geo. Brown, See Mr. R. re type_

10:00 _Staff meeting Editorial_

10:30 ____

11:00 _Mr. R. call to Paris_

11:30 _Mr. R. - dentist 11:45_

12:00 _Me - lunch with Anne - Brass Rail_

12:30 _Mr. R. lunch with Mr. Lyon and Mr. Cone —_

1:00 _Armondo's 12:45_

1:30 ____

2:00 ____

2:30 _Exec. Comm. - Conf. Room_

3:00 ____

3:30 ____

4:00 ____

4:30 _Me - Mrs Smith Accounting_

5:00 ____

5:30 _Mr. R. - Theater with Mr. & Mrs. Owens - Baltimore_

Notes

Sort Mail
Get Wed. letters signed
Check on Mr. Lyon - re lunch
Get info on magazine rate
Check order #3721 when back from printer!
Productions cost on #7878
Staff memo URGENT
Lists from accounting
Call travel agent —
Re: Paris Trip
Call Insurance - RE: Policy

Continue letters to Outlets
Continue data on markets
Reservation - Friday - Armondo's
1:00 Mr. Owens, Mr. R
anyone else? - ck. Mr. R.
Info for George - call back
Appt. for Ed Ross - call back
Letters - Univ. Printing (1)
Mrs. MacArthur (2)
Jenson (3)
File carbons (Fri. ok.)

A typical desk calendar/memo pad might look like this:

through to be sure that there is no misunderstanding. If the appointment is canceled, she must make arrangements for a new appointment. If the employer leaves his appointment book with the secretary and she prepares a listing of the day's activities for him, as in the system mentioned above, the list should be placed on his desk with appropriate notes and materials each morning. This, therefore, is one of those day-ahead-of-time assignments.

Preparing and maintaining the appointment pad is not only a real service but also a privilege. Every effort should be made to avoid errors in this service.

THE TELEPHONE-ADDRESS BOOK

Blessed is the employer whose secretary knows who to call for what. One executive faced with the need of acquiring some hard-to-find item, was heard to boast, "I'll ask my secretary. She'd know where to get snowballs in July."

A secretary's telephone-address book should include not only the names of those she most frequently calls for her employer, but also names, addresses and phone numbers for services, emergencies, office personnel and sources of information.

The secretary who can, on short notice, call upon a reliable florist, ticket agent, travel agent or other such supplier is an asset to any company.

She would do well to become familiar with the yellow pages of her city's telephone directory and with the various sources of information listed in the section on references (Part 5).

WORK ORGANIZATION

Time is one of a business person's most precious commodities. The secretary who learns to organize her work well and plan her time wisely will save minutes out of every hour, hours out of every week. Here are a few time- and work-saving suggestions:

1) *Make efficient use of your desk.* Keep the surface clear of everything except your immediate work so you won't have to hunt through piles of other materials when you want page 2. Form the habit of using filing folders for anything of a temporary nature—work in progress, incoming or outgoing communications, work being held for additional information—and keep these folders in the file drawer of your desk where they are instantly accessible but not in the way.

2) *Plan your time, don't waste it.* When things are slow, plan ahead. Do

what can be done to relieve the work load at peak periods. Try to learn more about your company's operation. Consider what you can do to make your part of it run smoother. Bone up on reference materials. Bring your address book up to date. Get to know the filing system.

3) *Learn to schedule your time realistically.* It may take you an hour to type that stack of letters, provided you are not interrupted. But you will be. The phone will ring, your employer will call upon you to take care of something urgent, people will stop at your desk to ask questions, visitors will arrive. That one hour may become two or three. If you learn to expect interruptions, you won't be flustered by them or lose time trying to pick up where you left off. Interruptions are also part of your work and require a place in your schedule.

4) *Don't be a clock-watcher.* When the work load is heavy, when your employer and other members of the staff are up against a deadline to get a job done, be willing to pitch in and help even if it is a little after closing time. If you must leave promptly for any reason, inform your employer of the fact enough in advance so that he can plan his work accordingly. Your cooperation will be remembered when you have a favor to ask, or at promotion time.

Chapter 3

Ordering and Handling Supplies

A. E. KLEIN, ELIZABETH T. VAN DERVEER TONNE, MARION WOOD

THE RESPONSIBILITY for selecting and ordering supplies, for keeping inventories of quantities on hand, and for arranging stock in storage frequently falls on the shoulders of the secretary.

SELECTION AND ORDERING

In large companies orders are generally placed by a special purchasing department, and the secretary obtains supplies for her own office needs by sending a purchase requisition to that department. In small companies she may deal directly with the suppliers. She must learn first about the supplies being currently used on the job and then become familiar with others as they appear on the market. For example, inventions and improvements in the types of correctable bond paper and typing-correction paper have simplified typing considerably; developments in transparent tape have made it useful for a variety of purposes; and file labels are now available with adhesive backing. Such facts help the secretary in purchasing supplies for the job to be done efficiently and satisfactorily. By investigating the files a new secretary can find out the quantity, quality, and price of the items normally used and the names of the suppliers from whom purchases are usually made. She should become acquainted with the representatives of the various suppliers, for they are the best source of information on the characteristics of the materials she needs and on new developments in the manufacturing of office supplies.

PAPER

Among the paper supplies needed are letterheads, second sheets, carbon paper, envelopes, stenographers' notebooks, interoffice memoranda, and

28

forms. Certain questions must be answered before paper orders are placed. Is Corrasable bond used for letterheads? Are letterheads ever used for duplicated material, and, if so, is the duplicating process offset, mimeograph, or spirit? What kind of carbon is used—carbon sets or carbon sheets? What impression is intended to be created by the paper? (Paper from the president's desk, for example, is usually more impressive than that from the service department.) How long is the paper likely to be kept in the files? (Some grades of paper do not last well enough for permanent filing.) Is the paper to be used for two-sided work? Will it be subject to excessive creasing? Is it to be mailed? Such considerations as these affect the decision as to quality, size, and weight.

Quality. Letterhead paper is usually made from cotton or flax fiber or wood pulp or some combination of these. The higher the fiber (rag) content, the better the quality of the paper and the higher the cost. Some law offices and banks prefer 100 percent rag paper, because it is long-lasting. For the same reason a high rag content is desirable for papers to be permanently filed. Most of the letterhead paper used in business today contains about 25 percent fiber and 75 percent wood pulp or sulphite. The better quality of bond paper also bears a watermark, an emblem, slogan, or symbol manufactured in the texture of the paper and visible when the sheet is held up to the light. The letterhead should be printed on the side of the paper on which the watermark can be read. Paper for additional pages of a letter should be of the same quality as the letterhead paper.

Weight. The weight of paper used in business correspondence is determined by the weight of a manufacturer's ream (500 sheets) measuring 17 $\times$ 22 inches. The classification of paper as 20-pound means that the manufacturer's ream weighed 20 pounds. This number is sometimes referred to as the "substance number." Four reams of 8½ $\times$ 11 sheets can be cut from a manufacturer's ream. Paper for general office typing may be purchased in reams of 16-, 20-, and 24-pound weights. The greater the weight, the more expensive the paper. Heavier weights are also available for special purposes, such as offset; this stock is quoted in 40-, 60-, 70-, and 80-pound weights. For ordinary correspondence 20- or 24-pound stock is generally used. For two-sided work a heavy, opaque paper is needed. If paper is to be mailed, it is important to know how many sheets make up an ounce.

Erasing qualities. Another factor to be considered is the ease with which paper may be erased. Several companies are now manufacturing letterhead paper and second sheets which may be easily erased with a few light strokes of a pencil eraser. Such paper may be easily smudged, however, because the ink from the typewriter ribbon remains on the surface of the paper for about half an hour. Once the ink is absorbed, this paper is as smudgeproof as any of the ordinary bond papers.

The cheaper quality of paper, made solely of wood pulp or sulphite, pinpoints erasure spots and therefore should not be used for correspondence purposes. Today it costs two dollars or more for the production of a business letter. The additional fraction of a penny that may be spent on good letterhead paper is therefore almost insignificant. Being penny-wise and pound-foolish in the purchase of letterhead paper can result in the loss of valuable business.

Color. White is the most widely used color, but some companies are now using other colors. Advertising concerns sometimes use tan or blue letterhead paper. Color has also proved effective for sales-promotion letters.

Size of letterhead paper. The most economical and also the most widely used is the Standard, or business, size of letterhead paper, which is 8½ × 11 inches. For brief messages, half sheets, 8½ × 5½ inches, are sometimes used. Executives frequently use a letterhead paper that is 7½ × 10½ inches for personal business letters and business-social notes. Professional people also use this size, which is referred to as "Executive" or "Monarch" stationery. The Baronial letterhead sheet, 5½ × 8½ inches, 2 inches narrower than the Monarch, is also used for the same purposes. For legal documents, sheets measuring from 8½ × 14 to 13 × 16 are sometimes required.

Envelopes. The quality of the paper used for envelopes should match exactly that used for the letterhead. Envelopes come in different sizes and are designated by number. The following list shows the names of the letterheads and the envelope numbers that should be used for the different sizes of letterhead sheets:

Letterhead name	Envelope number
Standard	6¾ (small) or 10 (large)
Half sheet	6¾
Executive or Monarch	7
Baronial	5⅜

Manila envelopes are available in various sizes and with various types of closures on the flap (adhesive, metal tab, corded tab). They may also have protective padding or stiffening for enclosures that should not be bent.The firm name and address may be printed on the envelope, but for the address a mailing label is frequently used. The supplier should be consulted about the size and special features suited to the purposes.

Second sheets. The sheets that are used for making carbon copies of letters for filing purposes are referred to as "tissue," "onionskin," "manifold," or "second sheets." Three basic finishes are available (glazed, smooth, and cockle), and the normal weights range from 8- to 13-pound stock, but it may be as light as 4½ pounds. Frequently, when only one carbon copy is required, a coarse, inexpensive yellow sheet is used. For copies of letters and other material to be mailed, second sheets with the word "COPY" may be needed. The greater the number of copies required, the lighter the weight of the tissue should be. Usually 9- or 11-pound stock is satisfactory.

Carbon paper. Carbon paper comes in a variety of sizes, colors, weights, and finishes and is manufactured with many features for the convenience of the typist. The more expensive carbon papers have a tougher and more absorbent tissue. They are coated with a better ink formula and often have a special coating on the back that prevents curling and wrinkling. In selecting carbon, a factor to bear in mind is the number of times a sheet may be used; the more expensive the carbon paper, the more times it may be used. The decision as to weight depends upon the number of copies needed; the lighter the weight, the more copies can be made at a single typing. The choice of finish to be purchased depends on such factors as the hardness of the typewriter cylinder, the typing touch, and the action of the typewriter keys. The accompanying chart will help in choosing the weight and finish suitable for the three different kinds of typewriter and the number of copies desired.

For ease of removal, some carbon sheets are manufactured with an uncoated band at the bottom, some are slightly longer than 11 inches, and some have clipped corners.

To aid the typist in determining how many lines of typing remain, there is a carbon paper on the market with a strip about ¼ inch wide bearing numbers from 66 to 1, showing how deep the typing has run on the page.

Some firms are now using carbon sets, which consist of second sheets interleaved with carbon paper. To use such sets, the secretary should count off the number of copies needed, place a letterhead over the first carbon sheet, and begin typing. The carbon paper, known as "one-time" carbon paper, may be used only once. Carbon sets are great timesavers when there is much typing of multiple copies, because they eliminate assembling the carbon pack, but they may involve some sacrifice of quality in the copies.

Carbon paper is also available with a binder device. The binder fastens the carbon stack at the top and eliminates the problem of realigning the carbons after they are in the typewriter. Furthermore, binders make it possible to prepare carbon packs of two, three, four, or five copies in advance for use in rush periods.

CARBON-COPY CHART

Typewriter	1–4 Copies	5–9 Copies	10–12 Copies	Over 12
Electric	Standard weight Hard finish	Medium weight Hard finish	Light weight Hard finish	Feather weight Hard or sharp finish
Regular	Standard weight Sharp finish	Medium weight Sharp finish	Light weight Sharp finish	Feather weight Sharp finish
Noiseless	Standard weight Medium finish	Medium weight Medium finish	Light weight Medium finish	Feather weight Medium finish

Electric machines: For darker copies, sharp finish can be used.
Regular machines: For darker copies, medium finish can be used.
Noiseless machines: For darker copies, intense finish can be used.

The supplier can assist in the selection of the correct carbon paper for the secretary's needs and in solving any problems she may have with carbon copies. The secretary should make up a sample pack for him to analyze if she is having difficulty. The cost of carbon paper compared with her time is negligible, about one-tenth of 1 percent of the cost of the entire letter.

TYPEWRITER RIBBONS

Many brands of typewriter ribbons are on the market, and unless the secretary knows something of their uses, selection may be difficult. Fabric ribbons are made of nylon, silk, or cotton.

Nylon ribbons are used almost exclusively on electric typewriters, if a fabric ribbon is to be used at all. Other fabrics wear too quickly and do not give good service.

Silk and cotton both give good service. The office with heavy-duty work generally orders cotton. For beautiful, fine-line production silk is used. The more particular the job is, the finer the ribbon should be. As the silk ribbon has more yardage to the spool and holds ink well, the difference in price may be inconsequential, except in the most budget-minded office.

The one-time carbon ribbon is increasingly popular. It consists of carbon backed by film or paper. The film-backed type is frequently referred to by the trade names Mylar or Polyethylene carbon ribbon. The Mylar or Polyethylene type will stretch when put under tension, but the paper-backed variety may tear. For this reason the latter, though less expensive, is fast disappearing. The carbon ribbon is a one-time typing ribbon with a writing surface similar to a very hard, one-time carbon paper. It produces a fine even quality of print. Inasmuch as the type bar of the typewriter never comes into contact with an inked or carbon surface, the type remains bright and shining, even though used for a number of years. This feature eliminates the need for brushing and cleaning the type, which sometimes is injurious to the type surface.

Whether the secretary uses fabric or carbon ribbon, she must be able to indicate what density of inking she prefers. This she will probably be able to decide only after some experimentation. A good stationer or supplies salesman will answer questions and offer suggestions, but full understanding comes only with some experience in making the choice.

In making inquiry as to the best ribbon for the work to be done, the secretary must provide information as to the number of copies usually typed, the density of copy desired, the type of paper being used for original copy, the condition of the typing platen, the type style of the typewriter, and the kind of effect wanted.

One rule must be followed: the ribbon should be purchased to fit the machine being used. The mechanism which switches the ribbon from one direction to the other differs with every make of machine. Some mechanisms require a metal spot on the ribbon a certain distance from the end. Typewriter spools vary in style. Any variation from the standard for the machine being used can cause the ribbon to cease moving and the type to hit again and again on the same spot. This action soon ruins the ribbon and may damage the ribbon mechanism, because it strains to accommodate the ineffective ribbon.

Cheaper ribbons swell with use. It is sometimes necessary to remove several feet shortly after placing a new ribbon of poor quality in a machine in order to keep the ribbon from overflowing the spool. If the machine is not working well, a careful check-up of the ribbon may sometimes reveal the reason. Any pile-up of ribbon should be the signal to call a service man.

Use of colored typing ribbons is a matter of office preference. The bichrome red-and-black is probably the most desirable for figure work. Ribbons can be purchased in almost any color desired, and some offices match ribbon to the colors in the letterhead.

The condition of the ribbon is probably one of the major indications of the service the secretary is giving her employer. It reflects true concern about the appearance of the completed work. In large offices with service contracts for all equipment, typewriter ribbons are changed regularly at specified times. However, the secretary is more likely to be satisfied with her production if she chooses her own ribbon for the job she has to do and the machine she is using.

KEYS

Among the miscellaneous equipment under the control of the secretary may be keys. Keys to special cabinets or closets should be plainly tagged with large pieces of cardboard or plywood and stored in a safe place. Such keys usually present no problem, because only a limited number of persons use them.

However, in a suite of offices or in a school office, for example, there may be keys for most of the rooms. It may be the secretary's duty to circulate and control all these keys. One form suggested for handling keys calls for the serial number of each key to be matched on the record with the location of door, cabinet, or room, the number of keys available, and the name of each person holding a key. Admittedly, this record accounts only for the keys known to be available. Any person can have a duplicate key made. For this reason master keys must be very carefully handled. Any suspicion of misuse or loss of a master key involves notifying the employer and obtaining his permission to change all locks affected—a time-consuming and expensive process.

When keys are being made, each should be marked with the number or name of the room to which it belongs. It may be necessary to allow keys in circulation, but this arrangement weakens control of the system. Therefore keys should be issued only when necessary, and all master keys should be kept under personal control.

FIRE EQUIPMENT

No discussion of supplies can be dismissed without consideration of fire extinguishers or other fire-safety devices. In a large office the responsibility for fire protection rests with building maintenance, but in a small office someone in the executive office may have to remind the executive of the need for refill or replacement. The secretary, regardless of who else may be checking the equipment, also should be sure that it is kept in working order. If safety precautions are being violated, the secretary should tactfully remind her employer of the potential danger or suggest methods for better fire protection. This is another topic that deserves some study on her part.

MISCELLANEOUS

Other supplies which should be in the desk or on the supply shelf are dictation notebooks; pencils; memorandum pads; erasers; scissors; rulers; date stamp; ink pad; clips; staples; stapler; transparent and perhaps opaque tape; supplies for dictating equipment, according to the machine being used; wooden, leather, or wire file baskets; file folders; binders; file labels; address labels; postage stamps; perhaps adding-machine tape; dusting paper; type cleaner; type brush; and typewriter oil.

If the secretary is responsible for special processes such as copying and other forms of duplicating, she will need to become familiar with the supplies for these uses. As each process requires specialized materials, no attempt will be made to list them here.

As new equipment is purchased, the secretary will find it advisable to ascertain from the salesman what supplies the machine requires and how to keep it in the best order. Some duplicating machines, for example, may give fair service with standard duplicating supplies but operate much better when fluids, paper, carbon master sets, mats, or stencils are of a particular type. The person using the machine and ordering the supplies should know this so that the quality of the work produced is excellent.

When ordering, the secretary should be specific. In requesting a supply of letterheads, for example, she should be sure to specify the number of sheets, the weight, the grain, the size, the color, and, if this is a repeat order, the previous order number.

KEEPING INVENTORY

A card record should be kept for each item. This record should include name of supplier, name of salesman, quantities usually purchased, sizes, weights, colors, and other details. The cards may be filed alphabetically by supplier or by item. They may be used as inventory records, showing the quantities coming in, the quantities distributed, and the minimum quantity to be kept in stock. As the record approaches the minimum, the item should be added to an order list or immediately placed on order. The minimum quantity should be high enough so that the stock is never exhausted and yet does not result in an overload of the item, for paper, inks, and typing ribbons deteriorate with age.

STORAGE

Stock in storage should be arranged according to age, with the oldest stock in front for immediate use. Only one box of a single item should be opened at a time. Like items may be stacked one in front of the other on shelves. Unlike items should be kept separate to ensure that no stock is concealed from sight and forgotten. Shelves, boxes, and packages should be plainly marked to show contents and date of purchase. It is important to store supplies so that humidity and temperature are as close to ideal as possible. Paper and carbon paper should be kept flat. Carbon paper should be laid carbon side down and away from excessive temperatures. Definition of ideal storage conditions can be given by the salesperson from whom the purchase is made. All supplies should be stored promptly and not allowed to clutter the office area.

Chapter 4

Dictation and Transcription

MARY E. CONNELLY

MUCH OF THE SECRETARY'S TIME in the office is spent in taking and transcribing dictation. Many employers have a regular time of the day for dictation. Others have to fit in their dictation time between meetings or other office activities during the day. No matter when the employer plans to dictate, the secretary must be ready to take dictation and must have at hand the necessary tools and references.

DICTATION TOOLS

1. A spiral-bound notebook, with a rubber band around the used portion, should be ready at all times. The notebook should be dated at the bottom of the page to facilitate locating old dictation. The efficient secretary usually keeps two notebooks, one for dictation and one for unexpected memos, special notices, and unusual notations.

2. Because pen notes are easier to read, the secretary usually uses a fountain pen, which she keeps filled, or a good ball-point pen. It is wise to have several sharpened pencils ready to use if the pen goes dry or the ball-point pen does not write on some parts of the notebook paper.

3. A file folder will help to keep papers and reference material organized. Notes on items that should be discussed with the employer, reports on telephone calls, or memos on additional appointments may be clipped in the file folder.

4. Paper clips may be used to mark something unusual in the dictation or to help the secretary to locate points in the dictation that need special attention. Memos, cards, small notes, enclosures, and so on, may be clipped to letters or in the notebook.

5. A colored pencil should be used to flag important items in the

dictation or to call attention to deletions, additions, or long insertions. A caret or a star is used for small insertions, and for longer insertions capital A, capital B, and so on, in a circle. If the dictator makes many changes, the secretary should take the dictation in the left-hand column of the notebook and make the corrections or insertions in the right-hand column on the line where the correction or insertion is to take place. The word "RUSH" may be written in colored pencil to call attention to urgent letters.

TAKING DICTATION

When the secretary takes dictation, she remains very quiet but always ready to follow the dictator's directions. A shorthand speed of 100 words a minute is adequate to handle the dictation of most employers. However, top executives may require speeds of 120 or more words a minute. Many dictators hesitate in their dictation while they are thinking how to express an idea. Once they have organized their ideas, they dictate at a very rapid rate of speed. While the dictator is thinking, the secretary uses that time to read over her notes, making any changes that are necessary, indicating words to be looked up in the dictionary, inserting punctuation that was omitted in taking dictation, encircling enclosures that are to be inserted with the finished letter or writing the word "ENCLOSURE" at the end of the letter, and noting other items that may need attention before the letter is typed or mailed.

If the dictation is not clear or the dictator's directions are not understood, the secretary should ask questions to clarify all matters before leaving, so that she will not have to interrupt her employer later. The secretary should not interrupt the dictator while he is dictating; she should wait until the end of the letter and then politely ask any questions she may have about doubtful words, sentences, or meanings.

Many times the dictator wishes the dictation read back. If the secretary has written good shorthand notes, this will be very easy for her. If she has made good use of periods of interruption in the dictation, she has polished her notes so that there is no hesitation in reading them back. If she is not certain of a word or of the construction of a dictated sentence, she should ask to read it back and make any corrections. If the secretary cannot keep up with the dictation, she should ask the dictator to slow down until she can catch up with him or to repeat the last sentence or the last few words. The dictator would rather dictate at the secretary's rate than repeat everything. If the secretary is new to the job, she should ask the dictator to spell any unusual or unfamiliar word. Before the secretary leaves her employer's office, she should ask any questions she needs to about the correspondence. She should take all her materials with her when she leaves.

If a letter is to have more than one carbon copy, the number should be noted at the top of the shorthand notes; otherwise the transcriber may neglect to make the extra copies. If a letter is to be sent air mail, special delivery, or registered, the classification of service should be typed on the letterhead as well as on the envelope.

UNFAMILIAR TERMS

An employer will take it for granted that his secretary's shorthand speed and typing technique are adequate for the job. The secretary can increase her shorthand speed by devising shortcuts for frequently used names and terms. It is helpful to keep a word list of unfamiliar terms with their shorthand outlines, such as those used by an engineer, a scientist, or other professional. Practice the shorthand outlines and memorize the spelling of these terms when there is a lull in the day's work.

NAMES AND ADDRESSES

The employer may give the secretary the original letter he is answering, from which she may secure the correct name and address, but it is helpful to keep a card file of names and addresses of correspondents. The card should be typed, with the telephone number of the firm, the extension number, if any, of the person in the firm with whom the employer corresponds, and any other pertinent data.

TRANSCRIBING

The efficient secretary estimates the length of the letter from her shorthand notes to determine the correct margins and the correct size of letterhead (see Chap. 3). In planning the placement of the letter, the secretary should consider the length of the message, the length of the inside address, and any special lines, such as attention line, subject line, or a tabulation within the letter (see Chap. 6). If it is necessary to use off-size stationery, the secretary may have a problem with margins. A well-placed letter should be centered on the paper. A margin of 1, 1½, or 2 inches may be used to accommodate a one-page letter. A two-page letter should have a 1-inch margin.

Every letter or report should be typed without strikeovers, misspelled words, or misspelled names, and a standard procedure for the closing of the letter should be followed. Ask the employer which letter format he prefers and use that one. Proofread every letter very carefully, and make any necessary corrections. Type the envelope as soon as the letter is typed. When a letter is removed from the machine, it should be placed face down on the desk or in a folder. When the letters are presented to `the dictator for his signature, they should be in a folder marked "FOR YOUR SIGNATURE." Some employers like to see the carbon copies and the envelopes. However, if the employer wishes only the letters, keep the envelopes and carbon copies in the same order as the original letters in a separate folder on the desk so that they are ready for letter insertion or for quick corrections on both original and carbon copies. If the dictator wishes to see the carbon copies, place the outgoing letters in one pile and the carbon copies in another pile. Thus the backs of the outgoing letters will be kept clean of carbon smudges.

If the secretary has permission to sign the dictator's name to letters in his absence, she should write her initials clearly and neatly at the end of the written name unless otherwise directed.

Before a letter is mailed, it should be checked for accuracy of dates, figures, and names. The enclosures should be inserted; the name on the letter and on the envelope should be the same; any special notation should appear on both the letterhead and the envelope. If the letter has an attention line, this should be typed on the envelope. If the letter is to be sent air mail, use an air-mail envelope or type or stamp "AIR MAIL" in the lower right-hand corner of the envelope. Letters addressed to foreign countries should be marked in a special way so that the correct postage will be affixed.

DICTATING MACHINES

Many employers use dictating machines to record some of their dictation material. The secretary should become familiar with various recording and transcribing machines and learn how to use them efficiently. Whether the voice-recording machine uses a wax disk, a plastic belt, a magnetic belt, a magnetic disk, magnetic paper, or tape, the operating principles are very similar. The dictator speaks into a microphone, and his voice is recorded on the disk or on the belt or tape. The machine is usually equipped with an indicator slip on which to mark the beginning and the end of the letter or message and any point at which a correction is to be made. The dictator must speak distinctly, spell out any unusual words, and record the punctuation, capitalization, and paragraphs. He indicates at the beginning of the dictation the number of carbons required and any other instructions he wishes the transcriber to follow.

The transcriber must learn to adjust the speed, volume, and tone controls, as well as the start and stop mechanisms. Transcribing machines are equipped with either a thumb or a foot control to start and stop the machine and a backspacer to replay the dictation when necessary. For good letter placement the transcriber should use the indicator slip as a guide to the letter length. Look at the indicator slip for corrections; if there are any, listen to them before typing the letter. In many instances this precaution will eliminate the need for retyping the entire letter. Check the indicator slip to locate rush items, telegrams, or telephone calls that must be made before typing the letters.

When a secretary uses the transcribing machine for the first time, she should make sure of the kind of material that has been dictated on the belt or disk. She should check the spelling of unfamiliar words and verify prices, quantities, and other facts. If the words are not clear, the dictator should be asked to supply the correct words or space should be left on the paper for their inclusion later. The beginning transcriber usually starts the transcribing machine, listens to a few words or a phrase, stops the machine, and types the words or phrases. Then she starts the machine and repeats the four steps—start, listen, stop, type. It may be necessary to repeat the dictation at first, but this step will be eliminated as the transcriber becomes familiar with the voice and with the nature of the material. The goal of a good machine transcriber is to start the machine, listen, type, and keep the typewriter moving with very few interruptions of the typing process.

As with all transcribing material, the finished transcripts should be proofread carefully for correct spelling, punctuation, capitalization, paragraphing, and meaning. As each letter is transcribed, a check mark should be made at the proper point on the indicator slip. This will ensure the transcription of every item on the recording. If the belt or disk is not completely used, a mark with a wax pencil will indicate to the dictator the portion of the disk that has been transcribed. All letters, with envelopes, enclosures, and other required material, should be placed in a folder on the dictator's desk for his signature.

Chapter 5

Typewriter Techniques and Typing Problems

MARION WOOD

HOW TO IMPROVE SPEED AND ACCURACY

It is the stops in typing that make you inaccurate. If you question this statement, ask a friend to count the number of stops you make in typing any paragraph for one minute. If you make three stops, the chances are that you will have three errors. The secret of accurate typing is to adopt a speed that allows you to keep the typewriter carriage moving constantly. Avoid speeding up on easy combinations of letters and then stopping just before typing the more difficult combinations.

Typing speed is obtained by quick key release. Only a light tap is needed when you let the typewriter mechanism carry the stroke for you. Use a quick, resilient touch and relax the finger the moment you feel contact with the key. A relaxed finger movement is probably the most important element in becoming a fast typist. One of the best ways to perfect your touch is to practice frequently used words and phrases over and over until you acquire a feel for typing them with a smooth, even rhythm. The more letter combinations you learn to type automatically, the greater your speed and control.

Many typing errors can be overcome by improving your posture. Adjust the typewriter so that the front edge of the frame is even with your typing desk. Let the chair comfortably support the center of your back so that your arms hang freely from the shoulders. Elbows should be in line with your hips or slightly ahead of the hip line. Wrists should be lower than your knuckles and the palms of your hands parallel to the keyboard slope. Keep your feet flat on the floor.

You can quickly determine whether or not you have the proper finger position if you place a penny on each wrist and then type any 70-space line. If the action is centered in the fingers, where it should be, and you are holding your fingers close to the keys, the pennies will remain in position. With an electric typewriter you should be able to type a complete page without dropping the pennies. This is a good check on whether or not you are lifting your fingers too high and whether or not you have the resilience in your stroke that makes for relaxed typing.

The ability to analyze and correct your own errors will do wonders for your typing. The accompanying list shows common errors and the possible reasons for them.

Error	Analysis
Misstroke	Typing too fast, reading copy too fast, or possibly difficulty with spelling.
Omission when typing double letters	Overemphasis of the first letter; roll into the second letter by giving it greater emphasis.
Omissions at the beginning and ending of words	Reading too far ahead in copy.
Inserting and rewriting letters	Watching letters as they are typed, faulty vision, poor light, reading too fast.
Transposition errors	Misreading, poor vision, bad light, typing too fast.
Adjacent key errors	Fingers not in correct position, improper position at typewriter, typewriter not at correct height, fingernails too long, not stroking the center of the key.
Failure to space	Poor concentration, hand movement in space bar stroke, swinging the thumb outward.

Nimble fingers are best developed through a daily practice plan. Begin each day's work with a rhythm drill, typing three copies in a 70-space line. Follow with three copies of this number drill:

1 and 2 and 3 and 4 and 5 and 6 and 7 and 8 and 9 and 0

Then type an alphabet sentence, such as: "Just by working with intelligence and zeal typists quickly become experts and avoid fatigue." Regulate your speed of typing according to how rapidly and accurately you can locate all the letters of the alphabet.

Each week select 12 or 15 lines of some straight copy material that fingers easily. Because you are working for smooth, continuous typing, the material should have few capitalizations and technical expressions. Test yourself the first day to see how long it takes you to type these lines. Record your time so that you can check your improvement. On each succeeding day practice the material in groups of three 70-space lines. Type each line over and over until you type it without error. Now type the same three lines in a group, starting at a slow rate and gradually building your speed on the second and third copies. Each day add a new group of three lines. At the end of the week test yourself again. How long has it taken you to type all the lines this time? You should realize a 10 percent improvement; 15 to 20 percent would be good, and 25 percent, tops. The slower your rate of speed, the greater your percentage of improvement.

HOW TO ERASE NEATLY

Expert as you may be in handling the typewriter, there are times when you may welcome hints on how to make erasing fast, clean, and inconspicuous. Did you know that if you blot the error just before using your eraser, much of the surplus ink clinging to the top fibers is removed? The remaining portion of the error can be easily removed with a soft eraser. You have an erasing touch, just as you have a typing touch. If yours is a light touch, use a hard eraser; if you have a hard touch, use a softer eraser.

Manufacturers make a great effort to provide erasers suited to the different papers we use, as well as to the inks. Smooth-finished papers require a less abrasive eraser, the soft eraser. Linen-finished papers are not so easily damaged, and therefore erasing on these papers is easier. Impressions on onionskin paper are also easily removed; use a soft eraser with a light, lifting motion. On colored papers use the pencil-stick eraser with as light a motion as possible to avoid removing the color. Should you remove the color, cover it lightly with a pencil of the same color as the paper. Blend in the penciled area by brushing over it lightly with a soft eraser. You may find that the Multilith eraser makes a good, clean correction on green paper. Cockle-finished papers are not easily penetrated, and the soft eraser usually removes the ink impression readily. The pencil stick is best for cards and manila stock. To erase on this stock you need to protect the glazed surface. Manufacturers will be happy to test your stationery and recommend the eraser that gives you good correction.

The paper-manufacturing process causes the fibers to run in a given direction; this effect is called the "grain" of the paper. The watermark, if there is one, usually indicates the grain. If the grain is horizontal (and it usually is on typewriting papers), the paper bends more easily around the platen. Erase with the grain of paper, and you are less likely to rough up its fibers. If the fibers do become roughened in erasing, smooth them back by pressing the thumb or fingernail against the nap of the paper. Chalking the surface helps to cover the spot.

There are many ways to obtain clean corrections. Keep the eraser clean by rubbing it on sandpaper or filing it with an emery board. When erasing, protect the surrounding copy by using the shields provided by equipment firms. These shields have small openings that match the space to be corrected. Frame the error with the shield and blot off the wet ink with either blotting paper, a soft eraser, or a plastic type cleaner. Kneaded rubber may also be used for blotting. Remove only the necessary portion of the misstroke. If an "o" is struck for a "p," on most typewriters only the left side of the "o" needs to be erased, because the "p" fits over the "o." Other characters that fit easily over one another are "h" over "n," "m" over "n," "s" over "e," "y" over "v," and "u" over "n." Roll your paper far enough forward to make the spot easily accessible and to secure good light on the spot to be corrected. Engage the automatic line-position reset before you roll the copy up or down; re-engage it as you return to the line of writing. This ensures accurate realignment. Avoid smearing the surrounding characters by using either the pencil type of eraser or an eraser with a sharp edge. If you are erasing near the bottom edge, roll the sheet back to free it from the platen. If your typewriter has a copy guide, bring the bottom edge over this guide, erase, and then roll the page into typing position; otherwise, secure the sheets by rolling an extra piece of paper behind the pages in the typewriter. Now roll up, erase, return, and correct.

There are a number of erasing aids with which you may wish to experiment. One is a coated paper that can be inserted in front of your error. Simply backspace to the letter typed in error and retype the same error on the coated paper. Remove the coated paper and type in the correction. This works very well when the stationery and coating match. The coated paper is not so effective with carbon-paper ribbon as with fabric ribbons, and reproduction processes using heat reproduce both characters, sometimes making it difficult to determine which letter is correct.

For rough-draft work you may like to use one of the opaque white correction fluids that are available. With these, you paint over the error and then retype over the painted area. This is a quick way of handling errors and is satisfactory for materials to be photographed.

HOW TO CORRECT CARBONS

In correcting carbons, erase the original first. It is your most important copy. Back the original with a plastic card or regular 3 × 5 card. Some secretaries use a piece of old film. One card serves for all copies. Put the card on top of the carbon paper, not behind it, and erase one copy at a time. Move the card back after each erasure. The card gives you a smooth surface to erase against and protects the copies and carbon sheets from damage.

If the correction on the carbon copy is lighter than the surrounding type, tap the key with the ribbon in stencil position. This leaves a darker impression on the carbon copy but keeps the original blank. You may want to match the retyped stroke to surrounding copy by inserting a small piece of carbon paper (carbon side facing carbon copy) between the type guide and the copy.

If the carbons have been removed from the typewriter before the correction is made, insert each carbon separately. To make the correction match the other typed characters, build a miniature carbon stack with the original, carbon paper, and copy paper. When you correct the first carbon copy, insert your miniature carbon stack between the type guide and your first carbon sheet so that you will strike through the original. When correcting the second carbon copy, place your miniature carbon stack over the correction and strike through the original and one carbon.

HOW TO CROWD AND EXPAND SPACES AND CORRECTIONS

Did you leave out a word? On rough drafts use this quick way of inserting it. Underscore the last letter of the word preceding the omission, tap the diagonal, and center the missing word above the line.

```
          be
He will/there
```

If you leave off the last letter of a word and have already typed the next word, position the carriage so that the printing point is at the space immediately following the incomplete word, depress the backspacer halfway, and type in the missing letter. On an electric typewriter without a half-space key, push the carriage back half a space with the left platen knob and hold it in this position as you type the missing letter. If the machine has a half-space key, position the carriage so that the printing point is at the last letter of the incomplete word, depress the half-space key, and type the missing letter.

If you are spreading three letters over a space formerly occupied by four, type in the initial letter and final letter first; then center the middle letter between them.

HOW TO CORRECT BOUND COPIES

Copies that are bound across the top of the sheets may be corrected by front-feeding the bound pages, as follows: Insert a blank sheet around the platen an inch or so above the type-bar guide. Lift the paper bail in upright position. Place the sheet to be corrected behind the top of the paper in front of the platen. Turn the platen back to the location of the error you wish to correct.

HOW TO USE THE TABULATOR KEY

The tab key is one of the most useful service features on the typewriter. Use it for indentations, for centering, for positioning the date line and the closing line of your letters, and for addressing envelopes.

On some electric typewriters you can use the tab key together with the carriage-return key to return the carriage to any desired point without returning it first to the left margin. Flick the carriage-return key and, as the carriage passes the tab stop setting, touch the tab key. Use this procedure in addressing envelopes, in positioning the carriage for the closing line of the letter, and in columnar typing.

HOW TO ALIGN PAPER

To reinsert copy accurately into the typewriter, you must know the relationship between the typed copy and the aligning scale. The aligning scale is on the card holder; on type-bar machines it is on each side of the point where the type bars strike the paper. On most typewriters the white marks on the scale are in line with the straight-line letters, "i," "l," "r," and "t," and the writing usually rests on the top of the scale. Typing the sentence, "It is thinking time," several times across the page will quickly show the relation of your typing to the alignment scale. Use the variable spacer on the left platen knob to align the typing so that it rests on this scale; use the paper release to slide the paper from left to right.

Correcting an error after you have taken the paper from the typewriter is always a little more difficult. It is even harder to make the erasure. When the paper is around the platen, the curve of the platen makes it easy to get the eraser right at the point of correction; this is not so easy when the paper is on a flat surface. Put the page on a hard, smooth surface and frame the error with the smallest usable opening of the erasure shield. Erase as little as possible, using a light, lifting motion.

Now reinsert the paper in the typewriter. Make certain that it is straight. Roll the sheet forward to the line on which the correction appears. Use the ratchet release and adjust the paper so that the line is resting on the top of the aligning scale. Leave the ratchet release engaged as you continue to work. If the paper is a trifle out of horizontal alignment, shift it slightly from left to right by using the paper release. Another way is to switch the ribbon-control lever to stencil position and position the correction to the left of the printing-point indicator. Move the carriage back slowly to the space where your eye tells you the key should be struck. Hold the carriage there as you tap the key just hard enough to produce a faint impression. If the first attempt is slightly out of alignment, try moving the carriage a bit more. The second trial is usually sufficient to center the stroke perfectly. Hold the carriage in that position, return the stencil lever to black, and tap the correct key. Strike lightly at first and repeat the tapping until the correction matches the rest of the material. Some secretaries secure their alignment by using the period as a gauge. With the ribbon in stencil position, they strike over a period near the correction. If the periods match, they then roll to the location of the correction and proceed to fill in the missing characters.

HOW TO TYPE SMALL CARDS

Make a pleat horizontally in the center of a sheet of bond paper. The depth of the pleat will determine how far down you can type on the card; that is, the depth of the pleat is equal to the margin to be left at the bottom of the card. Insert this sheet in the typewriter. Line up the folded edge of the pleat with the edge of the type guide. Place the bottom edge of the card in the pleat and roll back the platen to typing position. If you secure the pleat with transparent tape, it is easier to insert it in the machine. A pencil mark against the left edge of the first card can serve as a margin guide for all cards to be inserted in the typewriter.

Side margins on post cards should be ½ inch. Leave two blank lines for top and bottom margins. Type the return address on the front of the card if there is not room to type it with the date. If the message is long, single-space between paragraphs and omit the salutation and closing.

If you have many post cards to type, chain-feed them from the front of the platen. After you type the first card, feed backward until the card has a ¾-inch margin. Insert the next card so that the bottom is held in place by the first card. Each succeeding card will be held in position by the preceding card. The cards will pile up against the paper table as they are typed, and they will be in the same order in which they were inserted in the typewriter. This method is particularly useful when cards are stiff and smooth. You may also use this method for addressing envelopes in quantity.

CARBON PAPER AND ITS USE

Choose a carbon with as hard a finish and heavy a weight as you can use and still obtain good results. There are many variables that affect the quality of the carbon copy, such as make of typewriter and model, number of copies to be made, desired darkness of carbon copies, weight and finish of the copy paper, kind of type, kind of platen (soft or hard), weight of letterhead, and quality of carbon paper. (See Chap. 3.)

Some secretaries (or their employers) prefer black copies; others like a medium-black, and still others, a light-gray copy. Actually the grayer copies are more legible, and the writing is usually sharper. To obtain the effect that pleases you, select a finish that produces the desired degree of blackness. The intense finishes make an extremely black copy. If your typewriter has the small type (elite), it is best to sacrifice some blackness for a sharper impression and to select either a medium- or a light-finished carbon paper. Use the medium or light finishes also with the electric typewriter. The more forceful the type blow, the more ink is deposited on the characters. Too much ink can fill in the round letters, making them difficult to read.

Platens make a difference, too. Typing on a soft platen is like writing with a pencil on a linoleum desk top; typing on a hard platen is like writing with a pencil on a page laid over glass. Most suppliers suggest a medium platen for general work. If you want more sharpness in your impression, back your carbon pack with a plastic backer, which may be obtained from your office-equipment supplier. Using the backer is like having a second platen. To avoid cutting and excessive wear of the ribbon, use a platen that is no harder than is necessary for the quality of writing desired.

Sometimes you may make only one carbon; at other times you may have 12 to do. Each type of job calls for a different weight of carbon paper. (See the carbon chart in Chap. 3.)

Observe these considerations in using carbon paper:

Never pick up the carbon sheet by a pinch of the thumb and forefinger. You will crease the paper and cause "treeing" of your copies (that is, branching, treelike marks created by the creases). If you use a hard or extra hard platen, you will obtain more copies and a sharper impression.

Use the hardest finish and heaviest weight consistent with good results.

Use the rougher side of the sheet when you are using glazed second sheets, because carbon ink adheres best to rough surfaces.

Should you have trouble with curling of the carbon paper, attach a strip of plastic tape along the top and bottom edges of the uninked side of the sheet.

If you want sharp, legible copies, you must select second sheets of the correct weight (see Chap. 3). The number of legible copies decreases as the weight of the second sheets is increased.

Use the glazed finish for second sheets when the maximum number of carbon copies is your foremost requirement; use the smooth finish when high quality of impression and the number of carbons are of equal importance. The cockle finish is the least desirable for maximum carbon-copy results.

To feed a large number of carbons into the typewriter, disengage the paper release and start the pack under the platen; if your typewriter has a multiple-copy control lever, move the lever back several notches to start the pack under the platen, thus eliminating the necessity for aligning the pages after they are in the typewriter. Papers without a binder sometimes feed more easily if you insert a lead sheet first. Insert a half sheet of paper until it has a margin of 1 inch. Now put the pack between the bottom edge of this paper and the platen. The half sheet pulls in the carbon pack. Another method is to insert the original and copy sheets, roll them in for two spaces, let the paper bail support the copy sheets and the original, and interleave the carbon sheets.

To type a rush message or a telegram when a carbon pack is already in the typewriter, it is not necessary to remove the letter. Instead, roll the letter back until 1 inch is left in the front of the platen, put the telegraph blank or message sheet against the paper table and one sheet behind each carbon, roll the material into typing position and type your message, and then roll the material back and remove the message and its carbon copies. Position your letter and continue with your typing.

The accompanying list shows a number of carbon-copy problems and how to solve them.

Problem	*Solution*
Smudging	Use a harder-finish carbon paper and softer-finish copy sheet.
Offsetting	Use a lighter weight of paper; if you have a multiple-carbon-copy control lever on your typewriter, move the platen back a notch. Avoid snapping the paper release back into position.
Treeing	Insert carbon pack with binder. Avoid stretching carbons when you remove them from pack. Check the adjustment on the feed rollers. Don't pick up the carbon by pinching it between thumb and forefinger.
Cutting	Use a heavier weight of paper, especially for the first two papers in the pack. A better quality of paper will give a tougher tissue.
Short life	Alternate carbons as they are used, from top to bottom and from front to back. Softer finishes usually give longer life.
Copies light	Use a more intense finish and lighter carbon paper. On the electric typewriter, check the impression indicator.
Curling	Keep paper away from excessive temperatures and store flat.
Slipping	Use carbon papers with less gloss and back the stack with a white sheet of paper.
Illegibility	Use a harder finish and platen to give a sharper impression.

HOW TO CENTER PAPER

CENTERING HORIZONTALLY

For best paper feeding, center the paper in the typewriter and then move the paper-edge guide to the left edge of the paper. Determine the center point of your writing line by noting the figures on the writing scale against which the left and right edges of your paper rest, adding these figures, and dividing by 2. The result is the center of your page. Set a tab stop here. From this point backspace once for every two spaces in the line to be centered. If there is an extra letter, disregard it.

CENTERING VERTICALLY

There is a short cut to vertical centering, too. It is based on the same principle as the one used in the backspace method of centering horizontally (backspacing once for every two spaces in the typed line). Start at the vertical center of your page and turn the platen back once for each two lines you plan to type on the page.

To do this you must determine in advance the vertical center of the paper. Crease the paper straight across in the vertical center. Insert this creased sheet into the typewriter so that the top and bottom edges meet when you hold them together straight up. Turn the platen forward line by line until you come to the crease, counting the lines as you space. The number of lines to the creased line is your guide number for vertical centering. Remember this number. Now you will always be able to find the vertical center of the paper by using this number. Each paper size, of course, will have its own number of lines to the vertical center.

PIVOTING

Making lines end where you want them to end is called "pivoting." Set your carriage one space after the point where you wish to end the copy; backspace once for each letter and space in the line you are typing. If there are certain headings you frequently type, keep a list of them with the numbers on which you start them. With this reference list you can whizz through the headings of your typed reports.

TYPEWRITER CARRIAGE LENGTHS

Both manual and electric typewriters come with carriages that vary in length from 11 to 32 inches. If you are using a typewriter with a long carriage, center the paper by folding a sheet in half, lengthwise, opening it, and inserting it into the machine so that the fold lines up with the center point of the platen. Adjust the paper-edge guide so that it is flush with the left edge of the paper. Margin stops are easy to locate if you always think of them as being based on one inch.

Some long carriages have a bar in the center of the margin rail, preventing you from moving the right margin stop beyond the center point of the carriage. This is why you should always type with the paper centered; besides, the paper will feed better because the little rollers under the platen will pull evenly on the sheet as it is inserted.

TYPE STYLES

Not only do typewriter carriages differ in length, but type styles vary also. Although elite and pica are probably still the most commonly used type styles, a number of other styles are available. Some have a broad face and others produce a very sharp write. Some look like printing and one, Script Type, resembles handwriting. No single type style can meet every typing requirement, so you should select the one best suited to the work you are doing. Ask your typewriter company representative for advice.

HOW TO TYPE TABLES

Most tables have three parts, the title, columnar headings, and the figures in the columns. Tables can also have what some authorities call the "stub" (headings down the left side). Titles should be brief but specific. Allow three spaces between the title and the subheadings or columnar headings. Put two line spaces between the subheadings and the columnar headings as well as between the columnar headings and the items in the column. Headings may be centered with the backspace method. One caution: make an allowance if part of the left margin is used for binding.

If you are making a revision of a table already set up, insert the copy of the table in your typewriter and determine your margins and tab settings from the old copy. If you are typing a new table, select the longest line in each column as your guideline. Allow six spaces between columns. Clear your typewriter of all adjustments and determine your left margin by centering the line that is equivalent to the longest line in each column plus the six spaces for each division between columns. From the left margin, tap out the longest line in each column plus the six spaces between columns to locate each tab setting.

The following information is helpful in typing tables:

Generally, the title is written in capitals and centered over the table. However, some authorities prefer lower case for titles, because it is easier to read.
Arrange columnar headings for compactness.

Place the dollar sign only before the first figure in each column and before the totals.

Use leaders (a series of periods) to indicate omissions in a column.

Side headings are generally longer than top headings.

Use boxings of different kinds to bring out the subheadings.

Align figures on the right and words on the left.

If the table is short, use double spacing.

If you know that you are going to type this same table each month, keep a list of the number on which to set the tabs for each column.

Tables should be close to the discussion of their contents.

Put tables of more than 30 lines on separate pages.

When possible, place tables vertically on the page.

Use abbreviations in tables, such as lb., ft., %.

To avoid confusion with figures in the table, indicate references or footnotes by the symbol * or letters "a," "b," "c," etc.

Footnotes should be placed two or three spaces beneath the table.

Type credit lines at the left corner beneath the table.

Long, single-spaced titles should have a space break every sixth line.

There are six lines of typing to one vertical inch.

There are 10 pica spaces to a horizontal inch.

There are 12 elite spaces to a horizontal inch.

There are 85 pica spaces and 102 elite spaces on an 8½ - x 11-inch page.

There are 66 vertical line spaces on an 8½ - x 11-inch page.

When the columnar heading and the longest line in the column are the same length or differ by only one space, both lines can begin at the same point. If the heading is shorter, determine how many spaces shorter and then indent the heading half that number of spaces from the beginning of the column. If the heading is longer than the longest line in the column, let the heading extend beyond each end of the column. The heading should be your guideline for planning the table. The column is indented under it.

TYPING TABLES ON THE PROPORTIONAL-SPACED TYPEWRITER

On the proportional-spaced typewriter, tab stops can be set only on every four units or on the white lines of the writing scale, even though the carriage can be moved between these lines. Figures, the comma, the period, and the dollar sign are all three units. Use the three-unit space bar when spacing between the figures and remember to use the figure 1.

You can easily rule for a table while your work is in the machine. For horizontal lines move the carriage to the place at which the line should start; rest your pencil on the type guide, with the point against the paper; and hold the pencil in position as you move the carriage from left to right. For vertical lines, position the carriage where you want to begin the line, hold the pencil in the middle of the type guide, and turn the platen away from you until the line is as long as you want it.

Use a ruler to guide you as you type your tables. Put a couple of rubber bands around the ruler to keep it in place as you type.

TYPEWRITER UPKEEP AND MAINTENANCE

THE DAILY TWO-MINUTE CHECK

Spend two minutes each day wiping all exposed parts of your typewriter with a soft, dry cloth. Use a long-handled brush to get into the corners and brush toward you. Move the carriage all the way to the left or right and brush out any erasure dirt that may be there. A soft paintbrush is good for this kind of dusting. Do not oil your typewriter; let the service engineer do this for you.

CLEANING THE TYPE

Use a stiff, dry brush and brush out and away from the typewriter. If the "o's" and "e's" are filled up, tap them gently with your brush. Clean type at the end of the day's work. The ink is more easily removed then. If you are using nylon ribbons, leave a slight deposit of ink on the type bars. When you use a plastic type cleaner, do not press down on the keys too hard. With one finger lift a few keys at a time and apply the cleaner.

PLATEN CARE

A damp cloth will take off the excess carbon from the platen. If you clean the platen with alcohol, use it sparingly, because it has a tendency to harden the rubber. Disengage the paper release when you leave your typewriter for the night.

When erasing, move the carriage of the typewriter to keep the erasure dust from falling between the type bars.

If the keys jam, separate them carefully one at a time. Do not force them, or you may bend the type bars out of alignment.

Center the carriage and cover your typewriter when it is not in use. The cover protects the machine from dust and should be used whether the typewriter is on a desk or put away in a typewriter desk.

Record needed typewriter repairs as you notice them. Put your list on the underside of the typewriter cover. When the service man comes, he will have your list handy and will not need to disturb you.

Chapter 6

The Business Letter: Format and Structural Parts

A. E. KLEIN

EVERY LETTER emanating from a business office, no matter how insignificant its contents, should be considered an ambassador of good will. The impression it creates may sometimes mean the difference between the gain or loss of a prospective customer, a client, or a friend for your company. This impression depends as much on the appearance of the letter as on the tone.

Just suppose you were to receive in the morning's mail a letter that contained several sloppy erasures and one or two pen-written corrections, had an extremely uneven right-hand margin, and was completely off center, both horizontally and vertically. What would you think? Probably your immediate reaction would be that a firm incapable of producing so simple an item as a carefully typed business letter must also be incapable of handling more complex business activities with efficiency and dispatch. Your lack of confidence created by this first impression would incline you not to do business with this organization.

Because of their importance, this chapter will be concerned with those details of appearance and form of the letter which serve to create the most favorable impression. The next chapter will deal with the tone and spirit of the various types of communications that the secretary may be called upon to compose.

LETTER STYLES

It has often been said that a letter should look like a picture in a frame, but in the daily practice of business it is a luxury to think only of appearance; the practical aspects must also be considered.

The balanced effect achieved through the use of the indented form of letter (Fig. 4) is costly in time, which is the main reason it is rarely used today. The streamlined form proposed by the National Office Management Association (the NOMA letter, Fig. 5), although the quickest of all forms to type, is completely unbalanced and, therefore, not to everyone's taste. As a compromise, most businesses still prefer to use either the block style (Fig. 3) or a modified block, the semiblock style (Fig. 2). Other styles in current use are shown in Figs. 1 and 6.

PUNCTUATION

In the typing of end-of-line punctuation of those parts of the business letter above and below the body, the following three styles are recognized:

STANDARD PUNCTUATION

In this style, sometimes referred to as "mixed punctuation," a colon is placed after the salutation and a comma after the complimentary close (Fig. 2). Of all the punctuation styles, this is the most popular.

OPEN PUNCTUATION

No punctuation is used after any of the lines above and below the body of the letter (Fig. 1). This style, though the most practical, is still viewed as too radical by most business concerns.

CLOSE PUNCTUATION

When strict rules of punctuation were closely adhered to, it was mandatory that a period be placed at the end of the date line, a comma after each line but the last of the inside address and closing section, and a period at the end of the last line of each of these sections (Fig. 4). This style of punctuation, which is still in use in a few government offices, is seldom, if ever, seen in the business office.

BASIC PARTS OF THE BUSINESS LETTER

The discussion of letter placement and form can best be begun by identifying those elements which are usually found in every business letter. These parts have been labeled in Fig. 1.

PURPOSE OF EACH ELEMENT

Each of the elements of a business letter performs a definite function. The letterhead, for example, serves to identify the company transmitting the communication. The date usually indicates the day on which the letter

Date	January 20, 19—
Inside address	The Modern Book Store 200 Beechwright Road Waco, Texas 76703
Salutation	Gentlemen
	The publication THE CROWN AND THE CROSS, about which you inquired in your letter of January 12, is out of stock indefinitely.
Body	I have enclosed a return authorization for the ten #602z RAINBOW BIBLES. After we receive these volumes from you, we will send you a replacement order of ten #603 Bibles and a credit adjustment.
	Thank you very much for your cooperation. We are very glad to be of service to you.
Complimentary close	Sincerely yours
Company name	THE WORLD PUBLISHING COMPANY
Signature	
Typed signature Title	Howard J. Miller Trade Sales Manager
Reference initials Enclosure line	HJM:dh Enclosure
Carbon-copy notation	cc: Leonard Hathaway

FIG. 1. Full, or extreme, block style, with open punctuation. In this style all lines begin flush with the left margin. When open punctuation is used, the colon after the salutation and the comma after the complimentary close are omitted.

WORLD PUBLISHING
TIMES MIRROR

April 24, 19--

Mr. Fred Lane, Manager
Lawrence Book Shop
180 Fifth Avenue
New York, N. Y.   10010

Dear Mr. Lane:

Subject: Promotion of BENNY'S FLAG

Your order for 250 copies of BENNY'S FLAG has been entered
for processing, and it will be shipped according to your instructions.

We will be happy to cooperate in your promotion on this
title on a 50-50 basis up to a total of 10 per cent of the
net price of this order. This is our standard promotional
allowance, and we hope that it will be acceptable to you.

Thank you for your continued interest in the promotion
of our titles.

Sincerely yours,

Howard J. Miller
Trade Sales Manager

HJM:dh

cc: W. Taylor

2080 WEST 117TH STREET, CLEVELAND, OHIO 44111, TELEPHONE: (216) 941-6930, CABLES: "WORLDPUB"

FIG. 2.   Semiblock style, with standard punctuation and subject line. The essential features of the semiblock style are the blocked inside address; the blocked
closing section, each line of which starts at the center of the sheet; the five-space
indention at the beginning of each paragraph; and the position of the date line,
either ending flush with the right-hand margin or, as above, starting at the center
of the letter sheet.

WORLD PUBLISHING
TIMES MIRROR

February 9, 19--

Wright News, Incorporated
15 Main Street   File No. 2365
Utica, New York   13503

Gentlemen:

The 235 copies of No. 2711, DISCOTHEQUE DANCES, covered by
our return authorization No. 33508 were received yesterday.

Our Adjustment Department will issue a credit to cover the
return of these books; however, we are sorry to say that we
cannot accept the collect freight charges. · If you will read
your copy of the invoice for this order, you will see printed
at the bottom a statement of our policy regarding returns--
all transportation charges on returned merchandise are to be
paid by the customer.

Thank you for your continued interest in WORLD publications.
If we can be of any further service to you, please let us
know.

Very truly yours,

Howard J. Miller
Trade Sales Manager

HJM:af

cc: Mr. L. Hathaway
     Adjustment Department

2080 WEST 117TH STREET, CLEVELAND, OHIO 44111, TELEPHONE: (216) 941-6930, CABLES: "WORLDPUB"

FIG. 3.   Regular block letter, with standard punctuation and file number.
This style of letter is typed with block paragraphs. The date line may start at
the same point as the closing section, or it may be centered or typed to end
flush with the right-hand margin. The file number or notations such as "In re"
or "Re" should be placed to the right of the inside address.

WORLD PUBLISHING
TIMES MIRROR

December 7, 19--.

The Smith Public Library,
   500 Stanley Avenue,
      Miami, Florida   33106.

               Attention: Miss Mary Lane.

Gentlemen:

     As you requested in your letter of November 24, we have
checked with our Editorial Department and find that it is
not contemplating a book concerning the life or works of
IGNACE HENRI J. T. FANTIN-LATOUR, 1836-1904.

     We thank you for your interest in our company and regret
that we are unable to supply any additional information for
you.

            Yours very truly,

              THE WORLD PUBLISHING COMPANY,

                Howard J. Miller.

HJM:dh

2080 WEST 117TH STREET, CLEVELAND, OHIO 44111, TELEPHONE: (216) 941-6930, CABLES: "WORLDPUB"

FIG. 4. Indented style, with full, or close, punctuation. In this style the lines of the inside address and the closing section are each indented five spaces from the line above. In order to avoid having a long company name project into the right-hand margin, the complimentary close should be started five or more spaces to the left of the horizontal center. Note that each line of typing above and below the body of the letter ends with a punctuation mark. The last line of the inside address and the last line of the closing section end with periods, and the lines preceding these end with commas.

60

WORLD PUBLISHING

TIMES MIRROR

December 9, 19--

Johnson Wholesale Drug Company
750 Herkimer Avenue
Chicago, Illinois   60613

PRICE OF BIBLE NO. 751

Thank you for sending us your recent bulletin on World Bibles
that you mailed to your customers in the Chicago area.

In looking over this bulletin, we notice there is one Bible
that will be changed by our price increase effective January 1.
The Black Imitation Leather No. 751 will increase from $6.75
to $7.00 on that date.

You will naturally be able to buy this Bible at $6.75 until
December 31, and we will allow one stock order before February 1
of next year at the old price.

Perhaps you will want to make a price correction in a future
bulletin to your customers. Again, thank you for sending a
copy of your bulletin, and we sincerely hope it will be bene-
ficial.

HOWARD J. MILLER, Trade Sales Manager

HJM:dh

2080 WEST 117TH STREET, CLEVELAND, OHIO 44111, TELEPHONE: (216) 941-6930, CABLES: "WORLDPUB"

FIG. 5.   NOMA simplified style. The NOMA letter is typed in the full, or
extreme, block form. Note that there is no salutation and no complimentary
close. A subject line is always used, but the word "subject" is omitted. A triple
space is left above and below the subject line. The signature line is typed four
spaces below the body.

WORLD PUBLISHING
TIMES MIRROR

January 16, 19--

Dear Bookseller:

This Spring is different. The ecumenical movement, the "God is dead"
controversy, the stirrings of change in the churches, all reflect
a broad increase in religious interest. Not in decades have the
general news media given so much space to religion and the Bible.

So you can expect this year's World Bible Spring Promotion to bring you
more Bible sales than ever before.

"Because the Bible is such a special gift . . ." is the theme, attuned
to the important gift occasions of Spring---Easter, Mother's Day,
confirmation, graduation, and weddings.

You can mount your own full-scale Spring Bible promotion with these
merchandising aids, yours free for the asking:

  FULL-COLOR LECTERN DISPLAY for counter use or as a
  centerpiece for a window display.

  FULL-COLOR WINDOW BANNERS tying in with the display--
  one for your window, one for your Bible Department.

  TWO-COLOR, SIX-PAGE STATEMENT INSERT, supplied with
  your imprint, showing an assortment of best-
  selling World Bibles carefully selected for
  Spring gift occasions, from $2.95 to $17.50.

  TWO SIZES OF NEWSPAPER MATS, 2 col. x 5" and 2 col.
  x 10", for each of the three Spring gift seasons.
  World's cooperative advertising plan can pay up
  to 50 per cent of your ad cost.

Be sure to order an ample stock of World Bibles for a big Spring season.
Order forms for both Bibles and promotion materials are enclosed.

    Very truly yours,

    Howard J. Miller
    Trade Sales Manager

HJM/dh
Enc.

2080 WEST 117TH STREET, CLEVELAND, OHIO 44111, TELEPHONE: (216) 941-6930, CABLES: "WORLDPUB"

FIG. 6. Hanging indentation, or inverted-paragraph, style. This style, mainly
used for advertising letters, is the reverse of the indented style shown in Fig. 2;
that is, the first line of each paragraph is typed starting at the left margin, and
the remaining lines are uniformly indented.

was dictated, which is frequently of significance in transactions of a contractual nature and of great help in chronological filing. The salutation is a polite way of saying "Hello." The body of the letter contains the message the writer desires to convey. "Good-by" is expressed in such phrases as "Very truly yours," and "Sincerely yours."

LETTERHEAD

The term "letterhead" is frequently used to refer to both the printed heading and the paper on which the printed heading appears. In the following discussion the word "letterhead" refers to the printed heading, and "letterhead paper" refers to the paper on which the printed heading appears.

In order to reply to a letter it is necessary to know the name and address of the sender. In business correspondence this important information usually appears as part of the letterhead. Frequently the letterhead also contains the names of the most important officers in the concern, such as the president, vice-president, and treasurer. Sometimes a list of the sponsors of an organization or a list of products manufactured by the company is printed down the left-hand side of the letterhead paper.

Letterheads are usually from 1½ to 2 inches in depth; some are slightly deeper.

Should you find it necessary to write a personal business letter on plain paper, type your name and address above the date line.

DATE

Every business communication should be dated. The date to use in transcribing a business letter sometimes presents a problem for the secretary, because she may be given the dictation one day and not type it until the following day. Under such circumstances, unless otherwise instructed, the secretary should use the date on which the letter was dictated. This obviates the necessity for changing such expressions as "this morning" and "yesterday" to "yesterday morning" and "day before yesterday."

Form. The order in which the date is usually typed is month, day, year: February 28, 1968. In this form, the month is spelled out, and the day is always followed by a comma. It is now accepted in many offices that the month may be abbreviated. Such endings as "st," "d," "nd," and "rd," after the day, should not be used. In military and some government offices, the following style is used: 6 April 1968, or 6 Apr. 1968. It is desirable practice to avoid abbreviating in business letters, but if abbreviations are preferred by the executive, use the first three letters of each month, except June, which is rarely abbreviated.

Vertical placement. Generally the date should be typed 14 spaces down from the top of the sheet or a double space below the last line of the letterhead, whichever is lower. After typing the date a few times with this spacing, the typist or secretary should be able to find the correct vertical distance by judgment.

Typing the date a fixed number of spaces from the top of the letterhead paper is referred to as using a "fixed date line." Some individuals like to use a "floating date line," one that is changed according to the size of the letter. No matter which system is used, the purpose remains the same—to give the letter the appearance of a picture in a frame. In the author's experience, the fixed date line method is simpler to use.

Horizontal placement. The horizontal starting point of the date line depends on these factors: style of letter used, ease of filing, ease of typing, and pleasing appearance.

With two styles of letters, the full block and the NOMA (Figs. 1 and 5), the date must start at the left margin. With the other letter forms (Figs. 2, 3, 4, 6), the typist has a choice. If ease of filing is the major consideration, then the date line should be typed so as to end with the right-hand margin. In this position, the date is the first typed line seen when searching the files. When ease of typing is the objective, the date may begin at the same point as the closing lines of the letter, for this requires the use of but one tabular setting. With some letterheads a pleasing appearance and better balance are achieved by centering the date line or starting it some distance to the right of center.

INSIDE ADDRESS

Ordinarily included in this division of the business letter are the name of the addressee, the street address, and the city and state. Most addresses occupy three or four lines.

```
The New York Times
229 West 43 Street
New York, New York    10036

Mr. Joseph H. Uhrig
World Executives, Inc.
919 North Michigan Avenue
Chicago, Illinois    60611
```

No address should occupy less than three lines. If an individual or a company has no street address, make a three-line address by typing the city and state on separate lines.

                    Mr. James Harmon
                    Monterey
                    Massachusetts 01245

Position. The first line of the inside address is typed from four to eight lines below the date line, depending upon the length of the letter. The address is usually placed before the salutation. However, when writing a personal letter, a formal letter to a public official or other honored person, or a letter of appreciation, sympathy, or congratulations, place the inside address a double space below the typed signature and flush with the left margin.

Form. In most instances the block form is used; that is, each line of the inside address is typed starting at the left margin. When the indented style of letter is used, the first line starts at the left margin, and each succeeding line is indented five spaces from the line above (Fig. 4).

Names of individuals. Be sure to type the name of the addressee exactly as he spells it. Nothing is more annoying to an individual than to see his name misspelled. If his first name is Lewis, do not spell it "Louis." Always type a courtesy title, such as Mr., Mrs., Miss, Professor, Doctor, or Honorable, with the name.

Forms of address. For the titles to be used when addressing dignitaries, several individuals, and so forth, see Appendix 5.

Titles of office. A title of office, such as President or Secretary, follows the name of the addressee. It should be placed in a position that will help keep the lines of the inside address as even in length as possible. Therefore it may appear on the same line as the name of the addressee, on a line by itself, or on the same line as the company name.

              Mr. W. D. Haskell, Sales Manager
              The Black-Clawson Company, Inc.

                 Mr. M. C. Gravely, Jr.
                 Executive Vice-President
                 Briston Corporation

              Mr. Bartholomew J. Anderson
              Manager, The Johnson Hotel

Company names. As with individual names, spell company names just as they appear on the stationery. If a name appears with a hyphen, even though it may appear incorrect to you, type it that way; for example, New-York Historical Society. If an individual uses Jr. in his signature, be sure not to omit the Jr.

Include the word "The" only if it is part of the corporate name; for example, The World Publishing Company. When words such as "Company" and "Incorporated" are abbreviated, as in James C. Sinnigen & Co., Inc., you should use the same abbreviations in your letters.

Departments and divisions. When addressing a letter to a particular department or division, type the name of the company first, for it is more important, especially for filing purposes.

Federal Savings Association
Mortgage Division

Street address. The following rules should be observed in typing the street address:

If you are requested to address mail to a post-office box number, do not use a street address, for the mail will be delivered to the box number.

Use figures for the house, apartment, and room numbers. The word "number" or its abbreviations, No. and #, are never used before such figures.

450 Third Avenue   Apartment 3b   Room 1304

Write out street names that consist of numbers below ten and use figures for those of ten and above.

350 Fifth Avenue   425 West 72d Street
330 East 10th Street

Some firms omit the endings "st," "d," "nd," "rd," and "th" after the street number, because it is more legible without these endings.

918 East 47 Street   One West 22 Street

Always spell out the words "East," "West," "North," "South," "Northeast," and so forth, when they appear in street addresses, but initials representing sections of the city are abbreviated.

520 East 35 Street   346 South 32d Street, N.W.

Leave a space before and after a hyphen used to separate a house number from a street number.

25 - 36th Street

City and state. Always type the city and state in full, unless there is a strong reason for abbreviating. The word "Saint" is an exception to the rule and may be abbreviated, as in St. Louis. District of Columbia is also abbreviated, as D.C.

Names of foreign countries are spelled in full, with the exception of U.S.S.R. (Union of Soviet Socialist Republics).

ZIP numbers. ZIP numbers pinpoint the mailing address, thus speeding letters to their destination in record time. The number consists of five digits and is placed three spaces after the state name, with no punctuation after the state name.

```
Flushing, New York    11365
```

In some instances, in order to keep all the lines of the inside address as nearly equal in length as possible, it may be necessary to abbreviate the state name.

```
Mr. R. T. Colton
Personnel Director
James Hart & Company
Boston, MA    02115
```

SALUTATION

The salutation is placed underneath the inside address, preceded and followed by one blank line. It is always typed starting at the left margin.

In the NOMA style of letter, the salutation is omitted, and a subject line is used in its place (Fig. 5).

When a letter is addressed to a business firm, the salutation is "Gentlemen."

Degrees of formality. In addressing a business letter to an individual, four degrees of formality are recognized:

1. *Least formal:* Dear Mr. Stark, Dear Mrs. Randolph, Dear Miss Clark
2. *More formal:* My dear Mr. Frank, My dear Miss Tate, My dear Professor Saidel
3. *Formal:* Dear Sir, Dear Madam
4. *Very formal:* Sir, Madam

The very formal salutation is used in writing letters to government officials and other dignitaries.

Forms of salutation. For the forms of salutation to use in addressing church and government dignitaries, lawyers, doctors, partnerships, firms consisting solely of women, and so forth, see Appendix 5.

Capitalization. Capitalize the first word, the title, and any noun in the salutation: Dear Mr. Black, My dear Professor Clark, Dear Doctor Morgan.

Abbreviations. Mr., Ms., Mrs., Messrs., and Mmes. are abbreviated. Write out other titles, such as Captain, Professor, and Ambassador.

BODY OF THE LETTER

That part of the letter containing the message is known as the "body." It is typed a double space below the salutation. The paragraphs should be blocked or indented in accordance with the style of letter used. The paragraphs are single-spaced, except for very short letters, those of 50 words or less, which are double-spaced.

Whether the lines are single- or double-spaced, use only double spacing between paragraphs.

There is one style, effectively used in advertising letters, in which the first line of each paragraph starts at the margin and the remaining lines are indented five spaces. This is the inverted, or hanging, indentation style (Fig. 6).

For the sake of appearance and emphasis, try to use short paragraphs, particularly the opening and closing ones.

COMPLIMENTARY CLOSE

The "good-by" of the business letter is known as the "complimentary close."

Vertical placement. Like the date line, the complimentary close may appear in different positions—flush with the left margin (extreme block, or NOMA style), starting at the center or to the right of center (regular block and semiblock styles), or, when necessary, starting about five spaces to the left of center (indented style). These varied horizontal positions of the complimentary close may be seen in the illustrations of the various styles of letters.

Degrees of formality. As with the salutation, there are also degrees of formality recognized in complimentary closings.

1. *Formal:* This is the impersonal closing used frequently when addressing business letters to firms: Yours truly, Yours very truly, Very truly yours.

2. *More formal:* This is the type of closing used in writing for a favor

or writing to a dignitary: Respectfully yours, Yours respectfully, Very respectfully yours, Yours very respectfully.

3. *Less formal* and more personal in tone: Sincerely yours, Yours sincerely, Very sincerely yours, Very cordially yours, Yours very sincerely, Yours very cordially.

Punctuation. A comma follows the complimentary close, except when the open style of punctuation is used.

Capitalization. Only the first word of the complimentary close is capitalized.

TYPED SIGNATURE

It is customary in most business letters to type the name of the dictator or the person responsible for the letter.

Vertical placement. In many business letters this signature appears on the fourth line below the complimentary close. The penned signature is placed in the intervening space. If the dictator's handwriting is unusually large, the signature should be typed on the fifth or sixth line below the complimentary close.

Horizontal placement. Start typing the signature directly under the first letter of the complimentary close. In the indented style the typed signature starts five spaces to the right of this position.

Title. A title usually appears with the typed signature. If it is short, it may be typed on the same line with the typed signature, which is followed by a comma.

Yours very truly,

Clarence Brown, Manager

Longer titles are placed on the following line.

Very truly yours,

Albert Storch
Director of Research

When the individual signing the letter has no title, the word "By" may be used, followed by a solid line, on which the dictator signs his name.

Yours truly,

By_____
                Peter Small

Company name. When the name of the company appears as part of the signature, it is typed in all caps a double space below the complimentary close, and the signature is typed four spaces below it.

Yours truly,

YUMA CHAMBER OF COMMERCE

C. R. Spensley
President

Some firms desire the firm name to appear in the signature section, because they believe that it fixes legal responsibility on the company, rather than on the individual signing the letter, especially on formal or contractual letters. Other firms prefer to omit the firm name, because it already appears on the letterhead.

Division or department. Frequently a division or department is used in the closing lines of a letter; it is typed below the typed signature and title.

Very truly yours,

R. M. Brown, Supervisor
Plastics Division

Courtesy titles. A courtesy title is never used by a man before his pen-written or typed signature. Unless the recipient knows the marital status of a woman signing a business letter, it is customary for her to indicate such status by using "Miss" or "Mrs." before her typed signature.

Loretta Simpson

Miss Loretta Simpson

Francine Booth

Mrs. Francine Booth

If she prefers to be addressed by her husband's given name and initial, the form is the following:

Francine Booth

Mrs. Paul A. Booth

Instead of the above forms, it is also permissible to write "Miss" or "Mrs." in parentheses preceding the pen-written signature.

(Miss) Loretta Simpson

Loretta Simpson

(Mrs.) Francine Booth

Francine Booth

A divorced woman may sign her name in any of the following three ways:
1. She may use her given and maiden names and her former husband's.

Sandra Paley Appleton

Mrs. Sandra Paley Appleton

2. She may use her maiden name and her former husband's last name.

Sandra Paley Appleton

Mrs. Paley Appleton

3. She may use her maiden name, if she has resumed it, in which case she may use "Miss" in either of the two forms described above.

In recent years the use of Ms. in place of Miss or Mrs. has become increasingly popular and its general acceptance seems to be assured. The same rules that apply to the use of the title Mr. would apply to Ms.

Signature for the employer. If, as a secretary, you are required to sign a letter for your employer, use the following style:

Myra Lane

Secretary to Mr. Clarke

When the individual signing a letter for another person is not his secretary, use this form:

Gilda Thompson

For Mr. Clarke

When one individual signs for another in an official capacity, "By" is sometimes used.

Thomas M. Clancy, President

By_____
                    Milton Trout
                    General Manager

Signing someone else's name. When signing someone else's name, it is not necessary to write "Per" or "By." Simply sign the individual's name and then use your initials.

Sam Smith tm

Sam Smith, General Manager

Identifying initials. All typed business letters should contain identifying initials in order to fix responsibility. The simplest form to use is solid caps for both the dictator's and typist's initials, with a colon separating them.

BTS:RM

The secretary or typist never uses more than two of her initials. Other forms that are equally acceptable are:

```
BTS:rm   bts:rm            BTS  B. T. Sholes  BTS-4
BTS/RM   BTS/rm  bts/rm    RT   RT
```

In order to save time, some businessmen request that only the initials of the typist appear on the stationery, because the dictator is already identified through his pen-written and typed signatures. Others prefer to have the full name typed in place of their initials.

Yours truly,

President

Charles Brown/rt

You will recall that in formal letters to honored persons, personal letters, and letters of appreciation, sympathy, and congratulations, the inside address is placed a double space below the typed signature. Initials do not appear on the original of these letters but should be typed on the carbon copy used for filing.

Authorship of letter. Ordinarily the first set of initials indicate the author and signer of the letter. If the secretary composes the letter for the signature of the executive who is to sign it, her responsibility as the author of the letter may be indicated by the use of her initials only.

Very truly yours,

John Payne, General Manager

rt

When she is charged with composing, typing, and signing a letter, the secretary may also use her initials only.

Another device sometimes used to indicate that the secretary composed a letter for the employer's signature is to transpose the two sets of initials.

                              Very sincerely yours,

                              William Slaughter
                              President

        rt/ws

OCCASIONAL ELEMENTS IN BUSINESS LETTERS

ATTENTION LINE

In most business firms a letter addressed to a particular individual is considered personal and is delivered to him unopened. Should such mail arrive while the addressee is away from the office, it remains unopened until his return. Therefore, in order to avoid any delay when writing to a particular person whom you know to be capable of handling a specific matter, the wisest procedure is to address it to the company but to bring it to the attention of the individual involved. This is best accomplished by means of an "attention line," which appears as part of the inside address as well as on the envelope. The fact that such a letter has been addressed to the attention of a particular person indicates to the receiver or to the mailing department that the letter in the sealed envelope concerns company business. Such a letter will be opened by the employee of the company who has been designated to act for the addressee, should he be on vacation, away on a business trip, ill at home, or no longer associated with the concern.

Vertical placement. Since it is part of the inside address, the attention line is placed in proximity to this portion of the letter. The preferred vertical position is a double space below the inside address and a double space above the salutation.

        The Dawson Excavating Company
        11748 East 120th Street
        Philadelphia, PA   19104

        Attention Mr. Philip Barnes

        Gentlemen:

Because the letter is addressed to a company, the salutation used is "Gentlemen."

Horizontal placement. For ease of typing, the most practical position for the salutation is flush with the left margin. Some firms prefer to have this line centered, because it makes for better appearance and draws attention more quickly. The attention line may also be indented five spaces from the left margin.

Form. Any one of the following forms is acceptable:

```
Attention: Mr. John Little, General Manager
Attention: Mr. John Little, General Manager
Attention: Mr. John Little, General Manager
Attention of Mr. John Little, General Manager
ATTENTION: Mr. John Little, General Manager
ATTENTION OF MR. JOHN LITTLE, GENERAL MANAGER
```

It is now considered unnecessary to use the word "of" after "Attention." In fact, some persons go so far as to say that even the word "Attention" should be omitted, because the name placed in the position described above is sufficient to indicate that it is being brought to a particular person's attention. However, in cases of this sort, it is wise to heed Alexander Pope's sage advice:

> Be not the first by whom the new are tried,
> Nor yet the last to lay the old aside.

At present, therefore, you will be on the safe side if you decide on any one of the above forms.

SUBJECT LINE

The subject line informs the recipient at a glance of the nature of the contents of the letter. For the reader, this facilitates his referring to other correspondence on the same subject; for the writer, it means eliminating the writing of an opening sentence to explain the subject of the letter; and for both the reader and the writer, it facilitates the filing of the letter.

Vertical position. Because the subject line informs the reader of the nature of the contents of the body of the letter, it is placed in proximity to this section. The most commonly used position is between the salutation and the body, one blank line being left before and after the subject line.

Horizontal position. With most styles of letter the subject line may be typed starting at the left margin, centered, or indented five spaces. If the extreme, or full-block, letter is used, this line also must be blocked.

Form. Use any of the following forms:

```
Subject:   Employee Upgrading
Subject:   Employee Upgrading
Subject:   Employee Upgrading
Subject:   Employee Upgrading
SUBJECT:   EMPLOYEE UPGRADING
SUBJECT:   EMPLOYEE UPGRADING
```

Re and In re. Instead of the word "Subject," some companies prefer to use the Latin word, *"Re"* or *"In re."* Other companies use both "Subject" and *"In re,"* reserving the latter for use with policy, mortgage, and other types of numbers. When both a subject line and reference number appear in the same letter, *"Re"* or *"In re"* is placed on the right-hand side of the letter about on the same level as the inside address.

File or reference number. These words followed by a number may be placed in the position described above under *Re and In re.* In the extreme, or full-block, form of letter, they are typed starting at the left margin.

Subject line in the NOMA letter. In this style of letter, the subject line is typed in the position usually occupied by the salutation, and the word "Subject" is omitted. This is in accord with the idea that the position of the subject and attention lines is sufficient to indicate their purpose.

ENCLOSURE NOTATION

Whenever an item, such as a check, a contract, or a postcard, is to be enclosed with a letter to be mailed, this fact is noted on the letter by typing any one of the following notations one or two lines below the reference initials:

```
Enclosure     Enc.      Encl.
```

While the abbreviations shown are not preferred, they are in common use because of their timesaving nature.

The purpose of the enclosure notation is to remind both the sender, who may be a third person, not directly involved in either the dictation or transcription of the original letter, and the recipient that something in addition to the letter is enclosed in the envelope. Without this warning signal there exists a greater possibility of failing to make the required insertion or of discarding the envelope before the entire contents are removed.

When more than one item is enclosed, the following forms of notation may be used:

```
Enclosures  2
Enclosures:  (3)
Enclosures--3
3 Encls.
2 Enc.
Enc. 4
```

Important enclosures are enumerated.

```
Enclosures:              Enclosures:
  Check                    1. Check
  Contract                 2. Contract
```

CARBON-COPY NOTATION

When carbon copies are being sent to persons other than the addressee of the letter, a notation to this effect is placed two spaces below the identifying initials or below the enclosure notation, if there is one. Any one of the following styles may be used:

```
cc H. R. Leonard

CC H. R. Leonard
   P. T. Bryant

cc--Fisher

c.c. Stone
     Bryant

CC: Mr. K. C. Fisher

cc to A. T. Kane
```

Blind carbon copies. There are instances when it is deemed wise to send a carbon copy of a letter to a second person and to omit any indication of this on the original letter. Such notations are usually placed at the top-left corner of the file copy. This position makes it immediately apparent that the notation did not appear on the original. A further distinction is now frequently made by using the letters "bcc." These may be typed in any of the styles mentioned in conjunction with the typing of the regular carbon-copy notations.

To type a BCC notation, simply remove the original letter and the first carbon, reinsert the carbon pack, and type the notation, starting at the left margin and about one inch from the top of the page.

POSTSCRIPTS

Postscripts, as afterthoughts, are unnecessary in business-letter writing. Should the dictator forget to include a thought, he can simply dictate the missing paragraph and request his secretary to insert it at the appropriate place before she begins transcribing.

However, the postscript is often used in the business letter for the purpose of emphasis or sales effect. Important facts are given prominence by using them as a postscript, which is typed a double space below the last notation in the letter. If the paragraphs of the letter are indented, the postscript is likewise indented; if they are blocked, so is the postscript.

The letters "PS" may be used in any one of the various forms shown, or they may be omitted.

P. S.   P.S.   PS.   PS: PS--

A typical postscript will look like this:

```
JPS:nt
Enclosures

P.S.  Since you may also be interested in John-
son's training and supervisory development
services, I am enclosing an inquiry card that
briefly describes them.
```

Post-postscripts. Should it become necessary to add a second postscript, use the letters "PPS" in any of the approved postscript styles shown above, leaving a double space after the last paragraph of the first postscript.

MAILING NOTATIONS

When letters are sent by other than regular mail, questions frequently arise regarding their delivery; therefore notations on the letters themselves are of considerable help in tracing them or in determining delivery dates. These notations should be typed in all caps below the last typed line of the letter. If so preferred, they may appear on the carbon copies only.

```
AIR MAIL     REGISTERED     SPECIAL DELIVERY
             BY MESSENGER
```

LETTERS OVER ONE PAGE

Should additional pages of a letter become separated from the first page in the files or elsewhere, it may be difficult and time-consuming to match them. Therefore it is important that an appropriate heading be typed on succeeding sheets. For these pages it is customary to use plain bond paper of the same quality as the letterhead sheet. The margins should conform to those of the first page, and the heading should start six spaces from the top edge (1 inch). The first line of the second page should start on the fourth line below the heading.

Heading. This consists of the name of the addressee, "page 2," and the date.

Styles. The style to be used depends on the objective in mind. If ease of typing is the prime objective, the following style may be used:

```
Mr. Frank T. Ryan, October 30, 19--, page 2
```

If ease of filing and finding is the objective, then type the heading at the right-hand margin in the following style:

```
                                    Mr. Frank T. Ryan
                                    Page 2
                                    Date
```

If ease of collating is the objective, type the lines of the heading one under the other, starting at the left-hand margin:

```
Mr. Frank T. Ryan
Page 2
Date
```

Continuation of letter. Start the first line of the continued page four spaces below the heading. Try to start the page with a new paragraph. If this is impracticable, end the first page with at least two lines of a new paragraph and carry over at least two lines to the next page.

Division of the last word on the first page is forbidden, for invariably the reader is forced to return his gaze to the first page to recall the beginning of the hyphenated word.

If you are aware that you are going to use two or more pages for a letter, be sure to make a very light pencil mark about one inch from the bottom of the page and to stop typing when you reach this point. If your typewriter is equipped with a line meter that tells you how many typing lines you have left or how much space in inches is left, use this device to warn you to stop at least one inch from the bottom.

COPIES

Second sheets with the word "COPY" printed on them are used to identify copies of letters and other material that are mailed from the office. When a sheet used for making a copy does not contain this word, it should be typed in all caps near the top of the sheet. Some copying machines make such perfect replicas of typewritten and printed material that it becomes extremely important that they, too, be labeled as copies.

TYPING ENVELOPES

The post office prefers that envelopes be typed in indented style (Fig. 7), but the rule commonly followed in business offices is to use the same style in typing the envelope as is used in typing the inside address of the letter. Double spacing is also preferred by the post office, but the rule generally followed is to double-space three-line addresses and to single-space addresses of four or more lines.

Never use a two-line address on an envelope. If no street address is used, place the city or town and the state on separate lines.

The first line of the address should appear centered and should start just below the vertical center of the envelope. On a small envelope (No. 6¾) start approximately twelve lines from the top, and on the large envelope (No. 10) start about fourteen lines from the top. These distances should, of course, be approximated by eye.

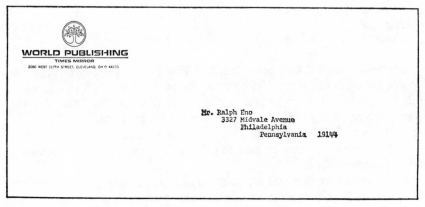

WORLD PUBLISHING
TIMES MIRROR
2080 WEST 117TH STREET, CLEVELAND, OHIO 44111

Mr. Ralph Eno
3327 Midvale Avenue
Philadelphia
Pennsylvania   19144

FIG. 7.   Envelope addressed in indented style.

Should the typing of the city, state name, and ZIP number on one line bring you close to the edge of the envelope, place the state and ZIP number on a separate line.

Mailing directions such as "AIR MAIL," "SPECIAL DELIVERY," or "REGIS-TERED" are typed beneath the position for the stamp. Other notations such as "HOLD FOR ARRIVAL," "PLEASE FORWARD," "CARE OF," and "PER-SONAL" are typed in the lower left-hand corner. Start such notations two or three lines below the last line of the address and about four to six spaces from the left edge of the envelope. The attention line or the name of the division of a company, such as "Mortgage Division," is also placed in the lower left-hand corner.

SPACING USED WITH PUNCTUATION MARKS

Period. Space twice after a period at the end of a sentence, once after the period following an abbreviation.

Comma. Space once after a comma.

Question mark. Space twice after a question mark at the end of a sentence, once after a question mark within a sentence.

Exclamation point. Two spaces are left after an exclamation point at the end of a sentence and one space if the exclamation point occurs within a sentence.

Semicolon. Space once after a semicolon.

Colon. Space twice after a colon. However, no space is used in expressions of time, such as 7:25.

In expressing proportions by the use of a colon, space once before and after the colon (4 : 1).

Quotation marks. No space is left between the quotation marks and the material they enclose. When typing a list or quoting lines of poetry, leave the first quotation mark to the left of all the items or lines, so that the first words line up at the left.

Double quotation marks. For a quotation within a quotation, single quotation marks are used. No space is left between the single and double quotation marks.

Parentheses. If the material in parentheses falls within a sentence, leave one space *before* the opening parenthesis mark, two spaces when the material in parentheses follows a sentence, and no space *after* the opening parenthesis. The closing parenthesis mark requires no space before it, one space after it when the material in parentheses falls within a sentence, and two spaces when the material in parentheses constitutes a complete sentence and is followed by another sentence.

Apostrophe. No space is left after an apostrophe within a word; one space is left after an apostrophe at the end of a word within a sentence.

Asterisk. The asterisk, used to refer a reader to a footnote, is typed immediately after a word or a punctuation mark with no space before it. In the footnote, one space is left after the asterisk.

Diagonal. No space precedes or follows the diagonal.

Dash. No space is used before or after a dash made up of two hyphens. The dash should never be used at the beginning of a line.

For rules on the use of punctuation in writing, see Chapter 18.

Chapter 7

Business Letters
Composed by the Secretary

A. E. KLEIN

A MARK of a good secretary is her ability to free the executive of routine tasks so that he can devote his energies to creative work. One of these onerous tasks is the answering of routine correspondence. The purpose of this chapter is to help you to develop the techniques that will enable you to handle this phase of secretarial work confidently and competently.

MAIN PRINCIPLES

There are essentially two broad categories of business letters—letters of inquiry, or "asking" letters, and letters of response, or "answering" letters. No matter which type you are called upon to write, the following guiding principles will simplify your task.

LENGTH

Use only those words which will help you to say what you need to say clearly and straightforwardly. An 8½ × 11-inch letterhead may invite the writer to fill the sheet. Beware of the temptation. A quarter- or half-filled blank sheet need not be displeasing to the eye. To make the short letter attractive, simply use wide margins and double spacing.

If you pad your message by repeating yourself or using superfluous words, you are wasting precious time—your time in composing the letter and the recipient's in reading it. It may be trite to say that time is money, but the saying is very true of business-letter writing. Few people realize that every business letter mailed today costs over $2. From this standpoint it becomes important to the business director to see that correspondence costs are kept to a minimum. Keeping business letters and interoffice correspondence brief will aid immensely in achieving this goal.

Blaise Pascal, the famous French mathematician, physicist, and philosopher, apologized for writing a long letter, saying that he *did not have time to write a shorter one.* Writing a brief letter takes careful planning.

Here are a few tips that will help you to keep your letters as brief as possible.

Do not repeat the information contained in the letter you are answering. This is a common weakness in business-letter writing, as illustrated in the following example: "This will acknowledge receipt of your letter of January 5, in which you state that you wish to purchase a Scott amplifier, a Scott tuner, two Wharfedale speakers, and a Garrard record changer, as advertised in yesterday's *Times.*"

The writer of the original letter remembers what he ordered. All that is needed, therefore, is to identify his order in the briefest manner possible. In this case it would be enough to say, "Thank you for your order for the stereo high-fidelity set we advertised in the Sunday *Times,*" and then continue with your reply. In other words, simply indicate in your identification of the sender's letter that you understand his aims and questions.

Another form of repetition is to quote or paraphrase an earlier letter to which the writer is referring. The recipient will, no doubt, refer to his files for the original anyway. All you need do in making such reference is to write, "Please refer to our letter dated March 5."

Avoid using phrases when a single word will serve the same function. Many such phrases used regularly add-up to a large number of unnecessary words.

Phrase	Single word
in order to	to
in reference to	about
in the amount of	for, of
in a number of cases	some
in view of	because
with regard to	about, in

Avoid the use of adjectives and nouns that are formed from verbs. For instance, using nouns such as "adjustment" and "replacement" requires the use of verbs. If, instead, you use the verbs "adjust" and "replace," you can eliminate the use of additional words and make your writing more vivid and alive. Note the following:

Noun form	Verb form
We *made an adjustment on* our books.	We *adjusted* our books.
We are sorry that we cannot *make a replacement of* . . .	We are sorry that we cannot *replace* . . .

Notice that in each case one verb replaces four words. Using the verb form instead of the noun form can result in a saving of three words. Over a period of several months the saving in time and space can be considerable.

Be on the lookout for unnecessary adjectives and adverbs. Some writers tend to sprinkle them generously throughout their letters, in the mistaken belief that such words improve their style. Actually they distract the reader and make it harder for him to see the point of the letter.

Here is a typical example, in which the superfluous adjectives appear in italics: "You will be *very much* interested to know that the *exceedingly large* number of reservations we are now making indicates that there is *very* likely to be an *extremely large* shortage of safe-deposit boxes because of the *great* additional demand which will come with the *grand* opening of the London Guarantee Building."

SIMPLICITY AND CLARITY

Make it as easy as possible for the reader to grasp quickly the thought of your letter by using short words, sentences, and paragraphs. For clarity keep closely related parts of your sentences together and place the sentences and paragraphs in an order that will enable the reader to follow your thoughts without getting lost.

THE HUMAN TOUCH

Make your letters sound personal. Instead of saying, "It is with regret that the Personnel Department must inform you that the above-mentioned party is no longer in the employ of the Jackson Manufacturing Company," you can infuse warmth into this fact by writing, "We are sorry to tell you, Mr. Jones, that Frank Bigelow is no longer with us. He left our company about a month ago and is now sales manager for Riley and Sons." Put flesh on bare-boned facts by using names and personal pronouns.

CONCRETENESS

Avoid using abstract words and making generalized statements. We think in terms of the sights and sounds experienced in our daily lives. Use names of objects and verbs of action instead of abstract nouns and verbs in the passive form. Instead of stating, "Mr. Smith's background and experience qualify him for the position," use concrete words that will conjure up in the reader's imagination a picture of Mr. Smith's experience:

```
    Mr. Smith was formerly assistant manager in
charge of production for the Johnson Bakelite
```

Company and is now manager of production for Clark
and Sons. He tells me that the men at the factory
are perfectly happy and that their working conditions are excellent. All machines at the factory
now have improved guards, so that it is practically
impossible for anyone to get hurt. The men have
two rest periods a day, and the pay rate is the
highest in the nation. Since he has taken charge,
production has tripled. From what I have seen, I
would say that Mr. Smith is doing a splendid job.

Use strong, active verbs in place of weak, passive ones. Instead of "The report *was written* by Mrs. Lane," say, "Mrs. Lane *wrote* the report."

NATURAL TONE

The moment some people put pen to paper, they are transformed. Their best friends would never associate them with their business letters. They sound hard, cold, and unnatural. The following is typical of the letters they write: "Referring to your letter of March 5, in regard to the matter of the shipment of goods via the Erie Railroad, I beg to advise you that the goods were shipped as requested."

By employing a natural, unaffected form of expression and judiciously using personal pronouns, the writer can achieve a warm, personal tone.

I am very sorry to hear that you failed to
receive the caps you ordered on February 25.
We shipped them the day after your letter
arrived, and you should have received them by
March 1 at the latest.
I am sending a tracer after them, and as soon
as I have word from the railroad company, I will
let you know what happened.
In the meantime, I am rushing a replacement
order to you, which you should receive in a day or
two. Should the original order arrive in the meantime, please return the replacement at our expense.
We are sorry about this delay and assure you
that we will do everything in our power to see
that this does not happen again.

Being yourself does not mean writing exactly as you talk. In our everyday conversation we tend to ramble, to repeat ourselves, and to use colloquialisms frequently. Also, in conversation we can be questioned directly concerning any unclear or ambiguous statements we make. In writing letters we must choose our words carefully, so as to avoid repetition, and we must arrange our thoughts so that they develop in an orderly fashion. Nevertheless, the expression and development of our ideas should sound natural and give the impression of informal speech.

PLANNING THE REPLY

Much time and effort are wasted by plunging in to answer a letter without any thought or plan. By keeping in mind the aphorism, "Plan your work; then work your plan," you can avoid such waste. If you will follow these few simple steps, you will eliminate the numerous false starts so typical of letter-writing beginners:

1. Read quickly the letter to be answered to get the gist.
2. Go back and underscore what you feel are the most important points.
3. Make an outline of the main points you wish to cover in your answer.
4. When necessary, gather the information you need to cover the points listed in 3.
5. Compose your answer and check to see that you have included the points in step 3.

Assume that you are employed as secretary for a book club and that the following letter of complaint was received:

Gentlemen:

If you will consult your records, you will see that I have already paid for the October selection. This has happened on two occasions recently, and I can see no reason for having to take my valuable time to write letters concerning charges for books for which I have already paid. From now on I would be very much obliged if you would check my account carefully to see that I am no longer annoyed with dunning letters for books already paid for.

Enclosed is my check for the November selection. Please credit my account accordingly.

Yours truly,

Applying the five steps, you would proceed as follows to answer this letter:

1. Read the letter quickly to get the gist. In this case it is the customer's annoyance at receiving invoices for books for which he has paid.
2. Underscore the important points. The words to be underscored are "already paid for the October selection" and "happened twice before."

3. Outline the main points to be covered in your answer:
   a. thanks for present payment
   b. expression of regret over the error
   c. reason for mistake: changeover from manual to automated record keeping and resulting confusion
   d. assurance that such errors will not happen again
   e. extra dividend due to savings from changeover
4. Check customer's account.
5. Compose your reply.

Your reply might then appear as follows:

Dear Mr. Wright:

    Thank you for your remittance of $2.50 for the book we shipped you on November 5. It has been credited to your account.

    Please accept our apology for the $2.50 invoice enclosed with your November book. This invoice and the duplicate invoices for August and September were sent to you and several other subscribers because of a radical change in our accounting methods. We have just completed the switch from manual to machine accounting, and I assure you that from now on you will not be billed twice for the same selection. I am sure you will understand that during such a period of rapid changeover mistakes are bound to occur.

    You will be glad to hear that, because of the savings resulting from the use of the new equipment, we are giving our subscribers an extra dividend. Enclosed is a list of books from which you may make a selection.

    Many thanks for your patience and loyalty to our Club during this most trying and hectic period.

                   Very sincerely yours,

PLANNING THE ORIGINAL LETTER

In composing an original letter, such as a letter of inquiry or a letter requesting room reservations at a hotel, you need simply apply steps 3 and 5 of the preceding plan.

Suppose your employer asks you to write a letter requesting Mr. Paul

Trent to be a guest speaker at the next luncheon of the local Chamber of Commerce. He would, of course, furnish you with all the essential details, such as the time, date, and place of the meeting; the nature of the audience to be addressed; and the nature of the talk. You would most likely proceed in this fashion:

1. List all the points to be covered:
   a. Give description of the meeting.
   b. Request Mr. Trent to be the guest speaker.
   c. Give time, date, and place of the meeting and topic.
   d. Request a reply to be received no later than one week after receipt of the letter.
2. Compose the letter, making sure you cover all the points listed in step 1.

WRITING STYLE

Do not use words and phrases that some employers believe are typical of the business world. Time-worn phrases such as "we beg to advise you," "yours of recent date," and "in answer to your request of the 15th instant" are frowned upon by modern authorities, who tell us to write simply, naturally, and straightforwardly. The following is a letter written in typical jargon or "businessese":

Dear Sir:

We are in receipt of your esteemed favor of the 9th instant and contents duly noted. We beg to advise you that we are not in a position to do anything about the matter today but we will advise you in due course of time of contemplated further action.

We take pleasure in drawing up plans to meet your wishes in the matter and to make them complete in every detail.

Kindly advise us concerning your wishes in the matter of the doors. Do we understand you to mean that the factory is to make them of oak? We presume that this will be settled in due time but we would like you to advise us in regard to the matter as soon as possible.

Awaiting the favor of your reply, we remain

Very truly yours,

Rewritten in a natural style, this becomes:

Dear Mr. Jackson:

Your letter dated April 9 arrived too late for us to make application for the permit today. We will take care of this matter the first thing tomorrow morning and will let you know at once when the permit arrives.

Please rest assured, Mr. Jackson, that the plans we are drawing up for you will be complete in every detail.

Just one question -- is the factory making the doors of oak? As our plans are dependent upon the type of wood you will use, please let us have this information as soon as you can.

Sincerely yours,

LETTER OPENINGS

Keep the opening paragraph short. Long paragraphs tend to repel the reader, and a short paragraph is more likely to catch and hold his attention. For this reason the first paragraph should contain at most two or three short sentences that will arouse the reader's attention and influence him to read the rest of the message.

To achieve this aim, announce the theme or point of your letter at once. Should it be necessary to refer to previous correspondence, place this reference in a subordinate position. Instead of starting with "In reference to your letter of January 15, we wish to state . . .," or "We wish to acknowledge receipt of your letter of March 5 in regard to . . .," why not go straight to the point and bring in the reference, if necessary, later in the sentence or in the following sentence? For example:

We are happy to furnish you with the figures you requested in your letter of January 15.

You will be interested to learn that this morning we shipped you the goods requested in your letter of March 5 and that they will be in your hands before the end of the week.

In the first of the opening sentences above, the date could be omitted, because it serves only to maintain continuity with the previous correspondence. In the second case the recipient may desire to check his copy with the acknowledgment you are sending, and therefore he will have to refer to the proper file folder. In this case the reference date will prove helpful.

Avoid stereotyped openings. Note the drabness of this stereotyped opening: "We acknowledge receipt of your letter of April 12, in which you asked for a copy of 'Insurance for All.' We are glad to send you a copy of this booklet."

The contrast between this and an immediate announcement of the theme is obvious from the following example:

```
We gladly enclose "Insurance for All," our
popular insurance manual. In it you will find the
answers to your questions about the several types
of insurance available for the protection of your
family.
```

When the occasion demands, try to be original in using openings and, when it is appropriate, clever.

LETTER CLOSINGS

As soon as you have made your point, you should end the letter. However, do not conclude it abruptly or impolitely. Though your aim is to bring the letter to a forceful conclusion, you must accomplish this in a courteous and friendly manner. Examples of effective closings might include:

```
As soon as I have a list of the courses you
need to complete your specialization, I will send
you the letter of permission.

The plan described will, when put into ef-
fect, result in a large increase in production.
```

Avoid hackneyed endings. The entire effect of a well-written business letter can be vitiated by using a hackneyed ending. Below are several weak participial letter endings and more effective rewordings.

Weak	*More effective*
Trusting this explanation makes the matter clear to you, we are	Should you have any further questions, we shall be happy to answer them.
Thanking you for past favors, I am	I thank you for your courtesy and consideration.
Thanking you for your order, we are	May we have the opportunity of serving you again soon.

Use a question to obtain a response. If your aim is to prod the recipient to respond to your request, you can very often achieve it by using a query. For example:

> What is the earliest date you can mail me the finished manuscript?

> At what time on Wednesday, January 12, can you make the presentation of your market analysis?

Date the action you wish taken. Telling the reader that you expect a response by a given date is also an effective method of triggering action. You might say:

> It is most important that we have your reply by November 15 at the latest.

> Please remember that this saving is yours only if you place your order before May 20.

Say "no" tactfully. Use positive words even when you must refuse a request. Do not leave the reader with a bad taste in his mouth. The following graceful refusal was used to conclude a letter in which the writer had to reject a manuscript because he believed that its sale would not be large enough to warrant publication by his firm.

> Your manuscript is written in such an interesting style that I am sure you will have no difficulty in placing it elsewhere.

End definitely. End the letter in a definite manner and with singleness of purpose. Avoid offering the reader alternative courses of action. When given a choice, he frequently chooses to do nothing. Instead of saying, "Write, wire, or phone us at once," or "Please mail me a check for the full amount of our overdue bill, or send me a letter of explanation," offer him only one suggested course of action. For example:

> Wire us collect and you will have the machine in a few days.

> Please mail us a check for $55 so that we can balance your account.

FORM LETTERS AND WHEN TO USE THEM

There are occasions when the same response can be made to many inquiries or requests. In that case much time can be saved by carefully preparing a standard reply that may be simply copied or duplicated. Such a reply is known as a "form letter." Sales letters or any communications employing identical messages fall into this category.

Sometimes a reply may be such that only a portion requires a unique response. For that portion which is routine in nature, a form paragraph or paragraphs may be composed and used when the occasion demands. If a sufficient variety is available, it may be possible to answer many inquiries by choosing the appropriate form paragraphs.

The following duplicated form letter is sent to new students by a preparatory school. Only the date, inside address, and salutation need be individually typed.

```
                              (Current date)
(Inside address)

(Salutation)  Dear Mary:

     We are happy to tell you that your applica-
tion for admission to Smith School has been ac-
cepted for the Spring, 1965, Term.  This accept-
ance is subject to the receipt of satisfactory
records and references.
     Enclosed are medical and dental certificates
that are to be completed by your physician and
dentist and returned to us as soon as possible.
Will you please send us a picture of yourself
(wallet size), so that we may complete your file.
     Kindly notify your school that you are en-
rolled at Smith so that we may obtain your record.
     We look forward to learning to know you per-
sonally as a student at Smith and hope that you
will find your stay pleasant and profitable.
                         Sincerely yours,


                         John A. Brown
                         Director

mc
Enc.
```

If a more personal-looking response is desired, an automatic typewriter or typewriters may be used to duplicate the letters. All that the tender of this machine need do is type the date, inside address, and salutation. From that point the typewriter will perform the rest.

INTEROFFICE MEMORANDA

The written communications passing between offices, departments, or branches of an organization are usually transmitted in a form known as an "interoffice memorandum." This form has the advantage of dispensing with the salutation, the complimentary close, and the signature of the dictator.

The four headings most frequently found on all interoffice memoranda are *To, From, Subject,* and *Date.* Other headings, such as *File* or *Reference No.,* may be added as needed. In firms where such memoranda are typed with frequency and in large quantities, these headings, together with the firm name and, perhaps, address, are printed. In typing interoffice memoranda, use margins for a 6-inch line unless the headings are printed, in which case, use margins corresponding to these headings. Signed initials are frequently placed on the memorandum to show that it has been read and approved. Sometimes the initials of the dictator and the typist appear on the memorandum, just as in a letter. Enclosures and attachments should be indicated.

The secretary who writes an interoffice memorandum need not rack her brains searching for an attention-getting opening sentence. She knows that the communication will not be tossed in the wastebasket before it is read. However, in writing an interoffice memorandum, she should try to include most of the essential characteristics of a good letter. She should use a considerate, courteous, and friendly tone; she should be clear, concise, and complete; in fact, she should follow most of the hints on letter writing given at the beginning of this section.

Memoranda may be sent to confirm conversations, to report actions taken at meetings, and to apprise the entire staff of an order from one of the administrators of the organization. Examples follow.

```
To: J. Blake, Comptroller    Subject: Computer System

From: F. Blaine, President   Date: October 31, 19--

     At the next meeting of the Board of Directors
to be held on November 5, I should like you to
present your ideas, which we have been discussing,
on the installation of the computer system.  Be
```

sure to emphasize the timesaving, as well as the money-saving, aspects of this system.

Please send to my office as soon as possible any of your presentation materials that will require duplicating, so that we can have them ready in time for the meeting.

To: All Tenure Members   Date: May 14, 19--

From: J. E. Frank, Chairman

Subject: Promotions

Please complete the information requested on the attached questionnaire in black ink and in good form for consideration by the appropriate Departmental Committee in the fall. You are to submit this information no later than October 1, 19--.

In completing the questionnaire, kindly enter information concerning only those accomplishments achieved since your last promotion.

JEF/ft

RESERVATION LETTERS

Often the secretary is asked to make reservations—hotel, motel, railroad, and plane. Examples of such letters and what they should include are given below. (See also Chap. 11.)

Gentlemen:

Please reserve a room away from the elevators for Mr. Albert Clark, who will arrive on Monday morning, February 8. He will probably leave before noon on Thursday, February 11.

May I please have a confirmation of this request at your early convenience, and will you also let me know the checking-out time.

Gentlemen:

Please reserve space on Flight No. 317, on
February 5, for Mr. Fred Lyons, vice-president of
the Drake Insurance Company. Our schedule shows
that this flight leaves Cleveland at 8:15 A.M.
and arrives in Kansas City at 12:57 P.M.   Mr.
Lyons holds air-travel card number 752.

May we have a confirmation of this reservation as soon as possible.

Gentlemen:

Please reserve a roomette for Mr. Frank
Evans, comptroller of the Atlantic Furniture Company, on the 20th Century Limited, from New York
to Chicago, on Tuesday, March 12.   Our schedule
shows that this train will leave New York at
6 P.M. and arrive in Chicago at 9 A.M.

As soon as your letter of confirmation is
received, Mr. Evans will arrange to have a mes-
senger pick up and pay for the tickets.

REFUND LETTERS

Because of unforeseen emergencies or inclement weather, plans for
travel must be canceled now and then. In order to secure a refund for
unused plane or railroad tickets, it is necessary to write a letter stating all
the facts and enclosing the tickets. The procedure to be followed in writing
for each type of cancellation is discussed in Chapter 11. Examples of
letters are as follows:

Gentlemen:

Enclosed is an unused ticket for Flight No.
317 from New York to Florida for August 5.   The
reservation was canceled at 10 A.M. on August 3.
The ticket was purchased on August 1 at the Airlines Building.

I should appreciate your making the proper
refund to:

        Pacific Furniture Company
        500 Jerusalem Avenue
        Merrick, New York

Gentlemen:

I am enclosing unused Pullman ticket No. 523
for Roomette 6, Car 4, on the 20th Century Limited, leaving New York for Chicago at 9 A.M. on
March 12. This ticket was canceled on March 11.
Kindly make refund of $ 0.00 to:

> Mr. James F. Lord
> Lord Rubber Company
> White Plains, New York

Gentlemen:

On March 15 I purchased the enclosed unused
ticket at the Grand Central Station for transportation from New York to Chicago. Kindly make the
refund payable to:

> Mr. James F. Lord
> Lord Rubber Company
> White Plains, New York

LETTERS REGARDING ERRORS

If you receive a shipment with missing or unordered items, or if you
receive an invoice with an incorrect total or a statement showing charges
for items never purchased or for items returned, point out the error without
"blowing your top." Remember, you or the company that employs you
may be guilty of similar mistakes.

When such errors occur, you should:

Identify the account by giving the name and number, where indicated.
Point out the error by describing the incorrect item, giving all pertinent information, and informing the recipient why it is incorrect.
Enclose a check for the correct amount and ask that the error in your record
be rectified or request a corrected statement.

Sample letters for such cases might be worded somewhat as follows:

Gentlemen:

On December 4, Mr. Albert Taylor bought one
raincoat and had it charged to Account No. 1572.
According to the sales slip received with the
garment, the cost of this article is $25.75. The

monthly statement just received shows a charge of
$35.73.

Enclosed is a check for $25.75, the sales
slip amount, which I presume to be the correct
charge. Please credit Mr. Taylor's account with
this amount as payment in full for the raincoat.

Gentlemen:

In the January statement, which we just received, there is a charge for $1,200 for four
Crane tape recorders. According to our records,
we never ordered these tape recorders and never
received them.

It is possible that a clerical error was
made, for we do have a record of receiving and
paying for four Crane tape recorders last September. Your invoice number for this order is 3689.
Should this prove to be the case, kindly cancel
the charge and send us a corrected statement.

APPOINTMENT LETTERS

There are five types of letters involving appointments:

1. arranging an appointment for someone who wishes to see the executive for
   whom you are employed
2. answering a request for an appointment with the executive
3. arranging an appointment for the executive to see someone
4. canceling an appointment
5. refusing a request for an appointment with the executive

In composing the first three types of letters, be sure to state the reason
for the appointment; make provision for the time, date, and place of
appointment; request a confirmation. The following letters exemplify respectively types 1, 2, and 3.

Dear Mr. Lane:

Mr. Thomas will be happy to see you in his
office on Thursday, April 12, at 3 p.m. to discuss
the Ryan situation. Please let me know if this
day and time are suitable.

Dear Miss Lindsay:

Mr. Thomas is eagerly looking forward to meeting you on February 23 at 1:30 p.m. in his office. He has read several of your exciting interviews with businessmen and is proud to be the subject of one of your articles.

Dear Mr. Sands:

Mr. Thomas is returning from London in a few days and would like to meet with you to discuss the purchase of your Smith Street property. He can come to your office on Wednesday, March 3, at 3 p.m.
Please let me know if this day and time are convenient.

In canceling an appointment (type 4) be sure to express regret for the cancellation and make some provision, albeit indefinite, for a future appointment.

Dear Mr. Kane:

Mr. Thomas was called out of town suddenly on urgent business and regrets exceedingly that he cannot keep the appointment for this coming Friday at 2 p.m.
Just as soon as he returns, I will let you know, so that arrangements may be made for another appointment on a day that will be mutually convenient.

All refusals for requests for appointments (type 5) should be made firmly but politely.

Dear Mr. Tracy:

After due deliberation, Mr. Thomas feels that further discussions of the Clancy matter will prove fruitless.
If there were any possibility of a meeting of the minds, he would be only too happy to see you again. It is his considered opinion, however,

that there is not the slightest chance that an
agreement can be reached, and he has asked me to
convey this message to you.

FOLLOW-UP LETTERS

The secretary should consult her follow-up file regularly to see which
replies to correspondence have not been answered. For each such piece of
correspondence, she usually writes a follow-up letter, and this requires that
she make reference to the contents of the unanswered letter.

Because of the widespread use of copying machines, the task of referring
to previous correspondence in follow-up letters has been greatly simplified.
Instead of laboriously recopying a letter or describing its contents fully, all
one need do is enclose a machine copy with the follow-up letter. Of course,
should a copying machine be unavailable or the contents of the letter too
long to quote or describe, then the secretary must make a typewritten copy.
The following is a typical reply in which a copy of the original letter is
being enclosed:

Dear Mr. Fisher:

    Because of the pressure of business, you
probably have not had time to answer the letter
we wrote you on March 11 concerning a contribution
from you on the topic, "Opportunities in the Field
of Programing"; or perhaps our letter went astray.
To refresh your recollection of our request, we
are enclosing a copy.
    We should very much like to publish your
ideas on this subject in the next issue of Modern
Business. We can do this if you can get your
manuscript to us by April 12.
    As time is of the essence, we would appreci-
ate your letting us know as soon as possible
whether you care to make this contribution.

Notice in the first sentence of the above letter that an excuse was made
for the recipient's failure to answer. Such a face-saving gesture is a must in
most follow-up letters.

If the contents of the original letter can be related in a very few words, a
copy of the original letter need not be enclosed. An example of this type
follows.

Dear Mrs. Beck:

Our letter of September 20 must have gone astray or else you are still in the process of making up your mind regarding the color of the draperies you ordered.

In order for us to have your draperies ready for hanging by October 15, as you requested, we must have your decision in this matter no later than October 1.

Chapter 8

Special Typing Projects

MARION WOOD

REPORTS

Secretaries wield an important influence in getting a report accepted. Editors are more likely to look with favor on the report that is well arranged and easy to read.

PAPER

Observe an accepted standard of style in typing reports and use a good quality of paper. Good paper is easier to handle, is easier to correct, and lends a more important look to the finished product. If you care enough to get the report read, you should care enough to put it on paper of high quality. Paper made from wood pulp, such as newspaper stock, has a short life; it just does not stand up under constant fingering and use. The higher the rag content of paper, the longer its life. Use either a 16- or a 20-pound paper. This weight is not easily embossed, and the typing does not show through on the opposite side. Reports on heavier paper are easier to read. Carbon copies that are to be widely circulated should also be on heavier paper, for readability is an aid in obtaining acceptance of a report.

Paper has a right and wrong side. If you are duplicating your report, make certain that you place it on the right side of the paper for best results. The manufacturer usually indicates which is the right side of the paper by the label attached to the end of the package.

MARGINS

Left and right margins of formal reports are usually an inch wide; many authors, however, prefer 1¼ inches. When the report is to be bound on the left side, allow for the binding by making the left margin 1½ inches wide. This makes the center point of your writing line three spaces to the right of

102

the present center; if you are centering lines at 50, you will now center them at 53. You can accomplish the same result by merely moving the paper ¼ inch to the left of the spot where you normally keep it.

Make the top margin 2 inches deep on the first page and 1 inch deep on the other pages. This means that you will begin on line 13 of page 1 and on line 7 of subsequent pages. Keep the bottom margins at least 1 inch deep; in some cases you may want to make them as much as 1½ inches deep. Put a light pencil mark at the left edge of your paper where you want the last line of typing to end, and then all bottom lines will be in exactly the same position on the page. After the page is typed, these marks can be easily removed.

Usually reports are double-spaced, and the first line of each paragraph is indented five spaces. Some typists use an eight-space indention, others a ten, but paragraph indention is always used.

When quotations are three lines or more long, indent the quoted material five spaces from the left and right margins or indent it the same number of spaces from these margins as you indent your paragraphs. Copy the indented quotation in single spacing and omit the quotation marks. The indention tells the reader that the material is quoted.

If listings are included in your report, single-space them. Center the items on the page. If the length of items varies, select the longest one to be centered and line up the others with it. If your listings contain widely separated columns, use leaders to assist the eye in reading the material. Make these leaders by alternating periods with spaces. Note whether the periods fall on the odd or even spaces in the first line, and then match the location of the periods accordingly in succeeding lines.

Never split a paragraph unless you can carry over at least two lines to the next page. The bottom margin may be one line narrower or wider to avoid carrying over the last line of the paragraph. A paragraph should not begin on the last line, and the last word on a page should not be hyphenated.

When pages are stapled or bound together, there is not much danger of their becoming separated. However, it is still good practice to identify each page by typing the author's name and address on the same line with the page number. Type the title of the report a double space below this line on all pages except the first page.

Leave three spaces between the title and the first line of the report. If the report has a subheading, separate it from the title with a double space. Leave an extra space before beginning the body of the material. Center subheadings or type them at the left margin in all capitals and indent them as you do your paragraphs. Actually they are the beginning of the paragraph.

The short report, one that contains less than 200 words, is typed double-spaced. Keep the top and bottom margins 2 inches deep. If the report is so short that it does not seem balanced on the page, use some kind of identifying line or reference source as a balancing line. Type the line 2 inches above the bottom edge, regardless of where the report ends. Of course, it is also permissible to center the report on the page.

NUMBERING SYSTEMS AND OUTLINES

The first page does not need to be numbered, because the 2-inch top margin shows it to be the first page. On other pages type the number down seven lines (1 inch from the top edge of the sheet) and in 1 inch from the right edge of the paper. You may or may not use the word "page" before the number. Unless the binding makes it necessary, avoid centering page numbers at the bottom of the page. Centered numbers are more inconvenient for the typists, the editor, and the proofreader to handle.

A numbering scheme is often used to make reading easier and to simplify the outlining of a report. Numerals and letters distinguish the main topics from subtopics. Roman numerals are used for the main headings and capital letters for the subtopics. Let the Arabic numerals represent secondary topics and lower-case letters their divisions. Place each subordinate topic directly under the first letter of the preceding heading. Double-space before each line carrying a number or letter. Put a period after the Roman and Arabic numerals, but omit it when the numbers or letters are written in parentheses. A sample numbering scheme is:

```
I. Roman numeral

   A. Capital letter

      1. Arabic number

         a. Small letter

            (1) Arabic number in parentheses

                (a) Small letter in parentheses
```

Indentions or a numbering system may be used in short outlines, but the above system is more specific and definite. Keep the number of headings and subheadings to a minimum; naturally, the longer the report, the more headings in your outline.

Numbered sequences should be typed so that the number stands alone. For instance, in typing this information regarding titles, you would type the numbers to stand by themselves:

A. A formal report may have several headings:

1. The main heading is typed in all capitals.

2. The subtitle is not always included, but it may tell more about the aim of the report than the main title.

3. The minor headings indicate main divisions in the report. These headings are under-scored and typed at the left margin.

4. The running head is the title of a book or chapter typed on every page, at the left margin in all capitals and on the same line with the page number.

BIBLIOGRAPHY

A bibliography includes the references used in the preparation of the report. Arrange it alphabetically by names of authors. When listing books, copy the information from the title page, rather than from the outside cover. If you are listing references from periodicals, take the title from the article itself.

Each reference lists the surname of the author, followed by his given name or initials; the title of the work; the publisher; the place of publication; and the date of publication. When using references from periodicals, one may include such identifying information as volume and page numbers. Observe these suggestions:

Underscore the titles of books and magazines.

Enclose the titles of magazine articles in quotation marks.

Type the author's initials after his surname. If some references use his full name and others his initials, be consistent, particularly when the references come close together. Usually it is better to use the full name.

If the author has written some books alone and collaborated with other authors on some materials, list those books he wrote alone first.

If the publication has more than three authors, list the publication under the name of the first mentioned author and use the words "and others."

If the publication is out of print, indicate this in parentheses following the reference.

Volume numbers of periodicals are written with Arabic numerals.

Give page references: 58–92; 275–80.

To make the author's name stand out, type the first line of the entry at the left margin and indent all other lines.

If there are many sources of reference material, classify them according to books, periodicals, pamphlets, or other documents.

When two or more books by the same author are listed in succession, instead of retyping the author's name each time, simply use a solid line of five spaces followed by a comma.

Hegarty, Edward J., How to Run Better Meetings, McGraw-Hill Book Company, Inc., New York, 1957, 300 pp.

_____, How to Write a Speech, McGraw-Hill Book Company, Inc., New York, 1951, 226 pp.

FOOTNOTES

Footnotes have a number of purposes: They may confirm or add meaning to the author's statements; they may refer to other parts of the report that have bearing on the topic discussed; or they sometimes make additional explanations of the content or terms used.

Footnotes are identified in the text by raised figures called "superior figures." The superior figure is typed one-half space above the line of writing immediately after the word or statement to which the footnote applies. To type this raised figure, engage your automatic line spacer and roll the paper down about one-third of the line. Type the figure and put the line-spacer lever back in typing position. Touch the platen knob gently, and the paper will resume its former position. It is more convenient to use the automatic line-spacer lever (sometimes called "line finder") than to use the variable spacer on the platen knob, because the former will automatically bring the platen back to its original line of writing.

Footnotes may be numbered in one of two ways: consecutively throughout the article or chapter, or consecutively on each page, beginning with the number 1 for each new page. Be uniform in numbering the references. In rough-draft work and thesis work it simplifies the typing if footnotes are numbered consecutively on each page. Then if there is an omission or correction, it can be accommodated without changing subsequent footnotes.

A footnote may be typed either on a separate line immediately following the material where the reference is made or at the bottom of the page. Sometimes footnotes are written on separate sheets immediately following the pages on which the references occur. If there are many footnotes, type them together, chapter by chapter, and separate them from the main text.

On rough-draft work, footnotes are sometimes written between two ruled lines directly after the line in which the reference is indicated. Type the footnote single-spaced, and double-space between the ruled lines and the contents of the copy. Also place a double space between the footnote and the ruled lines. The finished footnote looks like this:

---

1. American Association of School Administrators, <u>Building Americans in the Schools</u>, official report, Washington, D.C., 1960.

Some authorities consider that this style of handling the footnote makes it easier for the printer to follow the text and the references.

The more commonly used method is to type the footnote at the bottom of the page. Make certain to allow enough space for all footnotes, if there are more than one to the page. Usually you are safe if you allow three or four lines for each footnote.

Type a straight line of 12 or 15 spaces below the last line of your copy, starting at the left margin and extending the line toward the center. Type the footnote a double space below this line. Precede the footnote with the corresponding reference number. This number may be typed in regular position or as a superior number. In the interest of making the typists' work easier, there is a trend away from the raised position.

JUSTIFYING THE RIGHT MARGIN

There are three ways of justifying, that is, making lines come out even. You can change a word or sentence so that the lines end exactly at the same place, or you can put in some extra spaces between words to spread the line out. If you do this, avoid putting the extra spaces of one line directly under those of a preceding line. Also, of course, you may crowd letters and words to save spacing.

Select a line length that seems suitable for the job at hand. Draw a pencil line down the right side of your paper at this point. Set a tab stop five spaces beyond the penciled line. Type the copy line by line, making sure to end each line as close to the pencil mark as you can. Tab and record the number of spaces you need to increase or decrease. When your rough draft is completed, indicate with your pencil where you plan to expand or save spaces. Use the diagonal for increased spacing and the check mark to show where you wish to decrease spacing.

TITLE PAGE

A lengthy or formal report usually has a title page. If the report is to be bound, the title page is the first one after the cover. The title page includes the title of the report and the names of the persons to whom it is submitted and by whom it is written. It is always best to include the date. If the title is long, divide it into several lines, grouping key phrases. Never divide an adjective or an article from its modifier. Center the material and use adequate spacing between lines to give a balanced appearance to the page.

TABLE OF CONTENTS

The table of contents is one of the last things you prepare. It should be typed after all pages of the report are completed and numbered. The contents lists in order the numbers and titles of the sections or chapters in the report and the pages on which they begin. It should not be confused with the index, which is arranged alphabetically and includes more detail. Use Roman numerals for section numbers and Arabic numbers for page numbers. Center the table on the page. If it is a short table, double-space it. Chapter numbers are put on the left, page numbers on the right. Leaders may be used to assist the reader in finding page numbers.

INDEX

In long reports it may be necessary to prepare an index as well as a table of contents. Be extremely careful to see that the index is typed in alphabetical order. Put the entries first on 3 × 5 inch cards and then arrange them alphabetically. Then retype the index from the cards.

NEWS RELEASES

News releases are typed double-spaced on 8½ × 11 paper. Side margins should be generous, at least 1 inch or wider. Thus the editor has room for any notations that he may wish to make. Try to keep the release to one page, even if you have to use single spacing to do so.

The editor likes to see identifying information at the top of the sheet, including the date, the name of the person to whom he may turn for more information, and the address and telephone number of that person.

If the news release runs to more than one page, end each page with a complete paragraph and put the word "more" at the bottom. Copy is often divided so that it can be given to different typesetters. "More" tells the typesetters that there are more pages. End the news release with a concluding symbol such as # # # or -0-.

The editor appreciates having a word count at the logical stopping points in the story. Make certain that there are no errors in typing and that all information is accurate. An error in the copy causes the editor to doubt the reliability of the story, and when he is under pressure of deadlines, he may hesitate to print it.

Though you should endeavor to make the title of the news release tell the whole story at a glance, you need not worry too much about headlines. The newspapers have specialists whose job it is to create eye-catching headlines, and they will do this for you.

LEGAL DOCUMENTS

Even though you may not be employed in a legal office, at times you may find it necessary to type a legal document or, at least, to fill in a printed legal form. Accuracy is essential, because a changed word or correction may affect the validity of the paper. If you have any doubt about making a correction, consult your supervisor. When changes must be made in a document after it has been signed, all changes must be initialed by the signers.

Most legal documents are typed on "legal cap" paper. This paper is stronger than regular stationery and is usually slightly larger, measuring 8½ × 13 or 14 inches. It has a red, double-ruled line 1¼ inches from the left edge of the paper and a single ruled line ½ inch from the right edge. Not all legal documents are put on these ruled sheets. Many wills are written on plain sheets of paper.

To avoid crowding the information in the document, type it double-spaced and use generous side margins (at least two spaces within the red rulings). If your paper has no rulings, use a 1½-inch margin on the left and a ½-inch margin on the right. Start the first line of each page 2 inches from the top edge and end each page within an inch of the bottom. Indent all paragraphs ten spaces, and use only one side of the paper. Never end a page with the first line of a paragraph or begin a page with the last line of a paragraph. At least two lines of the document must appear on the same page with the signature lines.

Spell out sums of money and repeat them in figures enclosed within parentheses. Dates may either be spelled out or written in figures but not both ways.

Number each page except the first page. Type the page number either in the center of the paper at the bottom or in the upper right-hand corner. Do not place the number in parentheses or between hyphens, and do not follow it with a period. The words "and last" should be typed after the final page number.

Use the underscore for signature lines. The signature lines for the principal signers start at the center of the page and extend toward the right margin. The signature lines for witnesses begin at the left margin and extend toward the center. Lines should be at least four spaces apart. Lightly pencil the respective initials at the beginnings of the signature lines to guide the signers. If you prefer, use the small "x" to mark the spot where the parties sign. After the document is signed, insert the typed signatures and dates on the file copies. When copying the signature line, use the abbreviation "Sgd." for signed.

Type the introductory and closing phrases in all capitals. Put either a comma or a colon after the phrases, depending on how the phrase is used. Some of these phrases are:

```
KNOW ALL MEN BY THESE PRESENTS, That . . .
IN WITNESS WHEREOF, the parties . . .
THIS AGREEMENT, made June . . .
```

File copies can be made on onionskin paper. If carbon copies are to be signed, type the copies on the same quality of paper that you use for the original.

Most legal documents have cover sheets or binders. These are endorsed with a brief description of the document. To prepare the binder, lay it on the desk and bring the bottom edge up to within 1 inch of the top; crease. Bring the creased end up to approximately 1 inch from the top and fold again. Place a pencil mark in the upper left-hand corner of the surface that is uppermost as you make your last fold. Open this fold and insert the binder in the typewriter so that the pencil mark is now on the upper right-hand corner. Do not type beyond the crease. After typing the endorsement, turn the top edge of the backing sheet down, crease it, and insert the document in the crease. Staple it in place. Fold the document to fit the creases in the binder.

COPY FOR THE PRINTER

TYPING

When the copy is to be printed, keep the typewritten lines 6 inches long and use double spacing. If you make the right margin as even as possible, it is easier to determine the length of the copy. Type headings in the position they will occupy on the printed page and be consistent in style. Type on one side of the paper; make side margins at least 1 inch wide. Keep the pages equal in length. Do not staple pages together.

Proofread the material. It is a good idea to lay the material aside before giving it a final check. The second reading may reveal errors overlooked the first time. Sometimes the errors are seen more quickly on the first carbon copy than on the original. If this is true of your copy, proofread from the first carbon copy. Two heads are better than one for proofreading. When working with an assistant, the typist should follow the original and the assistant the final copy. The secretary is really a stand-in reader. It is her job to find those errors so elementary that they escape the author's attention.

A helpful check on the accuracy of figures is to total them on an adding machine, even though no total is necessary. A second total run off when you are proofreading your typing will assure you that the typing is accurate.

CORRECTING COPY

Use proofreading marks in making corrections. (See Appendix 7.) Short corrections can be made by crossing out the incorrect word and writing the correction over it. If the correction is lengthy, type it on a separate sheet of paper. If a whole paragraph needs correction, you may find it convenient to type the correction on a separate sheet and staple it over the original.

Here are three simple useful devices for making corrections:

Use the paragraph sign (¶) to indicate the beginning of a new paragraph.
Use the caret (∧) to indicate insertions.
Use a row of dots (...) under crossed-out material to show that it should remain and the word "stet" in the left margin beside the line.

The best time to number the pages of the manuscript is after the whole job has been typed and all corrections have been made. Pages are numbered consecutively, and the page number usually appears in the upper right-hand corner of each page, indented 1 inch from the right edge.

ART WORK

Identify all art work either by number or by some other system of labeling. If you use numbers, make certain that the numbering agrees with the order in which the items will appear in the finished job. Avoid writing on photographs with either pen or pencil, because the marks may break the finish on the photograph and show in the reproduction. Type the identification line on a separate label and attach it to the back of the exhibit. Make a list of all the exhibits you plan to use in the booklet, giving the description and location of each exhibit.

LAYOUT

Your printer will advise you on the layout and often will make up the dummy for you. A dummy is a set of blank sheets, cut and folded to the size of your booklet, showing the shape, size, and appearance of the finished job. In preparing the dummy, make allowances for necessary corrections and indicate the location of any art work.

ESTIMATING LENGTH

Often it is necessary to tell the printer the approximate length of the material. Select three or four lines of the copy and count the number of words in these lines. From this count determine the average number of words per line. Now count the number of lines on the page and multiply this by the number of words in each line. Suppose in four lines you count 44 words. This means that you have an average of 11 words to each line. If there are 27 lines on your page, 27 times 11 gives you 297 words, or nearly 300 words to the page. A report of ten full pages would be about 3,000 words long.

GALLEY PROOFS

The printer will return the original manuscript to you with two or more copies set up in the type you selected. Compare the printer's copy, word for word, with the original. Again, it is always safer if two people work together. Careful checking saves time and money, because the printer charges an extra fee for changes.

Reading the galley proofs is the next major step. This is the last chance to make corrections. However, if your revisions deviate much from the original, you pay a heavy penalty in time rates. Changes in the galley proof become very costly. Read material through for continuity in thought. Many people also read backward as an additional check for typographical errors. Some of the things to watch for in checking are:

Spelling and punctuation errors.
Inconsistencies in style, spelling, paragraphing.
Transposition of letters and lines.
Errors in page numbers.
Continuity from page to page. (Does the last word on a page make sense with the top of the next page?)

If your employer frequently publishes manuscripts, keep a record of each manuscript on a 3 × 5 card. You will want to record such facts as the title, the date it was submitted to the printer, and how many pages it contained.

MULTILITH MATS

HANDLING THE MAT

At times you will need to use offset duplication for reproducing copies of the typed report or manuscript you have been asked to handle. This requirement involves the preparation of a Multilith master. Handle the master with care, touching it only on the outside margins indicated by the guidelines printed there. If you use hand lotion or cold cream on your skin, avoid touching the body of the master in any way, because your finger contacts will be reproduced on the duplicated copy. When you insert the master into the typewriter, adjust the rubber rolls on the paper bail so that they run on the extreme right and left edges of the master or straddle the master entirely. Incorrect handling of the Multilith mats may result in wrinkling or creasing, which shows on the finished reproduction; in uneven inking, if a special ribbon is not used; in smudged letters, if the type is not clean or if erasing is not carefully done; and in dark fingerprints, if the body of the master is handled.

RIBBONS

The clearness of the image on the master is dependent on having a very heavy coating of ink deposited on the master. Therefore, although regular typewriter ribbon may sometimes be used, better copies result when you use Multilith ribbons especially prepared for this work. They may be used also for regular work. When the image on the master begins to look light, change to a new ribbon.

SERVICE ADJUSTMENTS

With electric typewriters the impression indicator should be adjusted to the lowest registration that still produces a clear impression on the master. Sometimes it helps to move the multiple-copy control back one notch, if your typewriter has this adjustment. Masters vary in thickness; it is necessary, therefore, to experiment to determine the best registration for machine-service adjustments.

CORRECTIONS

If you make an error, use a Multilith eraser and erase lightly in one direction. A few strokes are usually enough to remove the unwanted character from the surface of the master. You need remove only the ink deposited on the surface. Use a flicking motion rather than scrubbing action. The ghost image that remains will not print, and you may type over it without any fear that a strikeover will show. Keep the eraser clean by rubbing it on a piece of clean paper after each use to prevent the ink on the eraser from rubbing into the surface of the master. Only one erasure should be made in one spot. If you find it necessary to reinsert a typed master into the typewriter, lay a clean sheet of paper over the master, so that the feed rollers underneath the platen will not smear the previously typed material.

TIME INTERVAL BEFORE RUNNING MASTER

For best results in the duplicated copies, there should be a time interval of from ¼ to ½ hour between the typing and the running of the master. This interval allows the image to set. The time interval will vary, depending upon the freshness of the ribbon and the length of the run required. If only a few copies are needed, the master may be run soon after it is typed.

OFFICE COPIERS

Almost all companies—even one-man, one-secretary organizations—now own or rent a copying machine of the sort made by Xerox, Dennison, 3M, Royfax, Pitney Bowes, and other companies. For the most part, these machines reproduce electrostatically, on ordinary or special photocopy papers, any printed or written material—in moments. Charts and graphs are easily copied, and some equipment is sophisticated enough to reproduce photographs or art-work, even in color.

The copying machines vary enormously in size and abilities. Some models are small, table-top devices which require the user to feed the special copying paper in a sheet at a time. Others will supply dozens or hundreds of copies of a single page in minutes, separating the pages for automatic collation, and all at the press of one button and the changing of a dial. Equipment is available that permits copying from books or even of three-dimensional objects; some models reduce or enlarge printed documents, and make full-size reproductions from microfilm.

Since this range is so wide, the secretary using an office copier is best instructed in how to work her particular machine by the manual that comes with it, or by the representative of the company from which it has been secured. All the machines require routine upkeep—cleaning, for example, or use of a toner to control sharpness and depth of image, as well as occasional replacement of a pad or other parts. Often the secretary in a small office quickly learns routine upkeep techniques so that expensive service calls can be minimized. She may also be responsible for keeping sufficient special paper in stock so that supplies aren't exhausted at a crucial moment. In larger companies, of course, both upkeep and inventory of supplies is managed not by secretaries but by the office manager or his or her assistants.

It is so easy to use an office copier that many people tend to over-use it. The machine is frequently used for a few "carbon copies," when it would actually be easier (and far less expensive) to make actual carbons when the original is typed. That's particularly true in this day of carbon-packs and carbon-sets. The special paper used in an office-copier can cost as much as a dime a sheet; careless use, then, can mean the waste of many dollars a day.

But when used judiciously, the copying machine is so efficient and so dramatically time-saving that one wonders how business was conducted before the Xerox Corporation did us the favor of introducing the word and the practice of Xerography to the world of business. Complex reports can now be reproduced in a few minutes; copies of earlier correspondence can "back up" current letters and memos. Copies of checks, front and back, can be sent to help correct billing errors. As a typist, you'll be grateful throughout the day for your office copying equipment.

TECHNICAL SUBJECTS

The typing done for engineers, chemists, mathematicians, and other professional men is often referred to as "technical typing." The material often involves equation typing. In such work accuracy is extremely important, much more important than speed. Because you are typing symbols in patterns, spacing both horizontally and vertically becomes a consideration that may require some experimentation.

Equations generally include raised and lowered symbols. Those symbols written above the regular line of writing are called "superscripts"; those written below, "subscripts." It is essential, therefore, that technical reports be typed in double spacing to allow room for writing these subscripts and superscripts. Typewriters can be purchased with a 54-tooth ratchet that makes it very simple to half-space forward or back from the usual line of writing with one hand-turn of the platen. If you do not have this special ratchet, you will find it convenient to mark a strip of paper with the half spacing in red lines between the regular spacing marked in black ink around the left side of your platen. Make the strip about 1 inch wide, and fasten it firmly around the platen with a piece of transparent tape.

Typewriters can also be converted to have keys with the special mathematical symbols and Greek letters. If you are operating a Selectric typewriter, you may purchase a special symbol called the "universal symbol element." This element has the mathematical symbols and Greek alphabet used so frequently in equation typing.

For the larger symbols you will want a template. This is a small, plastic, rectangular guide that resembles the letter guides for stencil work, except that it provides outlines of symbols used in scientific reports. You trace the stencil symbol with a sharp-pointed pencil.

Always leave a space before and after the arithmetical operator symbol: $=$, $+$, $-$, $\div$, and $\times$. However, if the symbol is used adjectivally, as -3, there would be no space between the minus sign and the 3. Some authors prefer you to half-space the hyphen to show that the hyphen belongs with the figure 3. Here is a place for you to experiment. Type -3 with normal spacing; then try it with the minus sign a half space from the 3.

Multiplication is expressed by using the "$\times$" or the period or by parentheses inclosing an expression to be multiplied. Often the multiplication sign is omitted and the letters are typed together as ab. Thus, in the equation $7ad(x - y) = mx$, there is no space between d and the opening parenthesis, but there is a space before and after the equals sign.

In typing superscripts and subscripts a half space above or below the regular line of writing, first type all the symbols that are on the regular line, leaving spaces for all the subscripts and superscripts; then go back and type in all the subscripts, rolling the paper forward a half space; and finally insert the superscripts, moving the paper down a half space.

Fractions may be typed in two styles. If the equation is short, the fraction may be part of the running text and is typed in the shilling style, which looks like this: 4/5. If you use mixed numbers, it is safer to put a hyphen between the whole number and the shilling fraction, for example, 43-5/6. Since these fractions are difficult or may be confusing, many typists prefer to use the stacked or built-up fraction centered on the page. A built-up fraction looks like this: $\frac{4}{5}$. To type the stacked fraction, roll your paper back a half space, type the numerator, backspace, put in the division line (using the underscore), and then roll the platen up a half space below the regular writing line and type the denominator. Sometimes it is helpful to type the longest term first, because the division line must be as long as the longest term in the fraction.

Equations are numbered consecutively throughout a report to make it easy to refer to any equation in the text. Each equation number is put in parentheses at the right margin. Set a tab stop for this location. Arrange the tab setting so that the closing parenthesis will be just inside of the right margin of your page. When making reference to these equation numbers, abbreviate equation to "Eq." Your reference will look like this: "Eq. 5."

Usually punctuation is not used with equations. If your author requests punctuation in his equations, then observe these rules:

> Consider each equation as a clause of a complex sentence and follow it with either a comma or semicolon.

If the equation concludes the sentence, a period follows it.

If you have a series of equations, introduce them by a colon in the line preceding the equations.

Sometimes equations are too long for one line and must be placed on several lines. Break them before the equals sign when possible. Before any one of the operational signs ($+$, $-$, $\times$, $\div$) is another good place to divide an equation. You may also divide it between fractions or after brackets and parentheses. Do not put part of an equation on one page and the rest of it on the next page.

Some authors help their typists to read the symbols in an equation by writing all lower-case symbols and printing upper-case symbols. Why not suggest this to the man whose reports you are typing? You will also find it helpful to draft all the equations in the report before typing up the report. Let the author check your arrangement of the equations. If he has no objection, then you are ready to do the finished report and can proceed with confidence that the material is arranged in the very best form.

TYPING NUMBERS

Typing numbers involves the observance of certain rules established by manuals of style. The following list will enable you to apply these rules quickly. You may use the hyphen to represent the word "to," as 1865-1871.

Use figures for	*Use words for*
Exact numbers above ten	Exact numbers, ten and below
35 passengers	mail four cases
Amounts of money	Round or approximate numbers
$29.50, $24, 8 cents	nine hundred people
Percentages	Beginning of sentences
4 percent	Twelve years
Dimensions, measurements, etc.	Names of centuries and decades
15 feet	the twentieth century
size 6	
Exact age	Approximate age
10 years, 5 months, 4 days	sixteen years old
Time with A.M. or P.M.	Time with "o'clock"
3 P.M.	three o'clock
Street names above ten	Street names below ten
13 East 22 Street	Fifth Avenue
Word "number" followed by figure	Numbered sessions of Congress
Policy No. 46345	Seventy-eighth Congress

Use words for	*Use figures for*
Fractions standing alone	House or building numbers
send one-half of the order	45 Main Street
Two numbers coming together	Dates
six 4-inch bolts	December 12, 1966
213 eight-pound crates	26th of May
Mixed numbers	Plurals of numbers
three and three-fourths	64's
Shorter form in round numbers	Large even amounts
twelve hundred copies	10 million dollars

Chapter 9

Filing and Finding

MARY E. CONNELLY

ONE OF THE MOST IMPORTANT activities in the office is that of filing and finding papers, letters, and documents. Filing may be defined as the process of classifying office papers and storing them efficiently so that they can be found quickly when needed. The files represent the past history and current activities of the company, and they may determine its future policies and decisions. The importance of correct and efficient filing cannot be over-emphasized.

Whether there is a central file, as in a large organization, or a small personal file, as in a one- or two-man office, the secretary should know the basic filing systems. A file clerk must have an extensive knowledge of all the filing systems; the secretary must have a workable knowledge of the most used filing systems in today's offices.

FILING SYSTEMS

The basic filing systems in use in the modern office are: alphabetic, numeric, geographic, subject, and decimal.

ALPHABETIC

Almost 90 per cent of all the filing that is done in the office is alphabetic. The secretary usually files office correspondence and papers according to *name* or *subject,* in alphabetic order. Because a name file is arranged alphabetically, no cross-index file is necessary. It is very simple to expand a name file, because the new name or subject is filed alphabetically without disturbing the name before or after it. The alphabetic system of filing is known as a "direct" method of filing.

NUMERIC

The numeric system of filing is known as an "indirect" method, because a cross-index file is necessary. This cross-index file is usually arranged alphabetically and shows the name to which a number has been assigned. The correspondence is filed in a numbered folder and a card index is made for each folder. This card index, which is arranged alphabetically, must be referred to when filing or finding correspondence or papers. The numeric system is used when a confidential file is necessary. It is generally used in hospitals, in the offices of doctors, lawyers, construction companies, architects, and so on. The numeric file may be easily expanded by adding another folder with the next number and making out an index card for the new folder.

GEOGRAPHIC

In the geographic system the papers are filed alphabetically according to the name of the state; then alphabetically according to the town or city within that state; then alphabetically according to the name of the correspondent within the town or city. Mail-order houses, public-utility companies, publishing houses, and organizations that serve geographic districts or have branch offices in different areas use this system of filing. It is helpful to have a cross index by names to show the location of a given firm. These name cards are filed alphabetically. The geographic system of filing is an indirect method.

SUBJECT

When a company deals with products, supplies, materials, advertising, and so forth, the subject system is used. It is an indirect system, because a cross-index card file is used to save time in filing and finding material and in locating correspondence by firm name when the subject is doubtful. The folders in the subject file are arranged alphabetically by the name of the product. The material within the folders is arranged by date, with the latest date in the front of the folder.

Often a combination of subject file and name file is used. If there is not enough material to set up a separate subject file, the subject captions are set up in a name file.

DECIMAL

The decimal system of filing may be based on the Dewey decimal system, which is used by most public libraries (although many are switching to the Library of Congress Catalogue card system). This system is used only in highly specialized businesses. Other decimal or numeric systems that are used today are:

1. The "terminal-digit system," in which the numbers are read from right to left. Usually the last, or terminal, two digits are the drawer number, the next two digits are the folder number, and any other numbers

indicate the sequence within the folders. For example, an insurance policy numbered 567,123 would be stored in drawer 23, folder 71, and the 56 would refer to its sequence in the folder.

2. The "triple-digit system" is similar to the terminal-digit system, except that the numbers are read in three digits instead of two. The terminal three digits of a number are called the "primary" numbers, and the remaining digits refer to the sequence of the papers in the folders bearing the primary numbers. For example, the insurance policy numbered 567,123 would be found in folder 123, and 567 would refer to its sequence in the folder.

3. In the "middle-digit system" the third and fourth digits from the right of a number are separated from the last two digits on the right. For example, in the insurance policy number 567,123, the policy would be filed in folder 71, and 23 would refer to its sequence in the folder.

4. The "duplex-digit system" makes use of both numbers and letters of the alphabet. A digit is selected for the subject; this is followed by a dash and another digit for a division of the subject, plus a letter for a further subdivision. For example, the subject heading "Automobile Accessories" might be given the number 8; the division "Automobile Accessories: Tires" would be numbered 8-1; and a further subdivision "Automobile Accessories: Tires, White Wall" would be numbered 8-1A.

PHYSICAL SETUP OF FILES

The file drawer contains primary guides which divide the file into alphabetic sections. These primary guides are placed at the beginning of each section, and the tabs are usually on the left-hand side of the file drawer. Secondary guides are used to subdivide the section or to call attention to important names. Individual folders, arranged alphabetically, are placed directly behind the guides. Individual folders are used for correspondents who communicate frequently with the firm. When there are from five to eight pieces of correspondence from the same firm, an individual folder is set up. The full name of the correspondent is on the tab, which is usually twice as large as the guide tab. When material is placed in a miscellaneous folder, it should be arranged in alphabetic sequence, with the latest date in front. When material is arranged in an individual folder, the latest date is always in the front of the folder.

Miscellaneous folders follow the individual guides at the end of every group. They are used for correspondence that does not warrant individual folders. The tab on the miscellaneous folder is the same size as the tab on the primary guide for that section.

In preparing index tabs and labels for guides and folders, type the letter of the alphabet or the name whenever possible. The first typing space below the fold of the folder label should be used, and typing should start two spaces from the left of the folder. Use initial capitals and indent the second and each succeeding line two spaces, so that the first word on the top line will stand out. Use abbreviations if the name or subject is long. Use the largest type possible when typing file-drawer labels, or print these labels.

PREPARATION OF MATERIAL FOR FILING

Check all papers to see whether they are to be filed and have been released for filing. Sort the correspondence into personal, business, contracts, and the like. Remove all staples, paper clips, or other paper holders. Underline the name in colored pencil to indicate where the letter is to be filed. Indicate the guide number in the upper right-hand corner. Use a colored pencil to circle important words to help to locate a particular paper when it is needed. Make any cross-reference sheets that are required. A cross-reference sheet is made out when a letter or a record may be filed in one of two places. File the letter or record under the most important name and cross-reference the second name or subject. For example, a letter may be received from Jordan Marsh Company. It would be filed under Jordan (first unit) Marsh (second unit) Company (third unit), and a cross reference made out for Marsh, Jordan Company. The cross-reference sheet would read:

```
        Marsh, Jordan Company
        SEE
        Jordan Marsh Company
```

When it is necessary to take material from the files, replace the record or correspondence with an "out" guide or card. On the "out" guide record the date, the name of the record taken, who has it, and the date it is to be returned. The word "out" should be printed on the tab, and stock of a different color should be used so that the guide stands out. It is necessary to record the withdrawal of the material if it goes out of the office for a period of time, or if the employer is going to use it away from the office. Confidential records should be used in the office and returned to the files immediately.

FILING EQUIPMENT

A file drawer can take care of from 25 to 40 divisions. For efficient filing the drawers should not be overcrowded. No more than 40 divisions should be placed in one file drawer. A standard four-drawer correspondence file is most generally used. Each drawer will carry a load of from 60 to 70 pounds. The files should be arranged so that there is a minimum of walking required to and from the files. They should be arranged so that they fit the office work. The file drawers may be labeled in either vertical (top to bottom), or horizontal (from left to right) order. Space may be saved if the file cabinets are backed up against a wall. If there are many cabinets, it may be more efficient to arrange them in a cluster in the center of a room. Floor space is expensive; therefore, some consideration should be given to arranging cabinets economically. Adequate aisle space between cabinets must be allowed. At least 18 inches must be allowed for a file drawer when it is opened into the aisle. Thirty-six inches between two cabinets facing each other will allow for the file drawers to be opened and also allow for a passageway for two file workers. There should be gaps in long rows of cabinets to save time in getting from one row to another. This is particularly important for the file supervisor who has to make spot checks of the file drawers and to assist the file clerks.

INDEXING AND ALPHABETIZING

Indexing has to do with the arrangement of the names on the folder tab or on cards. The folders and cards are arranged alphabetically for simplicity of filing and finding. Secretaries should know the rules for indexing.

Individual names. Names of individuals are indexed by the last name (the surname) first, then the first name, and then the middle initial, if any.

Name	*Indexing order*
Alfred M. Amell	Amell, Alfred M.
Pete R. Gladd	Gladd, Pete R.
J. Thomas Williams	Williams, J. Thomas

Firm names. The names of firms, institutions, and organizations are indexed as they are written, unless they embody the name of an individual.

Name	*Indexing order*
Atlantic Service Station	Atlantic Service Station
General Department Store	General Department Store
Troy Sand and Gravel, Inc.	Troy Sand and Gravel, Inc.

When the firm name embodies the name of an individual, index the name by considering the last name first, then the first name, and the middle initial, if any.

Name	Indexing order
James A. Carson Company	Carson, James A. Company
J. M. Morgan Sign Company	Morgan, J. M. Sign Company
Thomas Stiles Florist Shop	Stiles, Thomas Florist Shop

Alphabetic order. Names are alphabetized by comparing each letter in the name. If the first units are alike, compare the second units. If there is no second unit, the single name is filed first. The rule of "nothing before something" applies here.

Name	Indexing order
Carson	Carson
Carson Brothers	Carson Brothers
J. Carson	Carson, J.
James Carson	Carson, James

Letters used as words. Consider one or more single letters as words.

Name	Indexing order
N A P A Jobbers	N A P A Jobbers
N C R Accounting Company	N C R Accounting Company
National Car Company	National Car Company
R E A Freight Service	R E A Freight Service

Article "the." When "the" is part of the name, it is disregarded in filing. If it is the initial word, it is placed at the end of the name in parentheses.

If "the" occurs in the body of the name, it is placed in parentheses and disregarded.

Name	Indexing order
The Crescent Boat Company	Crescent Boat Company (The)
Daley The Tailor	Daley (The) Tailor
Stanley of the Ritz	Stanley (of the) Ritz

(Such words or symbols as "and," "&," "for," "on," "in," "by," and "of the" are disregarded in indexing and filing. However, they are placed in parentheses when writing names on folders and cards.)

Hyphenated names. Hyphenated firm names are treated as separate names, because they represent separate individuals.

Name	Indexing order
Branch-Merrill Company	Branch Merrill Company
Richard I. Branch	Branch, Richard I.
William F. Wilson	Wilson, William F.
Wilson-Wyman, Inc.	Wilson Wyman, Inc.

Hyphenated individual names are treated as one name, because they represent one individual.

Name	Indexing order
Milton Burl-Cass	BurlCass, Milton
James A. Gladd-Monroe	GladdMonroe, James A.
John L. Marin-Jones	MarinJones, John L.

One- or two-word names. Names that may be spelled as one word or two words are usually considered as one word.

Name	Indexing order
Raybrook Cleaners	Raybrook Cleaners
Ray Brook Paint Company	RayBrook Paint Company
South East Electric Shop	SouthEast Electric Shop
Southeast Supply Company	Southeast Supply Company

Individual surnames with prefixes. Prefixes such as D', De, Del, Fitz, l', La, Mac, Mc, Van, Von, and so on, are indexed as written and treated as one word.

Index and file as

D'Aoust, James
Darling, John E.
De Lancett, Morris
DeLancey, Lincoln
MacDonald, George H.
McCasland, Raymond A.
Van Cour, Elsie A.
Von Ottenfeld, Oscar M.

Words ending in "s." When a name ends in "s' " the "s" is considered part of the name. When a name ends in " 's," the "s" is disregarded.

Index and file as

Bob's Sport Shop
Boy Scouts Camp
Boys' Clothing Store
William's Service Station
Williams' Dry Cleaning
Wilson, John M.

Titles. A personal or professional title or degree is usually not considered in indexing and filing. When the name is written, the title is placed in parentheses at the end of the name.

Name	Indexed as
Dr. Richard P. Bellaire	Bellaire, Richard P. (Dr.)
Miss Helen Hayles	Hayles, Helen (Miss)
Alfred Jason, D. D.	Jason, Alfred (D. D.)
Mr. George T. Nugent	Nugent, George T. (Mr.)

A religious or a foreign title is considered as the first indexing unit when it is followed by a given name only.

Indexed and filed as

Brother Francis
Madame Louise
Prince Charles
Princess Grace
Sister Mary Margaret

Married women's names. The name of a married woman is indexed according to her legal name (her given first name, her maiden surname, and her husband's surname). The name of a married woman is always cross-referenced under her husband's full name if it is known. The title "Mrs." is disregarded in filing, but it is placed in parentheses after her *legal* name.

Name	Indexed as
Mrs. John F. Watson (Mary Nason)	Watson, Mary Nason

The cross reference is Watson, John F. (Mrs.)

The name of the husband may be given in parentheses below the woman's legal name.

Name	Indexing order
Mrs. Lucien (Louise S.) Fritts	Fritts, Louise S. (Mrs.) (Mrs. Lucien Fritts)
Mrs. Robert (Mary Lee) Michael	Michael, Mary Lee (Mrs.) (Mrs. Robert Michael)

Names with numbers. When a name contains a number, it is considered as if it were written as one unit and is spelled as it is pronounced.

Name	Indexing order
A 1 Garage	A One Garage
The 400 Club	Fourhundred Club (The)
7th Ave. Building	Seventh Avenue Building

Geographic names. An easy rule to follow in arranging geographic names is to treat them as they are written. Each word in a compound geographic or location name is indexed as a separate unit.

Name	Indexing order
Mount Holly, New Jersey	Mount Holly, New Jersey
New Bedford, Massachusetts	New Bedford, Massachusetts
New York Central R. R.	New York Central Railroad
Newburgh, New York	Newburgh, New York

When the first part of a geographic name is not an English name, it is considered part of the first unit.

Name	Indexing order
Des Moines, Iowa	DesMoines, Iowa
Las Vegas Hotel	LasVegas Hotel
Los Angeles, California	LosAngeles, California
San Francisco, California	SanFrancisco, California

Government offices and departments. The name of a Federal government office is considered for indexing as follows:

1. United States Government (whether or not it is written as part of the name)
2. Principal word or words in the name of the department
3. Principal word or words in the name of the bureau
4. Principal word or words in the name of the division

"Department of," "Bureau of," and "Division of" are disregarded but are usually placed in parentheses.

Name	Indexing order
Bureau of the Census	United States Government
U.S. Department of Commerce	Commerce (Department of)
	Census (Bureau of the)
Office of Indian Affairs	United States Government
U.S. Department of the Interior	Interior (Department of the)
	Indian Affairs (Office of)
U.S. Postal Service	United States Government
Bureau of Accounts	Postal Service
Division of Cost Ascertainment	Accounts (Bureau of)
	Cost Ascertainment (Division of)

Banks. Banks are indexed under the cities in which they are located, then by bank name. The state is the last indexing unit.

Name	Indexing order
First National Bank Boston, Massachusetts	Boston: First National Bank, Massachusetts
Bank of New Jersey Newark	Newark: Bank of New Jersey
Wells Savings Bank Wells, Maine	Wells Savings Bank Maine

If the name of the city is a part of the name of the bank, the name of the city is considered the first unit.

Churches, schools, and other organizations. The names of churches, schools, and other organizations are indexed as they are written. Cross references may be used when necessary to file or find these names more efficiently.

Name	Indexing order
American Legion	American Legion
University of California	California, University (of)
Brockton Kiwanis Club	Kiwanis Club, Brockton
First Lutheran Church	Lutheran Church, First

TRANSFERRING RECORDS

When records become inactive in the file, they should be transferred to storage files. Thus, the expensive filing equipment is used only for active material. The material that is removed from the active files and placed in the inactive, or transfer, files should be well arranged, so that no time is wasted in locating this material if it is needed. Many firms plan to transfer the material in the files annually. The entire file drawer is transferred to the inactive file. The secretary needs to make new guides and prepare new folders for the new file.

If the guides and the folders are going to be kept in the file drawer, the transferred material may be placed in inexpensive folders that have been labeled with the same captions as those in the active-file drawer.

All transfer files or boxes should be labeled to indicate their contents, dates, and so forth, so that they can easily be located when needed.

Many business papers, correspondence, and some records that will not be needed in the future may be destroyed to conserve space and save time in transferring files. Material should not be destroyed without consideration of the statute of limitations in the state and other laws which require business firms to retain certain types of records.

MICROFILMING

Many offices use a process of making miniature copies of their business papers on film and storing the film on 100-foot reels. This system saves a great deal of time and space. To consult such files the films may be placed on a machine and enlarged to about their original size. Specially designed cabinets are used for filing boxes of microfilm.

Chapter 10

Communications — Mail, Telegrams and Cables, and the Telephone

ADELE F. SCHRAG

THIS CHAPTER covers communications—specifically, handling the mail; messages by telegraph, cable, and radio; and the use of the telephone, from ordinary uses to transmission of data. In short, here we are discussing the most important (other than face-to-face) communication systems of ordinary business.

I Handling the Mail

INCOMING MAIL

The system of handling mail differs among organizations. In a small office one person may sort and open all mail except that marked "Personal" or "Confidential." Letters so marked are delivered unopened to the person to whom they are addressed. A large organization usually has a mailing department, where both incoming and outgoing mail are handled according to a fixed system.

In an office where the secretary assumes the responsibility for opening the mail for the employer, a routinized procedure will permit rapid handling of each day's mail.

OPENING THE MAIL

To ensure that the contents will not be torn while the letter is being opened, tap the envelope firmly on the edge of the desk so that the contents will slip away from the top. Slit the upper edge of the envelope with a letter opener. Should the contents of a letter be cut by the opener, simply use transparent tape to paste the parts together.

130

Checking the contents. After removing the contents of an envelope, check whether it contains a return address. If not, staple the envelope containing the return address to the contents. (Caution: If the contents include a punched card, secure with a paper clip rather than a staple.) The envelope should also be retained if the signature on the letter is not easily distinguishable.

Another check should be made to determine that all enclosures stipulated in the letter are accounted for. If not, a notation should be made immediately on the face of the letter, indicating what is missing.

Dating the mail. It is always wise to affix each day's date on incoming mail. The easiest procedure is to use a rubber stamp. Such a procedure is helpful if the letter has arrived too late to meet a deadline requested therein, has been in transit longer than it should have been, or is undated. In either of the latter two cases, it is well to staple the envelope to the letter in addition to dating the letter. This will give evidence of the date of mailing as well as the date of receipt.

Envelopes. Generally the envelope may be destroyed after it has been ascertained that everything has been removed and that there are no problems concerned with the names, addresses, or dates.

PREPARATION OF MAIL FOR EMPLOYER

In order to save the employer's time, the efficient secretary should take the time to prepare the mail. This involves several steps.

1. Read each letter, underlining (in ink) important points which will aid you and your employer in answering the letter. Underline only those things which are of significance, such as names of people who are involved in the transaction, publications, dates.
2. Make annotations on each letter. This involves writing notes in the margins. Generally, annotations fall into three categories, namely:
   a. Action required by the letter—date of appointment for correspondent, reservations for a trip the employer may have to make as a result of the correspondence, etc.

   As the letters are being annotated, an efficient secretary will also make a list of files or pieces of correspondence and other information she must look up before presenting the correspondence to the employer.

   Some employers wish to see the mail as soon as it has been opened. In that case the secretary may give him the mail as soon as it has been annotated. While he is reading the mail, the secretary may take the compiled list and seek the necessary files, reports, and other information, for acting upon the urgent mail. To keep all papers pertaining to each piece of correspondence together, use file folders or small clips.

b. Procedures to be followed. These may depend upon former correspondence with the same person or related correspondence, which will have to be sought in the files.

c. Code indicating the priority the letter should receive. In an agreement with the employer a given place on each letter should be established for this code. For example, a red number may be written in the upper left corner. Such a code might include:

Code 1. Mail and reports with high priority and requiring a decision should be answered the same day they are received. It is assumed that personal or confidential mail is delivered unopened to the addressee as soon as it arrives on the secretary's desk.

Code 2. Mail for which additional information must be procured and for which answering may have to be deferred for a day or two while data are being collected. *All mail should be answered within 48 hours of receipt,* except under very unusual circumstances.

Code 3. Routine mail that the secretary may be able to handle. Many employers want to see all mail; it is wise to determine an employer's preference in this regard. After the relationship is well established, many secretaries have their employers' permission to reply to routine letters. In such instances it is usually good procedure to supply the employer with carbons of the letters sent and the original letter.

Code 4. Letters which require notations but no reply.

As the secretary reads and annotates the mail, it becomes a simple matter to encode and sort as she prepares the mail for the employer. A fifth or even a sixth category may be added as needed. Usually important reports require a special category, while weekly, monthly, or semimonthly periodicals may require no encoding. Most employers prefer to examine the periodicals before they are made available to others in the office.

Arranging the mail. After the sorting process has been completed, the secretary may arrange the mail either in one pile with the high-priority mail on top or in any other arrangement she and the employer agree upon. Whenever the mail is placed on the desk of the employer, a substantial weight should be placed on it to keep the letters from blowing off the desk, and some provision should be made so that no one can read the top letter. Some secretaries simply place the top letter face down.

Absence of the employer. Should the employer be away from the office, letters requiring immediate replies may be handled in either of two ways. First, if a decision must be made immediately, it may be necessary to give the mail to the next person in charge and ask him to respond. Second, if the employer will be in the office within a day or two and the decision can wait, the secretary should write the sender immediately and tell him when he may expect a reply and the reason for the delay.

The efficient secretary whose employer has entrusted her with the routine correspondence will maintain a file of materials handled during his absence. Upon his return, she presents the folder to him so that he may be made aware of what has transpired.

OUTGOING MAIL

If the secretary is responsible for the preparation of outgoing mail, as she may well be in a firm too small to have a separate mailing and shipping department, she can save time and expense by familiarizing herself with the various postal and shipping services available and with the general regulations and normal charges pertinent to these services.

An accurate scale for weighing postal matter is a worth-while addition to the office equipment, because it saves time and eliminates guesswork.

SOURCES OF MAIL INFORMATION

To obtain correct information on postal procedures and rates, which are subject to change, consult the local postal authorities. From them, or from the Superintendent of Documents, Government Printing Office, Washington, DC 20402, you can obtain a number of useful pamphlets which are periodically brought up to date. These are some of them:

How To Address Mail
How To Pack and Wrap Parcels for Mailing
Domestic Postage Rates and Fees
How To Prepare Second- and Third-Class Mailings
Mailing Permits
International Mail

Some of the information in those pamphlets is taken from the *Postal Manual,* which contains complete data on postal regulations and procedures. Chapters 1 and 2, which deal with domestic postal service and international mail, respectively, may be purchased separately.

Other publications that can be purchased through the Superintendent of Documents include the *Directory of United States Post Offices,* which lists all domestic post offices, branches, and stations, alphabetically by state, and the *Directory of International Mail,* which gives postal classifications, postage rates, special services, directions for preparing articles for mailing, and import restrictions for each country. A ZIP Code directory should be available to the secretary; it can be obtained from the government (see next page) or for about a dollar at any stationery shop.

STAMPS, STAMPED ENVELOPES, AND POSTCARDS

Postage stamps may be purchased in several forms—single stamps, sheets, books, and coils—and denominations for both regular mail and air mail. For the coil form, inexpensive dispensers are available at the post office. Envelopes printed with stamps for both regular and air-mail first-class postage are also sold at the post office; these may be obtained in two standard sizes. Postcards for both ordinary and air mail are available with the stamp printed on the address side. They come in single or double (reply) forms, with or without postage on the reply half.

Precanceled and meter stamps are two means of reducing the time and costs of mail handling. In order to use precanceled stamps (i.e., stamps canceled before mailing), a special permit must be obtained from the post office. For regulations applying to precanceled stamps, consult the *Postal Manual* or the local postal authorities.

Postage may be paid by printing meter stamps with a postage meter. Postage meters hasten the purchase, control, and attachment of postage and therefore facilitate mailing. Postage-meter machines may be leased from authorized manufacturers. Again, the *Postal Manual* or the local postal authorities should be consulted for regulations governing the leasing, use, and licensing of postal meters and also their manufacture and distribution.

ZIP CODE

The U.S. Postal Service relies heavily on ZIP codes in the processing of mail. While some letters (at this writing) are still delivered even if the ZIP code is not used, they may be delayed by lack of the five-digit code. On the other hand, the Postal Service will not accept quantity mailings of letters, circulars, brochures, catalogs, etc., unless the pieces to be mailed are ZIP coded and sorted by the code.

As you probably know, ZIP stands for Zoning Improvement Plan. And the ZIP itself is a five-digit designation that expedites mail deliveries by cutting down on the steps required to move a letter from sender to addressee. The digits identify state, city, and post office, enabling most efficient use of air, highway and rail transportation of the letter or parcel.

In addition to the ZIP code the Postal Service uses a set of two-letter abbreviations for all of the States and possessions of the United States. Although traditional abbreviations, such as Calif. for California and Mich. for Michigan, are still probably more common the Postal Service suggests the use of these abbreviations with ZIP code.

AK	Alaska	IL	Illinois	ND	North	SC	South
AL	Alabama	IN	Indiana		Dakota		Carolina
AR	Arkansas	KS	Kansas	NH	New	SD	South
AZ	Arizona	KY	Kentucky		Hampshire		Dakota
CA	California	LA	Louisiana	NJ	New Jersey	TN	Tennessee
CO	Colorado	MA	Massachusetts	NM	New Mexico	TX	Texas
CT	Connecticut	MD	Maryland	NV	Nevada	UT	Utah
CZ	Canal Zone	ME	Maine	NY	New York	VA	Virginia
DC	District of	MI	Michigan	OH	Ohio	VI	Virgin
	Columbia	MN	Minnesota	OK	Oklahoma		Islands
DE	Delaware	MO	Missouri	OR	Oregon	VT	Vermont
FL	Florida	MS	Mississippi	PA	Pennsylvania	WA	Washington
GA	Georgia	MT	Montana	PR	Puerto	WI	Wisconsin
HI	Hawaii	NB	Nebraska		Rico	WV	West
IA	Iowa	NC	North	RI	Rhode		Virginia
ID	Idaho		Carolina		Island	WY	Wyoming

A directory of ZIP codes is available from the Information Service, U.S. Postal Service, Washington, DC 20260. Your local telephone directory will generally show local ZIPs.

CLASSES OF MAIL

There are four classes of domestic mail, and these will be discussed later in general terms. Because postal regulations and rates change quite frequently, few details will here be given. If you are to be responsible for mailing packages and parcels, or large quantities of advertising material, or cards or letters of unusual size, you will want to acquire a copy of the appropriate *Leonard's Guide* for your city, available by mail; write to 2121 Shermer Road, Northbrook, Illinois 60062. The *Guide* is also carried in many stationery stores.

While it is unlikely that you will have to exercise such choices, you should know that private, commercial "mail" services are now springing up as a result of the U.S. Postal System's problems in effecting speedy delivery. Often such services operate only within a metropolitan area, but a few nationwide services also exist. All of these will be listed in the Yellow Pages, generally under "Delivery Services." There too you will find a listing of companies that will pick up your mail and deliver it to the post office for speedier handling, or will make pickups of mail directed to a box number at a post office.

First class: all handwritten or typewritten material and all material sealed against postal inspection.

Second class: newspapers and periodicals.

Third class: circulars, books, catalogs, and other printed matter, and merchandise not included in first or second class and weighing less than 16 ounces.

Fourth class, or parcel post: all mailable matter not included in first, second, or third class and weighing 8 ounces or more, but no more than 40 pounds, and not exceeding 84 inches in combined length and girth. (In some circumstances, 70 pounds and 100 inches.)

FIRST-CLASS MAIL

The rate for first-class mail is determined by weight (the ounce or fraction thereof), without regard to distance.

Address. Instructions for typing envelopes are given in Chapter 6. To ensure prompt delivery, observe these precautions regarding the address:

Write the address clearly and legibly, if it cannot be typewritten.

Mail addressed for delivery through a city-delivery post office must include the street and number, or post-office box number, or general delivery, or rural or star route designation. Mail for patrons on a rural route may be addressed to street names and numbers, provided that this type of address has been approved by the Regional Director of the Post Office Department. The rural route number or the words "Rural Delivery" should be used in such addresses.

All mail should bear the name and address of the sender, either in the upper-left corner or on the back flap.

Include the ZIP code on all mail.

Matter bearing more than one address or more than one post office in the return address or in the recipient's address is not acceptable for mailing.

Matter bearing instructions to return to point of mailing (postmark) is not acceptable for mailing.

Envelope size. All envelopes other than the standard size (3⅝ $\times$ 6½ inches) and the legal size (4⅛ $\times$ 9½ inches) should be marked "FIRST CLASS." A rubber stamp is generally used for this purpose, although it is not essential.

Envelopes less than 3 inches high or 4¼ inches long are not acceptable for mailing; those more than 9 inches high or 12 inches long are not recommended.

Postcards. Post, or postal, cards usually measure 3½ $\times$ 5½ inches. In order to be mailed at the postcard rate, which is lower than the first-class letter rate, cards cannot be larger than 4¼ $\times$ 6 inches; nor can they be

FIG. 8. Acceptable form for address side of business-reply mail sent by surface carriers.

FIG. 9. Alternate acceptable form for address side of business-reply mail sent by surface carriers.

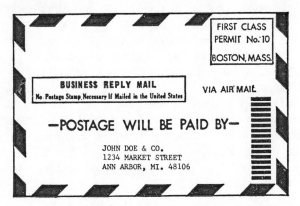

FIG. 10. Acceptable form for address side of business-reply mail sent by air. The border consists of alternate red and blue parallelograms.

enclosed in envelopes. Cards less than 3 inches high or 4¼ inches long are not acceptable for mailing.

Double postal cards are two attached cards, one of which is to be detached by the receiver and returned through the mail as a reply. The reply portion does not have to bear postage when originally mailed. Double cards must have the address of the reply portion on the inside.

Business-reply mail. Specially printed business-reply cards, envelopes, cartons, and labels may be distributed so that they can be returned to the original mailer without prepayment of postage. A permit must be obtained from the local postmaster in order to distribute such mail. There is no charge for the permit. Postage is collected on each piece of business-reply mail at the time it is delivered to the original mailer. The rates are the regular postage rates, plus an additional fee. No special services may be included in these rates.

No limitation is made on the quantity of business-reply mail, but it may not be returned by air mail without full prepayment of postage, and it cannot be sent to any foreign country except to U.S. military post offices overseas.

The forms of imprint and address for business-reply mail must conform to the requirements of the Post Office Department. The address side must be printed in one of the forms illustrated (Figs. 8, 9, 10). No extraneous matter may be added.

SECOND-CLASS MAIL

Since the category of second-class mail is restricted to newspapers and other periodical publications, the mailing of such matter would rarely fall to the lot of the secretary. Special rates apply, according to the nature of the publication, the frequency of publication, and so on.

Publications issued by, and in the interest of, nonprofit organizations and associations, such as religious, educational, scientific, philanthropic, agricultural, labor, and fraternal groups, are categorized for mailing under a special-rate structure.

Because of the variation and specialization of postal regulations in this category, the secretary who finds herself responsible for handling this kind of mail should get specific information from the post office on the particulars applying to the publication with which her office is concerned. However, a few general rules on the wrapping or covering of second-class matter may be useful here.

Preparation for mailing. Second-class mail must be prepared so that it can be easily examined. Even if envelopes, wrappers, or other covers are sealed, the use of second-class postage rates indicates that the sender consents to postal inspection of the contents.

Sealed or unsealed envelopes used as wrappers and sealed wrappers or covers must show in the upper-right corner a notice of entry and in the upper-left corner the name of the publication and the mailing address to which undeliverable copies or change-of-address notices are to be sent.

Special instructions must be followed for the sorting for mailing. These are available through the local post office.

THIRD-CLASS MAIL

All pieces in the third-class category—circulars, books, catalogs, and other printed matter, and merchandise weighing less than 16 ounces—must be legibly marked "Third Class," whether they are sealed or not. They may be mailed and charged by the single piece or in bulk (see *Printed Matter* and *Bulk Mailing,* below). All the pieces in a bulk mailing must be identical in size, weight, and number of enclosures, although the printed textual matter need not be identical. Special rates are available for non-profit organizations.

Preparation for mailing. Third-class mail must be prepared by the sender so that it can be easily examined. It need not be marked "May Be Opened for Postal Inspection," for this is implied in the sending of mail under this class.

Mailers must sort, face, and tie bulk mail into packages, both lengthwise and crosswise, with twine strong enough to withstand handling in the mail. Labels should be large enough to cover the address on the exposed piece of mail and to keep from sliding out from under the twine. Mailers should follow special instructions from the post office. Wrapping, in general, should be handled as for fourth-class mail, or parcel post (see below).

Writing permitted. Other than the address, the only writing permitted on the wrapper of third-class mail is in the form of instructions, such as "Printed Matter"; "Photograph—DO NOT BEND"; "Do Not Open until Christmas."

Enclosures. With catalogs or booklets, one order form, a business-reply card or envelope, and one circular concerning the product being sent may be enclosed.

A letter may also be enclosed in the package if separate first-class postage is paid and the wrapper is marked "Letter Enclosed."

FOURTH-CLASS MAIL (PARCEL POST AND AIR PARCEL POST)

Fourth-class mail includes merchandise, printed matter, mailable live animals, and all other matter not included in first, second, or third class. Rates are determined by weight (fractions of a pound are computed as a full pound) and by distance or zone. To find which zone the place of destination is in, and also to learn of weight and size limitations on parcels, call the post office or consult *Leonard's Guide*.

Special rates apply to library materials, educational materials, and catalogues and similar advertising matter. Educational materials include all bound books; 16-millimeter films and 16-millimeter film catalogs (except films and catalogs mailed to commercial theaters); printed music; printed objective-test materials; sound recordings; manuscripts of books, periodical articles, and music; printed educational reference charts processed for preservation; and loose-leaf pages, and their binders, consisting of medical information for distribution to doctors, hospitals, medical schools, and medical students. The outside of packages containing books or other educational materials must be labeled "BOOK" or "EDUCATIONAL MATERIALS."

There is also a special single-piece rate for catalogs containing 24 pages or more (at least 22 of which are printed) and weighing at least 16 ounces.

Wrapping. Fourth-class mail should be so wrapped that it can be examined easily. If a package is sealed, it is implied that the sender consents to the inspection of the contents.

Two or more packages may be mailed as a single parcel if they are about the same size or shape or if they are parts of one article. They must be securely wrapped or fastened together and must not, together, exceed the weight and size limits.

Packages may be excluded from the mail unless they are wrapped in such a way as to ensure safe transport.

Shipping containers. Containers in which the goods are to be shipped should be strong enough to retain and protect the contents from the weight of other parcels in the mail.

Cushioning contents. Excelsior, flexible corrugated fiberboard, or felt is generally used to protect the contents. Cellulose materials, cotton, clothing, shredded paper, or tissue paper may be used for lighter items.

Outside wrapper. Nonfragile materials may be wrapped in heavy paper and tied with strong twine. Thin paper bags are not acceptable.

Articles that are self-contained may be mailed without outside packaging or wrapping. However, the post office is not responsible if the surface or finish of the article becomes marred or damaged.

A fiberboard carton in good condition may be wrapped and tied with twine or simply tied with twine.

Mailing instructions. All parcel-post packages should be delivered to the post office and not deposited in mailboxes.

1. The return address of the sender must be shown on the face of each package. It is always wise to include inside each package the name and address of the sender as well as of the addressee. If the two addresses are close together, label the return address "from" and the addressee's "to."

Addresses should always be written with ink or an indelible marking pencil or typewritten on a label that is affixed to the package. Tied-on tags should be used only with packages too small to contain the information. It is not necessary to repeat the address on the back of the package.

2. Special inscriptions, such as "Merry Christmas," "Do Not Open until Christmas," or "Happy Birthday," may be written on the wrapper or placed on the contents.

3. Fragile packages, such as those containing glass, china, jewelry, and so forth, must be labeled "FRAGILE."

4. Products which may decay quickly, such as fresh meat or fresh produce, must be labeled "PERISHABLE."

5. The label "DO NOT BEND" may be used only when the contents are fully protected with fiberboard or corrugated fiberboard.

Enclosures. Handwritten and typewritten materials to be included in surface parcel post are limited to the following:

1. Invoices and customers' orders may be enclosed with the merchandise stipulated thereon.

2. A letter may be enclosed, provided that the wrapper is marked "Letter Enclosed" or "First-Class Enclosure" immediately below the postage location. Separate first-class postage is charged for such an enclosure.

Special handling. To ensure that a parcel-post package receives the fastest handling and transportation, the special-handling service may be used, for an additional fee. It does not include special-delivery service.

PRINTED MATTER

Books and catalogs of 24 or more bound pages (at least 22 of which are printed) and weighing less than 16 ounces apiece are considered third-class mail. So are circulars and other printed matter, such as proof sheets, corrected proof sheets with related manuscript copy, and bills or statements of account produced by any photographic or mechanical process.

All other matter wholly or partly in writing, except authorized additions to second-, third-, and fourth-class mail, should be sent as first-class mail.

Such items as printed price lists with written-in changes and applications for licenses, e.g., automobile and drivers' licenses, fall into this classification.

BULK MAILING

Items that are to be mailed at the special bulk-mailing rate should be enclosed in mail sacks or other suitable containers and separated according to route, state, city, or other distribution point; the containers must be taken to the post office.

Postage is computed by rates per pound on the entire bulk mailed at one time, except that the payment can never be less than the minimum charge per piece. An annual bulk-mailing fee must be paid at or before the first mailing of each calendar year. In addition, a postage permit is required for mail to be sent under the imprint system. Under this permit, which may be obtained from the post office for a fee, mail must be prepaid.

The permit imprint may be made by printing press, hand stamp, lithograph, mimeograph, multigraph, addressograph, or similar device. It may not be typewritten or hand-drawn. The style must conform to the specifications set forth by the Post Office Department. Each imprint must show the name of the post office and the permit number. Also, the words "BULK CATALOG RATE" must appear, and a special postal form, or mailing statement, must accompany each mailing.

For detailed instructions on folding, wrapping, labeling, and addressing all classes of mail to be sent at the bulk rate, consult the post office.

AIR MAIL

Mail of all classes, except that which may be damaged by low temperatures or high altitudes, is accepted for air mail. Air mail is transported by airplane and by the fastest connecting surface carriers, and it receives expeditious handling in dispatch and delivery.

Postage for air mail is charged according to weight; for air parcel post, rates take into account both weight and distance, or zone. Postage on air mail may be paid by regular postage stamps, air-mail stamps, stamped cards or envelopes, meter stamps, or permit imprints. In order to have air mail given special delivery to the addressee, the regular special-delivery fee must be paid in addition to the air-mail postage.

The words "AIR MAIL" should be written, stamped, or typed on the face of the envelope, above the address and to the right of the center, slightly below the stamps. On parcels, "AIR MAIL" should appear on the top, bottom, and sides. An adhesive label for this purpose is available without charge at the post office. The return address of the sender must be shown on the address side of each air parcel mailed at zone rates.

SPECIAL POSTAL SERVICES

Insurance. To assure the sender that payment may be obtained for loss of, rifling of, or damage to domestic mail, insurance is available. The fee, which is charged in addition to the regular postage, is based on the liability. By paying a service charge, the sender may be certain that an insured package will be delivered only to the addressee.

Only third- and fourth-class mail may be insured. Insured mail may contain incidental first-class enclosures, so long as they are noted on the face of the package and paid for at the first-class rate. The mail must bear the complete names and addresses of sender and addressee. Articles not sufficiently well packed and wrapped to withstand normal handling are not acceptable for insurance.

Collect on delivery. Collect-on-delivery service permits patrons to mail an article for which they have not been paid and to have the price and the cost of the postage collected from the addressee when the article is delivered. The amount collected is returned to the mailer by a postal money order. Fees for C.O.D. vary according to the amount to be collected and they include insurance.

Registered mail. Additional protection for valuable mail and evidence of mailing and delivery may be obtained by registering it. The sender is required by law to tell the postal clerk or, if the sender is a company, to enter on the company mailing bill the full value of mail presented for registry. The following list offers a guide to the required declaration of values of various types of valuable mail:

Kind of mail	*Value to be declared*
Negotiable instruments Instruments payable to bearer and matured interest coupons	Market value

Nonnegotiable instruments
   All registered bonds, warehouse receipts, checks, drafts, deeds, wills, abstracts, and similar documents
   Certificates of stock, including those endorsed in blank
	No value or replacement cost if postal insurance coverage is desired

Money	Full value
Jewelry, gems, precious metals	Market value or cost
Merchandise	Market value or cost

All classes of mail may be registered except air mail that is likely to be damaged by freezing. First-class postage must be prepaid in registering fourth-class mail. The registry fees are in addition to postage. In the registry of international mail, the indemnity varies according to the country of the addressee.

Special delivery and special handling. Immediate delivery at the address of the recipient during prescribed hours and within certain distance limits may be assured by payment of a special-delivery fee. Payment of this fee does not insure the safety of delivery or provide for payment of indemnity; therefore, money or other valuables sent special delivery should be registered also. Insured, certified, and C.O.D. mail may be sent special delivery.

Fees for special-delivery mail sent by regular first class or by air are based on weight. For all other classes of mail, fixed special-delivery fees apply. Prepayment of fees may be made by special-delivery stamps, ordinary postage stamps, or meter stamps.

Special-handling service is available for fourth-class mail only. It provides for the fastest and most efficient handling and delivery possible, but not for special delivery. Special handling is for those parcels that must be given special attention in handling and delivery, e.g., baby chicks, packaged bees. The fees are based on weight.

Special-delivery and special-handling fees must be paid in addition to regular postage.

Certified mail. Certified-mail service provides a receipt for the person mailing the item and a record of the delivery of the item from the post office from which it is delivered. No record is kept at the post office at which it is mailed. Certified mail is handled in the ordinary mails and is not covered by insurance. If the matter mailed has no intrinsic value, but the sender wishes to be sure that it has been sent to the correct point of receipt, this service is worthwhile.

Any item on which first-class postage has been paid will be accepted as certified mail. This matter may be sent air mail or special delivery if the required postage is also paid. An additional fee is involved if delivery is restricted (i.e., delivery only to the person named in the address) or if a return receipt is requested.

Certificates of mailing. At a fee somewhat lower than that for certified mail, certificates of mailing furnish evidence of mailing only. No receipt is obtained upon delivery of mail to the addressee. The fee does not insure the article against loss or damage.

Return receipt. For certified, insured, and registered mail the sender may wish to have evidence that the mail was received. When such proof of delivery is desired, a return receipt should be requested at the time of mailing. Fees are in addition to the regular postage.

Money orders. A practical method of sending money, if you do not wish to remit by check, is by postal money order. The fees vary according to the amount sent and also according to whether the order is domestic or international. Up to $100 may be sent by a single postal money order, but there is usually no limitation on the number of orders that can be purchased at one time.

INTERNATIONAL MAIL

International mail is divided into two general categories: International Postal Union mail and parcel post. The Postal Union mail includes two classes of matter:

1. LC mail (letters and cards): letters, letter packages, aerograms (air letters), and postcards.
2. AO mail (other articles): printed matter, samples, commercial papers, matter for the blind, and small packets.

The special postal services which apply to Postal Union mail are registration, insurance (though not to all countries), and special delivery in some countries. Consult the post office for details.

In addition, someone who wishes to prepay a reply letter from another country may do so by sending his correspondent one or more international reply coupons, which may be purchased at U.S. post offices. Inquiry should be made at the post office.

To avoid delay and inconvenience, postage on all foreign mail should be prepaid according to weight.

Prohibited articles. Certain articles of a dangerous or objectionable nature are generally prohibited in the international mail: poisons, narcotics, intoxicating liquors, most live animals, explosive or inflammable articles, obscene or libelous matter, and so on. Each country prohibits or restricts the importation of various articles, in addition to those generally prohibited. Such information may be obtained at the post office, provided the country named has made its restrictions known to the post office.

Preparation of Postal Union mail. The address on all articles must be legible and complete, showing the street name and house number, or post-office box number, the name of the post office, province (if known), and the country (on the last line). If the item is addressed in a foreign language, the name of the post office, province, and country must also be shown in English. The sender's name and address should be shown in the upper-left corner of the address side.

All Postal Union articles except letters and letter packages are required to be left unsealed, even if registered.

Mailers must endorse the envelopes or wrappers of all Postal Union articles except letters and post cards to show the classification under which they are being mailed; for example, "Printed Matter," "Printed Matter—Books." The words "Letter (Lettre)" should be written on the address side of letters or letter packages which, because of their size or manner of preparation, may be mistaken for mail of another classification.

In addition, air-mail articles should be plainly endorsed "Par Avion" or have such a label affixed; articles intended for special delivery should be marked boldly as "Express" or "Special Delivery."

International parcel post. Parcel-post packages that exceed certain size limitations are not accepted for mailing to foreign countries. Consult the post office about these and other restrictions.

Special services are subject to variation, but in certain cases registration and insurance are possible. Special handling, with the same provisions as for domestic mail, may be secured.

Packages for overseas mailing must be even more carefully packed and wrapped than those being sent within the confines of the United States. Containers should be strong enough to protect the contents from damage caused by pressures of other packages in the mail and by variations in climate and altitude.

Registered or insured parcels must be sealed. Consult the post office to determine restrictions of individual countries.

Customs declarations and other forms. A parcel-post sticker and at least one customs declaration are required for parcel-post packages (surface or air) mailed to another country. To some countries a dispatch note or more than one declaration form may be required. Detailed information may be obtained at the post office.

FORWARDING MAIL

First-class mail. The only class of mail that may be forwarded from one city or town to another without the payment of additional postage is first class. It may also be reforwarded without the payment of additional postage. Should the person forwarding the mail wish to send it by air mail, this may be done by simply affixing postage amounting to the difference between the surface-mail and the air-mail rates.

Second-class mail. If the addressee has moved from the address on the letter and left instructions that he agrees to pay forwarding postage, or if he has moved within a town and left a forwarding address, the mail will be sent to the new address. If mail is sent to the old address more than three months after the person has moved, the mailer will receive a notice giving the addressee's new address. If the new address is not known, the sender will receive a statement indicating why the mail was not delivered. This notice costs the mailer a small fee.

Third-class mail. A locally addressed circular or pamphlet mailed to a person who has moved from his former address will be destroyed unless the mailer marks it "Return Requested." Should the mailing piece be a package and apparently of some value, it will be forwarded, and the addressee will be charged the forwarding rate.

Mail marked "Return Requested" will be returned to the sender with a notation advising him of the new address or an explanation of why it could not be delivered. This notice costs a small fee.

Fourth-class mail. If the addressee has left a forwarding address, the package will be delivered and the addressee will be charged additional postage, depending upon the weight of the package and the distance forwarded. If there is no forwarding address, the package will be returned to the sender, and he will be charged for the return postage.

Forwarding foreign mail. Mail arriving in this country from a foreign country may be forwarded to any destination within the United States, or outside, without additional postage.

Surface mail may be forwarded by air if the full air-mail postage is affixed.

Mail arriving in the country may be forwarded "postage collect" to any destination within the United States or may have the new postage prepaid and affixed. Such mail may not be forwarded to another foreign country without rewrapping, procuring a customs declaration, and affixing new postage.

U.S. mail to be forwarded to a destination outside the country should always have any additional postage affixed before leaving the United States, because some countries charge double postage for mail arriving with postage due.

OTHER INSTRUCTIONS ABOUT MAIL

Recall of mail. At times it is desirable to recall a piece of mail that has already been delivered to a post office or dropped into a mailbox. In such instances the sender must go to the post office and complete a written application and present a similar envelope or wrapper to identify the piece of mail being recalled.

Change of address. Prior to moving, each individual or firm should procure from the post office and complete the change-of-address card. Change-of-address cards are available in quantity, so that all correspondents and publishers of periodicals regularly received may be notified of the new address and the date of its effect. It is wise to notify the publishers of periodicals at least one month before the move actually takes place, so that magazines and newspapers are not sent to the old address.

Undeliverable mail. First-class mail that bears no return address cannot be returned to the sender in the event that it is undeliverable; therefore, it is imperative that all mail have a return address typed or written on it.

Franked mail. The Federal government uses "franked" mail, that is, mail sent free of postage. The franked envelope may be used only for surface mail; it may not be used for air mail unless the air-mail postage is affixed. There is a Federal penalty for misuse of franked mail.

Unmailable items. The following items may not be sent through the U.S. mails. In fact, penalties are imposed on the mailers of these items.

Game, unlawfully killed, or prohibited from mailing.
Meat and meat-food products, without certificate of inspection.
Plants and plant products not accompanied by required certificate. Certain plants are prohibited from shipment into certain states by quarantine order. (Before attempting to mail plants, consult a postal authority.)
Poisons, except those for scientific use and those sent to licensed dealers.
Intoxicating liquors.
Explosive, flammable; corrosive, or toxic substances.
Live animals, except harmless, tiny ones that need no care, as day-old chicks or bees.
Foul-smelling articles.
Harmful articles, as sharp-pointed or sharp-edged tools insufficiently protected.
Firearms capable of being concealed on the person (with exceptions).
Matter tending to incite arson, murder, assassination, insurrection, or treason.
Indecent matter, written or other.
Defamatory, dunning, or threatening matter on post cards or on the outside of any piece of mail.
Lottery, gift, or endless-chain enterprises, or fraudulent matter.

Mail opened by mistake. At times mail is misdelivered and opened by mistake and has to be forwarded. When this happens, the person who opens it should simply reseal the envelope with tape and write "Opened by Mistake" and sign his name or initials. The mail should then be dropped into a mailbox or handed to the postman.

EXPRESS

Practically anything transportable may be sent by express. However, mail cannot be sent by express, nor can documents on which action is to be taken. An example is the punched card. If the cards are being transported from the office to storage, they may be shipped by express; yet, if the punched cards are to be further processed at their destination, they may not be shipped by that method.

Valuable papers, such as bonds, may be sent by express, provided that they can be replaced. Nothing irreplaceable should be sent by this means of transportation. Certain items are barred from express shipments, such as those containing explosives. Consult the nearest express agency office for other specific limitations.

Live animals may be sent by express and are entitled to receive special attention. In fact, a record form is completed to show the treatment of each animal sent by this means. For instance, dogs are fed; the kind of food, the day and the hour of feeding are recorded; dogs are also walked at intervals and a record is made of the service.

Pickup and delivery. REA Express (Railway Express Agency) offers pickup and inside-delivery service free of charge. Prepayment may be made to the driver, or the shipment may be sent "express collect." The express company then assumes full responsibility for collecting the express charges.

Rates. Express rates vary depending upon class, type of commodity, and distance. There are many commodity rates covering about 4,000 commodities. In many cases a commodity rate may be less than the general rate for sending a package by a given class of express. The local express company should be consulted for given rates on commodities, and also to determine which of the four classes of rates applies to a given shipment.

Shipments may be sent C.O.D.

Preparation for shipment. The following information must be given to the express company before a shipment can be made:

Consignee's name and local address
Value of shipment
Number of pieces of shipment and type of container
Weight
Description of articles shipped
Shipper's name and address
Information regarding payment

The address of the shipper and the consignee should both be written on the packing slip and enclosed in the package.

Packing containers. The express company provides, at no cost to the sender, containers in which goods may be shipped. A telephone call will trigger the delivery of containers according to a company's need. Two days are allowed for packing of the containers by the sender and two days for unpacking by the consignee. The basic rate for this service is 2,500 pounds, regardless of how light in weight the shipment is. Advantages of the container service are that (1) split lots are avoided, (2) multipiece handling is eliminated, and (3) pilferage is kept at a minimum.

The consignor should specify how he will accept payment (check or cash), and the express company will not release the shipment unless the correct form of payment is made.

Lot shipments, collect and prepaid. In many instances more than one package may be sent to one consignee. All pieces should be assembled so that one receipt may be given for the entire shipment. A lot-shipment label will be affixed to each piece and will carry on it information regarding the number of pieces, weight, declared value, and the number of the receipt.

Armed-guard service or armed surveillance. When valuable items or high-priority confidential materials are being shipped, two services are available to protect the shipment. First, whenever necessary, a shipment may be accompanied by an armed guard who will remain with the shipment, supervise the loading of the items, be locked in the car or truck with the shipment, and guard the items during delivery. Second, armed surveillance provides supervision of the shipment but without the same intense care as the former service. An armed guard supervises the loading at the point of origin, at transfer points, and when it is delivered to the consignee. These two services may be provided for air or surface transportation.

Special-care items. Special care is provided for items requiring refrigeration or icing. Refrigerated cars are, of course, standard equipment. In transporting some commodities it is essential that dry ice be used. There is no charge for the service of dry ice, but there is a charge if regular ice must be used. Items requiring use of ice are re-iced at transfer points.

Express money orders. Money orders may be handled by express. Like postal money orders, they are limited to $100 each.

DOMESTIC AIR EXPRESS

Air express offers the same pickup and inside delivery as surface express for those cities or towns having airports. This service is extended to the areas surrounding such towns, but an additional charge is made to "off-line" points outside the area served by the airport. The nearest express office should be queried as to the exact points to which delivery is made with no additional charge.

Air express for packages weighing from 5 pounds to 50 pounds and sent within the United States is often cheaper than surface express.

Shipments may be sent prepaid, collect, or collect on delivery.

INTERNATIONAL EXPRESS

International express (both surface and air) is provided by both Railway Express and American Express. Inquiries should be made at the express office to determine the feasibility of using international express carriers rather than parcel post. Pickup and delivery services are available at most points in the United States and Canada. Insurance is available for all international shipments. Rates may be procured at the nearest express office.

Surface. When surface transportation is used, shipments are routed to one of the following gateway cities:

Los Angeles, Calif.	New York, N.Y.
San Francisco, Calif.	Philadelphia, Pa.
Chicago, Ill.	Houston, Tex.
New Orleans, La.	Laredo, Tex.
Baltimore, Md.	Norfolk, Va.
Boston, Mass.	Seattle, Wash.
Detroit, Mich.	

Air. The Railway Express Agency also handles all air express. Surface express is used to transport shipments to the following air gateways:

Los Angeles, Calif.	St. Louis, Mo.
San Francisco, Calif.	New York, N.Y.
Washington, D.C.	Portland, Ore.
Miami, Fla.	Philadelphia, Pa.
Chicago, Ill.	Brownsville, Tex.
New Orleans, La.	Dallas, Tex.
Baltimore, Md.	Houston, Tex.
Boston, Mass.	San Antonio, Tex.
Detroit, Mich.	Seattle, Wash.
Minneapolis, Minn.	

Inquiries should be made at the nearest office concerning limitations of size and weight, as well as charges for shipment and insurance.

Complete customs-brokerage service is provided on import shipments, and arrangements are made for interior transportation.

PACKAGE EXPRESS BY BUS AND AIR

Bus lines offer package express within the United States and Canada. Consult them for information on rates, requirements, and restrictions, and for up-to-date schedules. Many airlines also accept small packages and envelopes for airport-to-airport delivery; the item will be held for pickup at the luggage-return area.

Prohibited articles. All packages are accepted for shipment by bus except those which contain the following:

Acids
Alcoholic beverages and liquors
Ammunition
Animals, live
Articles packed in wet ice or water
Batteries, electric-storage, wet
Birds
Dangerous articles
Explosives
Flammable materials
Fluorescent signs (fabricated)
Gases in cylinders
Jewelry, when the declared value is more than $50
Materials having disagreeable odor
Money
Motion-picture films (flammable)
Neon signs or bent neon tubing
Perishable shipments
Potted flowers or plants
Reptiles, live
Wild game
X-ray tubes

The following articles may be shipped by bus only under certain conditions, and special packing and marking requirements must be followed:

Fish and shellfish
Meat or meat products
Poultry or poultry products
Tires

Packing and marking. Shipments must be packed in containers made of material sufficiently strong to withstand the handling accompanying shipment. The names and addresses of the sender and the addressee should be shown in the same way as they are for parcel-post shipments.

For shipments to Canada the shipper must prepare the U.S. Customs export declaration forms and the Canadian Customs invoice. These forms should be placed in the special international envelope and fastened securely to the shipment. Also, an "INTERNATIONAL" sticker must be affixed to each package.

II *Telegrams, Cables, and Radio Messages*

When speed is of key importance in delivering a written message at home or abroad, you will probably instantly think of sending a telegram or cable.

However, doing this does not necessarily imply that your message will be delivered within minutes or hours. You must be aware that there are different classes of service, some considerably faster than others; and that often a phone call is not only much faster but also less expensive. Even an overseas call may cost only a few dollars more than a brief cable, and if the message can be delivered verbally rather than in writing, the additional expense may be justified by speed and certainty of receipt.

A key question, then, is whether the message *must* be delivered in print on paper with a record of when sent (and in some cases when received). Many companies and organizations understandably insist that such information as prices and specifications be submitted in a form that can be kept by them as a record—e.g., by telegram or cable if not in letter form, or by the system (to be discussed later) known as Telex. In such cases, however, the person who sends the telegram *must specify* that it be actually delivered to the recipient; otherwise, the message may simply be telephoned by the local Western Union to the recipient, with actual delivery of the printed message following by local mail.

Another key question is whether one message to one person is involved, or whether the same message will go to many people—for example, to all the men and women on a large sales force, or to all the dealers who sell a particular product. Western Union has effective systems for wide distribution of a specific message, including a comparatively inexpensive overnight service. (The overnight service can also be used to assure quick delivery of important messages in all parts of the country.)

If a response is desired, it is advisable to specify how that response should be sent. For example, you may ask a travel agency to send a cable requesting a hotel room; and he will ask for a cabled response. But if the agent sends the cable by reduced-rate night service, and if the hotel responds by similarly delayed service, the exchange of cables may take three days rather than a few hours.

Because the rates and rules of telegraph, cable, and radio change frequently, we will not attempt to specify costs or to provide detailed instructions as to the number of words transmitted at various base rates. Where such details appear, they are to be taken as examples rather than as specifics. Your local Western Union office will provide the latest printed material to you on request (along with blank forms for your use). The companies handling cable and radio services, named in the appropriate sections of this part of the chapter, will also furnish you with current information and materials.

TELEGRAPH SERVICE

Time of day. The time of day at which a telegram is sent is of vital importance. When a New York business office closes, a Chicago (Central Time) office has one hour left in the business day; a Denver (Mountain Time) office, two more hours; and a San Francisco (Pacific Time) office, three more hours. At 4:45 P.M. in New York there is time left to complete a pending deal in Chicago, thereby perhaps saving the company dollars that a day's delay may cost. (See Table 1, Appendix 8.)

CLASSES OF SERVICE

Full-rate or fast message (speed service). No abbreviation or indicator is used for the full-rate telegram. The omission of a class-of-service indicator on a telegraphic message means that the message will be sent as a full-rate telegram. The characteristics of this class of service are as follows:

15 words to start with
Additional words charged at low extra-word rate
Address and signature not charged for
Immediate transmission and delivery
May be sent in plain language or code

Day letter (DL). A day letter may be sent at any time of the day or night and is delivered during any hours the recipient's office is open. If it is desirable to have the day-letter message delivered to a business address at night, put "DLR TONIGHT" or "PHONE" and the telephone number (if known) with the addressee's name and address. Day letters are delivered at night whenever offices are open. A 50-word message or less costs approximately the same as a 25-word full-rate message. Additional words are counted in units of five. Transmission is deferred only for full-rate messages.

Night letter (NL). A night letter may be sent at any time up to 2 A.M. for delivery on the morning of the next business day. On weekends or holidays deliveries are made to business offices when open, and other disposition will be made if instructions from the addressee are on file or if the sender specifically requests. Deliveries are made to residences on any day. The minimum rate begins at 50 words or less. Additional words are counted in units of five.

SELECTING THE CLASS OF SERVICE

Fast messages usually provide the most efficient service. Night letters are the least expensive and are used when the speed of delivery is not an important consideration. Night letters can be used effectively to send information on which action is not required until the following morning or messages going out late in the business day.

When speed of service is important, a choice must be made between a fast message and a day letter. Generally, for messages of less than 25 words the fast message is less expensive and more efficient. For messages over 25 words, it is generally less expensive to select day-letter service.

Code words as well as plain language may be sent in full-rate messages, day letters, and night letters at the prevailing rates.

PREPARING THE TELEGRAPH FORM

A correctly prepared telegram is shown in Fig. 11. In filling out telegraph forms, the following points should be observed:

Use telegraph blanks provided by Western Union.
Prepare to type at least three copies of the message—one to be sent, one to be retained in the company file, and one to be filed with copies of all other messages sent so that they may be checked against Western Union's bill.
In the box in the upper left-hand corner check the class of service to be used —day letter or night letter. Unless the class is indicated, the message will be sent as a full-rate or fast telegram.

Point of origin should be written on the right-hand side immediately above the date.

Always date the message. In business questions often arise as to when a message was sent and when it was received.

Type in double space, using capital letters or, if you prefer, capital and lower-case letters.

Type the full name and address of the recipient. Use as many words in the address as are necessary to the location of the addressee.

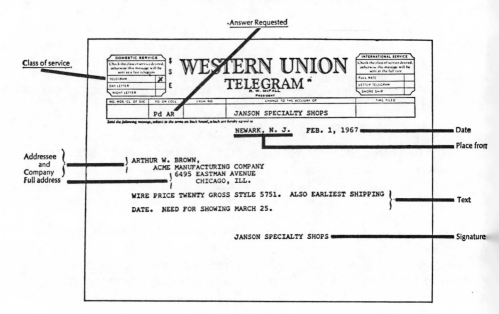

FIG. 11.   Western Union telegram form correctly filled out. Every telegram prepared should include each of the elements labeled in the margins around the sending blank.

The telegraph company charges nothing for the name and address of the addressee, unless more than one name is given (for example, "Henry Adams or Jeffrey Rose"). If two alternative names are used, a charge is made for the second name. The full name and address should be used, as:

```
Lawrence Allen
Todd Leather Company
1616 West Berk Street
New York, N.Y.
```

When sending a telegram to an individual in a large office building, be sure to include either the name of the company or the room number of the office.

"Mrs." "Ms.," or "Miss" is generally used to signify that the recipient is a woman, while "Mr." is not used in telegrams unless no first name or initial is given. The titles "Dr.," "Rev.," "Major," "Hon.," and so forth may be used.

"Care of" may be sent without additional charge.

"Hold for Arrival," followed by the time or a date, may be sent without additional charge.

```
      Leon P. Adams, Hold for Arrival, 6 p.m.
         (or June 15)
      Summit Hotel
      New York, N.Y.
```

A telephone number may be sent free of charge when it accompanies the address. The receiving telegraph office will then telephone the message and later mail a copy of the message to the addressee, if the request is made.

ZIP code is unnecessary in sending telegrams.

Code addresses are not acceptable on domestic telegraph messages.

Report delivery. If a report of delivery of the message is desired, the words "Report Delivery" should be written following the addressee's name:

```
      William B. Warren, Report Delivery
      393 Bates Road
      Lenox, Mass.
```

The words "Report Delivery" are charged for. Immediately following delivery, a telegram is sent "collect" to the sender, indicating the time of delivery. If desired, the indicator "Report Delivery and Address" may be used, in which event the time and address at which delivery is made will be reported.

Personal delivery. "*Only*" may be stipulated if the sender wishes to assure that delivery of the message will be made only to the addressee and to no one else. (This service corresponds to "restricted delivery" in postal services.)

"Will Call" should be written immediately after the name in the address if someone is going to call at the telegraph office for a given message. The message will be held at the central telegraph station, but it may be called for at any branch office.

"Do Not Phone" may be written in the address at no extra charge.

Two addresses may be given, if desirable, and a charge will be made for the alternate address.

Multiple addressees. If copies of a message are to be sent to different persons, it is necessary to furnish only one copy of the message text and a list of the names and addresses. The required number of copies of the message will be made in the telegraph office, and the names and addresses of the multiple addressees will be added from the list.

Message to a passenger on a train. Give full details:

Name of passenger	Leonard Morris, en route Miami
Care of conductor	Care of conductor
Pullman reservation (if known)	Car 16, Roomette B
Train name and number	Silver Star
Arrival time and station	12:12 P.M., Miami, Fla.

If not all information is known, give as much as is available. It is not charged for. Arrival time is most important. If it is not known, telephone the railroad for the information.

Any passenger who expects a message should tell the conductor. Should a conductor be unable to locate the addressee, the message will be returned to the telegraph company at the next station. The sender will then be notified that the message was not delivered.

Message to a passenger on a plane. Messages may be transmitted to the airports and delivered to passengers emplaning or deplaning. Give full details:

Name of passenger	Woodrow Lewis, passenger
Name of air line	Trans World Airlines, Inc.
Flight number and direction traveling	Flight 34, eastbound
Arrival time and airport	11:10 A.M., O'Hare Airport, Chicago, Ill.

Message to a passenger on a ship. Messages may be transmitted to sailing or arriving ships and delivered to passengers. Give full details:

Name of passenger	Frederick Yerkes, passenger
Name of steamship line	Woodson Line
Name of ship and stateroom number (if known)	SS Calgary, Stateroom B202
Time of sailing and pier	4 P.M. sailing Pier 97
Departure port	New York, N.Y.

Message to a passenger on a ship at sea (see below, *Radio Marine Service*).

PREPARING THE MESSAGE

A well-written telegraph message is concise. Because the charges are based upon the number of words sent, each word in the message should convey meaning, and no word necessary to the meaning should be omitted.

Use nouns and verbs freely to convey the message. Often prepositions, pro-
nouns, adjectives, and adverbs may be omitted without affecting the mean-
ing of the message.
Omit salutations and complimentary closes.
Do not divide words at the end of the line.
Paragraphing used in the original message is followed by the sending office.
Paragraphs should be used when they contribute to the clarity of the
message.

Identification initials. It is just as important on telegrams as on letters to identify the sender of the message by initials. They are not transmitted as part of the message, but they provide a record should a question arise regarding the composer of the message or the transcriber. Therefore it is important to have both sets of initials.

Charge or collect. If a message is to be charged to the account of a business or an individual, the name of the account should be indicated in the space provided for that purpose. If a message is to be sent collect, "Collect" should be written above the date.

Address of sender. The sender's name, address, and telephone number should be placed on the lower left-hand side of each wire. This permits the telegraph company to notify the sender immediately of an undelivered message; also, the information may assist in the telegraph company's billing procedure.

Second page of message. If a message is too long to be completed on one telegraph blank, a second telegraph blank is not necessary. A sheet of plain stationery should be used, headed in the same manner as a second sheet of a letter, except for the deletion of "Mr."

<pre>
     Samuel Jones   2   April 16, 19--
</pre>

When using a second page, begin the heading about two inches from the top of the page so that the telegraph company may paste the telegraph form and the second page together to display a continuous message.

Before sending a two-page message to the telegraph company, staple the pages together to prevent separation.

Confirmation copy. Wise secretaries routinely mail confirmation copies of certain telegrams to the addressee. A regular telegraph blank may be used for this copy, but the sender must be sure to type "CONFIRMATION" at the top of the blank.

Billing copy. In addition to the file copy of each telegram, a second carbon copy should be retained in a separate file for checking against the bill from Western Union. After the monthly bill is checked, such copies are destroyed.

Typing rush telegrams. When an emergency message must take precedence over what is in the typewriter, it is simple to complete the line being typed and remove the paper from the typewriter; but the paper in the machine need not be removed if the method explained in Chapter 6 is used.

WORD COUNT

Any word listed in the dictionary is counted as one word. That rule can be applied to all telegraphic messages. Nondictionary words or expressions are counted as one word for every five letters.

An abbreviation of five letters or less is counted as one word, provided it is written with no spacing: "COD" or "C.O.D.," "AM" or "A.M."

Geographical names are counted according to the number of words as normally written. Examples:

New York City, 3 words	N.Y.C., 1 word
St. Augustine, 2 words	
United States, 2 words	U.S., 1 word
North Carolina, 2 words	N.C., 1 word

Proper names are counted by the number of words and initials they contain:

Van de Perle, 3 words
Vanderbilt, 1 word
P. Conners, 2 words
T. H. Hanlon, 3 words

Each initial in a name is counted as a separate word:

A. F. Miller, 3 words
Sidney B. Wolf, 3 words

A surname prefix, such as "De" in De Berendinis or "Mac" in Mac-Dougall, is not counted as a separate word when it is written without separation by a space.

Punctuation. Punctuation marks are free. Punctuation marks such as the period, comma, colon, semicolon, dash, hyphen, decimal point, parentheses, question mark, quotation marks, and apostrophe are neither counted nor charged for. On the other hand, an apostrophe used in a figure group to designate "feet" or a quotation mark used to designate "inches" is counted as a chargeable character.

All words are counted; "stop," "comma," and "quote" are charged for as words when they are spelled out.

Figures and characters. Figures are counted as one word for a group of five figures or less:

    67,383 = 1 word
    1,343,682 = 2 words
    1–12–65 = 1 word

Figures that are written out are counted as they are written:

thirty-six, 2 words
one hundred five, 3 words

Signs such as #, $, &, and the / (diagonal) for fractions are counted and charged for in figure groups, but the diagonal counts as a separate word in expressions such as "and/or."

    #22 (3 characters), 1 word
    $36.42 (5 characters), 1 word
    2½ (transmitted 2-½), 1 word
    and/or, 3 words
    12/2/68 (7 characters), 2 words

The symbols ¢ and @ cannot be transmitted and should be written out. The per cent sign, %, is transmitted as o/o and counts as three characters.

Signatures. Only one individual's name is carried without extra charge, but a title, a department name, or the name of a firm added to an individual's name will be carried without charge. Examples:

Ruth M. Henderson, Treasurer
Ruth M. Henderson, Credit Department
Ruth M. Henderson, Woodrow Lumber Company

When an individual's name is followed by a title and a firm name, the title is charged for. "Sales Manager" would be charged for in the following example:

Ruth M. Henderson, Sales Manager
Woodrow Lumber Company

If two persons' names are sent, one is charged for:

Mary Brown and George Ace

In family signatures such as the following, no extra charge is made:

Mary and Bill
Mary and Bill Jones and family

An address following a signature is charged for.

TELEPHONING A TELEGRAM

Messages are frequently telephoned to a Western Union office and charged to the monthly telephone bill. The person answering at Western Union will take any message given. Simply give the following information:

Calling telephone number (for billing purposes)
Class of service
Addressee's name and address
Message
Sender's name and address

When dictating a message over the telephone, pronounce each letter of a difficult word.

TELEGRAPHIC COSTS

To calculate in advance the cost of telegraphic messages, the secretary must have the rate sheets, which can be obtained from Western Union. Because rates are subject to change, it is important to check with the telegraph company to be sure that the rate sheets on file in the office are up to date.

Credit cards. Western Union credit cards are useful for traveling business-men. Holders may charge domestic and international messages to the account name and number.

MEANS OF TRANSMITTING MESSAGES

The secretary may have several choices as to how the domestic telegram may be filed with the telegraph company.

Desk-Fax. The Desk-Fax is a unit of facsimile equipment. The sender may either write or type the message and place it around the drum of the Desk-Fax. Inside the machine an electric eye then scans the telegraph message and automatically sends an exact reproduction of it directly to the Western Union office in the area.

Private-wire system. Regardless of size or complexity, the function of any private-wire system furnished and maintained by Western Union is to provide instantaneous, continuous communication between stations on the system.

The simplest private-wire system is a two-point channel with a teleprinter at each end that both sends and receives messages. These machines may be on two different floors of the same building or hundreds of miles apart, perhaps connecting the company with a branch office or a correspondent.

Large private-wire systems may be thought of as roughly resembling a huge wagon wheel in their physical layout. Around the rim of the wheel are the stations that send and receive messages. These stations are linked to each other by a switching center at the wheel's hub. In addition, if there is a large volume of communications between two points on the rim, these points can also be connected with each other by direct circuits as well as to the switching center at the hub. A major advantage of such a system is that it permits a message to be routed instantly from any station on the system to any or all of the other stations through the central switching station at the hub. Just as in the case of simple two-point circuits, the extensive private-wire systems are engineered to provide two-way record communication between any two stations on the system.

Because of such technological advancements as integrated data processing (IDP) and electronic computers, greater importance has devolved upon high-speed, reliable communications. Through private-wire systems it is possible to provide sufficient volumes of data at a centralized processing center to utilize the full potential benefits to be derived from a computer installation. Private-wire systems are engineered to handle either administrative messages or bits of data in machine language over the same system with equal facility.

SERVICES OFFERED

Telex service. Telex is a dial-direct subscriber-to-subscriber service for record and data communications made available by Western Union within the United States and, through connections with other carriers, to Canada, to Mexico, and to most overseas countries. A subscriber to this Western Union service is provided with a console-mounted teleprinter, supplemented with dial and automatic answer-back equipment. Connection with another subscriber in the United States, Canada, or Mexico is established within eight seconds by dialing the distant subscriber's station number. The automatic answer-back feature enables the subscriber to confirm the correctness of the connection established, thus permitting transmission even though the called subscriber's station is unattended. A small, fixed monthly service charge applies, and for each Telex call placed only the amount of actual time used during the connection is charged for. There is no minimum period charged for on Telex calls to stations in the United States, Canada, and Mexico. For subscribers desiring to prepare their communications in advance, and thereby keep their Telex call usage time to a minimum, Western Union offers, at a nominal additional charge, alternate equipment that enables the subscriber to prepare and transmit perforated tape.

Tel(T)ex service. An additional service available to Western Union Telex subscribers permits the subscriber to send messages to nonsubscribers at major cities in the United States and Canada. The Telex subscriber dials and transmits his message to the destination city telegraph office, where delivery is made to the addressee. A flat-rate delivery fee is made for each Tel(T)ex message, plus the usual charge for the time used in the Telex transmission of the Tel(T)ex message.

Teletypewriter exchange service (TWX). Subscribed to by many companies for direct subscriber-to-subscriber transmission of telegraph messages, TWX service is made possible by the installation in the subscriber's office of a teletype machine which can be connected by wire to teletype machines of other TWX subscribers within the United States. A small monthly rental is made for the equipment, and the subscriber is billed by the telephone company for each three-minute period of usage, with an additional charge made for each additional minute or fraction of a minute of usage. TWX service is also available to Canadian subscribers, the basic charge being for one minute.

Personal opinion message (POM) service. A special service offering reduced rates permits the sender to send telegraph messages expressing his views on current issues to the President of the United States, the Vice President, senators, and congressmen in Washington, or to the governor, lieutenant governor, and legislators at a state capital.

Speedata. At the point of origin, data on sales, payrolls, and inventory are sent on regular telegraph forms and converted to punched tape before being delivered to the recipient. The customer may select the speed of service desired and send data as a fast telegram, day letter, or night letter.

Wirefax. A public facsimile service between major cities provides direct transmission of letters, drawings, or any graphic materials.

Tie-line discount. For customers who have private tie-line connections to the telegraph company's operating room, a discount is applicable on each paid message over 100 messages per month filed over the tie line.

Recall of wires. The sender may stop a message by calling the telegraph office, provided that the telephone message reaches the office before the message has been transmitted. If the message has already been transmitted, a paid telegraph message requesting cancellation of the previous message may be sent to the telegraph company at the destination. If the sender requests, a collect reply can be sent, indicating whether the cancellation was effectuated.

Report delivery. Whenever a report of delivery is desired, the sender simply writes "Report Delivery" beside the address. A charge is made for the two words, and a report will then be made in the form of a collect message.

Should a message be undeliverable for any reason, such as a wrong address or the inability of the telegraph company to locate the addressee, a report to the sender will automatically be sent by the telegraph company without charge.

Telegraphic money orders. Money may be sent quickly and safely by telegraph, and payment is made during the open hours of the destination office. Money-order payments in foreign countries are usually made in the currency of the country of destination and are subject to prevailing exchange rates. In addition to the charges for a message to the destination city, a money-order fee applies, depending on the amount of money transmitted.

To send money by telegraph, complete a telegraphic money-order form, giving the name and address of the recipient, any message, and the sender's name and address; then deliver to the telegraph office the money and the completed form.

At the destination the telegraph office will deliver a money-order draft or notify the recipient that the money may be called for at the telegraph office. Before a money-order draft can be cashed, the person is asked to present evidence of his identity.

Special greetings. Suggested texts for greeting messages are available at the telegraph office, or the sender may compose an original message. Appropriate telegraph blanks are available for all major holidays and other occasions.

INTERNATIONAL COMMUNICATIONS

Technological improvements in communications have resulted in increased speed and capacity, as well as in reduction of costs for sending cablegrams. The use of sophisticated computers now permits automatic electronic handling of messages through one or more of the following: high-frequency radio channels, submarine cable, or radio satellite.

Two classes of service are available: full-rate cables (FR) and letter telegrams (LT). In addition, there are two other services: Telex and leased-channel service.

Telex. Telex service (see above) is available for overseas written communications over either a Bell System TWX or Western Union Telex. The service is offered by ITT World Communications, Inc., RCA Communications, Inc., and Western Union International, Inc. To communicate with firms having Telex equipment in their offices overseas, the procedure is to call the Telex Center of any one of the three international carriers, identify yourself, and give the area code for the country being called, plus the Telex number of the correspondent.

By means of Data Telex, it is now possible to send some 1,500 words per minute over special broad-band channels of the international carriers for the transmission of intelligence of any type. Special computers and data equipment must be installed at both ends of these circuits in the carrier's and the correspondents' offices in order to take advantage of this high-speed service. The rates for Data Telex service, where it is available, carry a minimum charge for each connection. Special arrangements must be made with the international carriers, as this service is limited and must be scheduled in advance.

Leased-channel service. Through one of the major companies providing international communication service, leased-channel service provides instantaneous two-way communication 24 hours a day for firms whose volume of international messages warrants it. Service may be leased for a month or longer.

The company renting the service may transmit quickly and efficiently messages which would otherwise be handled by cable, air mail, or telephone.

Full-rate messages (FR). A full-rate message may be written in any language that can be expressed in Roman letters or in secret language. A minimum charge is based on seven words, including the address and signature. Twenty-four-hour service is available for rapid transmission of messages. Each secret-language, nondictionary word is counted at the rate of five characters, or fraction of five characters, to the word. For sending messages of eight text words or less, FR service is faster and costs less.

Letter telegrams (LT). The letter telegram is an overnight service for plain-language messages. A minimum charge is made for 22 words. Any number of words may be sent at half the rate of the full-rate message.

SENDING INTERNATIONAL MESSAGES

ITT World Communications, Inc., issues a *Pocket Guide* and periodically revised rate folders, which serve as a handy reference for sending
international telegraph and Telex messages to virtually all parts of the
world. Free copies may be obtained from ITT World Communications,
Inc., 67 Broad Street, New York, New York 10004.

Collect messages may not be used for countries which are not United
States possessions, except for Canada and Mexico.

The basic regulations are:

Each word of the address, text, and signature is counted and charged for.

Each plain-language dictionary word is counted at the rate of 15 characters,
or fraction of 15 characters, to the word. (See FR for count of secret language.)

Figures, letters, signs, or combinations of them are counted as five characters
per word.

If the name of a place is a compound word (e.g., Stratford on Avon), the
name of destination point is joined and counted as one word, regardless of
length.

In figure or letter groups, punctuation is counted as one character each.

Examples	No. of characters	Words charged
15,545	6	2
6,121	5	1
127,545	7	2

Punctuation used in conjunction with words is counted as one word each
and transmitted only on special request of the sender. Exceptions are the
two signs forming the parentheses ( ) and quotation marks (" " or ' '),
which are counted as one word.

Examples	Words charged
( )	1
" "	1
' '	1

Those punctuation marks and signs acceptable for transmission upon the
sender's recommendation are:

period (.)
comma (,)
colon (:)
division sign (÷)
question mark (?)
apostrophe or feet or minutes (')

inches or seconds (")
hyphen, dash, or subtraction sign (–)
diagonal (/)

Cable code address. A company which sends a volume of cable messages will find it economical to register a cable code address of its choice at any Western Union office. Such an address enables a company to economize on words in the signature of a message, thus reducing the cost.

Prepaid messages. A sender of a FR or LT message may wish to prepay the charges for a reply to the original message. When this is done, the indicator "RP" (reply paid) and figures showing the amount prepaid are inserted before the addressee's name.

Forwarding messages. Both FR and LT messages may be forwarded to an addressee who has left the place to which the message was addressed. If the sender wishes to assure delivery in such cases, the indicator "FS" is placed before the addressee's name. A charge is made for the additional word.

Delivery after business hours. If the sender wishes to be assured that the message will be delivered by the foreign telegraph office after the close of the regular business day, the word "NUIT" should be indicated before the addressee's name. An additional charge is made for the one word. (For time differences in various parts of the world, see Appendix 11.)

Report of time of delivery. When the sender wishes to receive a report as to the time of delivery of the cable, the indicator "PC" should be inserted before the addressee's name. The cost is for one word plus a six-word reply.

RADIO MARINE SERVICE

SHORE TO SHIP

Only full-rate telegraphic service is available from the United States to ships anywhere in the world.

Plain or secret language or a combination of both may be used. Plain language words are counted at 15 characters to the word; secret language words are counted at five characters to the word. Addresses and signatures are charged for.

Preparing messages. Write "INTL" above the name and address to stipulate "international message." The address must include the name of passenger, name of ship, ship's general location, and radio station.

```
INTL
William Alberts
SS United States
North Atlantic
Newyorkradio
```

Marine Radio stations are written as one word, as SANFRANCISCORADIO or PORTARTHURRADIO.

Speeding messages. When speed is a primary factor, messages may be filed directly with the coast station serving the general vicinity of the ship. If the sender is not familiar with the coast station, the message may be telephoned or filed TWX (see above) by indicating CHATHAMRADIO for ships in the Atlantic Ocean and SANFRANCISCORADIO for ships in the Pacific Ocean.

RECEIVING TELEGRAMS AND CABLEGRAMS

A message of such urgency that the sender selected telegraphic service should be delivered immediately to the addressee. In cases when the addressee is not in the office, the message may be read by the secretary or some other person given the responsibility of attending to urgent messages.

Code messages. If a code word is included in a message, the meaning of the word should be written above it. Should a major part of the message be in code, the decoded message should be typed on a separate sheet and attached to the original message.

Copies. When a copy of a telegraphic message is desired, a facsimile may be made on any photographic duplicator.

III *Telephone Techniques*

The telephone has become one of the most frequently used audio-communication media in the business world today. From the time of its invention, when Alexander Graham Bell proved that sounds could be transmitted by wire, the dependence upon this instrument has grown so that currently over 500 million telephone calls are made daily. Not only has the number of telephone calls increased, but so have the kinds of services and the telephone equipment now made available by the telephone company.

A secretary in an organization is expected to be knowledgeable in the use of this means of communication as well as in the telephone services and equipment that may fill the needs of her employer. The reputation and good will of the employer and the firm may depend upon the secretary's approach and skill in using the telephone. It is amazing that, although the average person begins to use the telephone in early childhood, most people need to be trained in proper telephone techniques. An impressive way to point out defects in techniques, and one that results in a rapid and desirable change, is to make a recording of a telephone conversation. Such a recording emphasizes the faults in telephone techniques and vividly points out the areas for improvement. Many organizations, even though they are efficiently organized, lose customers, money, and goodwill simply because employees answering calls are incoherent, curt, or impolite.

It must be remembered at all times that the caller at the other end of the phone cannot see to whom he is talking. Therefore he has no visual image on which to base his impressions. The telephone caller's attention is focused entirely upon the audio impressions coming to him over the wires. If these sounds are jarring or unpleasant, a busy executive may quickly lose patience and discontinue his association with the firm in question. On the other hand, a pleasant and understanding voice coming over an inanimate instrument can accomplish wonders. The power of the spoken word can and does exert a great impact upon the listener.

The telephone is not a nuisance instrument placed upon the secretary's desk to interrupt her when she is in the midst of some important or complicated task. It is, rather, a vital business-communication facility that assists her in carrying out her duties and responsibilities to her employer.

In order to enhance your telephone personality, it is necessary to inject variety and flexibility into your voice, so as to convey mood and attitude in telephone conversations. These qualities can be obtained through pitch, inflection, and emphasis. The development of these qualities is individual. A high-pitched voice may convey an impression of childishness and immaturity or of impatience and irritability. On the other hand, a voice that is well modulated carries the impression of culture and polish. "Pitch" in speaking, like "pitch" in music, refers to the key in which one speaks. Everyone has a range of tone within which a pleasant speaking voice is possible. However, each person must be conscious of his own range and practice utilizing it effectively. An individual is said to speak in a "modulated" voice when the pitch is in the lower half of his range. This tonal range carries best and is easiest to hear over the telephone.

Enunciation. In cultivating an interesting individual telephone personality, voice development alone is insufficient; it is essential also that the speaker enunciate clearly and distinctly. A garbled and indistinct speech pattern will annoy the listener who cannot understand what is being said. Do not be afraid to move your lips. One cannot form rounded vowel sounds or distinct consonants unless the lips accomplish their function. It is not necessary to exaggerate or to become stilted; clear enunciation should be made a part of the secretary's natural, daily speech pattern, because it is just as important in face-to-face conversations as in telephone conversations. Above all, be sure that your voice reflects your personality, that it transmits alertness and pleasantness, that it is natural, distinct, and expressive, and neither too loud nor too soft. Avoid repetitious, mechanical words and phrases, and try to enunciate in a manner that is neither too fast nor too slow.

ANSWER PROMPTLY

Answering a business telephone call is similar to welcoming a visitor. Therefore it is essential that each call be greeted by a prompt, effective, and pleasing answer.

The telephone should be placed on the secretary's desk so that it is readily accessible. A pad and pencil or pen should be kept handy in order to jot down necessary information. These should not be used for doodling when speaking on the phone; this habit distracts the secretary from the business at hand and interferes with giving the caller her undivided attention.

When the telephone rings, answer it promptly—at the first ring, if possible. Otherwise the caller may hang up and take his business elsewhere.

If the secretary finds it necessary to leave her desk for urgent, immediate duties, she should arrange to have someone else answer the telephone and take the messages until she returns. The instrument should never be left unattended for even an instant. Frequently a task that seems likely to take but a moment becomes so involved that moments stretch into precious minutes and hours, and the unanswered telephone becomes an instrument of failure—failure to the company because of the loss of customers and failure of the individuals responsible. It is well to make a practice of informing the person who covers the telephone why the secretary will be away from her desk and for how long. Armed with this information, the one who answers the telephone can be more helpful to the caller.

This courtesy, of course, should be extended in both directions. When the secretary is at her desk and one of her colleagues needs to be away, she should take her colleague's calls.

IDENTIFY WHO IS ANSWERING

The efficient secretary always identifies herself and her office when she answers the telephone. She may say, "Mr. Wright's office, Miss White," or she may use the firm' name, as, "Smith and Grey, Miss Jones." The identification formula depends upon the size and structure of the organization for whom she works. In this way she assures the caller that he has reached the proper office and person with whom to transact his business. Avoid answering the business telephone by saying, "Hello." Using this form of greeting is much like saying, "Guess who this is," and is unbusinesslike. Business people have no time to play guessing games, and this form of address can become irritating, particularly if it is necessary to call the office several times.

In answering calls for others, the secretary should identify herself and the office of the person whose calls she is taking. For example, "Miss Jones's office, Miss Smith speaking." Unless she does so, the caller will not know whether he has reached the right person at all. He expects to hear Miss Jones's voice and is taken aback when an unfamiliar voice and name come to him over the wires. Precious minutes are wasted in explanation, and perhaps by that time he has changed his mind about the matter in hand.

IDENTIFY WHO IS CALLING

The wise secretary develops a keen ear and learns to recognize the voices of important or frequent callers. However, a word of caution is necessary at this point. Do not become too sure that your ear is infallible, or you may overlook the fact that voices over the telephone can be misleading. If you know the voice beyond a doubt, use the caller's name when speaking to him. If you have identified the voice correctly, the caller will be pleased to be recognized and addressed by name. Then, speak *to the person* at the other end of the wire, not *at the telephone*. If you were incorrect in identifying the voice before you divulged any information, little harm was done, since the caller will correct you. You can then tactfully apologize and take up the business at hand. However, when the caller does not reveal his name and/or the nature of the business, your skill at diplomacy comes into play. Many executives prefer their secretaries to screen incoming calls (see below). This must be done with tact and discretion. In some cases the executive will speak with anyone who calls but would like to know beforehand who is calling and the nature of his business. It is the secretary's duty to obtain this information before transferring the call to the executive. She must avoid curtness and rudeness in doing so. She may say, for example, "May I tell Mr. Black who is calling?" or "Mr. Black is talking on another telephone. Would you care to wait, or may I have him call you, since I believe it will take some time?" or "Mr. Black is engaged with someone in his office. May I help you?" Be sincere and courteous in your explanation, but do not divulge information unnecessarily. Your goal is to find out who is calling.

SCREENING CALLS

Although some executives answer the telephone themselves, many depend upon their secretaries to answer all incoming calls. The secretary must, therefore, be familiar with her executive's preferences. She must learn which calls he expects her to handle herself, which he wants referred to him, and which should be transferred to someone else. Consequently, the secretary must classify telephone callers accurately and quickly. Every call is important. Enough information must be ascertained to classify the call. A caller cannot be allowed to get to the end of a long conversation before he is referred to the proper person.

Generally the calls that the secretary can handle herself are as follows:

Requests for information. If the information is not confidential, and if the secretary is certain of the facts, she can handle this type of call. Sometimes she may have to check with her employer before imparting information. If any complications arise, it is always wiser to turn the call over to the executive.

Requests for appointments. The secretary is usually authorized to make appointments for her employer. However, she should check his diary as well as her own before making an appointment. If her employer is out of the office, she should verify the appointment with him as soon as he returns, so that no conflict arises. He may have made a commitment about which he has forgotten to inform her or has not yet had the opportunity to tell her.

Receiving information. Often the secretary can conserve her employer's time by taking down telephone information. If she takes the message in shorthand, this must be transcribed as soon as possible and placed on her employer's desk.

Transferring calls. If the call cannot be handled by the secretary or her employer, it should be transferred to the office that can give the caller the information he seeks. This should be done only with the caller's permission, however. If he refuses to be transferred, she should obtain the information and call him back, after explaining to him why his call must be transferred. If the caller agrees to the transfer, she should make sure that the right office is reached before hanging up and give the attendant sufficient information so that the caller will not need to repeat it.

In taking calls from persons who wish to speak to the executive directly, the secretary must know how to handle the following situations tactfully, discreetly, and diplomatically.

1. The employer is in and free. She informs her executive who is calling. On occasion, if the caller is well known to her employer and someone to whom he talks frequently, she may signal for him to pick up the telephone.

2. The employer is in but does not want to be disturbed. She tells the caller that the executive is engaged at the moment and asks whether she can take a message. If the caller insists on speaking to him personally, she may ask to call him back as soon as her employer is free.

3. The employer is in another office in the building. The secretary should ascertain whether he will be available for telephone calls when he is away from his office. Generally only the most urgent call should be transferred to him under such circumstances.

TAKING MESSAGES

It is good practice to keep a written record of all incoming calls, particularly when the executive is away from the office. In recording the call, the secretary should indicate the time the call was received; the name, business affiliation, and telephone number of the caller; and the message. She should sign the note with her initials. If the message is from an out-of-town caller, the area code or the telephone operator's number should also be recorded, so that the executive can return the call within the minimum time and without confusion. It is best when taking a message to read it back to the caller in order to avoid errors or misunderstandings in interpretations. Messages should always be taken verbatim. The memorandum slips should be placed on the executive's desk immediately. The secretary will also anticipate his needs by attaching to the slips any material (possibly annotated) that may be necessary for reference in order to conclude the transaction successfully—back correspondence, a bill, price lists, or whatever may assist the executive in handling the call intelligently.

To be able to handle the incoming calls more efficiently, the secretary should know where her executive will be when he is away from the office, whether he can be reached for urgent messages, and when he expects to return to the office.

Also, in taking calls for other persons in the office, as suggested above, it is helpful if one can state when the person called will return or whether he can be reached somewhere else. It is best to offer what information one can; otherwise the caller may get the impression that he is being put off with an excuse. Be courteous, and use discretion in explaining an absence from the office. It is less offensive to say, "Miss Jones is away from her desk just now. May I have her call you, or would you prefer to leave a message?" than to say bluntly, "She's out," or "This is her coffee break," or "I don't know where she is." The secretary must always use tact in her dealing with callers, whether it be for her own executive or for another secretary whose calls she is taking.

TAKING ACTION

The secretary should promise the caller some definite action and see to it that she keeps her promise. If she tells the caller that her executive will call him back, then she must convey this information to her employer so that he can do so. A broken promise can result in a canceled order or a lost customer, and it may take many months to regain his goodwill.

On some calls that the secretary can handle herself she may need to obtain more information than she has at her finger tips. If she must leave the telephone to look up the necessary information, she should inform the caller of this fact and of the length of time it may take her to obtain the material. She should offer him a choice of waiting or of being called back. The customer should never be left dangling at the other end of the wire. If a promise is made to call back with the needed information, this promise must be honored.

If the caller is waiting to speak to the executive, the secretary should leave the receiver off the cradle and every quarter-minute or so tell the caller that she has not forgotten that he is waiting and will connect his call as soon as the employer is ready to speak to him. Otherwise the caller will be uncertain as to whether he is still connected, and a minute's silent delay will seem to him like a half-hour's wait. When the secretary is ready to transfer the call, she should thank the customer for waiting.

COMPLETING THE INCOMING CALL

At the completion of the call, indicate that you are ready to terminate your conversation by summing up the details. Use the caller's name as you say a pleasant "Good-by." It is courteous to wait for the caller to terminate the call first; the secretary who is too hasty in hanging up the receiver may cost the firm money. She leaves the caller breathless and with the impression that she is too busy to have the time or the interest to speak to him. He is made to feel that his business is of no importance to the organization, because they cut him short when he calls. Permitting the caller to say "Good-by" first allows him time for last-minute orders or special instructions that may have slipped his mind. The receiver should be replaced gently in its cradle, for the pleasantest "Good-by" can be spoiled by the jarring sound of a receiver dropped into position. It is like slamming the door after a visitor. The abruptness may not be intentional, but the effect is the same. Do not hang up until your caller has done so first.

PERSONAL CALLS

Because of her status and the prestige of her position, the secretary should set an example for the office personnel by refraining from making and accepting personal calls during business hours except in cases of emergency. The secretary sets the pattern for those whom she supervises. She is the model upon whom they mold their own office conduct and office etiquette.

TELEPHONE DICTATION

Frequently the secretary is called upon to take dictation over the telephone. For this reason a shorthand notebook and pen should be placed near the telephone and ready for use. The caller is always informed of the fact that the conversation will be taken by the secretary. She picks up her telephone and indicates to the parties concerned that she is ready to record the proceedings. In the case of telephone dictation, unlike dictation taken at the employer's desk, the dictator cannot tell whether the secretary is getting all the information. Therefore it is necessary for the secretary to repeat the material phrase by phrase as she takes it down in shorthand. This informs the dictator as to the rate of dictation, clarity of reception, and errors in grammar or facts. He can then make corrections immediately, instead of waiting until the end of the dictation, which may lead to confusion. If the dictation is too fast, it is best to indicate this immediately. It is a good practice to read back the notes at the termination of the dictation to ensure that the correct information was received and recorded and to correct any misinterpretations. The notes should be transcribed as soon as possible, and a copy should be sent to the telephone dictator. Of course, if your transcription equipment is one of those which can be used for recording telephoned dictation, the caller will be able to complete the dictation far more rapidly.

TELEPHONE REFERENCE MATERIALS

The efficient secretary must be cognizant of the available sources of information that will aid her in placing a call expeditiously, skillfully, and economically. She familiarizes herself with the directories and booklets published by the telephone company, which contain source materials and reference information. Telephone directories contain three general sections —the introductory pages, the alphabetical listing of subscribers, and the classified section, familiarly known as "the yellow pages." In many areas of the country all three sections appear in one volume of the telephone directory. However, in metropolitan areas where the listings are voluminous, the classified section is a separate book.

The introductory section gives instructions on what to do in an emergency, where to place service and other calls, how to use the dial system, how to use the table of contents, how to call the information operator. It also provides data on the different types of calls that can be made and on mobile and marine calls. It lists the area codes for faster calling and sample rates for long-distance and person-to-person calls. It explains how to make collect calls; how to call the telephone company's business office and the managers who handle customer information; how to find message-unit charges; where to pay bills and transact business in person; and what modern telephone services are available to the customer. A map illustrates the postal zones and localities of the particular area covered by the telephone directory.

The subscribers section lists in alphabetical sequence the names, addresses, and telephone numbers of all the telephone subscribers in a locality, borough, town, village, city, or county. Sometimes the kind of business or the occupation of a subscriber is also shown. At the top-outside corner of each page guide names, or "telltales," indicate the first and last listings on the page for quick location of the page on which a particular name appears. If a name might be spelled in several ways, a cross-reference spelling directs the user to additional listings. The divisions, departments, or branch offices of an organization with separate telephone listings are usually indented under the firm name. Alternate call listings can likewise be found in the telephone directory. These listings indicate telephone numbers to be called when no one answers the regular numbers. Furthermore, the nature of a company's business is generally shown after the firm name. However, if the company's name reveals the nature of its work, no further designation is given; for example, "Thomas & Sons" requires a designation and might appear as "Thomas & Sons, typwrtr svce"; whereas, "Thomas Typwrtr Svce" does not require identification, since the firm name clearly indicates the nature of its business. On the other hand, governmental agencies and state, county, and municipal offices are shown with major headings for the principal listing and indented entries for subordinate departments and divisions.

Information of the following types can be found in the classified directory: advertising service in the yellow pages, sample listings and advertisements, telephone equipment and services, calendars, key to street numbers, public transportation lines maps, postal services and rates, postal zone map for the locality, shopping guide ("Where To Buy It"), restaurant guide, school guide, and emergency services. This directory lists all businesses under the classifications that describe them most accurately. A company name can be verified, provided that the nature of its business and address are known, by searching under the proper business classification and then identifying the street address. The classification headings are placed at the top of each page next to the page number and represent the business headings listed on that page. Brand-name advertising is also featured, distributors and dealers being listed under trademark headings. Often a telephone listing is more quickly found in the classified directory or section than in the local alphabetical directory.

These reference books are brought up to date periodically to reflect changes in telephone numbers, addresses, and names of the subscribers; to delete the names of those who have discontinued service; and to add the necessary information for new subscribers.

Generally the local alphabetical and classified directories are distributed to all subscribers. Out-of-town directories may be obtained by calling the telephone business office and asking for these books.

In some cities street-address directories are available and may be rented from the telephone company. These directories list telephone numbers according to the alphabetical and numerical arrangements of streets in that city. They are of special value and usefulness to credit and collection agencies and for companies or organizations who desire to make up mailing lists.

DESK TELEPHONE FILES

The efficient secretary sets up a desk telephone file of numbers and area codes that both she and her executive call frequently. This list consists of (1) business numbers the employer calls frequently and, possibly, taxi, bus-terminal, railroad-terminal, and airlines numbers; (2) emergency numbers for ambulance service, fire department, police department, and so on; (3) personal numbers of the employer's family, doctor, lawyer, dentist, tailor, barber, and dry cleaner; (4) extension numbers in other offices; and (5) frequently called long-distance numbers, with notations indicating the difference in time belts.

Unlisted numbers should be added to this list, with an identifying mark indicating the nature of such a number. Unlisted numbers are never revealed without specific instructions from the executive to do so. They were given to the employer for his personal use, and this fact should be respected.

It is a good idea when compiling a desk telephone list to make it as informative as possible. The secretary should identify individual names by noting title and company affiliation in addition to the address and tele-phone number and area code. If she is entering the name, address, and telephone number of an organization, she should also indicate the name and title or department of the individual or individuals with whom she and her employer talk most frequently.

The placement of the desk telephone list depends upon its size. If very short, it may be taped neatly to the top or the slide panel of the desk; if long, it may be kept in a book or on a rotary file attached to the telephone.

ASSEMBLING DATA FOR OUTGOING CALLS

In order to place outgoing calls quickly for her employer, the secretary should master all the telephone techniques that enable her to perform this function skillfully. She should be absolutely sure of the telephone number before calling. It will save considerable time, trouble, and irritation to check the number with the desk list, telephone directory, or correspond-ence file before dialing.

Then she should assemble all the information that may be necessary to conduct the business transaction when the call is put through. It may be necessary to obtain materials from the files to refresh the executive's memory on previous business or other information that will assist him in making a successful call. All pertinent material should be placed on his desk before the call is made.

It is also a good practice to arrange with the executive that he be free and available to take the call as soon as it goes through. No one likes to be called and then find that he has to wait because the caller is talking on the other telephone or not ready to take the call immediately. Delay may not only lower the prestige of the company and the executive and cause annoyance but also prove costly to the firm making the call. The question frequently arises as to which executive should answer first. Courtesy prescribes that the caller should be on the line, ready to talk, when the person he is calling answers, particularly if the latter outranks him. The secretary should put her executive on the line immediately, if possible. This can be done readily if the secretary identifies herself and her employer when the call is answered. The secretary at the other end will then be able to transfer the call to her own employer without delay or immediately inform the caller how to reach the person called.

TELEPHONE SERVICES

In addition to business calls within the local community or surrounding areas, it frequently becomes necessary to place calls to more distant points.

The secretary who can handle long-distance calls capably will enhance her value to her employer.

TOLL CALLS

Toll calls are those made from one town or city to another town or city. A charge is made for such calls in addition to the charge for the regular telephone service. The amount of the charge depends upon the distance, the type of service requested, the time of day or night the call is made, and the time taken for the conversation.

There are two classes of toll calls—station-to-station and person-to-person.

Station-to-station calls. Almost any state in the United States can be reached by direct dialing today. The telephone directory carries a listing of cities and states and their area codes. In order to place a call to any of these localities, dial the area code and then the local telephone number of the individual to be reached. If the city or town is not listed at the front of the telephone directory, call the operator and give her the name of the city and state and the number of the telephone you want to reach. A station-to-station call is made to a particular telephone number, and the caller speaks to anyone who answers the telephone. Therefore, if someone answers the ring, the individual making the call is charged for it, and the charges start as soon as the call is answered. However, this type of call is less costly, is more frequently made, and is usually faster than the person-to-person call. In order to take advantage of the lower rates for station-to-station calls, some firms write in advance to the person with whom they wish to speak and ask that he be at his telephone at a certain time to take the call when it is put through. In this way, they have the advantages of the person-to-person call without paying the higher rate.

Person-to-person calls. To place a person-to-person call, the secretary dials zero, dials the three-digit area code, and then dials the telephone number; at this point the operator intercepts and the secretary gives her the name of the individual being called. Then she must wait for the call to be put through, because, if the person called is not present or available to take the call, she may have to decide whether someone else at that number can handle the transaction. A person-to-person call is made to a particular person only, and the caller is not charged for the call unless he speaks to the person called or consents to speak to some other specifically identified individual. Charges start as soon as the person called is reached; therefore, the secretary should not start a conversation herself but must make sure that her employer is ready to take the call immediately.

Direct distance dialing. Almost all calls in the United States and abroad should now be put through by means of direct distance dialing. A list of the area codes you must use for direct dialing is found at the beginning of the telephone directory. If the area does not appear on this list, the call must be given to the local or toll operator. The direct dialing system works on a three-digit area code, which is dialed first, followed by the local telephone number. There are no two areas that have the same area code, nor are there two identical telephone numbers in an area. It was necessary to change telephone numbers in many cities and towns in order to make this service possible. It is a quick and accurate system. If a wrong number is reached, the secretary, before disconnecting, should ascertain the name of the city that was reached. Then she should promptly dial the operator and tell her that she has reached an incorrect destination, so that the telephone bill will not reflect a charge for the wrong number.

The phone directory also explains how to use direct dialing for person-to-person, credit card, or collect calls.

TIME DIFFERENCES

It is vital to check the difference in time when planning to place a long-distance call. One must be aware not only that this country is divided into time zones, but also that certain regions change to daylight-saving time during the summer months and that differences in time exist in all countries. For example, the United States (excluding Alaska and Hawaii) is divided into four standard-time zones: Eastern, Central, Mountain, and Pacific. Each zone is one hour earlier than the zone immediately to the east of it; for example, when it is 12 P.M. Eastern Standard Time, it is 11 A.M. in the Central zone, 10 A.M. in the Mountain zone, and 9 A.M. Pacific Time. Greenwich Mean Time, which is the mean solar time of the meridian at Greenwich, England, is used as the basis for standard time throughout most of the world. For specific time information, consult the tables in Appendix 8.

Long-distance calls are charged at a flat rate for the first three minutes, and an additional fee is levied for each minute or fraction of a minute thereafter. The rates vary with the distance from the point at which the call was placed to the point called. After 6 P.M., 8:00 P.M., and midnight, further reduced rates go into effect. These same costs apply all day on Saturday and Sunday and on holidays.

APPOINTMENT CALLS

The telephone operator is asked to put through a person-to-person call at a specified hour. She will establish contact at the time indicated and will then notify the caller that the connection has been made. The charges for such calls are the same as those for an ordinary person-to-person call.

SEQUENCE CALLS

The sequence-calls service is of value when a number of calls are to be made to out-of-town points. Much time is saved by furnishing the operator with a list, oral or written, of the calls to be made at the specified times. The secretary should supply the names of the individuals to be called, the city and state where they are located, their telephone numbers, if known, and the hour at which the executive wishes to speak to each person on the list. The operator then keeps the lines clear for this operation and places the calls as arranged.

CONFERENCE CALLS

Another instance of the various accommodations that the telephone company offers its subscribers is the conference service. It is of particular value to executives of organizations with branches and/or plants located over a wide area who find it necessary to confer speedily with those at the different branches. The telephone company provides two methods for setting up a telephone conference.

1. An arrangement can be made with the conference operator to connect several people in various cities simultaneously for a conference or discussion. No special equipment is required for this hookup.

2. An arrangement can be made with the conference operator whereby a conference call can be placed to a large group of employees. This type of call requires setting up a loudspeaker at the called point in a different city, so that the executive can talk by phone to the entire group at one time.

When placing such a call, the secretary should signal the operator, ask her for the conference operator, describe the setup desired, and furnish the names of the individuals to be called, their telephone numbers, if known, the city and state where each is located, and the time of the conference.

COLLECT CALLS

Calls can be charged to the phone of the person who is being called. He may either accept the call and be charged for it or refuse the call and not be charged. The rate is the regular rate for a long-distance call, and there is no additional charge for this service. Since the telephone company is aware of the competition existing in the business world and the fact that friendlier and faster service plays an important role in beating competition, it has made available a series of call-collect labels, which subscribers can attach to their correspondence, price lists, catalogs, bills, and so on. These labels remind customers that they can call the subscriber free. This speedy and convenient service appeals to them. Furthermore, a subscriber can also charge to his own phone toll calls placed from other phones. However, someone has to be present to accept the charges, because the operator will call the number to find out whether charges will be accepted before putting through the call. Therefore it behooves the efficient secretary to discuss with her employer when she should accept collect charges. He will determine from whom collect charges will be honored. If in doubt, she should ask the operator to wait while she checks with the executive.

OVERSEAS CALLS

You can "direct dial" many overseas points. Information on such calls can be obtained from the long-distance operator. For person-to-person overseas calls, the secretary must dial the long-distance operator and ask for the overseas operator. She then must provide the name of the person called and the telephone number, if known. The charges for this service are higher than those for domestic calls; however, there are reduced rates that apply to calls made to many countries during certain night hours and during the weekend.

CALLS TO SHIPS, PLANES, TRAINS, AND AUTOMOBILES

Telephone calls to mobile conveyances by way of radio telephone are similarly made by the operator. Such service is not available without the installation of special equipment by the telephone company in the car, plane or ship, of course. Calls can then be placed direct from the office telephone to the destination desired.

RETURNING LONG-DISTANCE CALLS

Frequently a long-distance call is received when the executive is not in the office to take it. In such a case, the long-distance operator will give the secretary the operator's number, the city calling, and the name and telephone number of the person calling. To return the call, the secretary should dial the operator in her city, ask by number for the operator who called her, and identify the city from which the call originated. When the connection is made with the proper operator, the secretary should give her the name and telephone number of the person who placed the call to her employer.

RECORD KEEPING

Many organizations require that a record be kept of all toll calls made, in order to verify the telephone bill, and have special printed forms for this purpose. The secretary should institute the practice of asking the telephone operator, when placing such calls, to give her the charges when the call is completed. The operator will do this readily and courteously, because, when a long-distance call is made, the toll operator generally makes a record of the call and also obtains the desired connection. However, the request for charges must be made in advance, not after the call is completed.

SPECIAL TELEPHONE EQUIPMENT AND SYSTEMS

A good secretary should be familiar with the various types of telephone equipment available, in order to facilitate the needs of the company and those of her executive. Tremendous strides have been made in the field of telephone research. Not only business but also the world in general benefits from the discoveries made by telephone technicians and telephone researchers.

Call Director. A pushbutton telephone which provides the capacity of several ordinary pushbutton phones in one compact, attractive unit is known as the Call Director. It can handle up to 29 lines and is available in 18- to 30-button models, which can be adjusted as needs change. The Call Director can be combined with the Speakerphone feature (see below), which makes it possible to telephone with the hands free when needed. A plug-in headset model is also available; this frees the hands so that the secretary can take notes, consult records, and so forth.

The telephone company has also added the conference feature to the Call Director. This permits an executive to set up an intercom conference merely by dialing a code or pushing a button.

Speakerphone set. The Speakerphone consists of a microphone and a loudspeaker and permits the user to carry on a telephone conversation clearly from anywhere in an office without lifting the receiver from its rest. The microphone picks up the individual's voice, and the loudspeaker, with an adjustable volume control, broadcasts it. By sitting around the microphone, a group can engage in a telephone conversation at one time. Everybody can talk and give his viewpoint, and everybody can hear and understand fully what is being discussed.

Rapidial. An automatic mechanism, Rapidial, is available for fast, convenient, and accurate dialing. The name and telephone number are written with a special pencil in the desired space in the name directory of the instrument. The number is then dialed to record it on Rapidial's magnetic memory tape. Thereafter, to make a call, the subscriber merely turns the selector knob until the desired name appears between the black lines in the window, lifts the telephone receiver, waits until the dial tone is heard, and then pushes the start bar; the number will be dialed automatically. If the line is busy, the caller replaces the receiver; when ready to try again, he lifts the receiver and simply pushes the start bar again. Rapidial can be used with any dial or Speakerphone telephone for local, long-distance, or extension-to-extension calls. Its memory tape stores up to 290 numbers. Old numbers can be erased at will and new ones added. It was designed especially for business and the telephone needs of business.

Wide-area telephone service(WATS). A special service permits area calling with cost control. With wide-area telephone service an executive can have direct access to all telephones in any area or areas from his telephone through special access lines. These lines automatically tie the office telephone into the long-distance network, and the executive simply calls the number he wants. Lines may be added as needed and may be on either full-time or measured-time service. Full-time service is 24 hours a day, every day of the month, whereas measured-time service is 15 hours at any time during the month. WATS may also be used for data transmission by connecting it to the Bell System Data-Phone service.

Direct inward dialing. A setup is available whereby an outside caller can dial the central office designation, followed by the extension he wants, and thereby put the call directly to the office desired instead of to the switchboard operator.

Data-Phone. The Data-Phone is a telephone-computer setup which enables office machines to talk to one another and transmit data at tremendous speeds in various machine-usable forms.

Key-Lite. The Key-Lite is a compact switchboard dial system for medium-sized businesses and comes in two sizes—the 50-line and 100-line systems.

Chapter 11

Special Secretarial Functions

JEANETTE L. BELY

MAKING TRAVEL ARRANGEMENTS

Many firms today have extended and expanded their interests and scope into the international picture. This broadening of the horizons makes it imperative for the executive to travel in order to maintain his contacts with the firm's branches and customers, to attend meetings and conventions, to lecture, or just to relax. Commensurate with the need for increased travel, means of transportation have become more convenient and many-faceted. In order to ensure a smooth and enjoyable trip for her employer, the secretary should be familiar with the various means of transportation that are available. It is her responsibility to make sure that the executive gets where he is going on time, well-fed, in comfort, and accommodated, and that he has at his disposal the supplies and documents necessary to make his trip successful.

PREPARATORY INFORMATION

Before the secretary can make any arrangements for the trip, she will need to compile certain facts. She should inquire of the executive when he will leave, the cities he expects to visit, the length of time he will remain in each locality, the purpose of each visit, the time and day he must arrive in each city in order to keep his appointments, his preferences as to the means of travel, and whether he will be traveling alone. Supplied with this information, the secretary can take the next step in making travel arrangements, the compiling of an itinerary.

COMPILING AN ITINERARY

At first, as pieces and bits of information are gathered, it is a good practice to draw up a tentative itinerary or a work sheet on which notations of alternate flights, waiting lists, alternate train travel, costs, and so forth can be presented for the executive's approval and selection. Such a work sheet might contain the following information: dates, destination, airport, railroad station, bus depot, departure time, time of arrival, dining-car service, hotel accommodations, appointment (where and with whom), reference materials.

The secretary should start her preliminary planning of the itinerary from the dates and times provided by the executive. Then a listing of whatever travel methods the employer prefers that are available at the times he indicated should be added to the work sheet. If he leaves the means of transportation open, complete information on all air lines, railways, or buses servicing the city of destination, with arrival and departure times and the costs of each, should be obtained. It is wise to indicate all possible choices available and permit him to make the decision as to which means of travel he prefers. The work sheet should be revised continually with the approval of the executive until the decisions are complete and the itinerary is ready for final typing.

In planning an itinerary, the secretary must bear in mind that the traveler is a human being and must eat regularly while traveling, must rest, must have enough time to get from his terminal of destination to the place of his appointment, and so forth. Therefore, she should be alert and include in his schedule:

Eating locations (plane, train, hotel, restaurant, etc.)

Allowance of time to go from the point of arrival to his appointment at the designated hour and without pressure

Applicable time belt, noted in indicated time on the itinerary (EST, EDST, etc.)

All confirmations for hotel accommodations, attached to the itinerary

All confirmations for transportation accommodations, attached to the itinerary

Multiple copies of the final draft should be prepared by the secretary: one for her, one or two for the executive, one for his family, and, if customary, several copies for key men in the organization. The typed form of the itinerary would appear as follows:

Mr. Realson's Itinerary February 19, 19__

Raleigh-Winston-Greenville-Columbia

Tuesday, February 19 (Newark to Raleigh)
10:00 a.m.   Leave West Side Airlines Terminal, New York, by limousine for Newark Airport.

11:00 a.m.   Leave Newark Airport on Eastern Airlines Flight #75 (tourist class,
propeller aircraft, luncheon).
(Ticket attached.)

1:00 p.m.   Arrive Raleigh. Hotel Hilton. (Reservation attached.)

2:00 p.m.   Robert Lee, Office Manager at Raleigh
branch, will pick you up at the Hil-
ton. Conference scheduled at branch
offices. (File #1 in your briefcase.)

Wednesday, February 20 (Raleigh)

9:00 a.m.   You are to inspect the Raleigh plant
this morning. Robert Lee will pick
you up at the hotel. (File #2 in
your briefcase contains facts and
statistics on plant operations.)

8:00 p.m.   Company dinner will be held at the
Hotel Hilton. (File #3 in your
briefcase contains a copy of the
speech for this occasion.) Citations
were mailed to Hotel Hilton for signature and presentation.

Thursday, February 21 (Raleigh to Winston via
Greensboro)

9:00 a.m.   Robert Lee will pick you up at the
hotel and drive you to the airport.

9:30 a.m.   Leave Raleigh on PI Flight #101
(first class, propeller). (Ticket
attached.)

11:00 a.m.   Arrive Greensboro Airport. Limousine
will take you to Winston. Hotel
Winston-Salem. (Reservation attached.)
Have luncheon at the hotel.

3:00 p.m.   Appointment with John Spaaks, Office
Manager at Winston branch; Joseph
Wilson, Personnel Director; Bob Mere-

dith, Production Director; and
Al Smith, Sales Director. Hotel
Winston-Salem, Green Room. (File #4
in your briefcase.)

7:00 p.m. Dinner appointment at Bill Lawson's
home. (Telephone SA 2-1234.)

Friday, February 22 (Winston)

9:00 a.m. Golf with Bill Lawson.

1:00 p.m. Conference with staff at Winston offices. (File #5 in your briefcase.)

8:00 p.m. Company dinner at Hotel Winston-Salem.
(Speech File #6 in your briefcase.)

Saturday, February 23 (Winston to Greenville' via Asheville)

10:00 a.m. Leave Winston on PI Flight #501
(first class, propeller). (Ticket
attached.)

11:35 a.m. Arrive Asheville. Limousine will take
you to Greenville. Hotel Greenville.
(Reservation attached.)

2:00 p.m. Conference with Greenville branch
managers at Hotel Greenville, Mezza-
nine Lounge. (File #7 in your briefcase.)

7:00 p.m. Company dinner at hotel. (Speech in
File #8 in your briefcase.)

Sunday, February 24 (Greenville)

Free day.

Monday, February 25 (Greenville to Columbia)

9:00 a.m. Visit Greenville offices for inspection. Martin Blank, Office Manager,
will pick you up at the hotel.
Have lunch before boarding plane.

3:00 p.m, Leave Greenville on Southern Airlines
Flight #138 (first class, propeller).
(Ticket attached.)

5:00 p.m.   Arrive Columbia. George Lewis, Of-
            fice Manager of Columbia branch, will
            meet you at airport. Hotel Magnolia.
            (Reservation attached.)

Tuesday, February 26 (Columbia)
9:00 a.m.   Conference at Columbia offices.
            George Lewis will pick you up at your
            hotel. (File #9 in your briefcase
            contains statistics and reports of
            progress of this branch.)
7:00 p.m.   Dinner meeting of Columbia staff at
            Hotel Magnolia. Speech to be deliv-
            ered at dinner. (File #10 in brief-
            case.)

Wednesday, February 27 (Columbia to Newark)
10:00 a.m. George Lewis will pick you up to take
            you to the airport.
11:00 a.m. Leave Columbia on Eastern Airlines
            Flight #666 (tourist, propeller,
            lunch). (Ticket attached.)
2:00 p.m.   Arrive Newark Airport. Fred Grant
            will pick you up at airport and drive
            you to New York offices.

DATA AND SUPPLIES FOR TRIP

If the executive's trip is entirely for business or part business and part pleasure, the secretary's duties in making travel arrangements do not terminate with the completion of the itinerary. She is responsible for the preparation of an appointments calendar of all the calls he will make while traveling. Such a schedule is made only for the executive and the secretary and is not to be distributed to anyone else. It can be either combined with the itinerary or prepared as a separate schedule, depending upon the executive's preference. Regardless of which choice is made, the appointments schedule should include the following data: the city and state in which the call is to be made; the date and time of the appointment; the name and address of the firm to which the executive is going; the name of the individual with whom he has the appointment; the telephone number (if known); remarks or special reminders about each visit; and a reference to the file number of the data he is taking with him for each call.

The executive will not rely on memory alone for information pertaining to past associations he has had with the individual or the firm he plans to visit. He will expect his secretary to have prepared a file for each firm that he will call on, so that he can refresh his memory of the data he will need to make his call productive. A separate folder should be prepared for each call, and each folder should bear a reference number that is keyed to the schedule of appointments. In such folders the secretary should include carbons of past correspondence; letters or memos concerning the problem to be discussed; a list of the persons to see and their positions in the company; perhaps a list of the officers and executives of the organization; a list of the persons with whom the executive has had contact in the past, other than those whom he intends to see, and the circumstances of those contacts; and every other bit of information, regardless of how insignificant it may seem. These folders should be arranged in the order in which the executive will see the customers.

In addition to the files of correspondence and other data that the executive will take with him, he will also need some stationery and supplies so that he will be able to communicate with the office and with others while he is traveling. For this purpose the secretary should draw up a check list of those supplies that he should take, assemble all the materials, and pack them in his dispatch case, brief case, or carryall. Supplies that the executive might require include company stationery, plain paper, onionskin or copy paper, carbon paper, envelopes of all kinds (air-mail, plain, and self-addressed), large manila envelopes, memo paper or pads, legal pad, address book, legal-size folders, letter-size folders, business cards, dictation equipment (portable recorder), tapes or belts for recorder, mailing folders or boxes for dictation tapes or belts, cash, personal checkbook, office account checks, expense forms, other office forms, pens and pencils, erasers, clips, scissors, rubber bands, blotters, transparent tape, paste, calendar, pins, bottle opener, ruler, first-aid items, aspirin, aviation guide, timetable, stamp pad and stamps, postage stamps. The materials that the executive selects from the check list should be assembled by the secretary, checked by the executive, and made ready for packing at least the day before he leaves on his trip.

The expense record forms or expense book should be packed on top, so that the executive can record the expenses he incurs in his travels. This is a very important detail, because the expense record is needed for income-tax and accounting purposes. Generally the following information is needed if the executive is to be reimbursed in part or whole for his trip or to be able to deduct business-incurred travel expense from his income tax: date of trip; description of how expense was incurred; types of expense (transportation, entertainment, breakfast, lunch, dinner, and so forth); amount reimbursed by company. In some instances receipts must be obtained for travel expenses; therefore a secretary should familiarize herself with the company and income-tax requirements in this area and attach a reminder to the expense forms or expense book for the executive to obtain these receipts as he travels.

ARRANGEMENTS FOR DOMESTIC TRIPS

Large organizations generally have traffic departments which make all the arrangements pertinent to the trip. If the company has a traffic department, the executive's secretary submits to this department the pertinent data that she has obtained from the executive about the trip and the department takes over. It works out the itinerary with the traveler's approval, makes all the reservations for transportation and accommodations, and obtains the confirmations. This information is sent to the executive's office well in advance of his departure date.

Where there is no traffic department in an organization, the secretary may either call on the services of a reliable travel agency or take care of the arrangements herself.

Using a travel agency. The easiest method for obtaining reservations for domestic and foreign travel is through the services of a reliable travel agency. Many executives rely on these services to plan their trips and to make their reservations. This method saves the secretary considerable time. Furthermore, travel agencies can usually obtain better and faster services than an individual who lacks their specialized experience and knowledge.

If the secretary or the executive does not know the name of a good travel agency, she could contact other firms whose executives travel, or she can get a list from The American Society of Travel Agents, Inc., at 501 Fifth Avenue, New York, N.Y. However, not all of the good travel agencies belong to this society. Others may be listed in the classified telephone directory.

The secretary must provide the travel agent with the executive's name, his business and home telephone numbers, detailed information on dates, times of arrival and departure at each city, and the type of transportation preferred. Although the agent will report periodically the progress made, it is the secretary's responsibility to keep in touch with him and to see to it that tickets and reservations arrive at the office in plenty of time for her to check the dates, times, destinations, and so forth, before she turns them over to the traveler.

These agencies do not charge for making airline or hotel reservations, since they receive a commission from the hotel or airline with which the reservation is placed. There is a charge, however, for rail reservations unless they are part of a prearranged package tour, and usually for telephone calls and telegrams. Refunds for any unused tickets are obtained by the agency and should be reflected as deductions from the charges made on bills. The agency should be instructed that all bills should be sent to the attention of the executive or his secretary, so that they can be checked before being forwarded to the accounting department.

MAKING RESERVATIONS FOR TRANSPORTATION

When the secretary takes care of the travel arrangements herself, she should assemble all the information she can obtain in regard to air lines, railways, bus schedules, and the like before placing any reservations. She should learn what each type of service offers and the relative merits of each accommodation.

Plane travel. The types of plane service available are first class and economy. Both types of accommodation are usually available on the same plane. The differences between first class and economy are the size and comfort of the seats and the type of meals. First-class passengers enjoy wider seats and more leg room. They are served luxury meals and complimentary alcoholic beverages. The economy section of the plane is larger and seats are closer together. The meals are less elaborate than in first class and alcoholic beverages must be purchased separately.

The secretary whose executive travels extensively should add an airline guidebook to her library for information on air lines servicing each city in the nation. She can get the *Official Airlines Guide* by writing to the American Aviation Publications, Inc., at 139 North Clark Street, Chicago, Ill. This book lists each city in the United States and its possessions and Canada, indicates the airlines that service each city, and gives information on car-rental and air-taxi service in each city.

Timetables of the airlines that service a city are available and may be obtained from the airlines terminal. However, once the choice of an airline is made, dependence on the timetable should cease, because flights may have been added or canceled. It is wiser to obtain definite flight information from the reservation clerk.

To make reservations for a seat on a plane, the secretary should call the reservation desk of the airline chosen by the executive, give her name, the executive's name, the name and address of the firm, the executive's home telephone number, the desired flight number, the city of departure and the city of destination, and the time she assumes that the flight leaves. If the flight is already filled, the secretary should ask for alternative suggestions. If none of the suggestions is acceptable to the executive, she should ask to be placed on the waiting list and then try to make reservations on some other airline. As soon as a reservation is available and a definite confirmation is received, the secretary should immediately cancel all the other pending alternative arrangements. This will ensure the goodwill of the persons she deals with.

In placing airline reservations, the secretary should always get the name of the airline clerk who makes the original reservations. It is he who will handle the reservations for every lap of the trip, even though it may be broken by intervening alternative accommodations, such as train or bus. (This system is not followed by the railroads.) Furthermore, the secretary may find it necessary to speak with the airline clerk several times before the reservations are confirmed and the executive boards his plane. If she knows the clerk's name, she can avoid the necessity of repeating all the preliminary steps to different persons at the reservation desk when she calls for clarification of flight information.

Payment for airline tickets may be made in various ways. Generally they must be paid for at the time they are picked up. However, in order to eliminate the rush and nuisance of standing in a long line to pay for tickets, most airlines recognize various credit card plans. Either the traveler or the company can be billed once a month for the trips taken. Furthermore, the bill constitutes written evidence for accounting and tax purposes.

The tickets should be picked up as soon as they are available and well in advance of the departure date. These tickets must be checked carefully against the information on the itinerary as to the correctness of flight numbers, the type of flight, the time of departure, the departure airport, and the city of destination. If any discrepancies are noted, the secretary must immediately notify the reservation clerk with whom the flight arrangements were placed originally.

For international flights, reservations must be confirmed 24 hours or more before flight time. A reminder will call the executive's attention to this important procedure.

Train travel. The choice of available train accommodations may be dependent upon the length of the trip and the price of the accommodation. The least expensive way of traveling is by coach. For long trips the traveler may prefer a Pullman accommodation. The costs for such traveling space increase in sequential order of the means indicated below. For the most part, Pullman accommodations offered are:

Roomette: a private room, usually for one person, with a bed folding into the wall, a sofa seat for daytime use, and toilet facilities in the same room.
Bedroom: a private room with lower and upper berths, the lower berth serving as a sofa for daytime use, and toilet facilities in the same room.

The secretary should be aware of the fact that not all trains provide all the above accommodations and that some trains have, in addition to

Pullman space, dining cars, club cars, and observation cars. Moreover, railroad connections to many destinations are increasingly limited. Such information can be obtained from various sources, such as timetables, the railway reservation desk, and travel agencies. Data on all services offered on a train should be procured before submitting the recommended means of travel to the executive for his approval.

Information about train travel can be obtained from the *Official Guide of the Railways,* a publication issued monthly by the National Railway Publications Company in New York. It contains all the schedules and timetables of all the railroads and steamship lines in the United States, Canada, Mexico, Cuba, and Puerto Rico; describes the accommodations available on each train; and shows the mileage between stations and maps of individual roads. This guide can be obtained through yearly subscriptions or may be purchased as single copies. Facts about the railroads that service a particular route and the timetables for those roads can be obtained from the local railroad offices.

In planning a trip by railroad, the secretary should study the timetable and make a tentative plan of the trip. This plan should then be submitted to the executive for his approval. When it is approved, she can then call the passenger representative or the reservation desk. It is always wise for the secretary to give the passenger representative her name and to learn his name when placing reservations or when difficulties arise in planning the trip. In all probability, he can suggest something else that is available if the desired space is not open. However, it should be borne in mind that, unlike air lines, railroads make reservations for train travel only. If a trip is broken by plane travel, for example, railroads will not make reservations for the entire trip. Consequently, when seeking reservations, the secretary should be prepared to supply the following data: complete and clear information on day, date, time, point of departure and destination, train number or name, and accommodation desired.

The tickets for train travel may be paid for when they are picked up, or an account service, the same as that used on air lines, may be obtained for those who travel extensively. Before attaching the tickets to the itinerary, the secretary should check them against her records for date, time, departure, destination, railway station, Pullman service and number, and car number.

Automobile travel. Some men prefer to travel by automobile, rather than by the means previously mentioned. In that case, and if the executive is a member of the American Automobile Association (A.A.A.), help can be obtained from its travel department in planning the route that should be followed on the trip. The A.A.A. will prepare a "Triptik," which is a detailed, up-to-the-minute strip map of the entire trip, listing recommended hotels and A.A.A. service stations along the route. This association also assists members in obtaining hotel and resort accommodations.

If the executive is not a member of the A.A.A. but nevertheless prefers to travel by automobile, the secretary's task is more complicated. She must obtain route maps from gasoline stations and study them carefully, choosing those roads which are main arteries and will bring the traveler to his destination by the shortest and most direct route possible. This planned mapping of the trip should be presented to the executive for his approval.

If the executive cannot take his own car, for some reason, but, nonetheless, needs one for the trip or even part of the trip, a car can be rented from one of the car-rental services that can be found throughout the country. Arrangements can be made in advance with any of these car-rental organizations for a rented car to be placed at the executive's disposal, ready and waiting for his use, at the point of destination at the time specified. A rented car can be left at any of the branch offices of the firm from which it was rented, in any city. Such automobiles are covered by accident insurance for the driver as well as the renting agency. This method of supplementing travel makes it easier to get from the hotel to field jobs or from one town to another, if plants or organizations are situated in outlying areas.

Bus travel. With the improvements in the equipment and services offered by bus lines, the economy-minded traveler may choose to use this means of travel for all or intervening portions of his trip. Reservations for bus transportation can be arranged by calling the reservation desk at the bus depot in the local city. Bus lines have passenger service agents who will assist in planning either long or short trips. However, timetables should be obtained and the route laid out well before reservations are placed for a bus trip.

REFUNDS FOR UNUSED TICKETS

On occasion the executive may need to change his travel plans en route. In such a case the traveler is entitled to a refund on the unused portion of his ticket, provided the railroad or air line is notified of the cancellation of the reserved space. Some lines require a specific time allowance for cancellation notices; however, most do not, but the transportation lines should be informed at once when the need for cancellation becomes apparent. In other words, as much notice as possible should be given, so that the space can be resold and the railroad or air line will not lose money on it.

Refunds on unused Pullman reservations may be obtained by sending the tickets with a covering letter to The Pullman Company, Passenger

Department, 79 East Adams Street, Chicago, Ill. This letter should indicate the name of the traveler, the date of departure, the city of departure, the city of destination, the Pullman accommodation, the train number or name, the car and accommodation numbers, the ticket number, if any, and the cost.

Unused air-transportation tickets can be cashed in at the airline office in the city where the executive happens to be, because air lines usually make refunds en route. However, if the executive prefers, he may bring the unused ticket back to the office with him and still obtain a refund. In that case the secretary can either return the ticket to the airline at the point of purchase or send it with a covering letter to the Refund Accounting Department at the address given in the *Official Airlines Guide*. In the letter the secretary should mention the date of the flight that the executive was to have taken, the city of departure, the city of destination, the ticket number, the flight number, and the cost of the ticket.

MAKING HOTEL RESERVATIONS

Reservations for hotel accommodations should be made as soon as possible. Delay can cause the executive to arrive in a strange city without any place to stay. Therefore the secretary must be certain that reservations for all hotel accommodations have been made and confirmations for the room received before the executive leaves on his trip.

There are several sources from which the secretary can obtain information on hotels and hotel accommodations:

Local hotel association. The hotel organization in the locality can supply the names of and information about hotels in other cities.

Hotel Red Book, published annually by the American Hotel Association Directory Corporation, 221 West 57 Street, New York, N.Y. This book contains the hotel associations for each state; lists the hotels by city and state; indicates the number of rooms, rates, and plans under which they operate (American, with meals; European, without meals); gives telephone and teletype numbers for each hotel; and indicates whether the hotel belongs to a chain.

Leahy's Hotel Guide and Travel Atlas of the United States, Canada, and Mexico, published by the American Hotel Register Company, Chicago, Ill.

Chamber of Commerce in city of destination.

Folders from the American Automobile Association and the guidebook, *Lodging for a Night,* published by Duncan Hines, Inc., New York. These publications list good hotels, inns, motels, and overnight guest houses for automobile travelers.

If enough time is available, the secretary should write directly to the hotel for reservations. If the hotel has a listed telephone number in the local city or a service whereby the hotel (usually part of a chain) in the local city will make reservations at the city of destination, the secretary may telephone for accommodations. Reservations may also be placed by telegraph or teletype, and Western Union has a reservation service available for handling such arrangements.

In making reservations for overnight accommodations, the following information must be supplied to the reservations clerk at the hotel: the name and address of the traveler, the type of accommodation desired, the date of arrival, the approximate time of day of arrival, and the probable departure date. The secretary should be sure to obtain the check-out time, since this varies from hotel to hotel, and to request the hotel to wire or write a confirmation of the reservation. These confirmations should be attached to the traveler's itinerary. Unless a request for accommodations has been confirmed, there is no assurance that a room will be held for the traveler. A hotel need not furnish accommodations simply because a request for a reservation was made, but it cannot turn an individual away if it confirmed a reservation.

Generally if a reservation is not picked up by 6 P.M., the room is given to someone else. Therefore, if the traveler will arrive later than 6 P.M. or is delayed in transit or his arrival time is uncertain, the hotel should be asked to hold the reservation for his arrival. In order to be sure that the room is held, it is a good idea to make a "guaranteed reservation." In this case, include the company's name and address as well as the traveler's and indicate that the accommodations will be paid for whether the traveler arrives or not. This is most important when the traveler is likely to arrive late at night, since hotels may otherwise consider him a "no show" and will rent the space held for him. On the other hand, if the traveler changes his mind about the itinerary or the hotel after the reservation has been made, the secretary should write to the hotel canceling the reservation. This courteous gesture preserves the good will between the organization and the hotel and ensures future consideration for reservation requests.

ARRANGEMENTS FOR FOREIGN TRAVEL

Preparations for foreign travel should be made far in advance of the departure date. There are many more details to be considered than in domestic travel arrangements, and many phases of such an undertaking involve much time. Before any arrangements for travel accommodations are started, the traveler should know (1) whom he wants to see in what countries and for how long, (2) the U.S. government requirements governing travel to foreign countries, (3) the requirements of the government of the country or countries he is going to visit, (4) the conditions that are imposed on business travelers and not on tourists, and (5) something about the countries he will visit.

Using a travel agency. It is advisable that the arrangements for foreign travel be made by a reliable travel agency, unless the organization has a traffic department and foreign branches in the countries to be visited. Under any circumstance, the executive secretary must know where she can obtain information in preparation for the executive's trip abroad and the data that will be needed for such a trip. A travel agency can be chosen as suggested earlier in the chapter. It should be one that will work out a personal itinerary for the traveling executive, rather than an agency that specializes in package tours. A reliable agency will take care of all of the details pertaining to the trip and will perform the following services for its clientele:

Prepare a tentative itinerary, which the executive can approve or change.

Handle all the arrangements for traveling, for hotels, and perhaps for sightseeing for the entire trip.

Provide information as to exactly which documents will be needed (passport, visas, health and police certificates, etc.) and how to obtain them.

Obtain all the documents that they can (for certain ones the executive must appear in person for issuance).

Provide a small amount of currency in the denominations of the country or countries that he is to visit in exchange for the equivalent in U.S. dollars.

Help in obtaining a letter of credit or traveler's checks.

Arrange to have a foreign correspondent meet the employer on arrival, to help take care of the baggage and go through customs.

Arrange to have a self-drive car waiting for the executive at his destination if he so desires.

Handle both personal and baggage insurance.

If the executive is uncertain about where he will stay and is unable to make arrangements before he leaves, the agent will supply the name of a desirable hotel in the country of his destination, as well as a letter of introduction to the manager of the hotel, and will write to the hotel to request every assistance to the traveler.

Preliminary preparations. For help in arranging a foreign business trip for the executive, the secretary should write to the Washington Bureau of Foreign Commerce in the Department of Commerce. This department maintains a staff of specialists on individual countries and can contact foreign-trade experts who are stationed at each of the Department's field offices. This bureau will supply information on economic developments, regulations and trade statistics on any country, distribution methods, foreign costs and their effect on sales prices, types of distributors, and names of key commercial officers to contact both in the United States and in the countries to be visited. It will also set up the executive's overseas appointments and will notify all U.S. Foreign Service posts, such as the embassies, consulates, and consuls general, that the executive is coming to those countries and alert them as to the purpose of his visit. They will request that these posts give him any assistance that he needs. Furthermore, the Washington Bureau of Foreign Commerce maintains a trade complaint service, with which a traveler can communicate if he becomes involved in any dispute with a foreign country, and safeguards and protects the industrial property rights to patents, trademarks, and copyrights abroad.

A very important secretarial duty in making preparations for the executive's trip abroad is to write letters to pave the way for his reception in the countries to be visited. She should write to the firms that he will visit in order to confirm his appointments, giving the time of his arrival, the length of time he expects to stay, the address where he will be staying, and any other pertinent information that will make it possible to locate the executive in the country of his destination. The secretary should not overlook checking the holiday dates of the countries to be visited (see Appendix 6), so that an appointment will not be planned for a day when the offices will be closed. It should be borne in mind that many countries celebrate holidays that differ from those in the United States.

Foreign visas. Some, but not all, countries require that visitors obtain permission to enter the country through a document referred to as a "visa." Therefore the secretary should call the consulates of the countries that the executive intends to visit and find out whether a visa is necessary. If it is, the traveler must present his passport at the consulate and fill out a visa form. Since the length of time it takes to process a visa varies with the country to be visited, this must be done well in advance of the set departure date. The secretary should also find out from the consulate what the fee for the visa will be, since a charge for this document is generally made.

Customs regulations. In order to avoid difficulties upon the traveler's return to this country, the secretary should obtain information about the customs regulations for travelers abroad and present it to the executive. Such information can be procured from pamphlets issued by the U.S. Treasury Department, Bureau of Commerce, Washington, D.C., and from the travel agent who is arranging the trip.

The secretary should remind the executive that if he is taking abroad a watch, a camera, or any other item of foreign manufacture that was purchased in the United States, he will need to have in his possession the sales slip for each of such items. Such possessions should also be registered with the U.S. Customs officials before the executive leaves, in order to eliminate possible customs problems upon reentry.

During the trip, the executive will expect to be kept posted on events occurring at the home office. She must find out which items he wants her to handle herself, which he wants her to refer to others in the organization, and which he wants forwarded to him. Some employers request that the secretary keep a log of daily events and send it on to them at specific times. If the secretary keeps abreast of the traveler's itinerary and uses the air-mail services, she can keep the traveler informed, no matter where he is. The secretary should keep a duplicate copy of all correspondence that is forwarded and number each packet sent, so that any loss can be detected.

If it is necessary to send a package to the executive when he is in some foreign country, the secretary should first check with the post office the mailing regulations, restrictions, and requirements (see Chapter 10).

For urgent messages that need immediate attention, the secretary can rely on telephone, telegram, or cablegram services, which are described in Chapter 10.

THE TRAVELING SECRETARY

At times it is necessary for the executive to take along a secretary on a business trip. Although today the businessman has several means to facilitate his business needs, such as portable recorders, public stenographers, and the like, an employer may prefer to have his secretary along with him, because she knows his work, can take the dictation easily, and is more efficient than a strange worker would be.

The traveling secretary must know the rules of etiquette that guide her behavior on a business trip and must adhere to them without exception. She is expected to stay in the same hotel as the executive, but etiquette demands that her accommodations be on a different floor and less expensive than those of the executive. A room with bath is adequate.

A secretary's behavior on a business trip is open to criticism. Whether the verdict will be favorable or otherwise depends upon how she handles herself during and after business hours. Therefore her behavior should be more circumspect than it might be at home and such that it will reflect to the credit of the executive. She must remember never to discuss business after hours, because one never knows who is listening. Etiquette also demands that she arrange for her own entertainment in the evenings and not give the executive the uncomfortable feeling that he must look after her. Of course, if she may be needed in the evening, as during a convention, she should be on call.

More than likely the traveling secretary will be asked to do her work in a strange office, among strange people. Her personality, tact, diplomacy, and friendliness will pave the way for a pleasanter work situation. She cannot demand that the regular staff surrender their conveniences to oblige her.

She must remember that, as a guest in a strange office, she may not be permitted to return to the office after hours; therefore she must take with her when she leaves the office all the supplies and data that she will need for outside work.

A secretary who travels with her employer should be prepared for and try to foresee all contingencies that may arise during the trip. She should assemble supplies and materials, in addition to those she ordinarily packs for the executive, that she will need in carrying out her functions. Among the items she may need are several shorthand notebooks, a supply of the firm's letterhead paper, onionskin paper, and regular plain typing paper, as well as the firm's envelopes, plain envelopes, carbon paper, pencils, a colored pencil, pens, a typing eraser, a pencil eraser, a pencil sharpener, several scratch pads, and a supply of postage stamps. Most important of all the tools of her profession is the typewriter. If the organization has a portable machine available, she should suggest that it be taken along on the trip; with a machine at hand at all times, the secretary can carry out her duties readily as needed. Otherwise, she may have to make arrangements with the hotel, before arrival, for the rental of a typewriter, particularly if she has to work evenings. Hotels generally do provide this service for their guests, but such service does not help if the executive likes to take care of business matters en route.

Not the least part of her preparations for the trip is the consideration the secretary gives to assembling her wardrobe. First, the climate she will meet at the destination will govern the kind of clothing she will take. Under any circumstances it is always most sensible to travel light. A suit is always appropriate for traveling, but one should not live in it throughout the trip. The dresses she takes should be crease-resistant, so that they will stay fresh and neat looking; basic, so that they can be made to look like different costumes simply by changing accessories; and appropriate for business. A bathing suit is appropriate if the destination is a resort area. The secretary must remember that she is expected to be well-dressed, well-groomed, and conservative in her dress at all times, since she represents the executive and the company on the business trip.

SOCIAL AMENITIES

The secretary is responsible for the social amenities that are business-connected.

VISITING CARDS

All executives find occasions to use both business and personal calling cards. These cards should be uncluttered in the information they contain, yet informative and dignified. Frequently the secretary is called upon to act as a consultant in choosing the format and type of card to order, or the entire job is turned over to her good judgment. Therefore she should know the standard requirements for visiting cards.

Personal calling cards are usually 3 × 1½ inches in size, of heavy, white card paper called "two-sheet board." The legend on such cards is generally engraved in black ink in Roman letter style, which is considered in good taste. Matching envelopes generally accompany personal calling cards. Names should be written out in their entirety and initials avoided where possible. On this type of card it is permissible to include titles such as Mr., Mrs., and Dr. before names. The identifications of junior and senior may be abbreviated, if the name is long, or written out in full in small lettering. The use of the individual's residence address is a matter of choice; if the executive desires to have his address appear on his personal visiting cards, good taste prescribes that it should appear in the lower right-hand corner.

Business calling cards are slightly larger than personal cards. Customarily they are cut 3½ × 2 inches in size, but for top executives they may be 3½ × 2½ inches. It is considered good form to use Roman letters in black or gray ink on white pasteboard of good quality. Middle initials can properly be used on these cards. The word "company" in the name of the firm is always written out, unless the abbreviation "Co." is part of the legal name of the firm; "Inc." is always abbreviated. The name of the company is generally placed in the lower left-hand corner. The arrangement of the company address depends upon the location of the firm: if the company offices are in a small town, the name of the town and the state are shown on the same line; but if the company offices are situated in a large city, the street address is placed on one line and the name of the city on the next line, the name of the state being omitted. If the title of the executive is to be shown on the card, it should be placed above the name of the company in the lower left-hand corner, and the firm's address should be placed in the lower right-hand corner.

Women's business cards follow the same basic principles as those for men, except that a woman's name may be preceded by "Miss," "Mrs.," or "Ms."

A secretary encloses an executive's business card when a present goes to someone he knows through business. However, if the individual becomes a personal friend—that is, one who is seen outside of business hours—the executive's personal calling card should be used. The secretary should also enclose the executive's personal visiting card in greetings and presents that are sent to his friends and relatives.

DONATIONS

An executive usually receives many requests for donations annually, and many individuals respond to these pleas. It is not the secretary's responsibility to screen such requests before submitting them to the employer. Every request for a donation must be submitted for the executive's attention and decision. However, it is the secretary's responsibility to keep a record, and (if possible) a receipt, for all donations or contributions made by the executive to educational, religious, and philanthropic organizations. These records are very important for income-tax purposes and for the donor's own information. When a request for a donation or contribution comes into the office, it will aid the executive if the secretary will note on each request the amount given to that organization in the preceding year and the total amount of contributions made during the current year. If a pledge was made that is payable in installments, the due dates of the payments should be entered on the secretary's calendar or in the card tickler and brought to the executive's attention as they occur. At the end of the year a list should be compiled of all the organizations to which the executive has contributed, with the amounts of the donations given to each organization clearly shown.

INVITATIONS

Invitations extended by the executive to two types of functions are of particular concern to the secretary. These functions are formal dinners that he gives personally and official entertainments given by him in his official capacity.

Etiquette decrees that invitations to either of these functions be formal in nature. This means that they should be written in the third person and may be engraved for the occasion, partly engraved, or handwritten.

Engraved invitations should be of traditional size, usually three units by four units, with the lettering in black. It is considered proper form and makes a very elegant-looking invitation to use a white or light-cream paper of a kid finish. No address, monogram, or initial should appear on an engraved invitation. If the family has a coat of arms, however, this may be embossed, but without color. The space for the name of the guest that is generally provided on invitations is omitted on official invitations from executives.

If a reply is expected, this is indicated on the bottom left-hand corner with the letters R.S.V.P. and directly underneath, the address (if it differs from that where the entertainment will take place).

Mr. Harold Jones
requests the pleasure of your company
at a reception
on Wednesday, the third of January
at half past six o'clock
The Executive Club
700 Elm Road

If the entertainment is given in someone's honor, a line would be inserted before the date:

in honor of Mr. George Brown
or
to meet Mr. George Brown

If the reception is being given at the executive's home with his wife acting as hostess, the invitation would read:

To meet Mr. George Brown
Mr. and Mrs. Harold Jones
at home
Wednesday, the third of January
from six until eight o'clock
35 Woodland Drive

entertainment, and the time and date can be filled in by hand. A partially engraved invitation generally follows this form:

Mr. and Mrs. Harold Jones
request the pleasure of
(name written in)
company at
on
at   o'clock
35 Woodlane Drive

only on engraved invitations. On partially engraved invitations, the phrase "in honor of" or "to meet" may be handwritten at the top.

Etiquette prescribes that formal invitations should follow a standard acceptable format. The full name of both the sender and the guest should appear on invitations. However, on answers the full name of the person answering the invitation should appear, whereas only the last name of the person who sent the invitation need be mentioned. If the invitation enumerates more than one name, all the names mentioned should be shown in the reply. Good form calls for the omission of the year in both the invitation and the answer. The date and the hour that the function is to take place should be specified in an acceptance, but only the date need be mentioned in a regret. Furthermore, when referring to the invitation in a reply, it is courteous to refer to it as a "very kind invitation."

"Excellency," never appear on invitations except when referring to the guest of honor:

To meet the Honorable George Brown

or

In honor of His Excellency,
the Governor of Pennsylvania

The time of day of the function is usually written out in full. If the function begins at any time after the hour, the fraction of the hour should also be written out and worded as "so much past the hour," for example, "half past seven o'clock."

ANSWERS TO INVITATIONS

Etiquette requires that an invitation be answered promptly in the same form in which it was issued; that is, if the invitation was issued in the third person, it should be answered in the third person, and so forth. Formal answers are used in reply to formal invitations and are written by hand on personal writing paper.

Mr. and Mrs. John Smith
accept with pleasure
the kind invitation of
Mr. and Mrs. Harold Jones
for Wednesday, the third of January
from six until eight o'clock

Mr. Harold Jones
regrets that he is unable to accept
Mr. and Mrs. Harding's
kind invitation for dinner
on Saturday, the second of September

Answers to invitations to social business functions, such as luncheons, dinners, or receptions, should also be written by hand but they should be on business letterhead paper. If it is necessary to explain the reason for declining such an invitation, a letter of explanation should follow the formal note of regret. (See *Invitations,* above, for correct forms of names and dates on replies to invitations.) Generally no reason need be given unless the invitation was issued by the White House or by royalty.

A secretary who performs her functions efficiently will make a record of every invitation that her executive receives. This will enable her to remind him when the time to participate in the affair draws near. Also, if the employer should take the invitation home to consult with his wife about attending, the secretary will have a record of the host, time, place, and date of the affair, so that she can answer it correctly when the decision on attendance is made.

If the invitation originates with the executive, the secretary should type a list of the guests to whom the invitations were sent. As the acceptances and regrets come in, a notation should be made next to the name of each guest, and the letters should be attached to the list. It is also extremely helpful to make a daily summary of the total number of acceptances, regrets, and no replies to the invitations sent out. This summary should be placed on the executive's desk at the end of each day.

When dinner or luncheon invitations have specified a definite return date for reply and no reply has been received from some of the guests on the list, it is perfectly permissible for the secretary to telephone or telegraph the invited guests three or four days before the event. This is done generally in order to determine the number of guests who will be present and/or their choices of entrees. A good reference library will contain at least one book on etiquette which should be consulted whenever there is a question of social form. (See Section Five.)

THEATER TICKETS

One of those little, but vital, extras that a secretary is sometimes called upon to perform is that of obtaining theater tickets for the executive and his guests. For this purpose she must know about the shows that are currently offered in the theaters. A little information about the shows and the critics' opinions will help the executive in the choice of shows. The executive generally names several shows, in order of preference, and asks his secretary to procure the tickets. It is generally difficult to obtain tickets for hit shows unless they are ordered far in advance. However, advance notice is not always possible. The secretary, therefore, should familiarize herself with the reliable theater-ticket agencies in her locality, make contact with an agent who will take care of her needs, and establish an account. In this way tickets can often be obtained on short notice, since agents prefer to take care of their regular customers.

When the tickets arrive at the office, the secretary should enclose them in an envelope on which she has typed the date and day of the week of the performance, the curtain time, the name and address of the theater, the name of the show, and the seat numbers.

If the tickets must be sent through the mail for any reason, the secretary should enclose with them a letter of transmittal in which she has referred to the name of the show, the name and address of the theater, the date of the performance, and the seat number. Thus, if the tickets are lost, and particularly if her executive has planned to attend several different shows, she has on the carbon copy all the information necessary for follow-up. The letter also provides all the pertinent information to the individual receiving the tickets and acts as a reminder of the date.

GIFT AND CARD LISTS

Another of the secretary's responsibilities is to call the executive's attention to approaching occasions such as a birthday, anniversary, or graduation, or to the sending of holiday remembrances, and so forth. For this purpose she must keep a record of these events and lists of the persons to whom the executive sends cards and presents. Separate lists should be maintained for friends, relatives, and business acquaintances to whom the executive sends his own Christmas cards, those to whom he sends cards jointly with his wife, those who receive company cards, those to whom he gives gifts at Christmas, and those to whom he gives gifts at other times throughout the year.

These lists and records should be kept up to date, with names added or deleted and addresses checked periodically. It will aid the executive in the selection of gifts if the secretary keeps a cumulative record of the gifts previously given the individual, the cost of the gifts, and the occasion for such gifts. Furthermore, since the secretary in many cases is asked to select and purchase the cards and gifts and address and mail them, she should submit these lists to the employer well in advance of the occasion, so that sufficient time will be allowed for shopping, preparation, and mailing.

Christmas lists for cards and gifts should be submitted to the employer at least six weeks before Christmas for additions, deletions, and suggestions. Often the secretary must see to it that the gifts are appropriately wrapped or must do the wrapping herself and then mail them. Time must be allowed for mailing, particularly if the gift is to be sent abroad or to some distant point. It is somewhat embarrassing to have a gift or card arrive after the occasion for which it was intended. An appropriate

Christmas card (and not the executive's visiting card) should be enclosed in a Christmas gift before it is wrapped.

AT TIME OF DEATH

At the time of a death a friend or acquaintance of the deceased usually expresses his or her sympathy by sending a token remembrance to the bereaved family. The form of this expression of sympathy depends upon the religious affiliation of the deceased. Since no one wants to create a feeling of disrespect and disharmony on this most sensitive occasion, the secretary should know the correct procedure to follow in expressions of sympathy, so that she can advise her executive if the need should arise. These expressions may take any one or a combination of several of the following forms:

Flowers. It is customary to send flowers to the bereaved family except in the Orthodox Jewish faith. A fruit basket or an assortment of cookies is generally considered a proper and accepted expression of sympathy to Orthodox Jewish families. Flowers may take the form of a floral piece, that is, a spray or a wreath, but cut flowers should never be sent on such occasions. It is also considered appropriate to send a floral piece to memorial services for someone lost at sea or when the deceased is cremated. A card should always accompany a sympathy piece. If a visiting card is used for this purpose, the engraved name should be crossed out in ink and a few words of sympathy added. The floral piece is usually ordered by the secretary from the florist by telephone, and he supplies an appropriate card on which he writes the name of the person sending the flowers and any message the sender desires. When ordering the floral piece, the secretary must be prepared to tell the florist the name of the deceased, where the deceased reposes, the time and date of the funeral, and the kind and size of floral piece desired.

Letters of sympathy. Letters expressing sympathy to the bereaved family may be sent to people of any faith and may be sent in addition to flowers or any of the other expressions noted herein. Such letters are usually sent to close members of one's family or personal friends when an individual wishes to express a feeling of a deep and personal loss.

Mass cards. Mass cards indicate that arrangements have been made to have a mass or masses said in memory of the deceased and for the repose of his soul. It is considered appropriate to send such cards to a Roman Catholic family. They may be sent by either a Roman Catholic or a non-Catholic. The cards may be obtained from a priest. It is customary to make an offering when such cards are obtained. Although a Roman Catholic could ask a priest to say mass for a non-Catholic, it is not deemed to be in good taste to send a mass card to a non-Catholic family.

Charitable contributions. Some families specify that, instead of flowers, they would prefer friends to send contributions to charities or organizations in which the deceased was interested. If this is done, the charitable organization that receives these donations in the name of the deceased should notify the bereaved family that such contributions were received. The donor can also write to the family of a close friend or relative and inform them that he is sending a donation to the charitable institution in the name of the deceased.

Death of a member of the executive's family. The secretary may be called upon to keep for the executive a record of those who sent expressions of sympathy and what was sent when a member of his family has died. She should write a description of the floral piece that was received on the back of each accompanying card. In addition, a separate alphabetic file of all mass cards and letters should be kept. From these data, in order to facilitate sending acknowledgments, she should make separate lists indicating the names of those who sent flowers alone, of those who sent both mass cards and flowers, of those who wrote and also sent flowers or mass cards, and of those who sent contributions to charitable institutions.

Two opinions exist as to the type of acknowledgment that is appropriate at this time. According to one, the cards acknowledging expressions of sympathy should be formal and engraved. According to the other, it is perfectly proper to have the acknowledgments typed. Acknowledgments may be written out in longhand if only a few need to be sent, but if the deceased was a prominent person and hundreds of remembrances were received, engraved cards should be sent only to those who are unknown to the bereaved, not to acquaintances. The type of remembrance sent— flowers, mass cards, or contributions—should be mentioned in the acknowledgment.

The secretary should also keep a list of the names and addresses of those who performed outstanding services, such as doctors, nurses, a priest or minister, editorial writers, and the like, so that letters of appreciation can be sent to them for their kindness and understanding. Also, thank you letters should be sent to those who sent memorial contributions to charitable organizations.

All the lists should be submitted to the executive, who will select therefrom the persons to whom he wants to dictate letters, those to whom he wants to write in longhand, and those for whom he wishes the secretary to draft and type acknowledgments.

Death of the executive. The details that the secretary takes care of in the event of the executive's death depend upon his family. She should ask the family what they want her to do; generally they are very appreciative of any help that may be forthcoming. The secretary can be most helpful in several areas, particularly in taking care of the following items and thereby relieving the bereaved family of much worry and detail.

She could notify a mortician and make arrangements as to where the body will be kept—at home or in a funeral chapel, depending upon the family's wishes.

She could find out the church affiliation of the deceased and ascertain from the clergyman the time that is available for services.

She could notify the insurance company or companies of the death of the executive.

She could speak to the mortician about funeral notices to the newspapers. He may prepare these from information she provides, or she may prepare the notices herself and telephone them to all the papers in which the family wants them to appear. If the deceased was well known, she could call the city editors of the big papers and give them the information directly.

She could send wires to the friends of the deceased and to the secretaries of all the organizations to which he belonged. The time and place of the funeral and the interment should be clearly stated in these wires.

She could ask the family whom they would like to act as honorary pallbearers and then telephone or wire these people for their acceptances.

She should keep a file of clippings from all the papers bearing items about the deceased.

An important detail, and one which many people overlook, is the notification of the Social Security Administration of the executive's death. The secretary should remind the family of this necessity and offer to write the letter. This notification is important, because the one who pays the funeral expenses may be entitled to some remuneration from the Social Security Administration, and unless this agency is notified of the death, this remuneration will not be forthcoming.

PART THREE

Advanced Procedures and Techniques

Chapter 12

The Employer's Personal Funds

GERALD CROWNINGSHIELD

THE SECRETARY who handles her employer's personal funds will receive cash, prepare bank deposits, draw checks for her employer's signature in payment of his personal obligations, reconcile bank accounts, and take charge of the office fund. In addition, she may be asked to take care of some of his personal record keeping. This could involve making entries in a cash record and keeping expense records and investment records that will be needed when income-tax returns are being prepared. It is the purpose of this chapter to provide a background of information that will enable the secretary to carry out these duties proficiently.

HANDLING THE BANK ACCOUNT

RECEIVING CASH

The secretary who is taking care of her employer's personal funds will handle cash receipts from such items as salary, interest and dividends on investments, and rents from income-producing property. Usually receipts are in the form of checks; occasionally cash itself is received. Checks should be examined to determine whether they are properly made out. Attention should be paid to the date; postdated checks cannot be deposited or cashed before the date written on the check. Checks that are irregularly made out should be set aside to be discussed with the employer. Whenever cash is received, the secretary should prepare a receipt in duplicate (blank forms are available at any stationery store), one copy to be given to the person making payment and the other to be retained as a record of the transaction.

If the secretary's duties include record keeping, entries should be made in the proper records. After the entries have been recorded, all cash receipts should be deposited in the bank as soon as possible. Arrangements for night deposits should be made if funds cannot be deposited before the bank closes.

MAKING BANK DEPOSITS

When cash is to be deposited in a bank, a deposit slip is made out (Fig. 12). Although banks do accept deposit slips improperly prepared, the competent secretary is careful to do the job correctly. The date is entered,

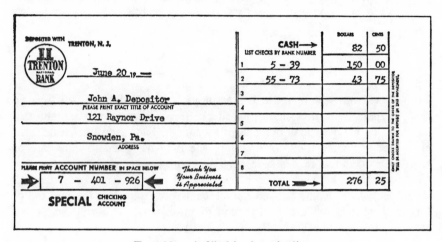

FIG. 12.   A filled-in deposit slip.

the name of the depositor is written *exactly* as it appears on the bank records, and the account number is filled in. The account number is important, since it is the number, rather than the name, that the bank uses to enter the deposit on its records. Currency is counted, and the total is entered on the slip. Large amounts of silver should be rolled in wrappers provided by the bank. Each check included in the deposit is listed separately and identified by the number assigned to the bank on which it

was written. On the check illustrated (Fig. 13), the bank number is $\frac{55\text{-}73}{312}$.

Only the top portion of the number need be placed on the deposit slip. Occasionally traveler's checks or money orders may be a part of the deposit. These are entered in the same manner as ordinary checks. After all checks have been listed, the amounts on the slip are added and the total is placed in the space provided.

Deposit slips are printed so that they may be prepared in triplicate. After being stamped by the teller, one copy is returned to the depositor as a receipt. Copies of deposit slips should be retained to be checked against the statement that will be rendered by the bank. When it has been ascertained that the bank has properly recorded all deposits, the slips may be discarded.

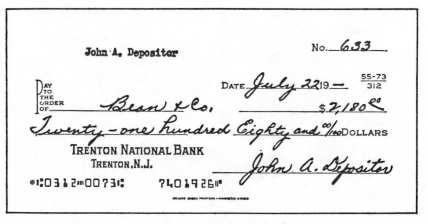

FIG. 13.   A completed check.

ENDORSING CHECKS

Checks are written orders by which the depositor, known as the "drawer," directs the bank, referred to as the "drawee," to pay money to the "payee" or to a third party designated by him. Checks are sometimes made payable to "bearer," a practice generally frowned upon because they are negotiated by simple delivery and can be cashed by persons who wrongfully receive them. Checks need not be made payable to real persons. Business checks are frequently made out to "Petty Cash" or to "Payroll." A check is made payable to Payroll, for example, when money is needed in making up pay envelopes.

If a check is made out to a definite payee, he must write on the back of the check directions for its disposition and sign his name. This is known as an "endorsement." Endorsements are placed on the back of the check on the *left-hand side*. The endorser should sign exactly as the name is written on the face of the check. If his name is misspelled or differs in any manner from the way it appears on the bank records, he should sign twice, first as it is written on the face and then correctly. There are three principal forms of endorsement: (1) in blank; (2) in full; and (3) restrictive (Fig. 14).

In a blank endorsement the endorser simply writes his name across the back of the check. The effect of a blank endorsement is to make the check payable to the bearer. If it is lost or stolen, it can be cashed by the holder without further endorsement. Although they are commonly used, blank endorsements are not to be recommended. They should be made only at the time a check is being cashed or deposited at the bank.

In an endorsement in full the endorser transfers the check to a designated party by writing the words "Pay to the order of" followed by the name of the person to whom payment is to be made ahead of his signature.

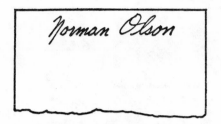

Blank Endorsement
Payable to bearer
without further endorsement

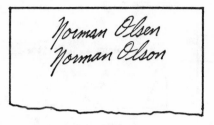

Blank Endorsement
Name misspelled

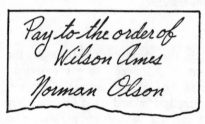

Endorsement in Full
Payable as Wilson Ames directs

FOR DEPOSIT ONLY IN
MECHANICS NATIONAL BANK
TO THE CREDIT OF
Norman Olson

Restrictive Endorsement
Further negotiation prohibited

FIG. 14.   Types of endorsements.

A check so endorsed can be cashed or negotiated only after the person named in the endorsement has signed it. It is not good in the hands of a person who wrongfully possesses it.

In a restrictive endorsement the endorser limits further negotiation of the check by writing above his signature definite instructions on what may be done with it. Thus, a check might be made payable to one person *only* or it might be endorsed "For deposit only." Except when checks are being deposited in the bank, restrictive endorsements are almost never used. Business checks are usually endorsed for deposit with a rubber stamp; no written signature is needed.

DISHONORED CHECKS

A bank accepts checks for deposit subject to their final payment. If the drawer has directed his bank to refuse payment or if he has insufficient funds on deposit, the bank will return the check and charge it to the depositor's account. Such a check is known as a "dishonored check."

Informal arrangements for payment or redeposit of a dishonored check are usually made with the drawer. However, if the drawer is a stranger, it would be advisable for the holder of a dishonored check to take legal steps and file a formal notice of protest. In this way, he is assured of protecting his full rights against the drawer.

Dishonored checks that have been returned by the bank should be deducted from the bank balance on the depositor's cash records and then be redeposited or filed for safekeeping until the drawer has made settlement. Any fees that may have been paid for the protest or collection can rightfully be collected from the drawer.

COLLECTING BOND COUPONS

Interest on most bonds is collected by tearing off coupons that are attached to the bonds and presenting them to the issuing corporation or its agent for payment on the due date. Bondholders generally accomplish this through their banks. Since banks differ in the manner in which they process bond coupons for deposit, the secretary should consult with the head teller to determine how bond coupons are to be handled.

Some banks accept bond coupons as collection items and credit the depositor's account *after* collection has been made; others accept bond coupons as regular cash deposits. In the first instance the coupons are left with the collection department, and the bank notifies the depositor when the account has been credited. In the second instance the bond coupons are listed on the deposit slip and the bank makes an immediate credit to the depositor's account. In both cases the coupons are enclosed in envelopes that are supplied by the bank (Fig. 15). Only one kind of coupon is enclosed in a single envelope; if coupons are clipped from several issues, a separate envelope should be used for each issue. Unless different arrangements have been made, the bank requires that a certificate of ownership be filled in and submitted with the coupons (Fig. 16). One exception is made. Certificates are not required with U.S. government bonds.

The secretary who has the responsibility of collecting bond coupons should keep some kind of record or file as a reminder of dates on which interest coupons are due. Coupons are not paid until they are presented. Failure to make presentment at the proper time results in a delay in securing cash.

BANK STATEMENT

At regular intervals, or sometimes upon request of the depositor, the bank renders a bank statement, showing what has taken place in the account since the last statement was prepared and the present balance

THE PHILADELPHIA NATIONAL BANK
PHILADELPHIA 1, PA.

NAME OF
COUPON_____PAYABLE AT_____

ENCLOSE BUT ONE KIND OF COUPON OF SAME ISSUE AND MATURITY IN THIS ENVELOPE.

REMARKS:	NO.	EACH	AMOUNT	
		$	$	
RETURN UNPAID COUPONS IN THIS ENVELOPE	DUE	TOTAL	$	

IF COUPONS ARE OWNED BY A DOMESTIC CORPORATION PLEASE SO STATE.

NAME OF OWNER_____
PRINT NAME

LEGAL ADDRESS OF OWNER_____
PRINT ADDRESS

IF DEPOSITOR IS OTHER THAN OWNER PLACE NAME HERE_____

SEE REVERSE SIDE FOR CERTIFICATE INSTRUCTIONS

Form 1102 E

CERTIFICATE INSTRUCTIONS

If enclosed coupons were detached from bonds issued by a DOMESTIC or RESIDENT Corporation prior to January 1, 1934, and the bonds contain a tax free covenant clause and they are owned by a citizen or resident individual, fiduciary or partnership, execute a United States Internal Revenue certificate form No. 1000, placing the amount on that line which indicates whether or not the owner pays an income tax. If coupons are OWNED by a Domestic Corporation or Charitable organization the above certificate is not required. This certificate is not required with coupons detached from obligations of the United States Government or the political sub-divisions such as a State, County, Municipality, Borough, Township or School District. If this certificate is executed by owner, he may take credit on his Income Tax return for the amount of his tax on the enclosed coupons paid by the Corporation.

If the owner is a non-resident alien, a foreign partnership or corporation, United States Internal Revenue certificate form No. 1001 or one of its variations must be enclosed. This certificate is required if the interest is in connection with obligations of the United States Government or the political sub-divisions or a Domestic or resident Corporation.

If neither of the above forms is required, but the bonds were issued by a PENNSYL-VANIA corporation, enclose a memorandum certificate Form No. PC279 (obtainable at Teller's window) showing the name and legal address of owner. This information is necessary so that the debtor corporation will be able to ascertain its tax liability under the laws of the Commonwealth of Pennsylvania. This certificate is required whether the owner is or is not a resident of the State of Pennsylvania.

Consult the Receiving Teller for further information.

THIS SPACE FOR BANK ENDORSEMENT

FIG. 15.   Envelope for deposit of bond coupons.

according to the bank's records (Fig. 17). The statement shows the balance carried forward from the previous statement, all deposits and all charges made to the account during the period, and the balance on the date the statement was rendered. Sent along with the statements are canceled checks, credit memos, and debit memos. Canceled checks are the depositor's checks that have been returned to the bank, charged against the

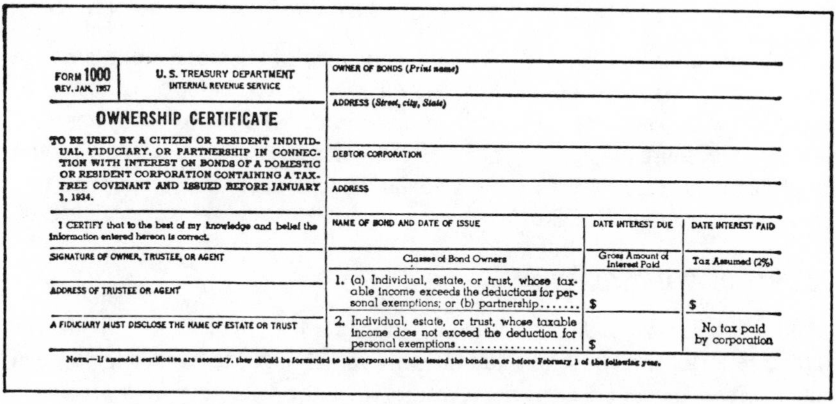

FORM 1000
REV. JAN. 1957

U. S. TREASURY DEPARTMENT
INTERNAL REVENUE SERVICE

OWNERSHIP CERTIFICATE

TO BE USED BY A CITIZEN OR RESIDENT INDIVIDUAL, FIDUCIARY, OR PARTNERSHIP IN CONNECTION WITH INTEREST ON BONDS OF A DOMESTIC OR RESIDENT CORPORATION CONTAINING A TAX-FREE COVENANT AND ISSUED BEFORE JANUARY 1, 1934.

I CERTIFY that to the best of my knowledge and belief the information entered hereon is correct.

SIGNATURE OF OWNER, TRUSTEE, OR AGENT

ADDRESS OF TRUSTEE OR AGENT

A FIDUCIARY MUST DISCLOSE THE NAME OF ESTATE OR TRUST

OWNER OF BONDS (*Print name*)

ADDRESS (*Street, city, State*)

DEBTOR CORPORATION

ADDRESS

NAME OF BOND AND DATE OF ISSUE	DATE INTEREST DUE	DATE INTEREST PAID
Classes of Bond Owners	Gross Amount of Interest Paid	Tax Assumed (2%)
1. (a) Individual, estate, or trust, whose taxable income exceeds the deductions for personal exemptions; or (b) partnership.......	$	$
2. Individual, estate, or trust, whose taxable income does not exceed the deduction for personal exemptions....................	$	No tax paid by corporation

NOTE.—If amended certificates are necessary, they should be forwarded to the corporation which issued the bonds on or before February 1 of the following year.

FIG. 16. Ownership certificate to be submitted with bond coupons.

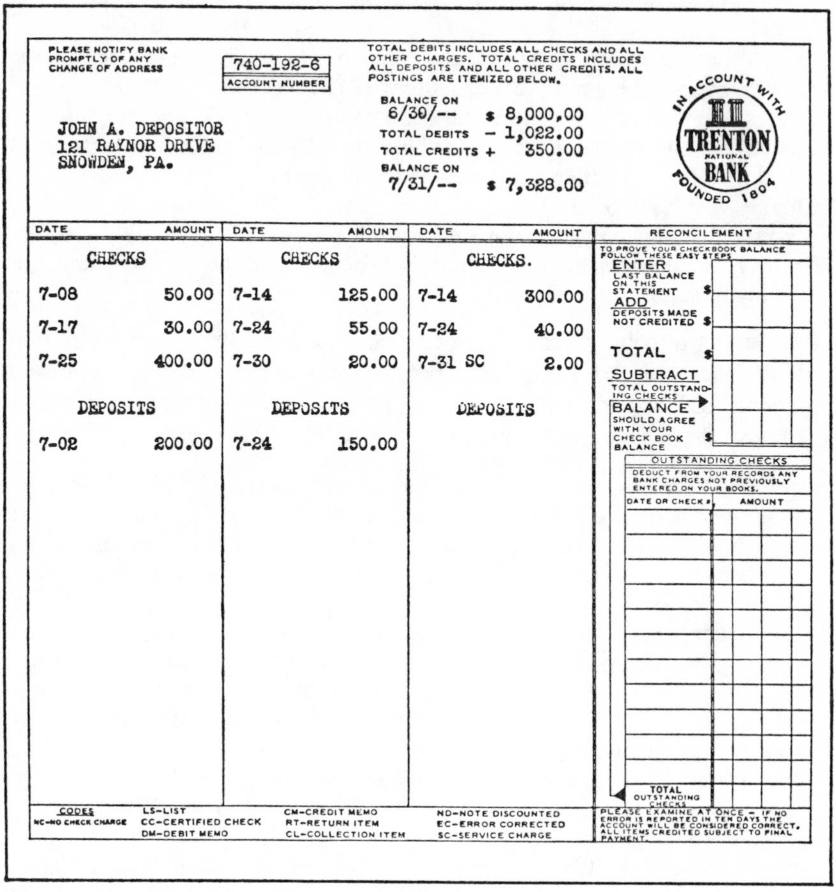

PLEASE NOTIFY BANK PROMPTLY OF ANY CHANGE OF ADDRESS

740-192-6
ACCOUNT NUMBER

TOTAL DEBITS INCLUDES ALL CHECKS AND ALL OTHER CHARGES. TOTAL CREDITS INCLUDES ALL DEPOSITS AND ALL OTHER CREDITS. ALL POSTINGS ARE ITEMIZED BELOW.

JOHN A. DEPOSITOR
121 RAYNOR DRIVE
SNOWDEN, PA.

BALANCE ON 6/30/-- $ 8,000.00
TOTAL DEBITS − 1,022.00
TOTAL CREDITS + 350.00
BALANCE ON 7/31/-- $ 7,328.00

IN ACCOUNT WITH TRENTON NATIONAL BANK FOUNDED 1804

DATE	AMOUNT	DATE	AMOUNT	DATE	AMOUNT
CHECKS		CHECKS		CHECKS.	
7-08	50.00	7-14	125.00	7-14	300.00
7-17	30.00	7-24	55.00	7-24	40.00
7-25	400.00	7-30	20.00	7-31 SC	2.00
DEPOSITS		DEPOSITS		DEPOSITS	
7-02	200.00	7-24	150.00		

RECONCILEMENT

TO PROVE YOUR CHECKBOOK BALANCE FOLLOW THESE EASY STEPS

ENTER LAST BALANCE ON THIS STATEMENT $
ADD DEPOSITS MADE NOT CREDITED $
TOTAL $
SUBTRACT TOTAL OUTSTANDING CHECKS
BALANCE SHOULD AGREE WITH YOUR CHECK BOOK BALANCE $

OUTSTANDING CHECKS
DEDUCT FROM YOUR RECORDS ANY BANK CHARGES NOT PREVIOUSLY ENTERED ON YOUR BOOKS.

DATE OR CHECK #	AMOUNT
TOTAL OUTSTANDING CHECKS	

CODES
NC—NO CHECK CHARGE
LS—LIST
CC—CERTIFIED CHECK
DM—DEBIT MEMO
CM—CREDIT MEMO
RT—RETURN ITEM
CL—COLLECTION ITEM
ND—NOTE DISCOUNTED
EC—ERROR CORRECTED
SC—SERVICE CHARGE

PLEASE EXAMINE AT ONCE — IF NO ERROR IS REPORTED IN TEN DAYS THE ACCOUNT WILL BE CONSIDERED CORRECT. ALL ITEMS CREDITED SUBJECT TO FINAL PAYMENT.

FIG. 17. Bank statement.

account, and stamped "PAID." Credit memos are notices of amounts *added* to the account for such sums as interest allowed by the bank or proceeds of items left with the bank for collection—notes and bond coupons, for example. Debit memos are notices of *deductions* made from the account for service charges, interest on bank loans, checks accepted for deposit that were dishonored, and the like.

BANK RECONCILIATION

Seldom will the balance showing in the checkbook agree with the balance reported on the bank statement, even though no errors have been made in either place. Disagreement results from the following causes:

> Deposits that were made near or after the date of the statement have not yet been posted on the bank records. They do, however, appear in the checkbook.
>
> Credits that have been made to the account by the bank, as indicated on the credit memos, have not yet been entered in the checkbook.
>
> Checks issued by the depositor and deducted in the checkbook are still outstanding; that is, they have not yet been presented to the bank for payment and therefore do not appear on the bank statement.
>
> Charges that have been made against the account by the bank, as indicated on the debit memos, have not yet been entered in the checkbook.
>
> Errors have been made either in the checkbook or on the bank's records, or in both places.

As soon as possible after he receives his statement, the depositor should locate the reasons for differences between the bank statement and the checkbook and find the correct balance in the account. This is done on a bank reconciliation statement, prepared by the following steps:

> Compare deposits entered in the checkbook with those recorded on the bank statement. Check discrepancies against duplicate deposit slips to determine which record is correct. Make a note of deposits that do not appear on the bank statement and credits made by the bank that have not been added in the checkbook.
>
> Arrange checks returned by bank in numerical order and compare them with their stubs, taking careful notice to see whether the amounts agree. Make a note of differences. Place a check mark, or other symbol, on stubs of the checks that have been returned. Prepare a list of the outstanding checks, noting the check number, the date, and the name of the payee. Do not include certified checks on this list, since they have already been charged against the account. Make a note of any bank charges that have not been entered in the checkbook.
>
> Arrange the information that has been assembled on a bank reconciliation statement. The form and preparation of this statement are explained and illustrated below.

If the checkbook and bank statement are both correct, the balances can be brought into agreement and the reconciliation is complete. If the accounts cannot be reconciled after adjustments have been made for omissions, an error in addition or subtraction in the checkbook is indicated. The check stubs should be checked, with particular attention to the balances carried forward from one stub to another.

BANK RECONCILIATION STATEMENT

Bank reconciliation statements are prepared in three ways:

Adjustments are made to the balance reported by the bank to bring it into agreement with the checkbook balance.
Adjustments are made in the checkbook balance to bring it into agreement with the balance according to the bank statement.
Adjustments are made to both balances to get the correct balance.

Since neither of the first two methods provides the correct balance, the third method is the preferred procedure and is the one illustrated and explained here. Data for the bank reconciliation statement in Fig. 18 were taken from the cash record illustrated in Fig. 24 and the bank statement illustrated in Fig. 17.

John A. Depositor
Bank Reconciliation Statement
July 31, 19—

Balance according to bank statement.....................$7,328

Add deposit of July 31 not recorded on bank statement.. 1,000

$8,328

Deduct outstanding checks:

Check No.	Date	Payee	Amount	
633	7/22/19—	Bean & Co.	$2,180	
634	7/28/19—	Blue Cross	50	2,230

Corrected bank balance............................... $6,098

Balance according to checkbook....................... $6,100
Deduct service charge not recorded................... 2
Corrected checkbook balance.......................... $6,098

Fig. 18. Bank reconciliation statement.

Comparison of the deposits that were made during the month with those · recorded on the bank statement reveals that the bank has not entered a deposit of $1,000 made on July 31; this amount is added to the balance reported by the bank. Comparison of the canceled checks returned by the bank with the checks drawn during the period shows that the following checks are still outstanding:

Check No.	Date	Payee	Amount
633	7/22/—	Bean & Co.	$2,180
634	7/28/—	Blue Cross	50
			$2,230

The total of the outstanding checks is deducted from the balance reported on the bank statement. Adding the unrecorded deposits and deducting the outstanding checks take care of all omissions on the bank statement. The correct bank balance is determined to be $6,098.

The bank statement shows a service charge of $2.00 which has not been entered in the cash records; this amount is deducted from the checkbook balance. Now the corrected checkbook balance is also $6,098, and it has been proved that no errors have been made.

After the reconciliation has been completed, errors should be corrected and entries should be made in the depositor's cash records and checkbook for any omissions, such as the service charge discussed above, so that the records will reflect the correct balance. Adjustments in the checkbook can be made on the stub for the last check drawn. It is not necessary to correct all preceding balances. Any bank errors uncovered in the reconciliation should be reported to the bank immediately.

The bank reconciliation statement should be filed for future reference. It will prove useful when the next reconciliation is made. The canceled checks are receipts for payments that have been made. They should be kept on file for as long as proof of payment might be necessary.

INVESTIGATING OUTSTANDING CHECKS

Ordinarily checks should clear through the bank and be returned to the depositor within a few weeks after issue. Checks that have been outstanding for unreasonably long periods of time should be investigated. Outstanding checks are not only annoying when bank accounts are being reconciled but they also pose a question as to what may have happened to them. Perhaps the checks have been lost or mislaid by the payee. Communication with the payee is in order.

If the payee claims that he has not received a check, a new one will have to be issued in its place. This should be done, however, only *after* a stop-payment notice has been filed on the old check. How to stop payment on a check is described later in this chapter.

BANK LOANS

There are several types of bank loans. Small amounts are usually borrowed on so-called "personal loans," which require no collateral and no co-signers. The amount received on the loan is less than the amount to be repaid, and repayment is generally made on a monthly basis. Thus, a bank might advance the borrower $576 on his promise to pay $600 in installments of $50 per month for 12 months. The interest rate on personal loans is high, sometimes as much as 2 per cent per month.

Larger amounts are borrowed on promissory notes, which may be secured or unsecured. Stocks, bonds, and insurance policies are the most common types of collateral used as security. In some cases interest is payable at maturity. For example, the borrower receives $1,000 and signs a note to repay $1,000 at the end of one year, plus interest at 6 per cent. He will repay $1,060 one year later. Very often interest is paid in advance. For instance, the borrower signs a note promising to pay $1,000 one year after date. The bank deducts interest at 6 per cent and advances him $940. The interest rate in this case is actually slightly more than 6 per cent. Another form of loan is the demand note, which bears interest at a fixed rate but does not require repayment of the principal at any predetermined date. The borrower can make repayments as he wishes, and the bank can call for payment of the principal at any time. Interest is payable at regular intervals on the unpaid balance.

The secretary who is handling her employer's personal affairs may be given the responsibility of seeing that payments of principal and interest are made on their due dates. In case the loan is secured, she may be asked to handle the details involved in making an assignment of the collateral posted as security.

HANDLING CASH PAYMENTS

PAYING THE EMPLOYER'S PERSONAL BILLS

The secretary who takes care of her employer's personal bills accepts responsibility for paying the *correct amount* at the *right time*. To ensure proper payment, she should (1) check to make sure that bills submitted to the employer are correct and (2) take measures to ensure that bills come to her attention for payment when they are due.

Before drawing checks for her employer's signature, the secretary should thoroughly check the accuracy of the statements received. She should compare the charges listed on the statement with the sales slips that are attached or other supporting evidence and make sure that proper credits have been allowed for returns and for payments that have been made on the account. The mathematical accuracy of all calculations on the statement should be verified.

Prompt payment of all bills is desirable; on some bills, payment on or before a given date is essential. Particular attention must be paid to insurance premiums, because policies lapse if premiums are not paid before a certain date, and to those bills that are subject to some form of additional charge if payment is not made within a stated period. One method of ensuring payment at the right time is a "tickler" file, in which bills are filed by the dates on which they should be paid.

Occasionally payments must be made in a foreign currency (see Appendix 3). The easiest means of making remittances to foreign countries is a draft payable in the funds of the country to which it is to be sent; drafts can be purchased at any bank. Personal checks could be used in some instances; however, this poses the problem of exchange rates and presents the possibility of over- or underpayment. The exchange rates fluctuate.

WRITING CHECKS

Care should be exercised in writing checks. It is good policy to fill in the check stub *first,* to prevent the possibility of drawing a check without recording it. The date, the check number, the name of the payee, and the reason for the payment should all be listed on the stub (Fig. 19). The reason for payment should contain enough information to permit later entry in the cash records. The check is filled in with the number, the date, the name of payee, the amount in both figures and words, and the signature.

DEPOSITS			CHECKS DRAWN	AMOUNT	
BALANCE FORWARD	7200	00	No. 632 DATE July 21 19—		
DATE			FAVOR OF Windsor Pharmacy		
7 23	150	00	FOR Drugs	20	00
7 31	1000	00	No. 633 DATE July 22 19—		
			FAVOR OF Bean & Co.		
			FOR 200 shares – a. Co. stock	2180	00
			No. 634 DATE July 28 19—		
TOTAL DEPOSITS	8350	00	FAVOR OF Blue Cross of N. J.		
TOTAL CHECKS DRAWN	2250	00	FOR Quarterly premium	50	00
BALANCE	6100	00	TOTAL CHECKS DRAWN	2250	00

FIG. 19. Page of checkbook stubs.

Checks should be written legibly. No blank spaces which might be used to alter the check should be left. The amount in figures is placed close to the dollar sign, and the amount in words is started close to the left-hand side. Writing the amount in hundreds is usually less cumbersome than in thousands. Thus, $3,150 becomes "Thirty-one hundred fifty dollars" rather than "Three thousand one hundred and fifty dollars." The amount in words should agree with the amount in figures. In case of disagreement, the bank may refuse to honor the check. If the check is honored, the amount written in words governs. If the amount of the check is less than one dollar, it is customary to cross out the word "Dollars" and write "Only . . . cents."

Titles such as "Dr." or "Rev." are not used; it is "Ben Kildare," not "Dr. Ben Kildare." "Mrs." is used only in connection with the husband's name; it is either "Mrs. Roy Roe" or "Ruth Roe." Checks issued to organizations should be made payable to the organization, not to some individual in the organization. Likewise, checks should be made payable to companies, rather than to their agents. Checks for insurance premiums, for example, would be drawn in favor of the insurance company, rather than the agent who handles the account.

It is not wise to sign blank checks. Should this be necessary when the employer will be absent from the office, the checkbook should be kept in a place where it will be safe from theft. Checks, like money, are a medium of exchange and should be guarded as carefully as money.

Erasures and alterations should never be made on checks. Banks are reluctant to accept checks if there is any suspicion that they have been tampered with. If mistakes are made in preparing a check, the word "VOID" should be written across the face of the check and on its stub. If the check has already been signed, the signature should be lined out. If checks are prenumbered, spoiled checks should not be discarded; they should be pasted back into the checkbook so that there can be no question concerning the whereabouts of a missing check.

CERTIFIED CHECKS

Often checks for large amounts drawn by a person whose financial status is unknown to the payee must be certified by the bank before they are issued. To secure certification, the depositor takes a completed check to the bank. After the cashier has ascertained that the account has sufficient funds to cover it, he stamps the check "CERTIFIED" and signs his name. Immediately upon certification, the amount of the check is charged against the depositor's account. There can be no question of funds being available for payment when it is presented. So far as the bank is concerned, it has already been paid.

Certified checks should never be destroyed. In the event that they are not sent to the payee, they should be redeposited in the bank.

STOPPING PAYMENT ON A CHECK

The drawer of a check has the power to stop payment on it at any time prior to its presentation to the bank for payment. This is accomplished by filing a stop-payment notice at the bank on a form that the bank will provide. Oral notice is insufficient. So that the bank can identify the check when it is presented, it will ask for such information as the number of the check, its date, the name of the payee, and the amount. Stop-payment notices should be filed immediately in case a check is lost.

As soon as the stop-payment notice is filed with the bank, the check stub should be marked "Payment stopped." The amount of the check should then be added to the current balance. This can be done on the check stub open at the time; it is not necessary to go back and correct all preceding balances.

PETTY-CASH FUND

Although it is good policy to make all payments by check, since a check provides a written record of the transaction and serves as a receipt, it is impractical to write checks for small amounts to cover items such as collect telegrams, postage due, carfare, supper money, and incidental purchases of office supplies. In some instances, too, cash is needed immediately. To meet these needs, it is customary to set up what is generally called a "petty-cash fund." Operation of the petty-cash fund is described in the following paragraphs.

Establishing the petty-cash fund. First, it is decided how much cash should be placed in the fund. This is determined by the expenditures that are anticipated. The amount should not be too high, yet it should not be so low that too frequent reimbursements are required. When the amount has been set, a check is drawn payable to Petty Cash. The check is cashed and the funds are placed in a locked cash box or drawer, generally referred to as the petty-cash drawer. Responsibility for the fund should be placed in one person, and he alone should have access to it.

Payments from the petty-cash fund. All payments from the petty-cash fund should be supported by documentary evidence in the form of a petty-cash voucher, showing the date of payment, the name of the payee, the reason for payment, and the amount paid out (Fig. 20). The petty-cash voucher is initialed by the person making payment and signed by the person who has received the cash. Printed forms for this purpose can be purchased at any stationery store.

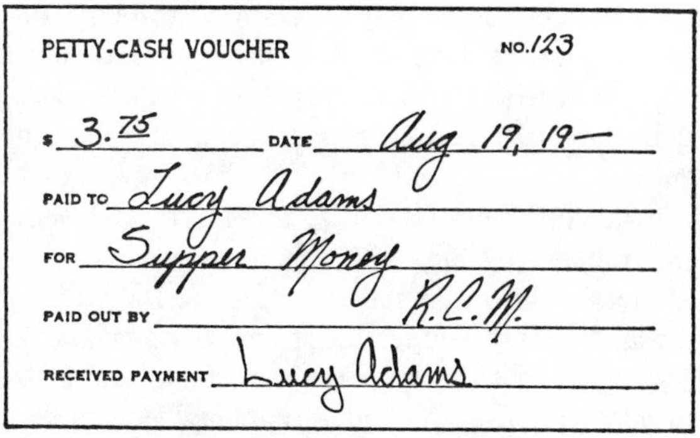

```
┌─────────────────────────────────────────────────────┐
│                                                       │
│   PETTY-CASH VOUCHER                  NO. 123         │
│                                                       │
│   $ 3.75          DATE   Aug 19, 19—                  │
│                                                       │
│   PAID TO  Lucy Adams                                 │
│                                                       │
│   FOR   Supper Money                                  │
│                                                       │
│   PAID OUT BY              R.C.M.                      │
│                                                       │
│   RECEIVED PAYMENT   Lucy Adams                       │
│                                                       │
└─────────────────────────────────────────────────────┘
```

FIG. 20.   Petty-cash voucher.

Paid vouchers are placed in the petty-cash drawer or in a special envelope kept for this purpose. In addition, some firms maintain a petty-cash record. This is simply a form on which paid vouchers can be summarized. Columns are provided for the voucher number, date, name of payee, explanation of payment, and a summary of the expenditures made. Seldom is there a real need for such a record; the petty-cash vouchers themselves usually provide an adequate record.

Replenishing the petty-cash fund. Whenever the cash in the petty-cash fund gets low, the fund is replenished. A check is written payable to Petty Cash for the amount that has been spent from the fund. The check is cashed and the proceeds are placed in the petty-cash drawer. After replenishment, the cash in the fund should amount to the fund originally established.

SECRETARY'S RECORD-KEEPING DUTIES

The record-keeping duties of the secretary are varied, depending upon the kind of information the employer desires and the nature of his investments. Since income taxes are a primary concern of many employers, it may be assumed that personal records which facilitate the preparation of tax returns are the ones he most desires. These would include expense records and diaries and records that reflect his income and expenditures in connection with his investments in stocks and bonds and real estate. Keeping records such as these is discussed in the following paragraphs.

EXPENSE DIARY

Taxpayers in business for themselves who incur expenses in carrying on their trade, business, or profession, and employees who incur expenses while away from home in connection with their employment, are allowed to take income-tax deductions if they can support their expenditures with proper records and prove that the expenses were both reasonable and necessary. Employees who receive expense allowances must keep expense records so that they can render proper accounting to their employers whenever required.

Starting with the taxable year 1962, the Internal Revenue Service put into effect a "crackdown" on entertainment and travel expenses. The taxpayer must clearly show that the expenses are for business reasons, not pleasure, and that they are neither lavish nor extravagant. Under the new rules, record keeping has become all-important. As never before, the taxpayer who claims travel or entertainment deductions has to be a meticulous bookkeeper. He must produce an accurate record of the who, the why, the when, the where, the what, and the how much.

```
                              EXPENSE DIARY

   DATE  July 29-30, 19—    WHERE HELD  Seaside Inn, Atlantic City, N. J.

   OCCASION    Annual convention—Institute of Purchasing Agents

   GUESTS  _____
   PRESENT _____

   BUSINESS _____
   DISCUSSED _____

   REMARKS. _____


                              EXPENSES
   TRAVEL:
     . Fares paid                                $
       Automobile expenses  200  miles  @  12 ¢      24.00
       Lodging                                       30.00
       Meals                                         36.00
       Incidentals (taxis, tips, etc.)                8.00

                                                              $  98.00

   ENTERTAINMENT:
                                                $



   OTHER:
       Convention registration fee             $   50.00

                                                              50.00

                               TOTAL EXPENSES   $ 148.00
```

FIG. 21.   Page from employer's expense diary.

Although the Internal Revenue Service does not prescribe a definite form that the expense record must take, it does recommend that the taxpayer keep a contemporaneous diary of expenses showing the following information: the time, the place, the business purpose or business relationship, a list of persons involved or a guest list, in case of entertainment, and the cost. The Service further requires that all disbursements of $10 or more must be substantiated with documentary evidence, such as itemized receipts, paid bills, and the like.

An expense diary that seems to meet income-tax needs is illustrated in Fig. 21. This is a form that could be easily ruled up, duplicated, and kept in a loose-leaf binder. Entries are made by the secretary from information supplied by her employer. Since memories are short, the diary should be made out as soon as possible after the event has taken place and should be a detailed record. It is better to write down too much information than too little; it is better to be safe than sorry. The employer dictates the information for the top of the form and gives the secretary the vouchers and paid bills for entry on the bottom. The diary should be kept for as long as the employer's tax return might be questioned. All supporting vouchers should also be retained.

The expense diary illustrated is filled in for an employer who attended a convention of a professional organization at his own expense. Note how the expenses have been itemized. Had the form been prepared to cover entertainment, the following information would have been filled in:

DATE July 30, 19– WHERE HELD Crystal Restaurant
OCCASION   Dinner conference
GUESTS John Doe and Richard Roe of Eastland Steel
BUSINESS DISCUSSED Subcontract for lunar missile

EXPENSES

ENTERTAINMENT:
    Dinner and cocktails $30.00
    Tips and taxi fares   7.50 $37.50

AUTOMOBILE-EXPENSE RECORD

The taxpayer who uses his automobile in connection with his business or employment is entitled to deduct automobile expenses (in whole if the auto is used exclusively for business, or in part if it is used for both business and pleasure) on his income-tax return. Expenses include not only all the operating costs but also a reasonable allowance for depreciation. To ensure that he receives full benefit from his allowable deductions, the taxpayer would be wise to keep careful account of expenses and mileage on an automobile-expense record. A simple form for this purpose, set up to accumulate expenses on an annual basis, is illustrated (Fig. 22).

AUTOMOBILE MILEAGE AND EXPENSE RECORD				YEAR __19—__	

Mileage Record:
    Speedometer reading—end   42,000
    Speedometer reading—beginning   22,000
    Mileage for year   20,000

Expenses	Jan.	Feb.	March	Dec.	Year
Gasoline	30.00	28.00	32.00	31.00	360.00
Oil & lubrication	10.00	10.00	10.00	10.00	120.00
Maintenance & repairs	25.00		7.00	12.00	110.00
Tires & other supplies		15.00	75.00	18.00	125.00
Washing	3.00	3.00	3.00	3.00	36.00
Garage rent	12.00	12.00	12.00	12.00	144.00
State inspection	4.00				8.00
Insurance		150.00			150.00
Totals	84.00	218.00	139.00	86.00	1,053.00

FIG. 22.   Automobile-expense record.

The secretary can keep the record by using information supplied by her employer or, better yet, by making entries from bills that he turns over to her. It is undoubtedly true that many taxpayers do not bother with detailed records and have to rely on "reasonable and realistic" approximations on their tax returns. It is probably true that most of these estimates are understated. Automobile-expense records are well worth the little trouble involved in keeping them.

REAL-ESTATE RECORD

A real-estate record similar to the one illustrated in Fig. 23 might be kept by the secretary for an employer who owns property that he leases to tenants. The form is set up to accumulate information for income-tax reporting. On the front the secretary posts entries for expenditures made in connection with the property, using information supplied by invoices and tax bills. The back of the form is ruled as a record of rents received. Rent checks are posted as they are received.

A word of explanation is needed concerning entries in the *Improvements* and *Expenses* columns. Improvements represent *extraordinary* expenditures that add something to the value of the property or extend its life. Examples are a new roof, new siding, additions, and alterations. Expenses are the *ordinary* outlays necessary to maintain the property in good condition. Included are such items as painting and decorating, ordinary repairs,

REAL ESTATE RECORD

PROPERTY One-family dwelling 50 Runyon Drive, City   DATE ACQUIRED Jan. 12, 19--

COST   LOT $ 2,000
        HOUSE $ 13,000   ASSESSED VALUATION $ 6,000

Improvements				Expenses			Depreciation	
Date	Description	Amount	Date	Description	Amount		Year	Amount
7/1/--	New siding	2,000	3/1/--	Redecorating	200		19--	750
			4/1/--	Plumbing	20			
			8/1/--	Real estate taxes	450			
			9/3/--	Water & sewer tax	60			

(Front)

(Back)

Rents Received

Date	Amount	Date	Amount	Date	Amount
2/3/--	130				
3/5/--	130				
4/4/--	130				

FIG. 23. Real-estate record.

and taxes. In case of doubt as to where an entry should be made, the secretary should consult with the tax accountant.

INVESTMENT RECORD

Secretaries are often asked to keep records of their employer's investments in stocks and bonds. These are ruled forms on which purchases and sales of securities are recorded and interest and dividend payments are entered.

RECORD OF CASH RECEIVED AND PAID OUT

Many employers rely on their secretaries to keep a detailed record of cash received and paid out. First, they desire such a record for their own personal use; second, they need a detailed record of income and expenses for income-tax purposes.

The kind of cash record kept by the secretary depends upon the kind of information her employer desires. A record kept for an employer who is primarily concerned with keeping track of household expenses would be quite different from the record maintained for an employer who is interested only in securing data for tax returns. The secretary must first find out what sort of information is wanted; then a cash record can be set up to suit the need. In the discussion that follows it is assumed that securing tax data is the primary objective.

The cash record illustrated in Fig. 24 presumes that the employer deposits all cash received from salary, rents, interest, dividends, and the like, and that he makes all payments by check. The columns on the left provide a bank record. Deposits are entered in the *Deposits* column and added to the previous balance; the number and amount of each check issued are entered in the *Checks Drawn* columns and the amount is deducted from the previous balance. An explanation of each entry is written in the *Description* column. The columns on the right-hand side of the record provide an analysis of the expenditures which have been made. Expenditures are divided into two main groups: those that are deductible for tax purposes and those that are nondeductible. Deductible expenditures are further broken down into the five major categories that appear on the income-tax return: *Contributions, Interest, Taxes, Medical and Dental,* and *Other.* Checks are entered in the proper columns at the time they are issued. At the end of the year, arriving at amounts for the tax return is a simple matter of taking figures from the cash record. Without such a record, securing figures for the return would involve a tedious tabulation from the check stubs.

CASH RECORD											
Bank Record						Deductible Expenditures					Non-deductible Expend.
Deposits	Checks Drawn No.	Amount	Balance	Date	Description	Contributions	Interest	Taxes	Medical & Dental	Other	
			8,000.00	7/1	Balance forward						
200.00			8,200.00	7/2	Dividends—X Co. stock						
	625	50.00	8,150.00	7/4	County College	50.00					
	626	125.00	8,025.00	7/6	City Bank—mtge on home		40.00				85.00
	627	300.00	7,725.00	7/10	Nu Appliances—refrigerator			15.00			285.00
	628	30.00	7,695.00	7/12	Dr. Kildare				30.00		
	629	55.00	7,640.00	7/16	Travel expenses—convention					55.00	
	630	40.00	7,600.00	7/18	City Dept. Store—on account						40.00
	631	400.00	7,200.00	7/20	Mutual Ins. Co.—premium						400.00
	632	20.00	7,180.00	7/21	Windsor Pharmacy—drugs				20.00		
	633	2,180.00	5,000.00	7/22	Bean & Co.—A Co. stock						2,180.00
150.00			5,150.00	7/23	Interest—Y Co. bonds						
	634	50.00	5,100.00	7/28	Blue Cross—quarterly payment				50.00		
1,000.00			6,100.00	7/31	Salary—July						
1,350.00		3,250.00			Monthly totals	50.00	40.00	15.00	100.00	55.00	2,990.00

FIG. 24.   Employer's personal cash record.

A few illustrative entries have been made in the cash records. Note that some of the payments had to be split into two parts when the expenditure was being recorded. The check covering a payment on the mortgage on a residence was entered in two columns. The part that represented interest was entered in the *Interest* column; the remainder is a personal expense which is not deductible for tax purposes. Likewise, the cost of a refrigerator was entered as a nondeductible expenditure, whereas the state and city sales taxes paid on the purchase were entered in the *Taxes* column.

Some employers might want more detailed information on the nondeductible expenditures. If so, the cash record illustrated could be expanded to meet the need. The *Nondeductible Expenditure* column, for example, could be broken up to show household expenses, food, clothing, entertainment, and so on.

Chapter 13

Business Law

HARRY KATZ

IN A BUSINESS WORLD that grows more complex each day, an essential part of the secretary's equipment is a knowledge of at least some of the basic legal rules that govern the day's business transactions. This information is important not to enable the secretary to make decisions on legal problems but to permit her to perform her duties with more understanding and thus with greater efficiency. Equally important is the fact that familiarity with the basic facts about business law will help the secretary to recognize when she is faced with a legal problem that requires the attention of the company's attorney.

Business law is a term used to describe the legal rules that apply to business transactions. This chapter will discuss the rules of business law that are useful not only to the secretary in a commercial office but also to the law secretary. The actual preparation and typewriting of legal papers is discussed in Chapter 8.

In this chapter different kinds of legal forms and documents are mentioned or discussed. Some of the most important of these are shown in detail. For the secretary who is interested in familiarizing herself with the content of the others, the common forms may be purchased in stationery stores that carry legal blanks in stock.

CONTRACTS

The law of contracts is the foundation of all business law, because most business transactions are based on a contract between two or more parties. Contracts are made for a variety of purposes—to buy or sell merchandise or real estate or stocks and bonds, to lease or mortgage property, to obtain insurance, to designate agents or representatives. The broad rules that apply to most contracts in determining whether they are legally enforceable should be known to the secretary.

236

REQUIREMENTS OF CONTRACTS

In general, a contract between two parties is an agreement that the courts will enforce. To be binding, a contract should satisfy the following conditions:

1. *The parties must be legally capable of entering into an agreement.* Although most persons meet this requirement without question, some persons are not considered to be legally competent to enter into a contract. These include "infants" (persons under 21 years of age), insane persons, or intoxicated persons. Any such person can refuse to perform a contract made by him, without incurring any liability to the other contracting party, unless the contract involves the purchase of "necessaries," that is, food, clothing, shelter, and medical services. Even in the case of necessaries, however, he can be held liable only for the reasonable value of the necessaries if that value is less than the price he agreed to pay.

An infant is liable upon any contract if he ratifies it after he becomes 21 years of age. Ratification consists of his express approval of the contract, or his receipt of benefits under it, or his failure to disaffirm the contract within a reasonable time after reaching 21.

2. *The parties must mutually agree upon the terms of the contract.* This is frequently called a "meeting of the minds." However, if a person's consent to a proposal is obtained by the practice of fraud or misrepresentation upon him or by coercion or undue influence, he may refuse to perform the agreement.

3. *A "consideration" must be given in exchange for the other party's promise.* In most business transactions consideration consists of the payment of a sum of money by one contracting party to the other; in return, the latter either makes a promise or performs an act.

4. *The agreement must have a lawful purpose.* A contract meeting all the conditions thus far mentioned will, nevertheless, be unenforceable if its purpose is contrary to law. Some examples of illegal contracts are (a) bets or wagers, (b) lotteries, (c) usurious agreements (which require payment of a higher rate of interest on loans than the maximum allowed by law), (d) contracts which *unreasonably* restrain the conduct of a trade or business, as happens in some cases when a person selling a business agrees not to compete with the buyer or an employee agrees not to compete with his employer after the employment ends, and (e) agreements for services by unlicensed persons, if a license to perform such services is required by law, as in the case of real-estate brokers.

Must a contract be in writing? Contrary to common belief, it is the general rule that an agreement need not be in writing to be enforceable. A written statement is, nevertheless, helpful in showing that an agreement was actually reached by the parties or in specifying what the terms of the agreement are, so that doubt or ambiguity is eliminated. For these reasons, it is desirable to have evidence of a business agreement in some written form, even though it may not be a formal legal document. Ordinary letters or memoranda between parties, or purchase orders or confirmations, or other writings, can effectively show both the existence of an agreement and its terms.

By statute some types of contract *must* be proven by a writing to be enforced by the courts. The most important contracts in this group are:

A contract for the sale of personal property for more than $500. However, if the buyer has made a part payment or has accepted delivery of at least part of the goods, or if the buyer or seller has signed a memorandum of the agreement, an oral contract of this type will be enforced.

A contract for the sale of real estate, regardless of the amount of the purchase price.

A lease of real property for more than a specified period, in most cases one year.

A guarantee to pay a third person's debt or obligation.

A promise that is not to be performed within one year from the time the promise is made.

SIGNING OF CONTRACTS

If a contract is in writing, an individual party to it should sign his name at the end of the contract. If he is incapable of signing his name, he should show his assent to the agreement by making a mark or sign at the place for signature, and the mark or sign should then be witnessed by another person.

The absence of the attestation and the corporate seal will not nullify the signature of a corporation, but the presence of these elements gives some assurance that the signing is genuine and properly authorized.

The letters "L.S.," sometimes printed after a signature of a person on a document, represents that person's "seal." Formerly a seal was placed on contracts to denote the existence of "consideration." Today the seal generally has no legal significance, except in the case of corporations, as just noted.

NOTARIZATION OF PAPERS

In the case of some documents, such as deeds or mortgages, which are recorded in a public office, the law requires that the identity of the person who signs the paper be established or that such person acknowledge that he signed the document. Even when not required by law, it may be of benefit

The signature of a partnership should be made in the following form:

ABC Associates

By_____
            (Partner)

A corporation should execute a document in the following form:

XYZ Corporation

By_____
            (Officer)

(Corporate Seal)

ATTEST:

_____
        (Officer)

in some cases to have the person's identity shown, in order to assure the genuineness of the signature on a legal document. In those instances, identity of the signer is proven by means of an acknowledgment, which is a statement signed by a notary public appearing on the contract after the signature of the contracting party.

Forms of acknowledgment. The form of the acknowledgment differs according to whether the signer is an individual, a partnership, or a corporation.

When an individual has signed the instrument:

State of _____)
) ss.:
County of_____)

On this ____ day of _____, 19 ____, before me personally came _____, to me known and known to me to be the individual described in and who executed the foregoing instrument, and he acknowledged that he executed the same.

_____
        Notary Public

When a partnership has signed the instrument:

```
State of _____)
                              ) ss.:
County of_____)
```

On this ___ day of _____, 19 ___, before me personally came _____, to me known and known to me to be a member of _____, and the person described in and who executed the foregoing instrument in the firm name of _____, and he duly acknowledged to me that he executed the same as and for the act and deed of said firm of _____.

```
          _____
                 Notary Public
```

When a corporation has signed the instrument:

```
State of _____)
                              ) ss.:
County of_____)
```

On this ___ day of _____, 19 ___, before me personally came _____, to me known, who, being by me duly sworn, did depose and say that he resides at _____, that he is the (title or position) of _____ Corporation, the corporation described in and which executed the foregoing instrument; that he knows the seal of said corporation; that the seal affixed to said instrument is such corporate seal; that it was so affixed by order of the board of directors of said corporation, and that he signed his name thereto by like order.

```
          _____
                 Notary Public
```

In addition to acknowledgments, a notary's signature appears on affidavits. An affidavit is a sworn statement in writing, signed in the presence of a notary public by the person who makes the statement. It is customary for the sworn statement to be preceded by these words:

```
State of _____)
                              ) ss.:
County of_____)
```

The statement is ended by the signature of the person making it, and is followed by these words:

```
Sworn to before me this
_____ day of _____, 19 ___


                        _____
                               Notary Public
```

A notary public is a person authorized by law to take the acknowledgments and oaths of persons who sign documents. One may apply for appointment as a notary public by filing a completed form of application in a designated public office and paying the required fee.

SUNDAY CONTRACTS

A contract made on a Sunday or to be performed on that day is generally held to be lawful unless a state law expressly declares it to be illegal. The same rule applies to promissory notes or checks drawn or delivered on a Sunday.

STATUTE OF LIMITATIONS

The law requires that a person asserting a claim against another must pursue it with reasonable diligence. Thus, statutes in all states fix time limits within which a claimant must sue, if he intends to enforce his claim by suit. These are called "statutes of limitation," and the periods of limitation vary according to the nature of the claim (for example, whether it is a claim for breach of contract or for slander).

If a debtor makes a part payment on a claim or a written promise to pay it, the computation of the period begins anew from the time of the part payment or the written promise. If the statutory period elapses without a suit having been brought, the claim is said to be "barred" or "outlawed."

THE SALE OF GOODS

A sale is an agreement by which one person transfers the ownership of goods to another person. If the seller does not own the goods, or if he has only a limited interest in them, the buyer will acquire only such right as the seller has and no more.

In general, the term "goods" means personal property. However, it does not include negotiable documents such as promissory notes, drafts, checks, stock certificates, bills of lading, and warehouse receipts, which will be discussed later.

FORM OF SALE CONTRACT

As noted above, no writing is necessary to render a contract for the sale of goods enforceable, unless the price is $500 or more. Even if the price is $500 or more, the sale is enforceable if the buyer has paid part of the price or has accepted delivery of all or a part of the goods.

On occasion a buyer may require the seller to furnish written proof of the sale, so that he (the buyer) will have evidence of ownership. In such a case a bill of sale is delivered by the seller to the buyer. A bill need not be in a special form; even a letter or simple statement indicating that a sale is being made will suffice. However, printed forms of bill of sale are available in stationery stores, on which the blanks may be filled in to show the names of the seller and the buyer, a description of the goods, the price, and the seller's signature.

SELLER'S DUTIES

A seller of goods is required to deliver (1) the kind of goods ordered, (2) in the quantities requested, (3) for the price agreed upon, and (4) at the time and place agreed upon by the parties. If the seller fails to do this, the buyer may, depending upon circumstances, sue the seller for money damages or even cancel the sale entirely.

If goods delivered by a seller are not of the quality ordered (for example, they are not of fast color), or if a seller has made untrue statements about the quality of the goods (for example, "this coat is 100 percent wool" when it is not that), the law treats this as a breach of warranty by the seller. If the seller has breached a warranty, the buyer may return the goods and cancel the sale. If the buyer chooses to keep the goods in spite of the defect or inferior quality of the goods, he is entitled to be compensated because of the lesser value of the goods. If a warranty is breached, the buyer must notify the seller promptly of his claim; otherwise he will be considered to have waived the seller's breach.

When goods are sold by sample, the lot delivered to the buyer must conform to the sample exhibited to the buyer. If a sample shown to a buyer has a defect that can be observed on examination, it is not a breach of warranty by the seller if the same defect appears in the goods delivered to the buyer.

BUYER'S DUTIES

In general, a buyer is obligated to take and pay the agreed price for goods purchased by him. If no specific price has been fixed by the agreement, the buyer is bound to pay the prevailing market price. If the buyer fails to fulfill these duties, the seller may sue him for damages for breach of contract.

SELLER'S RIGHTS

In addition to a seller's right to sue for damages, as just noted, he is given other rights under the law to protect him in case of a breach of contract by the buyer.

1. A seller has a lien on the goods sold, if he still has possession of the goods and the buyer has not paid the price as required by the contract. This means that the seller need not deliver the goods to the buyer until the price is paid. However, such a lien does not exist in the seller's favor if the contract of sale requires him to deliver the goods before the time fixed for payment by the buyer.

2. If a seller has turned over the goods to a carrier for delivery to the buyer and the buyer is insolvent or repudiates the contract, the seller may notify the carrier to stop the goods in transit and thus prevent delivery to the buyer. The seller's notice to the carrier must be given while the goods are still in the course of transit; otherwise the right to stop the goods is lost.

3. A seller may cancel the contract of sale.

4. A seller may resell the goods. If the goods are resold for a price below the contract price, the buyer may be held liable for the difference. If they bring more on a resale, the seller may retain the additional amount.

BUYER'S RIGHTS

As mentioned above, if a seller has breached a warranty, the buyer may rescind the sale or may claim damages from the seller.

In addition, the buyer has a right to recover damages from the seller if the latter refuses to deliver the goods as agreed. If the market price is higher than the contract price, the buyer will be entitled to recover the difference between the two amounts.

BULK SALES

If a businessman whose main business is the sale of merchandise from stock proposes to sell a major part of his merchandise or fixtures outside the ordinary course of trade, notice of the proposed sale must be given to his creditors by registered mail. This is required in order to prevent unscrupulous businessmen from absconding with the proceeds of sale, leaving their creditors unpaid. If notice of sale is not given to the seller's creditors as required by law, the buyer of the business assets is held liable to those creditors, to the extent of the value of the assets he has purchased.

BUSINESS ORGANIZATIONS

The three common forms under which businesses conduct their affairs are (1) the individual proprietorship, (2) the general partnership, and (3) the corporation.

INDIVIDUAL PROPRIETORSHIP

As its name indicates, the individual-proprietorship form of business organization represents the ownership of a business by an individual person. He manages its operations and is personally liable to creditors for all debts of the business.

GENERAL PARTNERSHIP

In a general partnership two or more persons associate with each other for the purpose of conducting business. Each partner has a voice in managing the business, and each partner is personally liable to partnership creditors for the payment of all debts of the partnership business. Differences among partners arising in the usual course of business are settled by a majority vote. However, if a partnership transaction is one that is not in the ordinary course of business (for example, selling the business or admitting a new partner to the firm), the consent of all partners is necessary; otherwise the action is not legally effective.

Each partner may make contracts with third persons that will be binding on the firm if the contracts appear to be made in the usual course of business. If a contract made by a partner is outside the normal scope of partnership business, only the acting partner will be liable on the contract, and not his copartners.

A partnership is legally dissolved if (1) the agreed term of the partnership expires, (2) the partners mutually agree to dissolve the firm, (3) a partner dies, (4) a partner or the partnership is in bankruptcy, (5) the partnership business is unlawful, or (6) a court directs that the partnership be dissolved.

In case of a dissolution, unless there is an agreement that provides otherwise, the assets of the firm must be liquidated and its affairs wound up, and distribution must be made first to creditors and then to partners.

CORPORATION

A corporation is an artificial person created under law, which has some of the attributes of a natural person, such as the right to make contracts, to receive and hold and dispose of property, and to sue and to be sued. As a legal person, a corporation is separate and distinct from those who own it, that is, its members or stockholders. Even if *all* shares of stock in a corporation are owned by a single individual, the law recognizes that the corporation is a different legal person from its stockholder. Thus, an individual who owns 100 percent of the stock of a corporation cannot, in his own name, sell property owned by the corporation.

Organizing a corporation. When persons desire to form a corporation, they execute a certificate of incorporation, which is then filed in a public office designated by law. This certificate contains specific information required by law, such as the name of the corporation (which is not to resemble closely the name of another corporation), the business purposes of the corporation and the powers it is to exercise, the amount of capital stock, the number of shares of stock, and the location of the corporation's principal office. A corporation may issue one or more classes of stock, depending upon its particular business needs. The rights of stockholders of each class of stock are fully described in the certificate of incorporation.

A distinction should be noted between shares of stock in a corporation, which represent the ownership of an interest in the corporation, and bonds issued by the corporation, which constitute a debt of the corporation.

Stockholders. In general, a stockholder is entitled to participate in and vote at stockholders' meetings (see also Chapter 14), to inspect the books and records of the corporation, to exercise the right to buy shares of a new issue of stock put out by the corporation (called the "preemptive right"), to transfer the shares held by him, to receive dividends when declared by the board of directors, and to share in the corporate assets when the corporation is dissolved.

Board of directors. Members of the board are elected by the stock-holders. The board is entrusted with the general management of the corporate business and the setting of its policies. However, if action to be taken is of an extraordinary nature, such as changing the capital stock, or merging or consolidating with another corporation, or dissolving the corporation, the board of directors cannot act alone. Such action, to be effective, must be adopted by the stockholders.

One of the most important functions of the board of directors is the declaration of dividends. This is a matter entrusted to the business judgment and discretion of the directors. Even if the corporation has profits or enjoys a surplus, directors need not declare dividends if they determine that a dividend payment will not be in the best business interests of the corporation. Dividends may be paid in the form of money, shares of stock, or other property.

Every director must use reasonable business judgment and care in performing his duties and cannot take advantage of his official position to obtain personal benefits.

The board of directors appoints the officers of the corporation, such as president, vice-president, secretary, and treasurer, who exercise the powers given to them in the corporate bylaws.

Officers. The president is the principal officer of the corporation. He is generally authorized to make and sign contracts, deeds, and other docu-ments on behalf of the corporation. He presides at stockholders' meetings.

The vice-president is empowered to act during the absence or disability of the president.

The secretary keeps records of the corporation, other than its financial records. He records the minutes of meetings of the board of directors and of stockholders. He usually has custody of the corporate seal, and he witnesses the signature of the president on documents signed on behalf of the corporation.

The treasurer is the finance officer of the corporation. He is in charge of its financial records and may sign checks or promissory notes issued by the corporation.

In large corporations, there may be several vice-presidents, each of whom is entrusted with a particular function, such as law, labor relations, personnel, or sales. Similarly, the secretary and the treasurer may be aided by assistant secretaries and assistant treasurers, respectively, who are charged with carrying out specific functions.

LIMITED PARTNERSHIPS

A limited partnership is a hybrid kind of business organization in that it consists of one or more general partners, who have the same powers and obligations as partners in the ordinary partnership, discussed above, and of one or more limited (or special) partners, who have the characteristics of stockholders of a corporation. The general partners manage the business and are personally liable for its debts; the limited partners are in the nature of investors in the enterprise, without power to manage, whose liability is limited to the amount of their investments. If a limited partner participates in managing the business, he becomes personally liable for its obligations.

A limited partnership can conduct any form of business open to a general partnership.

Limited partnerships, like corporations, are created pursuant to statutory authorization. The certificate of limited partnership must be recorded in a public office.

PRINCIPAL AND AGENT

In every form of business organization it becomes necessary at some time to designate persons who will be authorized to act on behalf of the organization in transacting its affairs. A corporation, for example, being an artificial entity, can act only through the agency of others; in a partnership, the firm conducts business through its partners and possibly other persons. A representative appointed for the business organization, with the authority to bring his employer into a contractual arrangement with a third party, is called an "agent." The employer whom he represents is known as the "principal." Agents are of various kinds, such as salesmen, real-estate brokers, consignees, commission merchants, and sales representatives. The authority of each type of agent may depend upon the circumstances in which he is called upon to act for his principal.

When an agent acts in accordance with the authority given to him by his principal, the principal is bound by contracts made for him by the agent with third persons.

APPOINTMENT OF AGENTS

The appointment of an agent by a principal creates a contractual relationship between them. An agency contract ordinarily need not be in writing to be enforceable, but if an agent is appointed to sell real estate belonging to his principal, the law generally requires that the agent's appointment be in writing. In any event, it is considered advisable for a principal to spell out his agent's authority in a written document, which is notarized. Such a document is called a "power of attorney." It states that the principal designates a named person as his agent, and it specifies the particular acts that the agent is authorized to perform for the principal.

A form that may be used for this purpose is as follows:

POWER OF ATTORNEY

Know All Men By These Presents, that I, (principal's name and address) do hereby appoint (agent's name and address) as my attorney-in-fact to (set forth the powers given to the agent)

Dated: _____ 19 __

_____ (Seal)
(Principal's Signature)
(Acknowledgment in presence of notary public)

AUTHORITY OF AGENT TO ACT FOR PRINCIPAL

Since a principal is liable for his agent's contracts only if the agent acts within the authority given to him, it is important to determine under what circumstances an agent's authority will be found to exist. Of course, if the agent's authority is expressly defined by the principal, as in a power of attorney, the agent's acts in accordance with such express authority will be binding on the principal. Similarly, if the agent performs acts that are necessary in order to carry out the express authority given to him by the principal, the principal will also be bound, on the basis that such acts are in accordance with "implied" authority given to the agent.

In addition, an agent is held to possess such authority as is customary and usual in the particular trade or such authority as the principal appears to have allowed the agent, either by the principal's words or conduct. This type of authority is called "apparent" authority.

When an agent is entrusted by his principal with the performance of a particular transaction, a third person dealing with the agent should make inquiry into the exact nature of the agent's special authority. If it develops that the agent is exceeding his authority, the third person dealing with the agent will be unable to hold the principal liable for the agent's acts.

RATIFICATION

As noted above, if an agent makes an unauthorized contract for his principal with a third party, the principal is not bound by the contract unless he has given the agent an apparent authority on which the third party has relied. In any event, however, a principal can approve an act carried out in his name but without his authority by the agent, either by expressing his approval in words or by acting in such a way as to show that he approves the agent's act. This approval of an unauthorized act is called "ratification." It renders the principal liable for the agent's act as if the agent had been expressly authorized to do it. If the principal does not ratify an unauthorized act, the agent can be held personally liable to the third party for having made an unauthorized contract.

PRINCIPAL'S DUTIES TO AGENT

If the agreement between a principal and agent specifically covers their rights and duties to each other, the terms of that agreement will prevail. However, certain general rules are applied in fixing the parties' relationship, even if their agreement does not cover the matter.

Thus, a principal is bound to compensate his agent for the latter's services. If no particular rate of compensation has been fixed by the parties, an agent is entitled to be compensated at a reasonable rate in view of the nature of the services rendered by him.

In addition, a principal is under a duty to reimburse his agent for any outlay of moneys made by the agent on the principal's behalf. Also, if an agent has become liable to a third person in performing his duties according to the principal's instructions, he is entitled to be protected by the principal against such liability to the third person.

AGENT'S DUTIES TO PRINCIPAL

An agent is generally held to occupy a fiduciary position—one of trust— toward his principal. He must, therefore, conduct himself toward his principal with the highest standards of good faith and fair dealing. He cannot, for example, reap a personal gain because of his position as agent or because of information he has acquired as an agent. He is not permitted to act for his principal and for another party in the same transaction, unless he does so with their consent. He may not sell his own property to his principal or buy his principal's property for himself.

An agent must obey his principal's instructions in performing his duties as an agent. He is also bound to use reasonable care and skill in carrying out the functions entrusted to him by the principal. If he fails to follow instructions or is careless in the performance of his tasks, he will be answerable for a loss sustained by the principal because of the disobedience or carelessness.

Further, an agent must keep proper records of his acts in performing the agency. If he comes into possession of money or property belonging to his principal, he is required to keep those assets separate and apart from his own. He is not permitted to mix them or to deposit his own funds and the funds of his principal in a single bank account.

PRINCIPAL'S LIABILITY TO THIRD PARTIES

A principal is liable to third parties according to the terms of the contract made for him with the third party by his agent, if the contract was within the agent's authority. A principal's liability exists in such circumstances even if, at the time the contract was made, the agent did not inform the third party that he was representing a principal. Actually, in such a case the agent enters into the contract in his own name, and he, too, is liable for the performance of the contract. However, it is the general rule that once the third party becomes aware of the existence of a principal for whom the agent was acting, he must make a binding choice whether he will hold the principal or the agent liable for the performance of the contract.

AGENT'S LIABILITY TO THIRD PARTIES

If an agent, acting within his authority, makes a contract with a third party in the name of his principal, the agent is not personally liable on the contract. However, there are some circumstances in which an agent is held responsible to third persons because of acts performed by him in the course of the agency. These are: (1) when he acts beyond his authority in making a contract; (2) when he acts for an undisclosed principal, thereby actually making the contract in his own name; (3) when he commits a tort (civil wrong), such as fraud, slander, or assault; (4) when he acts for a nonexistent principal (e.g., a promoter of a corporation to be formed enters into a contract for the ultimate benefit of the corporation before it is lawfully organized).

TERMINATION OF AGENCY

An agency relationship is terminated if:

The purpose of the agency is fulfilled, or if the period for which the agent was appointed expires.

The principal or the agent terminates the relationship. If the termination is in violation of the agreement, however, the person ending the relationship will be liable to the other party for damages.

The principal or the agent dies.

The principal or the agent is insane.

The agent becomes disabled so that he is prevented from performing his duties.

CREDITS AND SECURITY

Negotiable instruments are documents entailing the payment of money which may be transferred by one person to another, in effect, instead of money. The most important types of negotiable instruments are promissory notes, bills of exchange (drafts), and checks.

A promissory note is a written statement in which one person (the maker) unconditionally promises to pay a sum of money to bearer or to the order of another person (the payee), on demand or at a particular time.

A bill of exchange is a document in which one person (the drawer) gives an order to another person (the drawee) to pay a sum of money to bearer or to the order of a third person (the payee), on demand or at a particular time. If the drawee agrees to honor the bill of exchange, he accepts it by writing "Accepted" on it. He is then known as the "acceptor." A trade acceptance is a form of bill of exchange in which a seller of goods draws on the buyer for the amount of the sale price, and the buyer accepts the order to pay.

A check is a form of bill of exchange in which the drawee is a bank and which is payable only on demand. In this type of bill, the order to pay is given by a depositor to his bank. The bank is not liable to a holder of a check who presents it to the bank for payment unless the bank has certified the check.

NEGOTIATION

The characteristic of negotiable instruments that lends them importance is negotiability. The person who holds such an instrument can pass it on to another, and the latter not only obtains legal title to the instrument and can therefore enforce payment but may even obtain a better title than the transferor had and thus may enforce a payment that his transferor could not obtain. The better title may be obtained if the transferee gives a consideration for the transfer of the instrument to him and is not at that time aware of any defects in the instrument or defenses to it.

In such a case, the defenses that cannot be used against a transferee (although they may be used against earlier parties) are fraud, coercion, and absence of consideration for the instrument. However, other defenses, which have the effect of destroying the instrument, will defeat the rights of even a purchaser in good faith. Those defenses include forgery, the maker's incompetency, and a material alteration of the instrument.

If an instrument is payable to bearer, or if the last endorsement on it consists only of the endorser's signature, it can be negotiated merely by delivering it to the transferee. If the instrument is payable to order, it is negotiated by the transferor's endorsement of the instrument, coupled with delivery to the transferee.

ENDORSEMENTS

Endorsements are generally made on the back of the instrument. A negotiable instrument may be endorsed in any of several ways.

The most usual form is the blank endorsement, made merely by the endorser's signature. No endorsee is named, and the instrument becomes payable to bearer.

By writing the name of the endorsee to whom payment should be made and then signing his own name, the endorser makes a special endorsement. To negotiate the instrument thereafter, the person who is named as endorsee must himself endorse the instrument before he delivers it to his transferee.

A restrictive endorsement is one stating that it is conditional or indicating a purpose to collect payment of the instrument by the use of words such as "for deposit" or "for collection," followed by the endorser's name.

LIABILITY OF PARTIES

The maker of a promissory note and the acceptor of a bill of exchange are primarily liable on those instruments. Either of those parties is liable for the payment of the instrument, even if the holder does not present it to him for payment.

The drawer of a bill of exchange is required to pay the bill (1) if the bill is presented to the drawee and is not accepted or paid (that is, if it is dishonored), and (2) if the holder gives prompt notice to the drawer of the dishonor of the instrument.

An endorser (unless he endorses "without recourse") must pay the instrument if it is dishonored by the party primarily liable on the instrument and if the holder gives him prompt notice of the dishonor.

All endorsers are liable if the instrument is not genuine, or if their title to the instrument is not good, or if any other party was not legally competent to make the instrument.

PRESENTMENT

In order to hold a drawer and the endorsers liable on a negotiable instrument, the holder must first properly present the instrument to the primary party, that is to the maker in the case of a promissory note or the acceptor of a bill of exchange.

In large communities presentment is usually made by the holder through a bank acting on his behalf.

Presentment for payment must be made on the date fixed for payment in the instrument. If that date is a Sunday or a holiday, payment is due on the next business day; if that date is a Saturday, payment is due on Monday. An instrument made payable on demand should be presented within a reasonable time after it was originally issued.

If the instrument specifies the place where it is to be paid, it should be presented at that place. Otherwise, it should be presented at the maker's or acceptor's place of business, or at his residence, or at his last known place of business or residence. If presentment cannot be made anywhere with the exercise of reasonable diligence, the necessity for presentment is excused.

NOTICE OF DISHONOR

The drawer and the endorsers of a negotiable instrument, to be held liable on the instrument, must also be given notice that the instrument has been dishonored. Notice of protest by a notary public is the usual method by which notice of dishonor is given. However, the notice may be given in a less formal way, in writing or by word of mouth, to show that the instrument has not been accepted or paid. Notice of dishonor is excused if it cannot be given in the exercise of reasonable diligence.

The giving of the notice may be waived by the drawer and endorsers, either orally or in writing. This is usually done at the time of endorsement by including words to indicate that protest or notice of dishonor is waived.

GUARANTY

A guaranty is a promise to answer for another person's debt or obligation. A promise of guaranty is required to be in writing in order to be enforceable against the person making it.

The person who makes the promise is called the "guarantor"; the debtor is called the "principal debtor"; the person to whom the promise is made is known as the "creditor." The words "surety" and "guarantor" are often used interchangeably.

A guarantor is liable on his promise according to its terms. He can, however, avoid liability: (1) if the principal debtor is released by the creditor, without the guarantor's consent; (2) if the creditor and the principal debtor agree to extend the debtor's time for payment without the guarantor's assent; (3) if the creditor and the principal debtor change the terms of their contract without the guarantor's assent; (4) if the contract between the creditor and the principal debtor is illegal; (5) if the guarantor dies or revokes his promise and the creditor has not yet acted upon the promise of guaranty.

When a guarantor has been required to pay the principal debtor's obligation on the creditor, he has the following remedies: (1) he may obtain reimbursement from the principal debtor; (2) he may obtain and enforce the collateral security that the creditor holds; (3) if there are also other guarantors on the same debt, he may obtain proportionate contributions from them.

SECURED TRANSACTIONS

Transactions are called "secured" if a debtor gives his creditor collateral security in personal property in order to assure the creditor that the debt will be paid. Secured transactions embrace all security interests known as chattel mortgages, conditional sales, pledges, assignments of accounts receivable, and other business arrangements intended as security.

The written instrument that describes the nature and type of collateral security in a given transaction is called the "security agreement." It must be signed by the debtor. Although a creditor's security in goods is protected by taking the property into his actual possession (as in the case of a pledge), the most common and important method of safeguarding a security interest is the filing of the agreement in a public office, as explained below. Instead of filing the agreement itself, the secured party (creditor) may file a short form of statement known as a "financing statement," which is generally required to be signed by both the debtor and the secured party. Such forms of statement are prescribed by the public officials who are charged by law with the responsibility of keeping the statements on file.

Filing should be accomplished as soon as possible after the security interest has been given to the creditor. This is done in order to protect the latter from possible claims against the property by other creditors of the debtor or by persons who purchase the property from the debtor.

To be fully effective, the filing must be made in the proper public office designated by law for that purpose. In general business transactions involving security, if the debtor has but one place of business in the state, the instrument must be filed both in a central state filing office (the department of state) and with the filing officer of the county in which the debtor is located; if the debtor has more than one place of business in the state, the security agreement or financing statement should be filed in the state office prescribed. If the collateral security consists of fixtures, the document must be filed with the filing officer of the county in which the property is located. If the collateral consists of property used in farming operations (livestock or crops) filing should be made in the county in which the debtor resides.

Should the debtor default in payment of the obligation, the creditor may take possession of the property if this can be accomplished peaceably. Otherwise, resort to court proceedings will be required to obtain custody of the property. The creditor may then dispose of all or a part of the collateral to satisfy his claim. The proceeds from the sale of the property are used to pay the balance due on the debt. If the sale price is more than sufficient for this purpose, the secured party must account for the surplus proceeds. If there is a deficiency after sale, the debtor is liable for that deficiency.

It should be noted that the rules regarding secured transactions that are discussed above do not apply to security arrangements involving insurance policies, savings-bank passbooks, and real-estate mortgages given as collateral to secure the creditor.

BILLS OF LADING

A bill of lading is a written instrument issued by a carrier of goods. It represents both a receipt for the goods delivered to the carrier and an agreement by the carrier to transport the goods between two designated points. A bill of lading may be negotiable (if the goods are deliverable to bearer or to the order of a person) or not negotiable (if the goods are deliverable to a named person).

In issuing a bill of lading, the carrier acknowledges that it has possession of the goods described in the bill.

If a bill of lading is negotiable, it must be surrendered to the carrier by the person holding it before the carrier can be required to give up the goods. This rule affords some security to a seller of goods that he will be able to collect the sale price. Thus, when a seller consigns the goods to his own order and attaches to the bill of lading a draft drawn on the buyer for the amount of the sale price, both documents are sent to a bank for collection of the draft. If the buyer honors the draft, he is entitled to receive the bill of lading, and only then will he be able to obtain the goods from the carrier.

WAREHOUSE RECEIPTS

A warehouse receipt is issued by a warehouseman who receives goods for storage. Such a receipt may be negotiable (if the goods deposited with the warehouseman are deliverable to bearer or to the order of a named person) or not negotiable (if the goods are deliverable to a specified person).

The negotiation of a warehouse receipt gives the transferee the right to claim the goods from the warehouseman. Such a receipt, if negotiable, must be surrendered to the warehouseman properly endorsed before the latter is bound to deliver the goods.

REAL PROPERTY

The term "real property" refers to land and anything permanently attached to the land. Examples of real property (or "real estate," as it is also sometimes called) are houses, fences, lakes, growing trees, and underground mineral deposits such as coal and iron.

Items that are considered real estate because they are connected with land may, however, become *personal property* (goods) by being removed from the land. For example, coal after having been mined, trees after being cut down, and fruit taken from crops are considered to be personal property. (The manner in which personal property may be sold is discussed above under the heading *The Sale of Goods.*)

SALE OF REAL PROPERTY

Contracts for the sale of real property must be in writing in order to be enforced. They are usually signed by both the seller and the purchaser.

Contracts of sale are generally completed on printed forms that are issued by title-insurance companies. The completion of a real-estate contract form is a technical matter that requires the services of an attorney. The contract states the names of the seller and the buyer of the property, a description of the property, the sale price, how the price is to be paid, and all the details of the bargain between the seller and purchaser, which vary from case to case.

After the parties have signed a contract of sale, it is customary for the purchaser to have a "search" made in order to assure himself that he will acquire a good title to the property. The search is made in the public records in the county where the property is located. It may be conducted by an attorney, or an abstract company, or a title-insurance company. If the search discloses that the title is defective, the purchaser may be justified in refusing to carry out the contract. Even if the search fails to reveal a defect in the title, a purchaser may obtain a title-insurance policy to protect himself against financial loss due to defects that may be discovered after the sale takes place.

Deeds. The actual transfer of ownership of real estate is made by the seller's delivering a deed to the purchaser. The delivery may take place in person or through agents of either or both parties.

A deed is a written document which states that the seller transfers title to real estate to the buyer. It is signed by the seller or his authorized agent, and it is also acknowledged before a notary public.

A purchaser should have the deed promptly recorded in a designated public office in the county where the real property is located. The purpose of recording a deed is to give public notice that the purchaser is the new owner of the property. If a purchaser fails to record his deed, a subsequent purchaser of the same property from the seller, unaware that the seller has previously transferred the property, may acquire a better title than the first purchaser.

MORTGAGES

In general, a mortgage is a lien held by a creditor on his debtor's property. The lien represents security to the creditor for repayment of a debt owed to him. The creditor is known as the "mortgagee," the debtor as the "mortgagor." The debt itself, which the mortgage secures, is usually a written document called a "bond."

If the debt is repaid, the mortgagor is entitled to have the mortgage canceled. If the debt is not paid when due, the mortgagee may foreclose the mortgage. Foreclosure is a court proceeding in which the property is sold at a public auction, in order to pay off the balance due on the mortgage. If a surplus remains after payment of the balance, it is turned over to the debtor. In case of foreclosure when the real property is subject to several mortgages, the mortgagees share in the proceeds of sale according to the order of time in which their mortgages were given.

A mortgagee should record his mortgage in the public office designated for this purpose, as in the case of deeds. Otherwise, he may lose the benefit of his lien if the mortgagor should subsequently sell or mortgage the same real property to another person who does not know that a prior mortgage exists as a lien on the property.

LANDLORD AND TENANT

One person may grant to another the right to use his real property, in exchange for the payment of rent. The grantor is known as the "landlord," the user as "tenant." If such right to use real property is evidenced by a written lease, the grantor is generally called the "lessor," and the latter is known as the "lessee." If a lease is for a period of more than one year, it is usually required to be in writing.

The rights and obligations of landlords and tenants are determined according to their agreement. A tenant has the right to assign his interest as a tenant or to sublet the leased property to a third person, unless the lease prohibits him from doing so.

In general, a tenant is obligated to maintain the leased premises in ordinary repair and to return them to the landlord at the end of the lease period in substantially the same condition as at the time the tenancy began.

However, a tenant is not bound to make structural repairs or permanent improvements or to repair halls or elevators that are also used by other tenants.

A lease terminates when: (1) the term of the lease expires; (2) the lessor and the lessee agree to end the tenancy before the lease period expires; (3) the premises are destroyed; (4) the lessor loses ownership of the property by foreclosure or seizure by public authority; or (5) the tenant forfeits the lease by commiting a breach under it.

PATENTS. COPYRIGHTS, AND TRADEMARKS

PATENTS

A patent is an exclusive right given by the Federal government to an inventor to make and sell an invention. A patent usually exists for a period of 17 years. It is not renewable. It may be transferred by a written assignment by the person holding a patent (the "patentee"). He may also license other persons to make and sell the patented invention and, in return for the license, may require a royalty to be paid to him.

Application for patent. The issuance of a patent is necessary in order to protect an inventor from infringement on his invention.

To be patentable, an invention must involve a new or useful process or composition of matter, a machine, a manufacture, or a design for an article that is manufactured. On request, the U.S. Patent Office, Washington, D.C., will supply general information concerning the filing of patents and the papers necessary for the application.

Before a patent is applied for, a search should be made of existing patents in the Patent Office to ascertain whether the invention is actually new. After the application has been filed, the words "Pat. pending" or "Pat. applied for" may be affixed to the article to afford notice that an application for a patent has been filed. These words are not required by law. They cannot be used to deceive the public.

After a patent has been issued, persons selling patented articles should affix to the article the patent number under which the article is manufactured.

COPYRIGHTS

A copyright is an exclusive right to make and sell copies of an intellectual composition, such as a book, song, map, work of art, photograph, drawing, or label. A copyright lasts for a period of 28 years, and it may be renewed and extended for an additional term of 28 years.

Certain material is not subject to copyright: names and slogans; ideas and plans, as distinguished from the manner in which they are expressed in a writing; information that is common property, such as height and weight charts, or schedules of sporting events. Copyrights are issued by the Register of Copyrights, Library of Congress, Washington, D.C., who will also furnish information concerning copyright procedures.

A copyright may be transferred by the owner to other persons by written assignment.

Registration. Immediately after publication, the owner of the copyright should file two copies of his work with the Register of Copyrights. The work must bear a copyright notice consisting of the word "Copyright" and the name of the owner and year of publication. This must appear on the title page, or on the page immediately following the title page, of the book or other composition. On works of art, maps, drawings, and labels the copyright notice may be in the form of the letter C enclosed in a circle, thus ©, with the name of the copyright owner.

TRADEMARKS

A trademark is a mark, symbol, name, or device that a seller uses in connection with his goods or his services to distinguish them from the goods of other persons. Although trademarks may be registered, title to a trademark is not acquired by registration but by the continued use of the mark in connection with the sale or the service before another person has used the same mark.

Words that merely describe an article and geographical words cannot become trademarks.

A trademark may be transferred by written assignment in connection with the sale of the good will of a business, or the sale of that part of the good will connected with the use of the mark.

The life of a trademark is indefinite, and, if registered, it may be renewed at the end of each 20-year period.

Registration. Although registration of a trademark is not necessary to confer ownership of a trademark, it does afford added protection to the owner, in that it gives him the right to sue infringers in the Federal courts and to prevent the importation of goods that bear an infringing mark.

An application for registration is filed in the name of the owner with the U.S. Patent Office, Washington, D.C. Forms of application will be supplied by the Patent Office on request, and information concerning the manner of registering trademarks is obtainable from that office. In addition to the application, the owner must file a drawing of the mark and five specimens.

In order to qualify for Federal registration a trademark must be applied in some manner to goods or their containers that are sold or shipped in interstate or foreign commerce.

After registration, an owner should give notice that his trade-mark is registered by displaying with the mark the words "Reg. U.S. Pat. Off." or the letter R enclosed in a circle, ®.

LABELS

A label may be a trademark in that it consists of a word or symbol, and thus it may be registered as such. If, in addition, the label has a distinctive physical appearance, it may also be copyrighted. Trademark registration affords protection to the distinctive features of a label, whereas copyright registration covers its visual features.

BANKRUPTCY

The term "bankruptcy" is sometimes used loosely to refer to any kind of financial difficulty that befalls a debtor. Actually, the term has a specific meaning: bankruptcy is a Federal court proceeding in which a debtor's assets are taken into custody and distributed to his creditors in payment of his obligations. If the debtor has not committed a wrongful act in relation to his creditors, he will be discharged from further liability.

In addition to bankruptcy, there are various types of insolvency laws under which a debtor's property is delivered to his creditors for distribution, sometimes in a court proceeding. However, under such insolvency laws a debtor will not receive a discharge from his debts, as he may in bankruptcy. The term "insolvency" usually means a debtor's inability to pay his debts as they fall due.

Bankruptcy proceedings should be distinguished from "arrangement proceedings," which are usually called "Chapter XI proceedings." The purpose of an arrangement proceeding, unlike a bankruptcy proceeding, is to reach a settlement between a debtor and the majority of his creditors in a court proceeding (that is binding even on minority creditors), without the necessity of liquidating the debtor's business.

It should be noted that a debtor may also reach an out-of-court settlement with his creditors, but in this case a creditor who does not agree to the settlement is not bound by it, and he may continue to attempt full collection of his claim from the debtor.

HOW BANKRUPTCY PROCEEDINGS START

A financially embarrassed debtor may voluntarily institute a bankruptcy proceeding by filing a petition for bankruptcy in the Federal court. Such a proceeding may also be commenced involuntarily, that is, by the creditors of a debtor. If creditors bring on the proceeding, they must show that the debtor has committed an "act of bankruptcy," which means, in general, that the debtor has been guilty of conduct with respect to his property that may interfere with the rights of his creditors. This may mean, for example, that the debtor has concealed his property or has given a preference to one creditor over the others.

TRUSTEE IN BANKRUPTCY

The management of a bankrupt estate is vested in a trustee in bankruptcy, who is chosen by the creditors. It is the trustee's duty to collect all money and property belonging to the bankrupt and, after converting the property into cash, to make distribution to creditors.

In order to determine whether the claim of a creditor is valid, the creditor is required to file a "proof of claim," which is a sworn statement showing the facts on which his claim is based and the amount of the claim. The trustee may accept or reject the claim or may settle it with the creditor. When a creditor's claim is allowed, he is entitled to share in the distribution made by the trustee.

HOW DISTRIBUTION IS MADE

The bankruptcy law establishes an order of priority in which distribution of available assets must be made. First, administration expenses must be paid, consisting of the costs and expenses of administering the estate in the bankruptcy proceeding. Next, distribution is made to the bankrupt's employees, for wages earned by them in the three-month period before the bankruptcy, up to a maximum of $600 per employee. Other priority claims are certain taxes owed to the Federal government and to any state or municipality and debts due to creditors who may have special priorities under law. The general unsecured creditors are paid after all others.

If a creditor holds valid security from the debtor for his claim, such as a mortgage or pledge, he is entitled to sell the security held by him and to use the proceeds from the sale to the extent necessary to pay his claim.

DISCHARGE IN BANKRUPTCY

A bankrupt will be discharged from his debt if he has acted honestly and complied with the court's directions. Otherwise, a discharge may be refused, in which case the bankrupt will continue to be indebted to his creditors if they have not received payment of their claims from the trustee in the bankruptcy proceeding.

Even when a bankrupt receives a discharge, however, some of his obligations are not erased. These include (1) certain taxes, (2) alimony, (3) liabilities for intentional injuries to others, (4) liabilities for obtaining money or property by false pretenses and for embezzlement, and (5) liabilities for employees' wages that were earned within three months before the bankruptcy proceeding was started.

ESTATES OF DECEDENTS

When a person owning real or personal property dies, some distribution of his property must be made to other persons. If the decedent made a will in which he expressed his intention as to how his property should be distributed after death, the will prevails. If he dies intestate (without a will), his property is distributed to his heirs in the manner provided by the laws in force in the state in which he resides at the time of death. The manner of distributing real property owned by him in another state is governed by the law of the state in which the real property is located.

THE MAKING OF A WILL

In general, a will is a written instrument signed by the person making it (the "testator"), in which he gives instructions for the disposition of his property upon his death. Although no prescribed form of words is necessary in order to make a will, a will can be one of the most technical documents known to the law, and it is certainly of far-reaching importance, since it speaks for the testator after his death. It should, therefore, be drawn with great care.

Most states impose strict requirements as to how wills must be executed. A will must be signed at its end by the testator in the presence of witnesses, usually two in number, who also sign the will as witnesses at the same time. The testator makes known to the witnesses that he is making his will and he asks them to witness it; he does not disclose to them the contents of the will. A person who is a beneficiary under the will should not act as a witness to its making.

If a testator is unable to sign his name personally, he may make his mark, or place his finger print on the will, or have another person guide his hand, or have another sign it for him at his request.

A will may be typewritten or written with a pen or a pencil, but it is the usual practice to typewrite wills. In addition to the signatures of the testator and the witnesses appearing at the end, it is advisable for the testator to place his initials at the bottom margin of each page so as to identify the page as being part of the whole instrument.

CODICILS

A codicil is a document which in some way changes or modifies a will previously made by the testator. It is similar to a will, in that it involves the disposition of property belonging to the testator, and it must be executed with the same formality as the will; that is, it must be signed at the end by the testator and witnessed by others.

REVOCATION OF WILLS

A testator may revoke his will at any time before he dies. This can be done by his destroying the will or merely by making a subsequent will with the intent to revoke the original will.

PROBATE PROCEEDINGS

Wills are "probated" by court proceedings brought to establish that a will is genuine and that the testator was competent (that is, of sound mind) when he made it. If a will is found by the court to satisfy those requirements and it is admitted to probate, the executor named in the will begins to perform his functions in carrying out the intentions of the testator as expressed in the will.

If a decedent has not left a will, the court appoints an administrator, who administers the estate by collecting all assets, paying the decedent's debts, and distributing the balance of the estate to the decedent's heirs entitled to receive them under the law.

TRUSTS

In a trust, a person turns over all or a part of his real or personal property to a trustee, for the benefit of third persons. The owner (known as the "creator" or "settlor" of the trust) may make himself the trustee of his property; he may even name himself as a beneficiary. However, a person cannot be both trustee and beneficiary in the same trust. A trust may be set up either by a will, to take effect on the maker's death, or it may be established in a trust instrument which becomes effective while the settlor is still living.

Some trusts provide for different classes of beneficiaries, such as "life tenants," who are to receive the income earned from the assets of the trust so long as they live, and "remaindermen," who receive the principal of the trust fund after the death of the life tenants.

A trustee's powers in the management of the trust depend upon the terms of the trust instrument. Usually a trustee is required to invest the trust property and to distribute it according to the intentions of the creator of the trust as expressed in the trust instrument. A trustee is responsible for handling the trust in a prudent manner. He is liable for financial loss resulting from his carelessness but not for a loss that is due to an error of judgment on his part. He is not permitted to mix trust funds with his individually owned assets.

ENFORCEMENT OF LEGAL RIGHTS

The legal rights that one person acquires in a contractual relationship with another can have value only if they are capable of being enforced. To ensure the existence of a method of enforcing rights and of remedying wrongs, a system of courts of law has been developed by society. The courts interpret the statutes enacted by the legislative branch of government, if statutes are applicable in a given case; if no legislative enactment applies in a particular instance, the courts create and apply rules of law independent of statute.

In the United States two separate court systems exist, those under the jurisdiction of the Federal government and those operating by the authority of the states. Apart from this distinction in the source of power of the two systems, their general scheme is similar. In either case, the first court to which a person seeking the enforcement of a legal right will apply is the trial court. From a decision of that court, a party may appeal first to an intermediate appellate court and then to a final appellate court.

Sometimes special types of cases are entrusted to separately established trial courts that are given special jurisdiction. For example, under state law the administration of decedents' estates is usually separated from other litigated matters and reserved for courts specially constituted to handle them. Under Federal law customs matters and claims against the Federal government are heard in courts separate from those having general jurisdiction.

In recent years, as the result of the enormous growth in complexity of business affairs, special administrative bodies outside the court systems have been established to interpret and apply particular laws regulating business. For example, under state law special administrative agencies exist with authority to resolve legal questions involving public utilities and liquor licensing. In the area of the Federal government, administrative bodies dealing with special regulations include authorities such as the Federal Trade Commission, which is concerned with unfair business practices, including price discrimination, false advertising, and mislabeling of goods.

Decisions made by administrative agencies may be appealed to the courts by any person aggrieved. However, the general tendency of the courts on such appeals is to rely on the expertness of the administrative bodies in their respective fields and not to overturn their decisions unless they are clearly wrong.

Chapter 14

Corporate Problems
HARRY KATZ

THE PRECEDING CHAPTER discussed in general terms the type of business organization known as the corporation. Today business is commonly transacted through the medium of corporations, rather than partnerships and other forms of business organization, not only because wider ownership of a business is facilitated if the business is in corporate form but also because a corporation affords the advantage of limited liability to its owners, the shareholders, who are not personally responsible for the payment of business debts, as are the members of a partnership. In a corporation the liability of shareholders is limited to the amounts invested by them in shares of stock and does not extend to funds or property owned by them outside of the business.

As explained in Chapter 13, a corporate business is managed and operated by a board of directors, which establishes the general policies for the enterprise, and by corporate officers, who act under the broad supervision and direction of the board of directors.

Since the basic management decisions in a corporate structure are normally reached at meetings held by persons with authority to participate in the making of such decisions, one of the most important tasks entrusted to a secretary in the employ of the corporation is that of handling all details necessary for planning and holding such meetings. A general understanding of the organization of corporations and of the system by which decisions are made in corporate life is therefore necessary for the proper performance of the secretary's duties pertaining to the conduct of meetings.

KINDS OF MEETINGS AND THEIR PURPOSES

Corporate meetings are of various kinds, as described below.

Stockholders' meetings, annual and special. The purpose of the stockholders' annual meeting, in general, is to elect directors of the corporation

266

for the ensuing year, to ratify such acts of the board of directors previously undertaken as require the approval of stockholders, and to consider such other business as may properly be presented at the meeting.

In this connection, it should be noted that certain acts and transactions of an unusual or extraordinary nature are required to be approved by stockholders in order that they may be considered lawfully done. Among such business transactions are changing the capital structure of the company or the number of directors, altering the purposes of the corporate business, and a merger, consolidation, or reorganization of the company. In such instances the approval of the board of directors alone is not legally sufficient.

Special meetings of stockholders are held from time to time when circumstances require action on the part of stockholders that the board of directors itself is not empowered to take.

Directors' meetings, regular and special. Regular meetings of the board of directors are usually held at periodic intervals. At such meetings the directors consider those matters requiring action on their part which arise between regular meetings or which are carried over from previous meetings.

Special meetings of the board are called when it is necessary for the board to take action on matters that require immediate attention and cannot await the holding of a regular meeting, or matters of sufficient importance to justify calling a special meeting at which the board will consider no other business.

Committee meetings. Committees are set up either under the bylaws of a corporation or on special order of the board. They are concerned with particular aspects of the corporation's affairs, such as finances. The number and kinds of committees vary with the size and the needs of a corporation. Committee meetings are held from time to time, either as fixed by rule or as circumstances require. The practice in this regard varies widely among corporations.

Meetings in small corporations. In certain small corporations whose shares of stock are owned by one or a few individuals (called "closed corporations"), meetings of stockholders and directors are conducted at irregular intervals, because there is only a limited need to hold meetings in such a corporation. As a practical matter, meetings in closed corporations are informal and are held only when some action is required by a provision of law or by a third party. (For example, banks require a resolution to be adopted by the board of directors designating the persons who are authorized to sign checks of the corporation.) In general, the fact that meetings of stockholders and directors are held infrequently does not affect the lawful existence of a corporation.

In corporations other than closed corporations, however, a regular system of formal internal management is indispensable for the proper functioning of the corporate enterprise. To explain the significance of the different aspects of the system, some of its more important phases will be described at this point.

BASIC CORPORATE RECORDS

Certificate of incorporation. The basic document under which a corporation is formed and carries on its business, a certificate of incorporation contains the following information: the legal name of the corporation; the purposes for which it was formed and the powers it may exercise; the capital structure of the corporation, including a description of the different classes of stock and the rights and duties of the shareholders of each class with respect to voting, dividends, etc.; the location of the company's principal office; the number of directors; and other incidental matters.

Bylaws. The more detailed rules under which the corporation operates from day to day, the bylaws are generally adopted by the stockholders. They must not be inconsistent with or change any provision of the certificate of incorporation; if so, the provisions of the certificate of incorporation will prevail. Some matters provided for under the bylaws of a corporation are, for example, fixing of the time and place for meetings of stockholders and directors, how notice of meetings is to be given, the number and titles of corporate officers, and the duties attached to each office.

Minute book or books. The minutes contain the transcribed and official record of meetings of stockholders, directors, and committees, showing the acts and proceedings taken at those meetings. Minute books are generally in loose-leaf form, although from time to time they are bound in permanent volumes.

Stock-certificate book. A special book contains blank forms of stock certificates, on which the name of the corporation is imprinted. When a stock certificate is issued to a stockholder, a blank form is removed from the stub at a perforated line and completed by filling in the name of the person entitled to the certificate (that is, the stockholder), the number of shares covered by the certificate, and the signatures of the corporate officers authorized to sign the certificate, usually the president and the secretary of the corporation. In common practice the stock-certificate book also contains a consecutive transfer record, showing transfers of stock of the corporation, and a stock ledger, which is an alphabetical record of shares owned by each stockholder. The stock ledger is used as the basis for sending notices of stockholders' meetings, for making dividend payments, and for determining the right to vote at stockholders' meetings. In some corporations the stock-transfer record and the ledger are kept in separate volumes.

HOW MEETINGS ARE CALLED

In general the bylaws of the corporation should be examined to ascertain the requirements as to when and where meetings of stockholders and directors are to be held and how notice of such meetings is to be given to the persons entitled to receive notice. These requirements must be strictly observed; otherwise the legal validity of a meeting may be open to question. In general, notice of adjournments of meetings need not be given.

STOCKHOLDERS' MEETINGS

The notice of a proposed meeting of stockholders should be in writing and sent to all stockholders entitled to vote. The notice should specify the date and hour of the meeting, the place where it is to be held, and the purposes for which it is called. In large corporations with numerous stockholders, it is customary for all official notices to be printed. A form of notice of annual meeting is as follows:

```
                NOTICE OF ANNUAL MEETING
                  OF STOCKHOLDERS OF
                    USA CORPORATION


        The annual meeting of stockholders of USA
Corporation will be held on (date) at (hour)
at (address).
The following business will be transacted:
        1. (Purpose of meeting)
        2. All other business that may properly come
before the meeting.
Dated:


                        _____
                                Secretary


(The proxy form enclosed for the convenience of
 stockholders who cannot attend the meeting
 in person should be signed and returned to the
 Secretary.)
```

If the meeting of stockholders is a special meeting, rather than the annual meeting, the notice should be adapted by the secretary to state that fact.

With regard to the insertion of a statement of the particular purposes for which the meeting of stockholders is called, the following statements of purposes commonly used in the case of stockholders' meetings may be used as a guide.

> To receive report: "To receive the report of (*specify officer and briefly state nature of report*), and to act upon such report."
>
> To appoint auditors: "To elect independent accountants to audit the books of the corporation at the close of the fiscal year ending (*date*)."
>
> To vote at special election: "To elect a director to fill the vacancy caused by the (*resignation, death*) of (*name*)."
>
> To approve directors' acts: "To approve and ratify, or disapprove, the acts and contracts of the Board of Directors since the last annual meeting of stockholders held (*date*)."
>
> To amend bylaws: "To act upon a proposal adopted by resolution of the Board of Directors on (*date*) to amend the bylaws by substituting in place of the present Article (*number*), the following Article (*number*): (Quote proposed amendment)."
>
> To authorize sale of assets: "To act upon a proposal for the sale of (*specify assets*) belonging to the corporation."

As appears from the above forms, a simple statement which briefly indicates the purpose of the meeting will be sufficient.

The sending of notice of a meeting to stockholders is not necessary if the stockholders waive such notice. Notice is usually waived in small corporations, where there only are a few stockholders. A waiver of notice should be in writing and signed by each stockholder. A form of such waiver is as follows:

WAIVER OF NOTICE OF ANNUAL MEETING
OF STOCKHOLDERS OF
USA CORPORATION

We, being all of the stockholders of USA Corporation, do hereby waive the giving of notice of the annual meeting of stockholders of the Corporation, and we hereby consent to the holding of such meeting on (date) at (hour) at (address), or on any adjournments thereof, for the following purposes: (purposes of meeting), and to transact all other

business that may lawfully come before the meeting.
Dated:

_____

_____

(Stockholders' signatures)

This form of waiver may also be adapted for use in case of special
meetings of stockholders.

DIRECTORS' MEETINGS

Written notice of meeting should be sent to all members of the board of
directors. The notice should specify the date and hour of the meeting, the
place where it is to be held, and the purposes of the meeting. A form of
notice of a regular meeting of directors is as follows:

NOTICE OF REGULAR MEETING
OF BOARD OF DIRECTORS OF
USA CORPORATION

A regular meeting of the Board of Directors of
USA Corporation will be held on (date) at (hour)
at (address), for the following purposes:
    1. (Purposes of meeting)
    2. To transact all other business that may
properly come before the meeting.
Dated:

_____
              Secretary

A statement of purposes is optional in case of a regular meeting of the
board, and such a statement may be omitted. However, it is usually included in a notice of a special meeting of directors. The above form may be
adapted for use in case of a special meeting.

Directors waive notice of meeting by signing a waiver of such notice,
which may be in the following form:

WAIVER OF NOTICE OF REGULAR MEETING
OF BOARD OF DIRECTORS OF
USA CORPORATION

We, being all of the directors of USA Corporation,
do hereby waive the giving of notice of a regular
meeting of the Board of Directors of the Corporation to be held on (date) at (hour) at (address),
for the purposes of (purposes of meeting), and for
the transaction of all other business that may
lawfully come before the meeting.
Dated:

_____

_____

(Directors' signatures)

This form of waiver may be adapted for use in the case of special meetings of the board of directors.

COMMITTEE MEETINGS

Generally speaking, no special form of meeting notice is necessary for committee meetings, nor need it be in writing. Notice may be given by any reasonable method, including interoffice memorandum or telephone. Of course, a written notice reduces the possibility of error or forgetfulness. Also, if particular requirements are fixed under the bylaws as to how notice of committee meetings must be given, such provisions are to be strictly followed.

HOW TO PREPARE FOR MEETINGS

NECESSARY DOCUMENTS

Certain kinds of written material should always be on hand at a meeting. Such material is gathered by the secretary in advance so that it will be available for reference at the meeting. For stockholders' and directors' meetings the following should be on hand:

The certificate of incorporation
The bylaws of the corporation
The minute books

A list or record of stockholders or directors, as the case may be
The seal of the corporation

In addition, there should be available a copy of the notice of meeting and the names of the persons to whom the notice was given. Other papers needed will depend upon the agenda of the meeting. These may include reports, contracts, leases, correspondence, and so on.

PREPARATION OF AGENDA

The secretary should undertake, in advance of the meeting, to prepare an agenda of business to be transacted at the meeting. For this purpose she should refer to records of previous meetings in order to ascertain whether any unfinished business has been carried over for consideration at the current meeting. In addition, the secretary should collect from available sources the items of new business to be presented to the meeting, including copies of reports, statements, and all other supporting writings which will be helpful to the participants at the meeting. From this basic material an agenda can be prepared. In the preparation of an agenda, reference should be made to the requirements of the corporate bylaws governing the order of business at meetings. A general form of agenda would read as follows:

1. Read minutes of last meeting.
2. Present reports and statements, listing those to be submitted.
3. Consider items of business carried over from earlier meetings, indicating each such item of business.
4. Take up new business, indicating, if possible, each item of business to be presented.

A sufficient number of copies of the agenda should be prepared for distribution to each person who is to participate in directors' or committee meetings. It will be helpful if the agenda can be conveniently accompanied by copies of reports or statements to be presented at the meeting.

In the case of stockholders' meetings, the data mentioned above should be made available to the officers and directors of the corporation, so that they will be directly familiar with this material and in a position to answer questions, if necessary.

MEETING-ROOM FACILITIES

The secretary should make all necessary arrangements well in advance of the meeting to have the meeting room available on the date and at the time fixed for the meeting. Adequate seating arrangements should be provided for, as well as necessary materials such as memorandum pads, pencils, ash trays, and any other conveniences that may be helpful in promoting the efficient conduct of the meeting.

MAKING A RECORD OF THE MEETING

Advance preparations should also be made for recording the business transacted at the meeting. For large meetings it is customary to engage the services of business concerns which furnish stenographic reporters to record the proceedings. In some instances meetings are electronically recorded on tapes, from which typewritten transcriptions are later made for the official record.

If the minutes of a meeting are to be taken by the secretary directly, it is not unusual to prepare an outline or a draft of the minutes in advance, so that the task of accurate reporting at the meeting itself is considerably simplified. Such an outline or draft is set up on the basis of the agenda, which specifies the.business to be transacted at the meeting. On the outline or draft of the minutes, spaces may be left blank to indicate, as required, the names of persons attending the meeting, the names of persons who propose resolutions, the votes for and against resolutions, and so on, which will be filled in by the secretary at the meeting.

On occasion the secretary may be asked to prepare a draft of a resolution to be offered at the meeting, if it is not of a technical or complicated nature. Such a draft should be submitted for approval, before the meeting is held, to the person making the request. If a resolution involves the opening of a bank account, the form of resolution, which appears on printed blanks, may be obtained from the bank on request.

The following wordings of resolutions, indicating the manner in which they are drawn, may be used as a guide.

To fix officer's salary: "Resolved, that the salary of (*name of officer*) as (*specify office*) of the corporation be fixed at (*amount*) for the year ending (*date*), payable in equal monthly installments."

To replace lost stock certificates: "Resolved, if a certificate of stock issued to a shareholder be lost, stolen, mutilated, or destroyed, a duplicate may be issued, provided that the owner of the original certificate furnishes the corporation with an affidavit setting forth the facts and a surety bond to protect the corporation in an amount to be specified by the Treasurer of the Corporation."

To declare dividend: "Resolved, there is declared a dividend of (*amount*) per share on the common stock of the corporation, to be paid on (*date*) to the holders of record of such shares on (*date*) at the close of business, and the Treasurer of the Corporation is directed to make payment of this dividend to all stockholders entitled to it."

To authorize loan: "Resolved, that (*specify officer and title*) is authorized to negotiate a loan to the corporation of (*amount*), for the use of the corporation in (*state general purposes*), on the terms and conditions to be approved by the Board of Directors."

There are occasions when it is necessary to furnish a third party with a copy of a resolution adopted by the corporation, the copy to be certified as true by the secretary of the corporation. The certificate to be given may be in the following form:

```
           CERTIFICATE OF SECRETARY
              OF USA CORPORATION
           AS TO RESOLUTION ADOPTED
            BY BOARD OF DIRECTORS
                 ON (DATE)


I, (name of Secretary of Corporation), hereby
certify that I am the duly authorized Secretary
of the Corporation, charged with keeping the
records and the seal of said Corporation, and that
the following is a true and correct copy of a
resolution adopted at a meeting of the Board of
Directors of the Corporation duly held (date),
which resolution is now in full force and effect.
     (Quote the resolution)
Witness my hand as Secretary, and the seal of
the Corporation, this (date).


                    _____
                                 Secretary
(Corporate seal)
Sworn to before me
this (day) of (month), 19__.


_____
     Notary Public
```

THE CONDUCT OF THE MEETING

QUORUM AND PROXIES

In order that a meeting of stockholders or of directors be considered as held in accordance with legal requirements, it is necessary that a quorum be represented at the meeting. The bylaws of the corporation fix the number which constitutes the quorum in both types of meeting. If a quorum is not in attendance, the meeting must be adjourned to a future date.

In the case of stockholders' meetings, a quorum is determined by the number of shares represented at the meeting, and not by the number of stockholders in attendance. Thus, a stockholder owning 100 shares of stock is counted as 100 votes, and not as a single vote. To ascertain the number of shares held by a stockholder, the stock ledger, mentioned above, should be examined.

Although the determination of whether a quorum exists depends upon the number of shares represented at a meeting, in some instances, for purposes of voting, a different method of crediting votes to stockholders may be employed. In the election of directors under the *ordinary* system of voting, a stockholder may cast for each candidate favored by him a number of votes equal to the number of shares he owns. However, under the system of *cumulative* voting, each stockholder is entitled to cast a total number of votes equal to the number of shares he owns multiplied by the number of directors to be elected, and this total he may cast in any way he wishes. Thus, a stockholder owning 100 shares, voting at an election in which three directors are to be chosen by a system of cumulative voting, is entitled to a total of 300 votes, which he may cast, if he chooses, for a single candidate. Cumulative voting is designed to afford minority stockholders an opportunity to achieve representation on the board of directors. This voting system is used only when it is authorized by statute or by the certificate of incorporation.

To cast his votes at a meeting, a stockholder need not attend in person. Any stockholder may authorize an agent to cast votes on his behalf at the meeting, and such authorization is known as a "proxy." Large corporations invariably send out proxy forms with notices of meeting; small corporations do so only rarely. However, if there is reason to anticipate that a quorum may be lacking because of the inability of stockholders to attend a meeting, such a form, together with a return envelope, should be enclosed with the meeting notice. A form of proxy for an annual meeting of stockholders is as follows:

PROXY FOR ANNUAL MEETING

The undersigned, owner of (<u>number</u>) shares of (<u>common</u>) stock of USA Corporation, hereby appoints _____ and _____, and each of them proxies, with power of substitution, to vote at the annual meeting of stockholders of USA Corporation on (<u>date</u>) and adjournments thereof,

with the same force and effect as if the undersigned were personally present, for the election
of directors and upon such other business as may
be presented at the meeting. This revokes all
proxies heretofore given by the undersigned for
said meeting and adjournments thereof. Witness
the hand and seal of the undersigned this (date).

_____ (L.S.)
        (Stockholder)

A proxy may be revoked at any time by a stockholder. The revocation
may be made verbally or in writing, and even when a stockholder attends
the meeting in person after having given a proxy.

When proxies signed by stockholders have been returned to the corporate secretary, note should be made by the secretary of each such proxy on
the list of stockholders, so that it will be known at the meeting how many
shares are represented by proxy.

In the case of directors' meetings, in contrast to stockholders' meetings,
a quorum depends on the number of directors present at the meeting.
Directors may act only in person. A director cannot appoint another
person as his proxy for the purpose of representing him at a directors'
meeting.

The proceedings at committee meetings are less formal than at stockholders' or directors' meetings and are ordinarily governed by provisions of
the bylaws or by committee rules.

TAKING AND TRANSCRIBING NOTES

If an outside agency is not engaged to make a verbatim report of the
proceedings at the meeting, the secretary will be required to record the
business of the meeting. If such is the case, the secretary need not take
down every statement made by speakers, word for word, unless a formal
resolution is presented or if it is requested that remarks of a speaker be
made a part of the record. If word-for-word reporting is necessary, the
secretary should ensure the accuracy of the report by asking for clarification when the proceedings cannot be heard or clearly understood.

In any case, it is important that the record be a complete one. This
means that if the secretary has a doubt whether certain statements should
be recorded, it is preferable that this material be included rather than
omitted.

As soon as possible after the meeting, the secretary should prepare a draft of the minutes from the notes taken at the meeting. In the draft the notes are extended to the form that is expected to be complete and final. It is not necessary to mention the names of persons voting for or against a resolution, unless this is required by the chairman. The draft should be submitted to the corporate secretary for examination and correction, and thereafter the minutes in final form are entered in the corporation's minute book and signed by the corporate secretary.

It should be noted that action taken at a meeting does not become ineffective merely because the minutes of the meeting have not been signed by the proper officer of the corporation.

MINUTES

The minutes of a meeting, regardless of their length, should be written as clearly and simply as possible. The following sample of the minutes of an annual stockholders' meeting (which can be adapted for use in connection with other meetings of stockholders, and of the board of directors) is set forth in order to indicate to the secretary an acceptable arrangement and form of minutes. The marginal notes, although optional, facilitate the task of locating particular items of business considered at a meeting after the minutes have been transcribed and formally entered in the corporation's minute book.

MINUTES OF ANNUAL MEETING
OF STOCKHOLDERS OF
USA CORPORATION

TIME AND
PLACE
    The annual meeting of the stockholders of USA Corporation was held (date) at (hour) at (place), pursuant to notice of meeting given by the Secretary.

PRESIDING
OFFICER;
SECRETARY
    (Insert name), President of the Corporation, presided as chairman of the meeting, and (insert name), Secretary of the Corporation, acted as secretary of the meeting.

NOTICE OF
MEETING
    The Secretary read the notice of meeting, a copy of which is attached to these minutes, and stated

that copies of the notice had been
mailed to each stockholder at his
address furnished to the Corporation.

QUORUM

An examination and call of the
list of stockholders of the Corporation and an inspection of the proxies filed with the Secretary of the
Corporation showed that stockholders owning (number) shares were
present in person and stockholders
owning (number) shares were represented by proxy, constituting a
quorum under the bylaws of the Corporation. The President thereupon
announced that notice of meeting
was lawfully given and a quorum was
present, and the meeting was now
regularly convened.

APPROVAL OF
PREVIOUS
MINUTES

The Secretary presented the
minutes of the annual meeting of
stockholders held (date), which were
read and approved.

ANNUAL
REPORT

The President submitted his annual report for the year ended
(date), copies of which had been
previously distributed to stockholders of record. Upon motion duly
made, seconded, and unanimously carried, it was RESOLVED, that the annual report of the President to the
stockholders be approved, and the
acts of the Board of Directors and
officers of the Corporation therein
described be ratified and confirmed.

INSPECTORS
OF ELECTION

Upon motion duly made and seconded, (insert name) and (insert
name) were elected as inspectors of
election to count the votes cast in
person or by proxy for directors of
the Corporation to be elected at
this meeting.

ELECTION
OF
DIRECTORS

The meeting thereupon proceeded with the election of directors. The President announced that three directors were to be elected, to fill terms which expire with this annual meeting, and to hold office for a term of (number) years and until their successors are elected and qualify for office.

The following persons were nominated to be directors and their nominations were seconded:

_____   _____

_____   _____

_____   _____

The ballots and proxies were thereupon counted by the inspectors of election, who submitted their report in writing, which was as follows: (Insert report)
The report was ordered filed by the Chairman and a copy thereof attached to these minutes. The Chairman thereupon announced that the three persons who received the highest number of votes, namely, _____, _____, and _____, had been elected directors of the Corporation to serve for the term of (number) years and until their successors are elected and qualify for office.

There being no further business, the meeting was, on motion duly made, seconded, and unanimously carried, ADJOURNED.

_____
Secretary

Some wordings of resolutions commonly made at board meetings may be used as a guide.

> Resignation of director or officer: "Resolved, that the resignation of (*insert name*) as (*designate office*) is accepted, to take effect (*date*)."
>
> Adoption of minutes: "Resolved, that the minutes of the meeting of the Board of Directors held (*date*) are adopted, except that (*indicate changes, if any*)."
>
> Election of officers: "(*Insert name*) was nominated for the office of (*designate office*). No other nominations having been made, on motion made, seconded, and unanimously carried, (*name*) was elected (*title*) of the corporation."

Correcting minutes. If at a meeting the minutes of an earlier meeting are read and ordered corrected, it is the duty of the secretary to make the necessary corrections. In doing this, the secretary should merely draw lines through that part of the minutes which is to be deleted, and insert the new matter, if any, to be substituted. In this way, it will be possible to ascertain exactly how the correction was made in the minutes. It would be improper to rewrite completely that portion of the minutes so that the change ordered to be made cannot be seen, unless it is directed at the meeting that a physical deletion be made so that only the corrected minutes shall appear.

DUTIES AFTER THE MEETING

A meeting of stockholders or directors or of a committee results in decisions which, to some degree, must thereafter be carried out by various personnel in the employ of the corporation.

After the meeting the secretary should review the minutes with the aim of notifying any officer or other person affected by a resolution or decision taken at the meeting so that he can carry out the projected action. If, for example, a resolution of the board of directors requires a committee to study a new advertising or sales procedure, the chairman of the appropriate committee should be notified of this decision so that he may act upon it. Or, if a particular officer is required to send a communication on behalf of the corporation to a third party, he should be notified of that fact.

Notice of this kind should always be in written form, to reduce the possibility of mistake or a failure to act. The notice may be given either on an official form, if one is in use by the company, or on an interoffice memorandum. A copy of the resolution should accompany the notice. The recipient should sign a copy of the notice, which is retained by the secretary as a matter of record, to enable a follow-up to be made before the next meeting. In that way a report as to how the matter is progressing can be presented at that time.

STOCK ISSUANCE AND TRANSFER

In large corporations the task of making and recording the issuance and transfer of shares of stock in the corporation is entrusted to banks and other organizations which act as registrars and transfer agents on behalf of the corporation. In smaller corporations, however, these activities are usually the function of the corporate secretary. The records involved in the issuance and transfer of shares are known as the stock-certificate book and the stock-transfer book and ledger.

The stock-certificate book contains blank certificates which may be separated from stubs on a perforated line, in the style of an ordinary checkbook. Stubs and certificates are consecutively numbered.

When a new certificate is to be issued, the blank spaces on the stub are to be filled in to show the number of shares covered by the certificate, the name and address of the person to whom the shares are issued, and the date of issue. The blank certificate is removed from the book. Information similar to that on the stub is typewritten on the certificate at the places indicated, the certificate is then signed by the president and secretary of the corporation, and the corporate seal is impressed on the certificate.

There is a form of receipt on the stub on which the stockholder receiving the certificate should be requested to acknowledge receipt of the certificate.

When a stockholder transfers his shares of stock to another person, he executes a form of assignment printed on the back of the certificate, and ordinarily his signature must be guaranteed by a bank. When this certificate and the assignment are presented to the corporation by the purchaser of the stock, the certificate is canceled by marking it "CANCELED" across its face, with the date of cancellation, and the canceled certificate is attached to the stub from which it was originally removed. A new certificate is then issued to the purchaser in accordance with the procedure described above.

Counsel for the company should be consulted as to the necessity for affixing documentary stamps on the issuance and transfer of shares.

Appropriate notations are to be made in the stock-transfer book and ledger of the name and address of the stockholder, the number of shares owned, and the date the shares were acquired.

SAFEKEEPING OF CORPORATE DOCUMENTS
AND RECORDS

In addition to the basic documents mentioned earlier, every business corporation acquires necessary papers of various kinds in the course of its operations. Such documents include, among other things, instruments such as contracts, leases, licenses and permits, union agreements, stocks and bonds, insurance policies, mortgages, deeds, and receipts.

All such documents and records must be kept safely, and in a place where they will be readily available if they are needed. The more important records should be kept in a safe. The others may be classified according to the type of document, placed in envelopes which bear identifying labels, and filed in cabinets. Unless the documents are exceedingly numerous or of secondary importance, it is advisable for the secretary to make a master list of corporate documents, classified by type of document and separately identified by serial number. By reference to the master list a document can be quickly and conveniently located. To illustrate, an envelope bearing the classification "Leases" will contain all lease agreements, which are filed in consecutive order according to a serial number assigned to each document in the group. A person seeking to locate, for example, a lease dated Jan. 12, 1958, covering a branch office of the company located at 77 Ludlow Street, would refer to the master list under the classification of "Leases" and examine the list for a description of the particular lease by its date and the location of the premises. Assuming that this lease is found to bear serial number L-13 on the master list, the document should be found filed in the envelope entitled "Leases" in consecutive order.

When it becomes necessary to remove a document or record from the safe or from a file, a receipt should be signed by the person receiving the paper. This receipt is inserted at the specific place where the document was filed. The receipt is removed only when the paper is restored to the safe or file. For a full discussion of filing systems, see Chapter 9.

KEEPING A DIARY

It cannot be emphasized too strongly that the secretary should keep a written record, in a diary book or other form of calendar, of all acts required to be performed at some future date (see Chap. 2). For example, in regard to a meeting of the board of directors, note should be made in the diary not only of the date of the meeting but also of the last day on which notice of the meeting may be given to directors under the requirements of· the bylaws. In matters of this nature, in which strict compliance with bylaws provisions or other rules and regulations of the corporation is mandatory, it is inadvisable to rely on one's memory, no matter how good. A written record tends to eliminate the small margin of error to which even the most diligent and precise secretary may be subject.

It is useful to start at the outset of each calendar year to make entries in the diary of those events which are known in advance. Thus, if the date of the annual stockholders' meeting is fixed by the bylaws of the corporation, an immediate record can be made of that date and of other dates related to it. A similar procedure should be followed in the case of other corporate activities that the secretary performs. Of course, throughout the year additional entries will be made as required.

Having made the required entries in advance, the secretary should periodically, perhaps each month, check those entries for the immediately ensuing period.

PART FOUR

Grammar and Usage

JOHN I. MC COLLUM

Introduction

CONTRARY TO THE VIEW held by a majority of people, grammar and rhetoric are not devices conjured by fiendish teachers to bedevil defenseless students. They are useful studies, the mastery of which is the mark of a sophisticated person. In general, it may be said that their value is both functional and esthetic. There is efficiency in a precisely worded statement, just as there may be pleasure in a well-turned phrase. The ability to use language is about all that distinguishes the human from some other animals. Possibly, the more highly developed one's ability to use language, the more distinct is his transcendence of the lower animal forms.

Of the various theories relative to the development of language the social view seems most reasonable. The theory that languages have arisen, developed, and modified as a result of social necessity or convenience is the one from which most of the advice contained in the following pages springs. That is to say, the statements as to practice reflect usage widely adopted by informed writers and speakers. "Good" English is, in general, a somewhat debatable issue. What may at one time or in one place be good English may vary significantly from what is so considered at another time or in another place. The assumptions here are based on practices that may currently be considered acceptable by those who use the language clearly, efficiently, effectively, and artistically.

This section of the book contains basically useful advice for the development of an acceptable writing and speaking style. No attempt has been made to give a complete survey of the intricacies of grammar and rhetoric, and there is little or no theorizing. In many ways the material here is in the nature of a reminder of what one should bring to his writing.

In matters of debate, and there are many, the practice is to adopt the more conservative position. To those who would argue that some of the best writers ignore, overlook, or transcend "mere rules," we offer the counterargument that in so doing such writers offer significant stylistic or artistic compensation and that they are generally capable of such compensation only after a long apprenticeship in which they acquired the tools with which to shape their greater achievement.

It may be argued, as well, that many decisions concerning propriety and style are essentially matters of taste. Indeed, such may be the case; one may, therefore, adopt a single rule: What is clearest, most precise, most useful, and most pleasing should prevail. One must learn to perceive and abhor vague, slovenly, impoverished, and inaccurate language.

The purpose of this section is to record useful statements of practice in the hope of leading secretaries easily and quickly through what is often considered a tangle of rule and rhetoric. What we generally call grammar is simply a description of the way words function and relate to one another in a sentence. This is to say that instead of prescribing a set of rules handed down by the gods of grammarians, rhetoricians, and linguists, we merely describe the way people have used their language in the past and thereby suggest possibilities for success through similar practice.

Effective communication is not easy, but we can reduce the difficulty somewhat by developing as great a familiarity with language as possible. The more we understand about how our sentences can be put together, how we can by punctuation marks pull together or separate a variety of ideas, how we can substitute one word for another to gain a more precise meaning or a more pleasing manner of expression, the easier and more successful our communication will be.

an immediate record can be made of that date and of other dates related to it. A similar procedure should be followed in the case of other corporate activities that the secretary performs. Of course, throughout the year additional entries will be made as required.

Having made the required entries in advance, the secretary should periodically, perhaps each month, check those entries for the immediately ensuing period.

Chapter 15

Parts of Speech

SENTENCES ARE COMPOSED by combining a series of words, each of which functions in a specific way within the particular context. That is to say, the word itself is called a *noun* or a *verb* or an *adjective* or an *adverb* because it functions as such in a sentence, not because it is arbitrarily a particular part of speech. In identifying parts of speech, always think of the *function* of the word (or word group) in a specific sentence. For example, the word *light* may function as a noun, a verb, an adverb, or an adjective.

The *light* shines in the night. (Noun)
Light the fire. (Verb)
She struck him a *light* blow. (Adjective)

Obviously, it is necessary to identify a word (or word group) not as a particular part of speech but as a *functioning* part of the sentence. In this sense words may be divided according to four general functions:

1. To name or identify—a word or word group (noun, pronoun, gerund, infinitive, noun phrase, or noun clause—all substantives) that names a person, place, thing, condition, quality, or action.

2. To assert—a word or word group (verb) that indicates action, state of being, or occurrence.

3. To modify—a word, phrase, or clause (adjective, adverb, or participle) that describes, limits, restricts, or qualifies the meaning of another word or word group.

4. To connect—a word (preposition) that may join a substantive to another word in the sentence; a word (conjunction) that may join words, phrases, or clauses.

NOUNS

A noun is a word that names a person, place, thing, action, idea, quality, group, etc.

1. CLASSIFICATION

All nouns belong to one of two main classifications:

a. Proper nouns name specific persons, groups, organizations, places, things, ideas.

John Smith, Hamlet, Pittsburgh, White House

b. Common nouns name members of a group of persons, places, things, ideas, or conditions.

book, health, house, man, children, city, liberty

Common nouns are variously classified according to what they name: *collective, concrete, abstract, mass.*

2. AGREEMENT

a. For consistency, every verb must agree in number with its subject.

FAULTY: In each room *is* ten *typists.*
IMPROVED: In each room *are* ten *typists.*
FAULTY: The *quality* of a company's products often *determine* the reputation of the company.
IMPROVED: The *quality* of a company's products often *determines* the reputation of the company.

b. Nouns or pronouns placed between the subject and the verb do not affect the number of the subject.

The *sound* of the violins *seems* very faint.

c. The number of the subject is not changed by the use of parenthetical expressions that begin with such terms as *as well as, no less than, including, together with,* etc.

Dr. Smith, together with his wife and two sons, *is* to arrive on the evening flight.

d. Usually subjects joined by *and* take a plural verb.

A *dictionary* and a *typewriter are* two tools of a secretary.
Mother, Father, and *I were* at home when he called.

When the words joined by *and* refer to the same person or thing, the verb is singular:

Your family *physician* and *friend is* the man to see.

e. When *each* or *every* precedes a singular subject, the verb is singular. When *each* follows the subject and the subject is plural, the verb is plural.

Each member of the class *has* been urged to vote.
Every person *is* to vote if he possibly can.
They *each want* to go.

f. Singular subjects joined by *or, nor, either . . . or,* and *neither . . . nor* generally take a singular verb.

Neither a doctor *nor* a nurse *was* available.
Either the teacher *or* the principal *attends* the conference.

When one part of the subject is singular and one is plural, the verb usually agrees with the one closer to it.

Neither Bill nor his *parents are* at home.
He did not know where his pencil or his *books were.*
Either the eggs or the *milk has* to be used.
Either the milk or the *eggs have* to be used.

When the two parts of the subject are pronouns in different persons, usage is generally according to the following: If the sense is singular, the verb is singular and agrees with the closer pronoun.

Either you or *I am* able to attend the conference.

If the sense is plural, the verb is plural.

Neither you nor I *are* able to attend the conference.

g. Special care must be taken with sentences beginning with *there is* or *there are. There* is an expletive, not a substantive, and therefore cannot serve as a subject.

There *are* to be at least ten *floats* in the parade. (*Floats,* not the expletive *there,* is the subject.)
There *is* no *point* in questioning him further.

h. A collective noun (*class, committee, jury*) may be either singular or plural, depending upon the meaning of the noun in the particular context: If the items or people are considered as a group, the noun takes a singular verb; if they are considered as separate individuals in a group, the noun takes a plural verb. (Remember, too, that a collective noun can also be used in the plural form when more than one group is meant: *classes, committees, juries.* For some collective nouns the plural form is the same as the singular: *offspring.*)

The *jury was* in session for two days. (A group)
The *jury come* from several areas of the city. (Separate individuals)

A collective noun should not be used in both the singular and plural numbers within the same sentence.

FAULTY: Since the school *board hires* the teachers, *they may* also *dismiss* them. (*Board* is singular with *hires,* then inconsistently *plural* with *they.*)
IMPROVED: Since the school *board hires* the teachers, *it may* also *dismiss* them.

i. Some nouns that are plural in form but singular in meaning take singular verbs. *Aesthetics, civics, economics, linguistics, mathematics, mumps, news,* and *semantics,* for example, are regularly singular. Verb agreement with words like *measles, physics,* and *politics* depends upon the specific use of the word.

Your *politics* are going to get you into trouble with the company. (Your political opinions are going to . . .)
Politics has always interested him. ([The subject of] politics has always interested him.)

A check with your dictionary will help you with similar words you are not sure of.

j. The title of a single published work or work of art takes a singular verb.

The *Canterbury Tales* was written by Chaucer.

k. A word used as a word, even when it is plural in form, takes a singular verb.

They is a pronoun.
Scissors comes before *scissortail* in the dictionary.

3. CASE

Differentiations between the nominative and objective cases of nouns are not observed in the English language. A few special rules, however, are generally applied to nouns in the possessive case.

a. The possessive case of nouns denoting inanimate objects is usually formed with an *of* phrase. (See also *Apostrophe* in Chap. 18, on punctuation.)

FAULTY: The room's ceiling
IMPROVED: The ceiling *of* the room

Exceptions to this practice are found in certain familiar expressions that are idiomatically correct.

a year's labor	his heart's content
a moment's notice	for heaven's sake
a stone's throw	a mile's end

b. A noun preceding a gerund is usually in the possessive case.

FAULTY: I don't understand William being gone so long.
IMPROVED: I don't understand William's being gone so long. (It is not *William* that is not understood; it is *being gone,* which is adjectivally identified by the word *William's.*)

Distinction should be made between gerunds and participles. (See *Verbals,* under *Verbs,* in this chapter.)

Everett doesn't like *Mary's working.* (Everett disapproves of the fact that Mary works. *Working* is a gerund here.)
Everett doesn't like *Mary working.* (Everett doesn't like Mary when she is at work. *Working* is a participle here.)

4. NOUNS USED AS ADJECTIVES

Although many nouns are used as adjectives effectively, especially when no suitable adjectives can be found, such forms should be avoided if they are awkward or ambiguous.

a. Nouns used acceptably as adjectives:

opera tickets   *automobile* race

b. Nouns used awkwardly or ambiguously as adjectives:

FAULTY: Many people now become seriously involved in a race argument. (Race is ambiguous; does the writer mean *racing* or *racial* issues?)
IMPROVED: Many people now become seriously involved in arguments about *racial issues.*
Many people now become seriously involved in arguments about *horse racing.*

PRONOUNS

A *pronoun* is a word that may be substituted for a noun. It performs all the functions of a noun but is not as specific. Because a pronoun is a substitute and depends on other words for its meaning, it must refer expressly or by clear implication to a noun or another pronoun previously mentioned (called the *antecedent*).

1. CLASSIFICATION

Pronouns are usually classified descriptively:

a. Personal pronouns designate the person speaking, the person spoken to, or the person or thing spoken of.

DECLENSION OF PERSONAL PRONOUNS

Person	Case	Singular	Plural
1st person	nominative	I	we
	objective	me	us
	possessive	my, mine	our, ours
2nd person	nominative	you	you
	objective	you	you
	possessive	your, yours	your, yours
3rd person	nominative	he, she, it	they
	objective	him, her, it	them
	possessive	his, her, hers, its	their, theirs

(Note that the possessive forms *ours, yours, hers, its,* and *theirs* are each written without the apostrophe.)

b. Demonstrative pronouns point out or identify specific objects (*this, that, these, those, such*). The choice of pronoun depends on the relative proximity of the speaker to the object.

this house, these houses (Near)
that house, those houses (Farther away)

c. Relative pronouns connect a subordinate clause to the main clause. *Who, whom, whose* (and the compounds *whoever, whomever, whosoever,* and *whomsoever*) refer to persons; *which* and *whichever* refer to things or objects and to living creatures (but not to persons except groups of people regarded impersonally or categories of persons regarded as such); *that* and *what* may refer to either persons or objects.

Homer, *who* is the first among the epic writers, has been called the father of heroic literature.
The writer of *whom* I speak is Ben Jonson.
Is he the man *whose* hat is on my desk?
Whoever is first receives the award.
James will admit *whomever* he sees first.
This is the book of *which* I spoke.
The television set, *which* was repaired only last week, is broken again.
You may have *whichever* book you want.

He is a man *that* we all admire.
Is this the face *that* launched a thousand ships?
He is *what* I call a genius.
This is about *what* I would expect of him.

d. The pronouns *who, whose, which,* and *what* (and the compounds *whoever* and *whatever*) become *interrogative* when used to introduce a question.

Who shall cast the first stone?
Whose gloves are these?
Which is yours?
What do you want?
Whoever told you that lie?
Whatever does he mean?

e. Indefinite pronouns are ones whose antecedents are not explicit or precise persons, places, or things. Some of the most frequently used indefinite pronouns are listed below.

all	each one	neither	other
another	either	nobody	some
any	everyone	none	somebody
anyone	everybody	no one	someone
anything	everything	nothing	something
both	few	one	such
each	much		

f. Reflexive pronouns direct or reflect the action back to the subject. In form they represent a compound of one of the personal pronouns and *self* or *selves.*

He taught *himself* to read.

g. Intensive pronouns appear in an appositive position and serve t emphasize or intensify a substantive. The forms are the same as the reflexive forms above.

The students *themselves* made the decision.

h. Reciprocal pronouns indicate an interchange or mutual action. *Each other* and *one another* are the only two such pronouns in English.

The two girls very seldom saw *each other.*
As they passed, all the soldiers nodded to *one another.*

2. CASE

The case of a pronoun is determined not by its antecedent but by the construction that it is a part of.

a. Personal pronouns have different forms for different cases. (See *Declension of Personal Pronouns,* above.)

(1) The subject of the verb is in the nominative case.

He and *I* are going.
Dave and *she* are going.

(2) The complements of all forms of the verb *to be* (except the infinitive) are in the nominative case.

This is *she* speaking.
The speaker was neither *he* nor *she.*
It is *they* whom you seek.
It is *we* who must remain to spread your message.

(3) The subject and the complement of the infinitive are in the objective case if the subject is also the object of a verb or preposition.

He invited *them* and *us* to go to the party.
We believed *him* to be wrong.
He asked *you* and *me* to be ready at noon.
The judges declared the winner to be *him.*

(4) The object of a preposition is in the objective case.

Let's keep this secret *between you* and *me.*
I bought birthday presents *for him* and *her.*
Come to lunch *with* Judy and *me.*
I typed the letters *for* Mr. Miller and *him.*

Note: In (1) through (4) above, when a pronoun follows *and,* it sometimes becomes a problem to choose the correct case (*I* or *me, he* or *him, she* or *her, we* or *us, they* or *them*). Very often the correct form can be determined if the sentence is tried out with the *pronoun in question used by itself.* Some of the sentences above would be tried out as follows:

Come to lunch *with* [Judy and] *me.*
I typed the letters *for* [Mr. Miller and] *him.*
He invited *them* [and us] to go to the party.
He invited [them and] *us* to go to the party.
He asked [you and] *me* to be ready at noon.

(5) The proper case for a pronoun used in an elliptical clause introduced by *than* or *as* can be determined by the meaning of the complete form of the clause.

He is more understanding than *I* [am understanding]. (*I* is the subject of the verb in the clause *I am understanding.*)

I can write as well as *he* [can write]. (*He* is the subject of the verb in the clause *he can write.*)

She speaks to Helen more often than [she speaks to] *me.* (*Me* is the object of the preposition *to.*)

She speaks to Helen more often than *I* [speak to Helen]. (*I* is the subject of the verb *speak* in the clause *I speak to* Helen.)

(6) With gerunds the possessive case is most often used, although the choice of case sometimes depends on the emphasis intended.

Your reading aloud disturbs me.

Have you ever thought about *his* leaving the company? (The *leaving* is emphasized here.)

Have you ever thought about *him* leaving the company? (The person named [*him*] is emphasized here.)

(See *Verbals,* under *Verbs,* in this chapter.)

(7) The possessive case of *it* has no apostrophe.

The bird built *its* nest in the tree.

b. The case of a relative pronoun is determined by the construction of the clause in which it appears. Difficulties frequently arise in the use of *who* and *whom.* In formal English *who* and *whoever* serve as subjects of a verb; *whom* and *whomever* serve as objects.

NOMINATIVE CASE	OBJECTIVE CASE	POSSESSIVE CASE
who	whom	whose
whoever	whomever	whosever
that	that	of that
which	which	of which, whose
what	what	of what

Jean, *who* lives next door, was married last week. (Subject of the verb *lives*)

Ann, *whom* I have known all my life, was there. (Object of the verb *have known*)

John, to *whom* we looked for help, was not at home. (Object of the preposition *to*)

He spoke to *whoever* answered the telephone. (Subject of the verb *answered* in a noun clause that serves as the object of the preposition *to*)

Whose is often used as the possessive of *which,* in place of *of which,* to avoid an awkward or formal-sounding construction.

I'd like to have a desk the drawers *of which* don't stick.

I'd like to have a desk *whose* drawers don't stick.

c. Some indefinite pronouns can be made possessive in form through the addition of an apostrophe and an *s.*

another's glove   anyone's house   everybody's responsibility

d. A pronoun used in apposition with a noun or another pronoun is in the same case as the noun or other pronoun.

We—James and *I*—will never betray your confidence. (*I,* in apposition with *we,* the subject, is in the nominative case.)
He asked three men—Bob, Joe, and *me*—to be ready. (*Me,* in apposition with *men,* the subject of the infinitive *to be,* is in the objective case.)
The men—Bob, Joe, and *I*—met him at the river. (*I,* in apposition with *men,* the subject, is in the nominative case.)

Note: The correct form may be determined easily by dropping the noun with which the pronoun is in apposition and allowing the pronoun to function alone; *e.g., I* met him at the river.

3. REFERENCE

A pronoun should refer clearly to its antecedent if the meaning is to be precise. The following conventions concerning reference of pronouns should be noted.

a. The masculine pronoun (*he, him, his*) may be used to refer to an antecedent that is both masculine and feminine.

Each employee soon learns that *he* must accept responsibility for *his* actions. (Includes girls and women)

b. Each pronoun should refer clearly to a definite person, place, or thing in order to avoid the following difficulties:

(1) Remote antecedent. The pronoun should be placed as close as possible to its antecedent.

FAULTY: He wore a flower in his lapel, *which* he had received from an admirer. (What had he received from an admirer, his lapel or a flower?)
IMPROVED: In his lapel he wore a flower, *which* he had received from an admirer.

(2) Ambiguous reference. There should be no question as to the specific antecedent for each pronoun; if the antecedent involves the possibility of choice, it is ambiguous and thus the reference is faulty.

FAULTY: Last Tuesday James told Mr. Adams that *he* must find the money or face bankruptcy. (Who is to find the money or face bankruptcy?)

IMPROVED: Last Tuesday James told Mr. Adams to find the money or face bankruptcy.

or:

IMPROVED: Last Tuesday James told Mr. Adams, "You must find the money or face bankruptcy."

or:

IMPROVED: Last Tuesday James told Mr. Adams, "I must find the money or face bankruptcy."

(3) Broad or weak reference. A pronoun should refer to a definite word, not to an entire clause, idea, action, modifier, or understood or unexpressed word.

FAULTY: Bill was the star of the game, *which* led to his promotion to the first string.

IMPROVED: Bill's starring in the game led to his promotion to the first string.

FAULTY: Helen is studying the piano because her mother is a good *one.*

IMPROVED: Helen is studying the piano because her mother is a good pianist.

FAULTY: Helen is learning to play the piano. *It* is a subject I know nothing about.

IMPROVED: Helen is learning to play the piano. I know nothing about piano music.

(4) Indefinite reference with second- and third-person pronouns. Consistency of reference must be applied, or the passive voice may be used.

FAULTY: If you hope to pass, you must study; however, *anybody* can get help if *you* ask for it.

IMPROVED: If you hope to pass, you must study; however, *you* can get help if *you* ask for it.

or:

IMPROVED: If one hopes to pass, he must study; however, *anyone* can get help if *he* asks for it.

FAULTY: *They* have no income-tax law in the state of Florida.

IMPROVED: Florida has no state income-tax law.

4. AGREEMENT

Although pronouns are effective instruments by which we can secure variety, emphasis, and economy, they may merely confuse if consistent grammatical patterns are not maintained. .

a. The pronoun should agree with its antecedent in number, person, and gender.

If a new *secretary* wants to succeed, *she* must work hard. (Singular antecedent requires a singular pronoun.)

He is one of those people *who hate* early morning appointments. (*Who* refers to *people;* it is therefore plural and thus takes the plural form of the verb *hate*.)

b. The indefinite pronouns (*each, one, someone, somebody, any, anyone, everyone, everybody, none, nobody, either, neither*) are usually considered singular.

If *anyone* wishes to speak, *he* may do so now.
Neither of the men would answer when *he* was questioned.
Everyone present cast *his* vote.
Everybody must turn in *his* expense account by Thursday.

VERBS

A verb is a word that makes a statement about a subject. Its function is to convey a positive assertion, to make a statement of condition or probability, to give a command, to ask a question, or to make an exclamation.

1. CLASSIFICATION

a. A *transitive verb* is one that requires a direct object to complete its meaning (as the word *transitive* suggests, the action passes from one thing to another).

I *carried* the *book.*
Donne *wrote* intriguing *poetry.*
Alice *closed* the *book* with a sigh of relief.

b. An *intransitive verb* simply states something about the subject; there is no direct object to receive the action.

The sun *rose* at six o'clock.
The old dog *lay* sleeping in the sun.
James *sat* for two hours waiting for the train.

c. A *linking verb,* or *copula,* is an intransitive verb that makes no complete statement itself, but links the subject with a subjective complement (predicate noun or predicate adjective). *To be* is the most common linking verb; other principal ones are *taste, smell, become, feel, seem,* and *appear.*

The coffee *tastes* good.
I *am* the victor.
His account *seems* improbable.
She *felt* bad.

d. Many verbs serve an *auxiliary,* or *helping,* function; that is, they are used with another verb to form a verb phrase. They help indicate tense, mood, and voice. (See *Properties,* below.) Among the more common auxiliaries are *be, have, do, may, can, shall,* and *will.*

I *am* going.
She *has been* ill.
I *do* want to go.

2. PROPERTIES

Verbs regularly show the following qualities, or properties: *person, number, mood, voice,* and *tense.*

a. Verbs (except *to be*) change in form to denote *person* and *number* only in the third person singular of the present tense.

To stop	Singular	Plural
1st person:	I stop	we stop
2nd person:	you stop	you stop
3rd person:	he, she, it stops	they stop

To be	Singular	Plural
1st person:	I am	we are
2nd person:	you are	you are
3rd person:	he, she, it is	they are

b. *Mood* (or *mode*) is the property of a verb that denotes the state of mind in which the action is conceived:

(1) The *indicative* mood makes a statement or asks a question.

He *closed* the door.
Who *is* the hero of the play?

(2) The *imperative* mood expresses a command or makes a request.

Take time to compose a letter.
Listen well; respect wisdom.
Stop!
Please *come* as early as you can.

(3) The *subjunctive* mood expresses a condition contrary to fact, a doubt, a regret or a wish, a concession, or a supposition.

If I *were* you, I would study more regularly.
I wish I *were* in command here.
I move that the treasurer *be* instructed to pay our debts.
Suppose she *were* too late to be considered.
He acts as though he *were* the only person present.
If this *be* treason, make the most of it.

In English, the subjunctive mood has largely been displaced by the indicative. The subjunctive occurs most frequently in the third person singular of the present tense (*I desire that he go at once,* instead of the indicative form, *I desire that he goes at once*) and in the verb *to be,* as indicated below:

Present Indicative		Present Subjunctive	
I am	we are	if I be	if we be
you are	you are	if you be	if you be
he is	they are	if he be	if they be

c. *Voice* is the property of the verb that indicates whether the subject of a sentence or of a clause is *acting* or *being acted upon.* When the subject performs the action, the verb is said to be in the *active voice.* When the subject is acted upon, it is said to be in the *passive voice;* the subject is literally passive and is a receiver rather than an actor. The passive is formed by the use of some form of the verb *to be* as an auxiliary to the past participle of another verb.

The ball *struck* the player. (Active)
The player *was struck* by the ball. (Passive)
Mary *started* a rumor about two of her co-workers. (Active)
A rumor *was started* about two of Mary's co-workers. (Passive)

Although the passive voice is sometimes weak and should be avoided as a general rule, it has certain uses that are worth consideration by the careful writer.

(1) The passive voice may be used when the subject is not known or is not to be revealed.

A bomb was found in the railway station.
The invoice was mailed under separate cover.

(2) It may be used to emphasize the *action* in a sentence rather than the *actor.*

Good health *is sought* by everyone.
This lesson *will be learned* before we leave.

(3) It may be used to achieve variety in sentence structure.

Inexperienced writers often use the passive in an attempt to create an impression of authority and learning, but excessive use of the passive often results in vague and wordy constructions. When possible, use the active voice.

d. The word *tense* comes from the Latin word *tempus* (time) and refers to the forms of verbs denoting the time and the distinct nature of the action or existence (continuing or completed). In English six tenses are commonly used: present, past, future, present perfect, past perfect, and future perfect. (For more information on tenses, see *Principal Parts, Conjugation,* and *Sequence of Tenses,* below.)

3. PRINCIPAL PARTS

The *principal parts* of a verb are the *present stem* (*infinitive*) (*jump*), the *past tense* (*jumped*), and the *past participle* (*jumped*). The past tense and past participle of most verbs in English are formed by adding —*ed* to the present stem; these verbs are called "regular" verbs. The principal parts of many other verbs in English are formed in an "irregular" manner—some through a vowel change (*sing, sang, sung*), others in some other "irregular" manner (*catch, caught, caught*). The principal parts are important because the six tenses are built from the three principal parts. From the present stem are formed the present and future tenses; from the past participle are formed the present perfect, past perfect, and future perfect tenses.

Appendix 10 gives the principal parts of all irregularly formed verbs. You may also consult this list to learn when the final consonant is doubled to form the past tense, past participle, and present participle of a verb (*hop, hopped, hopping*) and to learn when a final *e* is dropped before the —*ed* is added to form the past tense and past participle or before the —*ing* is added to form the present participle (*hope, hoped, hoping*).

4. VERBALS

Because *participles, gerunds,* and *infinitives* are derived from verbs, they are called *verbals.* They are like verbs in that they have different tenses, may have subjects and objects, and may be modified by adverbs; but they cannot make a statement and therefore cannot be used in the place of verbs.

a. A *participle* may be used as an adjective.

A *working* man is generally busy. (Present participle used as an adjective to modify the noun *man*)

Polished silver always looks elegant. (Past participle used as an adjective to modify the noun *silver*)

Having completed his work, he retired for the night. (Perfect participle used as an adjective to modify the pronoun *he*) *b.* A *gerund* ends in *–ing* and functions as a noun.

Your *working* is greatly appreciated. (Gerund used as the subject of the sentence)
He objected to my *speaking* without permission. (Gerund used as the object of the preposition *to*)

A noun or pronoun preceding a gerund is usually in the possessive case.

Most companies disapprove of an *employee's* being late.

However, a plural noun preceding a gerund is often not in the possessive case.

Most companies disapprove of *employees* being late.

When the noun preceding the gerund denotes an inanimate object or an abstract idea, the noun is usually not in the possessive case.

They blamed the plane crash on the *engine* falling in mid-air.

c. An *infinitive* is usually preceded by *to* and functions as a noun, an adjective, or an adverb.

To succeed was my greatest ambition. (Infinitive used as a noun, subject of the verb *was*)
The person *to choose* is the one now in office. (Infinitive used as an adjective to modify the noun *person*)
We came *to help*. (Infinitive used as an adverb to modify the verb *came*)

5. CONJUGATION

Following is the conjugation of the verb *to see* in its various forms (principal parts: *see, saw, seen*).

INDICATIVE MOOD

Present Tense

1st person
ACTIVE: I see   we see
PASSIVE: I am seen   we are seen

2nd person
ACTIVE: you see   you see
PASSIVE: you are seen   you are seen

3rd person
ACTIVE: he, she, it sees   they see
PASSIVE: he, she, it is seen   they are seen

Past Tense

1st person
ACTIVE: I saw   we saw
PASSIVE: I was seen   we were seen

2nd person
ACTIVE: you saw   you saw
PASSIVE: you were seen   you were seen

3rd person
ACTIVE: he saw   they saw
PASSIVE: he was seen   they were seen

Future Tense

1st person
ACTIVE: I shall see   we shall see
PASSIVE: I shall be seen   we shall be seen

2nd person
ACTIVE: you will see   you will see
PASSIVE: you will be seen   you will be seen

3rd person
ACTIVE: he will see   they will see
PASSIVE: he will be seen   they will be seen

Present Perfect Tense

1st person
ACTIVE: I have seen   we have seen
PASSIVE: I have been seen   we have been seen

2nd person
ACTIVE: you have seen   you have seen
PASSIVE: you have been seen   you have been seen

3rd person
ACTIVE: he has seen   they have seen
PASSIVE: he has been seen   they have been seen

Past Perfect Tense

1st person
ACTIVE: I had seen   we had seen
PASSIVE: I had been seen   we had been seen

2nd person
ACTIVE: you had seen   you had seen
PASSIVE: you had been seen   you had been seen

3rd person
ACTIVE: he had seen   they had seen
PASSIVE: he had been seen   they had been seen

Future Perfect Tense

1st person
ACTIVE: I shall have seen   we shall have seen
PASSIVE: I shall have been seen   we shall have been seen

2nd person
ACTIVE: you will have seen   you will have seen
PASSIVE: you will have been seen   you will have been seen

3rd person
ACTIVE: he will have seen   they will have seen
PASSIVE: he will have been seen   they will have been seen

SUBJUNCTIVE MOOD

Present Tense

    Active Voice   *Passive Voice*
SINGULAR: if I, you, he see   if I, you, he be seen
PLURAL: if we, you, they see   if we, you, they be seen

Past Tense

SINGULAR: if I, you, he saw   if I, you, he were seen
PLURAL: if we, you, they saw   if we, you, they were seen

Present Perfect Tense

SINGULAR: if I, you, he have seen   if I, you, he have been seen
PLURAL: if we, you, they have seen   if we, you, they have been seen

Past Perfect Tense
(Same as the Indicative Mood)

IMPERATIVE MOOD

Present Tense
see   be seen

INFINITIVES

Present Tense
to see   to be seen

Present Perfect Tense
to have seen   to have been seen

PARTICIPLES

Present Tense
seeing   being seen

Past Tense
seen   been seen

Present Perfect Tense
having seen   having been seen

GERUNDS

Present Tense

seeing   being seen

Present Perfect Tense

having seen   having been seen

In addition to the six simple tenses in English, there are two other forms that are frequently recognized:

a. Progressive verb forms show action in progress.

I *am seeing*
I *was seeing.*
I *am being seen.*

b. Emphatic verb forms employ *do* or *does* as an auxiliary. (These forms are used also for questions and negations.)

I *do see;* he *does see.*
Does he *see* it? *Did* he *see* it?
He *does* not *see* it; he *did* not *see* it.

6. SEQUENCE OF TENSES

Tense reveals not only the time of the action (present, past, and future) but also the continuity of related action. Shifts in tense must conform to the logical order or sequence of action. In most instances a knowledge of the denotation of time in the six tenses and the application of common sense will aid in developing consistent practices.

a. The tense of a verb in a subordinate element should *agree* logically with the thought suggested by the governing verb in the main clause. Note that statements regarded as universally or permanently true are expressed in the present.

FAULTY: This book is *written* for an audience which *felt* that political favors *are* to be dispensed without particular regard for merit or justice.

IMPROVED: This book *was written* for an audience which *feels* that political favors *are* to be dispensed without particular regard for merit or justice.

b. A major difficulty arises from the use of verbals.

(1) The *present infinitive* is used to express action of the same time as, or future to, that of the governing verb.

He wants *to read* each new book.
He wanted *to improve* his efficiency.

(2) The *perfect infinitive* is used to express action previous to that of the governing verb.

I *should* like *to have seen* his face when you told him.
I consider it a privilege *to have worked* with him in the recent political campaign.

(3) The *present participle* is used to express action simultaneous with that of the governing verb.

Looking up from her book, she was startled to see her supervisor enter the room.

(4) The *perfect participle* is used to express action prior to that of the governing verb.

Having found his place, he sat down hurriedly.

7. *SHALL* AND *WILL, SHOULD* AND *WOULD*

Although in informal usage the differences between *shall* and *will* and *should* and *would* are hardly discernible, careful writers still recognize the distinctions. In more conservative practice the use of *should* and *would* follows the same patterns as those established for *shall* and *will*.

a. In expressing expectation and in the simple future *shall* is used in the first person and *will* in the second and third persons.

I shall	we shall
you will	you will
he, she, it will	they will

I *shall* be in the office next Monday at 10 o'clock.
They said that they *would* be on time.
I *should* think that they *would* be more careful.

b. Will is used in the first person and *shall* in the second and third persons to express determination, command, or promise.

I *will* have my way in this matter.
I *would* do it if I could.
They *shall* not pass.

c. Should may be used in all persons to express obligation or condition.

I *should* follow your advice, but I'm too lazy.
If he *should* leave now, all work would stop.

d. Would may be used in all persons to express determination, habitual action, or a wish.

Only on one condition *would* we be willing to consider such a proposal.
I *would* read for an hour or two each night before going to sleep.
If he *would* leave now, all work would stop.

ADJECTIVES AND ADVERBS

Modifiers are words or groups of words that describe or qualify other words. *To modify* means to describe, limit, or in any other way make the meaning more precise or exact. The two kinds of modifiers are *adjectives* and *adverbs*.

1. An *adjective* is a word that *modifies a noun or pronoun*.

blue bird	*the* chair
easy assignment	*his* grade
crushed flower	*several* people
a book	*seventh* day
an apple	*former* employer

Some adjectives form the comparative degree by adding *–er* and the superlative by adding *–est;* others form the comparative degree by the use of *more* (*less*) and *most* (*least*) for the superlative degrees. Still others have an irregular comparison.

Positive	*Comparative*	*Superlative*
cool	cooler	coolest
tired	more tired	most tired
bad	worse	worst
good	better	best

The comparative degree should be used to indicate the relationship between two persons or things.

I am the *taller* of the two children in our family.
This book is *better* than that one.
I am *more optimistic* than he.

The superlative degree should be used when three or more persons or things are compared.

This is the *warmest* day of the year.
I am the *tallest* of the three boys.
This is the *most pleasant* experience I can recall.

2. An *adverb* is a word that *modifies an adjective, a verb, or another adverb.* Frequently, adverbs can be distinguished from adjectives only by the context in which they appear.

Children like books. (No modifier)
Young children *usually* like *story* books. (*Young* and *story* are adjectives; *usually* is an adverb.)
Very young children *almost always* like *highly illustrated* books, books *that can be read quickly.* (*Young, illustrated,* and the clause *that can be read quickly* are *adjectives; very, almost, always, highly,* and *quickly* are adverbs.)

In the comparison of adverbs, some shorter adverbs form the comparative degree by adding *–er* (*fast, faster*) and the superlative by adding *–est* (*fastest*), but most adverbs form the comparative degree by using *more* (*less*) and the superlative by adding *most* (*least*). Others are irregularly formed.

Positive	Comparative	Superlative
badly	worse	worst
well	better	best
calmly	more calmly	most calmly

Adverbs have certain distinguishing characteristics:

a. They are frequently distinguished from corresponding adjectives by ending in *–ly.* Although many adverbs end in *–ly,* this ending is not a certain device for recognizing this part of speech; some adverbs do not and some adjectives (*early, cowardly*) do end in *–ly.* Several common words that do not end in *–ly* may be either adjectives or adverbs depending on their function in a given context: *fast, little, near, late, well.*

b. Some adverbs are distinguished from corresponding nouns by *–wise* or *–ways* used as a suffix: *sideways, lengthwise.*

c. Some adverbs are distinguished from the same word used as a preposition in that they have no noun as an object.

The sun came *up.* (Adverb)
Henry came *up* the hill. (Preposition)

d. Adverbs, like adjectives, may be preceded by words that intensify their meaning.

The *very hastily* written paper was much better than the author had expected.
He walked *right by* without speaking.

PREPOSITIONS

1. A *simple preposition* shows the relationship of a noun or a pronoun (the object of the preposition) to some other word: stayed *at* school, lived *in* the house, the neighborhood *across* the way. The following list contains the words most commonly used as prepositions:

about	beside	in	since
above	besides	inside	through
across	between	into	throughout
after	beyond	like	till
against	but	near	to
along	by	of	toward
amid	concerning	off	until
among	despite	on	under
around	down	onto	underneath
at	during	outside	up
before	except	over	upon
behind	excepting	per	with
below	for	regarding	within
beneath	from	save	without

A preposition is usually followed by its object, which may be a noun, a pronoun, a noun phrase, or a noun clause. Occasionally, however, the object may appear earlier in the sentence:

Which church are you going *to?*
The company I am employed *by* is a reliable one.

Although some writers object to the use of a preposition at the end of a sentence, others accept such usage unless the final preposition is weakening. The practice should always depend upon its effectiveness.

This is the sort of foolishness which we will not put up with.
We will not put up with this sort of foolishness.

2. A *compound preposition* serves the same purpose as a single one:

as for	for fear of	in view of
as to	for the sake of	on account of
aside from	in accordance with	owing to
because of	in addition to	pertaining to
by means of	in behalf of	regardless of
by way of	in case of	with reference to
contrary to	in favor of	with regard to
due to	in regard to	with respect to
exclusive of	in spite of	with the exception of

CONJUNCTIONS

Conjunctions are used to connect words or groups of words in sentences; they are identified generally according to their function as *co-ordinating* or *subordinating* elements. If the words or word groups are of equal value in the sentence, the conjunction is said to be *co-ordinating;* if the words or word groups are unequal, the conjunction is said to be *subordinating.*

1. *Co-ordinating conjunctions* link words, phrases, clauses, or sentences of equal rank—elements that are not grammatically dependent on one another.

    a. Pure, or *simple,* conjunctions join two or more words, phrases, clauses, or sentences of equal rank—that is, having similar importance in the grammatical unit. The simple conjunctions are *and, but, for, or,* and *nor* (some writers include *yet* or *so*).

    b. Correlative conjunctions are words used in pairs to emphasize the relationship between two ideas. The most commonly used correlatives are *either . . . or, both . . . and, neither . . . nor,* and *not only . . . but also.*

2. *Subordinating conjunctions* relate a noun clause or an adverb clause to its independent clause. (The adjective clause is usually related by a relative pronoun.) Some common subordinating conjunctions are *because, if, since, as, while, although, unless, before, so that.*

    Although English grammar is not difficult, many students never master it.
    Peter cannot hope to buy a car *unless* he begins to save money.

3. *Conjunctive adverbs* are words or phrases that ordinarily are used parenthetically but also are often used to relate two independent clauses or two words, phrases, or sentences; the more common are *however, thus, in fact, for example, still, then.*

    I worked for three hours on the bookkeeping; *then* I began to review the correspondence.
    English grammar is not difficult; *however,* many students never master it.

INTERJECTIONS

An *interjection* is an exclamatory or parenthetic word that has little relation to the remainder of the sentence. Frequently it is a sentence in itself:

Ouch!
Oh, why didn't you come earlier?
Alas, youth too soon is fled.

Commonly used interjections include the following:

ah	bravo	hurrah	so
aha	encore	hush	tut
ahoy	gosh	indeed	what
alas	hallo	lo	whoa
amen	hello	O	whoopee
ay	hey	off	why
bah	hist	oh	woe
behold	ho	ouch	
boo	huh	pshaw	

Interjections should be used sparingly in serious writing because they are for the most part colloquial and conversational. When overused, they give the effect of a strained, melodramatic, or immature style.

Chapter 16

Clauses and Phrases

THE SENTENCE, which is in itself a group or cluster of words in a meaningful pattern, is often made up of a number of subordinate groups or clusters of words that form *clauses* and *phrases* and that function as individual parts of speech.

A *clause* is a closely related group of words containing a subject and a verb. There are two general types of clause:

1. An *independent* (principal or main) *clause* expresses a complete thought and may stand alone as a sentence. The underscored sections represent the independent clause.

Today's newspaper is on my desk.

The theater section, which begins on page 30, reviews the new play.

2. A *dependent* (subordinate) *clause* cannot stand alone as a sentence, although it contains a subject and a verb. Such a clause depends for its meaning upon the principal clause of the sentence in which it occurs; it functions as a noun or a modifier, and it is usually introduced by a subordinating conjunction, an adverb, or a relative pronoun. Dependent clauses are used as adverbs (adverbial clause), as adjectives (adjective clause), or as nouns (noun clause) and are identified according to their function.

a. An *adverbial clause* modifies a verb, an adjective, or an adverb.

When the humidity is high, we suffer from the heat. (The adverbial clause modifies the verb *suffer.*)

We are sorry *that he is ill.* (The adverbial clause modifies the adjective *sorry.*)

He does his work more quickly *than I do.* (The adverbial clause modifies the adverbs *more quickly.*)

314

b. An *adjective clause* modifies a noun or a pronoun.

We saw a replica of the capsule *that John Glenn used in his orbital flight.* (The adjective clause modifies the noun *capsule.*)

The employee *who applies himself* will succeed. (The adjective clause modifies the noun *employee.*)

The employee *who applies himself* will succeed. (The adjective clause modifies the noun *man.*)

Give the book to anyone *who may want to use it.* (The adjective clause modifies the pronoun *anyone.*)

c. A *noun clause* serves as a subject, a complement, or an object.

What we need most is more money. (The noun clause is the subject of the verb *is.*)

That is *what he had in mind.* (The noun clause is a predicate nominative following the linking verb *is.*)

Macbeth stated *that he was governed only by his vaulting ambition.* (The noun clause is the direct object of the verb *stated.*)

Give *whoever needs one* a book. (The noun clause is the indirect object of the verb *give.*)

I will speak to *whoever answers the telephone.* (The noun clause is the object of the preposition *to.*)

3. A *phrase* is a group of related words having no subject and predicate. It is used as a noun or as a modifier (adjective or adverb) and is connected to the rest of the sentence by a preposition, a participle, a gerund, or an infinitive.

His ambition was *to learn another language.* (The infinitive phrase is used as a noun, serving as a predicate nominative.)

Milton hoped *to write the great English epic.* (The infinitive phrase is used as a noun, serving as the direct object of the verb.)

To succeed was my greatest ambition. (The infinitive phrase is used as a noun, serving as the subject of the sentence.)

His energies were directed to *writing a notable epic.* (The gerund phrase is used as a noun, serving as the object of the preposition *to.*)

Fishing with his friends was his favorite pastime. (The gerund phrase is used as a noun, serving as the subject of the sentence.)

He considered *peddling old clothes* undignified. (The gerund phrase is used as a noun, serving as the object of the verb.)

The Greeks sailed *to Troy.* (The prepositional phrase is used as an adverb.)

We went *to visit our brother at camp.* (The infinitive phrase is used as an adverb.)

The cover *of the book* was blue. (The prepositional phrase is used as an adjective.)

His ambition *to climb the mountain* was never fulfilled. (The infinitive phrase is used as an adjective.)

The mysterious stranger, *wearing a black coat,* disappeared into the night. (The participial phrase is used as an adjective.)

The *absolute phrase* is somewhat unlike other kinds of phrases in that it usually consists of a noun followed and modified by a participle or participial phrase. Because it cannot stand alone as a sentence, it is a phrase; but it modifies no single word in the sentence, although it is closely related in thought to the rest of the sentence or to some part of it. The phrase is *absolute* in that it has no grammatical relationship to the main clause.

The dishes having been done, she curled up in the chair for a nap.
The king having died, the prince assumed the throne.

An *appositive phrase* is a group of words naming again a substantive previously mentioned.

Washington, *our first president,* was an astute politician.
Chicago, *an inland city,* has grown in importance as an ocean port since the opening of the St. Lawrence Seaway.

Chapter 17

Sentences

COMMUNICATION IN ENGLISH begins with the sentence. Depending on the circumstances, a sentence may be a fully developed statement, or it may contain implied elements. In many instances, our spoken language can be reduced to writing; however, the written statement does not have accompanying aids like gesture and vocal intonation, nor does it permit immediate questioning or requests for repetition when it is unclear. A good sentence, and thus effective communication, requires clarity, unity, and propriety. In order to achieve these qualities, writing generally follows a set of rules and conventions.

With the proper inflection a single word could be considered a sentence— or at least a sentence by implication.

Oh? (Is that so?)
Oh! (That hurts!)
Come! (You come here!)
[Who is that?] John. (That is John.)

As questions, exclamations, commands, and responses, such units may function satisfactorily as sentences. In general, however, it is convenient to define a sentence as *a group of words conveying a single complete thought.* If the group of words contains more than one statement, such statements should be so closely related that they convey a single impression.

1. The typical English sentence contains a *subject* and a *predicate.* As previously suggested, either the subject or the predicate may be expressed or implied. In order to work meaningfully with such matters, one must understand the structure of the sentence; one must recognize the function of words as they stand in a particular relationship with one another. The following comments are basic to that understanding.

a. The *subject* (*S*) is the person, thing, or idea about which an assertion is made. The *predicate* (*P*) (in its most expanded form composed of a verb, its modifiers, and its object and modifiers) makes an assertion (of action, state of being, or condition) about the subject.

I read a book.
S   P

The old man spoke softly.
S   P

b. Both the subject and the predicate may be simple or compound.

John and Mary read and sing well.
S (compound)   P (compound)

John stated his opinion and sat down.
S (simple)   P (compound)

John and Mary are present.
S (compound)   P (simple)

John's briefcase and hat were found beside the wreck.
S (compound)   P (simple)

Note: A simple device by which the subject may be located is to ask *who* or *what* of the verb. Observe the sentences above:

Who read and sing well? *John and Mary* are thus identified as the subject.
Who stated his opinion and sat down? *John.*
Who are present? *John and Mary.*
What were found beside the wreck? *John's briefcase and hat.*

c. Although a sentence needs only a subject and a verb to fulfill the requirement of the definition, many sentences contain other elements to complete their meanings. Among these are two general classifications: *objects* and *complements.*

(1) The *direct object* (*DO*) is a word or group of words that receives the action of a transitive verb.

DO
Joan typed the *letter.*
DO
I have read *War and Peace.*

(2) The *indirect object* (*IO*) identifies the person or thing receiving the action suggested by the verb and direct object. The indirect object usually precedes the direct object; the preposition *to* or *for* is implied.

IO   DO
He gave *her* a *box* of candy.
   IO   DO
She told *him* a bedtime *story*.
IO   DO
Bring *me* the *report*. (Subject *you* understood)

(3) The *object of a preposition* (*OP*) is the substantive that follows a preposition (*P*) and completes its meaning. The complete prepositional phrase functions either as an adjective or as an adverb.

        P   OP
She wore a dress *with lace trim*.
          P   OP
Your money is *in the bank*.
    P   OP
He spoke *to the manager*.
         P   OP
The boat was built *by three old men*.

(4) A *subjective complement* (*SC*) (also called a *predicate nominative* when a noun or pronoun, and a *predicate adjective* when an adjective) is a noun, pronoun, or adjective following a linking verb and completing the assertion made about the subject or modifying the subject. (For more about linking verbs, see *Verbs,* in Chap. 21.)

        SC (or *predicate nominative*)
Tom is the *hero* of the play.
     SC (or *predicate nominative*)
This is *he* speaking.
          SC (or *predicate adjective*)
This coffee smells *good*.

(5) The *objective complement* (*OC*) is a noun, pronoun, or adjective following the direct object and completing the assertion made about the object.

            OC
The president appointed him *chairman*.
        OC
He washed his face *clean*.

2. Sentences are commonly classified according to their purpose: *declarative, imperative, interrogative,* and *exclamatory*.

I enjoy my work. (A declaration or a statement)
Learn to write well. (An imperative request or command)
Have you read the *Odyssey?* (An interrogation or question)
Look out! (An exclamation)

3. Sentences may also be classified according to their *structure,* that is, according to the kind and number of clauses of which they are composed.
   a. A *simple sentence* contains one independent clause.

   I work in an office.

   b. A *compound sentence* contains two or more independent clauses.

   She works in the city, but John works on the farm.
   I like the theater; Bill, however, prefers the movies.

   c. A *complex sentence* contains one independent and at least one dependent clause.

   Although she has traveled a great deal, she still finds charm in new places.

   b. A *compound sentence* contains two or more independent clauses.
   and one or more dependent clauses.

   My black dress, which I wore to the party last week, is at the cleaner's, and my blue dress is not suitable for the occasion.

4. Usually, every sentence should be grammatically complete. Sometimes, however, a group of words stands alone as a sentence but is not grammatically complete and therefore not really a sentence in the strictest meaning. Such a group of words is called a *sentence fragment.*
   a. Although many skilled writers use fragments purposely to achieve particular effects, the inexperienced writer should be certain that he is able to write complete sentences when appropriate and that he uses fragments knowingly and purposefully. The following sentences, while grammatically incomplete, are not considered real fragments, for the reader understands the writer's intent and the communication is complete.

   QUESTIONS AND ANSWERS: Why are you going? Because I want to.
   　Do you want to speak with me? No.
   EXCLAMATIONS: Too bad!　　So sorry!

   The sentence fragments that should be avoided are those that have no specific meaning for the reader and do not communicate the intent of the author.

   Increasingly large numbers of young people are seeking admission to colleges and universities, which are already overcrowded with students who have difficulty completing their work. Business and professions are demanding men and women with college degrees. *Because of a widespread idea that everyone should have a college education.*

The fragment is not clearly related to the sentences preceding it. Are large numbers of young people seeking admission to colleges and universities because of the widespread idea that everyone should have a college education, or do businesses and professions demand men and women with college degrees for that reason? The ambiguity cannot be resolved without grammatically associating the fragment with one of the complete sentences.

b. Many fragments occur because the writer is careless in making dependent elements a part of the sentence to which they belong; correction can usually be made by *modifying the punctuation.*

FAULTY: He asked me to forgive him. *Although I don't know why.*
IMPROVED: He asked me to forgive him, although I don't know why.
FAULTY: I was unable to gain admittance to the supply room. *The door having been locked five minutes before my arrival.*
IMPROVED: I was unable to gain admittance to the supply room, the door having been locked five minutes before my arrival.

c. A sentence fragment is not to be confused with *elliptical construction* (also called *ellipsis*), an acceptable construction in which a word or more is omitted but whose meaning can be supplied from the rest of the sentence.

He is as tall as she [is tall].

5. Effective sentences must be more than grammatically correct; they must be unified, coherent, and skillfully arranged through the coordination and subordination of ideas and structure. Poor sentences frequently result from a failure to organize ideas in such a way as to indicate clearly their relationship and relative importance to one another.

a. Coordination

The basic principle of coordination is parallelism, a means of achieving unity, emphasis, and coherence. Ideas of equal importance and elements with similar functions in a sentence should be made structurally parallel; that is, coordinate elements in a compound structure are most effectively stated when given similar word patterns. In such compound constructions, nouns will be parallel with nouns, verbs with verbs, phrases with phrases, dependent clauses with dependent clauses, independent clauses with independent clauses.

(1) Coordinating conjunctions (*and, but, for, or, nor*) are definite indicators of parallel structure; they should warn the writer to

be careful in constructing the sentence and alert the reader to look for ideas or elements of equal importance in the statement.

FAULTY: I like *to read, to listen* to good music, and *watching* television.
(The conjunction *and* joins improperly in this sentence two infinitive phrases—*to read, to listen*—and a gerund—*watching*.)
IMPROVED: I like *to read, to listen* to good music, and *to watch* television.
or:
IMPROVED: I like *reading, listening* to good music, and *watching* television.
FAULTY: The duties of the president are *presiding* at meetings, *appointment* of committees, and *to call* special meetings.
IMPROVED: The duties of the president are *to preside* at meetings, *to appoint* committees, and *to call* special meetings.

(2) Comparisons should be stated in parallel structures.

FAULTY: A ditchdigger is a less rewarding occupation than teaching. (A ditchdigger is not an occupation; teaching is.)
IMPROVED: Ditchdigging is a less rewarding occupation than teaching.
FAULTY: He protested that his job was more rewarding than a common laborer.
IMPROVED: He protested that his job was more rewarding than a common laborer's [job].
or:
IMPROVED: He protested that his job was more rewarding than that of a common laborer.

(3) A frequent error in parallelism occurs in the improper use of correlative conjunctions (conjunctions occurring in pairs): *either . . . or, neither . . . nor, not only . . . but also, both . . . and.* Elements compared or contrasted through the use of such conjunctions are best stated in parallel form: The second conjunction should be followed by a construction parallel to that following the first; if a prepositional phrase follows one conjunction, a prepositional phrase should follow the other conjunction.

FAULTY: He is not only a *tennis player* but *plays baseball* as well.
IMPROVED: He is not only a *tennis player* but also a *baseball player*.
FAULTY: He either was *a successful industrialist* or *an accomplished liar*.
IMPROVED: He was either *a successful industrialist* or *an accomplished liar*.
FAULTY: I talked both *to the student* and *his parents*.
IMPROVED: I talked to both *the student* and *his parents*.

b. Subordination
The mature writer recognizes that not all details and thoughts are of equal importance. He learns to give certain details a primary or

secondary position in the sentence in order to communicate accurately to the reader; in other words, he learns to apply the principle of *subordination*. He thus reveals with greater exactness the relationship of the ideas he wishes to express. The main clause will convey the major idea, and the modifiers (words, phrases, dependent clauses) will convey additional and clarifying information. Effective subordination is a means of achieving not only clarity but also variety and coherence.

    (1) Short, choppy sentences (often a mark of immature writing) may be eliminated.

FAULTY: He is a man. He is fifty years old. He works hard. He wants to give his family a good home.

IMPROVED: He is a fifty-year-old man who works hard to give his family a good home.

    (2) Rambling sentences composed of short clauses joined by *and's* and *but's* may be improved.

FAULTY: The alarm rings and she sits up in bed and she rubs her eyes.
IMPROVED: When the alarm rings, she sits up in bed and rubs her eyes.

    (3) Important ideas may be expressed emphatically in main clauses, and less important ideas through subsidiary constructions (modifying words; prepositional, infinitive, participial, and gerund phrases; appositives; dependent clauses).

FAULTY: I came to the office and found that I was behind in my work.
IMPROVED: When I came to the office, I found that I was behind in my work.

    (4) Faulty subordination frequently results when conjunctions fail to express clearly the relationship between ideas. (*Like* is not a subordinating conjunction and is not used to join two clauses; *as* is ordinarily used to show time, not causal, relationships.)

FAULTY: I don't know *as* I want to go.
IMPROVED: I don't believe I want to go.
       or:
IMPROVED: I don't want to go.
FAULTY: It looked *like* he would win the match.
IMPROVED: It looked *as if* he would win the match.
FAULTY: I liked the play *while* I didn't care for the picture.
IMPROVED: *Although* I liked the play, I didn't care for the picture.
FAULTY: I read in the paper *where* he had been elected.
IMPROVED: I read in the paper *that* he had been elected.

    (5) *Because, where,* and *when* are subordinating elements and should not be used as the subject or the complement of a verb.

FAULTY: The reason he won is *because* he is fifty pounds heavier than his opponent.

IMPROVED: He won because he is fifty pounds heavier than his opponent.

FAULTY: Trusting him is *where* I made my mistake.

IMPROVED: My mistake was trusting him.

>   *or:*

IMPROVED: Trusting him was my mistake.

FAULTY: A quatrain is *when* you have a verse of four lines.

IMPROVED: A quatrain is a verse of four lines.

c. Consistent constructions

The careful writer avoids unnecessary or illogical shifts within the structure of an individual sentence or of closely related sentences. Although such a shift may not obscure the meaning, it may result in awkwardness, incongruity, and general loss of effectiveness and emphasis. In order to present his ideas clearly and appropriately, the writer must be as consistent as possible in the use of voice, tense, mood, person, number, and style.

FAULTY: When John returned to his home, a new car was found waiting for him. (Illogical shift from active to passive)

IMPROVED: When John returned to his home, he found a new car waiting for him.

FAULTY: When he hears that his friend is here, he hurried home. (Inconsistency in sequence of tenses)

IMPROVED: When he heard that his friend was there, he hurried home.

FAULTY: Everyone should be careful of their grammar. (Inconsistency of number)

IMPROVED: Everyone should be careful of his grammar.

FAULTY: If a man is to succeed, you must work hard. (Illogical shift in person)

IMPROVED: If a man is to succeed, he must work hard.

FAULTY: First prepare your notes carefully; then the report may be written. (Unnecessary shift in voice)

IMPROVED: The supervisor should first prepare his notes carefully and then write his report.

FAULTY: He asked me would I help him with his expense account. (Inappropriate shift from indirect to direct discourse)

IMPROVED: He asked me to help him with his expense account.

FAULTY: Although the party has made significant contributions to the community, its weakness is that the big wheels grab all the glory. (Inappropriate shift from formal to colloquial diction)

IMPROVED: Although the party has made significant contributions to the community, its weakness is that the leaders do not recognize the contributions of others.

d. Modifiers

Modifiers, for clarity, must refer to specific words and should be placed as close as possible to the words they modify. A modifier is *misplaced* if it seems to modify a word that it logically should not or cannot; it is considered *dangling* if it has nothing to modify.

(1) Misplaced modifiers may be corrected by revising the sentence to place the modifier in such a position that its object of modification may be clearly discerned.

FAULTY: After driving blindly for hours, a local resident helped us find our way back to the main road.

IMPROVED: A local resident helped us find our way back to the main road after we had driven blindly for hours.

FAULTY: I only need a few more minutes.

IMPROVED: I need only a few more minutes.

(2) Dangling modifiers may be corrected by supplying the word that the phrase logically describes or by revising the dangling construction to make a complete clause.

FAULTY: Having taken our seats, the players began the game. (Dangling participial phrase)

IMPROVED: After we had taken our seats, the players began the game.

FAULTY: To appreciate good music, vigorous study must be undertaken. (Dangling infinitive phrase)

IMPROVED: To appreciate good music, one must study vigorously.

Chapter 18

Punctuation

FORMAL WRITING generally employs close punctuation because the sentences are often long and tend to contain more involved construction than informal writing. Punctuation serves two purposes: to make the structure of the sentence readily apparent and to establish minor relationships within the sentence. The marks of punctuation with conventional applications are listed in alphabetical order below.

1. APOSTROPHE

The apostrophe is used to indicate possession, contraction, plurality of certain words and symbols.

a. To show possession in singular nouns and indefinite pronouns, add an apostrophe and *s*.

Tom's book   anybody's guess

b. To show possession in plural nouns ending in *s*, add only an apostrophe.

the students' grades   the soldiers' allegiance

c. To show possession in plural and collective nouns that end in a letter other than *s*, add an apostrophe and *s*.

the people's choice   the children's wishes

d. To show possession with names of inanimate objects, it is more common to use an "of" phrase, but the apostrophe with *s* is also used. Sound, meaning, rhythm in the sentence, and the emphasis desired determine the choice.

326

the brightness of the sun   the sun's brightness
the power of the state   the state's power
the lesson of today   today's lesson

e. To indicate measurement (of time, amount, degree, etc.) add an apostrophe (and with the singular an *s*).

one day's work   a week's time
two weeks' notice   three dollars' worth

f. To show joint possession, add an apostrophe and *s* only to the last element.

Tom and Robert's office (Both share one office.)

Note: Individual or alternative possession may be indicated by adding an apostrophe and *s* to each element.

Tom's and Robert's offices (Each has a separate office.)
Hitler's or Mussolini's dictatorship

g. To form the possessive of compounds, add an apostrophe and *s* to the last element of the unit only.

my brother-in-law's request   anyone else's belief

h. To indicate omission of letters in contractions, insert an apostrophe at the point of elision.

Can't, isn't, won't, haven't

Note: It's is a contraction of *it is; its* is the possessive pronoun.

i. To indicate the omission of the first figures from dates, insert an apostrophe at the point of elision.

Class of '09   Spirit of '76

j. To form the plural of a word used as a word, without regard to its meaning, add an apostrophe and *s*.

There are too many *but's* in this sentence.

k. To indicate the plural of symbols and letters, add an apostrophe and *s*.

10's, two 5's, H's, &'s

Note: The possessive forms of personal and relative pronouns do not require the apostrophe: *his, hers, its, ours, theirs, whose*. The possessive forms of indefinite pronouns do require an apostrophe: *one's* book, *anyone's* opinion, *somebody's* mistake.

2. BRACKETS

    a. Brackets are commonly used to enclose comments, insertions, correc-tions, etc., made by a person other than the author of the quoted material.

"He [Abraham Lincoln] became known as a great humanitarian."

    b. Brackets are used to enclose parenthetical material within parentheses to avoid the confusion of double parentheses.

The Voyages of the English Nation to America, before the Year 1600, from Hakluyt's Collection of Voyages (1598–1600 [III, 121–128]). Edited by Edmund Goldsmid.

3. COLON

    a. The colon is a formal mark indicating introduction or anticipation. It is used ordinarily to precede a series or a statement that has already been introduced by a completed statement.

There is only one course of action: We must work more conscientiously.
The library has ordered the following books: *Don Quixote, The Pilgrim's Progress,* and *Alice in Wonderland.*
There are several schools and colleges in the university system: arts and sciences, business administration, education, music, and engineering.

    b. The colon may be used to introduce an extended quotation.

In a long speech President Roosevelt said: "We have nothing to fear but . . ."

    c. The colon is conventionally used after a formal salutation in a letter.

Dear Sir:
Dear Mr. Adams:

    d. The colon is used to separate chapter and verse numbers in Biblical citations, and volume and page numbers in references containing Arabic numerals.

John 3:16   I Corinthians 13:1–12   *PMLA* 72:19–25

    e. The colon is regularly used between numerals designating hours and minutes.

12:15 A.M.

4. COMMA

The comma is the most frequently used mark of punctuation; its misuse often produces confusion and misunderstanding.

a. A comma is used to separate two independent clauses joined in a compound sentence by co-ordinating conjunctions (*and, but, for, or, nor*).

He spoke clearly, but his father did not hear him.

Note: In less formal writing the comma is frequently omitted between short clauses joined by *and;* it is rarely omitted before *or* or *but.*

b. The comma is used to set off nonrestrictive modifiers. (A nonrestrictive modifier is one that is not essential to the meaning of the sentence but that supplies incidental information about a word already identified. A restrictive modifier restricts, limits, or defines; it cannot be left out without changing the meaning of the sentence.)

NONRESTRICTIVE MODIFIER: Tom's father, *who is a grocer,* ran for the city council. (The clause *who is a grocer* can be eliminated without robbing the sentence of meaning.)

RESTRICTIVE MODIFIER: An employee *who is always late* may be fired. (The clause *who is always late* is necessary to the meaning of the sentence.)

c. The comma is used to separate elements (words, phrases, clauses) in a series of three or more.

The vegetables included corn, beans, tomatoes, and asparagus.
Tell me what you wore, where you went, and what you did.

Note: Commas should not be used before the first or after the last element in the series unless needed for other reasons.

d. The comma is used to set off terms of direct address.

Professor Jones, please be seated.

e. The comma is used after a long introductory phrase or clause. Such "signal" words as *when, although, as, if, while, since, because* usually indicate that a comma will occur before the main clause.

After setting up our tent and getting the camp in order, we took a swim.
Although I am no scholar, I enjoy historical research.

f. The comma is used both before and after a dependent clause that appears in the body of a sentence.

His car, although he bought it only last year, looked ready for the junk heap.

g. The comma is used to separate elements of a date, address, or other statistical details.

Monday, September 1, 1952, was an important day.
The address is 1172 Louis Plaza, Arlington, Kentucky.
The quotation occurs on page 16, line 6, of the manual.

h. The comma is used to set off direct quotations.

He said, "I am prepared."

i. The comma is used between coordinate adjectives (usually co-ordination can be tested by substituting *and* for the comma).

COORDINATE: He sat in a poorly made, old-fashioned chair.
NOT COORDINATE: He was a member of the large freshman class.

j. Commas should not be used to separate the subject from the verb or the verb from the complement.

FAULTY: Careful study, may produce good grades.
IMPROVED: Careful study may produce good grades.

k. One of the most common errors in punctuation is the *comma splice,* the separation of two independent clauses by only a comma. Fused or run-together sentences result when two or more independent clauses are included in a single sentence without punctuation to separate them. Independent clauses should be separated by a comma and a coordinating conjunction or by a semicolon.

FAULTY: It was raining, he could not walk to work.
IMPROVED: It was raining, and he could not walk to work.
   or:
IMPROVED: It was raining; he could not walk to work.

(1) Frequently a comma splice can be best corrected by effective subordination.

FAULTY: It was raining, he could not walk to work.
IMPROVED: Because it was raining, he could not walk to work. (The first clause is now a subordinate clause.)
   or:
IMPROVED: Because of the rain he could not walk to work. (The first clause is now a prepositional phrase.)
   or:
IMPROVED: The rain kept him from walking to work. (The two clauses are combined to form one simple sentence.)

(2) If the two independent clauses are not closely related in meaning, each may be made into a sentence.

FAULTY: Swimming is good exercise, I like to swim in the summer.
IMPROVED: Swimming is good exercise. I like to swim in the summer.

l. Conjunctive adverbs (such as *moreover, therefore, thus, hence, then, still*) should not be used to connect independent clauses unless a semicolon or a coordinating conjunction is also used.

FAULTY: The two boys meet each morning, then they spend the day together.
IMPROVED: The two boys meet each morning; then they spend the day together.
        or:
IMPROVED: The two boys meet each morning, and then they spend the day together.

m. When a conjunctive adverb of more than one syllable (*however, moreover, consequently, therefore,* etc.) is used to connect two independent clauses, a semicolon comes before the adverb and a comma after it. When a conjunctive adverb of only one syllable (*yet, then, still,* etc.) is used to connect two independent clauses, a semicolon comes before the adverb but a comma is not used after it.

The flood destroyed many houses; however, the church remained undamaged.
The flood destroyed many houses; yet the church remained undamaged.

n. The comma is used to set off conjunctive adverbs or short transitional phrases.

We do not, moreover, need your advice.

o. The comma is often used before the conjunction *for* to avoid faulty interpretation.

We hurried, for the plane was about to leave.

p. The comma is used after the complimentary close of a letter.

Very truly yours,   Sincerely,

q. The comma is used after the salutation of a personal letter.

Dear David,

5. DASH

Dashes are frequently overused by inexperienced writers; they are more emphatic than commas and less emphatic than parentheses.

a. The dash is used to emphasize or to indicate hesitation or a sharp break or change in thought.

I must tell you—now what was I going to tell you?
He ought to be satisfied—if he is ever to be satisfied.

b. The dash is used to set off parenthetical material when commas might be confusing or inadequately emphatic.

Three books—a dictionary, a grammar, and a novel—lay on the desk.

c. The dash is used before a statement or word that summarizes what has been said.

The mayor, the aldermen, the lesser officials, and the citizenry—all were gathered in front of the city hall.
Kindness, understanding, and honor—these are needed virtues.

6. ELLIPSIS

The ellipsis (. . .) is a mark used to indicate the omission of a part of quoted material or of words needed to complete a sentence. Three dots are used to indicate the omission; if the ellipsis occurs at the end of a sentence, a period is added.

The war, which had been in progress for ten years, was ended by mutual agreement.
The war . . . was ended by mutual agreement.
The war . . . was ended. . . .

7. EXCLAMATION POINT

The exclamation point is used to indicate an emphatic utterance.

For heaven's sake!   Ready, set, go!

8. HYPHEN

Whenever possible, avoid breaking words from one line to the next. When hyphenation is necessary, (a) the hyphen should be placed at the end of a line, never at the beginning; (b) only words of two or more syllables should be divided, with the division occurring only between syllables. The word list in Appendix 10 shows these syllable breaks.

a. The hyphen is used to divide at syllable breaks a word that must be carried over from one line to another. Words should be so divided that a single letter does not stand alone (*fault-y*, *a-bove*). Hyphenated words should be divided at the hyphen.

b. The hyphen is used to join compound numbers from twenty-one through ninety-nine.

c. The hyphen is used to join words that function as a single adjective before a substantive.

a broken-down nag
up-to-date methods

d. The hyphen is used to join such prefixes as *self-*, *ex-*, *anti-* (when it is followed by a capital letter).

self-help   anti-Truman   ex-governor

e. The hyphen is used in compounds containing forms like *-elect* and *-in-law*.

President-elect Wilson   sister-in-law

f. The hyphen may be employed to eliminate confusion in the meaning of words to which prefixes are added.

re-creation (in contrast to *recreation*)
re-form (in contrast to *reform*)

g. The hyphen is now frequently used to join a single capital letter to a noun.

H-bomb, I-beam, U-boat

h. The hyphen is used to join a verb modifier except when the adverb ends in *-ly* or following such common adverbs as *very* and *most*.

a *fast-paced* horse
a *widely known* author

Be careful to recognize that some words ending in *-ly* are adjectives (*cowardly*, *friendly*) and that there may be times when the adjective and another word should be joined with a hyphen to form a modifier of a noun.

a *friendly-acting* animal
a *cowardly-looking* bullfighter

i. Although many modifiers are hyphenated when they come before the word which they modify, they are usually not hyphenated when they are in the predicate position.

He is a *well-known* scientist. The scientist is *well known*.

Sometimes, however, the meaning of the modifier is such that the hyphen should be retained even in the predicate position.

That man is *big-hearted*.
His appearance was *awe-inspiring*.

j. Usage is divided on hyphenating noun phrases used as modifiers (*income tax* laws, *income-tax* laws; *life insurance* policies, *life-insurance* policies). Usually a hyphen is not needed when the significance of the compound modifier is so well established that no ambiguity can result (*public health* program).

k. Sometimes two words mean one thing hyphenated and quite another without the hyphen. Contrast the difference in meaning between:

a light green coat   and   *a light-green coat*

Be careful not to use hyphens in constructions like *a long telephone conversation,* where each word modifies the noun separately.

a new company policy
a large cardboard box

The hyphen should be used in two-word modifiers like the following:

a *four-year* term
a *first-class* cabin

9. ITALICS

Italics are indicated in manuscript and typescript by underlining.

a. Italics are used to identify the titles of books, magazines, newspapers; the names of ships and aircraft.

I have recently read Hemingway's novel *The Sun Also Rises*.
The *Queen Mary* was one of the world's finest ships.

b. Italics may be used to indicate emphasis.

I am *always* on time.

c. Italics are used to identify foreign words or phrases.

He is *persona non grata* in this country.
He lacks *joie de vivre*.

d. Italics (but frequently quotation marks) are used to identify words used as words (that is, without reference to their meanings).

The word *go* will be the signal.

10. PARENTHESES
Parentheses are used to set off explanatory or supplementary material (definitions, additional information, illustration) not essential to the meaning of the sentence, or to enclose numbers or letters in enumeration.

Many of our Presidents (Washington, Lincoln, Wilson, and Roosevelt, for example) rose above mere party politics.
(1), (a)

11. PERIOD
The period is used to indicate the end of a sentence and to mark abbreviations.

12. QUESTION MARK
a. The question mark is used to mark the end of a question.

Do you really care?

b. A question mark is used to show doubt, uncertainty, or approximation.

Sir Thomas Wyatt, the English poet, lived from 1503? to 1542.

c. Question marks are used in a series of questions.

Several questions remained to be answered: How many were going? How many cars would be needed? What time would we return?

d. The question mark is not needed at the end of a courteous request that is phrased as a question.

Will you please return the completed form as soon as possible.

e. A question mark is not used after an indirect question.

He asked whether he would be allowed to go.

f. When quotation marks and a question mark are used together, the question mark is placed *before* the closing quotation marks if the quoted material is a question and *after* the closing quotation marks if the whole sentence is a question. (If both are questions, only one question mark is used, *before* the closing quotation marks.)

He said, "Are you here?"
Did he say "I am here"?
Did he say, "Are you here?"

(See also *Quotation Marks,* below.)

13. QUOTATION MARKS

Quotation marks serve to indicate spoken dialogue and to acknowledge specifically reproduced material.

a. Quotation marks are used to enclose direct quotations.

The supervisor said, "Come to my desk, young man."

Note: Single quotation marks (' ') are used to enclose a quotation within a quotation.

The boy asked, "Who popularized the statement 'This is the best of all possible worlds'?"

b. Quotation marks should be used to enclose titles of short poems, stories, and articles that are usually printed as a part of a larger work.

He read "Ode on a Grecian Urn" from an anthology.

c. Quotation marks may be used to enclose a word used as a word (rather than for its meaning). (See also item *d* under *Italics.*)

The word "school" brings back pleasant memories.
Do not overuse the word "and" in formal writing.

Note: When other marks of punctuation are used with quotation marks, the following practices should be observed:

(1) A question mark or an exclamation point is placed inside the final quotation mark if it is a part of the quotation, outside if it is a part of the sentence that includes the quoted material.
(2) Periods and commas are always placed inside the closing quotation marks.
(3) Semicolons and colons are always placed outside the closing quotation marks.

14. SEMICOLON

a. A semicolon is used to separate two independent clauses not joined by a coordinating conjunction.

He annoyed me; I regretted having invited him.

b. A semicolon is used to separate two independent clauses which are joined by a coordinating conjunction when either or both of the clauses contain one or more commas.

The office manager, a woman I admired, was pleased with the results of the survey; but she was not happy to lose two of her best workers.

  c. A semicolon is used to separate two independent clauses joined by a conjunctive adverb.

We placed our order with your salesman two weeks ago; however, we have not yet received delivery.

  d. A semicolon is used to separate two independent clauses when the second is introduced by such expressions as *namely, for example, that is, in fact.*

He is a poor example of what we expect; that is, he just doesn't meet our requirements for a man in such a position.

  e. The semicolon may be used to separate items in a series containing internal punctuation.

His tour carried him to all parts of the country—from Seattle, Washington, to Miami, Florida; from El Paso, Texas, to Bangor, Maine.

Among our greatest Presidents we include George Washington, the father of our country; Abraham Lincoln, the great emancipator; and Theodore Roosevelt, the hero of San Juan.

Chapter 19

Capitalization

THE USE OF THE CAPITAL LETTER generally is standardized, but some situations call for personal judgment based on the writer's taste and the level of writing in question. The following conventions are generally employed in formal writing.

1. Capitalize the first word of a sentence and of each line of poetry.

2. Capitalize the first word of a direct quotation. No capitalization is required at the resumption of a quotation interrupted by such expressions as *he said, he responded.*

He said, "This is your last opportunity to change your mind."
"This is your last chance," he said, "and I advise you to take it."

3. Capitalize proper nouns and adjectives derived from such nouns.
   a. Specific persons and places, their nicknames and titles.

Winston Churchill, Professor Smith, Major Adams, Grandma Moses, Boston, Bostonians

   b. Some words that were originally proper names but are no longer identified with those names are not capitalized. (Check the dictionary when in doubt.)

manila paper   india ink

   c. Titles used with a name, as on the envelope or inside address of a letter, are capitalized; but they are not capitalized when used alone.

John Jones, Director of Training
ABC Company
. . . the director of training of the ABC Company . . .

d. Racial, religious, political designations.

Indian, Negro, Baptist, Republican

e. Names of languages.

French, English, Latin, Aramaic

f. Days of the week, the months, and the holidays.

Monday, July, Christmas, Labor Day, Easter

g. Names of organizations and membership designations.

Phi Beta Kappa, Boy Scouts, Rotary Club, Rotarians, Socialists

h. References to the deity.

Lord, Jehovah, Christ, Savior, Holy Ghost, God

i. Names of historical events and documents.

Renaissance, Monroe Doctrine, French Revolution, Magna Charta

j. Names of specific institutions, ships, airplanes, academic courses, geographical features, regions.

First National Bank of Miami, *Queen Mary, Columbine,* History 101 (as distinguished from *my history class*), World War II (as distinguished from *a world war*), the South (as distinguished from *turn south on Main Street*)

k. Words denoting a definite geographical region or locality are proper names and therefore should be capitalized. However, compass points or words designating mere direction or position are not proper names and therefore should not be capitalized.

the Far East
Traveling south, we arrived . . .

4. Capitalize the first word and all important subsequent words (nouns, pronouns, adjectives, adverbs, verbs) in the titles of books, articles, musical compositions, motion pictures, and works of art.

The Sun Also Rises   *A Place in the Sun*

5. Capitalize names of family relationship when used with the person's name or in place of the name, but not otherwise.

I bought Mother a box of candy.
I bought my mother a box of candy.

6. Capitalize the pronoun *I* and the interjection *O* (but not *oh,* except at the beginning of a sentence).

7. Capitalize the word *the* in the title of a company or organization only when it is actually part of the name.

The World Publishing Company
the Girl Scouts of America

8. Once an organization or group has been referred to by name in full in a letter or other piece of writing, a shortened version of the name, using one of the words in the name, should be capitalized.

Acme Life Insurance Company .... the Company
Federal Communications Commission .... the Commission
Federal Bureau of Investigation .... the Bureau

(In expressions such as *our company policy, company* is not capitalized.)

9. Names of the seasons are ordinarily not capitalized.

10. Government organizations are capitalized when they are referred to by specific name.

House of Representatives   Peace Corps
Senate   Internal Revenue Service

11. Capitalize the material that follows a colon if it is in the form of a complete sentence. Do not capitalize it when it is not a sentence (unless the first word following the colon is capitalized for some other reason).

We had two alternatives: We could either go to the movies or stay home and watch television.
We had two alternatives: to go to the movies or to stay home and watch television.
We had two alternatives: Aileen's plan or Marilyn's plan.

Chapter 20

Spelling

SPELLING RULES represent generalizations that are applicable to large numbers of words; however, it should be noted that exceptions often occur. Proper understanding of prefixes, suffixes, syllabification, pronunciation, and definition will eliminate many spelling errors. Appendix 10 of this book is a guide to the correct spelling and syllabification of the 33,000 most frequently used words in English.

1. When the sound is long *e* (as in believe), *i* is placed before *e* except after *c*.

achieve, chief, relief, yield, piece, receive, deceive, conceive, ceiling

EXCEPTIONS: *neither, either, seize, weird, leisure*

When the *ie* combination is pronounced as separate syllables, the rule does not apply.

society, deity, science

When the *ie* combination follows a *c* to produce the *sh* sound, *i* is placed before *e*.

deficient, efficient, conscience, ancient

2. The final *e* is dropped before a suffix beginning with a vowel, retained before a suffix beginning with a consonant.

hope——hoping	pure——purely
desire——desirable	use——useful
allure——alluring	state——statement

EXCEPTIONS: *true, truly; acknowledge, acknowledgment* (but also *acknowledgement*). With some words, both forms are used: *likable, likeable; lovable, loveable.*

341

After *c* or *g* the *e* is retained before a suffix beginning with *a, o,* or *u* to preserve the soft *c* or *g*.

peaceable, courageous, changeable, serviceable

3. Monosyllables and words accented on the last syllable ending in a single consonant preceded by a single vowel *double* the consonant before a suffix beginning with a vowel.

prefer——preferred   hop——hopped
occur——occurrence   forbid——forbidden
red——redder   control——controlled

When the accent shifts to another syllable with the addition of the suffix, the stress in the new word determines the application of the rule.

confer——conference   refer——reference   prefer——preference

4. Words ending in *y* usually change the *y* to *i* before all suffixes except *–ing*.

lonely——loneliness   try——tried   lady——ladies

The *y* is usually retained if preceded by a vowel.

valleys   plays

EXCEPTIONS: *lay——laid   pay——paid   say——said*

5. In the formation of plurals most nouns add *s* or *es*. Some ending in *s* or *z* double these letters.
   a. Nouns ending in *s, z, x, sh, ch* add *es*.

church——churches   box——boxes
quiz——quizzes   loss——losses

   b. Nouns ending in *y* preceded by a consonant or by *u* sounded as *w* change the *y* to *i* and add *es*.

fly——flies   lily——lilies
sky——skies   soliloquy——soliloquies

   c. Compound nouns usually form the plural by adding *s* or *es* to the principal word.

attorneys-at-law   brothers-in-law
consuls-general   master sergeants
commanders in chief

   d. When the noun ends in *fe,* the *fe* is usually changed to *ve* and *s* is added.

knife——knives   wife——wives

e. Nouns ending in *o* usually add *s* to form the plural.

radio——radios   cameo——cameos

EXCEPTIONS: echo——echoes   hero——heroes

6. When diacritical marks are a part of the foreign spelling, such marks are retained when the words are used in English sentences (fiancé, auto-da-fé, chargé d'affaires), but many words completely Anglicized no longer require diacritical marks.

cafe, canape, fete, habitue, naive, depot, denouement

7. Only one word ends in *sede* (supersede); three end in *ceed* (exceed, proceed, succeed); all other words with this final sound end in *cede* (precede, secede).

Chapter **21**

Usage

THIS CHAPTER contains a list of words and phrases that are often used incorrectly or for some other reason cause a writer or speaker difficulty. In addition, the word list in Appendix 10 has many cross references to help you decide which is the appropriate word to use when confusion might arise (for example, *adapt, adept, adopt*).

A, AN: *a* is used before words beginning with consonants or with initial vowels that have consonant sounds (*a* book, *a* one-way street, *a* historian, *a* uniform); *an* is used before words beginning with vowels or with a silent *h* (*an* apple, *an* hour). Before an abbreviation that consists of letters sounded separately, use the article that agrees with the *pronunciation* of the first letter of the abbreviation (an S O S, an FM radio, a UN committee).

ACCEPT, EXCEPT: *accept* means *to receive something offered; except,* as a verb, means *to exclude;* as a preposition, *except* means *with the exclusion of.*

ACCIDENTLY: used incorrectly for *accidentally;* the *–ly* suffix should be added to the adjective and not to the noun.

ACQUIRE: often pretentious for *get.*

AFFECT, EFFECT: *affect* is a verb meaning, in one sense, *to pretend* or *to assume* and, in another sense, *to influence* or *to move; effect,* as a verb, means *to bring about;* as a noun, *effect* means *result* or *consequence.*

AGGRAVATE: in formal English, *to make worse or more severe;* in colloquial English, *to annoy* or *irritate.*

ALL RIGHT, ALRIGHT: *all right* means *satisfactory, correct,* or *yes; alright* is a misspelling.

ALOT: used incorrectly for *a lot.*

ALREADY, ALL READY: frequently confused: *Already* means *before* or *before this time; all ready* means *completely ready.*

ALTOGETHER, ALL TOGETHER: frequently confused: *Altogether* means *completely, on the whole; all together* means *in a group.*

A.M., P.M., a.m., p.m.: should not be used as synonyms for *morning* and *afternoon;* the abbreviations should be used only with the figures designating the time.

AND ETC.: redundant: *Etc.* is an abbreviation of the Latin *et* (and) *cetera* (others); *and etc.* would mean *and and so forth.*

AND WHICH: correct only when the clause that follows *and which* is co-ordinate with a previous clause introduced by *which.*

ANECDOTE, ANTIDOTE: an *anecdote* is a short, entertaining account of some event; an *antidote* is a remedy for poison.

ANGRY: *at* a thing and *with* a person.

ANYPLACE, EVERY PLACE, NO PLACE, SOMEPLACE: colloquialisms for *anywhere, everywhere, nowhere, somewhere.*

ANYWAY, ANYWAYS: colloquialisms for *in any case, in any event, anyhow.*

ANYWHERES: a misspelling of *anywhere.*

AS: sometimes used as a weak synonym for *since* or *because;* used incorrectly as a conjunction in place of *for, that,* or *whether* in sentences like these: I didn't buy the hat, *as* [use *for*] red is not my color. I don't know *as* [use *that* or *whether*] I can go. See also LIKE.

AT: redundant in such sentences as "Where are we at?"

AWFUL, AWFULLY: overworked intensives for *very.*

AWHILE: an adverb improperly used as the object of the preposition *for;* the acceptable form is *for a while.* Use *awhile* without the preposition *for:* He has been gone *awhile.*

BAD, BADLY: linking verbs *appear, be, seem, sound, taste, smell, feel, look, become* are followed by an adjective; hence *bad* is the proper form in such sentences as "This coffee tastes *bad.*" Remember, however, that a linking verb can also be used as a transitive verb, and the modifier may be an adverb, as in "He sounded the bell *loudly.*"

BADLY: colloquial for *very much, greatly.*

BECAUSE: a conjunction should not be used as a subject, object, or complement; thus, the construction beginning "The reason is because . . ." is incorrect.

BEFORE: redundant in such usage as *"Before, I used to get sick if I saw blood."*

BEING THAT, BEING AS HOW: misused for *as, since, because.*

BESIDE, BESIDES: only *beside* can be used as a preposition (That is *beside* the point), but both *beside* and *besides* can be used as an adverb (*Besides,* there is no place to go. *Beside,* there is no place to go).

BIANNUAL, BIENNIAL: *biannual* means twice (at any two times) every year (as distinguished from *semiannual,* which means once regularly every six months); *biennial* means once every two years.

CONTINUAL, CONTINUOUS: *continual* means happening again and again; *continuous* means going on without interruption.

CUTE: overused as a vague term of approval.

DEFINITELY: overused as an intensive modifier.

DEPRECIATE IN VALUE: redundant: *depreciate* means *lessen in value.*

DIFFERENT THAN: improperly used for *different from* except when the object is a clause: This room is *different from* that one. This room is *different than* I expected.

DUE TO: controversy among authorities exists about the use of *due to.* Some insist that *due to* should be used only as an adjective (The leak was *due to* a break in the line.), never as a preposition (*Due to* a break in the line, there was a leak). *Owing to, because of,* or *as a result of* should be substituted for *due to* in the second example.

EACH AND EVERY: needless repetition; use one word or the other.

EDUCATIONAL: inaccurate and pretentious as a synonym for *instructive* or *informative.*

EFFECT: see AFFECT.

ENTHUSE: colloquially used as a verb; not acceptable in formal writing as a substitute for *be enthusiastic about.*

EQUALLY AS: redundant; use *equally* (Both men were *equally* guilty).

EXCEPT: improperly used for *unless.* See also ACCEPT.

EXCEPT FOR THE FACT THAT: wordy for *except that.*

FARTHER, FURTHER: now infrequently distinguished; in formal usage *farther* indicates distance and *further* indicates degree or extent.

FEWER, LESS: *fewer* refers to number; *less* refers to quantity or degree.

FIRST OFF: use instead *in the first place.*

FLAUNT, FLOUT: *flaunt* means to display defiantly or impudently (The little girl *flaunted* her new dress in front of her friends); *flout* means to show scorn or contempt for (The employee who continually reports late to work *flouts* discipline).

GOES ON TO SAY: wordy for *adds, continues.*

HARDLY: do not use a negative before *hardly* when you mean *with effort or difficulty* (I *can hardly* read his handwriting; not I *can't hardly* . . .).

HAVE: see OF.

IDEA: often vague for *belief, scheme, theory, conjecture, plan.*

INCREDIBLE, INCREDULOUS: *incredible,* said of a situation, means unbelievable (That he went swimming in the ocean in freezing weather is *incredible*); *incredulous,* said of a person, means unbelieving (I was *incredulous* that he would do such a thing).

INDULGE: often used improperly for *take part in.*

INFER, IMPLY: often confused: *Infer* means *to draw a conclusion from facts or premises; imply* means *to hint* or *suggest.*

IN MY ESTIMATION, IN MY OPINION: often unnecessary or pretentious for *I think, I believe.*

IN REGARDS TO: a confusion of the British idiom *as regards* with the American idiom *in regard to.*

INSIDE OF: colloquial for *within* when used in a time sense (I will see you *within* an hour).

Is WHEN, IS WHERE: frequently used erroneously in definitions; the verb *to be* requires a noun or an adjective as a complement.

IT BEING, THERE BEING: awkward for introducing a clause that should be introduced by *since* ("There being little time left, we hurried to the airport" should be changed to "Since there was little time left, . . .").

ITS, IT'S: *its* is the possessive form of the pronoun *it; it's* is a contraction of *it is.*

KIND OF: colloquial for *somewhat.*

LAY, LIE: often confused: *Lay* is a transitive verb meaning *to put* or *to place something* (*Lay* the book on the table); its principal parts are *lay, laid, laid. Lay* is also the past tense of the intransitive verb *lie,* meaning *to recline, to assume a position,* or *to remain in a position* (I will *lie* here until morning); the principal parts of the verb *lie* are *lie, lay, lain.*

LEARN: not to be confused with or used as a synonym for *teach.*

LEAVE, LET: *leave* should not be used as a synonym for *permit* or *let;* use *let me alone* to mean *do not bother me.*

LIABLE, LIKELY: *liable* means *subject to the possibility of,* but in a disagreeable way (He is *liable* to be caught if he continues stealing); *likely* means, simply, *subject to the possibility of* (If the Pirates continue to win games, they are *likely* to win the pennant this year).

LIKE: should not be used as a substitute for *as* or *as if; like* is a preposition and governs a noun or pronoun (He looks *like* me); *as* and *as if* introduce clauses (He looks *as if* he wants to speak to me).

–LOOKING: often a redundant or parasitic suffix to an adjective.

LOT, LOT OF: vague, colloquial terms suggesting *many* or *much.*

MANNER: often unnecessarily used in phrases such as "in a clumsy manner"; a single adverb or a "with" phrase would suffice.

MARVELOUS: overused as a vague word of approval.

METHOD: a vague word for *manner, plan, scheme, way.*

MINUS: colloquial for *lacking* or *without.*

MR., MRS.: in American usage the abbreviations are followed by a period and are now rarely written out except ironically.

MYSELF: often improperly used as a substitute for *I* or *me.*

NEVER-THE-LESS: should be written as one solid word (*nevertheless*).

NOT TOO: colloquial for *not very.*

NOWHERES: incorrect for *nowhere.*

OBTAIN: often pretentious for *get.*

OF: *could of, may of, might of, must of, should of, would of* are often used incorrectly for *could have, may have, might have, must have, should have, would have.*

OFF OF, OFF FROM: a doubling of prepositions that should be reduced to *off* (She stepped *off* the escalator). However, verb-adverb combinations ending with *off* may be followed by *of* or *from* (The helicopter *took off from* the roof).

ONE AND THE SAME: needless repetition.

ONLY: should be placed in the sentence according to the meaning intended;

contrast the following meanings: *Only* men work in these rooms. Men *only* work in these rooms. Men work in *only* these rooms.

OUTSIDE OF: *of* is usually superfluous; *outside of* should not be used as a sub; stitute for *aside from, except, besides.*

PERSONS, PEOPLE: *persons* is used when the separateness of the individuals in a group is stressed (Five *persons* applied for the job); *people* is used when a large, indefinite, and anonymous mass is meant (Jackson was a man of the *people*).

PLAN ON: the idiom is *plan to.*

PLENTY: should not be used adverbially as a substitute for *very,* as in *plenty good* or *plenty tired.*

PLUS: colloquial for *in addition to, having something added.*

PRACTICAL, PRACTICABLE: *practical* stresses effectiveness as tested by actual experience; *practicable* stresses capability of being put into effect (Before the era of electronics, television did not seem *practicable;* today, however, it is only one of the *practical* applications of the science).

PRETTY: colloquial for *rather, somewhat, very.* (Faulty: He is a *pretty* good clerk. Improved: He is a *rather* good clerk. He is a *very* good clerk.)

PRINCIPAL, PRINCIPLE: often confused: *Principal* may be used as a modifier meaning *first in importance,* or as a noun naming a person or a thing of chief importance; *principle* is always a noun meaning *fundamental truth* or *motive force.*

REASON WHY: *why* is redundant. See also BECAUSE.

SEEING THAT, SEEING AS HOW: an appropriate subordinating conjunction (*since, because,* etc.) should be substituted for these phrases.

SO: colloquial as a conjunction meaning *with the result that* between independent clauses. Colloquial as an intensive (He's *so* handsome); substitute *very.*

SOME TIME, SOMETIME, SOMETIMES: *some time* is used when a vague lapse of time is stressed (It has been *some time* since the objects were first sighted); *sometime,* used as an adverb, means at some unspecified time, usually in the future (He will come back *sometime*), and, used as an adjective, it means *having been formerly* (the *sometime* president of the company); *sometimes* means on various occasions, usually unspecified (*Sometimes* I wish I were still working there).

–STYLE, –TYPE: redundant or parasitic suffixes to adjectives.

SURE: an adjective used colloquially as an adverb, as in "He was *sure* thorough."

THEIR, THERE, THEY'RE: frequently confused in spelling: *Their* is the possessive form of *they; there* is an adverb meaning *in that place; they're* is a contraction of *they are.*

TOO: overused as a substitute for *very.*

TRY AND: colloquial for *try to.*

WHILE: frequently overused as a substitute for *although, but,* and *whereas.*

WITHOUT: improperly used for *unless* ("I can't go *without* I get some money" should be changed to "I can't go *unless* I get some money").

YOU: often improperly used indefinitely, in the sense of *a person, anyone, someone, one.*

PART FIVE

Finding Facts and Figures

"YOU'VE BEEN MADE the head of the plant in Jefferson City, Missouri? Er . . . just how big a city is it?"

"The number of chemical elements? Well, over a hundred, certainly. We'd better look it up."

"Will you get me a list of about ten good books on cost accounting?"

Students, secretaries, businessmen—all of us—are often faced with such questions. We "look up" the answers, and that's one form of research

The subject for research might be the history of shipbuilding, the habits of kangaroos, the advertising rates for a metropolitan newspaper, the best hotel in Sioux City, Iowa, or the airline schedule between Detroit and Nairobi.

Resourcefulness often brings greater recognition for a researcher than does any other quality. Besides being an important part of general efficiency, it enables one to build up a reputation for knowing virtually everything.

Digging out information is first a matter of knowing *where* to dig. Following are sources of information with which all of us should be acquainted:

REFERENCE WORKS

Dictionaries. Your dictionary is indispensable in finding definitions of words and phrases, synonyms, geographical names, the usage of words, the derivations of words from foreign languages, and the determination of spelling and hyphenation.

Desk-size American dictionaries, known as "college editions," will prove to be most useful to students and secretaries. The publishers of this volume are proud to be able to recommend their own highly praised book, available in several editions, entitled:

Webster's New World Dictionary of the American Language, Second College Edition.

Some offices, families, and most libraries will also have an unabridged dictionary, larger in vocabulary coverage than the "college" editions. The principal dictionary of this scope is *Webster's Third New International Dictionary of the English Language* (Merriam).

Books of Synonyms and Antonyms. Synonyms and antonyms are groups of words with like or opposite meanings, respectively. "Sharp" and "keen" are synonyms, while "sharp" and "dull" are antonyms. Here again your dictionary is a useful tool, but you may want a richer resource. A *thesaurus* ("a treasury or storehouse") of synonyms and antonyms is then recommended; the best known is *Roget's International Thesaurus,* but the publishers can also recommend their *Webster's New World Thesaurus,* edited by Charlton Laird.

Books of Quotations. Of the many volumes of quotations, the most useful are John Bartlett's *Familiar Quotations,* H. L. Mencken's *New Dictionary of Quotations on Historical Principles,* and the *Oxford Dictionary of Quotations.*

Books on Usage. The most concise advice on usage can be found in *Elements of Style* by William Strunk and E. B. White. The conservative view on usage is best represented by H. W. Fowler's *Dictionary of Modern English Usage,* while the liberal point of view is represented by Bergen and Cornelia Evans' *Dictionary of Contemporary American Usage.* Many writers use as their reference *The Careful Writer* by Theodore M. Bernstein.

Encyclopedias. A general encyclopedia is a good reference source because it summarizes what otherwise might take hours of reading to discover. Good encyclopedias also contain maps and lists of books on the subjects treated (bibliographies). Three of the standard multivolume works that are revised periodically are the *Encyclopaedia Britannica* (24 vols.), generally considered the finest reference set, *Collier's Encyclopedia* (24 vols.), and *Encyclopedia Americana* (30 vols.). A good one-volume work is the *Columbia Encyclopedia.*

Atlases and Gazetteers. The best atlases, or books of maps and geographical data, are constantly being revised to show changing boundaries and the formation of new countries. The best general reference atlases are the *Ambassador World Atlas* (Hammond), the *International Atlas* (Rand McNally), the *National Geographic Atlas of the World* (National Geographic Society), and the *Times Atlas of the World* (Houghton Mifflin).

Gazetteers, which are dictionaries or indexes of geographic names, include the *Columbia Lippincott Gazetteer of the World* and *Webster's Geographical Dictionary* (Merriam). Extensive listing of geographical names are also contained in the atlases noted above.

Yearbooks and Almanacs. Although an almanac was originally and primarily a book of tables with astronomical information, data on tides, sunrise, etc., a number of commercial yearbooks and almanacs of a much broader scope are on the market. *The World Almanac and Book of Facts* and the *Information Please Almanac* are perhaps the best known. Both books are handy, inexpensive annual guides which give summaries of world history and politics, economic and statistical data, and facts on scores of subjects of current interest, from sports to State histories.

Among the standard hardcover yearbooks available in most libraries are the *Facts on File Yearbook* (*Facts on File* is a weekly periodical with a single volume, the yearbook, published at the end of each year), the *International Yearbook and Statesman's Who's Who,* the *Statesman's Year-Book,* and the *Political Handbook and Atlas of the World.*

Directories. The volumes listing individuals and institutions in specialized fields are far too numerous to mention. The following titles—a few of the countless commercial, professional, biographical, and other types of directories—suggest the usefulness of these books:

Commercial directories (lists of companies or institutions)—

Thomas' Register of American Manufacturers

American Book Trade Directory

Kelley's Directory of Merchants, Manufacturers, and Shippers of the World

American Library Annual

Directory of American Firms Operating in Foreign Countries

National Trade and Professional Associations of the United States

Professional directories (lists of lawyers, doctors, teachers, and members of other recognized professions)—

American Medical Directory

Martindale-Hubbell Law Directory

Who's Who in Insurance

Who's Who in American Education

Leaders in Education

Who's Who in Engineering

The World of Learning

American Men and Women of Science

Who's Who in Finance and Industry

Who's Who in Computers and Data Processing

Biographical directories—
Who's Who in America
Who's Who (British version)
Who's Who of American Women
International Who's Who
Who's Who in the World
Italian-American Who's Who

City directories—These are intended to give the name, address, and occupation of each resident of the cities for which they are issued. They frequently become out of date shortly after publication. In the cross index at the back of the book, entries are made by street and number so that, by looking up a certain address, one can discover who lives there.

Telephone directories—In the larger cities, telephone directories of other large cities are usually on file at the central telephone offices and in libraries that have comprehensive reference departments. They are valuable not only for the telephone numbers listed, but for the street addresses as well. Telephone companies also publish directories in which entries are made under streets and numbers so that, given a certain address, they can tell whether there is a phone at that place. Although these directories are not issued to the public, the information is sometimes given out by the telephone operator.

If you had to secure a quantity of dry ice so that you could send a dozen brook trout in first-class condition to a friend or favored customer, the problem of finding a dealer in that unusual article might be difficult without the Classified Telephone Directory. These "yellow pages" list the names, addresses, and telephone numbers of business houses, merchants, and professionals according to their specialties. Most big-city directories have indexes.

Other directories and lists—
Congressional Directory for the Use of the United States Congress (Gives comprehensive information regarding the legislative, judicial, and executive departments of the government, including biographical sketches of members of Congress and lists of members of diplomatic and consular services.)

Education Directory (Published by the U.S. Office of Education, it lists educational institutions, national and state educational officials and associations, county, town, and district superintendents, college presidents, etc.)

Patterson's American Education (One of several lists of schools, colleges, and other educational institutions in the U.S.)

Handbook of Private Schools
Directory of Directors
Official Catholic Directory
Yearbook of American Churches
Yearbook of International Organizations
Directory of Special Libraries and Information Centers
Research Centers Directory

It is unwise to use these directories in compiling mailing lists, since even the best is not perfect or up-to-date. Professional mailing list agencies, though expensive, are more reliable for this task.

Indexes to Various Subjects. Recourse to the proper indexes will uncover many important newspaper and magazine articles that may answer questions arising in your work. Such indexes list thousands of subjects and the newspapers, periodicals, etc. where articles on those matters can be found. Individual subjects in various fields are indexed in the following reference books:

Cumulative Book Index (Lists all currently published books.)
The New York Times (Possibly the most comprehensive index of news, politics, scientific progress, international development, etc.)
Readers' Guide to Periodical Literature
United States Catalogue (Lists all books printed in the U.S., beginning in 1898; superseded by the *Cumulative Book Index.*)
Books in Print (Lists current books by title, author, and subject.)
Education Index
Book Review Digest
Index Medicus
Business Periodical Index
Applied Science and Technology Index
Social Sciences & Humanities Index
Biological and Agricultural Index
Funk & Scott Index of Corporations and Industries
Index to Periodical Articles By and About Negroes
Index to Little Magazines
Bibliography of Medical Reviews (Part of *Index Medicus,* but also published separately.)
Catholic Periodical and Literature Index

The question will arise as to how many of the reference books listed above should be purchased for home or business use. There can be no general answer. If you find that you must visit or phone the library frequently to get information from certain books, it might be wise to buy them. But a shelf of unused books serves the dubious purpose of decoration. It is more important for you to familiarize yourself with what is available and to know where to look.

If you are asked to get the name of a paper manufacturer in Calcutta, the digest of an article on fire hose that appeared in *The New York Times* sometime in August, 1908, or the rate for sending a telegram to Belgium, just remember that there are many research avenues open and many people and books to help you.

PUBLIC LIBRARIES

The public-library system of the United States has a high standard of helpfulness and courtesy. It is exceptional when a reference librarian is not alert to your requests for information. In any part of the country, the great majority of librarians are not only willing but eager to help.

At libraries you will find books on special subjects, both technical and general, including the reference books listed above. You will also find information on government activities, current events, current biographies, scientific advances, industrial and commercial developments, and many other subjects.

The larger libraries have photostat or microfilm departments which, at a moderate price, supply reproductions of newspaper and magazine articles and of illustrations from books and periodicals.

The habit of going to the library for research will uncover many hitherto unsuspected sources of information. In using reference books, always check the date of publication; if a book was published in 1934, the data it contains may have no particular value today.

In making notes for your future use, be sure to cite the year in which the book, magazine, or newspaper was published. In the case of a book, the publisher and the city in which it was published should be included.

U.S. GOVERNMENT

The United States Government is the largest publisher in the country. The Superintendent of Documents, United States Government Printing Office, Washington, D.C. 20402, has catalogues of available government publications which cover a wide range of subjects. Some of these bulletins and pamphlets are free, but for some a small charge is made. Write the Superintendent of Documents to receive a monthly listing or if you do not know which government department or agency is the source of the information you are seeking. Otherwise, address the department or agency itself:

Department of State. For information regarding the diplomatic relations of the United States with foreign countries; ambassadors, ministers, consuls, and their staffs; matters pertaining to the activities of American citizens in foreign countries; and passports for Americans traveling abroad.

Department of Defense. For information regarding the armed forces, training academies, and military installations of the United States.

Department of the Treasury. For information about revenues and moneys due the government, minting and coinage, income taxes, duties, prosecution of counterfeiters, the Federal Reserve System, and similar subjects. (Inquiries about smuggling, law enforcement in coastal and other navigable waters of the United States, and assistance to vessels in distress should be addressed to the United States Coast Guard in the Department of Transportation.) Also address the Treasury Department concerning United States Savings Bonds, the United States Secret Service, and narcotics regulations and their enforcement.

Department of Justice. For information regarding the administration of the system of Federal courts and the supervision of Federal prisons, immigration, naturalization, the violation of Federal laws, and the Federal Bureau of Investigation.

Department of the Interior. For information about government lands, national parks, national monuments, Indian reservations, national forests, the Geological Survey, reclamation of wastelands, control of mines, etc.

Department of Agriculture. For information regarding crops in general, statistics relating to agricultural production, the Forest Service, home economics, the combating of injurious insects and animal and plant pests and diseases, road building, marketing, farm prices, and other agricultural matters.

Department of Commerce. For information on the national census, standards of weights and measures, government fisheries, lighthouses, navigable waters, coast and geodetic surveys, aviation, radio and shipping, the Patent Office, the National Weather Service, etc.

Department of Labor. For information on the welfare and improvement of wage earners' conditions in the United States, statistics relating to labor, employees' compensation, wages and hours regulations, etc.

Department of Health, Education, and Welfare. For information on food and drug laws, education, social security, vocational rehabilitation, and the Public Health Service (for which, address the Surgeon General).

Department of Housing and Urban Development. For information on urban renewal and public and Federal housing.

Department of Transportation. For information about national transportation policies, including programs involving transportation by air, road, and rail as well as programs concerned with urban mass transportation. Also address the Transportation Department for information about the United States Coast Guard.

Postal Service. For information on postal rates, laws, and services.

PUBLIC ORGANIZATIONS AND FOUNDATIONS

The secretaries of organizations of a more or less public nature are usually willing to give information concerning that organization to the public. Directories of associations, such as *Foundation Directory, Encyclopedia of Associations,* or *Association Index: A Source-List of Directories and Other Publications Listing Associations,* list these organizations with addresses and, in many cases, the names of the secretaries. Some of the popular almanacs also list such associations.

PRIVATE INSTITUTIONS

Publicity Departments. Large corporations, groups supporting causes, and public institutions such as universities, generally maintain departments of public information which handle inquiries regarding their products, services, policies, and plans. It is obvious that the information they give out will seek to promote their own interests, but much valuable information may be secured from such sources. These organizations find it expedient to avoid giving out erroneous or misleading facts. Inquiries or requests for photographs should be addressed to the director of public relations of the company or organization.

Travel Agencies. In most cities and towns, full information regarding transportation schedules and rates is on file with airline, bus, railroad, or ship offices or agencies. Travel agencies give efficient service free.

Newspaper offices. Newspapers maintain libraries or "morgues" which are sometimes open to the public for reference work. Here are filed thousands of news clippings under alphabetically arranged subject headings. Editors of special departments, such as society, finance, sports, etc., keep their own files and are often helpful. As well, most photographic departments of newspapers make prints available to the public for a nominal cost. *The New York Times* has developed a computerized research system available to other newspapers, public libraries, business libraries, and so on.

Appendixes

ABBREVIATIONS

A

A, in *chemistry,* argon.

A., Academy; acre; America; American; angstrom unit; April; Artillery.

a., about; acre; acres; active; adjective; alto; ampere; anonymous; answer.

A.A., Associate in Arts.

AAA, Agricultural Adjustment Administration.

A.A.A., Amateur Athletic Association; American Automobile Association; Automobile Association of America.

A.A.A.L., American Academy of Arts and Letters.

A.A.A.S., American Academy of Arts and Sciences; American Association for the Advancement of Science.

A.A.E., American Association of Engineers.

A.A.S., American Academy of Sciences; (*Academiae Americanae Socius*), Fellow of the American Academy.

A.A.U., Amateur Athletic Union.

A.A.U.P., American Association of University Professors; Association of American University Presses.

A.A.U.W., American Association of University Women.

ab., about.

A.B. (*Artium Baccalaureus*), Bachelor of Arts.

A.B., a.b., able-bodied (seaman).

A.B.A., American Bankers Association; American Bar Association.

abb., abbess; abbot.

abbr., abbrev., abbreviated; abbreviation.

A.B.C., ABC, American Broadcasting Company.

abr., abridge; abridged; abridgment.

abs., absent; absolute; abstract.

Ac, in *chemistry,* actinium.

A/C, a/c, in *bookkeeping,* account; account current.

A.C., Air Corps; Armored Corps; Army Corps; (*Ante Christum*), before Christ.

A.C., a.c., in *electricity,* alternating current.

acad., academic; academy.

acc., acceptance; accompanied; according; account; accountant.

acct., account.

A.C.S., American Chemical Society; American College of Surgeons.

A/cs pay., accounts payable.

A/cs rec., accounts receivable.

act., active.

actg., acting.

ad., adverb; advertisement.

A.D. (*Anno Domini*), in the year of the Lord.

a.d., after date.

A.D.A., American Dental Association; Americans for Democratic Action.

A.D.C., aide-de-camp.

ad inf. (*ad infinitum*), endlessly; forever; without limit.

ad int. (*ad interim*), in the meantime.

adj., adjective; adjourned; adjudged.

Adjt., Adjutant.

ad-lib (*ad libitum*), to improvise; extemporize.

Adm., Admiral; Admiralty.

adm., administrator.

adv., adverb; adverbial; advertisement.

ad val. (*ad valorem*), according to value.

advt., advertisement.

AEC, Atomic Energy Commission.

A.E.F., American Expeditionary Force (or Forces).

AF, Air Force.

Af., Afr., Africa; African.

A.F., a.f., audio frequency.

A.F.A.M., Ancient Free and Accepted Masons.

AFL–CIO, American Federation of Labor and Congress of Industrial Organizations.

aft., afternoon.

Ag (*argentum*), in *chemistry,* silver.

A.G., Adjutant General; Attorney General.

agcy., agency.

agr., agric., agricultural; agriculture; agriculturist.

agt., agent.

A.I.C., American Institute of Chemists.

AID, Agency for International Development.

A.I.E.E., American Institute of Electrical Engineers.

A.I.G.A., American Institute of Graphic Arts.

A.I.M.E., American Institute of Mining Engineers; Associate of the Institute of Mechanical Engineers.

Al, in *chemistry,* aluminum.

A.L., American League; American Legion.

Ala., Alabama.

A.L.A., American Library Association.

Alas., Alaska.

Ald., Aldm., Alderman.

alg., algebra.

A.L.P., American Labor Party.

alt., alternate; alternating; altitude; alto.

Alta., Alberta.

alum., aluminum.

AM, A.M., amplitude modulation.

Am, in *chemistry,* americium.

Am., America; American.

A.M. (*anno mundi*), in the year of the world; (*Artium Magister*), Master of Arts.

A.M., a.m. (*ante meridiem*), before noon.

A.M.A., American Management Association; American Medical Association.

Amb., Ambassador.

Amer., America; American.

amp., amperage; ampere; amperes.

amt., amount.

an., anonymous; (*anno*), in the year.

anal., analogous; analogy; analysis.

anat., anatomical; anatomist; anatomy.

ANC, Army Nurse Corps.

anc., ancient; anciently.

and., andante.

ann., annual; annuity.

anon., anonymous.

ans., answer.

ant., antiquity; antiquities; antonym.

anthrop., anthropol., anthropological; anthropology.

antiq., antiqu., antiquarian; antiquities; antiquity.

AP, A.P., accounts payable; Associated Press.

Ap., Apostle; April.

APO, Army Post Office.

Apoc., Apocalypse; Apocrypha; Apocryphal.

app., appended; appendix; appointed; apprentice.

appar., apparently.

approx., approximate; approximately.

Apr., April.

Apt., apt., apartment.

Ar., Arabic; Aramaic.

a.r. (*anno regni*), in the year of the reign.

A.R.A., American Railway Association; Associate of the Royal Academy.

Arab., Arabian; Arabic.

ARC, American Red Cross.

Arch., Archbishop.

arch., archaic; archipelago; architect; architectural; architecture.

archaeol., archaeology.

Archd., Archdeacon; Archduke.

A.R.C.S., Associate of the Royal College of Science; Associate of Royal College of Surgeons.

Arg., Argentina; Argentine.

arith., arithmetic; arithmetical.

Ariz., Arizona.

Ark., Arkansas.

Arm., Armenian; Armoric.

arr., arranged; arrangements; arrival; arrives.

art., article; artificial; artillery; artist.

arty., artillery.

A.R.U., American Railway Union.

As, in *chemistry,* arsenic.

As., Asia; Asian; Asiatic.

A.S., Academy of Science; Air Service; Anglo-Saxon.

a.s., assistant secretary.

A.S.A., Acoustical Society of America; American Standards Association; American Statistical Association.

ASC, Army Service Corps.

ASCAP, American Society of Composers, Authors, and Publishers.

A.S.P.C.A., American Society for Prevention of Cruelty to Animals.

ass., assistant; association; assorted.

ASSC, Air Service Signal Corps.

assn., association.

assoc., associate; associated; association.
asst., assistant.
Assyr., Assyrian.
astr., astron., astronomer; astronomical; astronomy.
astrol., astrologer; astrological; astrology.
At, in *chemistry,* astatine.
at., atmosphere; atomic; attorney.
Atl., Atlantic.
atm., atmosphere; atmospheric.
at. no., atomic number.
ATS, Army Transport Service.
att., attorney.
atty., attorney.
Atty. Gen., Attorney General.
at. wt., atomic weight.
Au (*aurum*), in *chemistry,* gold.
aud., auditor.
Aug., August.
Aust., Austria; Austria-Hungary; Austrian.
auth., author; authoress; authorized.
Auth. Ver., A.V., Authorized Version (of the Bible).
aux., auxil., auxiliary.
a/v, ad valorem, according to value.
av., average; avoirdupois.
A.V.C., American Veterans Committee.
avdp., avoirdupois.
Ave., Av., Avenue.
avoir., avoirdupois.
AVS, Army Veterinary Service.
A.W.O.L., a.w.o.l., absent or (absence) without leave.

B

B, in *chemistry,* boron.
B., in *medicine,* bacillus; Bible; Boston; British; Brotherhood.
B., b., bachelor; battery; bay; bicuspid; bolivar; book; born; brother.
Ba, in *chemistry,* barium.
B.A. (*Baccalaureus Artium*), Bachelor of Arts.
bact., bacteriology.
B.Ag., B.Agr., Bachelor of Agriculture.
bal., balance; balancing.
bank., banking.
Bap., Bapt., Baptist.
bar., barometer; barrel; barrister.

B.Ar., B.Arch., Bachelor of Architecture.
B.A.S., B.A.Sc., Bachelor of Agricultural Science; Bachelor of Applied Science.
bat., batt., battalion; battery.
B.B., Blue Book.
B.B.A., Bachelor of Business Administration.
B.B.C., British Broadcasting Corporation.
bbl., barrel or barrels.
B.C., Bachelor of Chemistry; Bachelor of Commerce; before Christ; British Columbia.
BCC, bcc, blind carbon copy.
B.C.E., Bachelor of Chemical Engineering; Bachelor of Civil Engineering.
B.C.L., Bachelor of Civil Law.
B.C.S., Bachelor of Chemical Science.
bd., board; bond; bound; bundle.
B/D, bank draft; bills discounted.
B.D., Bachelor of Divinity; bills discounted.
bd.ft., board feet; board foot.
bdl., bundle.
bds., boards; bundles.
B.D.S., Bachelor of Dental Surgery.
Be, in *chemistry,* beryllium.
B.E., Bachelor of Education; Bachelor of Engineering; Bank of England; Board of Education.
B.E., B/E, b.e., bill of exchange.
B.E.E., Bachelor of Electrical Engineering.
bef., before.
B.E.F., British Expeditionary Force.
Bel., Belg., Belgian; Belgium.
bet., between.
bf, b.f., in *printing,* boldface.
B/F, in *bookkeeping,* brought forward.
B.F., Bachelor of Finance; Bachelor of Forestry.
B.F.A., Bachelor of Fine Arts.
bg., bag.
Bi, in *chemistry,* bismuth.
Bib., Bible; Biblical.
bibliog., bibliography.
bicarb., sodium bicarbonate; baking soda.
biog., biographer; biographical; biography.
biol., biological; biologist; biology.
Bk, in *chemistry,* berkelium.
bk., bank; block; book.

bkg., banking.
bkkpg., bookkeeping.
bkpt., bankrupt.
bkt., basket; bracket.
B/L, b.l., bill of lading.
bl., bale; bales; barrel; barrels; black.
B.L., Bachelor of Laws; Bachelor of Letters.
bldg., building.
B.Lit., B.Litt. (*Baccalaureus Lit[t]erarum*), Bachelor of Letters; Bachelor of Literature.
B.LL. (*Baccalaureus Legum*), Bachelor of Laws.
BLS, Bureau of Labor Statistics.
B.L.S., Bachelor of Library Science.
Blvd., Boulevard.
B.M. (*Baccalaureus Medicinae*), Bachelor of Medicine; (*Baccalaureus Musicae*), Bachelor of Music.
B.M.A., British Medical Association.
B.M.E., Bachelor of Mechanical Engineering; Bachelor of Mining Engineering.
B.Mus., Bachelor of Music.
B.N., bank note.
B/O, in *bookkeeping*, brought over.
B.O., Board of Ordnance; body odor.
b.o., back order; bad order; box office; branch office; broker's order; buyer's option.
Bol., Bolivia; Bolivian.
bor., boron; borough.
bot., botanical; botanist; botany; bottle.
B.O.T., Board of Trade.
bp., birthplace; bishop.
B.P. (*Baccalaureus Pharmaciae*), Bachelor of Pharmacy; (*Baccalaureus Philosophiae*), Bachelor of Philosophy.
b.p., below proof; boiling point.
b.p., B/P, bill of parcels; bills payable.
B. pay., bills payable.
B.P.E., Bachelor of Physical Education.
B.P.O.E., Benevolent and Protective Order of Elks.
Br, in *chemistry*, bromine.
Br., Britain; British.
br., branch; brig; bronze; brother.
b.r., B/R, B. Rec., b. rec., bills receivable.

Braz., Brazil; Brazilian.
B.R.C.S., British Red Cross Society.
Brig. Gen., Brigadier General.
Brit., Britain; Britannia; British.
bro., brother.
bros., brothers.
B.S., Bachelor of Science; Bachelor of Surgery; British Standard.
b.s., balance sheet.
b.s., B/S, bill of sale.
B.S.A., Boy Scouts of America.
B.Sc. (*Baccalaureus Scientiae*), Bachelor of Science.
B.S.Ed., Bachelor of Science in Education.
bskt., basket.
Bs/L, bills of lading.
B.S.P., Bachelor of Science in Pharmacy.
B.T., B.Th. (*Baccalaureus Theologiae*), Bachelor of Theology.
B.T.U., Btu, B.t.u., British thermal unit (or units).
bu., bureau; bushel; bushels.
bul., bull., bulletin.
Bulg., Bulgaria; Bulgarian.
B.W.I., British West Indies.
bx., box; boxes.
bx., boxes.
Bz., benzene.

C

C, in *chemistry*, carbon.
C., Catholic; Congress; Conservative; Corps; Court.
C., c., capacity; carbon; carton; case; cent or cents; centigrade; centimeter; century; chapter; circa; copy; copyright; corps; cost; cubic; hundredweight.
Ca, in *chemistry*, calcium.
ca., cathode; centiare; circa (about).
C/A, capital accountant; credit account; current account.
C.A., Central America; Coast Artillery; Court of Appeal.
C.A., c.a., chartered accountant; chief accountant; commercial agent; consular agent; controller of accounts.
CAA, Civil Aeronautics Authority.

CAB, Civil Aeronautics Board.

C.A.F., c.a.f., cost and freight; cost, assurance, and freight.

Cal., California; large calorie (or calories).

cal., calendar; caliber; small calorie (or calories).

Calif., California.

Can., Canada; Canadian.

cap., capital; capitalize; captain.

caps., capitals (capital letters).

Capt., Captain.

car., carat; carats.

Card., Cardinal.

CARE, Co-operative for American Remittances to Europe, Inc.

cat., catalogue; catechism.

Cath., Catholic; (also cath.), cathedral.

cav., cavalier; cavalry.

C/B, c.b., cashbook.

C.B.S., CBS, Columbia Broadcasting System.

cc., chapters.

cc., c.c., carbon copy; cubic centimeter; cubic centimeters.

C.C., c.c., carbon copy; cashier's check; chief clerk; circuit court; city council; civil court; county clerk; county commissioner; county council; county court.

C.C.A., Chief Clerk of the Admiralty; Circuit Court of Appeals; County Court of Appeals.

CCC, Commodity Credit Corporation.

ccm., centimeters.

C.C.P., Court of Common Pleas.

C.C.R., Commission on Civil Rights.

Cd, in chemistry, cadmium.

c.d., cash discount.

Ce, in chemistry, cerium.

C.E., Chemical Engineer; Chief Engineer; Church of England; Civil Engineer.

C.E.F., Canadian Expeditionary Force (or Forces).

cen., central; century.

cent., centigrade; centimeter; central; century.

cert., certif., certificate.

Cf, in chemistry, californium.

cf. (confer), compare.

c/f, in bookkeeping, carried forward.

C.F., c.f., cost and freight.

C.F.I., c.f.i., cost, freight, and insurance.

cg., centigram; centigrams.

C.G., Coast Guard; Consul General.

ch., chapter; chief; child; church.

c.h., courthouse; customhouse.

chap., chaplain; chapter.

Ch.E., Chem. E., Chemical Engineer.

chem., chemical; chemist; chemistry.

chg., charge.

chgd., charged.

chgs., charges.

Chin., China; Chinese.

chm., chmn., chairman.

Chr., Christ; Christian.

Chron., Chronicles.

chron., chronol., chronological; chronology.

chs., chapters.

CIA, Central Intelligence Agency.

C.I.C., Commander in Chief.

C.I.F., c.i.f., cost, insurance, and freight.

CIO, C.I.O., Congress of Industrial Organizations.

cit., citation; cited; citizen.

civ., civil; civilian.

ck., cask; check.

Cl, in chemistry, chlorine.

cl., centiliter; centiliters; claim; class; clause; clearance; clerk; cloth.

c.l., carload; carload lots; civil law.

C.L.D., Doctor of Civil Law.

clk., clerk; clock.

Cm, in chemistry, curium.

cm., centimeter; centimeters.

cml., commercial.

C/N, circular note; credit note.

Co, in chemistry, cobalt.

C/O, cash order.

c/o, c.o., care of; carried over.

Co., co., company; county.

C.O., Commanding Officer; Conscientious Objector.

coad., coadjutor.

C.O.D., c.o.d., cash on delivery; collect on delivery.

C. of S., Chief of Staff.

Col., Colombia; Colombian; Colonel; Colorado; Colossians.

col., collected; collector; college; colonial; colony; color; colored; column.

coll., colleague; collect; collection; collective; collector; college; colloquial.

collab., collaboration; collaborator.

collat., collateral; collaterally.

colloq., colloquial; colloquialism; colloquially.

Colo., Colorado.

Com., Commander; Commission; Commissioner; Committee; Commodore; Communist.

com., comedy; comma; commentary; commerce; commercial; common; commonly; commune; communication; community.

comb., combination.

comdg., commanding.

Comdr., Commander.

Comdt., Commandant.

comm., commander; commentary; commerce; commission; committee; communication.

comp., companion; comparative; compare; compiled; compiler; composer; composition; compound; compounded.

Comr., Commissioner.

con., concerto; conclusion; connection; consolidate; consul.

conc., concentrate; concentrated; concentration; concerning.

Confed., Confederate.

Cong., Congregational; Congregationalist; Congress; Congressional.

conj., conjugation; conjunction; conjunctive.

Conn., Connecticut.

cons., Cons., constable; constitution. nant; constitution; construction.

cons., Cons., constable; constitution.

Cont., Continental.

cont., containing; contents; continent; continue; continued; contra; contract.

contemp., contemporary.

contr., contract; contracted; contraction; contralto; contrary; contrasted; control; controller.

contrib., contributor.

co-op., coöp., coop., co-operative.

cop., copper; copyrighted.

Cor., Corinthians; Coroner.

cor., corner; coroner; correct; corrected; correction; correspondence; correspondent; corresponding.

Corp., Corporal.

corp., corpn., corporation.

corr., corrected; correspond; correspondence; correspondent; corrupt; corrupted; corruption.

cos, cosine.

Cos., cos., companies; counties.

cp., compare.

C.P., Chief Patriarch; Command Post; Common Pleas; Common Prayer; Communist Party.

c.p., candle power; chemically pure.

C.P.A., c.p.a., Certified Public Accountant.

C.P.H., Certificate in Public Health.

Cpl., Corporal.

C.P.O., Chief Petty Officer.

CPS, Certified Professional Secretary.

Cr, in *chemistry,* chromium.

cr., credit; creditor; creek; crown.

C.R., Costa Rica.

crim., criminal.

crit., critical; criticism; criticized.

cryst., crystalline; crystallography.

Cs, in *chemistry,* cesium.

C.S., Christian Science; Christian Scientist.

C.S., c.s., capital stock; civil service.

CSC, Civil Service Commission.

csk., cask.

C.S.T., Central Standard Time.

Ct., Connecticut; Count.

ct., cent; certificate; county; court.

c.t., certified teacher; commercial traveler.

ctf., certificate.

ctg., cartage.

ctr., center.

cts., cents.

Cu (*cuprum*), in *chemistry,* copper.

cu., cub., cubic.

cu. cm., cubic centimeter; cubic centimeters.

cur., currency; current (of the present day, week, month, or year).

CWA, Civil Works Administration.
cwt., hundredweight.
cyl., cylinder.
C.Z., Canal Zone.

D

D., December; Democrat; Democratic; Duchess; Duke; Dutch.
d., date; daughter; day; days; dead; degree; delete; density; deputy; deserter; diameter; died; dime; director; dividend; dollar; dorsal; dose.
da., daughter; day; days.
D.A., District Attorney.
Dan., Danish.
d. and s., demand and supply.
D.A.R., Daughters of the American Revolution.
D.Arch., Doctor of Architecture.
D.A.V., Disabled American Veterans.
db, decibel.
d.b., daybook.
dbl., double.
D.C., in *music, da capo;* Dental Corps; District of Columbia; Doctor of Chiropractic.
D.C., d.c., direct current.
D.C.L., Doctor of Civil Law.
D.Cn.L., Doctor of Canon Law.
D.C.S., Deputy Clerk of Sessions; Doctor of Christian Science; Doctor of Commercial Science.
dd., d/d, delivered.
D.D. (*Divinitatis Doctor*), Doctor of Divinity.
D.D., D/D, demand draft.
D.D.S., Doctor of Dental Surgery.
D.D.Sc., Doctor of Dental Science.
DDT, dichlorodiphenyltrichloroethane.
D.E., D.Eng., Doctor of Engineering.
deb., debenture.
Dec., December.
dec., deceased; decimeter; declaration; declension; declination; decrease.
decl., declension.
def., defendant; defense; deferred; defined; definite; definition.
deg., degree; degrees.
Del., Delaware.
del., delegate; delete.

Dem., Democrat; Democratic.
Den., Denmark.
dent., dental; dentist; dentistry.
dep., department; departs; departure; deponent; deposed; deposit; deputy.
dept., department; deponent; deputy.
der., deriv., derivation; derivative; derived.
Deut., Deuteronomy.
D.F.C., Distinguished Flying Cross.
di., dia., diameter.
diag., diagonal; diagram.
dial., dialect; dialectal; dialectic; dialectical.
diam., diameter.
dict., dictated (by); dictator; dictionary.
dif., diff., difference; different.
dig., digest.
dil., dilute.
dim., dimension; (*also* **dimin.**), diminuendo; diminutive.
dis., distance; distant; distribute.
disc., discount; discovered; discoverer.
dist., discount; distance; distant; distinguish; district.
Div., Divinity.
div., diversion, divide; dividend; divine; division; divisor; divorced.
DL, day letter.
D/L, demand loan.
DLF, Development Loan Fund.
D.Lit., D.Litt. (*Doctor Lit[t]erarum*), Doctor of Letters; Doctor of Literature.
D.L.S., Doctor of Library Science.
D.Mus., Doctor of Music.
D.N.B., Dictionary of National Biography.
D/O, d.o., delivery order.
do., ditto.
D.O., District Office; Doctor of Optometry; Doctor of Osteopathy.
dol., dollar.
dols., dollars.
dom., domestic; dominion.
Dom. Rep., Dominican Republic.
doz., dozen; dozens.
D.P., displaced person.
dpt., department; deponent.
D.P.W., Department of Public Works.

Dr., Doctor.
dr., debit; debtor; dram; drams; drawer.
d.r., dead reckoning; deposit receipt.
D.S., D.Sc., Doctor of Science.
D.S.C., Distinguished Service Cross.
D.S.M., Distinguished Service Medal.
D.S.O., District Staff Officer.
D.S.T., Daylight Saving Time.
d.t., delirium tremens; double time.
D.Th., D. Theol., Doctor of Theology.
dup., duplicate.
D.V.M., Doctor of Veterinary Medicine.
D.V.S., Doctor of Veterinary Surgery.
Dy, in *chemistry*, dysprosium.
dz., dozen; dozens.

E

E, in *chemistry*, einsteinium.
E, E., e, e., east; eastern.
E., Earl; Easter; English.
E., e., earth; eastern; engineer; engineering.
ea., each.
E. A., in *psychology*, educational age.
E. & O.E., e. & o.e., errors and omissions excepted.
E.C., Engineering Corps; Established Church.
eccl., eccles., ecclesiastical.
Eccles., Eccl., Ecclesiastes.
Ecclus., Ecclesiasticus.
econ., economic; economics; economy.
ed., edited; edition; editor.
Ed.B., Bachelor of Education.
Ed.D., Doctor of Education.
Ed.M., Master of Education.
educ., education; educational; educator.
E.E., Early English; Electrical Engineering.
e.e., errors excepted.
E.E.C., European Economic Community.
Eg., Egypt; Egyptian.
e.g. (*exempli gratia*), for example.
e.h.p., effective horsepower.
E.I., East India; East Indian; East Indies.
elec., elect., electric; electrical; electricity.
elem., element; elementary; elements.
Eliz., Elizabethan.

E.M.F., e.m.f., EMF, emf, electromotive force.
Emp., Emperor; Empire; Empress.
enc., enclosed; enclosure; encyclopedia.
Eng., England; English.
eng., engine; engineer; engineering; engraved; engraver; engraving.
enl., enlarge; enlarged; enlisted.
Ens., Ensign.
Eph., Ephes., Ephesians.
eq., equal; equalizer; equation; equator; equivalent.
Er, in *chemistry*, erbium.
Esk., Eskimo.
ESP, E.S.P., extrasensory perception.
esp., especially.
Esq., Esqr., Esquire.
est., established; estimated.
E.S.T., Eastern Standard Time.
Esth., Esther.
E.T.A., Estimated Time of Arrival.
et al. (*et alibi*), and elsewhere; (*et alii*), and others.
etc., &c, et cetera.
E.T.D., Estimated Time of Departure.
Eu, in *chemistry*, europium.
Eur., Europe; European.
Ex., Exod., Exodus.
ex., examined; example; except; excepted; exception; exchange; executive; export; extra; extract.
exam., examination.
Exc., Excellency.
exc., excellent; except; excepted; exception; exchange.
exch., exchange; exchequer.
exec., executive; executor.
exp., expenses; export; exported; express.
ext., extension; external; extinct; extra.
Ez., Ezr., Ezra.
Ezek., Ezekiel.

F

F, in *chemistry*, fluorine.
F., Fahrenheit; February; Fellow; France; French; Friday.
F., f., farad; farthing; father; fathom; feet; feminine; fine; fluid; folio; folios;

following; foot; form; in *music,* forte; franc; francs; from.

f.a., fire alarm; freight agent.

FAA, Federal Aviation Agency.

F.A.A.S., Fellow of the American Academy of Arts and Sciences; Fellow of the American Association for the Advancement of Science.

fac., facsimile.

Fah., Fahr., Fahrenheit.

F.A.M., Free and Accepted Masons.

FAO, Food and Agriculture Organization (UN).

f.a.s., free alongside ship.

f.b., freight bill.

FBI, F.B.I., Federal Bureau of Investigation; Federation of British Industries.

f.c., in *printing,* follow copy.

FCA, Farm Credit Administration.

FCC, Federal Communications Commission.

F.D., Fire Department.

FDA, Food and Drug Administration.

FDIC, Federal Deposit Insurance Corporation.

Fe (*ferrum*), in *chemistry,* iron.

Feb., February.

Fed., Federal; Federation.

fem., feminine.

FEPC, Fair Employment Practices Committee.

feud., feudal; feudalism.

ff., folios; following (pages); in *music,* fortissimo.

FFCA, Federal Farm Credit Administration.

FFMC, Federal Farm Mortgage Corporation.

F.F.V., First Families of Virginia.

FHA, Federal Housing Administration.

FHLBB, Federal Home Loan Bank Board.

fict., fiction.

fig., figurative; figuratively; figure; figures.

Fin., Finland; Finnish.

fin., finance; financial.

Finn., Finnish.

fl., floor; flourished; flower; fluid.

Fla., Flor., Florida.

fl. oz., fluid ounce; fluid ounces.

FM, frequency modulation.

Fm, in *chemistry,* fermium.

fm., fathom; from.

F.M., Field Marshall; Foreign Missions.

F.O., Foreign Office.

F.O.B., f.o.b., free on board.

F.O.E., Fraternal Order of Eagles.

fol., folio; following.

for., foreign; forestry.

F.O.R., f.o.r., free on rail.

fp., F.P., f.p., foot-pound; foot-pounds.

F.P., f.p., in *insurance,* fire policy, floating policy; fully paid.

f.p., fp, fp., freezing point.

FPC, Federal Power Commission.

FPO, Fleet Post Office.

FR, full-rate cable.

Fr, in *chemistry,* francium.

Fr., Father; France; *Frau;* French; Friar; Friday.

fr., fragment; franc; francs; frequent; from.

FRB, Federal Reserve Bank; Federal Reserve Board.

freq., frequent; frequently.

Fri., Friday.

frt., freight.

FSA, Farm Security Administration; Federal Security Agency.

FSCC, Federal Surplus Commodities Corporation.

FSR, F.S.R., Field Service Regulations.

ft., feet; foot; fortification.

FTC, Federal Trade Commission.

fth., fthm., fathom.

ft-lb, foot-pound.

fut., future.

F.Y.I., for your information.

G

G., German; Germany; specific gravity.

G., g., gauge; gold; grain; gram; grams; grand; guide; guinea; guineas; gulf.

g., gender; general; genitive.

Ga, in *chemistry,* gallium.

Ga., Gaelic; Gallic; Georgia.

G.A., General Agent; General Assembly.

G.A., G/A, g.a., in *insurance,* general average.

gal., gallon; gallons.

G.A.R., Grand Army of the Republic.

gaz., gazette; gazetteer.

G.B., Great Britain.

g-cal., gram calorie; gram calories.

G.C.D., g.c.d., greatest common divisor.

G.C.F., g.c.f., greatest common factor.

G.C.L.H., Grand Cross of the Legion of Honor.

G.C.M., g.c.m., greatest common measure.

Gd, in *chemistry*, gadolinium.

gds., goods.

Ge, in *chemistry*, germanium.

Gen., General; Genesis; Geneva.

gen., gender; genera; general; generally; generator; generic; genitive; genus.

geneal., genealogy.

genl., general.

Gent., gent., gentleman; gentlemen.

geog., geographer; geographical; geography.

geol., geologic; geological; geologist; geology.

geom., geometric; geometrical; geometrician; geometry.

Ger., German; Germany.

ger., gerund.

G.F.T.U., General Federation of Trade Unions.

g.gr., great gross.

GHQ, General Headquarters.

gi., gill; gills.

Gk., Greek.

gl., glass; gloss.

gloss., glossary.

gm., gram; grams.

G.M., general manager; Grand Master.

Gmc., Germanic.

G.M.T., Greenwich mean time.

GNP, gross national product.

G.O., g.o., general office; general order.

G.O.P., Grand Old Party (Republican Party).

Goth., goth., Gothic.

Gov., gov., government; governor.

Gov. Gen., Governor General.

govt., Govt., government.

G.P., g.p., general practitioner.

G.P.O., General Post Office; (*also* GPO), Government Printing Office.

Gr., Grecian; Greece; Greek.

gr., grade; grain or grains; gram or grams; grammar; great; gross; group.

grad., graduate; graduated.

gram., grammar; grammarian; grammatical.

Gr. Brit., Gr. Br., Great Britain.

gro., gross.

G.S.A., Girl Scouts of America.

GSC, General Staff Corps.

gt., gilt; great.

Gt. Brit., Gt. Br., Great Britain.

guar., guaranteed.

Guat., Guatemala; Guatemalan.

H

H, in *physics*, henry; in *chemistry*, hydrogen.

H., h., harbor; hard; hardness; height; hence; high; hour; hours; hundred; husband.

ha., hectare; hectares.

Hab., Habakkuk.

Hag., Haggai.

Hal., halogen.

Hb, hemoglobin.

H.B.M., His (or Her) Britannic Majesty.

H.C., House of Commons.

H.C.F., h.c.f., highest common factor.

h.c.l., h.c. of l., high cost of living.

hd., head.

hdqrs., headquarters.

HE, H.E., high explosive.

He, in *chemistry*, helium.

H.E., His Eminence; His Excellency.

Heb., Hebrew; Hebrews.

Hf, in *chemistry*, hafnium.

hf., half.

H.F., high frequency.

Hg (*hydrargyrum*), in *chemistry*, mercury.

H.G., His (or Her) Grace; Home Guard.

hgt., height.

H.H., His (or Her) Highness; His Holiness.

H.I., Hawaiian Islands.

H.I.H., His (or Her) Imperial Highness.

hist., historian; historical; history.

H.L., House of Lords.

H.M.S., His (or Her) Majesty's Service, Ship, or Steamer.

Ho, in *chemistry,* holmium.

H.O., head office.

HOLC, Home Owners' Loan Corporation.

Hon., hon., honorable; honorary.

Hond., Honduran; Honduras.

hor., horizon; horizontal.

Hos., Hosea.

hosp., hospital.

H.P., HP, h.p., hp, high pressure; horsepower.

H.Q., Hq., headquarters.

hr., hour; hours.

H.R., Home Rule; House of Representatives.

H.R.H., His (or Her) Royal Highness.

hrs., hours.

ht., heat; height; heights.

hts., heights.

hund., hundred; hundreds.

Hung., Hungarian; Hungary.

hyd., hydraulics; hydrostatics.

hyp., hypotenuse; hypothesis; hypothetical.

I

I, in *chemistry,* iodine.

I., Idaho; Independent; Iowa.

I., i., island; islands; isle; isles.

i., incisor; interest; intransitive.

Ia., Iowa.

i.a. (*in absentia*), in absence; absent.

I.A.M., International Association of Machinists.

ib., ibid. (*ibidem*), in the same place.

IBM, I.B.M., International Business Machines.

ICBM, intercontinental ballistic missile.

ICC, Interstate Commerce Commission.

Ice., Icel., Iceland; Icelandic.

Id., Idaho.

id. (*idem*), the same.

I.D., Intelligence Department.

Ida., Idaho.

IDP, integrated data processing.

i.e. (*id est*), that is.

I.F.S., Irish Free State.

I.G., Inspector General.

ign., ignition; (*ignotus*), unknown.

I.L.G.W.U., ILGWU, International Ladies' Garment Workers Union.

Ill., Illinois.

ill., illus., illust., illustrated; illustration.

ILO, International Labor Organization.

imp., imperative; imperfect; imperial; impersonal; import; imported; importer; imprimatur; imprint.

imper., impv., imperative.

imperf., impf., imperfect.

impers., impersonal.

In, in *chemistry,* indium.

in., inch or inches.

inc., inclosure; included; including; inclusive; income; incorporated; increase.

incl., inclosure; including; inclusive.

incog., incognito.

incorp., incor., incorporated.

Ind., India; Indian; Indiana; Indies.

ind., independent; index; indicative; industrial.

indef., indefinite.

indic., indicating; indicative; indicator.

individ., individual.

Inf., inf., infantry.

inf., infinitive; information; (*infra*), below.

infin., infinitive.

init., initial.

ins., inches; inscribed; insulated; insurance.

insp., inspector.

Inst., Institute; Institution.

inst., instant (the present month); instrumental; installment.

instr., instructor; instrument; instrumental.

int., interest; interim; interior; interjection; internal; international; intransitive.

inter., interrogation.

interj., interjection.

interrog., interrogation; interrogative.

intr., intransitive.

in trans. (*in transitu*), on the way.

Int. Rev., Internal Revenue.

introd., intro., introduction; introductory.
inv., invented; inventor; invoice.
invt., inventory.
Io., Iowa.
I.O.F., Independent Order of Foresters.
Ion., Ionic.
I.O.O.F., Independent Order of Odd Fellows.
I.O.R.M., Improved Order of Red Men.
IOU, I.O.U., I owe you.
IPA, International Phonetic Alphabet; International Phonetic Association.
IQ, I.Q., intelligence quotient.
Ir, in *chemistry,* iridium.
Ir., Ireland; Irish.
Iran., Iranian.
Ire., Ireland.
IRS, Internal Revenue Service.
Is., Isa., Isaiah.
is., isl., island; isle.
Ital., It., Italian; Italic; Italy.
ital., it., italic; italics.
I.W.W., Industrial Workers of the World.

J

J, in *physics,* joule.
J., James; Judge; Justice.
Ja., James; January.
J/A, j/a, joint account.
J.A., Joint Agent; Judge Advocate.
J.A.G., Judge Advocate General.
Jam., Jamaica.
Jan., January.
Jap., Japan; Japanese.
Jas., James.
J.C., Jesus Christ.
jct., junction.
J.D. (*Jurum Doctor*), Doctor of Laws.
Jer., Jeremiah; Jeremy.
Jew., Jewish.
j.g., jg, junior grade.
Josh., Joshua.
jour., journal; journeyman.
J.P., Justice of the Peace.
Jr., jr., junior.
Jud., Judges; Judith.
Judg., Judges.
Jul., July.
jus., justice.
J.W.V., Jewish War Veterans.

K

K (*kalium*), in *chemistry,* potassium.
K., k., in *electricity,* capacity; karat; kilo; kilogram; king; knight; kopeck or kopecks; krona; krone; kronen; kroner; kronor; in *nautical usage,* knot.
Kan., Kans., Kas., Kansas.
kc., kilocycle; kilocycles.
K.C., King's Counsel; Knight (or Knights) of Columbus.
K.D., in *commerce,* knocked down (not assembled).
Ken., Kentucky.
kg., keg; kegs; kilogram; kilograms.
Ki., Kings (book of the Bible).
kilo., kilogram; kilometer.
kilom., kilometer.
K.K.K., KKK, Ku Klux Klan.
kl., kiloliter; kiloliters.
km., kilometer or kilometers; kingdom.
K.O., KO, k.o., in *boxing,* knockout.
K. of C., Knight (or Knights) of Columbus.
K. of P., Knight (or Knights) of Pythias.
KP, K.P., kitchen police.
Kr, in *chemistry,* krypton.
kr., kreutzer; krona; krone; kronen; kroner; kronor.
kt., carat.
K.T., Knight (or Knights) Templar.
kw., kilowatt.
kwh., K.W.H., kw-h, kw-hr, kilowatt-hour.
Ky., Kentucky.

L

L., Latin.
L., l., lady; lake; land; latitude; law; leaf; league; left; length; liberal; (*libra*), pound; (*librae*), pounds; line; link; lira; lire; liter; liters; lord; low.
La, in *chemistry,* lanthanum.
La., Louisiana.
L.A., Legislative Assembly; Los Angeles.
Lab., Laborite; Labrador.
lab., laboratory.
Lam., Lamentations.
lang., language.

Lat., Latin.

lat., latitude.

lb. (*libra*), pound; (*librae*), pounds.

L.B. (*Litterarum Baccalaureus*), Bachelor of Letters; Bachelor of Literature.

lbs., pounds.

L/C, l/c, letter of credit.

l.c., in *printing*, lower case.

L.C.D., l.c.d., lowest (or least) common denominator.

L.C.F., l.c.f., lowest (or least) common factor.

L.C.L., l.c.l., in *commerce*, less than carload lot.

L.C.M., l.c.m., lowest (or least) common multiple.

lect., lecture; lecturer.

leg., legal; legend; legislative; legislature.

Lev., Levit., Leviticus.

lex., lexicon.

L.F., low frequency.

lgth., length.

lg. tn., long ton.

L.H.D. (*Litterarum Humaniorum Doctor*), Doctor of Humanities.

Li, in *chemistry*, lithium.

L.I., Light Infantry; Long Island.

Lib., Liberal; Liberia.

lib., librarian; library.

Lieut., Lieutenant.

lin., lineal; linear.

lit., liter or liters; literal; literally; literary; literature.

Litt.B. (*Litterarum Baccalaureus*), Bachelor of Letters; Bachelor of Literature.

Litt.D. (*Litterarum Doctor*), Doctor of Letters; Doctor of Literature.

ll., lines.

LL.B. (*Legum Baccalaureus*), Bachelor of Laws.

LL.D. (*Legum Doctor*), Doctor of Laws.

loc. cit. (*loco citato*), in the place cited.

log, logarithm.

log., logic.

long., longitude.

L.O.O.M., Loyal Order of Moose.

L.R., Lloyd's Register.

L.S. (*locus sigilli*), place of the seal.

LT, letter telegram.

Lt., Lieutenant.

l.t., long ton.

Lt. Col., Lieutenant Colonel.

Lt. Comdr., Lt.-Comm., Lieutenant Commander.

Ltd., ltd., limited.

Lt. Gen., Lieutenant General.

Lt. Gov., Lieutenant Governor.

Lu, in *chemistry*, lutetium.

Luth., Lutheran.

Lux., Luxemburg.

lv., leave; leaves.

Lw, in *chemistry*, lawrencium.

M

M., Manitoba; Marshal; Master; Medieval; Monday; Monsieur.

M., m., majesty; male; manual; married; masculine; medicine; medium; meridian; (*meridies*), noon; meter; meters; middle; mile; miles; mill; mills; minim; minute; minutes; month; moon; morning; mountain.

M.A. (*Magister Artium*), Master of Arts.

Mac., Macc., Maccabees.

mach., machine; machinery; machinist.

Maj., Major.

Maj. Gen., Major General.

Mal., Malachi; Malay; Malayan.

Man., Manit., Manitoba.

manuf., manufac., manufacture; manufacturer; manufacturing.

Mar., March.

mar., marine; maritime; married.

marg., margin; marginal.

masc., masculine.

Mass., Massachusetts.

math., mathematical; mathematician; mathematics.

Matt., Matthew.

max., maximum.

M.B.A., Master of Business Administration.

M.B.S., MBS, Mutual Broadcasting System.

M.B.S., M.B.Sc., Master of Business Science.

M.C., Master of Ceremonies; Medical Corps; Member of Congress; Member of Council.

Md., Maryland.
M.D. (*Medicinae Doctor*), Doctor of Medicine; Medical Department.
Mdlle., Mademoiselle.
Mdm., Madam.
Mdme., Madame.
M.D.S., Master of Dental Surgery.
mdse., merchandise.
Me., Maine.
M.E., Mechanical Engineer; Methodist Episcopal; Middle English; Military Engineer; Mining Engineer.
meas., measure.
mech., mechanical; mechanics; mechanism.
med., median; medical; medicine; medieval; medium.
Medit., Mediterranean.
mem., member; memoir; memoranda; memorandum; memorial.
Messrs., Messieurs.
met., metaphor; metaphysical; metropolitan.
metal., metallurgical; metallurgy.
Meth., Methodist.
Mex., Mexican; Mexico.
M.F.A., Master of Fine Arts.
mfd., manufactured.
mfg., manufacturing.
mfr., manufacture; manufacturer.
Mg, in *chemistry*, magnesium.
mg., milligram; milligrams.
Mgr., Manager; Monseigneur; Monsignor.
M.H.R., Member of the House of Representatives.
mi., mile; miles; mill; mills; minute; minor.
M.I., Military Intelligence; Mounted Infantry.
Mic., Micah.
Mich., Michigan.
mid., middle; midshipman.
mil., military; militia.
min., mineralogy; minimum; mining; minister; minor; minute; minutes.
Minn., Minnesota.
misc., miscellaneous; miscellany.
Miss., Mississippi.
mkt., market.
ml., mail; milliliter; milliliters.

Mlle., Mademoiselle.
Mlles., Mademoiselles.
M.L.S., Master of Library Science.
MM., Messieurs.
mm. (*millia*), thousands; millimeter; millimeters.
Mme., Madame.
Mmes., Mesdames.
Mn, in *chemistry*, manganese.
Mo, in *chemistry*, molybdenum.
Mo., Missouri; Monday.
mo., month.
M.O., mo., money order.
mod., moderate; modern.
Mon., Monastery; Monday; Monsignor.
Mont., Montana.
Mor., Morocco.
mos., months.
MP, M.P., Military Police.
M.P., Member of Parliament; Metropolitan Police; Mounted Police.
M.P., m.p., melting point.
mph, n..p.h., miles per hour.
Mr., Mister.
Mrs., Mistress.
MS, ms., manuscript.
M.S., M.Sc., Master of Science.
Msgr., Monsignor.
M.Sgt., M/Sgt, Master Sergeant.
MSS, mss., manuscripts.
M.S.T., Mountain Standard Time.
Mt., mt., mount; mountain.
mtg., meeting; mortgage.
mtn., mountain.
mts., mountains.
mun., municipal.
mus., museum; music; musical; musician.
mut., mutilated; mutual.
Mv, in *chemistry*, mendelevium.
myth., mythol., mythological; mythology.

N

N, in *chemistry*, nitrogen.
N, N., n, n., north; northern.
N., National; Nationalist; Norse; November.
N., n., nail; name; (*natus*), born; navy; neuter; new; nominative; noon; northern; noun.
n., nephew; net; note; number.

Na (*natrium*), in *chemistry*, sodium.

n/a, in *banking*, no account.

N.A., National Academy; National Army; North America.

N.A.A.C.P., NAACP, National Association for the Advancement of Colored People.

Nah., Nahum.

N.A.M., NAM, National Association of Manufacturers.

N.A.S., National Academy of Sciences.

NASA, National Aeronautics and Space Administration.

nat. (*natus*), born; national; native; natural; naturalist.

natl., national.

NATO, North Atlantic Treaty Organization.

naut., nautical.

Nb, in *chemistry*, niobium.

N.B., New Brunswick.

N.B., n.b. (*nota bene*), note well.

N.B.C., NBC, National Broadcasting Company.

N.C., North Carolina.

NCO, noncommissioned officer.

Nd, in *chemistry*, neodymium.

N.D., n.d., no date.

N.D., N. Dak., North Dakota.

Ne, in *chemistry*, neon.

N.E., Naval Engineer; New England.

N.E.A., National Education Association.

Neb., Nebr., Nebraska.

N.E.D., New English Dictionary (the Oxford English Dictionary).

neg., negative.

Neh., Nehemiah.

Neth., Netherlands.

neut., neuter.

Nev., Nevada.

Newf., N.F., Nfd., Nfld., Newfoundland.

New M., New Mexico.

N.F., n/f, in *banking*, no funds.

N.G., National Guard.

N.G., n.g., no good.

N.H., New Hampshire.

Ni, in *chemistry*, nickel.

NIRA, N.I.R.A., National Industrial Recovery Act.

N.J., New Jersey.

NL, night letter.

NLRB, National Labor Relations Board.

N.M., N. Mex., New Mexico.

N.M.U., NMU, National Maritime Union.

NNE, N.N.E., n.n.e., north-northeast.

NNW, N.N.W., n.n.w., north-northwest.

No, in *chemistry*, nobelium.

No., Noah; north; northern.

No., no., number.

nom., nominative.

NOMA, National Office Management Association.

Nor., Norman; North; Norway; Norwegian.

Nov., November.

Np, in *chemistry*, neptunium.

N.P., n.p., new paragraph; Notary Public.

NRA, National Recovery Administration.

N.S., New Series; New Style; Nova Scotia.

N/S, n/s, N.S.F., in *banking*, not sufficient funds.

NSA, National Secretaries Association; National Security Agency; National Shipping Authority.

N.S.P.C.A., National Society for the Prevention of Cruelty to Animals.

NT., N.T., New Testament.

nt. wt., net weight.

Num., Numb., Numbers (book of the Bible).

num., number; numeral; numerals.

N.Y., New York.

N.Y.C., New York Central; New York City.

N.Z., N. Zeal., New Zealand.

O

O, in *physics*, ohm; in *chemistry*, oxygen.

O., Ocean; October; Ohio; Ontario; Oregon.

o., off; only; order.

OAS, Organization of American States.

Ob., Obad., Obadiah.

obj., object; objection; objective.

Obs., obs., observatory; obsolete.

occas., occasion; occasional; occasionally.

Oct., October.

oct., octavo.

O.D., Doctor of Optometry; Officer of the Day; overdraft; overdrawn.

OE., O.E., Old English.
O.E., o.e., omissions excepted.
O.E.D., OED, Oxford English Dictionary.
OEO, Office of Economic Opportunity.
off., office; officer; official.
O.K., OK, o.k., approval; approved.
Okla., Oklahoma.
Ont., Ontario.
op., opera; operation; opposite; opus.
O.P., o.p., out of print.
op. cit. (*opere citato*), in the work cited.
opt., optician; optics; optional.
Or., Oregon; Oriental.
o.r., owner's risk.
orch., orchestra.
ord., ordained; order; ordinal; ordinance; ordinary; ordnance.
Ore., Oreg., Oregon.
org., organic; organization; organized.
orig., origin; original; originally.
Os, in *chemistry,* osmium.
O.S., Old Series; Old Style; ordinary seaman.
o.s., out of stock.
OSS, Office of Strategic Services.
O.T., OT, OT., Old Testament.
Ox., Oxf., Oxford.
oz., ounce.
ozs., ounces.

P

P, in *chemistry,* phosphorus; in *mechanics,* power, pressure.
P., p., pastor; post; power; president; pressure; priest; prince.
p., page; participle; past; penny; per; in *music,* piano; pint; pipe; population.
Pa, in *chemistry,* protactinium.
Pa., Pennsylvania.
P.A., Passenger Agent; public address (system); Purchasing Agent.
Pac., Pacif., Pacific.
Pan., Panama; Panamanian.
par., paragraph; parallel; parenthesis.
Para., Paraguay; Paraguayan.
paren., parenthesis.
Parl., Parliament; Parliamentary.
part., participial; participle; particular.

pass., passenger; passive; passim.
pat., patent; patented; pattern.
path., pathol., pathological; pathology.
Pat. Off., Patent Office.
pat. pend., patent pending.
Pb (*plumbum*), in *chemistry,* lead.
PBX, P.B.X., Private Branch Exchange.
P/C, p/c, petty cash; prices current.
pc., piece; prices.
p.c., per cent; postal card; post card.
pct., per cent.
Pd, in *chemistry,* palladium.
pd., paid.
P.D., Police Department; postal district; (*also* **p.d.**), per diem.
P.E., Presiding Elder; probable error; Protestant Episcopal.
Penn., Penna., Pennsylvania.
Per., Pers., Persia; Persian.
per., period; person.
perf., perfect; perforated.
pers., person; personal; personally.
pert., pertaining.
Peruv., Peruvian.
Pet., Peter.
pf., perfect; pianoforte; preferred.
Pfc., Private First Class.
pfd., preferred.
Pg., Portugal; Portuguese.
Phar., Pharm., pharmaceutical; pharmacy.
Ph.D. (*Philosophiae Doctor*), Doctor of Philosophy.
Phil., Philippians; Philippine.
phil., philosophy.
phot., photog., photograph; photographer; photographic; photography.
PHS, P.H.S., Public Health Service.
phys., physical; physician; physics; physiological; physiology.
P.I., Philippine Islands.
pk., pack; park; peak; peck.
pkg., package; packages.
pl., place; plate; plural.
plup., plupf., pluperfect.
Pm, in *chemistry,* promethium.
pm., premium.
P.M., Paymaster; Postmaster; Prime Minister.
P.M., p.m. (*post meridiem*), after noon.

p.m. (*post-mortem*), after death.
pmk., postmark.
P/N, p.n., promissory note.
Po, in *chemistry*, polonium.
P.O., p.o., petty officer; postal order; post office.
POD, Post Office Department.
poet., poetic; poetry.
Pol., Poland; Polish.
pol., polit., political; politics.
POM, Personal Opinion Message.
pop., popular; popularly; population.
Port., Portugal; Portuguese.
pos., positive; possessive.
poss., possession; possessive; possibly.
pp., pages; past participle.
P.P., p.p., parcel post; past participle; postpaid.
ppd., prepaid.
ppr., p. pr., present participle.
P.P.S., p.p.s. (*post postscriptum*), an additional postscript.
P.Q., previous question; Province of Quebec.
Pr, in *chemistry*, praseodymium.
pr., pair; power; preferred (stock); present; price; pronoun.
P.R., Puerto Rico; proportional representation; public relations.
pred., predicate.
pref., preface; prefatory; preference; preferred; prefix.
prelim., preliminary.
prep., preparatory; preposition.
Pres., Presbyterian; President.
pres., present; presidency.
prim., primary; primitive.
prin., principal; principally; principle.
priv., private; privative.
prob., probable; probably; problem.
Prof., Professor.
pron., pronoun; pronunciation.
prop., properly; property.
Prot., Protestant.
Prov., Provençal; Proverbs; Province.
Prus., Prussia; Prussian.
PS., P.S., p.s., postscript.
Ps., Psa., Psalm; Psalms.
ps., pieces; pseudonym.

P.S., passenger steamer; permanent secretary; Privy Seal; Public School.
pseud., pseudonym.
P.SS., postscripts.
P.S.T., Pacific Standard Time.
psych., psychological; psychology.
Pt, in *chemistry*, platinum.
pt., part; payment; pint; point.
p.t., past tense; pro tempore.
P.T.A., Parent–Teacher Association.
Pu, in *chemistry*, plutonium.
pub., public; publication; published; publisher; publishing.
Pvt., Private.
PWA, P.W.A., Public Works Administration.
PX, post exchange.

Q

Q., Quebec; Queen; Question.
q., quart; quarter; quarterly; quarto; quasi; queen; question; quintal; quire; quotient.
q.e. (*quod est*), which is.
Q.E.D. (*quod erat demonstrandum*), which was to be proved.
Q.M., Quartermaster.
qr., quarter; quire.
qrs., quarters.
qt., quantity; quart.
qto., quarto.
qts., quarts.
qu., quart; quarter; quarterly; queen; question.
quart., quarterly.
Que., Quebec.
quot., quotation.
q.v. (*quantum vis*), as much as you will; (*quod vide*), which see.
qy., query.

R

R, in *chemistry*, radical.
R., Radical; Republic; Republican.
R., r., rabbi; radius; railroad; railway; (*Regina*), queen; (*Rex*), king; right; river; road; ruble; rupee.
r., range; rare; received; residence; retired; rises; rod; rods; rubber.

RA, Regular Army.
Ra, in *chemistry,* radium.
rad., radial; radical; radius.
R.A.F., RAF, Royal Air Force.
Rb, in *chemistry,* rubidium.
R.C., Red Cross; Roman Catholic.
R.C.Ch., Roman Catholic Church.
rcd., received.
R.C.M.P., Royal Canadian Mounted Police.
R.C.P., Royal College of Physicians.
R.C.S., Royal College of Surgeons.
R/D, R.D., in *banking,* refer to drawer.
Rd., rd., road; rod; round.
R.D., Rural Delivery.
Re, in *chemistry,* rhenium.
R.E., real estate; Reformed Episcopal.
REA, R.E.A., Railway Express Agency; Rural Electrification Administration.
rec., receipt; received; recipe; record; recorded.
recd., rec'd., received.
Rec. Sec., rec. sec., recording secretary.
ref., referee; reference; referred; reformed.
Ref. Ch., Reformed Church.
refl., reflection; reflex; reflexive.
reg., regent; regiment; region; register; registered; registrar; regular; regulation.
Rep., Representative; Republic; Republican.
rep., repeat; report; reported; reporter.
res., research; reserve; residence; resides; resistance; resolution.
ret., retired; returned.
Rev., Revelation; Reverend.
rev., revenue; reverse; review; revise; revised; revision; revolution; revolving.
RFC, Reconstruction Finance Corporation.
RFD, R.F.D., Rural Free Delivery.
Rh, in *chemistry,* rhodium.
R.I., Rhode Island.
R.I.P. (*requiescat in pace*), may he (or she) rest in peace.
riv., river.
RM., r.m., reichsmark.
rm., ream; room.
rms., reams; rooms.

Rn, in *chemistry,* radon.
R.N., registered nurse; Royal Navy.
Rom., Roman; Romance; Romans.
Rom. Cath., Roman Catholic.
ROTC, Reserve Officers' Training Corps.
RP, reply paid.
r.p.m., revolutions per minute.
r.p.s., revolutions per second.
rpt., report.
R.R., railroad; Right Reverend.
Rs., reis; rupees.
R.S., Recording Secretary; Reformed Spelling.
RSV, R.S.V., Revised Standard Version (of the Bible).
R.S.V.P., r.s.v.p. (*répondez s'il vous plait*), please reply.
rt., right.
Ru, in *chemistry,* ruthenium.
Rum., Rumania; Rumanian.
Rus., Russ., Russia; Russian.
Ry., Railways.

S

S, in *chemistry,* sulfur.
S, S., s, s., south; southern.
S., Sabbath; Saturday; Saxon; Senate; September; *Signor;* Socialist; Sunday.
S., s., saint; school; society.
s., second; seconds; section; see; series; shilling; shillings; sign; silver; singular; son; steamer; substantive.
S.A., Salvation Army; South Africa; South America; South Australia.
SAC, Strategic Air Command.
S. Afr., South Africa; South African.
Salv., Salvador.
Sam., Saml., Sam'l., Samuel.
S. Am., S. Amer., South America; South American.
Sans., Sansk., Sanskrit.
Sask., Saskatchewan.
Sat., Saturday; Saturn.
Sb (*stibium*), in *chemistry,* antimony.
SBA, Small Business Administration.
Sc, in *chemistry,* scandium.
Sc., Scotch; Scots; Scottish.
sc., scale; scene; screw; scruple.
SC, Signal Corps; Staff Corps.

S.C., South Carolina; Supreme Court.
s.c., in *printing,* small capitals.
sch., school; schooner.
sci., science; scientific.
Scot., Scotch; Scotland; Scottish.
S/D, sight draft.
S.D., S. Dak., South Dakota.
Se, in *chemistry,* selenium.
SEATO, Southeast Asia Treaty Organization.
SEC, Securities and Exchange Commission.
sec., secant; second or seconds; secondary; secretary; section or sections; sector; security.
secy., sec'y., secretary.
sem., semicolon.
Sen., sen., Senate; Senator; senior.
Sep., Sept., September; Septuagint.
ser., series; sermon.
S.F., Sinking Fund.
s.g., specific gravity.
sgd., signed.
Sgt., sgt., Sergeant.
Shak., Shakespeare.
Si, in *chemistry,* silicon.
Sib., Siberia; Siberian.
Sic., Sicilian; Sicily.
Sig., sig., signal; signature; *Signor; Signore; Signori.*
Sig.na, *Signorina.*
Sig.ra, *Signora.*
sing., singular.
S.J., Society of Jesus.
Skr., Skrt., Skt., Sanskrit.
Slav., Slavic; Slavonian; Slavonic.
Sm, in *chemistry,* samarium.
Sn (*stannum*), in *chemistry,* tin.
So., South; southern.
Soc., Socialist; Society.
sociol., sociological; sociology.
sol., soluble; solution.
SOP, S.O.P., standard (or standing) operating procedure.
S O S, international distress signal.
Sp., Spain; Spaniard; Spanish.
sp., special; species; specific; spelling.
S.P., SP, Shore Patrol; Submarine Patrol.
Span., Spaniard; Spanish.

S.P.C.A., Society for Prevention of Cruelty to Animals.
S.P.C.C., Society for Prevention of Cruelty to Children.
spec., special; specifically; specification.
specif., specifically.
sp. gr., specific gravity.
spt., seaport.
Sq., sq., square.
Sr, in *chemistry,* strontium.
Sr., Senior; *Señor;* Sir.
Sra., *Señora.*
S.R.O., standing room only.
Srta., *Señorita.*
S.S., SS, S/S, steamship.
St., Saint; Strait; Street.
s.t., short ton.
Sta., Santa; Station.
ster., stg., sterling.
sub., substitute; substitutes; suburb; suburban.
subj., subject; subjective; subjunctive.
Sun., Sunday.
sup., superior; superlative; supplement; supplementary; supply; (*supra*), above; supreme.
Supt., supt., Superintendent.
surg., surgeon; surgery; surgical.
Sw., Swed., Sweden; Swedish.
syn., synonym; synonymous; synonymy.
Syr., Syria; Syriac; Syrian.
syst., system.

T

T., tablespoon; tablespoons; Testament; Tuesday; Turkish.
T., t., tenor; territorial; territory; ton; tons; (*tomus*), volume.
t., teaspoon; teaspoons; telephone; temperature; tense; time; tone; town; township; transitive; troy.
Ta, in *chemistry,* tantalum.
tan, tan., tangent.
Tasm., Tasmania.
TB, T.B., tb., t.b., tuberculosis.
Tb, in *chemistry,* terbium.
tbs., tbsp., tablespoon; tablespoons.
Tc, in *chemistry,* technetium.
Te, in *chemistry,* tellurium.
tech., technical; technically; technology.

tel., telegram; telegraph; telegraphic; telephone.

temp., temperature; temporary.

Tenn., Tennessee.

ter., terr., terrace; territory.

Test., Testament.

Teut., Teuton; Teutonic.

Tex., Texas.

Th, in *chemistry,* thorium.

Th., Thursday.

theol., theologian; theological; theology.

Thess., Thessalonians.

Thur., Thurs., Thursday.

Ti, in *chemistry,* titanium.

Tim., Timothy.

Tl, in *chemistry,* thallium.

Tm, in *chemistry,* thulium.

tn., ton; tons.

TNT, T.N.T., trinitrotoluene.

topog., topographical; topography.

tp., township.

t.p., title page.

tr., trace; transitive; translated; translation; translator; transpose; treasurer.

trans., transactions; transitive; translated; translation; translator; transportation; transpose.

transl., translated; translation.

treas., treasurer; treasury.

trig., trigon., trigonometric; trigonometry.

tsp., teaspoon; teaspoons.

Tu., Tues., Tuesday.

Turk., Turkey; Turkish.

TV, T.V., television.

TVA, Tennessee Valley Authority.

twp., township.

TWX, Teletypewriter Exchange Service.

U

U, in *chemistry,* uranium.

U., Uncle; Union; University.

U., u., upper.

U.A.W., UAW, United Automobile, Aerospace, and Agricultural Implement Workers of America.

U.C., Upper Canada.

u.c., in *printing,* upper case.

UFO, unidentified flying object.

UHF, ultrahigh frequency.

U.K., United Kingdom.

Ukr., Ukraine.

UL, Underwriters' Laboratories.

ult., ultimate; ultimately; ultimo.

UMT, Universal Military Training.

UMW, U.M.W., United Mine Workers of America.

UN, U.N., United Nations.

UNESCO, United Nations Educational, Scientific, and Cultural Organization.

UNICEF, United Nations Children's Fund.

Unit., Unitarian.

Univ., Universalist; University.

univ., universal; universally.

UPI, United Press International.

Uru., Uruguay; Uruguayan.

U.S., US, United States.

U.S.A., USA, United States of America; United States Army.

USAF, United States Air Force.

USCG, United States Coast Guard.

USIA, United States Information Agency.

USIS, United States Information Service.

U.S.M., United States Mail; United States Marines; United States Mint.

USMA, United States Military Academy.

USMC, United States Marine Corps.

USN, United States Navy.

USNA, United States Naval Academy.

USNG, United States National Guard.

USNR, United States Naval Reserve.

USO, U.S.O., United Service Organizations.

U.S.P., U.S. Pharm., United States Pharmacopoeia.

U.S.S., United States Senate; United States Ship; United States Steamer; United States Steamship.

U.S.S.R., USSR, Union of Soviet Socialist Republics.

Ut., Utah.

V

V, in *chemistry,* vanadium.

V, v, vector; velocity; volt; volts.

v., verb; verse; version; versus; (*vide*), see; village; violin; voice; voltage; volume.

VA, Veterans' Administration.

Va., Virginia.

var., variant; variation; variety; various.

vb., verb; verbal.

V.C., Vice-Chairman; Vice-Chancellor; Victoria Cross.

V.D., venereal disease.

Venez., Venezuela; Venezuelan.

vet., veteran; veterinarian; veterinary.

V.F.W., VFW, Veterans of Foreign Wars.

V.I., Virgin Islands.

v.i., intransitive verb; (*vide infra*), see below.

Vic., Vict., Victoria.

V.I.P., VIP, very important person.

VISTA, Volunteers in Service to America.

viz. (*videlicet*), namely; that is.

vocab., vocabulary.

vol., volcanic; volcano; volume.

vols., volumes.

V.P., Vice-President.

V. Rev., Very Reverend.

vs., versus.

Vt., Vermont.

v.t., transitive verb.

Vuĺ., Vulg., Vulgate.

vv., verses; violins.

v.v., vice versa.

W

W, in *chemistry*, tungsten; watt; watts; west; western; (*wolfram*).

W., Wales; Wednesday; Welsh; West; Western.

W., w., warehouse; watt; watts; weight; west; western; width.

W., week; weeks; wide; wife; with; won.

WAC, Women's Army Corps.

Wash., Washington.

WAVES, Women Accepted for Volunteer Emergency Service (Women's Reserve, USNR).

W.B., W/B, waybill.

W.C.T.U., Woman's Christian Temperance Union.

Wed., Wednesday.

w.f., wf, in *printing*, wrong font.

WFTU, W.F.T.U., World Federation of Trade Unions.

WHO, World Health Organization (UN).

W.I., West Indian; West Indies.

Wis., Wisc., Wisconsin.

wk., week; work.

wkly., weekly.

w.l., wave length.

WO, War Office; Warrant Officer.

wt., weight.

W.Va., West Virginia.

Wyo., Wy., Wyoming.

XYZ

x, in *mathematics*, an unknown quantity; a sign of multiplication.

Xe, in *chemistry*, xenon.

Y, in *chemistry*, yttrium.

Y., Young Men's Christian Association

y., yard; yards; year; years.

Yb, in *chemistry*, ytterbium.

yd., yard; yards.

Y.M.C.A., Young Men's Christian Association.

Y.M.Cath.A., Young Men's Catholic Association.

Y.M.H.A., Young Men's Hebrew Association.

yr., year; younger; your.

yrs., years; yours.

Y.W.C.A., Young Women's Christian Association.

Y.W.H.A., Young Women's Hebrew Association.

Z., in *chemistry*, atomic number; in *astronomy*, zenith distance.

Z., z., zone.

Zech., Zechariah.

Zeph., Zephaniah.

ZIP, Zoning Improvement Plan.

Zn, in *chemistry*, zinc.

zool., zoological; zoology.

Zr, in *chemistry*, zirconium.

BUSINESS TERMS

A

abatement, *n.* a deduction or rebate: the *order of abatement* establishes the order in which deficiencies in an estate are apportioned to the various types of bequest.

abeyance, *n.* a state of suspension: as, settlement of an estate is held in *abeyance* pending certain developments, such as proof of ownership.

abstract of title, a set of notes showing the history of transfers of ownership of real estate.

acceptance, *n.* 1. endorsement of a bill of exchange by the person on whom it is drawn committing him to payment when due: the endorsement is written on the face of the bill, with the word "accepted" accompanying the signature: the acceptor becomes responsible for payment: in event of his failure to pay, the original maker of the bill is responsible; thus, the acceptance is a transaction between these two parties. 2. an acknowledgment of receipt, as of goods, by a buyer. 3. an acknowledgment of agreement, as to a contract, thus binding the purchaser: see also **bank** or **banker's acceptance; trade acceptance.**

acceptor, *n.* a person who signs a promise to pay a draft, or bill of exchange: also *accepter.*

accommodation paper, a bill of exchange or a note made or endorsed without consideration by one or more persons to enable the drawer to get credit or raise money on it.

account, *n.* 1. an itemized record of transactions, showing credits and debits. 2. a business relation, especially one in which credit is used; charge account.

account book, a book in which business accounts are set down.

account current, a record of business dealings showing money owed.

accrued dividends, loosely, any unpaid dividends: strictly, dividends are not due until specifically declared.

accrued expense, charges incurred but not yet paid, as wages and other overhead for any period.

accrued income, income that has been earned but has not yet been received.

accrued interest, interest figured at a given time between the regular dates for payment: when a security is sold at a stated price "plus accrued interest," the buyer has to pay that price and the interest from the last interest date to the date of delivery: he is recompensed by receiving interest for the full term.

accumulative stock, see **cumulative preferred stock.**

acknowledgment, *n.* a legal avowal, especially a notarized declaration of responsibility.

active stock, 1. an issue of stock currently figuring in market transactions. 2. one for which there is a ready market.

addendum, *n.* something added or to be added.

adjudicate, *v.t.* 1. to submit (a contested matter) to judicial settlement. 2. to settle (such a matter).

admiralty court, a court having jurisdiction in maritime matters.

affiant, *n.* one who makes an affidavit; deponent.

affidavit, *n.* a statement made under oath and in writing.

agate line, a unit of type measurement used in buying and selling space for advertising in newspapers: one fourteenth of an inch in a column, varying somewhat according to the width of the column.

aggregate, *n.* a total amount.

agio, *n.* 1. percentage paid as premium for exchange of currency, or in exchange of depreciated money for money of full value. 2. agiotage.

agiotage, *n.* speculation on fluctuation of public securities.

alien, *v.t.* to transfer (land, etc.).

aliunde, *adv. & adj.* in *law,* from some other source: as, evidence clarifying a document, but not deriving from the document itself, is evidence *aliunde.*

allonge, *n.* a paper pasted on a note or bill of exchange to allow more endorsements than the bill has room for.

alodium, *n.* in *law,* land owned independently, without any rent, payment in service, etc.; a freehold estate.

amercement, *n.* 1. punishment, especially by fine. 2. the fine or penalty imposed.

American Federation of Labor, a federation of labor unions of the United States and Canada, founded in 1881: merged with the Congress of Industrial Organizations in 1955.

American Stock Exchange, one of the two major U.S. securities exchanges, dealing with stocks not listed on the New York Stock Exchange. Formerly called the *curb exchange.*

amortize, *v.t.* 1. to put money aside at intervals, as in a sinking fund, for gradual payment of (a debt, etc.). 2. in *accounting,* to write off (expenditures) by prorating over a fixed period. 3. in *law,* to transfer or sell (property) in mortmain.

amount gross, the total sum or aggregate.

amount net, total sum less proper deduction for expenses, discount, or charges.

and interest, a term used in bond sales to indicate that the purchaser pays the interest accrued to the time of the sale, in addition to the stated price.

annual interest, interest due yearly, rather than at more frequent intervals.

annuity, *n.* 1. a yearly payment of money. 2. the right to receive such a payment. 3. an investment yielding fixed payments during the holder's lifetime or for a stated number of years.

A1, 1. first class; best of its kind. 2. in *shipping registry,* a first-class rating: numerals are prefixed to indicate whether the ship is built of steel or wood.

appraisal, *n.* an estimate of the value of property or assets.

appraise, *v.t.* to examine and make an estimate of value.

appreciation, *n.* increase in value.

arbitrage, *n.* 1. arbitration. 2. purchase of securities or goods in one market for immediate sale in another market where the price is higher: such trading tends to level out price differences.

arbitration of exchange, in *international business,* the process of arriving at a mutual understanding as to rates of exchange in the currencies of different countries.

arrears, *n.pl.* sums due but not paid: as, an overdue account is in *arrears;* a delinquent customer is in *arrears.*

arson, *n.* the malicious burning of another's buildings or property, or of one's own, so as to collect insurance.

article, *n.* 1. the unit division of a document, as a constitution or a contract. 2. a single piece of any kind of goods.

assay office, a department of the Mint or private firm which tests metals and certifies them as to weight and fineness.

assessed valuation, value placed upon property by an official assessor, as for determination of tax: it is commonly less than the true or market value.

assessment, *n.* 1. a charge against the owner of a property to cover his proportionate share of the cost of public improvements, as for street paving, sewer, water main, sidewalks. 2. a demand upon owners of securities, in proportion to the amount of their individual holdings, for the purpose of raising new capital for the corporation issuing the securities: most corporation securities are not subject to assessment, but bank stocks usually are: owners of assessable stocks are commonly held responsible for debts of the institution if it becomes insolvent.

assignee, *n.* the person to whom any asset, as a contract, right, or security, has been made over.

assignment, *n.* the making over to another of ownership or interest in any property or right: it may be made to an individual person, a corporation, or one's creditors in general: if acceptable to the creditors, in shares in proportion to the claims of each, it saves the cost of bankruptcy proceedings; but if it is not satisfactory to all the creditors, any of them may override the assignment by instituting bankruptcy action.

assignment in blank, an assignment, as of bonds or shares of stock, in which the name of the new owner does not appear.

assume, *v.t.* to take over, as bonds of one company by another, as in case of a merger or a transfer of control.

assurance, *n.* 1. [chiefly British], insurance. 2. an agreement to pay on a contingency sure to occur.

at a premium, at a price above par: said of the price of a security.

attachment, *n.* 1. seizure of property or person by legal writ. 2. the writ authorizing such seizure.

at the market, term used in ordering a broker to buy or sell a security at its market price at a specified time, instead of naming a figure under or over which he shall not go.

attorn, *v.i.* to continue as tenant under a new landlord.

auditor, *n.* one who checks claims and adjusts accounts.

automation, *n.* in *manufacturing,* a system or method in which all or many of the processes of production, movement, or inspection are performed or controlled by self-operating machinery, electronic devices, etc.

available assets, unencumbered resources, especially those that can be converted into money through sale or can serve as security for a new obligation.

average down, to buy more shares of a security at a lower price than was paid for the first purchase, in order to reduce the average cost per share: thus if 100 shares were bought for $5,000, the average would be $50; another 100

shares at $30 would bring the investment to $8,000 for 200 shares, or $40 per share: compare **average up.**

average of payments, method of finding the time when payment may be made of several sums due at different dates, without loss to either party.

average up, to buy more goods or shares at a higher price, increasing the average payment per unit, in anticipation of a further advance in price and sale at a profit: compare **average down.**

avulsion, *n.* lands torn as by a current of water from one estate and added to another.

B

bailment, *n.* goods delivered in trust against an obligation and to be returned when that obligation is ended.

balance of trade, excess of a country's exports over its imports (*favorable balance*) or of imports over exports (*unfavorable balance*): the terms *favorable* and *unfavorable* are based upon the flow of gold into or out of a country.

balance sheet, a statement of assets and liabilities to show the standing of a business: it summarizes profits, losses, assets, liabilities, net worth, etc., and is usually figured at the close of a fiscal period.

bank acceptance, acceptance of a bill of exchange by a bank or other credit-loaning institution: see **acceptance.**

bank annuities, British government bonds; consols.

bank balance, the amount to a depositor's credit in a bank; the amount to which a bank or trust company is obligated to the depositor, and must hold subject to his order.

bank bill, 1. a bank note. 2. a bill of exchange issued or accepted by a bank: also called *banker's bill.*

bank discount, interest deducted by a bank from a loan when the loan is made: it is equal to the normal interest from the date of the loan to the date of the final payment.

bank draft, an order by one bank for payment by another.

banker's acceptance, acceptance of a bill of exchange by a bank or trust company: see **acceptance.**

bank holiday, a period when banks are not open for business; in Great Britain, any of six legal holidays: called *legal holiday* in the United States.

bank note, a bank's promise to pay bearer on demand, at face value: these notes circulate as money: in 1935 the privilege of issuing such notes was greatly restricted.

bank of deposit, any bank, and in most of the states any trust company, which accepts deposits of money subject to order by check.

bank of issue, any bank empowered by law to issue notes for use as currency; in the United States, a Federal Reserve Bank.

bank paper, bank notes or commercial paper which can be handled by banks, as notes subject to discount.

bank rate, rate of discount fixed for a system of banks.

bank statement, 1. a bank's public report of its condition. 2. a detailed report of financial condition given to a bank by an applicant for a loan. 3. popularly, a bank's summary of activity in a depositor's account for a certain period.

bank stock, shares in a banking company; paid-up capital of a bank divided into shares.

barratry, *n.* 1. in *maritime law,* an act by a shipmaster hurtful to the owners of the vessel or its cargo. 2. in common legal use, repeated deliberate attempts to cause resort to the courts.

barrister, *n.* British name for a lawyer who practices in the courts.

bear, *n.* 1. a person who views the business situation pessimistically. 2. a trader who gambles on prices going down; one who sells securities he does not own for future delivery at a certain price, counting on being able to buy the shares at a lower price before the delivery date.

bear market, a period of sustained downward tendency in prices on stock or commodity exchanges: see **cover; raid; short sale.**

bench warrant, order by a court that a certain person be brought before it.

billing terms, conditions, as of time and rate of discount, on which an order is accepted.

bill of entry, a list of incoming and outgoing goods entered at the customs.

bill of exceptions, a written list of exceptions to a court's decisions.

bill of lading, 1. originally, a cargo list. 2. a contract issued to a shipper by a transportation agency, listing the goods shipped, acknowledging their receipt, and promising delivery to the person named.

bill of particulars, specification of demands for which an action is brought.

bill of sale, a legally formal paper attesting transfer of title to goods or chattels and safeguarding the buyer in his ownership thereof.

bill of sight, a form of customhouse entry allowing consignee to see goods before paying duty: it may be used to permit unloading of goods on which the importer lacks the information for a bill of entry.

blank credit, permission to draw money on account, no sum being specified.

blank endorsement, endorsement of a check or other commercial paper with signature only, making the paper payable to bearer, not to a named individual or his order.

blue-sky law, any law protecting the investing public against exploitation by promoters to whom "the sky's the limit."

board, *n.* 1. a body of directors. 2. [Colloq.], the listing of current stocks and their prices, as at a stock exchange.

bona fide, in good faith; made or done in good faith; genuine: used in English as an adjective: as, a *bona fide* offer.

bond, *n.* 1. in *commerce, a)* an agreement by an agency holding taxable goods that taxes on them will be paid before they are sold. *b)* the condition of such goods. *c)* an insurance contract by which a bonding agency guarantees payment of a specified sum to an employer, etc., in the event of a financial loss caused him by the act of a specified employee or by some contingency over which the payee has no control. 2. in *finance,* an interest-bearing certificate issued by a government or business, promising to pay the holder a specified sum on a specified date: it is a common means of raising capital. 3. in *law, a)* a written obligation under seal to pay specified sums, or to do or not do specified things. *b)* a person acting as surety for another's action; payer of bail. *c)* an amount paid as surety or bail.

bond creditor, a creditor protected by bonds.

bonded debt, 1. amount of indebtedness, as of a corporation or government, represented by outstanding issues of bonds. 2. a long-term indebtedness, as distinguished from current indebtedness represented by short-term obligations, such as notes.

bonded goods, goods held in bond, senses 1 *a)* and *b)*: their place of storage is known as a *bonded warehouse.*

bondsman, *n.* one who gives security for the payment of money, performance of an act, or integrity of another.

book debts, accounts on the books of record.

books closed, 1. designating a period when the books of a corporation are closed, to provide a period of adjustment during which the list of stockholders is checked to determine who is entitled to vote in a stockholders' meeting, after which the books are opened again to record transfers of shares. 2. designating a period when the books are closed because an issue of shares has been fully subscribed and no more orders can be taken.

book value, 1. the worth of stock or any asset as shown in the financial records of the company that issues or owns it, as distinguished from par value or market value: it reflects the amount of capital invested per share of the stock. 2. the value of a company's assets as carried on its books.

bought-and-sold notes, notes given by a broker to the buyer and seller, respectively.

bounty, *n.* a bonus or premium given to encourage trade.

break in market, a sudden and extensive drop in prices, checking an extended rise.

break bulk, to open a package of goods in transit and remove a part.

broker, *n.* one who buys and sells for others on commission.

brokerage, *n.* the business or office of a broker; a broker's fee.

bull, *n.* a trader in stocks who buys in anticipation of a rising market.

bull market, a condition of sustained activity and rising prices in a stock market.

buyers' market, state of the market in which the buyer is at an advantage because supply is greater than demand: see **sellers' market.**

buyer's option, a buyer's privilege, when so stipulated in an agreement, to postpone completion of an order over a certain period but to demand delivery, should he so desire, on stated notice at any time within that period.

buy on margin, to buy (stocks, etc.) on credit established by a deposit with a broker who advances the rest.

buy outright, to pay full price for immediate delivery or delivery on a specified date: distinguished from *buying on margin.*

C

calendar year, 12 months beginning January 1 and ending December 31: distinguished from *fiscal year*.

call, *n.* 1. demand for payment. 2. privilege of demanding fulfillment of an order at a given price within a stated period of time. *v.t.* to redeem, as an issue of bonds, before maturity.

callable, *adj.* subject to call: said especially of bonds issued with reservation of the right to redeem on or after a specified date in advance of maturity.

call loan, a loan payable on demand of the lender or at the will of the borrower: commonly made by banks or brokers: this lending provides a profitable use for available funds and protects the bank against a shortage of cash.

call money, money borrowed subject to the lender's demand for payment at any time within a stated limit.

cancel, *v.t.* to annul or erase: often done by stamp or punch.

capital, *n.* money available for investment; wealth used to finance production.

capital gain, profit resulting from the sale of capital investment, as stocks, etc.

capital goods, goods used productively, as raw materials, machinery, buildings, etc.; producers' goods: distinguished from *consumers' goods*.

capitalize, *v.t.* 1. to calculate the present value of (a periodical payment, annuity, income, etc.); convert (an income, etc.) into one payment or sum equivalent to the computed present value. 2. to convert (floating debt) into stock or shares.

carrier, *n.* a person or firm that transports passengers or goods, or both, as a business: see **common carrier.**

carrying charges, a percentage paid by a customer making deferred payments on his debt, to cover interest on the seller's money, costs of service, etc., as in purchase of stock on margin or of goods on the installment plan.

carte blanche, a signed paper, as an order or other authorization, to be filled in as the holder may please.

cashier's check, a check drawn by a bank against itself and carrying the signature of the cashier.

cash sale, sale of goods for immediate payment, or payment in full within a certain short period of time.

certificate of deposit, a paper given by a bank acknowledging receipt of money to be held for the customer, subject to his demand, but not to be treated as a checking account: the holder of the certificate is not regarded as a depositor.

charter party, a written contract for the hire of a vessel or space on a vessel for a given voyage.

chattel mortgage, a lien on personal property, taken to secure a loan or to enable seizure and sale of property bought on the installment plan should the buyer default.

chose, *n.* a piece of personal property; chattel.

chose in action, a right, as to personal property which has not been taken into possession.

circular note, a letter of credit for a traveler's use abroad.

clearinghouse, *n.* an office maintained by a group of banks as a center for exchanging checks drawn against one another, balancing accounts, etc.

clearinghouse balance, the amount which a bank owes to the clearinghouse at the end of a day or is to receive from it in settlement of its part in the day's debits and credits.

close corporation, a corporation whose stock is owned and controlled by only a few persons, as a family group.

cognovit, *n.* in *law,* a written acknowledgment of his liability made by a defendant in a civil suit to avoid the expense of contending.

coinsurance, *n.* insurance on commercial property in which two or more insurers (*coinsurers*) carry the risk in proportion to the coverage of the full property value which each has insured: sometimes the insured stands as a coinsurer in assuming part of the risk.

collateral, *n.* property, such as securities, pledged by a borrower to protect a lender.

collateral note, a note secured by collateral: it is given by a borrower to a lending bank, stating the terms of deposit of security on the loan, to protect the bank against the borrower's possible attempt to sell the pledged security.

co-maker, *n.* a co-signer.

commerce, *n.* extended trade or traffic.

commercial agency, an organization which furnishes subscribers with information as to the financial standing and credit rating of individuals and corporations engaged in business: Dun and Bradstreet, Inc., of New York, is the foremost such agency in the United States: also called *mercantile agency*.

commercial paper, negotiable instruments, such as drafts and notes, issued by business houses: a large brokerage business is done in the notes of houses known to be reliable.

commission broker, one who buys or sells on commission.

commissioner of deeds, in certain states, an attorney or notary authorized to take acknowledgment of deeds.

commission house, a firm that handles transactions, as purchase or sale of securities or goods, for others, on a percentage basis.

commission merchant, a person who buys or sells goods for others and is paid a commission by them.

common carrier, a person or company engaged in the business of transporting passengers or goods, or both: railroads, ships, ferries, streetcar lines and bus lines, airlines, and trucking systems are common carriers: each state regulates their operation within its own boundaries, and the Federal Interstate Commerce Commission fixes rates and rules for operation across state lines: this supervision is exercised in the interest both of the carriers and of the public.

common law, the unwritten law based on established custom: it is now largely regularized by legislative definition.

common stock, stock which does not carry the privileges granted to holders of preferred issues, and which shares in the profits of a business only after the claims of the preferred have been satisfied: income on preferred stock is usually a fixed percentage of par, or face, value; that on common stock is proportionate to earnings and may be very high or nothing at all: there is no rigidly fixed arrangement as between the two kinds of stock: the conditions of each issue are set forth on its certificates.

composition, *n.* 1. a payment by an insolvent debtor of a percentage of his debts as settlement in full. 2. the sum offered and accepted in this way.

compound interest, interest on both principal and accumulated unpaid interest: distinguished from *simple interest*.

computer, *n.* an electronic machine which, by means of stored instructions and information, performs rapid, often complex calculations, or compiles, correlates, and selects data.

Congress of Industrial Organizations, a group of affiliated labor unions in the United States and Canada, established in 1938: merged with the American Federation of Labor in 1955.

consideration, *n.* that which is given or promised by the parties to a contract: it may be money or another thing of value, or an action of some kind.

consignee, *n.* the person to whom a shipment of goods is addressed.

consignment, *n.* 1. an order of goods shipped. 2. commitment of goods, especially to an agent or distributor, for sale: see **on consignment.**

consignor, *n.* one who ships goods, as to an agent or distributor; the maker of a consignment.

consolidation, *n.* the joining of two or more business houses under one management: technically distinguished from a *merger* in the details of financing and reorganizing.

consols, *n.pl.* funded government securities of Great Britain: abbreviation for *consolidated annuities* or *bonds*.

consumers' goods, goods, such as food, clothing, etc., for satisfying people's needs rather than for producing other goods or services: distinguished from *producers'*, or *capital, goods*.

contract, *n.* an agreement between two or more people to do something: a contract follows an *offer* and *acceptance* and implies a legal means and purpose, as well as a sufficient *consideration*.

convertible, *adj.* of bonds, subject to surrender in exchange for stock, either by act of the issuing company or of the holder, or as required under certain stated conditions.

corner, *n.* control of the market for a security or commodity, as wheat, through acquisition of a major part of the supply.

corporation, *n.* a group of persons legally empowered to act as a single personality in business.

co-signer, *n.* a person who signs a promissory note in addition to the maker, thus becoming responsible for the obligation if the maker should default: also called *co-maker*.

cost and freight, a term of sale indicating that transportation charges will be paid by the seller.

countinghouse, *n.* an office where business books are kept.

court of equity, a court having a chancery or equity jurisdiction: it is not limited by the common law.

cover, *v.t.* 1. to provide payment for. 2. to buy securities or commodities, after a short sale, in order to make good on a contract of future delivery: see **short sale.**

craft union, a labor union composed of workers belonging to a particular trade: also called *horizontal union*. See **industrial union.**

credit instrument, a paper (aside from paper currency) acknowledging obligation to pay, as a check or draft, a note, a bond coupon, etc.

credit standing, status of a person or firm as a trustworthy debtor, with ability to command credit.

cumulative preferred stock, a stock on which successive unpaid dividends accrue and have to be paid before any dividend can be paid on the common stock.

curbstone broker, a broker not a member of the regular stock exchange. Now, often, a member of the **American Stock Exchange,** which see. Also called *curb broker*.

current, *adj.* passing freely; now in progress; of this day: as, *current accounts*.

current assets, resources that can be converted into cash quickly and easily.

current expenses, day-to-day costs of doing business.

current liabilities, obligations attendant upon the day-to-day conduct of business, such as wages.

customs, *n.pl.* 1. duties or taxes imposed by a government on imported and, occasionally, exported goods. 2. the government agency in charge of collecting these duties.

customs union, a union of two or more nations that agree to eliminate customs restrictions among them and to follow a common tariff policy toward all other nations.

cutback, *n.* reduction or discontinuance, as of a contract, before the completion of what was originally called for.

D

dating, *n.* an extension of the period of credit by considering a transaction as made at a later date than that at which it actually was made: sometimes offered as an incentive to purchase, as during a slack season.

dead weight, freight for which charge is made by weight instead of bulk.

debenture bond, a bond not secured by a lien on property of the issuing corporation or backed by any security except the corporation's general assets and good faith.

deed, *n.* a paper in legal form conveying ownership of real estate.

deferred dividend, a dividend, as on cumulative preferred stock, not paid when due but permitted to accrue.

deficiency judgment, a judgment in favor of a mortgagee for the remainder of a debt not completely cleared by foreclosure of the mortgage.

demand deposit, a deposit in a bank, subject to withdrawal at any time: the usual form of checking account.

deposit slip, the printed form supplied by a bank on which the depositor makes an itemized statement of each deposit.

depreciation, *n.* 1. a decrease in the value of property through wear, deterioration, or obsolescence. 2. the allowance made for this in accounting, bookkeeping, etc. 3. a decrease in the purchasing power of money.

deviation, *n.* a change from a set or prearranged plan: as, the *deviation* of a ship from her regular course to stop at other ports.

discount broker, one who lends money on notes or bills.

discount rate, percentage at which commercial paper is discounted by the banks.

dollar exchange, bills of exchange drawn in other countries upon American banking houses and payable in United States money.

domestic exchange, issuance and acceptance of bills of exchange within the United States, chiefly in the form of bank drafts on Federal Reserve Banks.

double-entry bookkeeping, that system of bookkeeping in which every transaction is entered as both a debit and a credit.

double-name paper, a negotiable paper with an additional endorsement called

for by the bank: also called *two-name paper.*

double taxation, taxation of one person or property by two governments, as state and Federal, or by two states, as of a man who lives in one state on income derived from property in another state.

draft, *n.* a written order by which one person directs another to pay a certain sum to a third person, charging it to the maker of the draft: a check is a form of draft.

draw, *v.t.* to make a draft of or for; write (a check).

drawback, *n.* an allowance or return of duties paid at the customhouse, made when a shipment is re-exported.

drawing account, 1. an account showing money paid for expenses or as advances on salary, commissions, etc., as to a salesman. 2. the privilege of such an account.

drop shipment, an order for which the goods go to the retailer direct from the factory but the bill comes to him from the distributor or wholesale agent from whom he would normally receive the goods.

due bill, a paper given to a customer who returns ordered goods, granting him credit for the amount against a future purchase.

E

easement, *n.* a right to certain uses of another's land, as of passage over it to a highway.

easy, *adj.* 1. lacking firmness in prices: said of a market. 2. with funds plentiful and interest rates low: said of a money market: opposed to *tight.*

effects, *n.pl.* property; goods on hand; the possessions of a firm or an individual.

ejectment, *n.* dispossession of houses or land; a forcing out; eviction.

endorse, *v.t.* to place a signature on the back of a paper, as a check or note, in order to cash it or to assume responsibility for its payment: also *indorse*.

endorsee, *n.* one to whom a note or check is made over through endorsement by its holder: also *indorsee*.

endorsement, *n.* the act of writing on the back of a check, note, etc., or that which is written, as the signature of a payee, by which money or property is made over to someone. A *blank endorsement* or *endorsement in blank* is the usual form of endorsement, specifying no particular payee. A *restrictive endorsement* specifies the use to be made of the paper, as "Pay to X as agent," or "Deposit to the account of Y," with the maker's signature. A *special endorsement* designates the party to whom or to whose order payment is to be made. Also *indorsement*.

engrosser, *n.* 1. one who takes the whole of a line of goods. 2. one who corners the market on a commodity.

engrossing clerk, a copyist; a copying clerk.

entrapment, *n.* the arranging by a policeman, detective, etc., of circumstances that provide or encourage temptation to commit a felony or misdemeanor, as the encouragement of the offer of a bribe.

entry, *n.* 1. an item of record in an account. 2. the officially recognized and recorded arrival of a ship or goods at a port.

equity, *n.* 1. a body of laws supplementary to statute law, designed to correct injustices due to legal technicality: see **court of equity.** 2. a participation in ownership, as the share of a part owner.

equity of redemption, the right of a mortgagor to redeem his forfeited estate by payment of capital and interest within a reasonable time: it is granted by a court of equity.

escalator clause, a clause in a contract between an employer and a labor union providing for increases or decreases in pay, as in accordance with fluctuations in the cost of living.

estoppel, *n.* the prevention of a person from asserting a fact or doing an act inconsistent with previous acts or declarations.

examiner, *n.* 1. a person named by state or Federal authority to examine the records of a bank; bank examiner. 2. a customhouse officer who compares goods with invoices.

exchange, *v.i.* 1. to make an exchange; barter; trade. 2. in *finance,* to pass in exchange: as, the currency of this country *exchanges* at par. *n.* 1. *pl.* the checks, drafts, etc., presented for exchange and settlement between banks in a clearinghouse. 2. in *law,* a contract by which parties agree to exchange one thing for another. *adj.* having to do with an exchange: as, an *exchange broker.*

exchange broker, a broker who deals in foreign bills of exchange and currencies.

excise tax, a government tax on goods made and sold within its domain, as the Federal taxes on domestic liquors, automobiles, cigarettes, etc.: differentiated from *customs duties,* or *tariffs,* on imported goods.

ex parte, on, or in the interest of, one side only; one-sided.

export duty, a tax imposed on exports.

exports, *n.pl.* the goods or merchandise exported; especially, all of the goods sent from one country to another or others.

ex post facto, acting backward; retrospective: an *ex post facto law* is one that can be applied to offenses charged as occurring before the law's enactment.

express company, a corporation engaged in the business of transporting goods and money from one place to another more quickly than can be done by sending as ordinary freight.

express money order, a money order issued by an express company, to be cashed at any of its offices.

extension, *n.* 1. allowance of additional time for payment to a debtor. 2. a carrying out of items of a bill or account, as by multiplying units by a unit rate.

external loan, an issue of bonds for buyers in other countries, often made payable in currency of the country in which the bonds are sold: distinguished from a *domestic* or *internal loan.*

extinguish, *v.t.* to bring to an end; settle; finish: as, to *extinguish* an obligation.

F

facture, *n.* 1. the act or method of making something. 2. the thing made. 3. an invoice or bill of goods.

fair copy, an exact copy of a document after final corrections have been made on it.

Federal Deposit Insurance Corporation, a government corporation set up to protect bank depositors: all deposits are insured against loss, theft, etc., up to a limit of $10,000 for each account.

Federal Reserve Bank, any of the 12 district banks of the Federal Reserve System.

Federal Reserve Board, a board composed of seven (originally eight) members which directs the Federal Reserve System: in 1935, the name was changed to *Board of Governors of the Federal Reserve System.*

Federal Reserve notes, currency issued by the banks of the Federal Reserve System: most common form of legal tender.

Federal Reserve System, a centralized banking system in the U.S., consisting of 12 Federal Reserve Banks, each acting as the central bank for its district, and over 10,000 affiliated banks: it was established by the Federal Reserve Act of 1913 to develop a currency which would fluctuate with business demands and to regulate the member banks of each district.

fee, *n.* 1. originally, *a)* heritable land held from a feudal lord in return for service; fief; feudal benefice: also called *feud. b)* the right to hold such land. *c)* payment, service, or homage due to a superior. 2. a payment asked or given for professional services, admissions, licenses, tuition, etc.; charge. 3. a present of money; tip; gratuity. 4. in *law,* an inheritance in land.

fee simple, absolute ownership; ownership of property without limitations of heirs to whom it must descend: distinguished from *fee tail,* which limits the inheritance to a specified class of heirs.

feud, *n.* in the feudal system, land held from a lord in return for service given him: used in certain legal phrases: also *fee, fief.*

feudist, *n.* in *law,* a specialist in feudal law.

fiduciary, *n.* 1. a trustee of an estate or director of a corporation. 2. a person engaged in a confidential financial capacity, as an agent.

first-mortgage bond, a bond secured by a mortgage on part or all of a business property and having priority over other liens.

fiscal year, the 12-month period between settlements of financial accounts: in the United States, the government fiscal year legally ends June 30.

fixed charges, certain charges, as taxes, rent, interest, etc., which must be paid, usually at regular intervals, without being changed or shifted, and without reference to the amount of business done.

floating, *adj.* 1. not funded: said of a debt. 2. not set aside by holders as a permanent investment but held for speculation and frequently changing hands in the market: said of stock.

forced sale, sale of property, on legal order, to satisfy creditors' claims; foreclosure sale.

foreclosure, *n.* legal action for sale of mortgaged property to enable the mortgagee to recover his loaned money in case of default by the mortgator: if the sale realizes more than the claim, the surplus goes to the holders of secondary liens; if there are none, it is paid to the mortgagor: foreclosure sales may also be held on pledged property other than real estate, and by a government, local, state, or Federal, for unpaid taxes on lands and buildings. These general practices may be altered locally by state law.

foreign bill, a bill of exchange payable abroad: a bill payable in another state may also be classified under this head.

forestall, *v.t.* to interfere with the trading in (a market) by buying up goods in advance, getting sellers to raise prices, etc.

forwarder, *n.* a person or thing that forwards; specifically, a transmitting agent; person who receives goods and delivers them to the regular transportation agent for transmission to the proper destination.

fractional currency, currency of less than a dollar face value.

franchise, *n.* 1. right to operate a business in public service, granted by a government: as, a bus *franchise.* 2. the right to market a product, often exclusive in a specified area, as granted by the manufacturer.

franking privilege, right to send mail free.

free alongside ship (or vessel), delivered to the dock with freight charges paid by the shipper: said of goods to be hauled by ship.

free and clear, without encumbrance: said especially of title to real estate against which there is no mortgage or other legal lien.

free list, 1. a list of persons entitled to service without charge. 2. a list of goods not subject to duty.

free on board, delivered (by the seller) aboard the train, ship, etc., at the point of shipment, after which the buyer

pays all carriage charges. See also **cost and freight.**

free port, a port open to all ships and goods without payment of customs duties.

front foot, one foot of the edge of a plot of land facing on a road, street, or water front: used as a unit of valuation.

frozen assets, resources that cannot be quickly liquidated.

frozen credit, credit based upon security holdings that cannot be marketed advantageously on short notice.

funded debt, indebtedness in the form of long-term obligations: debt is frequently funded by transforming a number of short-term issues into long-term, interest-bearing bonds.

fungible, *adj.* in *law,* designating goods, as grain, coffee, etc., any unit or part of which can replace another unit, as in discharging a debt; capable of being used in place of another. *n.* a fungible thing.

futures, *n.pl.* securities or commodities bought and sold for delayed delivery: frequently done as speculation, selling of futures is a factor of business stability, enabling manufacturers to price their products with due regard to future cost of raw materials.

G

general average, in *marine insurance,* a proportionate contribution levied on ship and goods to cover necessary sacrifice of a part: all owners and shippers involved share in assuming this expense, even though the "necessary sacrifice" may have been goods belonging to only one of them.

gold basis, use of gold as a standard of prices; adjustment of prices to the gold standard.

gold bond, a bond payable in gold: such bonds were payable in gold money of the weight and fineness required by law at the time of their issue: they were intended as protection of the investor against inflation. In 1934 the dollar was devalued by act of Congress, and the Supreme Court held that the "gold clause" in such bonds was nonenforceable: they may still be offered by certain foreign governments.

gold certificate, formerly, a note certified as being backed by a deposit of gold in the United States Treasury: in 1933 all the country's gold was called in by the Federal Government, and the gold certificates were withdrawn from circulation as legal tender: the Federal Reserve Banks now hold them as evidence of their surrender of gold to the Government in 1933. Gold certificates are used within the Federal Reserve System but are not circulated.

gold point, the rate of foreign exchange which makes it cost no more to square accounts by shipping gold than to settle by buying or selling bills of exchange.

gold reserve, 1. the backing of gold held in the United States Treasury against United States notes and Treasury notes. 2. the volume of gold certificates held by the Federal Reserve Banks.

gold standard, 1. use of gold as base for measuring values, with a certain weight and fineness prescribed by law for the national unit of money: gold becomes the medium of exchange as represented by other forms of currency. 2. the legal weight and fineness of gold used in United States coins before 1934.

goodwill, *n.* favorable attitude of the buying public toward a business house, constituting an intangible asset in valuing the business: sometimes written *good will.*

grand larceny, in *law,* 1. theft in which the property stolen has a value equaling or exceeding a certain amount fixed by law: the amount varies from state to state but is usually between $25 and $50: distinguished from *petit* (or *petty*) *larceny.* 2. in some states,

the theft of property of any value directly from the person of the victim, but without the use of force.

great gross, 12 gross, i.e., 1,728 articles.

gross, *n.* 1. 12 dozen, i.e., 144. 2. total amount: opposed to *net.*

gross income, total receipts, without deductions: distinguished from *net income.*

gross profit, the amount by which receipts on sales exceed the cost of the goods, without deduction of costs of running the business.

gross receipts, total receipts from sale of goods, without expense deduction.

gross ton, a ton of 2,240 pounds: also called *long ton.*

groundage, *n.* a fee charged for permitting a ship to remain in port.

H

hand money, money given as part payment and pledge.

harbor dues, charges made for use of a harbor; groundage.

hedge, *v.t.* to buy or sell in order to balance threatened loss in other transactions.

holder in due course, one to whom a check, note, or other bill of exchange has come through earlier endorsements without protest or notice of defect.

holding company, a company organized to control subsidiary companies through possession of their stock issues.

horizontal union, see **craft union.**

I

import duty, a tax imposed on imports.

increment, *n.* increase: see **unearned increment.**

indenture, *n.* 1. a formal legal agreement, of which identical copies are held by each party: originally, the two copies had correspondingly notched edges. 2. an official, authenticated list, inventory, etc.

index numbers, statistics in a table or record showing fluctuations of prices, volume of trade, or production, etc., from an assumed base.

indulgence, *n.* extension of time for payment, considered as a favor.

industrial union, a labor union composed of members of an industry, regardless of specialized occupation: also called *vertical union.*

inland bill, a bill of exchange or draft drawn upon a person in the same state or country: also known as *domestic bill.*

insurable interest, a sufficient personal concern in the object of insurance to establish a reason for assuming responsibility for premium payment: for example, the *insurable interest* a company may have in the life of its chief executives.

insurance broker, one who negotiates insurance contracts.

insurance trust, an estate in the form of insurance policies, with a trustee to administer it in the beneficiary's interest.

inter alios, among other persons.

interest account, in *bookkeeping,* a separate account of sums paid and received as interest.

interfere, *v.i.* in *patent law,* to claim priority for an invention, as when two or more applications for its patent are pending.

interim certificate, a paper acknowledging deposit of stock to be held, as by a designated trust company, during a period of reorganization of the issuing corporation, to be exchanged for new securities when the reorganization is completed.

interplead, *v.i.* in *law,* to go to trial with each other in order to settle a dispute in which a third party is concerned; initiate an interpleader.

interpleader, *n.* a legal proceeding by which a person sued by two others having the same claim against him may compel them to go to trial with each other to determine what settlement should be made.

in transit, in the course of shipment.

investment banking, the business of buying all or part of new stock issues, for sale to the buying public. Investment banking does not include conventional banking services.

investment trust, a firm that invests money for others, distributing profits to holders of its shares: also called *investment company:* see **mutual fund.**

invoice book (or **register**), a book for entering copies of invoices.

J

job analysis, a study of a specific job, as in industry, with respect to operations and hazards involved, qualifications required of the worker, etc.

job printer, a printer who does various kinds of printing, such as letterheads, circulars, posters, etc.

joint and several note, a note with two or more signers: any or all signers can be held liable for performance of the pledge.

joint tenancy, tenure of property by two or more persons under which the holdings of any who die are held jointly by the survivors.

judgment debtor, one against whom a creditor has obtained a court ruling.

judgment note, a promissory note by the terms of which the holder is authorized, upon default, to take out and execute a judgment ex parte: it is illegal in some states: also called *cognovit note.*

jump a claim, to seize mining rights or land claimed by someone else.

K

key punch, a machine, operated from a keyboard, that records data by punching holes in cards that can then be fed into machines for sorting, accounting, etc.

knocked down, in *commerce,* not assembled: said of furniture, etc.

L

law merchant, all the rules and usages originating in the customs of merchants and now applied to dealings in trade and commerce.

letter of advice, a notification of completion of a commercial transaction; especially a letter in which the drawer of a bill of exchange notifies the drawee that he has issued the bill.

letter of credit, a letter from a bank asking that the holder of the letter be allowed to draw specified sums of money from other banks or agencies, to be charged to the account of the writer of the letter.

lien, *n.* a legal claim against property to protect a creditor, as one claiming pay for work done on the property.

limited, *adj.* having liability of stockholders coincide with the actual amount of their investment: as, a *limited* company.

limited partnership, a partnership differing from a general partnership in that the partner's liability is limited to an amount equal to his investment.

linage, lineage, *n.* amount of advertising space calculated in lines of print: see **agate line.**

line of credit, amount of credit to which a customer is entitled.

liquid assets, assets that can be quickly and easily converted into cash.

liquidation, *n.* conversion, either voluntary or forced, of assets into cash, either to take profits or to close out a business.

Lloyd's, *n.* an association of insurance underwriters in London formed in the 18th century to subscribe marine insurance policies and to publish shipping news: it now handles many kinds of insurance.

loan at a premium, in *stock-market usage,* when a borrower of securities is required to pay a charge for the service, the stock is said to be *loaned at a premium.*

loan flat, when no special charge is made for the service of lending stock, it is said to be *loaned flat:* used in the stock market.

loan office, an office where loans are negotiated.

loan society, a group of people who pay various sums into a fund which is then used as a source of loans to them and, sometimes, to others.

locum tenens [chiefly British], a person taking another's place for the time being; temporary substitute; lieutenant.

long dozen, 13 articles for the price of 12: it is sometimes given by way of effecting a discount: also called *baker's dozen.*

longshoreman, *n.* a laborer who loads and unloads vessels.

long-term bond, a bond of slow maturity, running over a longer period than the average.

long-term capital gain, a capital gain (which see) taxed at one half the regular rate because the asset on whose sale it was realized had been held for more than six months.

loss leader, an article that a store sells cheaply or below cost in order to attract customers.

M

managed currency, currency whose gold content (represented by the standard monetary unit) is varied in order to stabilize its purchasing power.

manifold writer, a contrivance by which several copies may be obtained at once: also *manifolder.*

manit, *n.* a standard unit expressing the amount of work that may be done or produced by a man in one minute: used in time study and production scales, and in incentive pay scales.

margin of profit, the difference between what is paid and what is received in sales.

market price, the price that a commodity brings when sold in a given market; prevailing price.

matched order, an order to buy and to sell equal amounts of securities or goods: it is a trick to give the market an air of activity and cause advance in prices, and is illegal.

maximum, *n.* the highest price or sum.

measurement goods, goods on which freight is charged by measurement.

mechanic's lien, a lien against property filed by one who has been engaged in its construction or repair and has not been paid for work done or materials supplied: to safeguard against double liability, the owner may require the contractor to give a bond pledging himself to satisfy those who work for him, thus confining the matter to the two principals, the owner and the contractor.

mercantile agency, an establishment that gathers and provides for clients information about the credit rating, financial status, etc., of individuals and firms.

mercantile paper, checks, promissory notes, bills of exchange, and other negotiable paper used in business: also called *commercial paper.*

merger, *n.* a unification of business houses by concentration of their properties under the name of the corporation taking over the business of all.

metallic currency, coinage of silver, gold, copper, and other metals.

milline, *n.* 1. a unit of measurement equal to a one-column agate line (of an advertisement) in one million copies of some publication. 2. the cost per milline of an advertisement.

money market, 1. the general system of cash loans. 2. the exchange of different kinds of currency.

moratorium, *n.* a period of postponement, either permitted or ordered by government, as a *bank moratorium* in which banking operations are temporarily suspended as a check against panic.

mortgage bond, a bond that is secured by a mortgage on property.

municipal bond, a bond issued by a municipality, as for schools, improvements, and other needs of town or city government.

mutual, *adj.* involving common interest: in *life insurance,* a *mutual company* is one in which the holders of policies elect the officers of the company and share the profits of the business.

mutual fund, a type of investment company formed by the pooling together of funds contributed by a number of investors: profits from the investment of this money are shared mutually by all concerned.

mutual savings bank, a savings bank in which the profits are distributed among the depositors: it has no capital.

N

negotiable, *adj.* capable of being transferred through endorsement or surrender to another: as, *negotiable paper* designates checks, drafts, bills of exchange, and bonds not registered but having coupons payable to bearer.

negotiations, *n.pl.* agreeing upon a mercantile transaction; making a bargain; fixing a price.

net, *adj.* left over after certain deductions or allowances have been made, as for expenses, weight of containers or waste materials, nonessential considerations, etc. *n.* a net amount, profit, weight, price, result, etc. *v.t.* to get or bring in as a net; gain.

net cash, sold not subject to discount.

net 30, to be paid, as per invoice, within 30 days, without discount.

nonassessable, *adj.* not subject to assessment: said of a stock whose holders cannot be required to participate in the raising of new capital for the issuing house.

no protest, note written on a check, draft, note, or other bill of exchange, to indicate to the one who cashes it that in case of nonpayment it is to be returned to the creditor and not protested.

note of hand, a written undertaking to pay money at a certain time; promissory note

O

odd lot, in the sale of securities and commodities, a lot of less than 100 shares of stock, or less than 10,000 dollars' worth of bonds, figuring in a sale: see **round lot.**

on consignment, shipped or turned over to an agent for sale, with the understanding that payment to the shipper will follow sale.

one-name paper, commercial paper that is not endorsed and has no co-signer: also called *single-name paper.*

open account, 1. an account that has not yet been balanced. 2. an account with credit privileges.

opening price, the figure at which the first sale of the day is made on a stock exchange.

open policy, in *marine insurance,* a policy which covers undefined risks either to a specific kind of goods or in a specific geographical location.

overbuy, *v.t. & v.i.* to buy more than is needed or justified by ability to pay.

overhead, *n.* cost of conducting a business; costs which do not come under particular expenses but belong to the whole business, as rent, taxes, insurance, depreciation of plant, etc.

overissue, *n.* an issue, as of bonds or stocks, that exceeds authorization, credit limit, etc.

oyer, *n.* a copy of a bond or other instrument that is the subject of a suit, given to the opposite party instead of being read aloud, as formerly.

P

paid-up shares, securities for which the full price has been delivered; nonassessable shares.

paid-up value, in *insurance,* value of a policy on which payments have ceased, in advance of maturity.

paper profits, profits showing on outstanding deals but not yet realized or taken.

par of exchange, the value of a unit of one country's coinage expressed in that of another: see also **rate of exchange.**

particular average, partial damage of a ship alone, or of cargo alone, arising from ordinary wear and tear or mishaps: see also **general average.**

past-due account, an account which has matured but has not been settled.

patentee, *n.* one who holds a patent giving sole right to manufacture and sell an invention.

payable to bearer, designating paper which need not be endorsed: such paper is not protected against theft or loss.

pay load, a cargo, or the part of a cargo, producing income.

peg, *v.t.* to maintain the price of, as a stock, by regulations or by buying and selling freely.

perpetual calendar, a calendar that is mathematically so arranged that the correct day of the week can be determined for any given date over a wide range of years. See Appendix 10, Table 3.

petitioning creditor, a creditor bringing bankruptcy proceedings against a debtor.

petty cash, a cash fund from which small incidental expenses are paid.

petty (or **petit**) **larceny,** theft involving a sum smaller than that which constitutes **grand larceny** (which see).

planned economy, the organization of the economy of a country by which all phases of production are planned as an interdependent whole by some central authority, usually the state: in most modern countries, the phrase may be applied to some parts of the economy.

pool, *n.* in the *stock market,* a combination of traders seeking market control; in *commodity trading,* a group posing as rivals but actually co-operating in an endeavor to control supply and prices.

post, *n.* a section of the floor of a trading room where trade in one stock is carried on.

posting, *n.* the transfer from a daybook or journal to the ledger.

post-obit, *n.* a bond given by a borrower, pledging to pay his debt upon the death of a specified person from whom he expects to inherit money.

power of attorney, a written statement legally authorizing a person to act for one.

preferred creditor, a creditor entitled to have his claims paid before those of others, such as the holder of a first mortgage, or of claims for personal services.

preferred stock, stock on which dividends must be paid before any are paid on the common stock, and whose holders have precedence when the assets of a dissolved corporation are distributed.

price current, 1. the price named in a list of prices at a certain time, such as dealers circulate among their salesmen and customers. 2. market price.

price fixing, artificial regulation of prices, as by a combination of sellers.

price index, a table of prices of commodities compiled as an indicator of the purchasing power of the dollar: see also **index numbers; price level.**

price level, average of prices of a number of commodities in relation to a price taken as base (an index number).

price maintenance, control, by manufacturer, of price to be charged by retailers; fair-trade agreement or control.

procuration, *n.* a power of attorney.

producers' goods, see **capital goods.**

profit-and-loss account, a ledger showing profits, losses, and expenses, with favorable or unfavorable balance: also called *income statement.*

program, *n.* 1. a logical sequence of operations to be performed by a computer in solving a problem or processing data. 2. the coded instructions and data for such a sequence. *v.t.* 1. to plan a computer program for (a task, problem, etc.). 2. to furnish (a computer) with a program.

promissory note, a written promise to pay a certain sum of money to a certain person or bearer on demand or on a specific date.

prorate, *v.t.* to divide in proportion to respective claims.

protest, *n.* 1. a formal declaration in writing made by a notary public in behalf of the holder of a bill or note, protesting against all parties liable for any loss or damage by nonpayment; a declaration and service of notice of dishonor. 2. declaration by a shipmaster that damage to ship or cargo was due to no fault of ship, officers, or crew.

proxy, *n.* authority in writing which gives a certain person the right to vote for the holder of shares or to act for him in the transaction of business.

public-service corporation, a corporation supplying services for the convenience of the public, as a street-railway company.

put, *n.* a contract calling upon the issuer to purchase a stock named in the agreement within a specified time at a fixed price, at the option of the purchaser.

put and call, see **straddle.**

Q

qualified endorsement, an endorsing signature, with the note "without recourse," or some other qualification.

quick assets, current assets; goods or other resources which can readily be converted into cash.

quitclaim deed, a deed of release of title, interest, or claim in property: distinguished from *warranty deed.*

quitrent, *n.* rent paid by a tenent of a freehold, discharging him from other rent: also *quit rent.*

quota, *n.* a proportional part: as, a foreign nation's *quota* of immigration.

R

raid, *n.* a concentrated endeavor by operators in the stock market to drive prices down.

rate of exchange, the ratio between currency of one country and that of another country: it fluctuates as conditions change and is regulated through stabilization funds by governments having managed currencies, as Great Britain and the United States.

rating, *n.* the credit standing of a person or firm, as set by mercantile agencies.

rating book, a commercial agency's book in which financial standings are given in a special code, with symbols for each rating.

real property, real estate; land, buildings, etc.

realtor, *n.* a real-estate broker holding membership in the National Association of Real Estate Boards.

receipt book, a book in which receipts are filed.

receiver, *n.* a person appointed by a court to manage the property and affairs of a person or business house while legal processes affecting the property or business are under way.

rediscount, *v.t.* to give a second discount, as the action of a Federal Reserve Bank in discounting commercial paper for a member bank.

rediscount rate, the rate of interest charged for discounting a note or acceptance that has already been discounted once.

register, *n.* 1. a ship's paper issued by the customhouse, stating description, name, tonnage, nationality, and ownership. 2. a listing of the names of ships, together with pertinent information regarding each.

registered bond, a bond with principal and interest payable only to a listed owner or on his order.

registrar, *n.* an official of a company recording placement and transfers of stock or bonds, and safeguarding against false transactions.

reinsurance, *n.* 1. renewed insurance. 2. insurance taken out by an insurer to protect himself against loss. 3. the amount of such insurance.

reloading, *n.* a device used by questionable security dealers to sell additional shares of stock to individuals who have already bought.

rental value, the sum for which a property can be rented.

repository, *n.* a warehouse or storehouse.

reserve ratio, percentage relation of reserves to liabilities, as in bank statements.

resources, *n.pl.* assets.

respondentia bond, a bond for a loan secured by the cargo of a ship, as well as the ship itself.

retailer, *n.* a dealer who sells single articles or small amounts to consumers: opposed to *wholesaler.*

return, *n.* 1. a statement of financial condition. 2. the yield of an investment.

reversion, *n.* the right to possess property after the happening of some event, as the death of a person.

risk, *n.* 1. the hazard of a new undertaking: as, a good *risk;* a poor *risk.* 2. degree of credit standing of an applicant for credit.

round lot, in the sale of securities and commodities, a lot of shares in a normal trading unit, as 100 shares: see also **odd lot.**

royalty, *n.* a percentage fee paid the holder of a patent or copyright for the right to make or sell, etc. the article in question.

running account, an account settled from time to time, and held open: also *open account.*

S

sag, *n.* a letdown in stock-market prices.

salvage, *n.* compensation given those who rescue a ship or cargo from loss.

saturation point, state of a market when normal demands are met and sales depend upon demand for replacement.

scrip, *n.* 1. certificate for a fractional share of stock: such fractional shares may be paid in lieu of a cash dividend. 2. a certificate of indebtedness, issued as currency.

secured creditor, a creditor whose safety is protected by pledge of property or by unquestionable guarantee in the form of pledged securities.

securities company, a company depend· ing for its supporting income on securities of other corporations held by it.

seigniorage, *n.* a government's charge for coining bullion: usually, the difference between face value and intrinsic value.

self-insurance, *n.* insurance of oneself or one's property, usually by providing a fund out of current income.

self-liquidating, *adj.* providing profit in a short time; converting itself into cash in the normal course of business.

sellers' market, state of the market in which the seller is at an advantage because demand exceeds supply: see **buyers' market.**

seller's option, a contract giving the seller of stock shares the privilege of delivering to the buyer on one day's notice during a specified period.

sell short, 1. to sell securities not owned, but borrowed in expectation of a favorable change in the market. 2. to sell a commodity, as wheat, for future delivery, in expectation of a drop in prices.

sequestrator, *n.* a person appointed to administer sequestrated, or confiscated, property.

settlement, *n.* full and final payment on an obligation.

settlor, *n.* in *law,* a person who makes a settlement of property.

severable, *adj.* in *law,* separable into distinct, independent obligations: said of a contract.

shade, *v.t.* to make a concession in the price of a commodity or security.

share, *n.* one of the unit parts of securities issued by a company.

shave, *v.t.* to buy a note at a rate higher than the legal rate of interest or to give a discount exceeding the legal figure.

shipping articles, articles of agreement between a captain and seamen: also *ship's articles.*

shipping clerk, one who oversees the forwarding of merchandise; one who prepares and enters goods for shipment.

shipping order, a form filled in with instructions for shipping.

ship's husband, one who attends to the requisite repairs of a ship while in port and does all the other necessary acts preparatory to a voyage.

ship's papers, all the documents that a merchant ship must carry to meet the requirements of port authorities, international law, etc.

ship's stores, provisions, fuel, cables, extra spars, etc.

short account, 1. the account of one who sells securities or commodities short. 2. the total short sales in a particular commodity or in the market as a whole.

short exchange, bills of exchange payable at sight or in a few days.

short sale, sale of a security not owned but borrowed, in expectation of buying at a lower price before the date of delivery as contracted.

shrinkage, *n.* a decrease due to shrinking of goods.

sight, *n.* the time when a bill is presented to the drawee; demand; presentation.

sight draft, a draft that is due to be paid when presented.

simple interest, interest on principal alone, not on previously accumulated interest: distinguished from *compound interest.*

single-entry bookkeeping, that system of bookkeeping which requires only one entry for a single transaction: the single account consists of debts owed to and by the concern in question.

single-name paper, commercial paper, unendorsed: also called *one-name paper.*

sinking fund, a fund made up of sums of money set aside at intervals, usually invested at interest, to pay a debt, meet expenses, etc.

slow assets, resources which require considerable time to be changed into cash: real estate, buildings, etc. belonging to and used by a firm might be considered thus.

slowdown, *n.* a slowing down or being slowed down; specifically, a planned slowing down of industrial production on the part of labor or management.

smart money, 1. money paid as compensation for injuries, wounds, etc. received in the line of duty. 2. money paid to cancel, or compensate for failure to keep the terms of, a contract, agreement, etc. 3. money paid over and above usual damages, as an extra penalty for gross negligence, cruelty, etc.

social insurance, any government measure, as a pension plan, health and accident insurance, etc., safeguarding people in low-income groups against economic and industrial hazards.

specialty, *n.* a written, sealed, and delivered contract.

speculation, *n.* buying and selling for immediate profit rather than for investment.

split commission, a commission shared, as with a customer.

stamp duty, a law requiring stamps to be affixed to checks and proprietary articles.

statement of account, presentation of an account since the last payment.

statute law, a body of laws established by legislative enactment: written, as opposed to *unwritten* or *common law.*

sterling exchange, exchange in terms of the British pound sterling.

stock, *n.* a debt owed to persons who have lent their money for interest, or the certificates representing this; the capital, or fund of invested money, used by a business firm in making its transactions; shares of corporate capital, or the certificates of ownership representing them. See **stock certificate.**

stockbroker, *n.* a person who acts as an agent in buying and selling stocks and bonds.

stock certificate, a paper evidencing ownership of shares: also *certificate of stock.*

stock dividend, a dividend paid in stock instead of cash.

stock in trade, goods kept on hand, ready for sale.

stockjobber, *n.* 1. in British usage, an operator in the stock exchange who deals only with brokers, not with the public. 2. a stockbroker or stock salesman: often contemptuous.

stocktaking, *n.* inventory.

stop-loss order, an order to a broker to sell when the price falls to a certain figure, or, if selling short, to buy at a certain point: its purpose is to reduce or stop any loss.

stop order, an order to buy or sell a certain stock when a specified price is reached.

stoppage in transit, the right of the seller to stop goods on which delivery has not yet been completed if the purchaser has become insolvent.

stop payment, order by a bank's customer to refuse payment on a check or draft that has been issued.

straddle, *n.* a combined put and call, giving the holder an option either to buy or sell at a fixed price within a specified period: see **put; call.**

straight bill of lading, a bill of lading with no requirement beyond that of delivery to the consignee.

subrogation, *n.* putting one thing in place of another; substituting one creditor for another.

sui juris, in *law,* legally competent to manage one's own affairs, because of legal age and of sound mind.

supercargo, *n.* an agent who accompanies cargo to care for and sell it.

surety, *n.* one who binds himself to pay money in case another person fails to pay, to fill a contract, or to serve with integrity: he may do this by endorsement or by posting a *surety bond,* as against losses due to malfeasance of employees.

surveyor, *n.* agent of an insurance company to examine and report on applications for marine or fire insurance.

suspense account, a ledger account containing the amounts of items in doubt, to be credited or debited later to the right accounts.

syndicate, *n.* a group of bankers or capitalists acting together for an agreed purpose, such as underwriting a new issue of securities.

T

tally, *n.* keeping account by checking off.

tallyman, *n.* one who accepts payment for goods in weekly installments.

tangible assets, resources consisting of real estate or chattels.

tare, *n.* 1. an allowance for the weight of a container. 2. the difference between gross and net weights of a shipment.

tariff, *n.* 1. a list or system of taxes placed by a government upon exports or, especially, imports. 2. a tax of this kind, or its rate. 3. any list or scale of prices, charges, etc. *v.t.* 1. to make a schedule of tariffs on; set a tariff on. 2. to fix the price according to a tariff.

taxpayer, *n.* 1. a person who pays a tax; a person subject to taxation. 2. a building for business use erected on land that is taxed for the purpose of defraying tax expenses.

tenants in common, persons holding the same property in common, i.e., by distinct titles and not as joint tenants: the shares held by the several tenants need not be equal.

tie-in, *adj.* designating a sale in which two or more articles are offered together, often at a reduced price, generally a scarce or desirable item with one of little value or interest. *n.* such a sale or item.

tierce, *n.* 1. an old liquid measure, equal to ⅓ pipe (42 gallons). 2. a cask of this capacity, between a barrel and a hogshead in size.

tight, *adj.* 1. difficult to get; scarce in relation to demand: said of commodities on a market. 2. characterized by such scarcity, as, a *tight* market: opposed to *easy.*

time bargain, a firm contract for the future sale of stock.

time deposit, a deposit not to be withdrawn until a certain period has elapsed or a specified number of days' notice of intention to withdraw has been given.

time draft, a draft payable at a future date specified on the draft.

time money, money borrowed or loaned for a specified period of time.

title deed, a document that establishes title to property.

token payment, a partial payment made as a token of intention to pay the remainder of a debt later.

trade acceptance, a bill of exchange in payment for goods, marked as accepted by the purchaser: when properly executed, it constitutes an acceptance of obligation to pay.

trade association, an association of merchants or business firms for the unified promotion of their common interests.

trade discount, percentage off from list prices allowed a dealer as his profit on reselling the goods.

trade sale, an auction by and for the trade, i.e., those in the same line of business.

transfer agent, 1. an officer of a corporation who keeps account of transfers of its stock and issues new certificates. 2. a bank or other financial institution performing this function.

transfer in blank, the signing over of a stock certificate without endorsement in the customary place on the back of the certificate.

transit duty, a tax imposed on goods passing through a country.

transportation, *n.* conveying goods from one place to another.

transshipment, *n.* removing goods from one ship or conveyance to another.

tret, *n.* an allowance formerly made to buyers of certain goods for waste, damage, or deterioration during transit; specifically, an allowance of 4 lbs. in every 100 lbs. by weight after the deduction for tare.

trover, *n.* 1. originally, an action against a person who found another's goods and refused to return them. 2. an action to recover damages for goods withheld or used by another illegally.

trust company, a corporation, under the laws of a state, which administers estates and acts as guardian or trustee, also as fiscal agent.

trust deed, 1. a deed by which power is given to a group of creditors to foreclose mortgages upon default. 2. a deed to property, serving as collateral for a bond issue, and held by a trustee.

U

ullage, *n.* 1. the amount by which a container of liquor falls short of being full. 2. the amount of grain, etc., lost through spilling or sifting through a bag. 3. the loss of liquor from a container through evaporation or leakage, or of grain, etc., through spilling or sifting.

ultra vires, beyond (legal) power; beyond authority (of a court, corporation, etc.).

underlying, *adj.* in *finance,* prior, as a claim.

underwriter, *n.* 1. a person who guarantees against losses or who guarantees loans, stock or bond issues, etc. 2. a person or agent who underwrites insurance.

unearned increment, increase in value

from causes other than those of management or direction.

upset price, 1. the minimum price at which the courts permit property to be sold at a receivership sale following foreclosure. 2. the lowest price an owner is willing to take at an auction sale of his property.

usance, *n.* 1. the time allowed by usage for the payment of a bill of exchange, as established by custom and excluding any period of grace. 2. income or other benefits derived from wealth or the use of wealth.

V

value received, a phrase used in notes and bills to express a consideration, without specifying its nature.

vertical union, see **industrial union.**

voidable, *adj.* that can be made or adjudged void, or of no effect.

voucher, *n.* 1. a receipt for a payment. 2. a check that has been paid and returned to its maker by the bank. 3. a document proving a transaction.

W

wages, *n.pl.* the share of the total product of industry that goes to labor, as distinguished from the share taken by capital.

wage scale, 1. a schedule of wages paid for the performance of related jobs or tasks in a given industry, plant, etc. 2. the schedule of wages paid by a given employer.

warehouse receipt, a receipt for goods deposited in a warehouse: sometimes it ·is made negotiable and traded in as representing ownership of the merchandise.

warrant, *n.* [British], a receipt for goods stored in a warehouse. *v.t.* in *law,* to guarantee the title of granted property to (the grantee).

warranty, *n.* 1. an undertaking that goods of title are as represented. 2. a guarantee by the insured that the facts are as stated in regard to an insurance risk, or that specified conditions shall be fulfilled; it constitutes a part of the contract and must be fulfilled to keep the contract in force. 3. a covenant by which the seller of real estate gives assurance of, and binds himself to defend, the security of the title: also called *covenant of warranty*.

warranty deed, a deed to real estate containing a covenant of warranty (see **warranty,** sense 3): distinguished from *quitclaim deed*.

wash sales, fake sales made to influence the market: see **matched order.**

watered stock, stock only partly covered by the capital of the issuing company.

wholesaler, *n.* one who buys in large quantities to sell to retailers.

without recourse, without liability on the part of an endorser of a promissory note to pay the amount of the note if the maker or any following endorser fails to do so.

working capital, capital needed for and used in actual operation of a business.

workmen's compensation, the compensation to an employee for injury or occupational disease suffered in connection with his employment, paid under a government-supervised insurance system contributed to by employers.

CURRENCY UNITS OF FOREIGN COUNTRIES

(For evaluation in U.S. dollars, check with local banks.)

Afghanistan: afghani
Albania: lek
Algeria: dinar
Andorra: franc; peseta
Argentina: peso
Australia: dollar
Austria: schilling

Bahrain: dinar
Bangladesh: taka
Barbados: dollar
Belgium: franc
Bhutan: rupee
Bolivia: peso boliviano
Botswana: rand
Brazil: cruzeiro
Bulgaria: lev
Burma: kyat
Burundi: franc

Cambodia: riel
Cameroon: CFA franc
Canada: dollar
Central African Republic: CFA franc
Ceylon: rupee
Chad: CFA franc
Chile: escudo
China (People's Republic of): yuan
Colombia: peso
Congo: CFA franc
Costa Rica: colon
Cuba: peso
Cyprus: pound
Czechoslovakia: koruna

Dahomey: CFA franc
Denmark: krone
Dominican Republic: peso

Ecuador: sucre
Egypt: pound
El Salvador: colon

Equatorial Guinea: peseta
Ethiopia: dollar

Fiji: dollar
Finland: markka
France: franc

Gabon: CFA franc
Gambia: dalasi
Germany (East): mark
Germany (West): deutsche mark
Ghana: cedi
Greece: drachma
Guatemala: quetzal
Guinea: franc
Guyana: dollar

Haiti: gourde
Honduras: lempira
Hungary: forint

Iceland: krona
India: rupee
Indonesia: rupiah
Iran: rial
Iraq: dinar
Ireland: pound
Israel: pound
Italy: lira
Ivory Coast: CFA franc

Jamaica: dollar
Japan: yen
Jordan: dinar

Kenya: shilling
Korea (North and South): won
Kuwait: dinar

Laos: kip
Lebanon: pound

Lesotho: rand
Liberia: dollar
Libya: dinar
Liechtenstein: franc
Luxembourg: franc

Malagasy Republic: franc
Malawi: kwacha
Malaysia: dollar
Maldive Islands: rupee
Mali: franc
Malta: pound
Mauritania: CFA franc
Mauritius: rupee
Mexico: peso
Monaco: franc
Mongolia: tugrik
Morocco: dirham

Nauru: dollar
Nepal: rupee
Netherlands: guilder
New Zealand: dollar
Nicaragua: cordoba
Niger: CFA franc
Nigeria: pound
Norway: krone

Oman: rial

Pakistan: rupee
Panama: balboa
Paraguay: guarani
Peru: sol
Philippines: peso
Poland: zloty
Portugal: escudo

Qatar: riyal

Rhodesia: dollar
Romania: leu
Rwanda: franc

San Marino: lira
Saudi Arabia: riyal
Senegal: CFA franc
Sierra Leone: leone
Singapore: dollar
Somalia: shilling
South Africa: rand
Spain: peseta
Sudan: pound
Swaziland: rand
Sweden: krona
Switzerland: franc
Syria: pound

Taiwan: dollar
Tanzania: shilling
Thailand: baht
Togo: CFA franc
Tonga: paanga
Trinidad and Tobago: dollar
Tunisia: dinar
Turkey: lira

Uganda: shilling
Union of Soviet Socialist Republics: ruble
United Kingdom: pound
Upper Volta: CFA franc
Uruguay: peso

Vatican City: lira
Venezuela: bolivar
Vietnam (North): dong
Vietnam (South): piaster

Western Samoa: dollar

Yemen (People's Democratic Republic of): dinar
Yemen Arab Republic: riyal
Yugoslavia: dinar

Zaire: zaire
Zambia: kwacha

APPENDIX 4

DISTANCES—AIR AND ROAD

TABLE 1. AIR MILEAGE BETWEEN PRINCIPAL CITIES OF THE UNITED STATES

	Amarillo, Tex.	Atlanta, Ga.	Billings, Mont.	Boston, Mass.	Buffalo, N.Y.	Charleston, S.C.	Cheyenne, Wyo.	Chicago, Ill.	Cincinnati, Ohio	Cleveland, Ohio	Dallas, Tex.	Denver, Colo.	Detroit, Mich.	El Paso, Tex.	Houston, Tex.	Indianapolis, Ind.	Jacksonville, Fla.	Kansas City, Mo.	Los Angeles, Calif.	Louisville, Ky.	Memphis, Tenn.	Miami, Fla.	Minneapolis, Minn.	New Orleans, La.	New York, N.Y.	Philadelphia, Pa.	Phoenix, Ariz.	Pittsburgh, Pa.	Portland, Ore.	St. Louis, Mo.	Salt Lake City, Utah	San Francisco, Calif.	Seattle, Wash.	Tulsa, Okla.	Washington D.C.
Amarillo, Tex.	—	999	809	1722	1338	1266	440	894	992	1173	334	358	1124	358	533	915	1219	481	937	915	667	1441	812	776	1560	1494	598	1244	1304	685	668	1157	1359	335	1391
Atlanta, Ga.	999	—	1519	937	697	267	1229	587	360	554	721	1212	596	1291	701	426	285	676	1936	319	337	604	907	424	748	666	1592	521	2172	467	1583	2139	2182	678	543
Billings, Mont.	809	1519	—	1861	1473	1761	370	1073	1304	1360	1092	453	1283	1204	1315	1204	1796	846	959	1275	1213	2083	742	1479	1760	1727	872	1479	686	1057	387	904	668	930	1669
Boston, Mass.	1722	937	1861	—	400	820	1735	851	740	551	1551	1769	613	2072	1605	807	1017	1251	2596	826	1137	1255	1123	1359	188	271	2300	483	2540	1038	2099	2699	2493	1398	393
Buffalo, N.Y.	1338	697	1473	400	—	699	1335	454	393	173	1198	1369	216	1692	1236	435	879	861	2198	483	881	1181	731	1086	292	279	1906	178	2156	662	1699	2300	2117	1023	292
Charleston, S.C.	1266	267	1761	820	699	—	1486	757	506	609	981	1474	681	1552	936	594	197	928	2203	500	604	482	1104	641	641	562	1857	528	2425	547	1845	2405	2428	945	453
Cheyenne, Wyo.	440	1229	370	1735	1335	1486	—	920	1094	1227	726	96	1125	653	947	986	1493	558	831	1038	879	1982	826	1082	1604	1556	917	1320	982	796	371	949	813	550	1477
Chicago, Ill.	894	587	1073	851	454	757	920	—	252	308	803	920	238	1252	940	165	863	414	1745	269	482	1188	355	833	713	666	1758	410	1737	262	1260	1858	1737	683	597
Cincinnati, Ohio	992	360	1304	740	393	506	1094	252	—	222	814	1094	235	1335	973	100	626	591	1897	90	482	948	605	706	570	503	1985	257	2055	309	1453	2043	1972	674	404
Cleveland, Ohio	1173	554	1360	551	173	609	1227	308	222	—	1240	1227	90	1525	1114	263	770	700	2049	311	630	1087	630	924	405	360	1749	115	2026	492	1568	2166	2026	853	300
Dallas, Tex.	334	721	1092	1551	1198	981	726	803	814	1240	—	663	999	572	225	763	905	451	1240	726	420	1111	862	443	1374	1299	887	1070	1633	547	999	1483	1681	236	1185
Denver, Colo.	358	1212	453	1769	1369	1474	96	920	1094	1227	663	—	1156	557	879	1000	1467	558	831	1038	879	1763	700	1082	1631	1579	586	1320	982	796	371	949	1021	550	1494
Detroit, Mich.	1124	596	1283	613	216	681	1125	238	235	90	999	1156	—	1479	1105	240	831	645	1983	316	623	1152	543	939	482	410	1690	205	1969	455	1492	2091	1972	826	396
El Paso, Tex.	358	1291	1204	2072	1692	1552	653	1252	1335	1525	572	557	1479	—	676	1264	1473	839	701	1254	976	1643	1157	983	1905	1836	346	1590	1286	1034	689	995	1376	674	1728
Houston, Tex.	533	701	1315	1605	1236	936	947	940	973	1114	225	879	1105	676	—	865	821	644	1374	803	484	968	1056	318	1420	1341	1017	1137	1836	679	1163	1645	1891	442	1220
Indianapolis, Ind.	915	426	1204	807	435	594	986	165	100	263	763	1000	240	1264	865	—	699	453	1809	107	384	1024	511	712	646	585	1499	330	1885	231	1356	1940	1872	591	494
Jacksonville, Fla.	1219	285	1796	1017	879	197	1493	863	626	770	905	1467	831	1473	821	699	—	950	2147	594	590	326	1191	504	838	758	1794	703	2439	751	1837	2374	2455	921	647
Kansas City, Mo.	481	676	846	1251	861	928	558	414	591	700	451	558	645	839	644	453	950	—	1356	480	369	1241	413	680	1097	1038	1049	781	1497	238	925	1506	1506	216	945
Los Angeles, Calif.	937	1936	959	2596	2198	2203	831	1745	1897	2049	1240	831	1983	701	1374	1809	2147	1356	—	1829	1603	2339	1524	1673	2451	2394	357	2136	825	1589	579	347	959	1231	2300
Louisville, Ky.	915	319	1275	826	483	500	1036	269	90	311	726	1038	316	1254	803	107	594	480	1829	—	320	919	605	623	652	582	1529	344	1950	242	1402	1986	1943	582	476
Memphis, Tenn.	667	337	1213	1137	881	604	879	482	482	630	420	879	623	976	484	384	590	369	1603	320	—	872	699	358	957	881	1263	703	1849	240	1250	1802	1867	341	765
Miami, Fla.	1441	604	2083	1255	1181	482	1982	1188	948	1087	1111	1763	1152	1643	968	1024	326	1241	2339	919	872	—	1511	669	1092	1019	1982	1010	2165	1061	2089	2594	2734	1286	923
Minneapolis, Minn.	812	907	742	1123	731	1104	826	355	605	630	862	700	543	1157	1056	511	1191	413	1524	605	699	1511	—	1051	1018	985	1280	743	1427	466	987	1584	1395	626	934
New Orleans, La.	776	424	1479	1359	1086	641	1082	833	706	924	443	1082	939	983	318	712	504	680	1673	623	358	669	1051	—	1171	1089	1280	919	2063	598	1434	1926	2101	548	966
New York, N.Y.	1560	748	1760	188	292	641	1604	713	570	405	1374	1631	482	1905	1420	646	838	1097	2451	652	957	1092	1018	1171	—	83	2145	317	2445	875	1972	2571	2408	1231	205
Philadelphia, Pa.	1494	666	1727	271	279	562	1556	666	503	360	1299	1579	410	1836	1341	585	758	1038	2394	582	881	1019	985	1089	83	—	2083	259	2412	811	1925	2523	2380	1163	123
Phoenix, Ariz.	598	1592	872	2300	1906	1857	917	1758	1985	1749	887	586	1690	346	1017	1499	1794	1049	357	1529	1263	1982	1280	1280	2145	2083	—	1828	1005	1272	504	653	1114	917	1983
Pittsburgh, Pa.	1244	521	1479	483	178	528	1320	410	257	115	1070	1320	205	1590	1137	330	703	781	2136	344	703	1010	743	919	317	259	1828	—	2165	559	1668	2264	2138	917	192
Portland, Ore.	1304	2172	686	2540	2156	2425	982	1737	2055	2026	1633	982	1969	1286	1836	1885	2439	1497	825	1950	1849	2165	1427	2063	2445	2412	1005	2165	—	1723	636	534	145	1531	2354
St. Louis, Mo.	685	467	1057	1038	662	547	796	262	309	492	547	796	455	1034	679	231	751	238	1589	242	240	1061	466	598	875	811	1272	559	1723	—	1162	1744	1724	361	712
Salt Lake City, Utah	668	1583	387	2099	1699	1845	371	1260	1453	1568	999	371	1492	689	1163	1356	1837	925	579	1402	1250	2089	987	1434	1972	1925	504	1668	636	1162	—	600	701	917	1848
San Francisco, Calif.	1157	2139	904	2699	2300	2405	949	1858	2043	2166	1483	949	2091	995	1645	1940	2374	1506	347	1986	1802	2594	1584	1926	2571	2523	653	2264	534	1744	600	—	678	1461	2442
Seattle, Wash.	1359	2182	668	2493	2117	2428	813	1737	1972	2026	1681	1021	1972	1376	1891	1872	2455	1506	959	1943	1867	2734	1395	2101	2408	2380	1114	2138	145	1724	701	678	—	1560	2329
Tulsa, Okla.	335	678	930	1398	1023	945	550	683	674	853	236	550	826	674	442	591	921	216	1231	582	341	1286	626	548	1231	1163	917	917	1531	361	917	1461	1560	—	1058
Washington D.C.	1391	543	1669	393	292	453	1477	597	404	300	1185	1494	396	1728	1220	494	647	945	2300	476	765	923	934	966	205	123	1983	192	2354	712	1848	2442	2329	1058	—

	ATLANTA, GA.	BOSTON, MASS.	CHICAGO, ILL.	CINCINNATI, OHIO	CLEVELAND, OHIO	DENVER, COLO.	DETROIT, MICH.	EL PASO, TEXAS	HOUSTON, TEXAS	KANSAS CITY, MO.	LOS ANGELES, CALIF.	MEMPHIS, TENN.	MIAMI, FLA.	MINNEAPOLIS-ST. PAUL, MINN.	MONTREAL, QUE., CAN.	NEW ORLEANS, LA.	NEW YORK, N. Y.	PHILADELPHIA, PA.	PITTSBURGH, PA.	PORTLAND, ORE.	ST. LOUIS, MO.	SALT LAKE CITY, UTAH	SAN FRANCISCO, CALIF.	SEATTLE, WASH.	WASHINGTON, D. C.
ALBANY, N. Y.	1059	169	800	717	471	1841	539	2261	1832	1275	2880	1239	1495	1209	231	1554	151	231	454	2995	1021	2252	3011	2935	358
ASHEVILLE, N. C.	207	965	656	386	603	1514	630	1662	1083	873	2409	533	771	1076	1067	744	748	652	586	2826	619	2009	2720	2840	505
ATLANTA, GA.	•	1084	715	481	727	1519	741	1450	875	882	2252	414	662	1136	1296	518	863	776	741	2873	582	1959	2554	2954	641
AUGUSTA, MAINE	1297	168	1113	1018	777	2142	840	2562	2129	1576	3264	1540	1733	1533	326	1793	387	481	755	3240	1322	2565	3332	3174	628
BALTIMORE, MD.	680	404	696	493	361	1624	524	2056	1555	1070	2724	955	1146	1106	586	1206	184	102	232	2892	800	2120	2899	2792	39
BIRMINGHAM, ALA.	160	1250	684	499	741	1364	755	1307	711	723	2091	242	783	1080	1335	358	990	893	812	2676	525	1855	2393	2707	759
BISMARCK, N. DAK.	1569	1850	871	1172	1220	710	1144	1454	1486	838	1723	1306	2231	428	1535	1721	1712	1630	1336	1379	1006	1000	1767	1313	1567
BOISE, IDAHO	2340	2797	1789	2018	2137	891	2056	1266	1889	1492	908	1957	2974	1582	2637	2167	2616	2531	2238	443	1744	375	662	552	2480
BOSTON, MASS.	1084	•	976	853	643	2008	706	2428	1961	1442	3130	1389	1547	1399	327	1625	217	308	595	3229	1188	2431	3198	3163	443
BUFFALO, N. Y.	963	466	553	430	203	1554	259	1974	1545	988	2676	952	1479	945	388	1321	380	365	240	2775	734	1977	2744	2709	379
CHARLESTON, W. VA.	549	786	498	198	277	1381	357	1778	1269	797	2398	689	1115	918	834	1051	567	477	227	2649	543	1868	2626	2609	364
CHATTANOOGA, TENN.	120	1088	603	387	597	1343	612	1453	873	702	2200	320	783	1003	1175	537	869	775	637	2655	448	1838	2511	2686	628
CHEYENNE, WYO.	1479	1955	982	1198	1312	102	1241	816	1151	656	1196	1124	2141	812	1822	1379	1791	1709	1426	1253	910	454	1230	1323	1646
CHICAGO, ILL.	715	976	•	301	349	1043	297	1519	1113	504	2189	545	1386	409	854	977	818	767	473	2250	292	1466	2233	2184	696
CINCINNATI, OHIO	481	853	301	•	239	1245	273	1590	1115	604	2292	492	1143	721	819	846	623	578	281	2495	348	1682	2449	2485	498
CLEVELAND, OHIO	727	643	349	239	•	1373	173	1785	1356	799	2487	763	1365	769	578	1132	502	425	128	2599	545	1796	2563	2533	358
COLUMBUS, OHIO	560	769	316	109	145	1236	180	1654	1212	668	2356	619	1236	736	722	988	555	473	183	2559	408	1746	2526	2500	389
DALLAS, TEXAS	826	1868	955	988	1225	805	1194	631	242	514	1431	470	1394	980	1775	509	1649	1561	1282	2145	657	1285	1791	2222	1414
DENVER, COLO.	1519	2008	1043	1245	1373	•	1302	657	1049	619	1189	1107	2126	855	1883	1314	1852	1770	1420	1347	895	514	1267	1426	1707
DES MOINES, IOWA	933	1313	350	582	678	695	607	1223	1013	206	1841	637	1595	252	1188	1056	1165	1083	789	1386	363	1118	1885	1962	1061
DETROIT, MICH.	741	706	297	273	173	1302	•	1754	1326	752	2448	751	1395	693	581	1143	632	588	294	2523	514	1725	2492	2457	525
DULUTH, MINN.	1199	1474	476	796	844	1065	768	1642	1361	637	2192	1004	1861	158	1056	1419	1336	1254	960	1840	695	1469	2155	1774	1191
EL PASO, TEXAS	1450	2428	1519	1590	1785	657	1754	•	762	1015	806	1130	2068	1483	2335	1130	2209	2127	1842	1747	1240	885	1209	1822	2052
FREDERICTON, N. B., CAN.	1534	405	1350	1255	1014	2379	1077	2799	2366	1813	3501	1777	1970	1684	490	2030	624	718	992	3404	1559	2802	3569	3338	865
GLACIER NAT'L PARK, MONT.	2378	2618	1639	1940	1988	951	1912	1573	2071	1500	1373	2023	3040	1203	2145	2352	2480	2398	2104	673	1809	690	1217	580	2335
GRAND CANYON NAT'L PARK, ARIZ.	1884	2718	1807	1880	2075	798	2044	581	1352	1303	542	1463	2515	1774	2625	1577	2499	2417	2132	1230	1530	389	831	1310	2340
GRAND RAPIDS, MICH.	790	833	183	309	284	1216	149	1683	1277	668	2362	723	1452	594	700	1138	759	700	406	2433	460	1639	2406	2367	637
HELENA, MONT.	2111	2479	1500	1789	1849	796	1773	1386	1845	1294	1321	1762	2773	1080	2187	2082	2341	2259	1965	709	1542	498	1134	622	2196
HOUSTON, TEXAS	875	1961	1113	1115	1356	1049	1326	762	•	754	1564	593	1306	1205	1907	376	1742	1648	1396	2368	817	1508	1984	2445	1501
INDIANAPOLIS, IND.	549	948	174	110	305	1064	273	1480	1052	494	2182	453	1219	611	855	845	729	647	364	2385	236	1572	2353	2375	572
JACKSON, MISS.	411	1497	779	739	980	1300	968	1060	461	685	1877	217	979	1091	1549	195	1278	1184	1020	2638	526	1789	2206	2669	1037
JACKSONVILLE, FLA.	356	1204	1032	791	1028	1789	1058	1722	960	1148	2539	672	346	1449	1395	568	982	888	924	3101	904	2284	2892	3132	756
KANSAS CITY, MO.	882	1442	504	604	799	619	752	1015	754	•	1631	468	1485	478	1333	887	1223	1141	856	1953	256	1136	1903	1984	1066
LAS VEGAS, NEV.	2004	2810	1866	1972	2167	907	2123	704	1484	1417	279	1637	2582	1688	2704	1740	2591	2509	2224	1027	1668	446	576	1204	2434
LITTLE ROCK, ARK.	560	1530	661	663	904	970	874	975	452	418	1701	139	1221	857	1455	445	1311	1217	944	2299	348	1464	2046	2334	1070
LOS ANGELES, CALIF.	2252	3130	2189	2292	2487	1189	2448	806	1564	1631	•	1877	2885	2033	3029	1947	2911	2829	2544	1016	1942	742	424	1193	2754
LOUISVILLE, KY.	432	989	309	109	352	1167	363	1512	1004	526	2214	373	1101	729	930	737	771	689	404	2479	268	1662	2433	2493	614
MEMPHIS, TENN.	414	1389	545	492	763	1107	751	1130	593	468	1877	•	1018	864	1332	411	1170	1076	803	2421	301	1600	2188	2452	929
MIAMI, FLA.	662	1547	1386	1143	1365	2126	1395	2068	1306	1485	2885	1018	•	1786	1732	881	1325	1231	1261	3438	1231	2621	3238	3469	1096
MILWAUKEE, WIS.	814	1069	90	391	439	1044	363	1574	1233	572	2149	652	1476	341	944	1067	931	849	555	2130	374	1428	2186	2043	786
MINNEAPOLIS-ST. PAUL, MINN.	1135	1399	409	721	769	855	693	1483	1205	478	2033	864	1786	•	1194	1279	1261	1179	885	1830	555	1310	2077	1691	1116
MONTREAL, QUE., CAN.	1296	327	854	819	578	1883	581	2335	1896	1333	3029	1332	1732	1194	•	1710	405	473	607	2914	1095	2306	3073	2848	618
NASHVILLE, TENN.	240	1168	458	291	542	1205	553	1351	814	564	2098	216	921	876	1120	549	949	855	582	2517	310	1700	2409	2548	708
NEW ORLEANS, LA.	518	1625	977	846	1132	1314	1143	1130	376	887	1947	411	881	1279	1710	•	1406	1312	1172	2654	724	1794	2300	2731	1165
NEW YORK, N. Y.	863	217	818	623	502	1852	632	2209	1742	1223	2911	1170	1325	1261	405	1406	•	89	376	3088	969	2275	3082	3025	232
OKLAHOMA CITY, OKLA.	911	1745	845	907	1102	619	1071	678	460	370	1350	511	1572	860	1652	683	1526	1444	1159	2076	557	1199	1695	2155	1369
OMAHA, NEB.	1027	1451	486	702	816	555	745	1038	937	209	1668	680	1686	379	1326	1086	1295	1213	919	1749	455	968	1726	1824	1150
OTTAWA, ONT., CAN.	1231	464	784	754	513	1798	511	2232	1837	1263	2867	1262	1985	1068	126	1645	434	453	542	2770	1025	2224	2982	2683	702
PHILADELPHIA, PA.	776	308	767	578	425	1770	588	2127	1648	1141	2829	1076	1231	1179	473	1312	89	•	284	3006	887	2193	2960	2943	141
PHOENIX, ARIZ.	1894	2746	1837	1908	2103	904	2072	440	1206	1333	390	1493	2491	1669	2653	1553	2527	2445	2160	1383	1543	716	806	1597	2370
PITTSBURGH, PA.	741	595	473	281	128	1420	294	1842	1396	856	2544	803	1261	885	607	1172	376	284	•	2712	602	1933	2710	2649	231
PORTLAND, MAINE	1237	111	1053	958	717	2082	780	2502	2073	1516	3204	1480	1673	1473	266	1733	327	421	695	3180	1262	2505	3272	3114	568
PORTLAND, ORE.	2873	3229	2250	2495	2599	1347	2523	1747	2368	1953	1016	2421	3438	1830	2914	2654	3088	3006	2712	•	2207	839	706	175	2943
PUEBLO, COLO.	1415	2086	1148	1248	1443	110	1396	611	939	644	1264	996	2076	965	1977	1198	1867	1785	1500	1330	898	582	1320	1515	1710
QUEBEC, QUE., CAN.	1468	392	1026	991	750	2055	753	2507	2079	1505	3201	1504	1904	1366	155	1882	563	652	779	3086	1267	2478	3245	3020	799
RALEIGH, N. C.	423	731	825	543	602	1773	689	1894	1347	1132	2668	792	834	1245	897	957	512	418	471	3038	878	2225	2979	3009	271
RAPID CITY, S. DAK.	1569	1922	943	1230	1292	403	1216	1039	1403	753	1409	1221	2231	582	1770	1571	1784	1702	1408	1275	1000	689	1447	1188	1630
RENO, NEV.	2611	2953	1980	2196	2310	1038	2239	1213	1975	1654	475	2087	3217	1782	2820	2350	2789	2707	2413	666	1908	530	222	856	2644
RICHMOND, VA.	549	549	788	543	454	1762	617	1993	1489	1121	2740	863	995	1205	737	1099	351	257	323	3018	867	2205	2972	2972	106
ST. LOUIS, MO.	582	1188	292	348	545	895	514	1240	817	256	1942	301	1231	555	1095	724	969	887	602	2207	•	1390	2157	2238	812
SALT LAKE CITY, UTAH	1959	2431	1466	1682	1796	514	1725	885	1508	1136	742	1600	2621	1310	2306	1794	2275	2193	1933	839	1390	•	752	924	2130
SAN ANTONIO, TEXAS	1022	2108	1245	1247	1488	975	1458	564	196	788	1388	725	1435	1188	2039	574	1889	1795	1528	2224	949	1364	1793	2301	1648
SAN DIEGO, CALIF.	2230	3119	2210	2281	2476	1243	2445	747	1578	1706	125	1866	2817	2138	3026	1879	2900	2818	2533	1137	1931	812	525	1314	2743
SAN FRANCISCO, CALIF.	2554	3198	2233	2449	2563	1267	2492	1209	1984	1903	424	2188	3238	2077	3073	2300	3082	2960	2710	706	2157	752	•	866	2897
SANTA FE, N. MEX	1461	2295	1372	1457	1652	386	1621	330	877	868	889	1042	2092	1150	2202	1154	2076	1994	1709	1464	1107	627	1200	1631	1919
SAVANNAH, GA.	263	1072	954	676	872	1741	952	1662	1062	1100	2479	676	493	1374	1239	672	853	759	768	3053	846	2236	2808	3084	597
SEATTLE, WASH.	2954	3163	2184	2485	2533	1426	2457	1822	2445	1984	1193	2452	3469	1691	2848	2731	3025	2943	2649	175	2238	924	866	•	2880
SHREVEPORT, LA.	643	1729	873	871	1112	973	1084	816	268	569	1614	349	1155	1020	1665	316	1510	1416	1152	2262	575	1417	1972	2340	1269
SIOUX CITY, IOWA	1129	1482	497	784	852	590	776	1163	1039	314	1736	774	1791	268	1357	1193	1344	1262	968	1804	560	1013	1780	1738	1199
SPOKANE, WASH.	2501	2857	1878	2179	2227	1143	2151	1622	2211	1678	1256	2146	3163	1405	2542	2471	2719	2637	2343	373	1932	732	929	284	2574
TAMPA, FLA.	469	1427	1215	972	1209	1933	1224	1807	1045	1292	2624	782	270	1615	1594	639	1208	1114	1123	3245	1060	2424	2977	3276	967
TOLEDO, OHIO	685	756	241	206	110	1267	56	1702	1274	708	2404	699	1342	661	634	1090	611	529	235	2487	462	1690	2457	2421	466
TORONTO, ONT., CAN.	963	582	503	482	304	1532	235	1984	1556	982	2678	981	1594	923	347	1373	495	480	333	2753	744	1955	2722	2687	494
TULSA, OKLA.	853	1627	720	773	984	736	953	813	529	252	1473	434	1514	730	1534	762	1408	1326	1041	2085	406	1225	1814	2162	1251
VANCOUVER, B. C., CAN.	3041	3215	2236	2525	2585	1537	2509	1940	2580	2209	1327	2776	3709	1816	2923	2783	3077	2995	2701	321	2465	1053	1017	149	2932
WASHINGTON, D. C.	641	443	696	498	358	1707	525	2052	1501	1066	2754	929	1096	1116	618	1165	232	141	231	2943	812	2130	2897	2880	•
WICHITA, KANS.	980	1660	722	822	1017	519	970	748	632	206	1383	561	1603	685	1551	842	1441	1359	1074	1856	472	1016	1759	1899	1284
WINNIPEG, MAN., CAN.	1584	1859	880	1181	1229	1089	1153	1652	1608	867	2067	1324	2246	452	1445	1739	1721	1639	1345	1550	1015	1323	1959	1463	1575
YELLOWSTONE NAT'L PARK, WYO.	1946	2333	1354	1624	1703	544	1609	1187	1647	1085	1079	1570	2608	1015	2089	1854	2195	2113	1819	889	1377	326	971	809	2050

10169 MILEAGES ARE APPROXIMATE AND ARE COMPUTED OVER COMMONLY TRAVELED THROUGH ROUTES

G © The H.M. Gousha Co.

TABLE 3. AIR MILEAGE BETWEEN PRINCIPAL CITIES OF THE WORLD

	Zanzibar, Afr.	Wellington, N.Z.	Valparaiso, Chile	Tokyo, Jap.	Singapore	Shanghai, Ch.	Seattle, U.S.A.	Rome, It.	Rio de Janeiro, Braz.	Reykjavik, Ice.	Quebec, Can.	Port Said, Eg.	Peking, Ch.	Paris, Fr.	Panama, Pan.	Oslo, Norw.	Nome, U.S.A.	New York, U.S.A.	Moscow, U.S.S.R.	Mexico City, Mex.	Melbourne, Austl.	Manila, P.I.	Los Angeles, U.S.A.	London, Eng.	Juneau, U.S.A.	Istanbul, Turk.	Honolulu, U.S.A.	Hong Kong	Gibraltar	Darwin, Austl.	Capetown, S.Afr.	Calcutta, Ind.	Buenos Aires, Arg.	Bombay, Ind.	Berlin, Ger.
Berlin, Ger.	4309	11265	7795	5538	6166	5215	5041	734	6114	1479	3583	1747	4567	542	5849	515	4342	3961	996	6037	9919	6128	5782	574	4560	1078	7305	5500	1453	8036	5977	4376	7376	3910	
Bombay, Ind.	2855	7677	10037	4188	2429	3133	7741	3843	8257	5191	7371	2659	2964	4359	9742	4130	5901	7794	3131	9722	6097	3133	8701	4462	6866	2991	8020	2673	4814	4503	5134	1041	9273		3910
Buenos Aires, Arg.	6421	6260	761	11400	9864	12197	6913	6929	1218	7099	5680	7362	11974	6877	3381	7613	8848	5297	8375	4633	7558	11042	6118	6918	7759	6918	8020	11463	5963	9127	4270	10242		9273	7376
Calcutta, Ind.	3859	7042	10993	3187	1791	2112	6913	4496	8190	5373	7481	3506	2024	4889	9495	4459	5101	7921	3447	9495	5547	2112	8172	4980	4954	3646	7037	2189	5963	3744	6026		10242	1041	4376
Capetown, S.Afr.	2346	7019	4998	9071	6016	8059	10199	5249	3769	7111	7857	4590	8045	5941	7014	6494	10107	7801	6294	8511	6412	7525	9969	6005	7234	6219	11532	7650	5076	6947		6026	4270	5134	5977
Darwin, Austl.	6409	3310	8961	3367	2075	3142	7619	8190	9960	8631	9724	7159	3728	8575	10352	8022	6235	9959	7046	9081	1964	1979	7835	8598	7105	7390	5355	2642	9265		6947	3744	9127	4503	8036
Gibraltar	4103	11682	6405	6988	7231	5710	6471	887	5772	2047	3101	1710	6009	964	4926	1791	5398	3627	2413	5629	10798	7483	5936	964	6294	1874	7433	8075		9265	5076	6026	6929	4814	1453
Hong Kong	5414	5833	12060	1796	1652	772	6471	5768	10995	6031	7650	4975	1226	5956	10084	5337	4547	8051	4439	8776	4607	693	7240	5981	5936	4980	5537		8075	2642	11532	2189	11463	2673	5500
Honolulu, U.S.A.	10869	4708	7042	3850	6710	4934	2678	8022	8190	6084	4644	8738	5067	7434	6248	6016	3004	4959	7033	3781	5513	5296	2557	7226	2815	8104		5537	8075	5355	11532	7037	7558	8020	7305
Istanbul, Turk.	3312	10663	8172	5556	6744	5005	6471	854	6395	3268	4644	693	4379	1401	6760	1518	5101	5009	1088	8422	5659	5551	6843	1551	4607		8104	4980	1874	7390	6219	3646	7234	2991	1078
Juneau, U.S.A.	8795	7475	7271	4011	7235	4869	899	5247	7598	3268	2660	6215	4522	4628	3495	4045	1094	2854	4534	3219	8035	5869	1842	4418		4607	2815	5936	5936	7105	7234	4954	7759	6866	4560
London, Eng.	4604	11682	7263	5470	6744	5710	4782	887	5772	1171	3101	2154	5054	213	5278	714	4381	3459	1549	5541	10501	6667	5439		4418	1551	7226	5981	1094	8598	6005	4954	6918	4462	574
Los Angeles, U.S.A.	10021	6714	5527	5470	6232	6477	959	6326	6296	4306	2557	7528	6250	213	3205	5325	2876	2451	6323	1542	7931	7269		5439	1842	6843	2557	7240	5936	7835	9969	8843	6118	8701	5782
Manila, P.I.	5763	5162	6793	1863	1479	1152	6759	6457	11254	6651	8124	5619	1770	6673	10283	6016	4817	8493	5130	8829	3941		7269	6667	5619	5659	8738	693	8172	1979	10107	2189	11042	2964	6128
Melbourne, Austl.	6802	1595	6998	5089	3761	5020	8136	9934	8186	10544	10497	8668	5667	10396	9022	9926	7558	10355	8963	8422		3941	7931	10501	8035	9088	5000	4607	10798	6482	6412	5547	7234	6097	9919
Mexico City, Mex.	9454	6899	4053	7011	10307	8039	2337	6353	7598	4622	2454	7671	7733	5706	1495	5706	4309	2085	5701		8422	8829	1542	5541	3219	8422	3781	8776	5629	9081	8511	9495	4633	9722	6037
Moscow, U.S.S.R.	4270	10279	8792	4650	5472	4235	5199	1474	7179	2056	3235	1541	3597	1541	6711	832	4574	4662		5701	8963	5130	6323	1549	4534	1016	7033	4439	3627	7046	6294	3447	8375	3131	996
New York, U.S.A.	7698	8946	5094	6739	9630	7357	2408	4273	4820	2576	6423	5590	6823	3622	2231	3672	3769		4662	2085	10355	8493	2451	3459	2854	5009	4959	8051	3627	9959	7801	7921	5297	7794	3961
Nome, U.S.A.	8209	7383	10079	2983	5088	5132	1976	5082	8586	3366	3489	5745	3428	3651	6146	3836		3769	1016	4309	8658	4817	2876	4381	3769	2876	3004	4036	5398	6235	4590	5271	8375	3004	4342
Oslo, Norw.	4803	10249	8360	5373	3761	5020	2353	1243	6395	1083	3263	5715	4360	5221	5691		3836	3672	832	5706	9926	6016	5325	714	4045	1518	5513	4547	1791	8022	6412	4459	7613	4130	515
Panama, Pan.	8245	7014	7914	5842	7160	5132	3614	5903	3294	4706	2659	7146	8906	5382		5691	6146	2231	6711	1495	9022	10283	3205	5278	3495	6750	5245	10084	4926	10352	7014	9495	3381	9742	5849
Paris, Fr.	4396	11791	7225	6033	6671	5752	4993	682	5703	1380	3235	1975	3622		5382	5221	3651	3622	1541	5706	10396	6673	7269	213	4628	1401	7434	5956	964	8575	5941	5271	6877	4359	542
Peking, Ch.	5803	6714	5527	1307	6232	662	6759	5047	10768	4903	5943	5703		3622	8906	4360	3428	6823	3597	7733	5667	1770	6250	5054	4522	4975	5067	1226	6009	3728	8045	2024	11974	2964	4567
Port Said, Eg.	2729	6230	7420	5842	6232	5703	6759	1317	6244	3227	2353		5703	1975	7146	5715	5745	5590	1710	7671	8658	5619	7528	2154	6215	693	8738	4975	2179	7619	4590	5271	6794	2659	1747
Quebec, Can.	7443	9228	6230	6417	9097	6981	2353	3943	5125	2189		2353	4360	3235	2659	5020	3489	439	4242	2454	10497	8124	2579	3101	2660	4644	5000	7650	3383	9724	7857	5547	5680	7371	3583
Reykjavik, Ice.	5757	10724	11774	4777	7160	5559	3614	2044	6118		2189	5088	4903	1380	4706	1083	3366	2576	2056	4622	10544	6651	4306	1171	3268	2558	6084	6031	2047	8631	7111	5373	7099	5191	1479
Rio de Janeiro, Braz.	5589	7349	1855	6033	9774	11340	5659	5684		6118	5125	6244	10768	5703	3294	6482	8586	4820	7179	4770	10768	11254	6296	5772	7598	854	8190	10995	5772	9960	3769	8190	1218	8257	6114
Rome, It.	3712	11594	8088	6133	6232	5677	5703		5684	2044	3943	1317	5047	682	5903	1243	5082	4273	1474	6353	9934	6457	6326	887	5247	854	8022	5768	887	8190	5249	4496	6929	3843	734
Seattle, U.S.A.	9359	8124	6230	4777	7160	5677		5703	5659	3614	2353	6759	6759	4993	3614	2353	1976	2408	5199	2337	8136	6759	959	4782	899	6471	2678	6471	6471	7619	10199	6913	6913	7741	5041
Shanghai, Ch.	5971	9228	11650	1094	5703		5677	5677	11340	5559	6981	5703	662	5752	5132	5020	5132	7357	4235	8039	5020	1152	6477	5710	4869	5005	4934	772	5710	3142	8059	2112	12197	3133	5215
Singapore	4490	5292	3304	3304		5703	7160	6232	9774	7160	9097	6232	6232	6671	7160	3761	5088	9630	5238	10307	3761	1479	6714	6744	7235	5373	6710	1652	7231	2075	6016	1791	9864	2429	6166
Tokyo, Jap.	7040	5760	10226		3304	1094	4777	6124	11535	5472	6417	1307	1307	6033	8423	6034	4650	6735	4650	7035	6998	1796	7349	6988	4011	5556	3850	1796	6988	3367	9071	3188	11400	4188	5538
Valparaiso, Chile	7184	10635		10226	10226	11650	7225	8088	1855	11774	6230	7420	5527	7225	7914	10074	7383	5094	10279	6899	6998	5853	6714	7263	7271	10663	6793	11607	12060	8961	7019	10993	761	10037	7795
Wellington, N.Z.	8122		10635	5760	5292	9228	8124	11594	7349	10724	9228	6230	6714	11791	7014	10249	7383	8946	10279	6899	1595	5162	6714	11682	7475	10663	4708	5833	11682	3310	7019	7042	6260	7677	11265
Zanzibar, Afr.		8122	7184	7040	4490	5971	9359	3712	5589	5757	7443	2729	5803	4396	8245	4803	8209	7698	4270	9454	6802	5763	10021	4604	8795	3312	10869	5414	4103	6409	2346	3859	6421	2855	4309

FORMS OF ADDRESS

PERSON BEING ADDRESSED	ENVELOPE ADDRESS	SALUTATION		IN SPEAKING
		FORMAL	LESS FORMAL OR PERSONAL	
Ambassador (United States)	The Honorable (full name), The Ambassador of the United States, American Embassy (city and country)	Sir (*or* Madam):	My dear Mr. (*or* Madam) Ambassador:	Mr. Ambassador (*or* Madam Ambassador)
Ambassador (Foreign)	His (*or* Her) Excellency (full name), Ambassador of (country), Washington, D.C.	Excellency:	My dear Mr. (*or* Madam) Ambassador:	Excellency *or* Mr. Ambassador (*or* Madam Ambassador) *or* Sir
Archbishop (Roman Catholic)	The Most Reverend (full name), Archbishop of (city), (city and state, etc.)	Your Excellency: *or* Most Reverend Sir:	Most Reverend and dear Sir:	Your Excellency
Bishop (Methodist)	Bishop (full name), (city and state, etc.)	My dear Bishop (surname):	Dear Bishop (surname):	Bishop (surname)

	Address	Salutation (formal)	Salutation (informal)	Spoken address
Bishop (Protestant Episcopal)	The Right Reverend (full name), Bishop of (diocese), (city and state, etc.)	Right Reverend Sir:	My dear Bishop (surname):	Bishop (surname)
Bishop (Roman Catholic)	The Most Reverend (full name), Address of Church, (city and state, etc.)	Most Reverend Sir:	My dear Bishop (surname):	Bishop (surname)
Cabinet Officer of the United States	The Honorable (full name), (title), Washington, D.C.	Sir (or Madam): or Dear Sir:	My dear Mr. (or Madam) Secretary: or Dear Mr. (surname):	Mr. (or Madam) Secretary or Sir
Cardinal (Roman Catholic)	His Eminence (given name) Cardinal (surname), Archbishop of (city, etc.), (city and state, etc.)	Your Eminence:	Dear Cardinal (surname):	Your Eminence
Common Form (Man)	Mr. (full name), (address, city, and state)	My dear Mr. (surname): or My dear Sir: in plural, Gentlemen:	Dear Mr. (surname): or Dear Sir:	Mr. (surname)
Common Form (Woman)	Mrs. (or Miss) (or Ms.) (full name), (address, city, and state)	My dear Mrs. (or Miss) (or Ms.) (surname): or My dear Madam: in plural, Ladies: or Mesdames:	Dear Mrs. (or Miss) (or Ms.) (surname): or Dear Madam:	Miss (or Mrs.) (or Ms.) (surname)

PERSON BEING ADDRESSED	ENVELOPE ADDRESS	SALUTATION		IN SPEAKING
		FORMAL	LESS FORMAL OR PERSONAL	
Congressman	The Honorable (full name), United States House of Representatives, Washington, D.C.	Sir (*or* Madam):	My dear Mr. (*or* Mrs. *or* Miss) (surname):	Mr. (*or* Mrs. *or* Miss) (surname)
Consul (United States or other)	(full name), Esq., American (or other) Consul, (city and country, or state)	Sir: *or* My dear Sir:	Dear Mr. (surname):	Mr. (surname) (*or* Mrs. *or* Miss)
Doctor (of Philosophy, Medicine, Divinity, etc.)	(full name), Ph.D., M.D., D.D., etc., *or* Dr. (full name), (address, city, and state)	My dear Dr. (surname): *or* My dear Sir:	Dear Dr. (surname):	Dr. (surname)
Governor (of a state)	The Honorable (full name), Governor of (state), (capital city and state)	Sir:	Dear Governor (surname):	Governor (surname) *or* Sir
Judge (see also Supreme Court)	The Honorable (full name), Justice (name of court), (city and state)	Sir (*or* Madam):	Dear Judge (surname):	Judge (surname)
Mayor	His (*or* Her Honor, The Mayor City Hall (city and state)	Sir (*or* Madam):	My dear Mr. (*or* Madam) Mayor: *or* My dear Mayor (surname):	Mr. (*or* Madam) Mayor

Military Officer (American)	(title of rank), (full name), (address)	Sir: *or* Dear Sir:	Dear General (*or* Colonel, Major, Captain, etc.) (surname): Dear Mr. (surname): (for rank below Second Lieutenant)	General (*or* Colonel, Major, Captain, etc.) Mr. (surname) (for rank below Second Lieutenant)
Minister (Protestant)	The Reverend (full name), (plus D.D. if applicable) (address, city, and state)	My dear Sir: *or or* Sir:	Dear Mr. (*or* Dr.) (surname):	Mr. (*or* Dr. *or, if a Lutheran,* Pastor) (surname)
Monsignor (Roman Catholic)	The Right Reverend Monsignor (surname), (church), (city and state)	Right Reverend and dear Monsignor (surname):	Reverend and dear Monsignor (surname):	Monsignor (surname)
Naval Officer (American)	(title of rank), (full name), (address)	Sir: *or* Dear Sir:	Dear Admiral (*or* Commodore, Captain, Commander, etc.) (surname): Dear Mr. (surname): (for rank below Commander)	Admiral (*or* Commodore, Captain, Commander, etc.) Mr. (surname) (for rank below Commander)
Nun	Sister (religious name), (initials of her order), (address, city, and state)	My dear Sister:	Dear Sister (religious name):	Sister (religious name)
Pope	His Holiness the Pope, Vatican City, Rome, Italy	Your Holiness:	Most Holy Father:	Your Holiness (*or* Most Holy Father)

PERSON BEING ADDRESSED	ENVELOPE ADDRESS	SALUTATION		IN SPEAKING
		FORMAL	LESS FORMAL OR PERSONAL	
President (of the United States)	The President, The White House, Washington, D.C.	Sir: *or* Mr. President:	My dear Mr. President: *or* Dear President (surname):	Mr. President *or* Sir
Priest (Roman Catholic)	The Reverend (full name plus initials of his order), (address, city, and state)	Reverend Father:	Dear Father (surname):	Father (surname) *or* Father
Professor	Prof. (*or* Dr. if Ph.D. or Mr.) (full name), Department of (mathematics, history, etc.), (name of university or college), (address, city, and state)	My dear Sir: *or* Dear Sir:	My dear Professor (surname): *or* Dear Dr. (surname): *or* Dear Mr. (surname):	Professor (*or* Dr. *or* Mr.) (surname). In certain universities (e.g., Harvard) all faculty members are orally addressed as Mr. (*or* Miss *or* Mrs.) (surname)
Rabbi	Rabbi (full name plus D.D. if he holds degree), (address, city, and state)	Dear Sir: (surname):	Dear Rabbi (*or* Dr.) (surname):	Rabbi (*or* Dr.) (surname)
Representative (of a state legislature)	The Honorable (full name), Member of Assembly (or other name of the legislature), (capital city and state)	Sir (*or* Madam):	My dear Mr. (*or* Mrs. *or* Miss) (surname):	Mr. (*or* Mrs. *or* Miss) (surname)

Senator (of the United States)	The Honorable (full name), United States Senate, Washington, D.C.	Sir (*or* Madam):	My dear Senator (surname):	Senator (surname) *or* Mr. (*or* Madam) Senator
Supreme Court (Associate Justice)	Mr. Justice (surname), The Supreme Court, Washington, D.C.	Sir:	My dear Mr. Justice (surname):	Mr. Justice *or* Mr. Justice (surname) *or* Sir
United Nations Delegate	His (*or* Her) Excellency, (Country) Representative to the United Nations, United Nations, New York	Sir (*or* Madam): *or* Your Excellency:	My dear Mr. (*or* Madam) Ambassador: *or* My dear Mr. (surname):	Your Excellency
Vice President (of the United States)	The Vice President, United States Senate, Washington, D.C.	Sir:	My dear Mr. Vice President:	Mr. Vice President *or* Sir
Chief Justice (Supreme Court)	The Chief Justice The Supreme Court Washington, D.C.	Sir:	My dear Mr. Chief Justice:	Mr. Chief Justice *or* Sir

HOLIDAYS

CHIEF LEGAL OR PUBLIC HOLIDAYS IN THE UNITED STATES

Each state has jurisdiction over holidays that will be observed in that state. They are designated either by the state legislature or by executive proclamation and, therefore, may be changed with each new state executive or legislature. There are no national holidays in the United States. The President and Congress designate holidays only for the District of Columbia and for Federal employees throughout the nation.

In 1971, Congress made changes in the observance days of certain holidays. In most states, holidays that fall on Sunday are observed on the following day.

Jan. 1—New Year's Day. All the states.

Jan. 18 or 19—Robert E. Lee Birthday. Ala., Miss., Va., Ark., Fla., Ga., La., S.C., Tex.

Jan. 20—Inauguration Day. Begun in 1937. Observed every 4th year in the District of Columbia only.

Feb. 12—Lincoln's Birthday. All the states except Ala., Ark., Fla., Ga., Hawaii, Idaho, Ky., La., Me., Mass., Miss., Nev., N.H., N.C., Ohio, Okla., R.I., S.C., Tenn., Tex., Va., and Wis.

February—Washington's Birthday. Third Monday in February. All the states except Okla. and Ky. In Hawaii, this day is called President's Day; in Minn. i* is called Washington/Lincoln Day; in Vt., it is observed on Feb. 9.

March or April—Good Friday. Friday before Easter. A public holiday in Cal., Conn., Del., Hawaii., Ill., Ind., Iowa, Ky., La., Md., N.J., N.D., Pa., Tenn., W. Va. and Wis. Easter is not a public holiday; it is a religious holiday which falls on the first Sunday after the full moon on or after Mar. 21st and no later than April 25th.

May—Memorial *or* Decoration Day. Last Monday in May. All the states except Ala., Miss., and S.C. In Arizona, this holiday is observed on May 31st.

July 4—Independence Day. All the states.

September—Labor Day. First Monday in Sept. All the states.

October—Columbus Day. Second Monday in Oct. All the states except Ala., Alas., Ark., Iowa, Ky., Me., Miss., Nev., Ohio, Okla., Ore., S.C., S.D., Tenn. and Wyo. In Ind. and N.D., this day is called Discovery Day; in Wis., it is called Landing Day.

October—Veteran's Day. Fourth Monday in Oct. All the states except Ariz., Ky. and Wis. In La., Miss., Okla., W. Va. and S.D., this holiday is observed on Nov. 11th.

November—Thanksgiving Day. Fourth Thursday in November. All the states.

Dec. 25—Christmas Day. All the states.

HOLIDAYS IN OTHER COUNTRIES

The following list is a sampling of the legal holidays observed in various countries. Business firms and banks are closed on these days. Travelers and others doing business in foreign countries should check with the individual consulates, cultural attachés, or United Nations delegations of the countries with which they are concerned to be sure of the calendar of legal holidays in any particular year. Furthermore, individual provinces and cities may celebrate holidays not included in the national calendar.

Canada—Jan. 1, New Year's Day; Good Friday; Easter Monday; the Monday before May 25, Victoria Day and Queen's Birthday; July 1, Dominion Day; Civic Holiday, as declared by municipalities (often first Monday in Aug.); first Monday in Sept., Labour Day; second Monday in Oct., Thanksgiving Day; Nov. 11, Remembrance Day; Dec. 25, Christmas.

Denmark—Jan. 1, New Year's Day; Holy Thursday; Good Friday; Easter Saturday; Easter Monday; General Prayer Day (13 days before Ascension); Ascension; Whit Monday; June 5, Constitution Day (half holiday); Dec. 24, Christmas Eve (half holiday); Dec. 25 and 26, Christmas; Dec. 31, New Year's Eve (half holiday).

England—Good Friday; Easter Monday; Whit Monday; first Monday in August, Bank Holiday; Dec. 25, Christmas; first weekday after Christmas, Boxing Day.

France—Jan. 1, New Year's Day; Easter Monday; May 1, Labor Day; Ascension; Whit Monday; July 14, Bastille Day; Aug. 14, Assumption; Nov. 1, All Saints' Day; Nov. 11, Armistice Day; Dec. 25, Christmas.

Germany, West—Jan. 1, New Year's Day; Good Friday; Easter Monday; May 1, Labor Day; Ascension; Whit Monday; Corpus Christi (in Catholic regions); June 17, German Unity Day; Nov. 1, All Saints' Day; Dec. 25 and 26, Christmas.

Italy—Jan. 1, New Year's Day; Jan. 6, Epiphany; Feb. 11, Conciliation Day; Mar. 19, St. Joseph's Day; Apr. 25, Liberation Day; May 1, Labor Day; Corpus Christi; June 2, Proclamation of the Republic; June 29, St. Peter and St. Paul; Aug. 15, Assumption; Nov. 1, All Saints' Day; Nov. 4, Victory Day; Dec. 8, Immaculate Conception; Dec. 24, Christmas Eve (half holiday); Dec. 25, Christmas; Dec. 26, St. Stephen's Day; Dec. 31, New Year's Eve (half holiday).

Japan—Jan. 1, New Year's Day; Jan. 15, Adults' Day; Feb. 11, National Founding Day; Mar. 21, Vernal Equinox Day; Apr. 29, Emperor's Birthday; May 3, Constitution Day; May 5, Children's Day; Sept. 15, Day of Respect for the Aged; Sept. 24, Autumnal Equinox Day; Oct. 10, Health—Sports Day; Nov. 3, Culture Day; Nov. 23, Labor-Thanksgiving Day.

Mexico—Jan. 1, New Year's Day; Feb. 5, Constitution Day; Mar. 18, Benito Juarez's Birthday; Good Friday; Easter Monday;

May 1, Labor Day; May 5, Battle of Puebla Day; Sept. 16, Independence Day; Oct. 12, Columbus Day; Nov. 20, Revolution Day; Dec. 12, Our Lady of Guadalupe; Dec. 25, Christmas.

Netherlands—Jan. 1, New Year's Day; Good Friday; Easter Monday; Apr. 30, Queen's Birthday; May 5, Liberation Day (observed every 10 years); Ascension; Whit Monday; Dec. 25 and 26, Christmas.

Norway—Jan 1, New Year's Day; Holy Thursday; Good Friday; Easter Monday; May 1, Labor Day; Ascension; May 17, Constitution Day; Dec. 25 and 26, Christmas.

Sweden—Jan. 1, New Year's Day; Jan. 6, Epiphany; Good Friday; Easter Monday; May 1, Labor Day; Ascension; Whit Monday; June 24, Midsummer Day; Nov. 1, All Saints' Day; Dec. 25 and 26, Christmas.

Switzerland—Jan. 1, New Year's Day; Good Friday; Easter Monday; May 1, Labor Day; Ascension; Whit Monday; Aug. 1, Independence Day; Dec. 25, Christmas; Dec. 26, St. Stephen's Day.

MAJOR JEWISH HOLIDAYS, 1973–1980

Holidays begin at sundown of the preceding day. For observances extending over several days only the first day of the celebration is noted here.

1973—Mar. 18, Purim; Apr. 17, Passover; June 6, Shabuoth; Sept. 27, Rosh Hashana; Oct. 6, Yom Kippur; Oct. 11, Sukkoth; Oct. 19, Simhath Torah; Dec. 20, Hanukkah.

1974—Mar. 8, Purim; Apr. 7, Passover; May 27, Shabuoth; Sept. 17, Rosh Hashana; Sept. 26, Yom Kippur; Oct. 1, Sukkoth; Oct. 9, Simhath Torah; Dec. 9, Hanukkah.

1975—Feb. 25, Purim; Mar. 27, Passover; May 16, Shabuoth; Sept. 6, Rosh Hashana; Sept. 15, Yom Kippur; Sept. 21, Sukkoth; Sept. 23, Simhath Torah; Nov. 29, Hanukkah.

1976—Mar. 23, Purim; Apr. 15, Passover; June 4, Shabuoth; Sept. 25, Rosh Hashana; Oct. 4, Yom Kippur; Oct. 9, Sukkoth; Oct. 17, Simhath Torah; Dec. 17, Hanukkah.

1977—Mar. 4, Purim; Apr. 3, Passover; May 23, Shabuoth; Sept. 13, Rosh Hashana; Sept. 22, Yom Kippur; Sept. 27, Sukkoth; Oct. 5, Simhath Torah; Dec. 5, Hanukkah.

1978—Mar. 23, Purim; Apr. 22, Passover; June 11, Shabuoth; Oct. 2, Rosh Hashana; Oct. 11, Yom Kippur; Oct. 16, Sukkoth; Oct. 24, Simhath Torah; Dec. 25, Hanukkah.

1979—Mar. 13, Purim; Apr. 12, Passover; June 1, Shabuoth; Sept. 22, Rosh Hashana; Oct. 1, Yom Kippur; Oct. 6, Sukkoth; Oct. 14, Simhath Torah; Dec. 15, Hanukkah.

1980—Mar. 2, Purim; Apr. 1, Passover; May 21, Shabuoth; Sept. 11, Rosh Hashana; Sept. 20, Yom Kippur; Sept. 25, Sukkoth; Oct. 3, Simhath Torah; Dec. 3, Hanukkah.

APPENDIX 7

SIGNS AND SYMBOLS

ASTRONOMY

1. SUN, MOON, PLANETS, ETC.

☉ (1) The Sun. (2) Sunday.

☾ or ☽ (1) The Moon. (2) Monday.

● New Moon.

☽, or ☾ First Quarter.

○ Full Moon.

☾, ●, or ☽ Last Quarter.

✶ or ✴ Fixed Star.

☿ (1) Mercury. (2) Wednesday.

♀ (1) Venus. (2) Friday.

⊕, or ♁ The Earth.

♂ (1) Mars. (2) Tuesday.

♃ (1) Jupiter. (2) Thursday.

♄ (1) Saturn. (2) Saturday.

♅ or ♆ Uranus.

♆ Neptune.

♇ Pluto.

☄ Comet.

☉, ☽, ☉, etc. Asteroids in the order of their discovery.

α, β, γ, etc. The stars (of a constellation) in the order of their brightness; the Greek letter is followed by the Latin genitive of the name of the constellation.

2. SIGNS OF THE ZODIAC

Spring Signs

1. ♈ Aries (the Ram).

2. ♉ Taurus (the Bull).

Summer Signs

4. ♋ or ⊙ Cancer (the Crab).

5. ♌ Leo (the Lion).

6. ♍ Virgo (the Virgin).

Autumn Signs

7. ♎ Libra (the Balance).

8. ♏ Scorpio (the Scorpion).

9. ♐ Sagittarius (the Archer).

Winter Signs

10. ♑ or ♑ Capricorn (the Goat).

11. ♒ Aquarius (the Water Bearer).

12. ♓ Pisces (the Fish).

3. ASPECTS AND NODES

☌ Conjunction;—with reference to bodies having the same longitude, or right ascension.

✶ Sextile;—being 60° apart in longitude, or right ascension.

□ Quadrature;—being 90° apart in longitude, or right ascension.

△ Trine;—being 120° apart in longitude, or right ascension.

☍ Opposition;—being 180° apart in longitude, or right ascension.

☊ Ascending Node.

☋ Descending Node.

4. SIGNS AND ABBREVIATIONS USED IN ASTRONOMICAL NOTATION

a. Mean distance.

A.R. Right ascension.

β Celestial latitude.

D. Diameter.

△ Distance.
E. East.
e Eccentricity.
h. or ʰ Hours: as, 5h. or 5ʰ.
Inclination to the ecliptic.
l, l, or ε Mean longitude in orbit.
λ Longitude.
M. Mass.
m. or ᵐ Minutes of time: as, 5m. or 5ᵐ.
μ or n Mean daily motion.
+ or N. North.
N.P.D. North polar distance.
ν, ☊, or L. Longitude of ascending node.
π or ϖ Longitude of perihelion.
q. Perihelion distance.
ρ or R. Radius or radius vector.
— or S. South.
s. or ˢ Seconds of time: as, 16s. or 16ˢ.
T. Periodic time.
W. West.
φ Angle of eccentricity; also, geographical latitude.
° Degrees of arc.
′ Minutes of arc.
″ Seconds of arc.

BIOLOGY

○, ⊙, ⊙ Annual plant.
⊙⊙, ⊙ ♂ Biennial plant.
♃ Perennial herb.
△ Evergreen plant.
⊙ Monocarpic plant, that bears fruit but once.
♄ Shrub.
♄ Treelike shrub.
♄ Tree.
(Climbing plant.

♂, ☌ (1) Male organism or cell. (2) Staminate plant or flower.
♀ (1) Female organism or cell. (2) Pistillate plant or flower.
☿ Perfect, or hermaphroditic, plant or flower.
○ Individual, especially female, organism.
□ Individual, especially male, organism.
☿ ♀ Unisexual; having male and female flowers separate.
☿—♀ Monoecious; having male and female flowers on the same plant.
☿ : ♀ Dioecious; having male and female flowers on different plants.
♀ ☿ Polygamous; having hermaphroditic and unisexual flowers on the same or different plants.
☿ or ∞ Indefinite number, as of stamens when there are more than twenty.
0 Lacking or absent, as a part.
) Turning or winding to the left.
(Turning or winding to the right.
× Crossed with: used of a hybrid.
P Parental (generation).
F Filial (generation); offspring.
F_1, F_2, F_3, etc. Offspring of the first, second, third, etc. filial generation.
+ | Possessing a (specified) characteristic.
— Lacking a (specified) characteristic.
☰ Northern hemisphere.
☰ Southern hemisphere.
|* Old World.
*| New World.
°, ″ Feet, inches, lines.
′, ″, ‴ Feet, inches, lines (in European usage).

COMMERCE AND FINANCE

$ Dollar or dollars: as, $100.
¢ Cent or cents: as, 13¢.
£ Pound or pounds sterling: as, £100.

Shilling or shillings: as, 2/8, two shillings and six-pence.

℔ Pound (in weight).

@ (1) At: as, 200 @ $1 each. (2) To: as, shoes per pr. $10 @ $15.

℀ Per.

% (1) Per cent: as, 5%. (2) Order of.

a/c Account.

B/L Bill of lading.

B/S Bill of sale.

c/d, C/D Carried down (in bookkeeping).

c/f, C/F Carried forward (in bookkeeping).

c/o (1) Care of. (2) Carried over (in bookkeeping).

d/a Days after acceptance.

d/s Days after sight.

L/C Letter of credit.

(1) Number (before a figure): as, #5 can. (2) Pounds (after a figure): as, 25#.

MATHEMATICS

1. NUMERATION

Capital letters were sometimes used for the Greek numerals, and lower-case letters are often used for the Roman. In the Roman notation, the value of a character to the right of a larger numeral is added to that of the numeral: as, VI = V + I = 6. I, X, and sometimes C, are also placed to the left of larger numerals and when so situated their value is subtracted from that of such numerals: as, IV, that is, V − I = 4. After the sign IↃ for D, when the character Ↄ was repeated, each repetition had the effect of multiplying IↃ by ten: as, IↃↃ, 5,000; IↃↃↃ, 50,000; and the like. In writing numbers twice as great as these, C was placed as many times before the stroke I as the Ↄ was written after it. Sometimes a line was drawn over a numeral to indicate thousands: as, C̄ = 100,000.

Arabic	Greek	Roman
0		...
1	α	I
2	β	II
3	γ	III
4	δ	IV or IIII
5	ε	V
6	ϛ	VI
7	ζ	VII
8	η	VIII or IIX
9	θ	IX or VIIII
10	ι	X
11	ια	XI
12	ιβ	XII
13	ιγ	XIII or XIIV
14	ιδ	XIIII or XIIII
15	ιε	XV
16	ιϛ	XVI
17	ιζ	XVII
18	ιη	XVIII or XIIX
19	ιθ	XIX or XVIIII
20	κ	XX
30	λ	XXX
40	μ	XL or XXXX
50	ν	L
60	ξ	LX
70	ο	LXX
80	π	LXXX or XXC
90	ϙ	XC or LXXXX
100	ρ	C
200	σ	CC
300	τ	CCC
400	υ	CD or CCCC
500	φ	D or IↃ
600	χ	DC or IↃC
700	ψ	DCC or IↃCC
800	ω	DCCC or IↃCCC
900	ϡ	CM, DCCCC, or IↃCCCC
1,000	͵α	M, CIↃ
2,000	͵β	MM or CIↃCIↃ

2. CALCULATION

+   (1) Plus, the sign of addition; used also to indicate that figures are only approximately exact; some figures being omitted at the end: as, 2.1557 +. (2) Positive.

−   (1) Minus, the sign of subtraction; used also to indicate that figures have been left off from the end of a number, and that the last figure has been increased by one: as, 2.9378 = 2.94 −. (2) Negative.

± or ∓   Plus or minus; indicating that either of the signs + or − may properly be used; also used to introduce the probable error after a figure obtained by experimentation, etc.

×   Multiplied by: $5 \times 4 = 20$; multiplication is also indicated by a centered dot ($5 \cdot 4 = 20$) or by placing the factors in immediate juxtaposition ($2ab = 2 \times a \times b$).

÷   Divided by; division is also indicated by the sign: ($x \div y = x : y$), by a straight line between the dividend and the divisor ($\frac{x}{y}$), or by an oblique line (x/y).

=   Is equal to; equals.

≠   Is not equal to.

>   Is greater than: as, $x > y$; that is, x is greater than y.

<   Is less than: as, $x < y$; that is, x is less than y.

≧, or ≥   Is not less than; is equal to or greater than.

≦, or ≤   Is not greater than; is equal to or less than.

≡   Is identical with.

≅   Is congruent to.

~   The difference between; used to designate the difference between two quantities without indicating which is the greater; as, $x \sim z$ = the difference between x and z.

∝   Varies as; is directly proportional to: as, $x \propto y$; that is, x varies as y.

∺   Geometric proportion: as, $\div x : y :: a : b$; that is, the geometric proportion, x is to y as a is to b.

:   Is to; the ratio of.

::   As; equals: used between ratios.

∞   Indefinitely great: the symbol for infinity.

! or ∟   The factorial of, or the continued product of numbers from one upward: as, $5! = 5 \times 4 \times 3 \times 2 \times 1$.

∴   Therefore.

∵   Since; because.

...   And so on.

∠   Angle: as, $\angle XYZ$.

∟   Right angle.

⊥   The perpendicular; is perpendicular to: as, EF ⊥ MN = EF is perpendicular to MN.

∥   Parallel; is parallel to: as, EF ∥ DG.

○   Circle; circumference; 360°.

⌒   Arc of a circle.

△   Triangle.

□   Square.

▭   Rectangle.

▱   Parallelogram.

√ or √   Radical sign; root, indicating, when used without a figure placed above it, the square root: as, $\sqrt{9} = 3$. When any other than the square root is meant, a figure (called the *index*) expressing the degree of the required root, is placed above the sign: as, $\sqrt[3]{27} = 3$.

1, 2, 3, *etc.*   Exponents, placed above and to the right of a quantity to indicate that it is raised to the first, second, third, etc. power: as, a^2, $(a + b)^3$.

', ", ''', *etc.*   Prime, double (or second) prime, triple (or third) prime, etc., used to distinguish between different values of the same variable: as, x', x'', x''', etc.

‾   Vinculum: as, $\overline{x + y}$
( )   Parentheses: as, $2(x + y)$
[ ]   Brackets: as, $a[2(x + y)]$
{ }   Braces: as, $b + (2 - a[2(x + y)]]$

These signs indicate that the quantities connected or enclosed by them are to be taken together, as a single quantity.

ƒ or F   Function; function of: as, $f(a)$, a function of a.

d — Differential of: as, *da*.

δ — Variation of: as, δ*a*.

Δ — Finite difference, or increment.

D — Differential coefficient, or derivative.

∫ — Integral; integral of, indicating that the expression following it is to be integrated: as, ∫*f(x)dx* indicates the indefinite integral of *f(x)* with respect to *x*.

$\int_a^b$ — Definite integral, indicating the limits of integration: as, $\int_a^b f(x)dx$ indicates the integral of *f(x)* with respect to *x*, between the limits *a* and *b*.

Σ — Sum; algebraic sum: when used to indicate the summation of finite differences, it has a sense similar to that of the symbol ∫.

Π — The continued product of all terms such as (those indicated).

π — Pi, the number 3.14159265+; the ratio of the circumference of a circle to its diameter, of a semicircle to its radius, and of the area of a circle to the square of its radius.

e or ε — The number 2.7182818+; the base of the Napierian system of logarithms; also, the eccentricity of a conic section.

M — The modulus of a system of logarithms, especially of the common system of logarithms, where it is equal to 0.43429448193+.

g — The acceleration of gravity.

° — Degrees: as, 90°.

′ — (1) Minutes of arc.   (2) Feet.

″ — (1) Seconds of arc.   (2) Inches.

h — Hours.

m — Minutes of time.

s — Seconds of time.

MEDICINE AND PHARMACY

ĀĀ, Ā, *or* aa [Gr. *ana*], of each.

a.c. [L. *ante cibum*], before meals.

ad [L.], up to; so as to make: as, *ad* ʒij, so as to make two drams.

ad [L. *adde*], let there be added; add.

ad lib. [L. *ad libitum*], at pleasure; as needed or desired.

aq. [L. *aqua*], water.

b. (i.) d. [L. *bis (in) die*], twice daily.

C. [L. *congius*], a gallon.

coch. [L. *cochleare*], a spoonful.

D. [L. *dosis*], a dose.

dil. [L. *dilue*], dilute or dissolve.

ess. [L. *essentia*], essence.

ft. mist. [L. *fiat mistura*], let a mixture be made.

ft. pulv. [L. *fiat pulvis*], let a powder be made.

gr. [L. *granum*], a grain.

gtt. [L. *guttae*], drops.

guttatim [L.], drop by drop.

haust. [L. *haustus*], a draft.

hor. decub. [L. *hora decubitus*], at bedtime.

lot. [L. *lotio*], a lotion.

M. [L. *misce*], mix.

mac. [L. *macera*], macerate.

O. *or* o. [L. *octarius*], a pint.

p.c. [L. *post cibum*], after meals.

pil. [L. *pilula(e)*], pill(s).

p.r.n. [L. *pro re natal*], as circumstances may require.

pulv. [L. *pulvis*], powder.

q. (i.) d. [L. *quater (in) die*], four times daily.

q.l. [L. *quantum libet*], as much as you please.

q.s. [L. *quantum sufficit*], as much as will suffice.

q.v. [L. *quantum vis*], as much as you like.

℞ [L. *recipe*] take: used at the beginning of a prescription.

S *or* Sig. [L. *signa*], write: used in prescriptions to indicate the directions to be placed on the label of the medicine.

t. (i.) d. [L. *ter (in) die*], three times daily.

℥ ounce: ℥i = one ounce; ℥ij = two ounces; ℥ss = half an ounce; ℥iss = one ounce and a half, etc.; f℥ = a fluid ounce.

ʒ dram; ʒi = one dram; ʒij = two drams; ʒss = half dram.

a dram; Ʒiss = one dram and a half, etc.; Ʒɓ = a fluid dram.

℈ scruple; ℈i = one scruple; ℈ij = two scruples; ℈ss = half a scruple; ℈iss = one scruple and a half, etc.

m or ℳ minim.

MISCELLANEOUS

& or & (the ampersand) and: as A. B. Smith & Co.

&c. [L. *et cetera*], and others; and so forth.

© copyrighted.

℞ response: in religious services, used to mark the part to be uttered by the congregation in answer to the officiant.

* in Roman Catholic service books, a mark used to divide each verse of a psalm into two parts, indicating where the response begins.

℣, V, or V. versicle: in religious services, used to mark the part to be uttered by the officiant.

⳨ (1) a sign of the cross used by the pope, by archbishops, and by bishops, before their names. (2) in religious services, used to mark the places where the sign of the cross is to be made.

† died: used in genealogies, etc.

X (1) by: used in dimensions, as paper 8 X 11 inches. (2) a mark representing a signature, as on a legal document, made by someone unable to write; the name is added by someone else; e.g.

his
John X Doe
mark

PROOFREADER'S MARKS

⊙ Insert period
⌃ Insert comma
⊙ or :; Insert colon
; Insert semicolon
! Insert exclamation point
⌄ Insert apostrophe or single quotation mark
⌄/⌄ Insert quotation marks
C⊃ Insert parentheses
[] Insert brackets
⊙⊙⊙⊙ Insert ellipsis
=/ Insert hyphen

en Insert en dash
em Insert em dash
?/ Insert question mark
⊙ Query to author
∧ Insert marginal addition
⌿ Delete
⌿ Delete and close up
◠ Close up
Insert space
⌵ Less space
∨ or Eq.# Equalize spacing
¶ Paragraph

No ¶ Run in same paragraph
⊏ or ⊐ Move to left or to right
⊓ or ⊔ Raise or lower
= Straighten type horizontally
‖ Align type vertically
⟋⟍ Transpose
stet Let crossed-out words stand
center or Ctr.. Center
l.c Set in lower-case letters
caps Set in capital letters
s.c. Set in small capitals
rom Set in roman type

ital. Set in italic type
bf Set in boldface type
X Replace imperfect letter
⊙ Reverse upside-down letter
⌐ Push down space that prints
wf Wrong font (wrong size or style of type)
SP Spell out word or figure
ld in Insert lead, or space, between lines
ld Delete lead, or space, between lines

TIME

TABLE 1.   TIME ZONES IN THE UNITED STATES

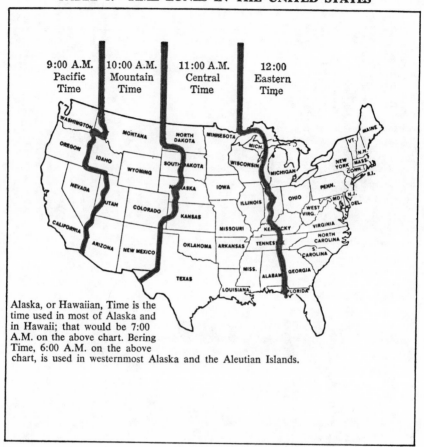

9:00 A.M.
Pacific
Time

10:00 A.M.
Mountain
Time

11:00 A.M.
Central
Time

12:00
Eastern
Time

Alaska, or Hawaiian, Time is the time used in most of Alaska and in Hawaii; that would be 7:00 A.M. on the above chart. Bering Time, 6:00 A.M. on the above chart, is used in westernmost Alaska and the Aleutian Islands.

TABLE 2.
STANDARD TIMES AT 12 NOON, EASTERN STANDARD TIME
(Selected Areas of the World)

AREA	TIME	AREA	TIME
Argentina	1 P.M.	Netherlands	6 P.M.
Austria	6 P.M.	Neth. Antilles (Aruba,	
Australia (Sydney)	3 A.M.	Bonaire, Curaçao)	1 P.M.
Bangladesh	12 midnight	New Zealand	
Belgium	6 P.M.	(Auckland)	5 A.M.
Brazil	2 P.M.	Newfoundland	12:30 P.M.
Burma	11:30 P.M.	Nigeria	6 P.M.
Canada (Toronto)	12 noon	Norway	6 P.M.
Canada (Vancouver)	9 A.M.	Pakistan	11 P.M.
China (Shanghai)	1 A.M.	Peru	12 noon
Columbia	12 noon	Philippines	1 A.M.
Costa Rica	11 A.M.	Poland	6 P.M.
Cuba	1 P.M.	Portugal	6 P.M.
Czechoslovakia	6 P.M.	Romania	7 P.M.
Denmark	6 P.M.	Singapore	12:30 A.M.
Dominican Republic	1 P.M.	Spain	6 P.M.
Egypt	7 P.M.	Sweden	6 P.M.
Finland	7 P.M.	Switzerland	6 P.M.
France	6 P.M.	Thailand	12 midnight
Germany	6 P.M.	Tunisia	6 P.M.
Gibraltar	6 P.M.	Turkey	7 P.M.
Greece	7 P.M.	South Africa	7 P.M.
Haiti	1 P.M.	United Kingdom	6 P.M.
India	10:30 P.M.	Uruguay	2 P.M.
Indonesia (Java)	12 midnight	U.S.A. (Chicago)	11 A.M.
Iran	8:30 P.M.	U.S.A. (Salt Lake City)	10 A.M.
Iraq	8 P.M.	U.S.A. (San Francisco)	9 A.M.
Ireland	6 P.M.	U.S.S.R. (Moscow, Lenin-	
Italy	6 P.M.	grad)	8 P.M.
Ivory Coast	6 P.M.	Venezuela	1 P.M.
Jamaica	1 P.M.	Vietnam	1 A.M.
Japan	2 A.M.	Zaire	6 P.M.
Morocco	6 P.M.		

CALENDAR TIME

The Julian calendar was instituted by Julius Caesar in 46 B.C. to measure calendar time. In 1582, Pope Gregory XIII decreed a new calendar to correct a cumulative error of about a day every 128 years. The Gregorian calendar, introduced into the United States in 1752, adds a day in February every fourth year (leap year) except those centesimal years which can be divided by 400.

A year is divided into 12 months, 52 weeks, or 365 days (except a leap year, which has 366 days):

January	31 days	July	31 days		
February	28 days	August	31 days		
	(leap year 29)				
March	31 days	September	30 days	1 week has 7 days	
April	30 days	October	31 days	1 day has 24 hours	
May	31 days	November	30 days	1 hour has 60 minutes	
June	30 days	December	31 days	1 minute has 60 seconds	

To compute actual days between two dates, find the number of days between months in the chart below and to that add the difference between the days (after February in a leap year, add one day).

FROM ANY DATE IN	TO THE SAME DATE IN											
	Jan.	Feb.	Mar.	Apr.	May	June	July	Aug.	Sept.	Oct.	Nov.	Dec.
January	365	31	59	90	120	151	181	212	243	273	304	334
February	334	365	28	59	89	120	150	181	212	242	273	303
March	306	337	365	31	61	92	122	153	184	214	245	275
April	275	306	334	365	30	61	91	122	153	183	214	244
May	245	276	304	335	365	31	61	92	123	153	184	214
June	214	245	273	304	334	365	30	61	92	122	153	183
July	184	215	243	274	304	335	365	31	62	92	123	153
August	153	184	212	243	273	304	334	365	31	61	92	122
September	122	153	181	212	242	273	303	334	365	30	61	91
October	92	123	151	182	212	243	273	304	335	365	31	61
November	61	92	120	151	181	212	242	273	304	334	365	30
December	31	62	90	121	151	182	212	243	274	304	335	365

TABLE 3. PERPETUAL CALENDAR (A.D. 1–2400)

To find calendar for any year, first find Dominical letter for the year in the upper section of table. Two letters are given for leap year; the first for January and February, the second for other months. In the lower section of table, find column in which the Dominical letter for the year is in the same line with the month for which the calendar is desired; this column gives the days of the week that are to be used with the month.

For example, in the table of Dominical Letters we find that the letter for 1960, a leap year, is CB; in the line with July, the letter B occurs in the third column; hence July 4, 1960, is Monday.

DOMINICAL LETTERS

Century				Julian Calendar 0 / 700 / 1400	100 / 800 / 1500†	200 / 900 / 1000	300 / 1100	400 / 1200	500 / 1300	600	Gregorian Calendar 1500‡ / 2000	1600 / 2100	1700 / 2200	1800 / 2300	1900
Year															
0				DC	ED	FE	GF	AG	BA	CB	—	BA	C	E	G
1	29	57	85	B	C	D	E	F	G	A	F	G	B	D	F
2	30	58	86	A	B	C	D	E	F	G	E	F	A	C	E
3	31	59	87	G	A	B	C	D	E	F	D	E	G	B	D
4	32	60	88	FE	GF	AG	BA	CB	DC	ED	CB	DC	FE	AG	CB
5	33	61	89	D	E	F	G	A	B	C	A	B	D	F	A
6	34	62	90	C	D	E	F	G	A	B	G	A	C	E	G
7	35	63	91	B	C	D	E	F	G	A	F	G	B	D	F
8	36	64	92	AG	BA	CB	DC	ED	FE	GF	ED	FE	AG	CB	ED
9	37	65	93	F	G	A	B	C	D	E	C	D	F	A	C
10	38	66	94	E	F	G	A	B	C	D	B	C	E	G	B
11	39	67	95	D	E	F	G	A	B	C	A	B	D	F	A
12	40	68	96	CB	DC	ED	FE	GF	AG	BA	GF	AG	CB	ED	GF
13	41	69	97	A	B	C	D	E	F	G	E	F	A	C	E
14	42	70	98	G	A	B	C	D	E	F	D	E	G	B	D
15	43	71	99	F	G	A	B	C	D	E	C	D	F	A	C
16	44	72		ED	FE	GF	AG	BA	CB	DC	—	CB	ED	GF	BA
17	45	73		C	D	E	F	G	A	B	—	A	C	E	G
18	46	74		B	C	D	E	F	G	A	—	G	B	D	F
19	47	75		A	B	C	D	E	F	G	—	F	A	C	E
20	48	76		GF	AG	BA	CB	DC	ED	FE	—	ED	GF	BA	DC
21	49	77		E	F	G	A	B	C	D	—	C	E	G	B
22	50	78		D	E	F	G	A	B	C	—	B	D	F	A
23	51	79		C	D	E	F	G	A	B	—	A	C	E	G
24	52	80		BA	CB	DC	ED	FE	GF	AG	—	GF	BA	DC	FE
25	53	81		G	A	B	C	D	E	F	—	E	G	B	D
26	54	82		F	G	A	B	C	D	E	C	D	F	A	C
27	55	83		E	F	G	A	B	C	D	B	C.	E	G	B
28	56	84		DC	ED	FE	GF	AG	BA	CB	AG	BA	DC	FE	AG

Month				Dominical letter						
Jan., Oct.				A	B	C	D	E	F	G
Feb., Mar., Nov.				D	E	F	G	A	B	C
Apr., July				G	A	B	C	D	E	F
May				B	C	D	E	F	G	A
June				E	F	G	A	B	C	D
Aug.				C	D	E	F	G	A	B
Sept., Dec.				F	G	A	B	C	D	E

Day										
8	15	22	29	Sun.	Sat.	Fri.	Thurs.	Wed.	Tues.	Mon.
9	16	23	30	Mon.	Sun.	Sat.	Fri.	Thurs.	Wed.	Tues.
10	17	24	31	Tues.	Mon.	Sun.	Sat.	Fri.	Thurs.	Wed.
11	18	25		Wed.	Tues.	Mon.	Sun.	Sat.	Fri.	Thurs.
12	19	26		Thurs.	Wed.	Tues.	Mon.	Sun.	Sat.	Fri.
13	20	27		Fri.	Thurs.	Wed.	Tues.	Mon.	Sun.	Sat.
14	21	28		Sat.	Fri.	Thurs.	Wed.	Tues.	Mon.	Sun.

† On and before 1582, Oct. 4 only. ‡ On and after 1582, Oct. 15 only.

This calendar was prepared by G. M. Clemence, U. S. Naval Observatory, and is reprinted from the Smithsonian Physical bles, Ninth Edition, by permission of the Smithsonian Institution.

WEIGHTS AND MEASURES

Linear Measure

1 inch		= 2.54	centimeters
12 inches	= 1 foot	= 0.3048	meter
3 feet	= 1 yard	= 0.9144	meter
5½ yards or 16½ feet	= 1 rod (or pole or perch)	= 5.029	meters
40 rods	= 1 furlong	= 201.17	meters
8 furlongs or 1,760 yards or 5,280 feet	= 1 (statute) mile	= 1,609.3	meters
3 miles	= 1 (land) league	= 4.83	kilometers

Square Measure

1 square inch		= 6.452	square centimeters
144 square inches	= 1 square foot	= 929	square centimeters
9 square feet	= 1 square yard	= 0.8361	square meter
30¼ square yards	= 1 square rod (or square pole or square perch)	= 25.29	square meters
160 square rods or 4,840 square yards or 43,560 square feet	= 1 acre	= 0.4047	hectare
640 acres	= 1 square mile	= 259	hectares or 2.59 square kilometers

Cubic Measure

1 cubic inch		= 16.387 cubic centimeters
1,728 cubic inches	= 1 cubic foot	= 0.0283 cubic meter
27 cubic feet	= 1 cubic yard	= 0.7646 cubic meter
	(in units for cordwood, etc.)	
16 cubic feet	= 1 cord foot	
8 cord feet	= 1 cord	= 3.625 cubic meters

Nautical Measure

6 feet	= 1 fathom	= 1.829 meters
100 fathoms	= 1 cable's length (ordinary)	
	(In the U.S. Navy 120 fathoms or 720 feet = 1 cable's length; in the British Navy, 608 feet = 1 cable's length.)	
10 cables' lengths	= 1 nautical mile (6,076.10333 feet, by international agreement in 1954)	= 1.852 kilometers
1 nautical mile (Also called geographical, sea, or air mile, and, in Great Britain, Admiralty mile.)	= 1.1508 statute miles (the length of a minute of longitude at the equator)	
3 nautical miles	= 1 marine league (3.45 statute miles)	= 5.56 kilometers
60 nautical miles	= 1 degree of a great circle of the earth	

Dry Measure

1 pint		= 33.60 cubic inches	= 0.5505 liter
2 pints	= 1 quart	= 67.20 cubic inches	= 1.1012 liters
8 quarts	= 1 peck	= 537.61 cubic inches	= 8.809ℓ liters
4 pecks	= 1 bushel	= 2,150.42 cubic inches	= 35.2383 liters
	1 British dry quart	= 1.032 U.S. dry quarts.	

According to United States government standards, the following are the weights avoirdupois for single bushels of the specified grains: for wheat, 60 pounds; for barley, 48 pounds; for oats, 32 pounds; for rye, 56 pounds; for corn, 56 pounds. Some States have specifications varying from these.

Liquid Measure

1 gill	= 4 fluid ounces	= 7.219 cubic inches	= 0.1183 liter
	(see next table)		
4 gills	= 1 pint	= 28.875 cubic inches	= 0.4732 liter
2 pints	= 1 quart	= 57.75 cubic inches	= 0.9463 liter
4 quarts	= 1 gallon	= 231 cubic inches	= 3.7853 liters

The British imperial gallon (4 imperial quarts) = 277.42 cubic inches = 4.546 liters. The barrel in Great Britain equals 36 imperial gallons, in the United States, usually 31½ gallons.

Apothecaries' Fluid Measure

1 minim		= 0.0038 cubic inch	= 0.0616 milliliter
60 minims	= 1 fluid dram	= 0.2256 cubic inch	= 3.6966 milliliters
8 fluid drams	= 1 fluid ounce	= 1.8047 cubic inches	= 0.0296 liter
16 fluid ounces	= 1 pint	= 28.875 cubic inches	= 0.4732 liter

See table immediately preceding for quart and gallon equivalents. The British pint = 20 fluid ounces.

Circular (or Angular) Measure

60 seconds (″)	= 1 minute (′)
60 minutes	= 1 degree (°)
90 degrees	= 1 quadrant or 1 right angle
4 quadrants or 360 degrees	= 1 circle

Avoirdupois Weight

(The grain, equal to 0.0648 gram, is the same in all three tables of weight)

1 dram or 27.34 grains		= 1.772	grams
16 drams or 437.5 grains	= 1 ounce	= 28.3495	grams
16 ounces or 7,000 grains	= 1 pound	= 453.59	grams
100 pounds	= 1 hundredweight	= 45.36	kilograms
2,000 pounds	= 1 ton	= 907.18	kilograms

In Great Britain, 14 pounds (6.35 kilograms) = 1 stone, 112 pounds (50.80 kilograms) = 1 hundredweight, and 2,240 pounds (1,016.05 kilograms) = 1 long ton.

Troy Weight

(The grain, equal to 0.0648 gram, is the same in all three tables of weight)

3.086 grains	= 1 carat	= 200	milligrams
24 grains	= 1 pennyweight	= 1.5552	grams
20 pennyweights or 480 grains	= 1 ounce	= 31.1035	grams
12 ounces or 5,760 grains	= 1 pound	= 373.24	grams

Apothecaries' Weight

(The grain, equal to 0.0648 gram, is the same in all three tables of weight)

20 grains	= 1 scruple	= 1.296	grams
3 scruples	= 1 dram	= 3.888	grams
8 drams or 480 grains	= 1 ounce	= 31.1035 grams
12 ounces or 5,760 grains	= 1 pound	= 373.24	grams

THE METRIC SYSTEM

Linear Measure

10 millimeters	=	1 centimeter	=	0.3937 inch
10 centimeters	=	1 decimeter	=	3.937 inches
10 decimeters	=	1 meter	=	39.37 inches or 3.28 feet
10 meters	=	1 decameter	=	393.7 inches
10 decameters	=	1 hectometer	=	328 feet 1 inch
10 hectometers	=	1 kilometer	=	0.621 mile
10 kilometers	=	1 myriameter	=	6.21 miles

Square Measure

100 square millimeters	=	1 square centimeter	=	0.15499 square inch
100 square centimeters	=	1 square decimeter	=	15.499 square inches
100 square decimeters	=	1 square meter	=	1,549.9 square inches or 1.196 square yards
100 square meters	=	1 square decameter	=	119.6 square yards
100 square decameters	=	1 square hectometer	=	2.471 acres
100 square hectometers	=	1 square kilometer	=	0.386 square mile

Land Measure

1 square meter	=	1 centiare	=	1,549.9 square inches
100 centiares	=	1 are	=	119.6 square yards
100 ares	=	1 hectare	=	2.471 acres
100 hectares	=	1 square kilometer	=	0.386 square mile

Volume Measure

1,000 cubic millimeters	=	1 cubic centimeter	=	.06102 cubic inch
1,000 cubic centimeters	=	1 cubic decimeter	=	61.02 cubic inches
1,000 cubic decimeters	=	1 cubic meter	=	35.314 cubic feet

(the unit is called a *stere* in measuring firewood)

Capacity Measure

10 milliliters	=	1 centiliter	=	.338 fluid ounce
10 centiliters	=	1 deciliter	=	3.38 fluid ounces
10 deciliters	=	1 liter	=	1.0567 liquid quarts or 0.9081 dry quart
10 liters	=	1 decaliter	=	2.64 gallons or 0.284 bushel
10 decaliters	=	1 hectoliter	=	26.418 gallons or 2.838 bushels
10 hectoliters	=	1 kiloliter	=	264.18 gallons or 35.315 cubic feet

Weights

10 milligrams	=	1 centigram	=	0.1543 grain
10 centigrams	=	1 decigram	=	1.5432 grains
10 decigrams	=	1 gram	=	15.432 grains
10 grams	=	1 decagram	=	0.3527 ounce
10 decagrams	=	1 hectogram	=	3.5274 ounces
10 hectograms	=	1 kilogram	=	2.2046 pounds
10 kilograms	=	1 myriagram	=	22.046 pounds
10 myriagrams	=	1 quintal	=	220.46 pounds
10 quintals	=	1 metric ton	=	2,204.6 pounds

33,000 WORDS SPELLED AND SYLLABIFIED

Each of the words listed alphabetically in the following list will be referred to here as an *entry* or an *entry word.*

1. CONTENT

This list is a quick, accurate, up-to-date guide to the correct spelling and syllabification of more than 33,000 words, based on the widely used *Webster's New World Dictionary of the American Language, Second College Edition.* A special feature is the *World Finder Table,* which will help you locate a word even though all you know about the word is how to pronounce it.

Many of the entries will settle questions as to whether a certain term is written as one word or with a hyphen or as two words. Answers to specific questions such as the following can be found easily: Do I want the word *anecdote* or *antidote?* When is *hanged* preferred as the past tense and past participle of *hang?* Is the word I want spelled *moot* or *mute?* When is *ringed* used correctly as a verb?

An almost infinite number of words can be formed through the addition of certain prefixes or suffixes to base words. Many of these derived words have been entered. Those that present any question of spelling have been included. For example:

a·gree′a·ble	di·ag′o·nal	di·dac′tic	gar′lic
a·gree′a·bly	di·ag′o·nal·ly	di·dac′ti·cal·ly	gar′lick·y

Obsolete, rare, and archaic forms have been omitted. Many technical terms, especially those in general use, and many colloquial words in common use have been included.

In all, this list has been designed to be as complete and timesaving an aid to spelling and syllabification as possible.

2. WORD DIVISION

All the entry words have been divided into syllables. Each syllable break is indicated by a centered dot, an accent mark, or, in certain cases, a hyphen. Wherever a hyphen *is* used in an entry word, that hyphen is part of the spelling of the word.

A word can be divided from one line to the next between any of its syllables except in the following cases:

a. Never separate from the rest of the word a first or last syllable of only one letter or, if you can avoid it, two letters.

b. Never divide a hyphenated word at any point other than the hyphen.

3. ACCENT MARKS

Accent marks are included to help you find words more quickly. In some cases the accent mark will distinguish one word from another word spelled almost the same way.

lo′cal / lo·cale′   kar′at / ka·ra′te

Two kinds of accent marks are used. The accent mark in heavy type shows that the syllable preceding it receives the main stress, **or** accent. The lighter one, wherever used, indicates that the preceding syllable receives less stress than the main one but somewhat more than an unmarked syllable.

ag′gra·vate′ / dem′on·stra′tion / su′per·vise′

4. PARTS OF SPEECH

Part-of-speech labels (*n.* = noun, *v.* = verb, *adj.* = adjective, *adv.* = adverb) are included here only in special cases. Sometimes this label will give you information about current usage. In all cases the main purpose is to help you be sure you have the word you are looking for. Two of these special cases are explained here.

a. Sometimes a word is accented and syllabified in one way as one part of speech and differently as another. These changes in accent and syllabification are indicated, and the word is appropriately labeled; for example: re·cord′ *v.* / rec′ord *n.*

b. Sometimes two words are related in meaning and close in spelling and pronunciation. A part-of-speech label is all that is needed to identify each word:

ad·vice′ *n.*	proph′e·cy *n.*
ad·vise′ *v.*	·cies
·vised′ ·vis′ing	proph′e·sy′ *v.*
	·sied′ ·sy′ing

5. INFLECTED FORMS

Inflected forms include the plurals of nouns, the parts of the verb, and the comparative and superlative forms of the adjective and adverb. All irregularly formed inflected forms have been entered as part of the entry for the base word. To save space, these forms have been shortened in most cases to show only those syllables that are different from the base word. For example:

please	li′a·bil′i·ty	pic′nic
pleased pleas′ing	·ties	·nicked ·nick·ing
fly	eas′y	date
flies	·i·er ·i·est	dat′ed dat′ing
flew flown fly′ing		

For verbs, when two forms are given, the first is the past tense and past participle and the second is the present participle. When three forms are given, the first is the past tense, the second is the past participle, and the third is the present participle. Noun, adjective, and adverb forms are easy to identify.

Again to save space, inflected forms of some compound words and derived words have been omitted. These forms can easily be found with the entry for the base word. For example:

po·lice′man   pre·pack′age   un′der·score′

Occasionally certain inflected forms are used for certain meanings. These are identified. For example:

staff

    staffs *or* staves

      (*stick; music*)

    staffs

      (*people*)

ring

    rang rung ring′ing

      (*sound . . .*)

ring

    ringed ring′ing

      (*circle . . .*)

This system of entering inflected forms as part of the entry for the base word accomplishes at least three things: (1) It helps you distinguish between words that might be confused if entered separately, as in:

hop

    hopped hop′ping

hope

    hoped hop′ing

(2) It saves the time and trouble of searching for a word you might think is spelled one way but is, in fact, spelled differently, as in:

swim

    swam swum swim′ming

(3) It establishes, without further identification under a separate entry, the specific inflected form that you are looking for (see *fly* above).

One last point: when an entry contains verb forms, this does not necessarily mean that the word is used only as a verb. On the contrary, many of the entries represent the spelling for more than one part of speech. If, for example, a word used as an adjective is already entered as a verb form, and the spelling and syllabification are exactly the same, this word is not entered again separately. You may accept the verb form as the correct spelling for the adjective (see *please* above). If, too, a noun has the same spelling as a verb, no special notation is given (see *picnic* above). Where confusion might exist, some kind of identification is given.

6. USE OF IDENTIFYING DEFINITIONS

It is no doubt clear that this list is not meant to replace the dictionary. It is also clear that in attempting to learn the correct spelling for a specific word, you may run into the difficulty of confusing another word with it. Many instances of such confusion are present in the English language. To help you find the exact word you are seeking, this list contains many cross-references. Each cross-reference supplies you with a very short *identifying definition* and refers you to another word that may be the one you want.

Confusion may result for any of several reasons. Two of the most common are: (1) similar (but not exactly the same) pronunciation:

mou′ton′

    (*fur;* SEE mutton)

mut′ton

    (*food;* SEE mouton)

(2) exactly the same pronunciation but, usually, a different spelling (such words are called *homonyms*):

la'ma	leak
(*monk;* SEE llama)	(*escape;* SEE leek)
lla'ma	leek
(*animal;* SEE lama)	(*vegetable;* SEE leak)

Often the words involved are very close alphabetically. In such cases only the identifying terms are given, as in:

less'en	les'son
(*make less*)	(*instruction*)
less'er	les'sor
(*smaller*)	(*one who leases*)

An important thing to note here is that these *identifying definitions* are meant only as an aid to your locating or identifying the word you want. They are not meant to replace or by any means cover the entire dictionary definition.

7. MORE THAN ONE ACCEPTED SPELLING

Many words in the English language have more than one accepted spelling in use today. Because of space limitations, only the variant spellings of the more common words have been included. To help you identify them as variants of the same word, they have, in most cases, been entered together, as part of the same entry. Usually, the first spelling given is the one more frequently used. Sometimes, if they are far apart alphabetically, they are entered as separate entries. Whichever variant spelling you decide on, it is advisable to be consistent and use that same spelling throughout any one piece of writing.

8. PREFIXES

Many derived words have been entered. Since all such words cannot possibly be included, the information given below about certain prefixes will be helpful.

The prefix . . . is usually added to the base word . . .

---

self . . . . with a hyphen.

out . . . . without a hyphen.

over . . . . without a hyphen.

anti . . . . . .⎫
pre . . . .⎪ without a hyphen *except* when the prefix is followed by a capital
pro . . . .⎬ letter.
semi . . . . . .⎪
un . . . .⎭

non . . . . .without a hyphen *except* when the prefix is followed by a capital letter or a word that has a hyphen in it.

re . . . . .without a hyphen *except* to distinguish between a word in which the prefix means *again* or *anew* and a word having a special meaning (*re-lay* and *relay*).

WORD FINDER TABLE

HAVE YOU EVER tried to look up a word in order to find its spelling when you don't have any idea how to find it—simply because you can't spell it? This *Word Finder Table,* which gives the most common spellings for sounds, will help you end this vicious circle.

Think of the word in terms of its pronounced syllables. *Be sure you are pronouncing the word correctly.*

If the sound is like the . . .	try also the spelling . . .	as in the words . . .
a in fat	ai, au	plaid, draught
a in lane	ai, ao, au, ay, ea, ei, eigh, et, ey	rain, gaol, gauge, ray, break, rein, weigh, sachet, they
a in care	ai, ay, e, ea, ei	air, prayer, there wear, their
a in father	au, e, ea	gaunt, sergeant, hearth
a in ago	e, i, o, u, *and combinations, as* ou	agent, sanity, comply, focus, vicious
b in big	bb	rubber
ch in chin	tch, ti, tu	catch, question, nature
d in do	dd, ed	puddle, called
e in get	a, ae, ai, ay, ea, ei, eo, ie, u	any, aesthete, said, says, bread, heifer, leopard, friend, bury
e in equal	ae, ay, ea, ee, ei, eo, ey, i, ie, oe	alumnae, quay, lean, free, deceit, people, key, machine, chief, phoebe
e in here	ea, ee, ei, ie	ear, cheer, weird, bier
er in over	ar, ir, or, our, re, ur, ure, yr	liar, elixir, author, glamour, acre, augur, measure, zephyr
f in fine	ff, gh, lf, ph	cliff, laugh, calf, phrase
g in go	gg, gh, gu, gue	egg, ghoul, guard, prologue
h in hat	wh	who
i in it	a, e, ee, ia, ie, o, u, ui, y	usage, English, been, carriage, sieve, women, busy, built, hymn
i in kite	ai, ay, ei, ey, ie, igh, uy, y, ye	aisle, aye, sleight, eye, tie, nigh, buy, fly, rye
j in jam	d, dg, di, dj, g, gg	graduate, judge, soldier, adjective, magic, exaggerate
k in keep	c, cc, ch, ck, cqu, cu, lk, q, qu, que	can, account, chorus, tack, lacquer, biscuit, walk, quick, liquor, baroque
l in let	ll, sl	call, isle
m in me	chm, gm, lm, mb, mm, mn	drachm, paradigm, calm, limb, drummer, hymn
n in no	gn, kn, mn, nn, pn	gnu, kneel, mnemonic, dinner, pneumatic

If the sound is like the . . .	try also the spelling . . .	as in the words . . .
ng in ring	n, ngue	pink, tongue
o in go	au, eau, eo, ew, oa, oe, oh, oo, ou, ough, ow	mauve, beau, yeoman, sew, boat, toe, oh, brooch, soul, dough, row
o in long	a, ah, au, aw, oa, ou	all, Utah, fraud, thaw, broad, ought
oo in tool	eu, ew, o, oe, ou, ough, u, ue, ui	maneuver, drew, move, shoe, group, through, rule, blue, fruit
oo in look	o, ou, u	wolf, would, pull
oi in oil	oy	toy
ou in out	ough, ow	bough, crowd
p in put	pp	clipper
r in red	rh, rr, wr	rhyme, berry, wrong
s in sew	c, ce, ps, sc, sch, ss	cent, rice, psychology, scene, schism, miss
sh in ship	ce, ch, ci, s, sch, sci, se, si, ss, ssi, ti	ocean, machine, facial, sure, schwa, conscience, nauseous, tension, issue, fission, nation
t in top	ed, ght, pt, th, tt	walked, bought, ptomaine, thyme, better
u in cuff	o, oe, oo, ou	son, does, flood, double
u in use	eau, eu, eue, ew, ieu, iew, ue, ui, you, yu	beauty, feud, queue, few, adieu, view, cue, suit, youth, yule
ur in fur	ear, er, eur, ir, or, our, yr	learn, germ, hauteur, bird, word, scourge, myrtle
v in vat	f, lv, ph	of, salve, Stephen
w in will	o, u, wh	choir, quaint, wheat
y in you	i, j	onion, hallelujah
z in zero	s, sc, ss, x, zz	busy, discern, scissors, xylophone, buzzer
z in azure	ge, s, si, zi	garage, leisure, fusion, glazier

Sometimes, certain letter combinations (rather than single sounds) cause problems when you are trying to find a word. Here are some common ones:

If you've tried . . .	then try . . .	If you've tried . . .	then try . . .	If you've tried . . .	then try . . .
pre	per, pro, pri, pra, pru	cks, gz	x	fiz	phys
		us	ous	ture	teur
per	pre, pir, pur, par, por	tion	sion, cion, cean, cian	tious	seous
				air	are
is	us, ace, ice	le	tle, el, al	ance	ence
ere	eir, ear, ier	kw	qu	ant	ent
wi	whi	cer	cre	able	ible
we	whe	ei	ie	sin	syn, cin, cyn
zi	xy	si	psy, ci		

A

aard'vark'
aard'wolf'
·wolves'
ab'a·cus'
·cus·es or ·ci'
ab'a·lo'ne
a·ban'don
a·base'
·based' ·bas'ing
a·bash'
a·bat'a·ble
a·bate'
·bat'ed ·bat'ing
ab'a·tis
ab'at·toir'
ab'ax'i·al
ab'ba·cy
·cies
ab'bé
ab'bess
ab'bey
ab'bot
ab·bre'vi·ate'
·at'ed ·at'ing
ab·bre'vi·a'tion
ab·bre'vi·a'tor
ab'di·cate'
·cat'ed ·cat'ing
ab'di·ca'tion
ab'di·ca'tor
ab'do·men
ab·dom'i·nal
ab·duct'
ab·duc'tion
ab·duc'tor
ab·er'rant
ab'er·ra'tion
a·bet'
·bet'ted ·bet'ting
a·bey'ance
ab·hor'
·horred' ·hor'ring
ab·hor'rence
ab·hor'rent
a·bide'
·bode' or ·bid'ed
·bid'ing
a·bil'i·ty
·ties
ab'ject
ab·jec'tion
ab'ju·ra'tion
ab·jure'
·jured' ·jur'ing
ab'la·tive
a·blaze'
a'ble
·bler ·blest
a'ble-bod'ied
ab·lu'tion
ab'ne·gate'
·gat'ed ·gat'ing
ab'ne·ga'tion

ab·nor'mal
ab'nor·mal'i·ty
·ties
ab·nor'mi·ty
·ties
a·board'
a·bode'
a·bol'ish
ab'o·li'tion
A'-bomb
a·bom'i·na·ble
a·bom'i·nate'
·nat'ed ·nat'ing
a·bom'i·na'tion
a·bom'i·na'tor
ab'o·rig'i·nal
ab'o·rig'i·ne
·nes
a·bort'
a·bor'ti·cide
a·bor'ti·fa'cient
a·bor'tion
a·bor'tive
a·bound'
a·bout'-face'
·faced' ·fac'ing
a·bove'board'
ab'ra·ca·dab'ra
ab·rade'
·rad'ed ·rad'ing
ab·ra'sion
ab·ra'sive
ab're·act'
ab're·ac'tion
a·breast'
a·bridge'
·bridged'
·bridg'ing
a·bridg'ment
or ·bridge'ment
a·broad'
ab'ro·gate'
·gat'ed ·gat'ing
ab'ro·ga'tion
ab'ro·ga·tor
a·brupt'
ab'scess
ab'scessed
ab·scis'sa
·sas or ·sae
ab·scond'
ab'sence
ab'sent adj.
ab·sent' v.
ab'sen·tee'ism
ab'sent-mind'ed
ab'sinthe or ·sinth
ab'so·lute'
ab'so·lu'tion
ab'so·lut'ism
ab·solve'
·solved' ·solv'ing
ab·solv'ent
ab·sorb'
·sorbed' ·sorb'ing
ab·sorb'a·ble
ab·sorb'en·cy
ab·sorb'ent

ab·sorp'tion
ab·stain'
ab·ste'mi·ous
ab·sten'tion
ab'sti·nence
ab'sti·nent
ab·stract'
ab·strac'tion
ab·struse'
ab·surd'
ab·surd'i·ty
·ties
a·bun'dance
a·bun'dant
a·buse'
·bused' ·bus'ing
a·bus'er
a·bu'sive
a·but'
·but'ted ·but'ting
a·but'ment
a·but'ter
a·bys'mal
a·bys'mal·ly
a·byss'
a·ca'cia
ac'a·de'mi·a
ac'a·dem'ic
ac'a·dem'i·cal
ac'a·dem'i·cal·ly
a·cad'e·mi'cian
ac'a·dem'i·cism
a·cad'e·my
·mies
ac'a·jou'
a·can'thus
·thus·es or ·thi
a' cap·pel'la
A'ca·pul'co
ac·cede'
·ced'ed ·ced'ing
(agree; SEE
exceed)
ac·cel'er·an'do
ac·cel'er·ant
ac·cel'er·ate'
·at'ed ·at'ing
ac·cel'er·a'tion
ac·cel'er·a'tor
ac·cel'er·om'e·ter
ac'cent
ac·cen'tu·al
ac·cen'tu·al·ly
ac·cen'tu·ate'
·at'ed ·at'ing
ac·cen'tu·a'tion
ac·cept'
(receive; SEE
except)
ac·cept'a·bil'i·ty
ac·cept'a·ble
ac·cept'a·bly
ac·cept'ance
ac'cep·ta'tion
ac·cept'ed
(approved; SEE
excepted)
ac·cep'tor

ac'cess
(approach; SEE
excess)
ac·ces'si·bil'i·ty
ac·ces'si·ble
ac·ces'sion
ac·ces'so·ry
or ·sa·ry
·ries
ac'ci·dent
ac'ci·den'tal
ac'ci·den'tal·ly
ac·claim'
ac'cla·ma'tion
ac'cli·mate'
·mat'ed ·mat'ing
ac·cli'ma·tize'
·tized' ·tiz'ing
ac·cliv'i·ty
ac·cli'vous
ac'co·lade'
ac·com'mo·date'
·dat'ed ·dat'ing
ac·com'mo·da'·
tion
ac·com'pa·ni·
ment
ac·com'pa·nist
ac·com'pa·ny
·nied ·ny·ing
ac·com'plice
ac·com'plish
ac·com'plished
ac·cord'
ac·cord'ance
ac·cord'ant·ly
ac·cord'ing
ac·cor'di·on
ac·cost'
ac·count'
ac·count'a·bil'·
i·ty
ac·count'a·ble
ac·count'a·bly
ac·count'ant
ac·count'ing
ac·cou'ter
ac·cou'ter·ments
ac·cred'it
ac·cred'it·a'tion
ac·cre'tion
ac·cru'al
ac·crue'
·crued' ·cru'ing
ac·cul'tu·rate'
·rat'ed ·rat'ing
ac·cul'tu·ra'tion
ac·cu'mu·la·ble
ac·cu'mu·late'
·lat'ed ·lat'ing
ac·cu'mu·la'tion
ac·cu'mu·la·tive
ac·cu'mu·la·tor
ac'cu·ra·cy
ac'cu·rate
ac'cu·rate·ly
ac·curs'ed or
ac·curst'

ac·cus'al
ac·cu'sa'tion
ac·cu'sa·tive
ac·cu'sa·to'ry
ac·cuse'
·cused' ·cus'ing
ac·cus'tom
ac·cus'tomed
a·cer'bi·ty
·ties
ac'e·tate'
ac'e·tone'
a·cet'y·lene'
ache
ached ach'ing
a·chiev'a·ble
a·chieve'
·chieved'
·chiev'ing
a·chieve'ment
ach'ro·mat'ic
a·chro'ma·tism
a·chro'ma·tize'
·tized' ·tiz'ing
A'chro·my'cin
ach'y
ach'i·er ach'i·est
ac'id-fast'
ac'id-form'ing
a·cid'ic
a·cid'i·fi'er
a·cid'i·fy'
·fied' ·fy'ing
a·cid'i·ty
ac'i·do'sis
a·cid'u·late'
·lat'ed ·lat'ing
a·cid'u·lous
ac·knowl'edge
·edged ·edg·ing
ac·knowl'edge·
a·ble
ac·knowl'edg·
ment or
·edge·ment
ac'me
ac'ne
ac'o·lyte'
ac'o·nite'
a'corn
a·cous'tic or
·ti·cal
a·cous'ti·cal·ly
ac·quaint'
ac·quaint'ance
ac'qui·esce'
·esced' ·esc'ing
ac'qui·es'cence
ac'qui·es'cent
ac·quir'a·ble
ac·quire'
·quired' ·quir'ing
ac·quire'ment
ac'qui·si'tion
ac·quis'i·tive
ac·quit'
·quit'ted
·quit'ting

ac·quit'tal
a'cre
a'cre·age
ac'rid
a·crid'i·ty
ac'ri·mo'ni·ous
ac'ri·mo'ny
ac'ro·bat'
ac'ro·bat'ic
ac'ro·bat'i·cal·ly
ac'ro·nym
ac'ro·pho'bi·a
a·crop'o·lis
a·cross'
a·cros'tic
a·cryl'ic
act'a·ble
act'a·bil'i·ty
act'ing
ac·tin'i·um
ac'ti·nom'e·ter
ac'ti·no·my'cin
ac'tion
ac'ti·vate'
·vat'ed ·vat'ing
ac'ti·va'tion
ac'ti·va'tor
ac'tive
ac'tiv·ism
ac'tiv·ist
ac·tiv'i·ty
·ties
ac'tiv·ize'
·ized' ·iz'ing
ac'tor
ac'tress
ac'tu·al
ac'tu·al'i·ty
·ties
ac'tu·al·ize'
·ized' ·iz'ing
ac'tu·al·ly
ac'tu·ar'i·al
ac'tu·ar'y
·ies
ac'tu·ate'
·at'ed ·at'ing
ac'tu·a'tion
ac'tu·a'tor
a·cu'i·ty
·ties
a·cu'men
ac'u·punc'ture
a·cute'
a·cute'ly
ad'age
a·da'gio
·gios
ad'a·mant
a·dapt'
(fit; SEE adept,
adopt)
a·dapt'a·bil'i·t-
a·dapt'a·ble
ad'ap·ta'tion
a·dap'tion
a·dapt'er or
a·dap'tor

a·dap'tive
add'a·ble *or* ·i·ble
ad·den'dum
·da
ad'der
(*snake*)
add'er
(*one who adds*)
ad'dict
ad·dic'tion
ad·dic'tive
ad·di'tion
(*an adding;* SEE edition)
ad·di'tion·al
ad·di'tion·al·ly
ad'di·tive
ad'dle
·dled ·dling
ad'dle·brained'
ad·dress'
ad·dress·ee'
ad·duce'
·duced' ·duc'ing
ad·duc'i·ble
ad·duc'tion
ad·e·noi'dal
ad'e·noids'
ad·ept'
(*skilled;* SEE adapt, adopt)
ad'e·qua·cy
ad'e·quate
ad'e·quate·ly
ad·here'
·hered' ·her'ing
ad·her'ence
ad·her'ent
ad·he'sion
ad·he'sive
ad' hoc'
ad' hom'i·nem'
·dieu'
ad in·fi'ni'tum
ad in'te·rim
ad'i·pose'
ad·ja'cen·cy
ad·ja'cent
ad'jec·tive
ad·join'
(*be next to*)
ad·journ'
(*suspend*)
ad·judge'
·judged'
·judg'ing
ad·ju'di·cate'
·cat·ed ·cat'ing
ad·ju'di·ca'tion
ad·ju'di·ca'tor
ad'junct
ad·ju·ra'tion
ad·jure'
·jured' ·jur'ing
ad·just'
ad·just'a·ble
ad·just'er *or*

·jus'tor
ad·just'ment
ad'ju·tant
ad'-lib'
·libbed' -lib'bing
ad'man'
·men'
ad·min'is·ter
ad·min'is·tra·ble
ad·min'is·trate'
·trat'ed ·trat'ing
ad·min'is·tra'tion
ad·min'is·tra'tive
ad·min'is·tra'tor
ad'mi·ra·ble
ad'mi·ra·bly
ad'mi·ral
ad'mi·ral·ty
·ties
ad·mi·ra'tion
ad·mire'
·mired' ·mir'ing
ad·mir'er
ad·mis·si·bil'i·ty
ad·mis'si·ble
ad·mis'si·bly
ad·mis'sion
ad·mit'
·mit'ted ·mit'ting
ad·mit'tance
ad·mit'ted·ly
ad·mix'
ad·mix'ture
ad·mon'ish
ad·mo·ni'tion
ad·mon'i·to'ry
ad' nau'se·am
a·do'
a·do'be
ad·o·les'cence
ad·o·les'cent
a·dopt'
(*choose;* SEE adapt, adept)
a·dop'tion
a·dop'tive
a·dor'a·ble
ad·o·ra'tion
a·dore'
·dored' ·dor'ing
a·dorn'
a·dorn'ment
ad·re'nal
ad·ren'al·in
a·drift'
a·droit'
ad·sorb'
ad·sor'bent
ad·sorp'tion
ad'u·late'
·lat'ed ·lat'ing
ad·u·la'tion
a·dul'ter·ant
a·dul'ter·ate'
·at'ed ·at'ing
a·dul'ter·a'tion
a·dul'ter·er
a·dul'ter·ess *n.*

a·dul'ter·ous *adj.*
a·dul'ter·y
a·dult'hood
ad·um'brate
·brat·ed ·brat·ing
ad' va·lo'rem
ad·vance'
·vanced'
·vanc'ing
ad·vance'ment
ad·van'tage
ad·van·ta'geous
ad·ven·ti'tious
ad·ven'ture
·tured ·tur·ing
ad·ven'tur·er
ad·ven'ture·some
ad·ven'tur·ous
ad'verb
ad·ver'bi·al
ad'ver·sar'y
·ies
ad·verse'
(*opposed;* SEE averse)
ad·verse'ly
ad·ver'si·ty
·ties
ad·vert'
ad·vert'ent
ad·ver·tise' *or*
·tize'
·tised' *or* ·tized'
·tis·ing *or*
·tiz'ing
ad·ver·tise'ment
or ·tize'ment
ad·vice' *n.*
ad·vis·a·bil'i·ty
ad·vis'a·ble
ad·vis'a·bly
ad·vise' *v.*
·vised' ·vis'ing
ad·vis'ed·ly
ad·vise'ment
ad·vis'er *or*
·vi'sor
ad·vi'so·ry
ad'vo·ca·cy
ad'vo·cate'
·cat'ed ·cat'ing
Ae·ge'an
ae'gis
ae'on
aer'ate'
·at'ed ·at'ing
aer·a'tion
aer·a'tor
aer'i·al
aer'i·al·ist
aer'ic *or* ·y
aer·o·bal·lis'tics
aer·o·bat'ics
aer'obe
aer·o·dy·nam'i·cal·ly
aer·o·dy·nam'ics
aer·o·me·chan'·ics

aer·o·med'i·cine
aer·o·nau'ti·cal
aer·o·nau'tics
aer·o·neu·ro'sis
aer'o·sol'
aer'o·space
aer·o·stat'ics
Ae'sop
aes'thete'
aes·thet'ic
aes·thet'i·cal·ly
aes·thet'i·cism
af·fa·bil'i·ty
af'fa·ble
af'fa·bly
af·fair'
af·fect'
(*to influence;* SEE effect)
af'fec·ta'tion
af·fect'ed
af·fec'tion
af·fec'tion·ate
af·fec'tive
(*of feelings;* SEE effective)
af·fi'ance
·anced ·anc·ing
af·fi·da'vit
af·fil'i·ate'
·at'ed ·at'ing
af·fil·i·a'tion
af·fin'i·ty
af·firm'
af·fir·ma'tion
af·firm'a·tive
af·firm'a·tive·ly
af·fix'
·fixed' *or* ·fixt'
·fix'ing
af·flict'
af·flic'tion
af·flu·ence
af·flu·ent
(*rich;* SEE effluent)
af·ford'
af·fray'
af·front'
af'ghan
a·fi'cio·na'do
a·field'
a·fire'
a·flame'
a·float'
a·fore'men'tioned
a·fore'said'
a·fore'thought'
a·fore'time'
a·foul'
a·fraid'
A'-frame'
a·fresh'
Af'ri·can
af'ter
af'ter·birth'
af'ter·burn'er
af'ter·damp'

af'ter·ef·fect'
af'ter·glow'
af'ter·im'age
af'ter·life'
af'ter·math'
af'ter·noon'
af'ter·shock'
af'ter·taste'
af'ter·thought'
af'ter·ward
a·gain'
a·gainst'
a·gape'
ag'ate
ag'ate·ware'
age
aged, ag'ing *or*
age'ing
age'less
age'long'
a'gen·cy
·cies
a·gen'da
a'gent
age'-old'
ag·glom'er·ate'
·at'ed ·at'ing
ag·glom'er·a'tion
ag·glu'ti·nant
ag·glu'ti·nate'
·nat'ed ·nat'ing
ag·glu'ti·na'tion
ag·gran'dize'
·dized' ·diz'ing
ag·gran'dize·ment
ag'gra·vate'
·vat'ed ·vat'ing
ag·gra·va'tion
ag'gre·gate'
·gat'ed ·gat'ing
ag·gre·ga'tion
ag·gres'sion
ag·gres'sive
ag·gres'sor
ag·grieve'
·grieved'
·griev'ing
a·ghast'
ag'ile
ag'ile·ly
a·gil'i·ty
ag'i·tate'
·tat'ed ·tat'ing
ag·i·ta'tion
ag'i·ta'tor
ag'it·prop'
a·gleam'
ag'let
a·glow'
ag·nos'tic
ag·nos'ti·cal·ly
ag·nos'ti·cism
a·gog'
ag'o·nize'
·nized' ·niz'ing
ag'o·ny
·nies

ag·o·ra·pho'bi·a
a·grar'i·an
a·gree'
·greed' ·gree'ing
a·gree·a·bil'i·ty
a·gree'a·ble
a·gree'a·bly
ag'ri·busi'ness
ag'ri·cul'tur·al
ag'ri·cul'ture
ag'ri·cul'tur·ist
or ·tur·al·ist
a·gron'o·my
a·ground'
a'gue
a'gu·ish
a·head'
aid
(*help*)
aide
(*assistant*)
aide'-de-camp' *or*
aid'-de-camp'
aides'- *or* aids'-
ail
(*be ill;* SEE ale)
ai'le·ron'
ail'ing
ail'ment
aim'less
air
(*gases;* SEE heir)
air base
air'borne'
air brake
air'bra'sive
air'brush'
air coach
air'-con·di'tion
air'-con·di'tioned
air conditioner
air conditioning
air'-cool'
air'-cooled'
air'craft'
air'drome'
air'drop'
·dropped'
·drop'ping
air'-dry'
-dried' -dry'ing
air express
air'field'
air'foil'
air force
air'frame'
air gun
air hole
air'i·ly
air'i·ness
air'ing
air lane
air'lift'
air'line'
air'lin'er
air lock
air'mail'

air'man
·men
air'-mind'ed
air'mo'bile
air'plane'
air'port
air pressure
air'proof'
air pump
air raid
air'scape'
air'ship'
air'sick'
air'space'
air'speed'
air'-sprayed'
air'stream'
air'strip'
air'tight'
air'waves'
air'wor'thy
air'y
  air'i·er air'i·est
aisle
  (passage; SEE isle)
a·kim'bo
Al'a·bam'a
al'a·bas'ter
a' la carte'
a·lac'ri·ty
à' la king'
a' la mode'
  or à' la mode'
a·larm'ing
a·larm'ist
A·las'ka
al'ba·core'
al'ba·tross'
al·be'it
al'bi·nism
al·bi'no
  ·nos
al'bum
al·bu'men
  (egg white)
al·bu'min
  (class of proteins)
Al'bu·quer'que
al'che·mist
al'che·my
al'co·hol'
al'co·hol'ic
al'co·hol'i·cal·ly
al'co·hol'ism
al'cove
al'der·man
·men
ale
  (a drink; SEE ail)
a'le·a·to'ry
ale'house'
a·lert'ly
A·leu'tian
ale'wife'
·wives'
al'fal'fa
al·fres'co
al'gae

al'gae·cide'
al'ge·bra
al'ge·bra'ic
al'ge·bra'i·cal·ly
a'li·as
al'i·bi'
·bis'
·bied' ·bi'ing
al'ien
al'ien·ate'
·at·ed ·at·ing
al'ien·a'tion
a·light'
·light'ed or ·lit'
·light'ing
a·lign' or a·line'
·ligned' or ·lined'
·lign'ing or
·lin'ing
a·lign'ment
or a·line'ment
a·like'
al'i·men'ta·ry
(nourishing; SEE
elementary)
al'i·mo'ny
al'i·quant
al'i·quot
a·live'
al'ka·li'
·lies' or ·lis'
al'ka·line
al'ka·lize'
·lized' ·liz'ing
al'ka·loid'
al'kyd
all'-A·mer'i·can
all'-a·round'
al·lay'
·layed' ·lay'ing
all'-clear'
al'le·ga'tion
al·lege'
·leged' ·leg'ing
al·leg'ed·ly
Al'le·ghe'ny
al·le'giance
al'le·gor'i·cal
al'le·go·rize'
·rized' ·riz'ing
al'le·go'ry
·ries
al·le·gret'to
al·le'gro
al·le·lu'ia
al'ler·gen
al'ler·gen'ic
al·ler'gic
al'ler·gist
al'ler·gy
·gies
al·le'vi·ate'
·at·ed ·at·ing
al·le'vi·a'tion
al'ley
·leys
(narrow lane;
SEE ally)

al'ley·way'
al·li'ance
al·lied'
al'li·ga'tor
all'-im·por'tant
all'-in·clu'sive
al·lit'er·ate'
·at·ed ·at·ing
al·lit'er·a'tion
al'lo·cate'
·cat·ed ·cat·ing
al·lo·ca'tion
al·lot'
·lot'ted ·lot'ting
al·lot'ment
al·lot'tee'
all'-out'
all'o·ver
al·low'
al·low'a·ble
al·low'ance
al·lowed'
(permitted; SEE
aloud)
al'loy
all'-pur'pose
all right
all'spice'
all'-star'
all'-time'
al·lude'
·lud'ed ·lud'ing
(refer to; SEE
elude)
al·lure'
·lured' ·lur'ing
al·lu'sion
(mention; SEE
elusion, illusion)
al·lu'sive
(mentioning; SEE
elusive, illusive)
al·lu'vi·al
al·lu'vi·um
·vi·ums or ·vi·a
al·ly' v. al'ly n.
·lied' ·ly'ing
·lies
(join; partner;
SEE alley)
al'ma ma'ter
al'ma·nac'
al·might'y
al'mond
al'mon·er
al'most
alms
a·loft'
a·lo'ha
a·long'shore'
a·long'side'
a·loof'
a·loud'
(loudly; SEE
allowed)
al·pac'a
al'pen·stock'
al'pha·bet'

al'pha·bet'i·cal
al'pha·bet'i·cal·ly
al'pha·bet·ize'
·ized' ·iz'ing
al·read'y
al'so·ran'
al'tar
(table for
worship)
al'ter
(to change)
al'ter·a'tion
al'ter·cate'
·cat·ed ·cat·ing
al·ter·ca'tion
al'ter·nate'
·nat·ed ·nat·ing
al·ter·na'tion
al·ter'na·tive
al'ter·na'tor
al·though'
al·tim'e·ter
al'ti·tude'
al'to
·tos
al·to·geth'er
al'tru·ism
al'tru·is'tic
a·lu'mi·num
a·lum'na n.fem.
·nae
a·lum'nus
n.masc.
·ni
al'ways
a·mal'ga·mate'
·mat·ed ·mat·ing
a·mal'ga·ma'tion
a·man'u·en'sis
·ses
am'a·ryl'lis
am'a·teur'
am'a·to'ry
a·maze'
·mazed'
·maz'ing
a·maze'ment
Am'a·zon'
am·bas'sa·dor
am·bas'sa·do'ri·al
am'ber
am'ber·gris'
am·bi·ance
am'bi·dex·ter'i·ty
am'bi·dex'trous
am'bi·ent
am·bi·gu'i·ty
am·big'u·ous
am·bi'tion
am·bi'tious
am·biv'a·lence
am'ble
·bled ·bling
am·bro'sia
am'bu·lance
am'bu·late'
·lat·ed ·lat'ing
am'bu·la·to'ry

am'bus·cade'
·cad·ed ·cad'ing
am'bush
a·me'ba
·bas or ·bae
a·mel'io·rate'
·rat·ed ·rat'ing
a·mel'io·ra'tion
a·mel'io·ra'tive
a·me'na·bil'i·ty
a·me'na·ble
a·mend'
(revise; SEE
emend)
a·mend'ment
a·men'i·ty
·ties
A·mer'i·can
A·mer'i·ca'na
A·mer'i·can·ism
A·mer'i·can·i·
za'tion
A·mer'i·can·ize'
·ized' ·iz'ing
Am'er·ind'
am'e·thyst
a'mi·a·bil'i·ty
a'mi·a·ble
a'mi·a·bly
am'i·ca·bil'i·ty
am'i·ca·ble
am'i·ca·bly
a·mid'
a·mid'ships
a·midst'
a·mi'no
Am'ish
a·miss'
am'i·ty
·ties
am'me·ter
am·mo'nia
am·mu·ni'tion
am·ne'sia
am·ne'si·ac' or
am·ne'sic
am'nes·ty
·ties, ·tied ·ty·ing
a·moe'ba
·bas or ·bae
a·mok'
a·mong'
a·mongst'
a·mon'til·la'do
a·mor'al
a·mor'al·i·ty
am'o·rous
a·mor'phous
am'or·ti·za'tion
am'or·tize'
·tized' ·tiz'ing
a·mount'
a·mour'
am'per·age
am'pere
am'per·sand'
am·phet'a·mine'
am·phib'i·an

am·phib'i·ous
am'phi·the·a'ter
am'pho·ra
·rae or ·ras
am'ple
am'pli·fi·ca'tion
am'pli·fi'er
am'pli·fy'
·fied' ·fy'ing
am'pli·tude'
am'ply
am'pul
am·pul'la
·las or ·lae
am'pu·tate'
·tat·ed ·tat'ing
am'pu·ta'tion
am'pu·tee'
a·muck'
am'u·let
a·muse'
·mused'
·mus'ing
a·muse'ment
a·nach'ro·nism
a·nach'ro·nis'tic
an'a·con'da
a·nae'mi·a
a·nae'mic
an·aes·the'sia
an·aes·thet'ic
an·aes'the·tize'
·tized' ·tiz'ing
an'a·gram'
a'nal
an'al·ge'si·a
an'al·ge'sic
an'a·log' compu
a·nal'o·gize'
·gized' ·giz'ing
a·nal'o·gous
a·nal'o·gy
·gies
a·nal'y·sis
·ses'
an'a·lyst
(one who
analyzes; SEE
annalist)
an'a·lyt'i·cal
or an·a·lyt'ic
an'a·lyt'i·cal·ly
an'a·lyze'
·lyzed' ·lyz'ing
an'a·pest'
an·ar'chic
or an·ar'chi·c
an'ar·chism
an'ar·chist
an·ar·chis'tic
an'ar·chy
·chies
an·as·tig·mat'ic
a·nas'tro·phe
a·nath'e·ma
·mas
a·nath'e·ma·tiz
·tized' ·tiz'ing

an·a·tom'i·cal
or an·a·tom'ic
an·a·tom'i·cal·ly
a·nat'o·mist
a·nat'o·mize'
·mized' ·miz'ing
a·nat'o·my
·mies
an·ces'tor
an·ces'tral
an·ces'tress
an·ces'try
·tries
an'chor
an'chor·age
an'cho·rite'
an'cho'vy
·vies
an'cient
an'cil·lar'y
an·dan'te
and'i'ron
and/or
an'dro·gen
an'ec·dot'al
an'ec·dote'
(story; SEE
antidote)
a·ne'mi·a
a·ne'mic
a·nem'o·graph'
an'e·mom'e·ter
a·nem'o·ne'
an'er·oid'
an'es·the'sia
an'es·the'si·
ol'o·gy
an'es·thet'ic
an'es·the·tist
an'es·the·tize'
·tized' ·tiz'ing
an'gel
(spirit; SEE angle)
an'gel·fish'
an·gel'ic
or an·gel'i·cal
an·gel'i·cal·ly
an'ge·lus
an'ger
an·gi'na
an'gle
an·gled ·gling
(corner; scheme;
EE angel)
an'gler
an'gle·worm'
an'gli·can
an'gli·cism
an'gli·cize'
·cized' ·ciz'ing
an'gling
an'glo-A·mer'i·
an
an'glo·ma'ni·a
an'glo·phile'
an'glo-Sax'on
an·go'ra
an'gos·tu'ra

an'gri·ly
an'gry
·gri·er ·gri·est
an'guish
an'gu·lar
an·gu·lar'i·ty
·ties
an'gu·la'tion
an·hy'drous
an'ile
a·nil'i·ty
an'i·mad·ver'
sion
an'i·mal
an'i·mal'cule
an'i·mal·ism
an'i·mal·is'tic
an'i·mal·ize'
·ized' ·iz'ing
an'i·mate'
·mat'ed ·mat'ing
an'i·ma'tor
or ·mat'er
an'i·ma'tion
an'i·mism
an'i·mos'i·ty
·ties
an'i·mus
an'i'on
an'ise
an'i·seed'
an'i·sette'
ankh
an'kle
an'kle·bone'
an'klet
an'nal·ist
(a writer of
annals; SEE
analyst)
an'nals
An·nap'o·lis
an·neal'
an'ne·lid
an·nex' v
an·nex n.
an·nex·a'tion
an·ni'hi·late'
·lat'ed ·lat'ing
an·ni'hi·la'tion
an·ni'hi·la'tor
an'ni·ver'sa·ry
·ries
an'no·tate'
·tat'ed ·tat'ing
an'no·ta'tion
an·nounce'
·nounced'
·nounc'ing
an·nounce'ment
an·nounc'er
an·noy'
an·noy'ance
an'nu·al
an'nu·al·ly
an·nu'i·tant
an·nu'i·ty
·ties

an·nul'
·nulled'
·nul'ling
an'nu·lar
an·nul'ment
an'nu·lus
·li' or ·lus·es
an·nun'ci·ate'
·at'ed ·at'ing
(announce; SEE
enunciate)
an·nun'ci·a'tor
an'ode
an'o·dize'
·dized' ·diz'ing
an'o·dyne'
a·noint'
a·nom'a·lous
a·nom'a·ly
·lies
an'o·mie
an·o·nym'i·ty
a·non'y·mous
a·noph'e·les'
an·oth'er
an'swer
ant·ac'id
an·tag'o·nism
an·tag'o·nis'tic
an·tag'o·nize'
·nized' ·niz'ing
ant·al'ka·li'
·lies' or ·lis'
ant·arc'tic
Ant·arc'ti·ca
an'te
·ted or ·teed
·te·ing
an'te- prefix
(before; SEE
anti-)
ant'eat'er
an'te·bel'lum
an'te·cede'
·ced'ed ·ced'ing
an'te·ced'ence
an'te·ced'ent
an'te·cham'ber
an'te·date'
an'te·di·lu'vi·an
an'te·lope'
an'te me·ri'di·em
an·ten'na
·nae or ·nas
an'te·pe'nult
an·te'ri·or
an'te·room'
an'them
an'ther
an·thol'o·gist
an·thol'o·gy
·gies
an'thra·cite'
an'thrax
·thra·ces'
an'thro·poid'
an'thro·pol'o·gist
an'thro·pol'o·gy

an'thro·po·mor'·
phic
an'ti- prefix
(against; SEE
ante-)
an'ti·air'craft
an'ti·bac·te'ri·al
an'ti·bi·ot'ic
an'ti·bod'y
·ies
an'tic
·ticked ·tick·ing
an·tic'i·pant
an·tic'i·pate'
·pat'ed ·pat'ing
an·tic'i·pa'tion
an·tic'i·pa·to'ry
an'ti·cli·mac'tic
an'ti·cli'max
an'ti·de·pres'sant
an'ti·dote'
(remedy; SEE
anecdote)
an'ti·freeze'
an'ti·gen
an'ti·he'ro
an'ti·his'ta·mine'
an'ti·knock'
an'ti·la'bor
An·til'les
an'ti·ma·cas'sar
an'ti·mat'ter
an'ti·mo'ny
an'ti·nov'el
an'ti·par'ti·cle
an'ti·pas'to
an'ti·pa·thet'ic
an·tip'a·thy
·thies
an'ti·per'son·nel'
an'ti·phon
an·tiph'o·nal
an'ti·pode'
an'ti·pode'
an·tip'o·des'
an'ti·quar'i·an
an'ti·quar'y
·ies
an'ti·quate'
·quat'ed
·quat'ing
an·tique'
·tiqued'
·tiqu'ing
an·tiq'ui·ty
·ties
an'ti-Sem'ite
an'ti-Se·mit'ic
an'ti-Sem'i·tism
an'ti·sep'sis
an'ti·sep'tic
an'ti·so'cial
an'ti·tith'e·sis
·ses'
an'ti·thet'i·cal
an'ti·thet'i·
cal·ly
an'ti·tox'in

an'ti·trust'
ant'ler
an'to·nym'
an'trum
·trums or ·tra
a'nus
·nus·es or ·ni
an'vil
anx·i'e·ty
·ties
anx'ious
an'y·bod'y
an'y·how'
an'y·one'
an'y·thing'
an'y·way'
an'y·where'
A'-OK' or
A'-O·kay'
a·or'ta
·tas or ·tae
a·pace'
a·part'heid
a·part'ment
ap'a·thet'ic
ap'a·thet'i·
cal·ly
ap'a·thy
·thies
a'pe·ri·tif'
ap'er·ture
a'pex
a'pex·es or
ap'i·ces
a·pha'si·a
aph'o·rism
aph'ro·dis'i·ac'
a'pi·ar'y
·ies
a·piece'
a·plomb'
a·poc'a·lypse'
a·poc'a·lyp'tic
a·poc'ry·phal
ap'o·gee'
a·pol'o·get'ic
a·pol'o·get'i·
cal·ly
a·pol'o·gi·a
a·pol'o·gize'
·gized' ·giz'ing
ap'o·logue'
a·pol'o·gy
·gies
ap'o·plec'tic
ap'o·plex'y
a·pos'ta·sy
a·pos'tate
a' pos·te'ri·o'ri
a·pos'tle
ap·os·tol'ic
a·pos'tro·phe
ap'os·troph'ic
a·pos'tro·phize'
·phized'
·phiz'ing
a·poth'e·car'y
·ies

ap'o·thegm'
(short saying)
ap'o·them'
(math. term)
a·poth'e·o'sis
·ses
Ap'pa·la'chi·an
ap·pall' or ·pal'
·palled' ·pal'ling
ap'pa·loo'sa
ap'pa·ra'tus
·tus or ·tus·es
ap·par'el
·eled or ·elled
·el·ing or ·el·ling
ap·par'ent
ap'pa·ri'tion
ap·peal'
ap·pear'ance
ap·peas'a·ble
ap·pease'
·peased'
·peas'ing
ap·pease'ment
ap·peas'er
ap·pel'lant
ap·pel'late
ap'pel·la'tion
ap·pend'
ap·pend'age
ap·pend'ant or
·ent
ap·pen·dec'to·my
·mies
ap·pen·di·ci'tis
ap·pen'dix
·dix·es or
·di·ces'
ap'per·cep'tion
ap·per·tain'
ap'pe·tite'
ap'pe·tiz'er
ap'pe·tiz'ing
ap·plaud'
ap·plause'
ap·ple·jack'
ap·ple·sauce'
ap·pli'ance
ap'pli·ca·bil'i·ty
ap'pli·ca·ble
ap'pli·cant
ap'pli·ca'tion
ap'pli·ca'tor
ap·plied'
ap'pli·qué'
·quéd' ·qué'ing
ap·ply'
·plied' ·ply'ing
ap·pog'gia·tu'ra
ap·point'
ap·point'ee'
ap·poin'tive
ap·point'ment
ap·por'tion
ap'po·site
ap'po·si'tion
ap·prais'a·ble
ap·prais'al

ap·praise'
·praised'
·prais'ing
(estimate; SEE
apprise)
ap·prais'er
ap·pre'ci·a·ble
ap·pre'ci·ate'
·at'ed ·at'ing
ap·pre'ci·a'tion
ap·pre'ci·a·tive
ap'pre·hend'
ap'pre·hen'sion
ap'pre·hen'sive
ap·pren'tice
·ticed ·tic·ing
ap·prise' or
·prize'
·prised' or
·prized'
·pris'ing or
·priz'ing
(inform; SEE
appraise)
ap·proach'
ap·proach'
a·ble
ap'pro·ba'tion
ap·pro'pri·ate'
·at'ed ·at'ing
ap·pro'pri·ate·ly
ap·pro'pri·a'tion
ap·prov'a·ble
ap·prov'al
ap·prove'
·proved'
·prov'ing
ap·prox'i·mate'
·mat'ed ·mat'ing
ap·prox'i·mate·ly
ap·prox'i·ma'·
tion
ap·pur'te·nance
a'pri·cot'
A'pril
a' pri·o'ri
ap'ro·pos'
ap'ti·tude'
apt'ly
aq'ua·cade'
aq'ua·lung'
aq'ua·ma·rine'
aq'ua·naut'
aq'ua·plane'
a·quar'i·um
·i·ums or ·i·a
a·quat'ic
aq'ua·tint'
aq'ue·duct'
a'que·ous
aq'ui·line'
ar'a·besque'
A·ra'bi·an
Ar'a·bic
ar'a·ble
a·rach'nid
ar'bi·ter
ar'bi·tra·ble

ar·bit'ra·ment
ar'bi·trar'i·ly
ar'bi·trar'i·ness
ar'bi·trar'y
ar'bi·trate'
·trat'ed ·trat'ing
ar'bi·tra'tion
ar'bi·tra'tor
ar'bor
ar·bo're·al
ar'bo·re'tum
·tums or ·ta
ar'bor·vi'tae
arc
arced or arcked
arc'ing or arck'ing
(curve; SEE ark)
ar·cade'
ar'chae·o·log'i·cal
ar'chae·ol'o·gy
ar·cha'ic
arch'an'gel
arch'bish'op
arch'dea'con
arch'di'o·cese
arch'duch'y
·ies
arch'duke'
arched
arch'en'e·my
·mies
ar'che·o·log'i·cal
ar'che·ol'o·gy
arch'er·y
ar'che·type'
arch'fiend'
ar'chi·pel'a·go'
·goes' or ·gos'
ar'chi·tect'
ar'chi·tec·ton'ics
ar'chi·tec'tur·al
ar'chi·tec'tur·
al·ly
ar'chi·tec'ture
ar'chi·trave'
ar'chives
arch'priest'
arch'way'
arc'tic
ar'dent
ar'dor
ar'du·ous
ar'e·a·way'
a·re'na
aren't
Ar'gen·ti'na
ar'gon
ar'got
ar'gu·a·ble
ar'gu·a·bly
ar'gue
·gued ·gu·ing
ar'gu·ment
ar'gu·men·
ta'tion
ar'gu·men'ta·
tive
a'ri·a

a·rid'i·ty
ar'id·ness
a·rise'
·rose' ·ris'en
·ris'ing
ar'is·toc'ra·cy
·cies
a·ris'to·crat'
a·ris'to·crat'ic
a·ris'to·crat'i·
cal·ly
Ar'is·to·te'li·an
Ar'is·tot'le
a·rith'me·tic' n.
ar'ith·met'ic adj.
ar'ith·met'i·cal
ar'ith·met'i·
cal·ly
ar'ith·me·ti'cian
Ar'i·zo'na
ark
(enclosure;
SEE arc)
Ar'kan·sas'
ar·ma'da
ar'ma·dil'lo
·los
ar'ma·ment
ar'ma·ture
arm'chair'
armed
arm'ful
·fuls
arm'hole'
ar'mi·stice
arm'let
ar'mor
ar'mored
ar'mor-plat'ed
ar'mor·y
·ies
arm'pit'
arm'rest'
ar'my
·mies
ar'ni·ca
a·ro'ma
ar'o·mat'ic
ar'o·mat'i·cal·ly
a·round'
a·rous'al
a·rouse'
·roused'
·rous'ing
ar·peg'gio
·gios
ar·raign'
ar·range'
·ranged'
·rang'ing
ar·range'ment
ar·rang'er
ar'rant
ar·ray'
ar·ray'al
ar·rear'age
ar·rears'
ar·rest'

ar·riv'al
ar·rive'
·rived' ·riv'ing
ar'ro·gance
ar'ro·gant
ar'ro·gate'
·gat'ed ·gat'ing
ar'ro·ga'tion
ar'row·head'
ar'row·root'
ar·roy'o
·os
ar'se·nal
ar'se·nic
ar'son
ar'son·ist
ar'te·fact'
ar·te'ri·al
ar·te'ri·o·scle·
ro'sis
ar·te'ri·o·scle·
rot'ic
ar'ter·y
·ies
ar·te'sian
art'ful
art'ful·ly
ar·thrit'ic
ar·thri'tis
Ar·thu'ri·an
ar'ti·choke'
ar'ti·cle
ar·tic'u·late'
·lat'ed ·lat'ing
ar·tic'u·late·ly
ar·tic'u·la'tion
ar'ti·fact'
ar'ti·fice
ar·tif'i·cer
ar'ti·fi'cial
ar'ti·fi'cial·ly
ar'ti·fi·ci·al'i·ty
·ties
ar·til'ler·y
art'i·ness
ar'ti·san
art'ist
ar·tiste'
ar·tis'tic
ar·tis'ti·cal·ly
art'ist·ry
art'less
art'mo·bile'
art'sy-craft'sy
art'y
·i·er ·i·est
Ar'y·an
as·bes'tos
as·cend'
as·cend'a·ble
as·cend'an·cy
as·cend'ant
as·cen'sion
as·cent'
(a rising; SEE
assent)
as'cer·tain'
as·cet'ic

as·cet'i·cal·ly
as·cet'i·cism
a·scor'bic
as'cot
as·crib'a·ble
as·cribe'
·cribed'
·crib'ing
as·crip'tion
a·sep'tic
a·sep'ti·cal·ly
a·sex'u·al
a·shamed'
ash'can'
ash'en
ash'es
a·shore'
ash'y
·i·er ·i·est
A'sia
A'si·at'ic
as'i·nine'
as'i·nin'i·ty
·ties
a·skance'
a·skew'
a·sleep'
a·so'cial
as·par'a·gus
as'pect
as'pen
as·per'i·ty
as·perse'
·persed' ·pers'ing
as·per'sion
as'phalt
as·phyx'i·a
as·phyx'i·ant
as·phyx'i·ate'
·at'ed ·at'ing
as·phyx'i·a'tion
as·phyx'i·a'tor
as'pic
as'pir·ant
as'pi·rate'
·rat'ed ·rat'ing
as'pi·ra'tion
as'pi·ra'tor
as·pire'
·pired' ·pir'ing
as'pi·rin
as·sail'
as·sail'ant
as·sas'sin
as·sas'si·nate'
·nat'ed ·nat'ing
as·sas'si·na'tion
as·sault'
as·say'
(analyze; SEE
essay)
as·sem'blage
as·sem'ble
·bled ·bling
as·sem'bly
·blies
as·sem'bly·man
·men

as·sent'
(consent; SEE ass[c])
as·sert'
as·ser'tion
as·ser'tive
as·sess'
as·ses'sor
as'set
as·sev'er·ate
·at'ed ·at'ing
as·sev'er·a'tion
as'si·du'i·ty
as·sid'u·ous
as·sign'
as·sign'a·ble
as·sig·na'tion
as·sign'ee'
as·sign'ment
as·sim'i·la·ble
as·sim'i·la'tion
as·sim'i·la'tive
as·sim'i·la'tor
as·sist'
as·sist'ance
as·sist'ant
as·size'
as·so'ci·ate'
·at'ed ·at'ing
as·so'ci·a'tion
as·so'ci·a'tive
as'so·nance
as'so·nant
as·sort'
as·sort'ed
as·sort'ment
as·suage'
·suaged'
·suag'ing
as·sua'sive
as·sum'a·ble
as·sume'
·sumed'
·sum'ing
as·sump'tion
as·sur'ance
as·sure'
·sured' ·sur'ing
as·sur'ed·ly
As·syr'i·a
as'ter·isk'
as'ter·oid'
asth'ma
asth·mat'ic
asth·mat'i·cal·l[y]
as'tig·mat'ic
as'tig·mat'i·cal·
a·stig'ma·tism
as·ton'ish
as·tound'
a·strad'dle
as'tra·khan
or ·chan
as'tral
a·stride'
as·trin'gen·cy
as·trin'gent

as'tro·dome'
as'tro·labe'
as·trol'o·ger
as·tro·log'i·cal
as·trol'o·gy
as'tro·naut'
as'tro·nau'ti·cal
as'tro·nau'tics
as·tron'o·mer
as·tro·nom'i·cal
 or ·nom'ic
as·tro·nom'i·cal·ly
as·tron'o·my
as'tro·phys'i·cal
as'tro·phys'i·cist
as'tro·phys'ics
as·tute'
a·sun'der
a·sy'lum
a·sym·met'ri·cal
 or ·met'ric
a·sym'me·try
as'ymp·tote'
at'a·vism
at'a·vis'tic
at·el·ier'
a'the·ism
a'the·ist
a'the·is'tic
ath·lete'
ath·let'ic
ath·let'i·cal·ly
at·home'
a·thwart'
a·tin'gle
At·lan'tic
at'las
at'mos·phere'
at'mos·pher'ic
at'mos·pher'i·
 cal·ly
at'oll
at'om
a·tom'ic
a·tom'ics
at'om·ize'
 ·ized' ·iz'ing
at'om·iz'er
a·ton'al
a·to·nal'i·ty
a·tone'
 ·toned' ·ton'ing
a·tone'ment
a'tri·um
 ·tri·a or ·tri·ums
a·tro'cious
a·troc'i·ty
 ·ties
at'ro·phy
 ·phied ·phy·ing
at·tach'
at·ta·ché'
at·tach'ment
at·tack'
at·tain'
at·tain'a·ble
at·tain'der
at·tain'ment

at·taint'
at'tar
at·tempt'
at·tend'
at·tend'ance
at·tend'ant
at·ten'tion
at·ten'tive
at·ten'u·ate'
 ·at'ed ·at'ing
at·ten'u·a'tion
at·ten'u·a'tor
at·test'
at'tes·ta'tion
at'tic
at·tire'
 ·tired' ·tir'ing
at'ti·tude'
at'ti·tu'di·nal
at·tor'ney
 ·neys
at·tract'
at·trac'tion
at·trac'tive
at·trib'ut·a·ble
at'tri·bute' n.
at·trib'ute v.
 ·ut·ed ·ut·ing
at'tri·bu'tion
at·trib'u·tive
at·tri'tion
at·tune'
 ·tuned' ·tun'ing
a·typ'i·cal
a·typ'i·cal·ly
au'burn
auc'tion
auc'tion·eer'
au·da'cious
au·dac'i·ty
 ·ties
au'di·bil'i·ty
au'di·ble
au'di·bly
au'di·ence
au'di·o
au'di·ol'o·gy
au'di·o·vis'u·al
au'di·phone'
au'dit
au·di'tion
au'di·tor
au·di·to'ri·um
au'di·to'ry
au'ger
 (tool; SEE augur)
aught
 (anything; SEE
 ought)
aug·ment'
aug'men·ta'tion
aug·ment'a·tive
au gra'tin
au'gur
 (soothsayer;
 SEE auger)
Au'gust
au jus'

au na·tu·rel'
au'ra
 ·ras or ·rae
au'ral
 (of the ear; SEE
 oral)
au're·ole'
Au're·o·my'cin
au' re·voir'
au'ri·cle
 (earlike part;
 SEE oracle)
au·ric'u·lar
au·ro'ra bo're·
 a'lis
aus·cul·ta'tion
aus'pi·ces'
aus·pi'cious
aus·tere'
aus·tere'ly
aus·ter'i·ty
 ·ties
Aus·tral'ia
au·then'tic
au·then'ti·cal·ly
au·then'ti·cate'
 ·cat·ed ·cat·ing
au·then'ti·ca'tion
au·then·tic'i·ty
au'thor
au·thor'i·tar'i·an
au·thor'i·ta'tive
au·thor'i·ty
 ·ties
au'thor·i·za'tion
au'thor·ize'
 ·ized' ·iz'ing
au'to
 ·tos
 ·toed ·to·ing
au'to·bi'o·
 graph'ic or
 graph'i·cal
au'to·bi·og'ra·
 phy
 ·phies
au·toc'ra·cy
 ·cies
au'to·crat'
au'to·crat'ic
au'to·crat'i·
 cal·ly
au'to·graph'
au'to·mat'
au'to·mate'
 ·mat'ed ·mat'ing
au'to·mat'ic
au'to·mat'i·cal·ly
au'to·ma'tion
au·tom'a·tism
au·tom'a·ton'
 ·tons' or ·ta
au'to·mo·bile'
au'to·mo'tive
au·to·nom'ic
au·ton'o·mous
au·ton'o·my
 ·mies

au'top'sy
 ·sies
au'to·sug·ges'·
 tion
au'tumn
au·tum'nal
aux·il'ia·ry
 ·ries
a·vail'a·bil'i·ty
a·vail'a·ble
a·vail'a·bly
av'a·lanche'
 ·lanched'
 ·lanch'ing
a·vant'-garde'
a·vant'-gard'ism
a·vant'-gard'ist
av'a·rice
av'a·ri'cious
a·venge'
 ·venged'
 ·veng'ing
a·veng'er
av'e·nue'
a·ver'
 ·verred'
 ·ver'ring
av'er·age
 ·aged ·ag·ing
a·verse'
 (unwilling; SEE
 adverse)
a·ver'sion
a·vert'
a'vi·ar'y
 ·ies
a'vi·a'tion
a'vi·a'tor
a'vi·a'trix
av'id·ly
av'o·ca'do
 ·dos
av'o·ca'tion
a·void'a·ble
a·void'a·bly
a·void'ance
av'oir·du·pois'
a·vow'al
a·vowed'
a·vun'cu·lar
a·wait'
a·wake'
 ·woke' or
 ·waked',
 ·waked',
 ·wak'ing
a·wak'en
a·wak'en·ing
a·ward'
a·ware'
a·weigh'
awe'some
awe'-struck'
aw'ful
aw'ful·ly
aw'ful·ness
a·while'
awk'ward

awn'ing
a·wry'
ax or axe
ax'es
axed ax'ing
ax'i·om
ax'i·o·mat'ic
ax'i·o·mat'i·
 cal·ly
ax'is
ax'es
ax'le
Ax'min·ster
a·zal'ea
az'i·muth
Az'tec
az'ure

B

bab'bitt
bab'ble
 ·bled ·bling
ba·boon'
ba·bush'ka
ba'by
 ·bies
 ·bied ·by·ing
ba'by-sit'
 ·sat' ·sit'ting
baby sitter
bac'ca·lau're·ate
bac'ca·rat'
bac'cha·nal
bac'cha·na'li·an
bac'chant
 ·chants or
 bac·chan'tes
bac·chan'te
bach'e·lor
ba·cil'lus
 ·li
back'ache'
back'bite'
 ·bit', ·bit'ten or
 ·bit', ·bit'ing
back'bend'
back'board'
back'bone'
back'break'ing
back'court'
back'date'
 ·dat'ed ·dat'ing
back'door'
back'drop'
back'field'
back'fire'
 ·fired' ·fir'ing
back'gam'mon
back'ground'
back'hand'
back'lash'
back'list'
back'log'
 ·logged'
 ·log'ging

back'rest'
back'side'
back'slide'
 ·slid', ·slid' or
 ·slid'den, ·slid'ing
back'space'
 ·spaced'
 ·spac'ing
back'spin'
back'stage'
back'stairs'
back'stop'
back'stretch'
back'stroke'
 ·stroked'
 ·strok'ing
back'track'
back'up' or
 back'-up'
back'ward
back'wash'
back'wa'ter
back'woods'man
 ·men
ba'con
bac·te'ri·a
 (sing. bac·te'ri·um)
bac·te'ri·cide'
bac·te'ri·o·log'i·
 cal·ly
bac·te'ri·ol'o·gist
bac·te'ri·ol'o·gy
bad
 worse worst
badge
 badged badg'ing
badg'er
bad'i·nage'
 ·naged' ·nag'ing
bad'lands'
bad'min·ton
bad'-tem'pered
baf'fle
 ·fled ·fling
bag
 bagged bag'ging
bag'a·telle'
ba'gel
bag'ful'
 ·fuls'
bag'gage
bag'gy
 ·gi·er ·gi·est
bag'pipe'
ba·guette' or
 ·guet'
Ba·hai'
Ba·ha'mas
bail
 (money; SEE
 bale)
bai'liff
bai'li·wick
bails'man
 ·men
bait'ed
 (lured; SEE
 bated)

bake
  baked bak'ing
bak'er
bak'er·y
  ·ies
bal'a·lai'ka
bal'ance
  ·anced ·anc·ing
bal'ance·a·ble
bal·brig'gan
bal'co·ny
  ·nies
bal'der·dash'
bald'faced'
bald'head'ed
bald'ness
bale
  baled bal'ing
  (bundle; SEE
  bail)
bale'ful
balk'y
  ·i·er ·i·est
ball
  (round object;
  SEE bawl)
bal'lad
bal'lad·eer'
bal'last
ball bearing
bal·le·ri'na
bal'let
bal·lis'tic
bal·loon'ist
bal'lot
ball'park'
ball'play'er
ball'room'
balm'y
  ·i·er ·i·est
ba·lo'ney
bal'sa
bal'sam
Bal'tic
Bal'ti·more'
bal'us·ter
bal'us·trade'
bam·bi'no
  ·nos or ·ni
bam·boo'
bam·boo'zle
  ·zled ·zling
ban
  banned ban'ning
ba'nal
ba·nal'i·ty
  ·ties
ba·nan'a
band'age
  ·aged ·ag·ing
band·aid' or
  band'aid'
ban·dan'na
band'box'
ban·deau'
  ·deaux'
ban'de·role'
ban'dit

band'mas'ter
ban'do·leer'
  or ·lier'
band saw
bands'man
  ·men
band'stand'
band'wag'on
ban'dy
  ·died ·dy·ing
ban'dy·leg'ged
bane'ful
ban'gle
bang'-up'
ban'ish
ban'is·ter
  or ban'nis·ter
ban'jo
  ·jos or ·joes
ban'jo·ist
bank'book'
bank note
bank'roll'
bank'rupt
bank'rupt·cy
  ·cies
ban'ner
banns or bans
  (marriage notice)
ban'quet
ban'tam
ban'tam·weight'
ban'ter
ban'zai'
bap'tism
bap·tis'mal
bap'tis·ter·y
  or ·tis·try
  ·ies or ·tries
bap'tize
  ·tized ·tiz·ing
bar
  barred bar'ring
bar·bar'i·an
bar·bar'ic
bar·ba·rism
bar·bar'i·ty
  ·ties
bar'ba·rous
bar'be·cue'
  ·cued ·cu'ing
barbed wire
bar'bel
  (hairlike growth)
bar'bell'
  (bar with weights)
bar'ber
bar'ber·shop'
bar'bi·tal'
bar·bi'tu·rate
bar'bule
bare
  bared bar'ing
  (uncover; SEE
  bear)
bare'back'
bare'faced'
bare'fac'ed·ly

bare'foot'
bare'foot'ed
bare'hand'ed
bare'head'ed
bare'leg'ged
bare'ly
bar'gain
barge
  barged barg'ing
bar'i·tone'
bar'keep'er
bark'en·tine'
bark'er
bar'ley·corn'
bar'maid'
bar'man
  ·men
bar mitz'vah or
  bar miz'vah
bar'na·cle
bar'na·cled
barn'storm'
barn'yard'
bar'o·graph'
ba·rom'e·ter
bar'o·met'ric
bar'on
  (nobleman; SEE
  barren)
bar'on·ess
bar'on·et
ba·ro'ni·al
ba·roque'
ba·rouche'
bar'racks
bar·ra·cu'da
bar·rage'
  ·raged ·rag'ing
barred
bar'rel
  ·reled or ·relled
  ·rel·ing or
  ·rel·ling
bar'ren
  (empty; SEE
  baron)
bar·rette'
  (hair clasp;
  SEE beret)
bar·ri·cade'
  ·cad·ed ·cad'ing
bar'ri·er
bar'ring
bar'ris·ter
bar'room'
bar'row
bar'tend'er
bar'ter
Bart'lett pear
bas'al
bas'al·ly
ba·salt'
bas'cule
base
  bas'es
  based bas'ing
  (foundation; vile;
  SEE bass)

base'ball'
base'board'
base'born'
base'burn'er
base hit
base'less
base line
base'ly
base'man
  ·men
base'ment
base'ness
bas'es
  (pl. of base)
ba'ses
  (pl. of basis)
bash'ful
bash'ful·ly
bash'ful·ness
bas'ic
bas'i·cal·ly
bas'il
ba·sil'i·ca
ba'sin
ba'sis
  ·ses
bas'ket
bas'ket·ball'
bas'ket·work'
bas'-re·lief'
bass
  (singer; SEE base)
bass
  (fish)
bass clef
bass drum
bas'set
bass horn
bas'si·net'
bas·soon'
bass viol
bass'wood'
bas'tard
baste
  bast'ed bast'ing
bas·tille'
bas'tion
bat
  bat'ted bat'ting
batch
bate
  bat'ed bat'ting
ba·teau'
  ·teaux'
bat'ed
  (held in; SEE
  baited)
bathe
  bathed bath'ing
bath'er
bath'house'
bath'i·nette'
ba'thos
bath'robe'
bath'room'
bath'tub'
bath'y·sphere'
ba·tik'

ba·tiste'
bat mitz'vah or
  bat miz'vah
ba·ton'
bat·tal'ion
bat'ten
bat'ter
bat'ter·y
  ·ies
bat'ting
bat'tle
  ·tled ·tling
bat'tle-ax' or -axe'
bat'tle·dore'
bat'tle·field'
bat'tle·ground'
bat'tle·ment
battle royal
battles royal
bat'tle-scarred'
bat'tle·ship'
bau'ble
baux'ite
bawd'y
  ·i·er ·i·est
bawl
  (shout; SEE ball)
bay'o·net'
  ·net·ed or ·net'ted
  ·net'ing or ·net'ting
bay'ou
ba·zaar'
  (market; SEE
  bizarre)
ba·zoo'ka
be
  was or were,
  been be'ing
beach
  (shore; SEE
  beech)
beach'comb'er
beach'head'
bea'con
bead'ing
bead'work
bead'y
  ·i·er ·i·est
bea'gle
beak'er
bean'bag'
bean'stalk'
bear
  (animal; SEE
  bare)
bear
  bore, borne or
  born,
  bear'ing
  (carry; SEE bare)
bear'a·ble
bear'a·bly
beard'ed
bear'ish
bear'skin'
beast'li·ness
beast'ly
  ·li·er ·li·est

beat
  beat beat'en
  beat'ing
be'a·tif'ic
be·at'i·fi·ca'tion
be·at'i·fy'
  ·fied' ·fy'ing
be·at'i·tude'
beat'nik
beau
  beaus or beaux
  (sweetheart; SEE
  bow)
beau'te·ous
beau·ti'cian
beau'ti·fi·ca'tion
beau'ti·fi'er
beau'ti·ful
beau'ti·ful·ly
beau'ti·fy'
  ·fied' ·fy'ing
beau'ty
  ·ties
bea'ver
bea'ver·board'
be·calm'
be·cause'
beck'on
be·come'
  ·came' ·come'
  ·com'ing
bed
  bed'ded
  bed'ding
bed'bug'
bed'cham'ber
bed'clothes'
bed'cov'er
be·dev'il
  ·iled or ·illed
  ·il·ing or ·il·ling
bed'fast'
bed'fel'low
bed'lam
Bed'ou·in
bed'pan'
bed'post'
be·drag'gle
  ·gled ·gling
bed'rid'den
bed'rock'
bed'roll'
bed'room'
bed'side'
bed'sore'
bed'spread'
bed'spring'
bed'stead'
bed'time'
beech
  (tree; SEE beach)
beech'nut'
beef
  beeves or beefs
beef'eat'er
beef'steak'
beef'y
  ·i·er ·i·est

bee'hive'
bee'keep'er
bee'line'
beer
(drink; SEE bier)
beer'i·ness
beer'y
·i·er ·i·est
bees'wax'
Bee'tho·ven
bee'tle
bee'tle-browed'
be·fall'
·fell' ·fall'en
·fall'ing
be·fit'
·fit'ted ·fit'ting
be·fog'
·fogged'
·fog'ging
be·fore'hand'
be·friend'
be·fud'dle
·dled ·dling
beg
begged beg'ging
be·get'
·got', ·got'ten or
·got', ·get'ting
beg'gar
be·gin'
·gan' ·gun'
gin'ning
(start; SEE beguine)
be·gin'ner
be·gird'
·girt' or ·gird'ed,
·girt', ·gird'ing
be·gone'
·gon'ia
be·grime'
·grimed'
·grim'ing
be·grudge'
·grudged'
·grudg'ing
be·guile'
·guiled' ·guil'ing
be·guine'
(dance; SEE begin)
be·half'
be·have'
·haved' ·hav'ing
be·hav'ior
be·head'
be'he·moth
be·hest'
be·hind'hand'
be·hold'
·held' ·hold'ing
be·hold'en
be·hoove'
·hooved'
·hoov'ing
beige
bejew'el
·ed or ·elled
·ing or ·el·ling

be·la'bor
be·lat'ed
be·lay'
·layed' ·lay'ing
belch
be·lea'guer
bel'fry
·fries
be·lie'
·lied' ·ly'ing
be·lief'
be·liev'a·bil'i·ty
be·liev'a·ble
be·liev'a·bly
be·lieve'
·lieved' ·liev'ing
be·liev'er
be·lit'tle
·tled ·tling
be·lit'tler
bel'la·don'na
bell'boy'
(errand boy)
bell buoy
(signal bell)
belle
(pretty girl)
belles-let'tres
bell'-bot'tom
bel'li·cose'
bel'li·cos'i·ty
·ties
bel·lig'er·ence
bel·lig'er·en·cy
bel·lig'er·ent
bell'-like'
bell'man
·men
bel'low
bell'weth'er
bel'ly
·lies
·lied ·ly·ing
bel'ly·band'
be·long'
be·lov'ed
be·low'
belt'ing
be·mire'
·mired' ·mir'ing
be·moan'
bend
bent bend'ing
be·neath'
ben'e·dict'
Ben'e·dic'tine
ben'e·dic'tion
ben'e·fac'tion
ben'e·fac'tor
ben'e·fac'tress
ben'e·fice
be·nef'i·cence
be·nef'i·cent
ben'e·fi'cial
ben'e·fi'ci·ar'y
·ar'ies
ben'e·fit
·fit·ed ·fit·ing
be·nev'o·lence

be·nev'o·lent
ben'ga·line'
be·night'ed
be·nign'
be·nig'nan·cy
be·nig'nant
be·nig'ni·ty
ben'i·son
be·numb'
ben'zene
(in chemistry)
ben'zine
(cleaning fluid)
be·queath'
·queathed'
·queath'ing
be·queath'al
be·quest'
be·rate'
·rat'ed ·rat'ing
be·reave'
·reaved' or ·reft'
·reav'ing
be·reave'ment
be·ret'
(flat cap; SEE
barrette)
ber'i·ber'i
Berke'ley
Ber·mu'da
ber'ry
·ries
·ried ·ry·ing
(fruit; SEE bury)
ber·serk'
berth
(bed; SEE birth)
ber'yl
be·ryl'li·um
be·seech'
·sought' or
·seeched'
·seech'ing
be·set'
·set' ·set'ting
be·side'
be·sides'
be·siege'
·sieged' ·sieg'ing
be·smirch'
be·sot'
·sot'ted ·sot'ting
Bes'se·mer
bes'tial
bes'ti·al'i·ty
·ties
be·stow'
best seller
bet
bet or bet'ted
bet'ting
be'ta·tron'
be·tray'al
be·troth'
be·troth'al
be·trothed'
bet'ter
(compar. of good)

bet'tor or ·ter
(one who bets)
be·tween'
be·twixt'
bev'a·tron'
bev'el
·eled or ·elled
·el·ing or ·el·ling
bev'er·age
bev'y
·ies
be·wail'
be·ware'
·wared' ·war'ing
be·wil'dered
be·witch'
be·yond'
bez'el
bi·an'nu·al
bi·an'nu·al·ly
bi'as
·ased or ·assed
·as·ing or ·as·sing
Bi'ble
Bib'li·cal
Bib'li·cal·ly
bib'li·og'ra·phy
·phies
bib'li·o·phile'
bib'u·lous
bi·cam'er·al
bi·car'bon·ate
bi·cen'te·nar·y
·ies
bi·cen·ten'ni·al
bi'ceps
·ceps or ·ceps·es
bick'er
bi·cus'pid
bi'cy·cle
·cled ·cling
bi'cy·clist
bid
bade or bid;
bid'den or bid,
bid'ding
bid'da·ble
bi·det'
bi·en'ni·al
bi·en'ni·al·ly
bier
(coffin stand; SEE
beer)
bi'fo'cals
bi'fur·cate'
·cat'ed ·cat'ing
big
big'ger big'gest
big'a·mist
big'a·mous
big'a·my
·mies
big'gish
big'heart'ed
big'horn'
big·no'ni·a
big'ot
big'ot·ed

big'ot·ry
·ries
bi'jou
·joux
bi·ki'ni
bi·la'bi·al
bi·lat'er·al
bilge
bi·lin'gual
bil'ious
bill'board'
bil'let
bil'let-doux'
bil'lets-doux'
bill'fold'
bill'head'
bil'liards
bil'ling
bil'lings·gate'
bil'lion
bil'lion·aire'
bill of fare
bill of lad'ing
bill of sale
bil'low
bil'low·i·ness
bil'low·y
·i·er ·i·est
bil'ly
·lies
bish'op
bish'op·ric
bi·man'u·al
bi·man'u·al·ly
bi·me·tal'lic
bi·met'al·lism
bi·month'ly
bin
binned bin'ning
bi'na·ry
bind
bound bind'ing
bind'er
bind'er·y
·ies
binge
bin'go
bin'na·cle
bin·oc'u·lars
bi·no'mi·al
bi·no'mi·al·ly
bi'o·as'tro·
nau'tics
bi'o·chem'ist
bi'o·chem'is·try
bi'o·cide'
bi'o·e·col'o·gy
bi·og'ra·pher
bi'o·graph'i·cal
bi'o·graph'i·cal·ly
bi·og'ra·phy
·phies
bi'o·log'i·cal
bi'o·log'i·cal·ly
bi·ol'o·gy
bi·on'ics
bi'o·phys'ics
bi'op·sy
·sies
bi'o·sat'el·lite'

bi·par'ti·san
bi·par'tite
bi'pro·pel'lant
bi·quar'ter·ly
bi·ra'cial
bird'bath'
bird'call'
bird'ie
bird'lime'
bird'man'
·men'
bird'seed'
bird's'-eye'
bi·ret'ta
birth
(being born; SEE
berth)
birth'day'
birth'mark'
birth'place'
birth'rate'
birth'right'
birth'stone'
bis'cuit
bi·sect'
bi·sec'tion
bi·sec'tor
bi·sex'u·al
bi·sex'u·al·ly
bish'op
bis'muth
bi'son
bisque
bis'tro
bitch
bite
bit, bit'ten or
bit, bit'ing
bit'ter
bit'tern
bit'ter·sweet'
bi·tu'men
bi·tu'mi·nous
bi·va'lent
bi'valve'
biv'ou·ac'
·acked' ·ack'ing
bi·week'ly
·lies
bi·year'ly
bi·zarre'
(odd; SEE bazaar)
bi·zarre'ly
black'-a·moor'
black'-and-blue'
black'ball'
black'ber'ry
·ries
black'bird'
black'board'
black'en
black'face'
black'guard
black'head'
black'heart'ed
black'jack'
black'list'

black'mail'
black'out'
black'smith'
black'top'
·topped'
·top'ping
blad'der
blam'a·ble or
blame'a·ble
blame
blamed blam'ing
blame'wor'thy
blanc·mange'
blan'dish
blan'ket
blare
blared blar'ing
blar'ney
bla·sé'
blas·pheme'
·phemed'
·phem'ing
blas'phe·mous
blas'phe·my
·mies
blast'off' or
blast'-off'
bla'tan·cy
·cies
bla'tant
blaze
blazed blaz'ing
blaz'er
bla'zon
bleach'ers
bleak'ly
blear'i·ness
blear'y
·i·er ·i·est
blear'y-eyed'
bleed
bled bleed'ing
blem'ish
blend
blend'ed or blent
blend'ing
blend'er
bless
blessed or blest
bless'ing
bless'ed·ness
blight
blind'fold'
blintz
bliss'ful
bliss'ful·ly
blis'ter
blithe
blithe'some
blitz'krieg'
bliz'zard
bloat'ed
bloc
(group)
block
(solid piece)
block·ade'
·ad'ed ·ad'ing

block'bust'ing
block'head'
block'house'
blond or blonde
blood bank
blood count
blood'cur'dling
blood'hound'
blood'i·ness
blood'i·ly
blood'less
blood'let'ting
blood'mo·bile'
blood pressure
blood'shed'
blood'shot'
blood'stained'
blood'stream'
blood test
blood'thirst'y
blood vessel
blood'y
·i·er ·i·est
·ied ·y·ing
Bloody Mary
blos'som
blot
blot'ted blot'ting
blotch'y
·i·er ·i·est
blot'ter
blouse
bloused
blous'ing
blous'on
blow
blew blown
blow'ing
blow'gun'
blow'hole'
blow'out'
blow'pipe'
blow'torch'
blow'up'
blow'y
·i·er ·i·est
blowz'y
·i·er ·i·est
blub'ber
blu'cher
bludg'eon
blue
blued, blu'ing or
blue'ing
blue'ber'ry
·ries
blue'bird'
blue'-blood'ed
blue book
blue'-chip'
blue'-col'lar
blue'fish'
blue'grass'
blue jay
blue law
blue'-pen'cil
·ciled or ·cilled
·cil·ing or ·cil·ling

blue'print'
blue'stock'ing
bluff'er
blu'ing or
blue'ing
blu'ish or
blue'ish
blun'der
blun'der·buss'
blunt'ly
blur
blurred blur'ring
blur'ri·ness
blur'ry
·ri·er ·ri·est
blus'ter
blus'ter·y
bo'a
boar
(hog; SEE bore)
board'er
board foot
board feet
board'ing·house'
boarding school
board'walk'
boast'ful
boast'ful·ly
boat'house'
boat'ing
boat'load'
boat'man
·men
boat'swain
bob'bin
bob'ble
·bled ·bling
bob'o·link'
bob'sled'
·sled'ded
·sled'ding
bob'white'
bode
bod'ed bod'ing
bod'ice
bod'ied
bod'i·ly
bod'kin
bod'y
·ies
bod'y·guard'
bo'gey
·geys
·geyed ·gey·ing
(golf term)
bog'gy
·gi·er ·gi·est
(like a bog)
bo'gus
bo'gy
·gies
(spirit)
boil'ing
bois'ter·ous
bold'face'
bold'faced'
bo·le'ro
·ros

boll
(pod; SEE bowl)
boll weevil
boll'worm'
bo·lo'gna
bol'ster
bom·bard'
bom'bar·dier'
bom'bast
bom·bas'tic
bom·bas'ti·cal·ly
bomb'proof'
bomb'shell'
bomb'sight'
bo'na fi'de
bo·nan'za
bon'bon'
bond'age
bonds'man
·men
bone'-dry'
bon'fire'
bon'go
·gos
bon'i·ness
bon' mot'
bons' mots'
bon'net
bon'ny
·ni·er ·ni·est
bon·sai'
bo'nus
bon' vi·vant'
bons' vi·vants'
bon' voy·age'
bon'y
·i·er ·i·est
boo'by
·bies
boo'hoo'
·hoos'
·hooed' ·hoo'ing
book'bind'er
book'case'
book club
book'end'
book'ish
book'keep'er
book'keep'ing
book'let
book'mak'er
book'mark'
book'mo·bile'
book'plate'
book'rack'
book'sell'er
book'shelf'
·shelves'
book'stack'
book'stall'
book'stand'
book'store'
book'worm'
boom'er·ang'
boom'let
boon'docks'
boon'dog'gle
·gled ·gling

boor'ish
boost'er
boot'black'
boot'ee
(baby's shoe; SEE
booty)
boot'leg'
·legged'
·leg'ging
boot'leg'ger
boot'strap'
boo'ty
·ties
(spoils; SEE
bootee)
bo'rax
bor'der
bor'der·line'
bore
(dull person;
SEE boar)
bore
bored bor'ing
bore'dom
born
(brought into
life)
borne
(participle of
bear)
bor'ough
(town; SEE burro,
burrow)
bor'row
borsch or borsht
bos'om
boss'i·ness
boss'y
·i·er ·i·est
bo·tan'i·cal
bot'a·nist
bot'a·ny
botch
both'er·some
bot'tle
·tled ·tling
bot'tle·neck'
bot'tle·nose'
bot'tom
bot'u·lism
bou·clé' or
bou·cle'
bou'doir
bouf·fant'
bough
(tree branch;
SEE bow)
bought
bouil'la·baisse'
bouil'lon
(broth; SEE
bullion)
boul'der
boul'e·vard'
bounce
bounced
bounc'ing
bounc'er

bound'a·ry
·ries
bound'en
bound'less
boun'te·ous
boun'ti·ful
boun'ti·ful·ly
boun'ty
·ties
bou·quet'
bour'bon
bour·geois'
bour'geoi·sie'
bourse
bou·tique'
bou'ton·niere'
bo'vine
bow
(curve; SEE beau)
bow
(of a ship; SEE
bough)
bowd'ler·ize'
·ized' ·iz'ing
bow'el
bow'er
Bow'er·y
bow'ie knife
bow'knot'
bowl
(dish; SEE boll)
bow'leg'ged
bow'line
bowl'ing
bow'sprit'
bow'string'
bow tie
box'car'
box'er
box office
box'wood'
boy
(child; SEE buoy
boy'cott
boy'friend'
boy'hood'
boy'ish
boy'sen·ber'ry
·ries
brace
braced brac'in
brace'let
brack'et
brack'ish
brad'awl'
brag
bragged
brag'ging
brag'ga·do'ci·
brag'gart
Brah'ma
Brah'man·ism
braid
Braille
brain'child'
brain'i·ness
brain'pow'er
brain'storm'

brain'wash'
brain wave
brain'y
·i·er ·i·est
braise
  braised brais'ing
  (cook; SEE braze)
brake
  braked brak'ing
  (stop; SEE break)
brake'man
  ·men
bram'ble
branch'ing
bran'dish
brand'-new'
bran'dy
·dies
·died ·dy·ing
bras'sard
brass'ie n.
bras·siere'
brass'i·ness
brass'ware'
brass'-wind' adj.
brass winds
brass'y adj.
·i·er ·i·est
braun'schwei'ger
bra·va'do
brave
  braved brav'ing
brave'ly
brav'er·y
bra'vo
·vos
brawl
brawn'y
·i·er ·i·est
braze
  brazed braz'ing
  (solder; SEE
  braise)
bra'zen
bra'zen·ness
bra'zen·faced'
bra'zier
Bra·zil'
bra·zil'wood'
breach
  (a gap; SEE
  breech)
bread'bas'ket
bread'board'
bread'box'
breadth
  (width; SEE
  breath)
breadth'ways'
bread'win'ner
break
  broke bro'ken
  break'ing
  (smash; SEE
  rake)
break'a·ble
break'age
break'down'

break'fast
break'front'
break'neck'
break'out'
break'through'
break'up'
break'wa'ter
breast'bone'
breast'-feed'
  -fed' -feed'ing
breast stroke
breast'work'
breath
  (air; SEE breadth)
breath'a·lyz'er
breathe
  breathed
  breath'ing
breath'er
breath'less
breath'tak'ing
breech
  (rear; SEE
  breach)
breech'cloth'
breech'es
breech'-load'ing
breed
  bred breed'ing
breez'i·ly
breez'i·ness
breeze'way'
breez'y
  ·i·er ·i·est
breth'ren
bre'vi·ar'y
·ies
brev'i·ty
brew'er·y
·ies
brib'a·ble
bribe
  bribed brib'ing
brib'er·y
·ies
bric'-a-brac'
brick'bat'
brick'lay'ing
brick'work'
brick'yard'
brid'al
  (wedding; SEE
  bridle)
bride'groom'
brides'maid'
bridge
  bridged
  bridg'ing
bridge'a·ble
bridge'head'
bridge'work'
bri'dle
  (harness; SEE
  bridal)
brief'case'
bri'er or bri'ar
bri·gade'
brig'a·dier'

brig'and
brig'an·tine'
bright'en
bril'liance
bril'liant
bril'lian·tine'
brim
  brimmed
  brim'ming
brim'ful'
brim'stone'
brin'dled
brine
  brined brin'ing
bring
  brought
  bring'ing
brin'i·ness
brink'man·ship'
brin'y
  ·i·er ·i·est
bri·oche'
bri·quette'
  or ·quet'
bris'ket
brisk'ly
bris'tle
  ·tled ·tling
bris'tli·ness
bris'tly
  ·tli·er ·tli·est
Bris'tol board
Brit'ain
  (place)
Brit'i·cism
Brit'on
  (person)
brit'tle
brit'tle·ly or
  brit'tly
broach
  (open; SEE
  brooch)
broad'ax' or ·axe'
broad'cast'
  ·cast' or ·cast'ed
  ·cast'ing
broad'cloth'
broad'leaf'
broad'-leaved'
broad'loom'
broad'-mind'ed
broad'side'
broad'sword'
bro·cade'
  ·cad'ed ·cad'ing
broc'co·li
bro·chette'
bro·chure'
bro'gan
brogue
broil'er
bro'ken-down'
bro'ken·heart'ed
bro'ker
bro'ker·age
bro'mide
bro·mid'ic

bro'mine
bro'mo selt'zer
bron'chi·al
bron·chi'tis
bron'chus
  ·chi
bron'co
  ·cos
bron'to·sau'rus
bronze
  bronzed
  bronz'ing
brooch
  (pin; SEE broach)
brood'i·ness
broom'stick'
broth'el
broth'er-in-law'
  broth'ers-in-law'
brougham
brought
brou'ha·ha'
brow'beat'
  ·beat' ·beat'en
  ·beat'ing
brown'ie
brown'out'
brown'stone'
browse
  browsed
  brows'ing
bruise
  bruised bruis'ing
bruis'er
bru·net' or
  bru·nette'
brush'wood'
brush'work'
brusque
brusque'ly
brusque'ness
Brus'sels sprouts
bru'tal
bru·tal'i·ty
  ·ties
bru'tal·ize'
  ·ized' ·iz'ing
brut'ish
bub'ble
  ·bled ·bling
bub'bler
bub'ble-top'
bub'bly
bu·bon'ic
buc'ca·neer'
buck'board'
buck'et·ful'
  ·fuls'
bucket seat
buck'le
  ·led ·ling
buck'-pass'er
buck'ram
buck'saw'
buck'shot'
buck'skin'
buck'tooth'
  ·teeth'

buck'toothed'
buck'wheat'
bu·col'ic
bud
  bud'ded bud'ding
Bud'dha
Bud'dhism
budge
  budged budg'ing
budg'et
budg'et·ar'y
buf'fa·lo'
  ·loes' or ·los'
buff'er
buf'fet
buf·foon'er·y
bug'bear'
bug'gy
  ·gies
  ·gi·er ·gi·est
bu'gle
  ·gled ·gling
build
  built build'ing
build'up' or
  build'-up'
built'-in'
built'-up'
bul'bar
bul'bous
bulge
  bulged bulg'ing
bulg'i·ness
bulk'i·ness
bulk'y
  ·i·er ·i·est
bull'dog'
bull'doze'
  ·dozed' ·doz'ing
bull'doz'er
bul'let
bul'le·tin
bul'let·proof'
bull'fight'er
bull'frog'
bull'head'ed
bull'horn'
bul'lion
  (gold; SEE
  bouillon)
bull'ish
bull'ock
bull'pen'
bull's'-eye'
bull'whip'
bul'ly
  ·lies
  ·lied ·ly·ing
bul'rush'
bul'wark
bum'ble·bee'
bum'bling
bump'er
bump'kin
bump'tious
bump'y
  ·i·er ·i·est
bun'combe

bun'dle
  ·dled ·dling
bun'ga·low'
bung'hole'
bun'gle
  ·gled ·gling
bun'ion
bunk'er
bun'ting
Bun'sen burner
buoy
  (marker; SEE boy)
buoy'an·cy
buoy'ant
bur'ble
  ·bled ·bling
bur'den·some
bu'reau
  ·reaus or ·reaux
bu·reau'cra·cy
  ·cies
bu'reau·crat'
bu·reau·crat'ic
bu·reau·crat'i·
  cal·ly
bu·rette' or ·ret'
bur'geon
bur'glar
bur'gla·rize'
  ·rized' ·riz'ing
bur'gla·ry
  ·ries
Bur'gun·dy
bur'i·al
bur'lap
bur·lesque'
  ·lesqued'
  ·lesqu'ing
bur'ley
  (tobacco)
bur'li·ness
bur'ly
  ·li·er ·li·est
  (muscular)
burn
  burned or burnt
  burn'ing
burn'a·ble
bur'nish
bur·noose'
burn'out'
bur'ro
  ·ros
  (donkey; SEE
  burrow, borough)
bur'row
  (hole; SEE burro,
  borough)
bur'sa
  ·sae or ·sas
bur'sar
bur·si'tis
burst
  burst burst'ing
bur'y
  ·ied ·y·ing
  (cover; SEE
  berry)

bus
bus′es *or* bus′ses
bused *or* bussed
bus′ing *or* bus′sing
(*motor coach;* SEE
buss)
bus′boy′
bus′by
·bies
bush′el·bas′ket
bush′ing
bush′man
·men
bush′rang·er
bush′whack′er
bush′y
·i·er ·i·est
bus′i·ly
busi′ness
busi′ness·like′
busi′ness·man′
·men′
busi′ness·wom·an
·wom·en
bus′kin
bus′man
·men
buss
(*kiss;* SEE bus)
bus′tle
·tled ·tling
bus′y
·i·er ·i·est
·ied ·y·ing
bus′y·bod′y
·ies
bus′y·ness
butch′er·y
but′ler
butte
but′ter·fat′
but′ter·fin′gers
but′ter·fly′
·flies′
but′ter·milk′
but′ter·nut′
but′ter·scotch′
but′ter·y
but′tocks
but′ton·down′
but′ton·hole′
·holed′ ·hol′ing
but′tress
bux′om
buy
bought buy′ing
buz′zard
buz′zer
by′gone′
by′law′
by′line′
by′pass′
by′path′
by′play′
by′prod′uct *or*
by′-prod′uct
by′road′
by′stand′er

by′way′
by′word′

C

ca·bal′
·balled′ ·bal′ling
cab′a·lism
ca′bal·le′ro
·ros
ca·ba′na
cab′a·ret′
cab′bage
cab′driv′er
cab′in
cab′i·net
cab′i·net·mak′er
cab′i·net·work′
ca′ble
·bled ·bling
ca′ble·gram′
ca·boose′
cab′ri·o·let′
cab′stand′
ca·ca′o
cac′ci·a·to′re
cache
cached cach′ing
ca·chet′
cach′in·nate′
nat′ed ·nat′ing
cach′in·na′tion
cack′le
·led ·ling
ca·cog′ra·phy
ca·coph′o·nous
ca·coph′o·ny
cac′tus
·tus·es *or* ·ti
ca·dav′er
ca·dav′er·ous
cad′die *or* ·dy
·dies
·died ·dy·ing
(*in golf*)
cad′dish
cad′dy
·dies
(*tea box*)
ca′dence
ca·den′za
ca·det′
cad′mi·um
ca′dre
ca·du′ce·us
·ce·i
Cae·sar′e·an
cae·su′ra
·ras *or* ·rae
ca·fé′ *or* ca·fe′
caf′e·te′ri·a
caf′fe·ine *or* ·in
cage
caged cag′ing
ca′gey *or* ca′gy
·gi·er ·gi·est

ca′gi·ly
ca′gi·ness
cais′son
cai′tiff
ca·jole′
·joled′ ·jol′ing
ca·jole′ment
ca·jol′er·y
cake
caked cak′ing
cal′a·bash′
ca·lam′i·tous
ca·lam′i·ty
·ties
cal·car′e·ous
cal′ci·fi·ca′tion
cal′ci·fy′
·fied′ ·fy′ing
cal′ci·mine′
·mined′ ·min′ing
cal′ci·um
cal′cu·la·ble
cal′cu·late′
·lat′ed ·lat′ing
cal′cu·la′tion
cal′cu·la′tor
cal′cu·lus
·li *or* ·lus·es
cal′dron
cal′en·dar
(*table of dates*)
cal′en·der
(*roller;* SEE
colander)
cal′ends
ca·les′cent
calf
calves
calf′skin′
cal′i·ber *or* ·bre
cal′i·brate′
·brat′ed ·brat′ing
cal′i·bra′tion
cal′i·co′
·coes′ *or* ·cos′
Cal′i·for′ni·a
cal′i·pers
ca′liph
cal·is·then′ics
calk
call′board′
cal·lig′ra·phy
cal′lous *adj.*
cal′low
call′-up′
cal′lus *n.*
·lus·es
calm′ly
ca·lor′ic
cal′o·rie *or* ·ry
·ries
cal′o·rim′e·ter
cal′u·met′
ca·lum′ni·ate′
·at′ed ·at′ing
ca·lum′ni·ous
cal′um·ny
·nies

Cal′va·ry
(*Biblical place;*
SEE cavalry)
calve
calved calv′ing
Cal′vin·ism
ca·lyp′so
ca′lyx
ca′lyx·es *or*
ca′ly·ces′
ca·ma·ra′de·rie
cam′ber
cam′bric
Cam′bridge
cam′el
ca·mel′li·a
Cam′em·bert′
cam′e·o′
·os′
cam′er·a
cam′er·a·man′
·men′
cam′er·a·shy′
cam′i·sole′
cam′o·mile′
cam′ou·flage′
·flaged′ ·flag′ing
cam·paign′
cam·pa·ni′le
·les *or* ·li
camp′er
camp′fire′
camp′ground′
cam′phor
cam′phor·ate′
·at′ed ·at′ing
camp·o·ree′
camp′site′
camp′stool′
camp′us
cam′shaft′
can
canned can′ning
Ca′naan
Can′a·da
Ca·na′di·an
ca·naille′
ca·nal′
ca·nal′boat′
ca·nal′ize′
·ized ·iz·ing
ca′na·pé
(*food;* SEE
canopy)
ca·nard′
ca·nar′y
·ies
ca·nas′ta
can′can′
can′cel
·celed *or* ·celled
·cel·ing *or*
·cel·ling
can′cel·la′tion
can′cer
can′cer·ous
can·de·la′bra
·bras

can·de·la′brum
·bra *or* ·brums
can·des′cence
can·des′cent
can′did
(*frank;* SEE
candied)
can′di·da·cy
·cies
can′di·date′
can′died
(*sugared;* SEE
candid)
can′dle·light′
candle power
can′dle·stick′
can′dle·wick′
can′dor
can′dy
·dies
·died ·dy·ing
can′dy-striped′
cane
caned can′ing
ca′nine
can′is·ter
can′ker
can′na·bis
can′ner·y
·ies
can′ni·bal
can′ni·bal·ize′
·ized ·iz′ing
can′ni·ly
can′ni·ness
can′non
(*gun;* SEE canon,
canyon)
can′non·ade′
·ad′ed ·ad′ing
can′not
can′ny
·ni·er ·ni·est
ca·noe′
·noed′ ·noe′ing
can′on
(*law;* SEE cannon,
canyon)
ca·non′i·cal
can′on·ize′
·ized′ ·iz′ing
can′o·py
·pies
(*hood;* SEE
canapé)
can·ta′bi·le′
can′ta·loupe′
or ·loup′
can·tan′ker·ous
can·ta′ta
can·teen′
can′ter
(*gallop;* SEE
cantor)
can′ti·cle
can′ti·le′ver
can′to
·tos

can′ton
can·ton′ment
can′tor
(*singer;* SEE
canter)
can′vas
(*cloth*)
can′vass
(*to solicit*)
can′yon *or* ca′ño
(*valley;* SEE
cannon, canon)
caou·tchouc′
cap
capped cap′ping
ca·pa·bil′i·ty
·ties
ca′pa·ble
ca′pa·bly
ca·pa′cious
ca·pac′i·tance
ca·pac′i·tor
ca·pac′i·ty
·ties
ca′per
cap′ful′
·fuls′
cap′il·lar′y
·ies
cap′i·tal
(*city; chief;* SEE
capitol)
cap′i·tal·ism
cap′i·tal·is′tic
cap′i·tal·is′ti-
cal·ly
cap′i·tal·i·za′tion
cap′i·tal·ize′
·ized′ ·iz′ing
cap′i·tal·ly
cap′i·ta′tion
cap′i·tol
(*building;* SEE
capital)
ca·pit′u·late′
·lat′ed ·lat′ing
ca·pit′u·la′tion
ca′pon
ca·price′
ca·pri′cious
cap′ri·ole′
·oled′ ·ol′ing
cap′size
·sized ·siz·ing
cap′stan
cap′stone′
cap′su·lar
cap′sule
·suled ·sul·ing
cap′su·lize′
·ized′ ·iz′ing
cap′tain
cap′tain·cy
·cies
cap′tion
cap′tious
cap′ti·vate′
·vat′ed ·vat′ing

cap'tive
cap·tiv'i·ty
·ties
cap'tor
cap'ture
·tured ·tur·ing
car'a·cul
ca·rafe'
car'a·mel
car'a·mel·ize'
·ized' ·iz'ing
ar'a·pace'
ar'at
(weight; SEE
caret, carrot)
ar'a·van'
ar·a·van'sa·ry
·ries
ar'a·way'
ar'bide
ar'bine
ar·bo·hy'drate
ar·bol'ic
ar'bon
ar·bo·na'ceous
ar'bon·ate'
·at'ed ·at'ing
ar·bon·a'tion
ar'bon-date'
·dat'ed -dat'ing
ar·bon·if'er·ous
r'bon·ize'
ized' ·iz'ing
ar'bo·run'dum
r'bun·cle
ar'bu·re'tion
r'bu·re'tor
r'cass
r·cin'o·gen
r'ci·no'ma
r'da·mom
rd'board'
rd'-car'ry·ing
r'di·ac'
r'di·gan
r'di·nal
r'di·o·gram'
r'di·o·graph'
d'sharp'
·e
red car'ing
reen'
reer'
e'free'
e'ful
e'ful·ly
e'less
ress'
res'sive·ly
'et
sert mark; SEE
rat, carrot)
e'tak'er
e'worn'
'fare'
'go
es or ·gos
'hop'

Car·ib·be'an
car'i·bou'
car'i·ca·ture
·tured ·tur·ing
car'i·ca·tur·ist
car'ies
(decay; SEE
carries)
car'il·lon'
car'load'
car'man
·men
car'mine
car'nage
car'nal
car'nal·ly
car·na'tion
car·nel'ian
car'ni·val
car'ni·vore'
car·niv'o·rous
car'ol
·oled or ·olled
·ol·ing or ·ol·ling
car'ol·er or ·ol·ler
Car'o·li'nas
Car'o·lin'i·an
car'om
car'o·tene' or ·tin
ca·rot'id
ca·rous'al
ca·rouse'
·roused'
·rous'ing
car'ou·sel'
car'pen·ter
car'pen·try
car'pet
car'pet·bag'ger
car'pet·ing
carp'ing
car'port'
car'ri·age
car'ri·er
car'ries
(form of carry;
SEE caries)
car'ri·on
car'rot
(vegetable; SEE
carat, caret)
car'rou·sel'
car'ry
·ried ·ry·ing
car'ry·all'
car'ry·out'
car'ry-o'ver
car'sick'
cart'age
carte' blanche'
cartes' blanches'
car·tel'
car'ti·lage
car·ti·lag'i·nous
car'to·gram'
car·tog'ra·phy
car'ton
car·toon'

car·toon'ist
car'tridge
carve
carved carv'ing
car'wash'
car'y·at'id
·ids or ·i·des'
ca·sa'ba
or cas·sa'ba
cas'bah
cas·cade'
·cad'ed ·cad'ing
cas·car'a
case
cased cas'ing
case'book'
case'hard'ened
ca'se·in
case'load'
case'mate'
case'ment
case'work'er
cash'-and-car'ry
cash'book'
cash'ew
cash·ier'
cash'mere
cas'ing
ca·si'no
·nos
(gambling room)
cas'ket
cas·sa'va
cas'se·role'
cas·sette'
cas·si'no
(card game)
cas'sock
cas'so·war'y
·war'ies
cast
cast cast'ing
cas'ta·nets'
cast'a·way'
caste
(social class)
cas'tel·lat'ed
cast'er
cas'ti·gate'
·gat'ed ·gat'ing
cast'-i'ron
cas'tle
cast'off'
cas'tor
cas'trate
·trat·ed ·trat·ing
cas·tra'tion
cas'u·al
cas'u·al·ly
cas'u·al·ty
·ties
cas'u·ist
cas'u·is'tic
cas'u·ist·ry
cat'a·clysm
cat'a·comb'
cat'a·falque'
cat'a·lep'sy

cat'a·lep'tic
cat'a·lo'
·loes' or ·los'
cat'a·log' or
·logue'
·loged' or
·logued'
·log'ing or
·logu'ing
cat'a·log'er or
·logu'er
ca·tal'y·sis
·ses'
cat'a·lyst
cat'a·ma·ran'
cat'a·pult'
cat'a·ract'
ca·tarrh'
ca·tarrh'al
ca·tas'tro·phe
cat'a·stroph'ic
cat'a·stroph'i·
cal·ly
cat'a·to'ni·a
cat'call'
catch
caught catch'ing
catch'all'
catch'er
catch'ing
catch'pen'ny
·nies
catch'up
catch'word'
catch'y
·i·er ·i·est
cat'e·chism
cat'e·chize'
·chized' ·chiz'ing
cat'e·chu'men
cat'e·gor'i·cal
cat'e·go·rize'
·rized' ·riz'ing
cat'e·go'ry
·ries
ca'ter
cat'er-cor'nered
ca'ter·er
cat'er·pil'lar
cat'er·waul'
cat'gut'
ca·thar'sis
ca·thar'tic
ca·the'dral
cath'e·ter
cath'e·ter·ize'
·ized' ·iz'ing
cath'ode
cath'o·lic
Ca·thol'i·cism
cath·o·lic'i·ty
ca·thol'i·cize'
·cized' ·ciz'ing
cat'i'on
cat'-nap'
·napped'
·nap'ping
cat'nip

cat'-o'-nine'-tails'
cat's'-eye'
Cats'kill'
cat's'-paw'
cat'sup
cat'tail'
cat'ti·ly
cat'ti·ness
cat'tle
cat'tle·man
·men
cat'ty
·ti·er ·ti·est
cat'ty-cor'nered
cat'walk'
Cau·ca'sian
Cau'ca·soid'
cau'cus
cau'dal
cau'date
caul'dron
cau'li·flow'er
caulk
caus'a·ble
caus'al
caus'al·ly
cau·sal'i·ty
·ties
cau·sa'tion
caus'a·tive
cause
caused caus'ing
cau'se·rie'
cause'way'
caus'tic
cau'ter·i·za'tion
cau'ter·ize'
·ized' ·iz'ing
cau'ter·y
·ies
cau'tion
cau'tion·ar'y
cau'tious
cav'al·cade'
cav'a·lier'
cav'al·ry
(troops; SEE
Calvary)
cav'al·ry·man
·men
cave
caved cav'ing
ca've·at' emp'tor
cave'-in'
cav'ern
cav'ern·ous
cav'i·ar'
cav'il
·iled or ·illed
·il·ing or ·il·ling
cav'i·ty
·ties
ca·vort'
cay·enne'
cease
ceased ceas'ing
cease'-fire'

cease'less
ce'dar
cede
ced'ed ced'ing
ce·dil'la
ceil'ing
ceil·om'e·ter
cel'e·brant
cel'e·brate'
·brat'ed ·brat'ing
cel'e·bra'tion
cel'e·bra'tor
ce·leb'ri·ty
·ties
ce·ler'i·ty
cel'e·ry
ce·les'ta
ce·les'tial
cel'i·ba·cy
cel'i·bate
cel'lar
cel'lar·et'
cel'lar·way'
cel'list
or 'cel'list
cell'-like'
cel'lo
or 'cel'lo
·los or ·li
cel'lo·phane'
cel'lu·lar
cel'lu·loid'
cel'lu·lose'
Cel'o·tex'
Cel'si·us
ce·ment'
cem'e·ter'y
·ies
cen'o·bite'
Ce'no·zo'ic
cen'ser
(incense box)
cen'sor
(prohibiter)
cen'sored
cen·so'ri·al
cen·so'ri·ous
cen'sor·ship'
cen'sur·a·ble
cen'sure
·sured ·sur·ing
(blame)
cen'sus
cen'taur
cen·ta'vo
cen·te·nar'i·an
cen'te·nar'y
cen·ten'ni·al
cen·ten'ni·al·ly
cen'ter
cen'ter·board'
cen'tered
cen'ter·piece'
cen·tes'i·mal
cen·tes'i·mal·ly
cen'ti·grade'
cen'ti·gram'
cen'ti·li'ter

cen'time
cen'ti·me'ter
cen'ti·pede'
cen'tral
cen'tral·i·za'tion
cen'tral·ize'
·ized' ·iz'ing
cen·trif'u·gal
cen'tri·fuge'
cen·trip'e·tal
cen'trist
cen'tu·ple
cen·tu'ri·on
cen'tu·ry
·ries
ce·phal'ic
ce·ram'ic
ce·ram'ist or
ce·ram'i·cist
ce're·al
(grain; SEE serial)
cer'e·bel'lum
·lums or ·la
cer'e·bral
cer·e'bral·ly
cer'e·brate'
·brat'ed ·brat'ing
cer'e·bro·spi'nal
cer'e·brum
·brums or ·bra
cer'e·ment
cer·e·mo'ni·al
cer·e·mo'ni·al·ly
cer·e·mo'ni·ous
cer'e·mo'ny
·nies
ce·rise'
cer'tain
cer'tain·ly
cer'tain·ty
·ties
cer'ti·fi'a·ble
cer'ti·fi'a·bly
cer·tif'i·cate
cer'ti·fi·ca'tion
cer'ti·fy'
·fied' ·fy'ing
cer'ti·o·ra'ri
cer'ti·tude'
ce·ru'le·an
ce·ru'men
cer'vi·cal
cer'vix
·vi·ces' or ·vix·es
ces·sa'tion
ces'sion
(a giving up; SEE
session)
cess'pool'
chafe
chafed chaf'ing
(rub)
chaff
(husks of grain)
chaf'finch
cha·grin'
·grined'
·grin'ing

chain'man
·men
chain'·re·act'
chain'-smoke'
chair'lift'
chair'man
·men
chair'wom'an
·wom'en
chaise longue
chaise or chaises
longues
chaise lounge
chaise lounges
chal·ced'o·ny
cha·let'
chal'ice
chalk'board'
chalk'i·ness
chalk'y
·i·er ·i·est
chal'lenge
·lenged ·leng·ing
chal'leng·er
chal'lis
cham'ber
cham'ber·lain
cham'ber·maid'
cham'bray
cha·me'le·on
cham'fer
cham'ois
·ois
·oised ·ois·ing
cham'o·mile'
cham·pagne'
(wine)
cham·paign'
(open field)
cham'pi·on
chance
chanced
chanc'ing
chan'cel
chan'cel·ler·y
·ies
chan'cel·lor
chance'-med'ley
chan'cer·y
·ies
chan'cre
chan'croid
chanc'y
·i·er ·i·est
chan·de·lier'
chan·delle'
chan'dler·y
·ies
Cha·nel'
change
changed
chang'ing
change'a·bil'i·ty
change'a·ble
change'a·bly
change'ful
change'ful·ly
change'less

change'ling
change'o'ver
change'-up'
chan'nel
·neled or ·nelled
·nel·ing or
·nel·ling
chan'nel·ize'
·ized' ·iz'ing
chan·teuse'
chan'tey or ·ty
·teys or ·ties
Cha'nu·kah
cha'os
cha·ot'ic
cha·ot'i·cal·ly
chap
chapped
chap'ping
chap'ar·ral'
cha·peau'
·peaus' or
·peaux'
chap'el
chap'er·on'
or ·one'
·oned' ·on'ing
chap'fall'en
chap'lain
chap'let
chap'ter
char
charred
char'ring
char'ac·ter
char'ac·ter·is'tic
char'ac·ter·is'ti·
cal·ly
char'ac·ter·i·
za'tion
char'ac·ter·ize'
·ized' ·iz'ing
cha·rade'
char'coal'
chare
chared char'ing
charge
charged
charg'ing
charge'a·ble
charge plate or
charge'-a-plate'
charg'er
char'i·ly
char'i·ness
char'i·ot
char'i·ot·eer'
cha·ris'ma
char'is·mat'ic
char'i·ta·ble
char'i·ty
·ties
cha·ri'va·ri'
char'la·tan
charm'ing
char'nel
char'ry
·ri·er ·ri·est

char'ter
char·treuse'
char'wom'an
char'y
·i·er ·i·est
chase
chased chas'ing
chasm
chas·sé'
·séd' ·sé'ing
chas'sis
·sis
chaste'ly
chas'ten
chas·tise'
·tised' ·tis'ing
chas·tise'ment
chas'ti·ty
chas'u·ble
chat
chat'ted
chat'ting
châ·teau'
·teaux' or ·teaus'
chat'e·laine'
cha·toy'ant
chat'tel
chat'ty
·ti·er ·ti·est
Chau'cer
chauf'fer
(stove)
chauf'feur
(driver)
chau·tau'qua
chau'vin·ism
chau'vin·ist
chau'vin·is'tic
chau'vin·is'ti·
cal·ly
cheap
(low in cost;
SEE cheep)
cheap'en
cheat'er
check'book'
check'er·board'
check'ered
check'list' or
check list
check'mate'
·mat'ed ·mat'ing
check'off'
check'out' or
check'-out'
check'point'
check'rein'
check'room'
check'up'
Ched'dar
cheek'bone'
cheek'i·ly
cheek'i·ness
cheek'y
·i·er ·i·est
cheep
(sound; SEE cheap)
cheer'ful

cheer'ful·ly
cheer'i·ly
cheer'i·ness
cheer'lead'er
cheer'less
cheer'y
·i·er ·i·est
cheese'burg'er
cheese'cake'
cheese'cloth'
chees'i·ness
chees'y
·i·er ·i·est
chee'tah
chem'i·cal
che·mise'
chem'ist
chem'is·try
·tries
chem'ur·gy
che·nille'
cher'ish
Cher'o·kee'
che·root'
cher'ry
·ries
cher'ub
·ubs or ·u·bim
che·ru'bic
che·ru'bi·cal·ly
cher'vil
chess'board'
chess'man'
ches'ter·field'
chest'nut
chev'i·ot
chev'ron
chew'y
·i·er ·i·est
Chi·an'ti
chi·a'ro·scu'ro
·ros
chic
chic'quer
chic'quest
chi·can'er·y
chi'chi or chi'-chi
chick'en·heart'ed
chicken pox
chic'le
chic'o·ry
chide
chid'ed or chid,
chid'ed or chid
or chid'den,
chid'ing
chief'ly
chief'tain
chif·fon'
chif'fo·nier'
chig'ger
chi'gnon
chig'oe
·oes
Chi·hua'hua
chil'blain'
child
chil'dren

child'bear'ing
child'bed'
child'birth'
child'hood'
child'ish
child'like'
chil'i
·ies
chill'i·ness
chill'y
·i·er ·i·est
chime
chimed chim'ing
chi·me'ra
chi·mer'i·cal
chim'ney
·neys
chim'pan·zee'
chin
chinned
chin'ning
chi'na·ware'
chin·chil'la
Chi·nese'
chi'no
chin'qua·pin
chintz
chip
chipped
chip'ping
chip'munk'
chi·rog'ra·phy
chi·rop'o·dist
chi·rop'o·dy
chi'ro·prac'tic
chi'ro·prac'tor
chir'rup
chis'el
·eled or ·elled
·el·ing or ·el·ling
chis'el·er or
chis'el·ler
chi'-square'
chit'chat'
chit'ter·lings
chiv'al·rous
chiv'al·ry
chlor'dane
chlo'ric
chlo'ride
chlo'ri·nate'
·nat'ed ·nat'ing
chlo'ri·na'tion
chlo'rine
chlo'ro·form'
chlo'ro·phyll'
or ·phyl'
chlo'rous
chlor·tet'ra·cy'
cline
chock'a·block'
chock'-full'
choc'o·late
choice
choic'er choic'
choir
(singers; SEE
quire)

ke
oked chok'ing
k'er
l'er·a
l'er·ic
les'ter·ol'
ose
ose cho'sen
oos'ing
p
opped
op'ping
p'house'
p'pi·ness
p'py
er ·pi·est
p'sticks'
p su'ey
ral
a chorus)
·rale' or ·ral'
mn tune)
rd
usic; SEE cord)
re
·re'a
r'e·og'ra·pher
r'e·o·graph'ic
r'e·o·graph'·
al·ly
r'e·og'ra·phy
r'is·ter
r'tle
ed ·tling
'rus
'sen
w'der
w mein
ism
is'ten
is'ten·dom
is'tian
is·ti·an'i·ty
is'tian·ize'
ed' ·iz'ing
is'tie or ·ty
ist'like'
ist'mas
ist'mas·tide'
o·mat'ic
o'ma·tin
ome
o'mic
o'mi·um
o'mo·some'
on'ic
on'i·cle
ed ·cling
on'o·log'i·cal
o·nol'o·gy
o·nom'e·ter
o·nom'e·try
ys'a·lis
ys·an'the·
um
ys'o·lite'
ys'o·prase'
b'bi·ness

chub'by
·bi·er ·bi·est
chuck'-full'
chuck'hole'
chuck'le
·led ·ling
chug
chugged chug'ging
chuk'ka boot
chuk'ker or ·kar
chum'mi·ness
chum'my
·mi·er ·mi·est
chunk'i·ness
chunk'y
·i·er ·i·est
church'go'er
church'man
church'wom'an
church'yard'
churl'ish
churn
chute
chut'ney
chyle
chyme
ci·bo'ri·um
·ri·a
ci·ca'da
·das or ·dae
cic'a·trix
ci·cat'ri·ces
cic'e·ly
Cic'er·o'
ci'der
ci·gar'
cig'a·rette'
or ·ret'
cig'a·ril'lo
·los
cil'i·a
(sing. cil'i·um)
cil'i·ar'y
cin·cho'na
Cin'cin·nat'i
cinc'ture
·tured ·tur·ing
cin'der
cin'e·ma
cin'e·mat'o·
graph'
cin'e·rar'i·um
·rar'i·a
cin'er·a'tor
cin'na·bar'
cin'na·mon
cinque'foil'
ci'pher
cir'ca
cir'cle
·cled ·cling
cir'clet
cir'cuit
cir·cu'i·tous
cir'cuit·ry
cir'cu·lar
cir'cu·lar·i·
za'tion

cir'cu·lar·ize'
·ized' ·iz'ing
cir'cu·late'
·lat'ed ·lat'ing
cir'cu·la'tion
cir'cu·la·to'ry
cir'cum·cise'
·cised' ·cis'ing
cir'cum·ci'sion
cir·cum'fer·ence
cir'cum·flex'
cir'cum·lo·
cu'tion
cir'cum·nav'i·
gate'
·gat'ed ·gat'ing
cir'cum·po'lar
cir'cum·scribe'
·scribed' ·scrib'ing
cir'cum·
scrip'tion
cir'cum·spect'
cir'cum·spec'tion
cir'cum·stance'
cir'cum·stan'tial
cir'cum·stan'ti·
ate'
·at'ed ·at'ing
cir'cum·vent'
cir'cum·ven'tion
cir'cus
cir·rho'sis
cir·ro·cu'mu·lus
cir·ro·stra'tus
cir'rus
·ri
cis·al'pine
cis·at·lan'tic
cis'tern
cit'a·del
ci·ta'tion
cite
cit'ed cit'ing
(mention; SEE
sight)
cit'i·fied'
cit'i·zen
cit'i·zen·ry
cit'i·zen·ship'
cit'rate
cit'ric
cit'ron
cit'ron·el'la
cit'rous adj.
cit'rus n.
cit'y
·ies
cit'y·scape'
cit'y-state'
civ'et
civ'ic
civ'il
ci·vil'ian
ci·vil'i·ty
·ties
civ'i·li·za'tion
civ'i·lize'
·lized' ·liz'ing

civ'il·ly
civ'vies
claim'ant
clair·voy'ance
clair·voy'ant
clam
clammed
clam'ming
clam'bake'
clam'ber
clam'mi·ness
clam'my
·mi·er ·mi·est
clam'or
clam'or·ous
clan·des'tine
clan·des'tine·ly
clan'gor
clan'gor·ous
clan'nish
clans'man
clap
clapped
clap'ping
clap'board
clap'per
clap'trap'
claque
clar'et
clar·i·fi·ca'tion
clar'i·fi'er
clar'i·fy'
·fied' ·fy'ing
clar'i·net'
clar'i·net'ist or
clar'i·net'tist
clar'i·on
clar'i·ty
clas'sic
clas'si·cal
clas'si·cal·ly
clas'si·cism
clas'si·cist
clas'si·fi'a·ble
clas·si·fi·ca'tion
clas'si·fi'er
clas'si·fy'
·fied' ·fy'ing
class'mate'
class'room'
clat'ter
clause
claus'tro·
pho'bi·a
clav'i·chord'
clav'i·cle
cla·vier'
clay'ey
clay'i·er
clay'i·est
clean'a·ble
clean'-cut'
clean'er
clean'hand'ed
clean'li·ly
clean'li·ness
clean'ly
·li·er ·li·est

clean'ness
cleanse
cleansed
cleans'ing
cleans'er
clean'shav'en
clean'up'
clear'ance
clear'-cut'
clear'eyed'
clear'head'ed
clear'ing·house'
clear'sight'ed
cleats
cleav'age
cleave
cleaved or cleft
or clove, cleaved
or cleft or
clo'ven,
cleav'ing
(to split)
cleave
cleaved cleav'ing
(to cling)
cleav'er
clem'en·cy
clem'ent
clere'sto'ry
·ries
cler'gy
·gies
cler'gy·man
·men
cler'ic
cler'i·cal
cler'i·cal·ly
cler'i·cal·ism
clev'er
clew
cli·ché'
click
cli'ent
cli'en·tele'
cliff'-dwell'ing
cliff'hang'er or
cliff'-hang'er
cli·mac'ter·ic
cli·mac'tic
(of a climax)
cli·mac'ti·cal·ly
cli'mate
cli·mat'ic
(of climate)
cli·mat'i·cal·ly
cli·ma·tol'o·gy
cli'max
climb'er
clinch'er
cling
clung cling'ing
clin'ic
clin'i·cal
cli·ni'cian
clink'er
cli·nom'e·ter
clip
clipped clip'ping

clip'board'
clip'per
clique
cli'to·ris
clo·a'ca
·cae
cloak'room'
clob'ber
cloche
clock'wise'
clock'work'
clod'dish
clod'hop'per
clog
clogged
clog'ging
cloi·son·né'
clois'ter
close
closed clos'ing
close
clos'er clos'est
closed'-end'
close'fist'ed
close'fit'ting
close'grained'
close'-hauled'
close'ly
close'mouthed'
clos'et
close'-up'
clo'sure
clot
clot'ted clot'ting
cloth n.
clothe v.
clothed or clad
cloth'ing
clothes'line'
clothes'pin'
clothes'press'
cloth'ier
cloth'ing
clo'ture
cloud'burst'
cloud'i·ness
cloud'y
·i·er ·i·est
clo'ver·leaf'
·leafs'
cloy'ing·ly
clown'ish
club
clubbed
club'bing
club'foot'
club'house'
clue
clued clu'ing
clum'si·ly
clum'si·ness
clum'sy
·si·er ·si·est
clus'ter
clut'ter
coach'man
co·ad'ju·tor
co·ag'u·la·ble

co·ag'u·lant	cod'i·cil	co·li'tis	col'o·ni·za'tion	com'et	com·mis'sion·e(r)
co·ag'u·late'	cod'i·fi·ca'tion	col·lab'o·rate'	col'o·nize'	come'up'pance	com·mit'
·lat'ed ·lat'ing	cod'i·fy'	·rat'ed ·rat'ing	·nized' ·niz'ing	com'fit	·mit'ted ·mit'ti(ng)
co·ag·u·la'tion	·fied ·fy'ing	col·lab'o·ra'tion	col'on·nade'	com'fort	com·mit'ment
co·ag'u·la'tor	co'ed·u·ca'tion	col·lab'o·ra'tor	col'o·ny	com'fort·a·ble	com·mit'ta·ble
co'a·lesce'	co·ef·fi'cient	col·lage'	·nies	com'fort·a·bly	com·mit'tal
·lesced' ·lesc'ing	co·erce'	col·lapse'	col'o·phon'	com'fort·er	com·mit'tee
co'a·les'cence	·erced' ·erc'ing	·lapsed' ·laps'ing	col'or	com'ic	com·mit'tee·n(...)
co'a·les'cent	co·er'cion	col·laps'i·bil'i·ty	Col'o·rad'o	com'i·cal	com·mode'
co'a·li'tion	co·er'cive	col·laps'i·ble	col'o·rant	com'i·cal·ly	com·mo'di·ous
coarse	co·e'val	col'lar	col·or·a'tion	com'i·ty	com·mod'i·ty
(common; SEE	co'ex·ist'ence	col'lar·bone'	col'o·ra·tu'ra	·ties	·ties
course)	cof'fee·house'	col·late'	col'or·bear'er	com'ma	com'mo·dore'
coarse'grained'	cof'fee·pot'	·lat'ed ·lat'ing	col'or·blind'	(punctuation	com'mon·al·ty
coars'en	cof'fer	col·lat'er·al	col'or·cast'	mark; SEE coma)	·ties
coarse'ness	cof'fer·dam'	col·lat'er·al·ly	·cast' or cast'ed	com·mand'	com'mon·er
coast'al	cof'fin	col·la'tion	·cast'ing	com'man·dant'	com'mon·ness
coast'er	co'gen·cy	col·la'tor	col'ored	com·man·deer'	com'mon·place
coast guard	co'gent	col'league	col'or·fast'	com·mand'er	com'mon·weal'
coast'land'	cog'i·tate'	col·lect'a·ble	col'or·ful	com·mand'ment	com'mon·weal(...)
coast'line'	·tat'ed ·tat'ing	or ·i·ble	col'or·less	com·man'do	com·mo'tion
coat'ing	cog'i·ta'tion	col·lec'tion	co·los'sal	·dos or ·does	com'mu·nal
coat'tail'	co'gnac	col·lec'tive·ly	Col'os·se'um	com·mem'o·rate'	com'mu·nal·ly
co·au'thor	cog'nate	col·lec'tiv·ism	co·los'sus	·rat'ed ·rat'ing	com'mu·nal·is(...)
co·ax'i·al	cog·ni'tion	col·lec'tiv·is'tic	·los'si or	com·mem'o·	com·mune' v.
coax'ing·ly	cog'ni·tive	col·lec·tiv'i·ty	·los'sus·es	ra'tion	·muned'
co'balt	cog'ni·zance	col·lec'tiv·ize'	colt'ish	com·mem'o·	·mun'ing
cob'ble	cog'ni·zant	·ized' ·iz'ing	Co·lum'bi·a	ra'tive	com'mune n.
·bled ·bling	cog·no'men	col·lec'tor	col'umn	com·mence'	com·mu'ni·ca·(...)
cob'bler	·no'mens or	col'leen	co·lum'nar	·menced'	com·mu'ni·can(...)
cob'ble·stone'	·nom'i·na	col'lege	col'um·nist	·menc'ing	com·mu'ni·cat(e)
co'bel·lig'er·ent	cog'wheel'	col·le'gi·al'i·ty	co'ma	com·mence'	·cat'ed ·cat'ing
co'bra	co·hab'it	col·le'gi·an	(stupor; SEE	ment	com·mu'ni·
cob'web'	co·hab'i·ta'tion	col·le'giate	comma)	com·mend'	ca'tion
co·caine'	co'heir'	col·lide'	com'a·tose'	com·mend'a·ble	com·mu'ni·
or ·cain'	co·here'	·lid'ed ·lid'ing	com·bat'	com·mend'a·bly	ca'tive
coc'cus	·hered' ·her'ing	col'lie	·bat'ed or	com·men·da'tion	com·mu'ni·ca't(...)
coc'ci	co·her'ence	col'li·gate'	·bat'ted	com·mend'a·	com·mun'ion
coc'cyx	co·her'ent	·gat'ed ·gat'ing	·bat'ing or	to'ry	com·mu'ni·qué(')
coc·cy'ges	co·he'sion	col'li·mate'	·bat'ting	com·men'su·	com·mu'nism
cock'a·lo'rum	co·he'sive·ness	·mat'ed ·mat'ing	com'bat·ant	ra·ble	com'mu·nist
cock'boat'	co'hort	col·lin'e·ar	com·bat'ive	com·men'su·	com·mu·nis'tic
cock'crow'	coif·fure'	col·li'sion	comb'er	ra·bly	com·mu·nis'ti·
cock'er·el	coign	col'lo·ca'tion	com·bin'a·ble	com·men'su·rate	cal·ly
cock'eyed'	(position; SEE	col·lo'di·on	com·bi·na'tion	com'ment	com·mu'ni·ty
cock'i·ly	coin, quoin)	col'loid	com·bine'	com'men·tar'y	·ties
cock'i·ness	coin	col·loi'dal	·bined' ·bin'ing	·ies	com'mu·nize'
cock'ney	(metal money;	col·lo'qui·al	comb'ings	com'men·tate'	·nized' ·niz'ing
·neys	SEE coign, quoin)	col·lo'qui·al·ism	com·bus'ti·	·tat'ed ·tat'ing	com·mut'a·ble
cock'pit'	coin'age	col·lo'qui·um	bil'i·ty	com'men·ta·tor	com·mu·tate'
cock'roach'	co·in·cide'	·qui·a or ·qui·ums	com·bus'ti·ble	com'merce	·tat'ed ·tat'ing
cocks'comb'	·cid'ed ·cid'ing	col'lo·quy	com·bus'ti·bly	com·mer'cial	com·mu·ta'tion
cock'sure'	co·in'ci·dence	·quies	com·bus'tion	com·mer'cial·ism	com·mu·ta'tive
cock'tail'	co·in'ci·dent	col'lo·type'	com·bus'tor	com·mer'cial·i·	com·mu·ta'tor
co'coa	co·in·ci·den'tal	col·lude'	come	za'tion	com·mute'
co'co·nut'	co·in·ci·den'tal·ly	·lud'ed ·lud'ing	came come	com·mer'cial·ize'	·mut'ed
or co'coa·nut'	co·i'tion	col·lu'sion	com'ing	·ized' ·iz'ing	·mut'ing
co·coon'	co'i·tus	col·lu'sive	come'back'	com·min'gle	com·mut'er
cod'dle	col'an·der	co·lo'cate'	co·me'di·an	·gled ·gling	com·pact'
·dled ·dling	(draining pan;	·cat'ed ·cat'ing	co·me'dic	com·mis'er·ate'	com·pan'ion
code	SEE calender)	co'·lo·ca'tion	co·me'di·enne'	·at'ed ·at'ing	com·pan'ion·
cod'ed cod'ing	cold'blood'ed	co·logne'	come'down'	com·mis'er·	a·ble
co'de·fend'ant	cold'heart'ed	co'lon	com'e·dy	a'tion	com'pa·ny
co'deine'	co'le·op'ter·ous	colo'nel	·dies	com'mis·sar'	·nies
co'dex	cole'slaw'	(officer; SEE	come'li·ness	com'mis·sar'i·at	com'pa·ra·ble
·di·ces'	col'ic	kernel)	come'ly	com'mis·sar'y	com'pa·ra·bly
cod'fish'	col'ick·y	co·lo'ni·al	·li·er ·li·est	·ies	com·par'a·tive
codg'er	col'i·se'um	col'o·nist	co·mes'ti·ble	com·mis'sion	com·par'a·tive·(l)

com·pare′
·pared′ ·par′ing
com·par′i·son
com·part′ment
com·part′men′·
tal·ize′
·ized′ ·iz′ing
com′pass
com·pas′sion
com·pas′sion·ate
com·pat′i·bil′i·ty
com·pat′i·ble
com·pat′i·bly
com·pa′tri·ot
com′peer
com·pel′
·pelled′ ·pel′ling
com·pen′di·ous
com·pen′di·um
·ums or ·a
com·pen′sa·ble
com′pen·sate′
·sat′ed ·sat′ing
com′pen·sa′tion
com·pen′sa·tive
com·pen′sa·tor
com·pen′sa·to′ry
com·pete′
·pet′ed ·pet′ing
com·pe′tence
com′pe·ten·cy
com′pe·tent
com′pe·ti′tion
com·pet′i·tive
com·pet′i·tor
com·pi·la′tion
com·pile′
·piled′ ·pil′ing
com·pil′er
com·pla′cence
com·pla′cen·cy
com·pla′cent
(smug; SEE
complaisant)
com·plain′
com·plain′ant
com·plaint′
com·plai′sance
com·plai′sant
(obliging; SEE
complacent)
com′ple·ment
(completing part;
SEE compliment)
com′ple·
men′ta·ry
com·plete′
·plet′ed ·plet′ing
com·ple′tion
com·plex′
com·plex′ion
com·plex′i·ty
·ties
com·pli′ance
com·pli′ant
com′pli·cate′
·cat′ed ·cat′ing
com′pli·ca′tion

com·plic′i·ty
com·pli′er
com′pli·ment
(praise; SEE
complement)
com′pli·men′·
ta·ry
com′pli·men·
tar′i·ly
com·ply′
·plied′ ·ply′ing
com·po′nent
com·port′ment
com·pose′
·posed′ ·pos′ing
com·pos′er
com·pos′ite
com′po·si′tion
com·pos′i·tor
com′pos men′tis
com′post
com·po′sure
com′pote
com·pound′ v.
com′pound n.
com′pre·hend′
com′pre·hen′si·
ble
com′pre·hen′sion
com′pre·hen′sive
com·press′
com·pressed′
com·pres′si·ble
com·pres′sion
com·pres′sor
com·prise′
·prised′ ·pris′ing
com′pro·mise′
·mised′ ·mis′ing
comp·tom′e·ter
comp·trol′ler
com·pul′sion
com·pul′sive
com·pul′so·ri·ly
com·pul′so·ri·ness
com·pul′so·ry
com·punc′tion
com·punc′tious
com·put′a·bil′i·ty
com·put′a·ble
com·pu·ta′tion
com·pute′
·put′ed ·put′ing
com·put′er
com·put′er·ize′
·ized′ ·iz′ing
com·put′er·i·
za′tion
com′rade
con·cat·e·na′tion
con·cave′
con·cav′i·ty
·ties
con·ca′vo-con·
cave′
con·ca′vo-con·
vex′
con·ceal′

con·cede′
·ced′ed ·ced′ing
con·ceit′
con·ceit′ed
con·ceiv′a·
bil′i·ty
con·ceiv′a·ble
con·ceiv′a·bly
con·ceive′
·ceived′ ·ceiv′ing
con′cen·trate′
·trat′ed ·trat′ing
con·cen·tra′tion
con·cen′tric
con·cen′tri·cal·ly
con·cept′
con·cep′tion
con·cep′tu·al
con·cep′tu·al·ize′
·ized′ ·iz′ing
con·cep′tu·al·i·
za′tion
con·cep′tu·al·ly
con·cern′
con·cerned′
con·cern′ing
con·cert′
con·cert′ed
con·cer·ti′na
con·cert′mas·ter
con·cer′to
·tos or ·ti
con·ces′sion
con·ces′sion·aire′
conch
conchs or
conch′es
con·chol′o·gy
con′ci·erge′
con·cil′i·ar
con·cil′i·ate′
·at′ed ·at′ing
con·cil′i·a·to′ry
con·cise′
con·cise′ly
con·cise′ness
con′clave
con·clude′
·clud′ed
·clud′ing
con·clu′sion
con·clu′sive
con·coct′
con·coc′tion
con·com′i·tance
con·com′i·tant
con′cord
con·cord′ance
con·cor′dat
con′course
con·crete′
con·cre′tion
con·cu′bine′
con·cu′pis·cence
con·cu′pis·cent
con·cur′
·curred′
·cur′ring

con·cur′rence
con·cur′rent
con·cus′sion
con·demn′
con·dem′na·ble
con·dem′na′tion
con·dem′na·to′ry
con·demn′er
con·den′sa·ble
or ·si·ble
con·den·sa′tion
con·dense′
·densed′
·dens′ing
con·dens′er
con·de·scend′
con·de·scend′ing
con·de·scen′sion
con·dign′
con·di′ment
con·di′tion
con·di′tion·al
con·di′tion·al·ly
con·do′la·to′ry
con·dole′
·doled′ ·dol′ing
con·do′lence
con′dom
con·do·min′i·um
·i·ums or ·i·a
con·do·na′tion
con·done′
·doned′ ·don′ing
con′dor
con·duce′
·duced′ ·duc′ing
con·du′cive
con′duct′
con·duct′ance
con·duct′i·ble
con·duc′tion
con·duc·tiv′i·ty
con·duc′tor
con′duit
co′ney
·neys or ·nies
con·fab′u·late′
·lat′ed ·lat′ing
con·fec′tion
con·fec′tion·ar′y
adj.
con·fec′tion·er
con·fec′tion·er′y
n.
·ies
con·fed′er·a·cy
·cies
con·fed′er·ate′
·at′ed ·at′ing
con·fed′er·a′tion
con·fer′
·ferred′ ·fer′ring
con′fer·ee′
con′fer·ence
con·fer·en′tial
con·fer′ment
con·fer′ral
con·fess′

con·fes′sed·ly
con·fes′sion
con·fes′sion·al
con·fes′sor
con·fet′ti
con·fi·dant′ n.
con·fide′
·fid′ed ·fid′ing
con′fi·dence
con′fi·dent adj.
con′fi·den′tial
con′fi·den′tial·ly
con·fig′u·ra′tion
con·fin′a·ble or
con·fine′a·ble
con·fine′
·fined′ ·fin′ing
con·fine′ment
con·firm′
con·fir′mand′
con·fir·ma′tion
con·firm′a·to′ry
con·firmed′
con·fis′cate′
·cat′ed ·cat′ing
con·fis·ca′tion
con·fla·gra′tion
con·flict′
con·flic′tion
con′flu·ence
con·form′
con·form′a·ble
con·form′a·bly
con·form′ance
con·for·ma′tion
con·form′ist
con·form′i·ty
con·found′ed
con·front′
con·fron·ta′tion
Con·fu′cius
con·fuse′
·fused′ ·fus′ing
con·fu′sion
con·fu·ta′tion
con·fute′
·fut′ed ·fut′ing
con·geal′
con·gen′ial
con·gen′ial·ly
con·ge′ni·al′i·ty
con·gen′i·tal
con·gen′i·tal·ly
con·gest′
con·ges′tion
con·glom′er·ate′
·at′ed ·at′ing
con·glom·er·a′tion
con·grat′u·late′
·lat′ed ·lat′ing
con·grat′u·
la′tion
con·grat′u·
la·to′ry

con·gres′sion·al
con′gress·man
con′gru·ence
con′gru·ent
con·gru′i·ty
con′gru·ous
con′ic
con′i·cal
con′i·cal·ly
co′ni·fer
co·nif′er·ous
con·jec′tur·al
con·jec′ture
·tured ·tur·ing
con·join′
con·joint′ly
con′ju·gal
con′ju·gal·ly
con′ju·gate′
·gat′ed ·gat′ing
con·junc′tion
con·junc′tive
con·junc·ti·vi′tis
con·junc′ture
con′jure
·jured ·jur·ing
con·jur′er or ·or
con·nect′
Con·nect′i·cut
con·nec′tion
con·nec′tive
con·nec′tor
or ·nect′er
conn′ing tower
con·niv′ance
con·nive′
·nived′ ·niv′ing
con′nois·seur′
con·no·ta′tion
con′no·ta·tive
con·note′
·not′ed ·not′ing
con·nu′bi·al
con′quer
con′quer·or
con′quest
con·quis′ta·dor
·dors or ·dores
con′science
con·sci·en′tious
con′scious
con′script′
con′se·crate′
·crat′ed ·crat′ing
con·se·cra′tion
con·sec′u·tive
con·sen′sus
con·sent′
con′se·quence′
con′se·quen′tial
con′se·quent′ly
con·ser′van·cy
con′ser·va′tion
con·ser′va·tism
con·ser′va·tive
con·ser′va·to′ry
·ries

con·serve′
·served′
·serv′ing
con·sid′er
con·sid′er·a·ble
con·sid′er·a·bly
con·sid′er·ate
con·sid′er·a′tion
con·sid′ered
con·sign′
con·sign′a·ble
con·sign·ee′
con·sign′ment
con·sign′or
or ·er
con·sist′
con·sis′ten·cy
·cies
con·sis′tent
con·sis′to·ry
·ries
con·sol′a·ble
con·so·la′tion
con·sol′a·to′ry
con·sole′
·soled′ ·sol′ing
con′sole
con·sol′i·date′
·dat′ed ·dat′ing
con·sol′i·da′tion
con·sol′i·da′tor
con′som·mé′
con′so·nance
con′so·nant
con′so·nan′tal
con′sort
con·sor′ti·um
·ti·a
con·spec′tus
con·spic′u·ous
con·spir′a·cy
·cies
con·spir′a·tor
con·spire′
·spired′ ·spir′ing
con′sta·ble
con·stab′u·lar′y
·ies
con′stan·cy
con′stant
con·stel·la′tion
con′ster·na′tion
con′sti·pate′
·pat′ed ·pat′ing
con′sti·pa′tion
con·stit′u·en·cy
·cies
con·stit′u·ent
con′sti·tute′
·tut′ed ·tut′ing
con′sti·tu′tion
con′sti·tu′tion·al
con′sti·tu′tion·
al′i·ty
con′sti·tu′tion·
al·ly
con·strain′
con·straint′

con·strict′
con·stric′tion
con·stric′tor
con·stru′a·ble
con·struct′
con·struc′tion
con·struc′tive
con·struc′tor or
con·struct′er
con·strue′
·strued′ ·stru′ing
con′sul
con′sul·ar
con′sul·ate
con·sult′
con·sult′ant
con′sul·ta′tion
con·sul′ta·tive
con·sum′a·ble
con·sume′
·sumed′
·sum′ing
con·sum′er
con′sum·mate′
·mat′ed ·mat′ing
con·sum′mate·ly
con′sum·ma′tion
con′sum·ma′tor
con·sump′tion
con·sump′tive
con′tact
con·ta′gion
con·ta′gious
con·tain′er
con·tain′er·ize′
·ized′ ·iz′ing
con·tain′ment
con·tam′i·nant
con·tam′i·nate′
·nat′ed ·nat′ing
con·tam′i·na′tion
con·tam′i·na′tor
con·temn′
con′tem·plate′
·plat′ed
·plat′ing
con′tem·pla′tion
con′tem·pla′tive
con′tem·pla′tor
con·tem′po·
ra′ne·ous
con·tem′po·rar′y
con·tempt′
con·tempt′i·bil′·
i·ty
con·tempt′i·ble
con·tempt′i·bly
con·temp′tu·ous
con·tend′
con·tent′
con′tent
con·tent′ed·ly
con·ten′tion
con·ten′tious
con·tent′ment
con·test′
con·test′a·ble
con·test′ant

con′text
con·tex′tu·al
con·ti·gu′i·ty
con·tig′u·ous
con′ti·nence
con′ti·nent
con′ti·nen′tal
con·tin′gen·cy
·cies
con·tin′gent
con·tin′u·a·ble
con·tin′u·al
con·tin′u·ance
con·tin′u·a′tion
con·tin′ue
·ued ·u·ing
con·ti·nu′i·ty
·ties
con·tin′u·ous
con·tin′u·um
·u·a or ·u·ums
con·tort′
con·tor′tion
con′tour
con′tra·band′
con′tra·bass′
con′tra·cep′tion
con′tra·cep′tive
con′tract
con·tract′i·bil′i·ty
con·tract′i·ble
con·trac′tile
con·trac′tion
con·trac·tor
con·trac′tu·al
con·trac′tu·al·ly
con·tra·dict′
con′tra·dic′tion
con′tra·dic′to·ry
con′tra·dis·
tinc′tion
con′trail′
con·tral′to
·tos or ·ti
con′tra·pun′tal
con′trar·i·ly
con′trar·i·ness
con′trar·i·wise′
con′trar·y
con′trast
con′tra·vene′
·vened′ ·ven′ing
con′tra·ven′tion
con·trib′ute
·ut·ed ·ut·ing
con′tri·bu′tion
con·trib′u·tor
con·trib′u·to′ry
con·trite′
con·tri′tion
con·triv′a·ble
con·triv′ance
con·trive′
·trived′ ·triv′ing
con·trol′
·trolled′
·trol′ling
con·trol′la·bil′i·ty

con·trol′la·ble
con·trol′ler
con′tro·ver′sial
con′tro·ver′sy
·sies
con′tro·vert′
con′tro·vert′i·ble
con·tu·ma′cious
con′tu·ma·cy
con·tu·me′li·ous
con′tu·me·ly
con·tuse′
·tused′ ·tus′ing
con·tu′sion
co·nun′drum
con·ur·ba′tion
con′va·lesce′
·lesced′ ·lesc′ing
con′va·les′cence
con′va·les′cent
con·vec′tion
con·vec′tive
con·vec′tor
con·vene′
·vened′ ·ven′ing
con·ven′ience
con·ven′ient
con′vent
con·ven′ti·cle
con·ven′tion
con·ven′tion·al
con·ven′tion·
al′i·ty
·ties
con·ven′tion·
al·ize′
·ized′ ·iz′ing
con·ven′tion·eer′
con·verge′
·verged′
·verg′ing
con·ver′gence
con·vers′a·ble
con·ver′sant
con′ver·sa′tion
con′ver·sa′tion·al
con·verse′
·versed′ ·vers′ing
con′verse
con·ver′sion
con·vert′
con·vert′er
or ·ver′tor
con·vert′i·ble
con·vex′
con·vex′i·ty
con·vex′o-con·
cave′
con·vex′o-con·
vex′
con·vey′
con·vey′ance
con·vey′or or ·er
con·vict′
con·vic′tion
con·vince′
·vinced′
·vinc′ing

con·vin′ci·ble
con·viv′i·al
con·viv′i·al′i·ty
con′vo·ca′tion
con·voke′
·voked′ ·vok′ing
con′vo·lut′ed
con′vo·lu′tion
con′voy
con·vulse′
·vulsed′
·vuls′ing
con·vul′sion
con·vul′sive
cook′book′
cook′out′
cook′ie or ·y
·ies
cool′ant
cool′head′ed
cool′ie
(Oriental laborer;
SEE coolly,
coulee)
cool′ly
(in a cool manner;
SEE coolie,
coulee)
co′-op
co·op′er·ate′
or co-op′·
·at′ed ·at′ing
co·op′er·a′tion
or co-op′·
co·op′er·a·tive
or co-op′·
co-opt′
co·or′di·nate′
or co-or′·
·nat′ed ·nat′ing
co·or′di·na′tor
or co-or′·
co-part′ner
cope
coped cop′ing
cop′i·er
co′pi′lot
co′pi·ous
cop′-out′
cop′per
cop′per·plate′
co′pra
cop′u·late′
·lat′ed ·lat′ing
cop·u·la′tion
cop′y
·ies
·ied ·y·ing
cop′y·cat′
cop′y·hold′er
cop′y·ist
cop′y·read′er
cop′y·right′
cop′y·writ′er
co·quet′
·quet′ted ·quet′ting
co′quet·ry
co·quette′

co·quet′tish
co·quille′
cor′al
cor′bel
cord
(string; SEE
chord)
cord′age
cor′date
cor′dial
cor·di·al′i·ty
·ties
cor′dil·le′ra
cord′ite
cor′don
cor′do·van
cor′du·roy′
cord′wood′
core
cored cor′ing
co′re·spond′ent
(in law; SEE
correspondent)
Cor′fam
co′ri·an′der
Co·rin′thi·an
cork′screw′
cor′mo·rant
corn borer
corn bread
corn′cob′
cor′ne·a
cor′nered
cor′ner·stone′
cor′ner·wise′
cor′net′
cor·net′ist
or ·net′tist
corn′field′
corn′flow′er
corn′husk′ing
cor′nice
corn′meal′
corn′stalk′
corn′starch′
cor·nu·co′pi·a
corn′y
·i·er ·i·est
co·rol′la
cor′ol·lar′y
·ies
co·ro′na
·nas or ·nae
cor′o·nar′y
cor′o·na′tion
cor′o·ner
cor′o·net′
cor′po·ral
cor′po·rate
cor′po·ra′tion
cor′po·ra·tive
cor·po′re·al
corps
corps
(group of people
corpse
(dead body)
corps′man

cor'pu·lence
cor'pu·lent
cor'pus
  cor'po·ra
cor'pus·cle
cor·ral'
  ·ralled' ·ral'ling
cor·rect'
cor·rect'a·ble
cor·rec'tion
cor·rec'tive
cor·rec'tor
cor're·late'
  ·lat'ed ·lat'ing
cor're·la'tion
cor·rel'a·tive
cor're·spond'
cor're·
  spond'ence
cor're·
  spond'ent
  (writer; SEE
  corespondent)
cor'ri·dor
cor'ri·gi·ble
cor'ri·gi·bly
cor·rob'o·rate'
  ·rat'ed ·rat'ing
cor·rob'o·ra'tion
cor·rob'o·ra'tive
cor·rob'o·ra'tor
cor·rode'
  ·rod'ed ·rod'ing
cor·rod'i·ble
cor·ro'sion
cor·ro'sive
cor'ru·gate'
  ·gat'ed ·gat'ing
cor'ru·ga'tion
cor·rupt'
cor·rupt'i·bil'i·ty
cor·rupt'i·ble
cor·rupt'i·bly
cor·rup'tion
cor·rup'tive
cor·sage'
cor'sair
corse'let
cor'set
cor'se·tiere'
cor·tege' or ·tège'
cor'tex
  ·ti·ces'
cor'ti·cal
cor'ti·cal·ly
cor'ti·sone'
co·run'dum
cor'us·cate'
  ·cat'ed ·cat'ing
cor·vette'
co·se'cant
co'sign'
co'sign'er
co·sig'na·to'ry
  ·ries
co'sine
cos·met'ic
cos·me·ti'cian

cos'me·tol'o·gy
cos'mic
cos'mi·cal·ly
cos·mog'o·ny
cos·mog'ra·phy
cos'mo·line'
cos·mol'o·gy
cos'mo·naut'
cos·mop'o·lis
cos·mo·pol'i·tan
cos·mop'o·lite'
cos'mos
cos'mo·tron'
co'spon'sor
cost
  cost cost'ing
cost'li·ness
cost'ly
  ·li·er ·li·est
cost'-plus'
cos'tume
  ·tumed ·tum·ing
cos·tum'er
co·tan'gent
co'te·rie
co·til'lion
cot'tage
cot'ton
cou'gar
cough
cou'lee
  (gulch; SEE
  coolie, coolly)
cou·lomb'
coun'cil
  (legislature; SEE
  counsel)
coun'cil·man
coun'ci·lor
  or ·cil·lor
  (council member;
  SEE counselor)
coun'sel
  ·seled or ·selled
  ·sel·ing or
  ·sel·ling
  (advice; advise;
  SEE council)
coun'se·lor
  or ·sel·lor
  (adviser; SEE
  councilor)
count'down'
coun'te·nance
count'er
  (one that counts)
coun'ter
  (opposite)
coun'ter·act'
coun'ter·ac'tion
coun'ter·at·tack'
coun'ter·bal'·
  ance
coun'ter·claim'
coun'ter·clock'
  wise
coun'ter·feit
coun'ter·foil'

coun'ter·ir'ri·
  tant
coun'ter·man'
coun'ter·mand'
coun'ter·march'
coun'ter·meas'·
  ure
coun'ter·move'
coun'ter·of·fen'
  sive
coun'ter·pane'
coun'ter·part'
coun'ter·plot'
coun'ter·point'
coun'ter·poise'
coun'ter·sign'
coun'ter·sink'
  ·sunk' ·sink'ing
coun'ter·spy'
coun'ter·weight'
count'ess
count'less
coun'tri·fied'
coun'try
  ·tries
coun'try·man
coun'try·side'
  ·ries
coun'ty
  ·ties
coup de grâce'
coup d'é·tat'
coupe
cou'ple
  ·pled ·pling
cou'pler
cou'plet
cou'pon
cour'age
cou·ra'geous
cou'ri·er
course
  coursed
  cours'ing
  (way; run; SEE
  coarse)
cour'te·ous
cour'te·san
cour'te·sy
  ·sies
  (polite act;
  SEE curtsy)
court'house'
cour'ti·er
court'li·ness
court'ly
  ·li·er ·li·est
court'-mar'tial
courts'-mar'tial
  ·tialed or
  ·tialled
  ·tial·ing or
  ·tial·ling
court'room'
court'yard'
cous'in
cou·ture'
cou·tu·rier'
cou·tu·rière'

cov'e·nant
Cov'en·try
cov'er·age
cov'er·alls'
cov'ered
cov'er·ing
cov'er·let
cov'ert
cov'er-up'
cov'et·ous
cov'ey
cow'ard
cow'ard·ice
cow'ard·li·ness
cow'ard·ly
cow'boy'
cow'catch'er
cow'er
cow'herd'
cow'hide'
  ·hid'ed ·hid'ing
cowled
cow'lick
cowl'ing
co'-work'er
cow'pox'
cow'rie or ·ry
  ·ries
cow'shed'
cox'comb'
cox'swain
coy'ly
coy·o'te
co'zi·ly
co'zi·ness
co'zy
  ·zies
  ·zi·er ·zi·est
crab
  crabbed crab'bing
crab'bed crab'bing
crab'bed
crab'bi·ness
crab'by
  ·bi·er ·bi·est
crack'brained'
crack'down'
cracked
crack'er
crack'ing
crack'le
  ·led ·ling
crack'lings
crack'up'
cra'dle
  ·dled ·dling
cra'dle·song'
craft'i·ly
craft'i·ness
crafts'man
craft'y
  ·i·er ·i·est
crag'gi·ness
crag'gy
  ·gi·er ·gi·est
cram
  crammed
  cram'ming
cramped

cram'pon
cran'ber'ry
  ·ries
crane
  craned cran'ing
cra'ni·al
cra'ni·ol'o·gy
cra'ni·um
  ·ni·ums or ·ni·a
crank'case'
crank'i·ness
crank'shaft'
crank'y
  ·i·er ·i·est
cran'ny
  ·nies
crap'u·lence
crash'-land'
crass'ly
crass'ness
cra'ter
cra·vat'
crave
  craved crav'ing
cra'ven
crawl'er
cray'fish'
cray'on
craze
  crazed craz'ing
cra'zi·ly
cra'zi·ness
cra'zy
  ·zi·er ·zi·est
creak
  (squeak; SEE
  creek)
creak'i·ness
creak'y
  ·i·er ·i·est
cream'er·y
  ·ies
cream'i·ness
cream'y
  ·i·er ·i·est
crease
  creased
  creas'ing
cre·ate'
  ·at'ed ·at'ing
cre·a'tion
cre·a'tive
cre'a·tiv'i·ty
cre·a'tor
crea'ture
cre'dence
cre·den'tial
cre·den'za
cred'i·bil'i·ty
cred'i·ble
cred'i·bly
cred'it·a·bil'i·ty
cred'it·a·ble
cred'it·a·bly
cred'i·tor
cre'do
  ·dos
cre·du'li·ty

cred'u·lous
creek
  (stream; SEE
  creak)
creep
  crept creep'ing
creep'i·ness
creep'y
  ·i·er ·i·est
cre'mate
  ·mat·ed ·mat·ing
cre·ma'tion
cre'ma·to'ry
  ·ries
cre'o·sote'
crepe or crêpe
cre·scen'do
  ·dos
cres'cent
crest'fall'en
cre'tin
cre'tonne
cre·vasse'
crev'ice
crew'el·work'
crib'bage
crick'et
cri'er
crim'i·nal
crim'i·nol'o·gy
crim'son
cringe
  cringed
cring'ing
crin'kle
  ·kled ·kling
crin'o·line
crip'ple
  ·pled ·pling
crip'pler
cri'sis
  ·ses
crisp'er
crisp'i·ness
crisp'y
  ·i·er ·i·est
criss'cross'
cri·ter'i·on
  ·i·a or ·i·ons
crit'ic
crit'i·cal
crit'i·cal·ly
crit'i·cism
crit'i·cize'
  ·cized' ·ciz'ing
cri·tique'
croak
cro·chet'
  ·cheted'
  ·chet'ing
crock'er·y
croc'o·dile'
cro'cus
crois·sant'
crom'lech
cro'ny
  ·nies
crook'ed·ness

croon'er
crop
  cropped
  crop'ping
crop'-dust'ing
cro·quet'
  ·queted'
  ·quet'ing
  (game)
cro·quette'
  (food)
cro'sier
cross'bar'
cross'beam'
cross'bow'
cross'breed'
  ·bred' ·breed'ing
cross'-check'
cross'-coun'try
cross'cut'
cross'-ex·am'i·na'tion
cross'-ex·am'ine
cross'-eyed'
cross'-fer'ti·lize'
cross'-grained'
cross'hatch'
cross'-in'dex
cross'ing
cross'-leg'ged
cross'o'ver
cross'piece'
cross'-pur'pose
cross'-re·fer'
cross'-ref'er·ence
cross'road'
cross'ruff'
cross section
cross'-stitch'
cross'tie'
cross'town'
cross'walk'
cross'wise'
cross'word'
crotch'et·i·ness
crotch'et·y
crou'pi·er'
crou'ton
crow'bar'
crowd'ed
crow's'-foot'
  ·feet'
crow's'-nest'
cru'cial
cru'cial·ly
cru'ci·ble
cru'ci·fix'
cru'ci·fix'ion
cru'ci·form'
cru'ci·fy'
  ·fied' ·fy'ing
crude'ly
cru'di·ty
  ·ties
cru'el·ly
cru'el·ty
  ·ties

cru'et
cruise
  cruised cruis'ing
cruis'er
crul'ler
crum'ble
  ·bled ·bling
crum'bly
  ·bli·er ·bli·est
crumb'y
  ·i·er ·i·est
crum'pet
crum'ple
  ·pled ·pling
crunch'i·ness
crunch'y
  ·i·er ·i·est
crup'per
cru·sade'
crush'a·ble
crus·ta'cean
crust'ed
crust'i·ness
crust'y
  ·i·er ·i·est
crux
  crux'es or cru'ces
cry
  cries
  cried cry'ing
cry'o·gen'ics
crypt
cryp'tic
cryp'ti·cal·ly
cryp'to·gram'
cryp'to·gram'mic
cryp'to·graph'ic
cryp'to·graph'i·cal·ly
cryp·tog'ra·phy
crys'tal
crys'tal·line
crys'tal·liz'a·ble
crys'tal·li·za'tion
crys'tal·lize'
  ·lized' ·liz'ing
crys'tal·log'ra·phy
cub'by·hole'
cube
  cubed cub'ing
cu'bic
cu'bi·cal
  (cube-shaped)
cu'bi·cal·ly
cu'bi·cle
  (compartment)
cu'bit
cuck'old
cuck'oo'
cu'cum·ber
cud'dle
  ·dled ·dling
cud'dly
  ·dli·er ·dli·est
cudg'el
  ·eled or ·elled
  ·el·ing or
  ·el·ling

cue
  cued cu'ing
  or cue'ing
  (signal; SEE queue)
cui·rass'
cui·sine'
cul'-de-sac'
cu'li·nar'y
cull
cul'mi·nate'
  ·nat'ed ·nat'ing
cul'mi·na'tion
cu·lottes'
cul'pa·bil'i·ty
cul'pa·ble
cul'pa·bly
cul'prit
cult'ist
cul'ti·va·ble
cul'ti·vate'
  ·vat'ed ·vat'ing
cul'ti·va'tion
cul'ti·va'tor
cul'tur·al
cul'ture
  ·tured ·tur·ing
cul'vert
cum'ber·some
cum'mer·bund'
cu'mu·late'
  ·lat'ed ·lat'ing
cu'mu·la'tive
cu'mu·lous adj.
cu'mu·lus n.
  ·li
cu·ne'i·form'
cun'ning·ly
cup'board
cup'ful'
  ·fuls'
cu·pid'i·ty
cu'po·la
cur'a·ble
cu'ra·çao'
cu'rate
cur'a·tive
cu·ra'tor
curb'stone'
cur'dle
  ·dled ·dling
cure
  cured cur'ing
cure'-all'
cur'few
cu'rie
cu'ri·o'
  ·os'
cu·ri·os'i·ty
  ·ties
cu'ri·ous
curl'i·cue'
curl'i·ness
curl'y
  ·i·er ·i·est
cur·mudg'eon
cur'rant
  (fruit)

cur'ren·cy
  ·cies
cur'rent
  (a flowing)
cur·ric'u·lar
cur·ric'u·lum
  ·u·la or ·u·lums
cur'ry
  ·ried ·ry·ing
cur'ry·comb'
curse
  cursed or curst
  curs'ing
cur'sive
cur·so·ri·ly
cur·so·ri·ness
cur'so·ry
cur·tail'
cur'tain
curt'ness
curt'sy
  ·sies
  ·sied ·sy·ing
  (knee bend;
  SEE courtesy)
cur'va·ture
curve
  curved curv'ing
cur'vi·lin'e·ar
curv'y
  ·i·er ·i·est
cush'ion
cus'pid
cus'pi·dor'
cus'tard
cus·to'di·al
cus·to'di·an
cus'to·dy
cus'tom
cus'tom·ar'i·ly
cus'tom·ar'y
cus'tom-built'
cus'tom·er
cus'tom·house'
cus'tom-made'
cut
  cut cut'ting
cu·ta'ne·ous
cut'a·way'
cut'back'
cut'i·cle
cut'lass or ·las
cut'ler·y
cut'let
cut'off'
cut'out'
cut'-rate'
cut'ter
cut'throat'
cy'a·nide'
cy'ber·cul'ture
cy'ber·na'tion
cy'ber·net'ics
cy'cla·mate'
cy'cle
  cy'cled cy'cling
cy'clic
cy'cli·cal

cy'clist
cy'cli·zine'
cy'clom'e·ter
cy'clone
cy'clo·pe'di·a
cy'clo·ra'ma
cy'clo·tron'
cyg'net
cyl'in·der
cy·lin'dri·cal
cym'bal
  (brass plate;
  SEE symbol)
cyn'ic
cyn'i·cal
cyn'i·cal·ly
cyn'i·cism
cy'no·sure'
cy'press
cyst'ic
cyst'oid
cy·tol'o·gy
cy'to·plasm
czar
Czech'o·slo·va'ki·a

D

dab'ble
  ·bled ·bling
dachs'hund
Da'cron
dac'tyl
dad'dy
  ·dies
da'do
  ·does
daf'fo·dil'
dag'ger
da·guerre'o·type'
dahl'ia
dai'ly
  ·lies
dain'ti·ly
dain'ti·ness
dain'ty
  ·ties
  ·ti·er ·ti·est
dai'qui·ri
dair'y
  ·ies
dair'y·maid'
dair'y·man
da'is
dai'sy
  ·sies
dal'li·ance
dal'ly
  ·lied ·ly·ing
Dal·ma'tian
dam
  dammed
  dam'ming
  (barrier; SEE damn)

dam'age
  ·aged ·ag·ing
dam'age·a·ble
dam'a·scene'
dam'ask
damn
  damned
  damn'ing
  (condemn; SEE dam)
dam'na·ble
dam'na·bly
dam·na'tion
dam'na·to'ry
damp'-dry'
  ·dried' ·dry'ing
damp'en
damp'er
dam'sel
dance
  danced danc'ing
danc'er
dan'de·li'on
dan'dle
  ·dled ·dling
dan'druff
dan'ger
dan'ger·ous
dan'gle
  ·gled ·gling
Dan'ish
dan·seuse'
dap'ple
  ·pled ·pling
dare
  dared dar'ing
dare'dev'il
Dar·jee'ling
dark'en
dark'room'
dar'ling
Dar·win'i·an
dash'board'
das'tard·li·ness
das'tard·ly
da'ta
  (sing. da'tum)
date
  dat'ed dat'ing
daugh'ter
daugh'ter-in-law'
  daugh'ters-in-law'
daunt'less
dav'en·port'
dav'it
daw'dle
  ·dled ·dling
day'bed'
day'book'
day'break'
day'dream'
day letter
day'long'
day'light'
day room
day'time'
day'-to-day'

day'work'
daze
  dazed daz'ing
daz'zle
  ·zled ·zling
D'-day'
dea'con
dea'con·ess
de·ac'ti·vate'
dead'en
dead'-end'
dead'head'
dead'line'
dead'li·ness
dead'lock'
dead'ly
  ·li·er ·li·est
dead'wood'
deaf'en·ing·ly
deaf'-mute'
deal
  dealt deal'ing
deal'er·ship'
dean'er·y
  ·ies
dear'ly
dearth
death'bed'
death'blow'
death'less
death'ly
death'trap'
death'watch'
de·ba'cle
de·bar'
  ·barred' ·bar'ring
de·bark'
de'bar·ka'tion
de·base'
  ·based' ·bas'ing
de·bate'
  ·bat'ed ·bat'ing
de·bauch'
de·bau'chee'
de·bauch'er·y
  ·ies
de·ben'ture
de·bil'i·tate'
  ·tat'ed ·tat'ing
de·bil'i·ta'tion
de·bil'i·ty
  ·ies
deb'it
deb'o·nair'
  or ·naire'
deb'o·nair'ly
de·brief'
de·bris'
debt'or
de·bunk'
de·but'
deb'u·tante'
dec'ade
dec'a·dence
dec'a·dent
dec'a·gon'
dec'a·gram'

dec'a·he'dron
  ·drons or ·dra
de·cal'ci·fy'
  ·fied' ·fy'ing
de·cal'co·ma'ni·a
dec'a·li'ter
Dec'a·logue'
  or ·log'
dec'a·me'ter
de·camp'
de·cant'
de·cant'er
de·cap'i·tate'
  ·tat'ed ·tat'ing
de·cap'i·ta'tion
de·cath'lon
de·cay'
de·cease'
  ·ceased'
  ·ceas'ing
de·ce'dent
de·ceit'ful
de·ceiv'a·ble
de·ceive'
  ·ceived'
  ·ceiv'ing
de·cel'er·ate'
  ·at'ed ·at'ing
de·cel'er·a'tion
de·cel'er·a'tor
de·cel'er·on'
De·cem'ber
de'cen·cy
  ·cies
de·cen'ni·al
de'cent
  (proper; SEE
  descent, dissent)
de·cen'tral·i·
za'tion
de·cen'tral·ize'
  ·ized' ·iz'ing
de·cep'tion
de·cep'tive·ly
dec'i·bel
de·cide'
  ·cid'ed ·cid'ing
de·cid'ed·ly
de·cid'u·ous
dec'i·mal
dec'i·mal·ize'
  ·ized' ·iz'ing
dec'i·mal·ly
dec'i·mate'
  ·mat'ed ·mat'ing
de·ci'pher
de·ci'sion
de·ci'sive
deck'le
de·claim'
dec'la·ma'tion
de·clam'a·to·ry
de·clar'a·ble
dec'la·ra'tion
de·clar'a·tive
de·clare'
  ·clared'
  ·clar'ing

de·clas'si·fy'
  ·fied' ·fy'ing
de·clen'sion
dec'li·na'tion
de·cline'
  ·clined' ·clin'ing
de·cliv'i·ty
  ·ties
de·code'
de·cod'er
dé·col'le·tage'
dé·col'le·té'
de'com·pos'a·ble
de'com·pose'
de'com·po·si'tion
de'com·pres'sion
de'con·gest'ant
de'con·tam'i·nate'
de'con·trol'
  ·trolled'
  ·trol'ling
dé·cor' or de·cor'
dec'o·rate'
  ·rat'ed ·rat'ing
dec'o·ra'tion
dec'o·ra·tive
dec'o·ra'tor
dec'o·rous
de·co'rum
de'cou·page'
de·coy'
de·crease'
  ·creased'
  ·creas'ing
de·cree'
  ·creed' ·cree'ing
de·crep'it
de·crep'i·tude'
de·cre·scen'do
de·cres'cent
de·cri'al
de·cry'
  ·cried' ·cry'ing
de·crypt'
de·cum'bent
ded'i·cate'
  ·cat'ed ·cat'ing
ded'i·ca'tion
ded'i·ca·to'ry
de·duce'
  ·duced' ·duc'ing
de·duc'i·ble
de·duct'
de·duct'i·ble
de·duc'tion
de·duc'tive
de·em'pha·sis
de·em'pha·size'
deep'-chest'ed
deep'-dyed'
deep'freeze'
  ·froze' or
  ·freezed'
  ·fro'zen or
  ·freezed'
  ·freez'ing
deep'-fry'
  ·fried' ·fry'ing

deep'-laid'
deep'-root'ed
deep'-seat'ed
deep'-set'
deer'skin'
de·es'ca·late'
de·es'ca·la'tion
de·face'
de fac'to
de·fal'cate'
  ·cat'ed ·cat'ing
def'a·ma'tion
de·fam'a·to'ry
de·fame'
  ·famed'
  ·fam'ing
de·fault'
de·fea'sance
de·feat'
de·feat'ist
def'e·cate'
  ·cat'ed ·cat'ing
def'e·ca'tion
de·fect'
de·fec'tion
de·fec'tive
de·fec'tor
de·fend'
de·fend'ant
de·fense'
de·fen'si·ble
de·fen'sive
de·fer'
  ·ferred' ·fer'ring
def'er·ence
def'er·en'tial
de·fer'ment
de·fi'ance
de·fi'ant
de·fi'cien·cy
  ·cies
de·fi'cient
def'i·cit
de·fi'er
de·file'
  ·filed' ·fil'ing
de·fin'a·ble
de·fine'
  ·fined' ·fin'ing
def'i·nite
def'i·ni'tion
de·fin'i·tive
de·flate'
  ·flat'ed ·flat'ing
de·fla'tion
de·fla'tion·ar'y
de·fla'tor
de·flect'
de·flec'tion
de·flec'tor
de·flow'er
de·fo'li·ate'
  ·at'ed ·at'ing
de'for·ma'tion
de·formed'
de·form'i·ty
  ·ties
de·fraud'

de·fray'
de·fray'al
de·frost'
de·funct'
de·fuse'
de·fy'
  ·fied' ·fy'ing
dé·ga·gé'
de·gen'er·a·cy
de·gen'er·ate'
  ·at'ed ·at'ing
de·gen'er·a'tion
de·gen'er·a·tive
de·grad'a·ble
deg'ra·da'tion
de·grade'
  ·grad'ed
  ·grad'ing
de·gree'
de·hu·mid'i·fy'
de·hy'drate
  ·drat·ed ·drat·ing
de·hy·dra'tion
de·hy'dra·tor
de·ic'er
de·i·fi·ca'tion
de'i·fy'
  ·fied' ·fy'ing
deign
de'ism
de'i·ty
  ·ties
de·ject'ed
de·jec'tion
Del'a·ware'
de·lay'
de·lec'ta·ble
del'e·gate'
  ·gat·ed ·gat'ing
del'e·ga'tion
de·lete'
  ·let'ed ·let'ing
del'e·te'ri·ous
de·le'tion
delft'ware'
de·lib'er·ate
de·lib'er·ate·ly
de·lib'er·a'tion
del'i·ca·cy
  ·cies
del'i·cate
del'i·cate·ly
del'i·ca·tes'sen
de·li'cious
de·light'ful
de·light'ful·ly
de·lin'e·ate'
  ·at'ed ·at'ing
de·lin'e·a'tion
de·lin'e·a'tor
de·lin'quen·cy
de·lin'quent
de·lir'i·ous
de·lir'i·um
de·liv'er·a·ble
de·liv'er·ance
de·liv'er·y
  ·ies

de·lude'
  ·lud'ed ·lud'ing
del'uge
  ·uged ·ug·ing
de·lu'sion
de·lu'sive
de·luxe'
delve
delved delv'ing
de·mag'net·ize'
dem'a·gog'ic
dem'a·gog'i·cal·ly
dem'a·gogue'
  or ·gog'
dem'a·gog'y
de·mand'ing
de·mar'cate
  ·cat·ed ·cat·ing
de·mar·ca'tion
de·mean'or
de·men'tia
de·mer'it
de·mesne'
dem'i·john'
de·mil'i·ta·rize'
de·mise'
dem'i·tasse'
de·mo'bi·lize'
de·moc'ra·cy
  ·cies
dem'o·crat'ic
dem'o·crat'i·cal·ly
de·moc'ra·ti·
za'tion
de·moc'ra·tize'
  ·tized' ·tiz'ing
de·mog'ra·phy
de·mol'ish
dem'o·li'tion
de'mon
de·mon'e·tize'
  ·tized' ·tiz'ing
de·mo'ni·ac'
de·mon'ic
de·mon'i·cal·ly
de·mon'stra·ble
dem'on·strate'
  ·strat'ed
  ·strat'ing
dem'on·stra'tion
de·mon'stra·tive
de·mon'stra·tor
de·mor'al·ize'
de·mote'
  ·mot'ed ·mot'ing
de·mo'tion
de·mount'
de·mul'cent
de·mur'
  ·murred'
  ·mur'ring
  (to object)
de·mure'
  (coy)
de·mur'rage
de·mur'rer
de·na'tion·al·ize'
de·nat'u·ral·ize'

de·na'ture
·tured ·tur·ing
de·ni'a·ble
de·ni'al
de·nier'
de·ni'er
den'im
den'i·zen
de·nom'i·nate'
·nat'ed ·nat'ing
de·nom'i·na'tion
de·nom'i·na'tor
de·no'ta'tion
de·note'
·not'ed ·not'ing
de·noue'ment
de·nounce'
·nounced'
·nounc'ing
dense
dens'er dens'est
dense'ly
den'si·ty
·ties
den'tal
den'tal·ly
den'ti·frice'
den'tin
den'tist
den'tist·ry
den'ture
de·nude'
·nud'ed ·nud'ing
de·nun'ci·a'tion
de·ny'
·nied' ·ny'ing
de·o'dor·ant
de·o'dor·ize'
·ized' ·iz'ing
de·o'dor·iz'er
de·part'ed
de·part'ment
de·part'men'tal
de·part'men'tal·
ize'
·ized' ·iz'ing
de·par'ture
de·pend'a·bil'i·ty
de·pend'a·ble
de·pend'a·bly
de·pend'ence
de·pend'en·cy
·cies
de·pend'ent
de·per'son·al·ize'
de·pict'
de·pic'tion
de·pil'a·to'ry
·ries
de·plane'
de·plete'
·plet'ed ·plet'ing
de·ple'tion
de·plor'a·ble
de·plore'
·plored'
·plor'ing
de·ploy'

de·pon'ent
de·pop'u·late'
de·port'a·ble
de·por'ta'tion
de·port'ment
de·pose'
de·pos'it
de·pos'i·tar'y
·ies
dep'o·si'tion
de·pos'i·tor
de·pos'i·to'ry
·ries
de'pot
dep'ra·va'tion
(a corrupting;
SEE deprivation)
de·prave'
·praved'
·prav'ing
de·prav'i·ty
·ties
dep're·cate'
·cat'ed ·cat'ing
dep're·ca'tion
dep're·ca·to'ry
de·pre'ci·a·ble
de·pre'ci·ate'
·at'ed ·at'ing
de·pre'ci·a'tion
dep're·da'tion
de·pres'sant
de·pressed'
de·press'ing
de·pres'sion
de·pres'sive·ly
dep'ri·va'tion
(a taking away;
SEE depravation)
de·prive'
·prived' ·priv'ing
depth
dep'u·ta'tion
'dep'u·tize'
·tized' ·tiz'ing
dep'u·ty
·ties
de·rail'
de·range'
·ranged'
·rang'ing
der'e·lict'
der'e·lic'tion
de·ride'
·rid'ed ·rid'ing
de ri·gueur'
de·ri'sion
de·ri'sive
de·riv'a·ble
der'i·va'tion
de·riv'a·tive
de·rive'
·rived' ·riv'ing
der'ma·tol'o·gist
der'o·ga'tion
de·rog'a·to'ri·ly
de·rog'a·to'ry
der'rick

der'ri·ère'
der'ring-do'
der'rin·ger
de·sal'i·na'tion
de·salt'
des'cant
de·scend'
de·scend'ant
de·scend'i·ble
de·scent'
(going down; SEE
decent, dissent)
de·scrib'a·ble
de·scribe'
·scribed'
·scrib'ing
de·scrip'tion
de·scrip'tive
de·scry'
·scried'
·scry'ing
des'e·crate'
·crat'ed ·crat'ing
des'e·cra'tion
de·seg're·gate'
·gat'ed ·gat'ing
de·seg're·ga'tion
de·sen'si·tize'
de·sen'si·tiz'er
de·sert'
(abandon; SEE
dessert)
des'ert
(dry area)
de·ser'tion
de·serts'
(reward, etc.)
de·serve'
·served'
·serv'ing
de·serv'ed·ly
des'ic·cant
des'ic·cate'
·cat'ed ·cat'ing
des'ic·ca'tion
de·sign'
des'ig·nate'
·nat'ed ·nat'ing
des'ig·na'tion
des'ig·na'tor
de·signed'
de·sign'er
de·sir'a·bil'i·ty
de·sir'a·ble
de·sir'a·bly
de·sire'
·sired' ·sir'ing
de·sir'ous
de·sist'
des'o·late'
·lat'ed ·lat'ing
des'o·la'tion
de·spair'
des'per·a'do
·does or ·dos
des'per·ate
(hopeless; SEE
disparate)

des'per·a'tion
des'pi·ca·ble
de·spise'
·spised'
·spis'ing
de·spite'
de·spoil'
de·spo'li·a'tion
de·spond'en·cy
de·spond'ent
des'pot
des·pot'ic
des·pot'i·cal·ly
des'pot·ism
des·sert'
(food; SEE desert)
des·sert'spoon'
des'ti·na'tion
des'tine
·tined ·tin·ing
des'tin·y
·ies
des'ti·tute'
des'ti·tu'tion
de·stroy'er
de·struct'
de·struct'i·bil'i·ty
de·struct'i·ble
de·struc'tion
de·struc'tive
de·struc'tor
des'ue·tude'
des'ul·to'ry
de·tach'
de·tach'a·ble
de·tach'ment
de·tail'
de·tain'
de·tect'
de·tect'a·ble
or ·i·ble
de·tec'tion
de·tec'tive
de·tec'tor
dé·tente'
de·ten'tion
de·ter'
·terred'
·ter'ring
de·ter'gent
de·te'ri·o·rate'
·rat'ed ·rat'ing
de·te'ri·o·ra'tion
de·ter'ment
de·ter'mi·na·ble
de·ter'mi·na·bly
de·ter'mi·nant
de·ter'mi·nate
de·ter'mi·na'tion
de·ter'mine
·mined ·min·ing
de·ter'min·ism
de·ter'rence
de·ter'rent
de·test'
de·test'a·ble
de·test'a·bly
de·tes'ta'tion

de·throne'
·throned'
·thron'ing
det'o·nate'
·nat'ed ·nat'ing
det'o·na'tion
det'o·na'tor
de'tour
de·tract'
de·trac'tor
det'ri·ment
det'ri·men'tal
de·tri'tus
deuce
de·val'u·a'tion
de·val'ue
dev'as·tate'
·tat'ed ·tat'ing
dev'as·ta'tion
de·vel'op·ment
de·vel'op·men'tal
de'vi·ant
de'vi·ate'
·at'ed ·at'ing
de'vi·a'tion
de·vice'
dev'il·ish
dev'il·ment
dev'il·try
·tries
de'vi·ous
de·vis'a·ble
(that can be devised;
SEE divisible)
de·vise'
·vised' ·vis'ing
de·vi'tal·ize'
de·void'
de·volve'
·volved'
·volv'ing
de·vote'
·vot'ed ·vot'ing
dev'o·tee'
de·vo'tion
de·vour'
de·vout'
dew'drop'
dew'lap'
dew'y
·i·er ·i·est
dex·ter'i·ty
dex'ter·ous
or dex'trous
dex'trose
di'a·be'tes
di'a·bet'ic
di'a·bol'ic
di'a·bol'i·cal
di'a·bol'i·cal·ly
di'a·crit'i·cal
di'a·dem'
di'ag·nos'a·ble
di'ag·nose'
·nosed' ·nos'ing
di'ag·no'sis
·no'ses
di'ag·nos'tic

di'ag·nos'ti·cal·ly
di'ag·nos·ti'cian
di·ag'o·nal
di·ag'o·nal·ly
di'a·gram'
·gramed' or
·grammed'
·gram'ing or
·gram'ming
di'a·gram·mat'ic
di'al
·aled or ·alled
·al·ing or ·al·ling
di'a·lect'
di'a·lec'tal
di'a·lec'tic
di'a·lec·ti'cian
di·al'o·gist
di'a·logue' or
·log'
di·am'e·ter
di'a·met'ri·cal
di'a·met'ri·cal·ly
di'a·mond
di'a·pa'son
di'a·per
di·aph'a·nous
di'a·phragm'
di'a·rist
di'ar·rhe'a
or ·rhoe'a
di'a·ry
·ries
di'a·stase'
di'a·ther'my
di'a·ton'ic
di'a·tribe'
dib'ble
·bled ·bling
dice
diced dic'ing
(sing. die or dice
di·chot'o·mize'
·mized' ·miz'ing
di·chot'o·my
dick'er
dick'ey
·eys
Dic'ta·phone'
dic'tate
·tat·ed ·tat·ing
dic·ta'tion
dic'ta·tor
dic·ta·to'ri·al
dic'tion·ar'y
·ies
Dic'to·graph'
dic'tum
·tums or ·ta
di·dac'tic
di·dac'ti·cal·ly
die
dice
(cube)
die
dies
died die'ing
(mold; stamp)

·die
died dy'ing
(*stop living;*
SEE dye)
die'-hard' *or*
die''hard'
diel'drin
di·e·lec'tric
di·er'e·sis
·ses'
die'sel
die'sink'er
di'e·sis
·ses'
di'e·tar'y
di'e·tet'ic
di'e·tet'i·cal·ly
di'e·ti'tian
or ·cian
dif'fer·ence
dif'fer·ent
dif'fer·en'tial
dif'fer·en'ti·ate'
·at'ed ·at'ing
dif'fer·en'ti·a'tion
dif'fi·cult
dif'fi·cul'ty
·ties
dif'fi·dence
dif'fi·dent
dif·fract'
dif·frac'tion
dif·fuse'
·fused' ·fus'ing
dif·fus'i·ble
dif·fu'sion
dif·fu'sive
dig
dug dig'ging
dig'a·my
di'gest
di·gest'i·ble
di·ges'tive
dig'ger
dig'it
dig'it·al
dig'i·tal'is
dig'i·ti·grade'
dig'ni·fy'
·fied' ·fy'ing
dig'ni·tar'y
·ies
dig'ni·ty
·ties
di·gress'
di·gres'sion
di·lan'tin
di·lap'i·date'
·dat'ed ·dat'ing
di·lat'a·ble
di·late'
·lat'ed ·lat'ing
di·la'tion
dil'a·to'ry
di·lem'ma
dil'et·tante'
·tantes' *or* ·tan'ti
dil'et·tant'ish

dil'i·gence
dil'i·gent
dil'ly·dal'ly
·lied ·ly·ing
dil'u·ent
di·lute'
·lut'ed ·lut'ing
di·lu'tion
di·lu'vi·al
dim
dim'mer
dim'mest
dimmed
dim'ming
di·men'sion
di·min'ish
di·min'u·en'do
dim'i·nu'tion
di·min'u·tive
dim'i·ty
dim'out'
dim'ple
·pled ·pling
din
dinned din'ning
dine
dined din'ing
din'er
(*person eating;*
SEE dinner)
din·ette'
din'ghy
·ghies
(*boat*)
din'gi·ness
din'gy
·gi·er ·gi·est
(*not bright*)
din'ner
(*meal;* SEE diner)
din'ner·ware'
di'no·saur'
di·oc'e·san
di'o·cese
di'o·ra'ma
di·ox'ide
dip
dipped dip'ping
diph·the'ri·a
diph'thong
di·plo'ma
di·plo'ma·cy
·cies
dip'lo·mat'
(*government
representative*)
dip'lo·mate'
(*doctor*)
dip'lo·mat'i·cal·ly
dip'so·ma'ni·a
di·rect'
di·rec'tion
di·rec'tive
di·rec'tor
di·rec'tor·ate
di·rec'to'ri·al
di·rec'to·ry
·ries

dire'ful
dirge
dir'i·gi·ble
dirn'dl
dirt'i·ness
dirt'y
·i·er ·i·est
dis·a·bil'i·ty
·ties
dis·a'ble
·bled ·bling
dis·a·buse'
·bused' ·bus'ing
dis'ad·van'tage
dis·ad·van·ta'·
geous
dis'af·fect'ed
dis·a·gree'
dis·a·gree'a·ble
dis·a·gree'a·bly
dis·a·gree'ment
dis·al·low'
dis·ap·pear'ance
dis·ap·point'ment
dis·ap·pro·ba'tion
dis·ap·prov'al
dis·ap·prove'
dis·ar'ma·ment
dis·arm'ing
dis·ar·range'
dis·ar·ray'
dis·as·sem'ble
dis·as·so'ci·ate'
dis·as'ter
dis·as'trous
dis·a·vow'
dis·a·vow'al
dis·band'
dis·bar'
dis·be·lief'
dis·be·lieve'
dis·be·liev'er
dis·burse'
·bursed'
·burs'ing
dis·burse'ment
disc
dis·card'
dis·cern'
dis·cern'i·ble
dis·cern'ing
dis·cern'ment
dis·charge'
dis·ci'ple
dis·ci·plin·a·ble
dis'ci·pli·nar'i·an
dis'ci·pli·nar'y
dis'ci·pline
·plined ·plin·ing
disc jockey
dis·claim'
dis·claim'er
dis·close'
dis·clo'sure
dis·cog'ra·phy
dis'coid
dis·col'or
dis·col'or·a'tion

dis·com'fit
dis·com'fi·ture
dis·com'fort
dis'com·pose'
dis'com·po'sure
dis·con·cert'
dis'con·nect'
dis'con'so·late
dis'con·tent'
dis'con·tin'u·ance
dis'con·tin'ue
dis'con·ti·nu'i·ty
dis'con·tin'u·ous
dis'co·phile'
dis'cord
dis·cord'ant
dis'co·thèque
dis'count
dis·cour'age
·aged ·ag·ing
dis·cour'age·ment
dis'course
dis·cour'te·ous
dis·cour'te·sy
dis·cov'er
dis·cov'er·er
dis·cov'er·y
·ies
dis·cred'it
dis·creet'
(*prudent;* SEE
discrete)
dis·crep'an·cy
·cies
dis·crete'
(*separate;* SEE
discreet)
dis·cre'tion
dis·cre'tion·ar'y
dis·crim'i·nate'
·nat'ed ·nat'ing
dis·crim'i·na'tion
dis·crim'i·na·
to'ry
dis·cur'sive
dis'cus
·cus·es *or* dis'ci
dis·cuss'
dis·cus'sion
dis·dain'ful
dis·ease'
·eased' ·eas'ing
dis'em·bark'
dis'em·bod'y
dis'em·bow'el
·eled *or* ·elled
·el·ing *or*
·el·ling
dis'en·chant'
dis'en·cum'ber
dis'en·gage'
dis'en·tan'gle
dis'es·tab'lish
dis·fa'vor
dis·fig'ure
dis·fig'ure·ment
dis·fran'chise
·chised ·chis·ing

dis·gorge'
dis·grace'
·graced'
·grac'ing
dis·grace'ful
dis·grun'tle
·tled ·tling
dis·guise'
·guised'
·guis'ing
dis·gust'
dis·ha·bille'
dis·har'mo·ny
dish'cloth'
dis·heart'en
di·shev'el
·eled *or* ·elled
·el·ing *or*
·el·ling
dis·hon'est
dis·hon'es·ty
dis·hon'or
dis·hon'or·a·ble
dish'pan'
dish towel
dish'wash'er
dish'wa'ter
dis'il·lu'sioned
dis'in·cli·na'tion
dis'in·cline'
dis'in·fect'
dis'in·fect'ant
dis'in·gen'u·ous
dis'in·her'it
dis·in'te·grate'
·grat'ed
·grat'ing
dis·in'te·gra'tion
dis·in'ter'
dis'in'ter·est·ed
dis·join'
dis·joint'
dis·junc'tion
disk
dis·like'
dis'lo·cate'
dis'lo·ca'tion
dis·lodge'
dis·loy'al
dis·loy'al·ty
dis'mal
dis'mal·ly
dis·man'tle
dis·may'
dis·mem'ber
dis·miss'
dis·miss'al
dis·mount'
dis'o·be'di·ence
dis'o·be'di·ent
dis'o·bey'
dis·or'der
dis·or'der·ly
dis·or'gan·i·za'·
tion
dis·or'gan·ize'
dis·o'ri·ent'
dis·own'

dis·par'age
·aged ·ag·ing
dis'pa·rate
(*not alike;* SEE
desperate)
dis·par'i·ty
dis·pas'sion·ate
dis·patch'
dis·patch'er
dis·pel'
·pelled' ·pel'ling
dis·pen'sa·bil'i·ty
dis·pen'sa·ble
dis·pen'sa·ry
·ries
dis·pen'sa'tion
dis·pense'
·pensed'
·pens'ing
dis·pen'ser
dis·per'sal
dis·perse'
·persed' ·pers'ing
dis·pers'i·ble
dis·per'sion
dis·pir'it·ed
dis·place'
dis·place'ment
dis·play'
dis·please'
dis·pleas'ure
dis·port'
dis·pos'a·ble
dis·pos'al
dis·pose'
·posed' ·pos'ing
dis'po·si'tion
dis'pos·sess'
dis·proof'
dis'pro·por'tion
dis'pro·por'tion·
ate
dis·prove'
dis·pu'ta·ble
dis·pu'tant
dis'pu·ta'tion
dis'pu·ta'tious
dis·pute'
·put'ed ·put'ing
dis·qual'i·fi·ca'·
tion
dis·qual'i·fy'
dis·qui'et
dis·qui'e·tude
dis'qui·si'tion
dis're·gard'
dis're·pair'
dis·rep'u·ta·ble
dis·rep'u·ta·bly
dis're·pute'
dis're·spect'ful
dis·robe'
dis·rupt'
dis·rup'tion
dis·rup'tive
dis·sat'is·fac'tion
dis·sat'is·fy'
·fied' ·fy'ing

dis·sect'
dis·sec'tion
dis·sec'tor
dis·sem'blance
dis·sem'ble
　bled ·bling
dis·sem'i·nate'
　·nat'ed ·nat'ing
dis·sem'i·na'tion
dis·sen'sion
dis·sent'
　(disagree; SEE
　decent, descent)
dis·sen'tient
dis·sen'tious
dis'ser·ta'tion
dis·serv'ice
dis·sev'er
dis'si·dence
dis'si·dent
dis·sim'i·lar
dis·sim'i·lar'i·ty
dis·sim'i·la'tion
dis·sim'u·late'
dis'si·pate'
　·pat'ed ·pat'ing
dis'si·pa'tion
dis·so'ci·ate'
　·at'ed ·at'ing
dis·so'ci·a'tion
dis·sol'u·ble
dis'so·lute'
dis'so·lu'tion
dis·solv'a·ble
dis·solve'
　·solved'
　·solv'ing
dis·sol'vent
dis'so·nance
dis'so·nant
dis·suade'
　·suad'ed
　·suad'ing
dis·sua'sion
dis·sym'me·try
dis'taff
dis'tance
dis'tant
dis·taste'ful
dis·tem'per
dis·tend'
dis·ten'si·ble
dis·ten'tion or
　dis·ten'sion
dis'tich
dis·till' or ·til'
　·tilled' ·till'ing
dis·til·late
dis'til·la'tion
dis·till'er
dis·till'er·y
　·ies
dis·tinct'
dis·tinc'tion
dis·tinc'tive
dis·tin·gué'
dis·tin'guish
dis·tin'guish·a·ble

dis·tin'guish·a·bly
dis·tort'
dis·tor'tion
dis·tract'
dis·tract'i·ble
dis·trac'tion
dis·trait'
dis·traught'
dis·tress'
dis·trib'ut·a·ble
dis·trib'ute
　·ut·ed ·ut·ing
dis'tri·bu'tion
dis·trib'u·tive
dis·trib'u·tor
dis'trict
dis·trust'ful
dis·turb'
dis·turb'ance
dis·un'ion
dis'u·nite'
dis·u'ni·ty
dis·use'
ditch
dith'er
dit'to
　·tos
　·toed ·to·ing
dit'ty
　·ties
di'u·ret'ic
di·ur'nal
di'va
di·van'
dive
　dived or dove
　dived div'ing
di·verge'
　·verged'
　·verg'ing
di·ver'gence
di·ver'gent
di'vers
　(sundry)
di·verse'
　(different)
di·ver'si·fi·ca'·
　tion
di·ver'si·form'
di·ver'si·fy'
　·fied' ·fy'ing
di·ver'sion
di·ver'sion·ar'y
di·ver'si·ty
di·vert'
di·ver'tisse·ment
di·vest'
di·vest'i·ture
di·vid'a·ble
di·vide'
　·vid'ed ·vid'ing
div'i·dend'
div'i·na'tion
di·vine'
　·vined' ·vin'ing
di·vin'i·ty
　·ties
di·vis'i·bil'i·ty

di·vis'i·ble
　(that can be divided;
　SEE devisable)
di·vi'sion
di·vi'sor
di·vorce'
　·vorced' ·vorc'ing
di·vor·cé' masc.
di·vor·cée' or
　·cee' fem.
div'ot
di·vulge'
　·vulged'
　·vulg'ing
di·vul'gence
diz'zi·ly
diz'zi·ness
diz'zy
　·zi·er ·zi·est
　·zied ·zy·ing
do'a·ble
dob'bin
do'cent
doc'ile
doc'ile·ly
do·cil'i·ty
dock'age
dock'et
dock'yard'
doc'tor
doc'tor·al
doc'tor·ate
doc'tri·naire'
doc'tri·nal
doc'trine
doc'u·ment
doc'u·men'tal
doc'u·men'ta·ry
　·ries
doc'u·men·ta'tion
dod'der·ing
dodge
　dodged
　dodg'ing
dodg'y
　·i·er ·i·est
do'er
does
doe'skin'
does'n't
dog'catch'er
dog'ear'
dog'ged·ly
dog'ger·el
dog'gy or ·gie
　·gies
　(dog)
do'gie or ·gy
　·gies
　(calf)
dog'ma
　·mas or ·ma·ta
dog·mat'ic
dog·mat'i·cal·ly
dog'ma·tism
dog'ma·tize'
　·tized' ·tiz'ing
dog'nap'

do'-good'er
dog'trot'
dog'watch'
dog'wood'
doi'ly
do'-it-your·self'
dol'ce
dol'drums
dole
　doled dol'ing
dole'ful
dol'lar
dol'lop
dol'man
　·mans
　(robe)
dol'men
　(tomb)
do'lor·ous
dol'phin
dolt'ish
do·main'
do·mes'tic
do·mes'ti·cate'
　·cat'ed ·cat'ing
do·mes·tic'i·ty
　·ties
dom'i·cile
dom'i·nance
dom'i·nant
dom'i·nate'
　·nat'ed ·nat'ing
dom'i·na'tion
dom'i·neer'ing
do·min'i·cal
do·min'ion
dom'i·no'
　·noes' or ·nos'
don
　donned don'ning
do'nate
　·nat·ed ·nat·ing
do·na'tion
do·nee'
Don' Ju'an
don'key
　·keys
don'ny·brook'
do'nor
do'-or-die'
Don' Qui·xo'te
don't
doo'dle
　·dled ·dling
doo'hick'ey
dooms'day'
door'bell'
do'-or-die'
door'jamb'
door'keep'er
door'knob'
door'man'
door'mat'
door'nail'
door'plate'
door'sill'
door'step'

door'stop'
door'-to-door'
door'way'
dope
　doped dop'ing
dor'man·cy
dor'mant
dor'mer
dor'mi·to'ry
　·ries
dor'mouse'
　·mice'
dor'sal
do'ry
　·ries
dos'-à-dos'
dos'age
dos'si·er'
dot
　dot'ted dot'ting
dot'age
dot'ard
dote
　dot'ed dot'ing
dou'ble
　·bled ·bling
dou'ble-bar'reled
dou'ble-breast'ed
dou'ble-check'
dou'ble-cross'
dou'ble-date'
dou'ble-deal'ing
dou'ble-deck'er
dou'ble-edged'
dou'ble-
　en·ten'dre
dou'ble-faced'
dou'ble-head'er
dou'ble-joint'ed
dou'ble-knit'
dou'ble-park'
dou'ble-quick'
dou'ble-space'
dou'blet
dou'ble-tongued'
dou'bly
doubt
doubt'ful
doubt'ful·ly
doubt'less
douche
　douched
　douch'ing
dough
dough'i·ness
dough'nut'
dough'y
　·i·er ·i·est
doup'pi·o'ni or
　dou'pi·o'ni
douse
　doused dous'ing
dove'cote'
dove'tail'
dow'a·ger
dow'di·ness
dow'dy
　·di·er ·di·est

dow'el
dow'er
down'beat'
down'cast'
down'fall'
down'grade'
down'heart'ed
down'hill'
down'i·ness
down'pour'
down'range'
down'right'
down'spout'
down'stage'
down'stairs'
down'state'
down'stream'
down'swing'
down'time'
down'-to-earth'
down'town'
down'trod'den
down'turn'
down'ward
down'wash'
down'wind'
down'y
　·i·er ·i·est
dow'ry
　·ries
dox·ol'o·gy
doze
　dozed doz'ing
doz'en
drab
drab'ber
drab'best
draft·ee'
draft'i·ness
drafts'man
draft'y
　·i·er ·i·est
drag
　dragged
　drag'ging
drag'gle
　·gled ·gling
drag'gy
　·gi·er ·gi·est
drag'net'
drag'o·man
　·mans or ·men
drag'on
drag'on·fly'
　·flies'
dra·goon'
drain'age
drain'pipe'
dra'ma
dra·mát'ic
dra·mat'i·cal·l
dram'a·tist
dram'a·ti·za'ti
dram'a·tize'
　·tized' ·tiz'ing
dram'a·tur'gy
drape
　draped drap'i

drap'er·y
·ies
dras'tic
dras'ti·cal·ly
draughts'man
·men
draw
drew drawn
draw'ing
draw'back'
draw'bridge'
draw·ee'
draw'er
draw'knife'
·knives'
drawl
drawn'work'
draw'string'
dray'age
dray'man
dread'ful
dread'ful·ly
dread'nought'
dream'i·ly
dream'i·ness
dream'y
·i·er ·i·est
drear'i·ly
drear'i·ness
drear'y
·i·er ·i·est
dredge
dredged
dredg'ing
drenched
dress
dressed or drest
dress'ing
dress'er
dress'i·ly
dress'i·ness
dress'ing-down'
dress'mak'er
dress'y
·i·er ·i·est
drib'ble
·bled ·bling
drib'let
drift'er or dry'er
drift'wood'
drill'mas'ter
drill press
drink
rank drunk
drink'ing
drink'a·ble
drip
dripped or dript
drip'ping
drip'-dry'
drive
drove driv'en

driv'er
drive'way'
driz'zle
·zled ·zling
driz'zly
droll'er·y
·ies
drol'ly
drom'e·dar'y
·ies
drone
droned dron'ing
droop'i·ly
droop'i·ness
droop'y
·i·er ·i·est
drop
dropped
drop'ping
drop'cloth'
drop'-forge'
-forged'
-forg'ing
drop'let
drop'out'
drop'per
dross
drought
or drouth
dro'ver
drown
drowse
drowsed
drows'ing
drow'si·ly
drow'si·ness
drow'sy
·si·er ·si·est
drub
drubbed
drub'bing
drudge
drudged
drudg'ing
drudg'er·y
drug
drugged
drug'ging
drug'gist
drug'store'
drum
drummed
drum'ming
drum'beat'
drum'head'
drum'mer
drum'stick'
drunk'ard
drunk'en·ness
drunk·o'me·ter
drupe'let
dry
dri'er dri'est
dried dry'ing
dry'as·dust'
dry'-clean'
dry cleaner
dry cleaning

dry'er
dry'-eyed'
dry ice
dry'ly or dri'ly
dry'ness
du'al
(of two; SEE duel)
du'al·ism
du'al·is'tic
du'al·ly
du'al-pur'pose
dub
dubbed dub'bing
du·bi'e·ty
du'bi·ous
du'cal
duc'at
duch'ess
duch'y
·ies
duck'ling
duck'pins'
duc'tile
duct'less
dudg'eon
due bill
du'el
·eled or ·elled
·el·ing or
·el·ling
(fight; SEE dual)
du·et'
duf'fel or ·fle
dug'out'
dul'cet
dul'ci·mer
dull'ard
dull'ness
dul'ly
(in a dull manner)
du'ly
(as due)
dumb'bell'
dumb'found' or
·dum'found'
dumb'ly
dumb'wait'er
dum'dum'
dum'my
·mies
dump'i·ness
dump'ling
dump'y
·i·er ·i·est
dun
dunned
dun'ning
dun'der·head'
dun'ga·ree'
dun'geon
dung'hill'
dun'nage
du'o
du'os or du'i
du'o·dec'i·mal
du'o·de'nal
du'o·logue'
du·op'o·ly

du'o·tone'
du'o·type'
dupe
duped dup'ing
du'ple
du'plex
du'pli·cate'
·cat'ed ·cat'ing
du'pli·ca'tion
du'pli·ca'tor
du·plic'i·ty
·ties
du'ra·bil'i·ty
du'ra·ble
du'ra·bly
dur'ance
du·ra'tion
du·ress'
dur'ing
du'rum
dusk'i·ness
dusk'y
·i·er ·i·est
dust'i·ness
dust'pan'
dust'y
·i·er ·i·est
du'te·ous
du'ti·a·ble
du'ti·ful
du'ti·ful·ly
du'ty
·ties
du'ty-free'
dwarf
dwarfs or
dwarves
dwell
dwelt or dwelled
dwell'ing
dwin'dle
·dled ·dling
dy'ad
dyb'buk
dye
dyed dye'ing
(color; SEE die)
dyed'-in-the-wool'
dy'er
dye'stuff'
dy·nam'ic
dy·nam'i·cal·ly
dy'na·mism
dy'na·mite'
·mit'ed ·mit'ing
dy'na·mo'
·mos'
dy'na·mom'e·ter
dy'na·mo'tor
dy'nas·ty
·ties
dyne
dy·nel'
dys'en·ter'y
dys·func'tion
dys·pep'si·a
dys·pep'tic
dys'tro·phy

E

ea'ger
ea'gle
ea'gle-eyed'
ear'ache'
ear'drum'
ear'ly
·li·er ·li·est
ear'mark'
ear'muffs'
ear'nest
earn'ings
ear'phone'
ear'plug'
ear'ring'
ear'shot'
earth'en·ware'
earth'i·ness
earth'ly
earth'quake'
earth'shak'ing
earth'ward
earth'y
·i·er ·i·est
ear'wax'
ease
eased eas'ing
ea'sel
ease'ment
eas'i·ly
eas'i·ness
east'er·ly
east'ern
east'ward
eas'y
·i·er ·i·est
eas'y-go'ing
eat
ate eat'en
eat'ing
eat'a·ble
eaves'drop'
ebb tide
eb'on·y
e·bul'lient
e'bul·li'tion
ec·cen'tric
ec·cen'tri·cal·ly
ec·cen·tric'i·ty
·ties
ec·cle'si·as'ti·cal
ech'e·lon'
ech'o
·oes
e·cho'ic
é·clair'
é·clat'
ec·lec'tic
ec·lec'ti·cism
e·clipse'
·clipsed'
·clips'ing
e·clip'tic
ec'o·log'i·cal

ec'o·log'i·cal·ly
e·col'o·gist
e·col'o·gy
e'co·nom'ic
e'co·nom'i·cal
e'co·nom'i·cal·ly
e·con'o·mist
e·con'o·mize'
·mized' ·miz'ing
e·con'o·my
·mies
e'co·sys'tem
e'co·tone'
ec'ru
ec'sta·sy
·sies
ec·stat'ic
ec·stat'i·cal·ly
ec·u·men'i·cal
ec'ze·ma
ed'dy
·dies
e'del·weiss'
e·de'ma
·mas or ·ma·ta
edge
edged edg'ing
edge'ways'
edge'wise'
edg'i·ly
edg'i·ness
edg'y
·i·er ·i·est
ed'i·bil'i·ty
ed'i·ble
e'dict
ed'i·fi·ca'tion
ed'i·fice
ed'i·fy'
·fied' ·fy'ing
e·di'tion
(form of book;
SEE addition)
ed'i·tor
ed'i·to'ri·al
ed·i·to'ri·al·ize'
·ized' ·iz'ing
ed'i·to'ri·al·ly
ed·u·ca·bil'i·ty
ed'u·ca·ble
ed'u·cate'
·cat'ed ·cat'ing
ed'u·ca'tion
ed'u·ca'tive
ed'u·ca'tor
e·duce'
·duced' ·duc'ing
e·duc'i·ble
ee'rie or ·ry
·ri·er ·ri·est
ee'ri·ly
ee'ri·ness
ef·face'
·faced' ·fac'ing
ef·face'a·ble
ef·fect'
(result; SEE
affect)

ef·fec'tive
(*having effect;*
SEE *affective*)
ef·fec'tu·al
ef·fec'tu·ate'
·at'ed ·at'ing
ef·fem'i·na·cy
ef·fem'i·nate
ef'fer·ent
ef'fer·vesce'
·vesced'
·vesc'ing
ef'fer·ves'cence
ef'fer·ves'cent
ef·fete'
ef·fi·ca'cious
ef'fi·ca·cy
ef·fi'cien·cy
ef·fi'cient
ef'fi·gy
·gies
ef'flo·resce'
·resced'
·resc'ing
ef'flo·res'cence
ef'flu·ence
ef'flu·ent
(*flowing;* SEE
affluent)
ef·flu'vi·um
·vi·a *or* ·vi·ums
ef'fort
ef·fron'ter·y
·ies
ef·ful'gence
ef·fu'sion
ef·fu'sive
e·gal'i·tar'i·an
egg'nog'
egg'shell'
e'go
e'go·cen'tric
e'go·cen'tri·cal·ly
e'go·ism
e'go·ist
e'go·ma'ni·a
e'go·tism
e'go·tist
e'go·tis'tic
e'go·tis'ti·cal·ly
e·gre'gious
e'gress
e'gret
ei'der·down'
ei·det'ic
eight'een'
eighth
eight'i·eth
eight'y
·ies
ei'ther
ei'ther-or'
e·jac'u·late'
·lat'ed ·lat'ing
e·jac'u·la'tion
e·jac'u·la'tor
e·ject'
e·jec'tion

e·jec'tor
eke
eked ek'ing
e·kis'tics
e·kis'ti·cal
e·lab'o·rate'
·rat'ed ·rat'ing
e·lab'o·rate·ly
e·lab'o·ra'tion
e·lapse'
·lapsed'
·laps'ing
e·las'tic
e·las'tic·i·ty
e·las'ti·cize'
·cized' ·ciz'ing
e·late'
·lat'ed ·lat'ing
e·la'tion
el'bow·room'
eld'er·ly
eld'est
e·lec'tion
e·lec'tion·eer'
e·lec'tive
e·lec'tor
e·lec'tor·al
e·lec'tor·ate
e·lec'tric
e·lec'tri·cal
e·lec'tri·cal·ly
e·lec·tri'cian
e·lec'tric·i·ty
e·lec'tri·fi·ca'tion
e·lec'tri·fy'
·fied' ·fy'ing
e·lec'tro·cute'
·cut'ed ·cut'ing
e·lec'tro·cu'tion
e·lec'trode
e·lec'trol'y·sis
e·lec'tro·lyte'
e·lec'tro·lyt'ic
e·lec'tro·lyze'
·lyzed' ·lyz'ing
e·lec'tro·mag'net
e·lec·trom'e·ter
e·lec'tro·mo'tive
e·lec'tron
e·lec·tron'ic
e·lec·tron'i·cal·ly
e·lec'tro·plate'
e·lec'tro·scope'
e·lec'tro·stat'ics
e·lec'tro·ther'a·py
e·lec'tro·type'
e·lec'tro·typ'y
el·ee·mos'y·nar'y
el'e·gance
el'e·gant
el'e·gi'ac
el'e·gize'
·gized' ·giz'ing
el'e·gy
·gies
el'e·ment
el'e·men'tal
el'e·men'ta·ri·ness

el'e·men'ta·ry
(*basic;* SEE
alimentary)
el'e·phant .
el'e·phan·ti'a·sis
el'e·phan'tine
El'eu·sin'i·an
el'e·vate'
·vat'ed ·vat'ing
el'e·va'tion
el'e·va'tor
e·lev'enth
elf
elves
elf'in
e·lic'it
(*draw forth;*
SEE *illicit*)
e·lide'
·lid'ed ·lid'ing
el'i·gi·bil'i·ty
el'i·gi·ble
el'i·gi·bly
e·lim'i·nate'
·nat'ed ·nat'ing
e·lim'i·na'tion
e·li'sion
e·lite' *or* é·lite'
e·lix'ir
E·liz'a·be'than
el·lipse'
el·lip'sis
·ses
el·lip'ti·cal
el·lip'ti·cal·ly
el'o·cu'tion
e·lon'gate
·gat'ed ·gat'ing
e·lon'ga'tion
e·lope'
·loped' ·lop'ing
e·lope'ment
el'o·quence
el'o·quent
else'where'
e·lu'ci·date'
·dat'ed ·dat'ing
e·lu'ci·da'tion
e·lude'
·lud'ed ·lud'ing
(*escape;* SEE
allude)
e·lu'sion
(*an escape;* SEE
allusion, illusion)
e·lu'sive
(*hard to grasp;*
SEE *allusive,
illusive*)
e·ma'ci·ate'
·at'ed ·at'ing
e·ma'ci·a'tion
em'a·nate'
·nat'ed ·nat'ing
em'a·na'tion
e·man'ci·pate'
·pat'ed ·pat'ing
e·man'ci·pa'tion

e·man'ci·pa'tor
e·mas'cu·late'
·lat'ed ·lat'ing
e·mas'cu·la'tion
e·mas'cu·la'tor
em·balm'
em·bank'ment
em·bar'go
·goes
·goed ·go·ing
em·bark'
em·bar·ka'tion
em·bar'rass
em·bar'rass·ment
em'bas·sy
·sies
em·bat'tle
·tled ·tling
em·bed'
em·bel'lish
em'ber
em·bez'zle
·zled ·zling
em·bez'zler
em·bla'zon
em'blem
em·blem·at'ic
em·bod'i·ment
em·bod'y
·ied ·y·ing
em·bold'en
em'bo·lism
em'bo·lus
·li
em·boss'
em·bou·chure'
em·brace'
·braced'
·brac'ing
em·brace'a·ble
em·bra'sure
em·broi'der
em·broi'der·y
·ies
em·broil'
em'bry·o'
·os'
em'bry·ol'o·gy
em'bry·on'ic
em·cee'
·ceed' ·cee'ing
e·mend'
(*to correct;*
SEE *amend*)
e'men·da'tion
em'er·ald
e·merge'
·merged'
·merg'ing
(*appear;* SEE
immerge)
e·mer'gence
e·mer'gen·cy
·cies
e·mer'i·tus
em'er·y
e·met'ic
em'i·grant

em'i·grate'
·grat'ed
·grat'ing
em'i·gra'tion
em'i·nence
em'i·nent
(*prominent;* SEE
imminent)
em'is·sar'y
·ies
e·mis'sion
e·mit'
·mit'ted
·mit'ting
e·mol'li·ent
e·mol'u·ment
e·mo'tion·al
e·mo'tion·al·ize'
·ized' ·iz'ing
em·path'ic
em'pa·thize'
·thized' ·thiz'ing
em'pa·thy
em'pen·nage'
em'per·or
em'pha·sis
·ses'
em'pha·size'
·sized' ·siz'ing
em·phat'ic
em·phy·se'ma
em'pire
em·pir'i·cal
em·pir'i·cism
em·place'ment
em·ploy'
em·ploy'a·ble
em·ploy'ee
em·ploy'er
em·ploy'ment
em·po'ri·um
·ri·ums *or* ·ri·a
em·pow'er
em'press
emp'ti·ly
emp'ti·ness
emp'ty
·ti·er ·ti·est
·ties
·tied ·ty·ing
emp'ty-hand'ed
emp'ty-head'ed
em'u·late'
·lat'ed ·lat'ing
em·u·la'tion
em'u·lous
e·mul'si·fi·ca'tion
e·mul'si·fi'er
e·mul'si·fy'
·fied' ·fy'ing
e·mul'sion
en·a'ble
·bled ·bling
en·act'ment
en·am'el
·eled *or* ·elled
·el·ing *or*
·el·ling

en·am'el·ware'
en·am'ored
en·camp'ment
en·case'
·cased' ·cas'ing
en·ceph'a·li'tis
en·chant'ment
en·chi·la'da
en·cir'cle
en'clave
en·close'
·closed'
·clos'ing
en·clo'sure
en·code'
en·co'mi·ast'
en·co'mi·um
·ums *or* ·a
en·com'pass
en'core
en·coun'ter
en·cour'age
·aged ·ag·ing
en·cour'age·ment
en·croach'
en·cum'ber
en·cum'brance
en·cyc'li·cal
en·cy'clo·pe'di·a
or ·pae'di·a
en·dan'ger
en·dear'
en·dear'ment
en·deav'or
en·dem'ic
end'ing
en'dive
end'less
end'most'
en·do·crine'
en·dog'a·my
en·do·me'tri·um
en·dorse'
·dorsed'
·dors'ing
en·dor·see'
en·dorse'ment
en·dors'er
en·dow'
en·dow'ment
end'pa'per
en·dur'a·ble
en·dur'a·bly
en·dur'ance
en·dure'
·dured' ·dur'ing
end'ways'
en·e·ma
en'e·my
·mies
en·er·get'ic
en·er·get'i·cal·ly
en'er·gize'
·gized' ·giz'ing
en'er·giz'er
en'er·gy
·gies

en'er·vate'
·vat'ed ·vat'ing
n·fee'ble
·bled ·bling
n'fi·lade'
·lad'ed ·lad'ing
n·fold'
n·force'
·forced'
·forc'ing
n·force'a·ble
n·fran'chise
·gage'
gaged' ·gag'ing
·gage'ment
·gen'der
'gine
'gi·neer'
ng'lish
·gorge'
gorged' ·gorg'ing
·grave'
graved'
grav'ing
·grav'er
·gross'
·gulf'
·hance'
·anced'
anc'ing
·ig'ma
ig·mat'ic
ig·mat'i·cal·ly
join'
joy'a·ble
joy'a·bly
joy'ment
kin'dle
·led ·dling
·lace'
·large'
·rged'
·rg'ing
·large'ment
·larg'er
ight'en
ight'en·ment
·ist'
·ist'ment
·iv'en
·nasse
·nesh'
·ni·ty
·s
·o'ble
·ed ·bling
·ui
·r'mi·ty
·s
·r'mous
·ugh'
·ane'
·age'
·ap'ture
·ed ·tur·ing
·ch'
·oll' or ·rol'
·led' ·roll'ing

en·roll'ee'
en·roll'ment or
en·rol'ment
en route'
en·sconce'
·sconced'
·sconc'ing
en·sem'ble
en·shrine'
·shrined'
·shrin'ing
en'sign
en·slave'
en·snare'
en·snarl'
en·sue'
·sued' ·su'ing
en·sure'
en·tail'
en·tan'gle
en·tente'
en'ter·prise'
en'ter·pris'ing
en'ter·tain'
en·thrall' or
en·thral'
·thralled'
·thrall'ing
en·throne'
en·thuse'
·thused'
·thus'ing
en·thu'si·asm
en·thu'si·as'tic
en·thu'si·as'ti·cal·ly
en·tice'
·ticed' ·tic'ing
en·tice'ment
en·tire'
en·tire'ly
en·tire'ty
·ties
en·ti'tle
·tled ·tling
en'ti·ty
·ties
en·tomb'
en·to·mol'o·gy
(insect study; SEE etymology)
en'tou·rage'
en·tr'acte'
en'trails
en·train'
en'trance
en·trance'
·tranced'
·tranc'ing
en'trant
en·trap'
en·treat'
en·treat'y
·ies
en·tree or ·trée
en·trench'ment
en·tre·pre·neur'
en·trust'

en'try
·tries
en·twine'
e·nu'mer·ate'
·at'ed ·at'ing
e·nu'mer·a'tion
e·nu'mer·a'tor
e·nun'ci·ate'
·at'ed ·at'ing
(pronounce; SEE annunciate)
e·nun'ci·a'tion
e·nun'ci·a'tor
en·vel'op v.
en've·lope' n.
en·ven'om
en'vi·a·ble
en'vi·a·bly
en'vi·ous
en·vi'ron·ment
en·vi'ron·men'tal
en·vi'rons
en·vis'age
·aged ·ag·ing
en·vi'sion
en'voy
en'vy
·vies
·vied ·vy·ing
en'zyme
e·o·lith'ic
e'on
ep'au·let' or ·lette'
e·pergne'
e·phem'er·al
ep'ic
(poem; SEE epoch)
ep'i·cen'ter
ep'i·cure'
ep'i·cu·re'an
ep'i·dem'ic
ep'i·der'mis
ep'i·glot'tis
ep'i·gram'
ep'i·gram·mat'ic
ep'i·gram·mat'i·cal·ly
ep'i·graph'
ep'i·graph'ic
ep'i·graph'i·cal·ly
ep'i·lep'sy
ep'i·lep'tic
ep'i·logue' or ·log'
E·piph'a·ny
e·pis'co·pal
E·pis'co·pa'li·an
ep'i·sode'
ep'i·sod'ic
ep'i·sod'i·cal·ly
e·pis'tle
e·pis'to·lar'y
ep'i·taph
ep'i·the'li·al
ep'i·the'li·um
·li·ums or ·li·a

ep'i·thet'
e·pit'o·me
e·pit'o·mize'
·mized' ·miz'ing
ep'och
(period; SEE epic)
ep'och·al
ep'o·nym'
ep·ox'y
ep'si·lon'
eq·ua·bil'i·ty
eq'ua·ble
eq'ua·bly
e'qual
·qualed or
·qualled
·qual·ing or
·qual·ling
e·qual'i·tar'i·an
e·qual'i·ty
·ties
e'qual·i·za'tion
e'qual·ize'
·ized' ·iz'ing
e'qual·ly
e'qua·nim'i·ty
e·quate'
·quat'ed
·quat'ing
e·qua'tion
e·qua'tor
e'qua·to'ri·al
eq'uer·ry
·ries
e·ques'tri·an
e·ques'tri·enne'
e'qui·an'gu·lar
e'qui·dis'tant
e'qui·lat'er·al
e·quil'i·brant
e·quil'i·brate'
·brat'ed ·brat'ing
e'qui·lib'ri·um
·ri·ums or ·ri·a
e'quine
e'qui·noc'tial
e'qui·nox'
e·quip'
·quipped'
·quip'ping
eq'ui·page
e·quip'ment
e·quip'tive
e'qui·poise'
e'qui·pol'lent
eq'ui·ta·ble
eq'ui·ta·bly
eq'ui·ty
·ties
e·quiv'a·lence
e·quiv'a·lent
e·quiv'o·cal
e·quiv'o·cal·ly
e·quiv'o·cate'
·cat'ed ·cat'ing
e·quiv'o·ca'tion
e·quiv'o·ca'tor
e'ra
e·rad'i·ca·ble

e·rad'i·cate'
·cat'ed ·cat'ing
e·rad'i·ca'tion
e·rad'i·ca'tor
e·ras'a·ble
e·rase'
·rased' ·ras'ing
e·ras'er
e·ra'sure
e·rec'tile
e·rec'tion
e·rec'tor
erg
er'go
er·gos'ter·ol'
er'got
er'mine
e·rode'
·rod'ed ·rod'ing
e·rog'e·nous
e·ro'sion
e·ro'sive
e·rot'ic
e·rot'i·ca
e·rot'i·cal·ly
e·rot'i·cism
er'o·tism
e·ro·to·gen'ic
err
er'ran·cy
·cies
er'rand
er'rant
er·ra'ta
(sing. er·ra'tum)
er·rat'ic
er·rat'i·cal·ly
er·ro'ne·ous
er'ror
er'satz
erst'while'
e·ruct'
e·ruc'tate
·tat'ed ·tat·ing
e·ruc·ta'tion
er'u·dite'
er·u·di'tion
e·rupt'
e·rupt'i·ble
e·rup'tion
e·rup'tive
e·ryth'ro·my'cin
es'ca·drille'
es'ca·lade'
·lad'ed ·lad'ing
es'ca·late'
·lat'ed ·lat'ing
es·ca·la'tion
es'ca·la'tor
es·cal'lop or ·op
es'ca·pade'
es·cape'
·caped' ·cap'ing
es·cap·ee'
es·cape'ment
es·cap'ism
es·cap'ist

es'ca·role'
es·carp'ment
es'cha·rot'ic
es·cha·tol'o·gy
es·cheat'
es·chew'
es·chew'al
es'cort
es·cri·toire'
es'crow
es'cu·lent
es·cutch'eon
Es'ki·mo'
·mos' or ·mo'
e·soph'a·gus
·a·gi'
es·o·ter'ic
es·o·ter'i·cal·ly
es'pa·drille'
es·pal'ier
es·pe'cial
es·pe'cial·ly
Es'pe·ran'to
es'pi·o·nage'
es'pla·nade'
es·pous'al
es·pouse'
·poused' ·pous'ing
es·pres'so
·sos
es·prit' de corps'
es·py'
·pied' ·py'ing
es'quire
es·say'
(try; SEE assay)
es'say·ist
es'sence
es·sen'tial
es·sen·ti·al'i·ty
es·sen'tial·ly
es·tab'lish
es·tab'lish·ment
es·tate'
es·teem'
es'thete
es·thet'ic
es·thet'i·cal·ly
es·thet'i·cism
es'ti·ma·ble
es'ti·mate'
·mat'ed ·mat'ing
es·ti·ma'tion
es'ti·ma'tor
es'ti·val
es'ti·vate'
·vat'ed ·vat'ing
es·trange'
·tranged'
·trang'ing
es·trange'ment
es'tro·gen
es'trous adj.
es'trus n.
es·tu·ar'i·al
es'tu·ar'y
·ies
et cet'er·a

et·cet'er·as
etch'ing
e·ter'nal
e·ter'nal·ly
e·ter'ni·ty
·ties
e'ther
e·the're·al
e·the're·al·ize'
·ized' ·iz'ing
e'ther·ize'
·ized' ·iz'ing
eth'i·cal
eth'i·cal·ly
eth'ics
eth'nic
eth'ni·cal·ly
eth'no·cen'tri·
cal·ly
eth'no·cen'trism
eth·nog'ra·phy
eth·no·log'i·cal
eth·nol'o·gy
e'thos
eth'yl
e·ti·ol'o·gy
et'i·quette
é'tude
et'y·mo·log'i·cal
et'y·mol'o·gy
·gies
(word study; SEE
entomology)
et'y·mon'
eu·ca·lyp'tus
·tus·es or ·ti
Eu'cha·rist
eu'chre
eu·gen'i·cal·ly
eu·gen'ics
eu'lo·gize'
·gized' ·giz'ing
eu'lo·gy
·gies
eu'nuch
eu'phe·mism
eu'phe·mis'tic
eu'phe·mis'ti·
cal·ly
eu'phe·mize'
·mized' ·miz'ing
eu·phon'ic
eu·pho'ni·ous
eu·pho'ni·um
eu'pho·ny
·nies
eu·pho'ri·a
eu·phor'ic
eu'phu·ism
eu'phu·is'tic
Eur·a'sian
Eur'a·tom'
eu·re'ka
Eu'ro·crat'
Eu'ro·dol'lars
Eu'ro·pe'an
eu·ryth'mics
eu·ryth'my

Eu·sta'chi·an
eu·tha·na'si·a
e·vac'u·ate'
·at'ed ·at'ing
e·vac'u·a'tion
e·vac'u·ee'
e·vade'
·vad'ed ·vad'ing
e·val'u·ate'
·at'ed ·at'ing
e·val'u·a'tion
ev'a·nesce'
·nesced' ·nesc'ing
ev'a·nes'cence
ev'a·nes'cent
e'van·gel'i·cal
e'van·gel'i·cal·ly
e·van'gel·ism
e·van'gel·ist
e·van'gel·is'tic
e·van'gel·ize'
·ized' ·iz'ing
e·vap'o·rate'
·rat'ed ·rat'ing
e·vap'o·ra'tion
e·va'sion
e·va'sive
e'ven·hand'ed
eve'ning
e'ven·ness
e·vent'
e'ven·tem'pered
e·vent'ful
e·ven'tu·al
e·ven'tu·al'i·ty
·ties
e·ven'tu·al·ly
e·ven'tu·ate'
·at'ed ·at'ing
ev'er·glade'
ev'er·green'
ev'er·last'ing
ev'er·more'
e·vert'
ev'er·y·bod'y
ev'er·y·day'
ev'er·y·one
ev'er·y·thing'
ev'er·y·where'
e·vict'
e·vic'tion
ev'i·dence
·denced ·denc·ing
ev'i·dent
ev'i·den'tial
e'vil·do'er
e'vil·ly
e'vil·mind'ed
e·vince'
·vinced'
·vinc'ing
e·vin'ci·ble
e·vis'cer·ate'
·at'ed ·at'ing
e·vis'cer·a'tion
ev'o·ca'tion
e·voke'
·voked' ·vok'ing

ev'o·lu'tion
ev'o·lu'tion·ar'y
ev'o·lu'tion·ist
e·volve'
·volved' ·volv'ing
ewe
(sheep; SEE yew)
ew'er
ex·ac'er·bate'
·bat'ed ·bat'ing
ex·ac'er·ba'tion
ex·act'
ex·act'ing
ex·ac'tion
ex·ac'ti·tude'
ex·act'ly
ex·ag'ger·ate'
·at'ed ·at'ing
ex·ag'ger·a'tion
ex·ag'ger·a'tor
ex·alt'
ex·al·ta'tion
ex·am'i·na'tion
ex·am'ine
·ined ·in·ing
ex·am'in·er
ex·am'ple
ex·as'per·ate'
·at'ed ·at'ing
ex·as'per·a'tion
ex' ca·the'dra
ex'ca·vate'
·vat'ed ·vat'ing
ex'ca·va'tion
ex'ca·va'tor
ex·ceed'
(surpass; SEE
accede)
ex·ceed'ing·ly
ex·cel'
·celled' ·cel'ling
ex'cel·lence
ex'cel·len·cy
·cies
ex'cel·lent
ex·cel'si·or'
ex·cept'
(omit; SEE accept)
ex·cept'ed
(left out; SEE
accepted)
ex·cep'tion
ex·cep'tion·a·ble
ex·cep'tion·al
ex·cep'tion·al·ly
ex·cerpt'
ex·cess'
(surplus; SEE
access)
ex·ces'sive
ex·ces'sive·ly
ex·change'
·changed'
·chang'ing
ex·change'·
a·bil'i·ty
ex·change'a·ble
ex·cheq'uer

ex·cis'a·ble
ex'cise
ex·cise'
·cised' ·cis'ing
ex·ci'sion
ex·cit'a·bil'i·ty
ex·cit'a·ble
ex·cit'a·bly
ex·ci·ta'tion
ex·cite'
·cit'ed ·cit'ing
ex·cite'ment
ex·claim'
ex·cla·ma'tion
ex·clam'a·to'ry
ex'clave
ex·clud'a·ble
ex·clude'
·clud'ed
·clud'ing
ex·clu'sion
ex·clu'sive
ex'clu·siv'i·ty
ex'com·mu'ni·
cate'
·cat'ed ·cat'ing
ex·co'ri·ate'
·at'ed ·at'ing
ex·co'ri·a'tion
ex'cre·ment
ex·cres'cence
ex·crete'
·cret'ed
·cret'ing
ex·cre'tion
ex·cre'to·ry
ex·cru'ci·ate'
·at'ed ·at'ing
ex'cul·pate'
·pat'ed ·pat'ing
ex'cul·pa'tion
ex·cur'sion
ex·cus'a·ble
ex·cus'a·bly
ex·cuse'
·cused' ·cus'ing
ex·e·cra·ble
ex'e·crate'
·crat'ed
·crat'ing
ex'e·cra'tion
ex'e·cute'
·cut'ed ·cut'ing
ex·e·cu'tion
ex·e·cu'tion·er
ex·ec'u·tive
ex·ec'u·tor
ex'e·ge'sis
ex·em'plar
ex·em·pla'ri·ly
ex·em'pla·ri·ness
ex·em'pla·ry
ex·em'pli·fi·
ca'tion
ex·em'pli·fy'
·fied' ·fy'ing
ex·empt'
ex·emp'tion

ex'er·cis'a·ble
ex'er·cise'
·cised' ·cis'ing
(use; SEE exorcise)
ex·ert'
ex·er'tion
ex'e·unt
ex'ha·la'tion
ex·hale'
·haled' ·hal'ing
ex·haust'
ex·haust'i·ble
ex·haus'tion
ex·haus'tive
ex·hib'it
ex·hi·bi'tion
ex·hi·bi'tion·ism
ex·hib'i·tor
ex·hil'a·rant
ex·hil'a·rate'
·rat'ed ·rat'ing
ex·hil'a·ra'tion
ex·hort'
ex'hor·ta'tion
ex·hu·ma'tion
ex·hume'
·humed'
·hum'ing
ex'i·gen·cy
·cies
ex'i·gent
ex'ile
ex·ist'
ex·ist'ence
ex·ist'ent
ex'is·ten'tial
ex'is·ten'tial·ism
ex'it
ex'o·dus
ex' of·fi'ci·o'
ex·og'a·my
ex·on'er·ate'
·at'ed ·at'ing
ex·on'er·a'tion
ex'o·ra·ble
ex·or'bi·tance
ex·or'bi·tant
ex'or·cise' or
·cize'
·cised' or ·cized'
·cis'ing or ·ciz'ing
(expel; SEE
exercise)
ex'or·cism
ex·o·ter'ic
ex·ot'ic
ex·ot'i·ca
ex·ot'i·cal·ly
ex·pand'
ex·panse'
ex·pan'si·ble
ex·pan'sion
ex·pan'sive
ex·pa'ti·ate'
·at'ed ·at'ing
ex·pa'ti·a'tion
ex·pa'tri·ate'
·at'ed ·at'ing

ex·pa'tri·a'tion
ex·pect'
ex·pect'an·cy
ex·pect'ant
ex·pec·ta'tion
ex·pec'to·rant
ex·pec'to·rate'
·rat'ed ·rat'ing
ex·pec'to·ra'tion
ex·pe'di·ence
ex·pe'di·en·cy
·cies
ex·pe'di·ent
ex'pe·dite'
·dit'ed ·dit'ing
ex'pe·dit'er
ex·pe·di'tion
ex·pe·di'tion·ar'y
ex·pe·di'tious
ex·pel'
·pelled' ·pel'ling
ex·pel'la·ble
ex·pel·lee'
ex·pend'
ex·pend'a·bil'i·ty
ex·pend'a·ble
ex·pend'i·ture
ex·pense'
ex·pen'sive
ex·pen'sive·ly
ex·pe'ri·ence
·enced ·enc·ing
ex·pe'ri·en'tial
ex·per'i·ment
ex·per'i·men'tal
ex·per'i·men·
ta'tion
ex'pert
ex'pert·ise'
ex'pi·a·ble
ex'pi·ate'
·at'ed ·at'ing
ex'pi·a'tion
ex'pi·a'tor
ex'pi·ra'tion
ex·pir'a·to'ry
ex·pire'
·pired' ·pir'ing
ex·plain'a·ble
ex'pla·na'tion
ex·plan'a·to'ry
ex'ple·tive
ex'pli·ca·ble
ex'pli·cate'
·cat'ed ·cat'ing
ex'pli·ca'tion
ex·plic'it
ex·plod'a·ble
ex·plode'
·plod'ed
·plod'ing
ex'ploit
ex'ploi·ta'tion
ex'plo·ra'tion
ex·plor'a·to'ry
ex·plore'
·plored'
·plor'ing

ex·plor'er
ex·plo'sion
ex·plo'sive
ex·po'nent
ex·po·nen'tial
ex·port'
ex·por·ta'tion
ex·pose'
·posed' ·pos'ing
ex'po·sé'
ex·po·si'tion
ex·pos'i·tor
ex·pos'i·to'ry
ex post fac'to
ex·pos'tu·late'
·lat'ed ·lat'ing
ex·pos'tu la'tion
ex·pos'tu la'tor
ex·po'sur
ex·pound'
ex·press'
ex·press'age
ex·press'i·ble
ex·pres'.ion
ex·pres'.ion·ism
ex·pre. sion·
  is'tic
ex·pre.'sive
ex·press'man
ex·press'way
ex·pr /'pri·ate'
·at'ed ·at'ing
ex·pro'pri·a'tion
ex·pul'sion
ex·punge'
·punged'
·pun_ing
x'pur·gate'
·gat'_d ·gat'ing
x'pu_ga'tion
x'qui site
x'tanι
(existing; SEE
extent)
x·tem'po·ra'ne·
ous
x·tem'po·re
x·tem'po·rize'
rized' ·riz'ing
x·tend'
x·ten'si·ble
x·ten'sion
x·ten'sive
.tent'
scope; SEE extant)
·ten'u·ate'
at'ed ·at'ing
·ten'u·a'tion
·te'ri·or
·ter'mi·nate'
nat'ed ·nat'ing
·ter'mi·na'tion
·ter'mi·na'tor
·ter'nal
·ter'nal·ize'
zed' ·iz'ing
·tinct'
·tinc'tion

ex·tin'guish
ex'tir·pate'
·pat'ed ·pat'ing
ex'tir·pa'tion
ex·tol' or ·toll'
·tolled' ·tol'ling
ex·tort'
ex·tor'tion
ex·tor'tion·ate
ex·tor'tion·er
ex·tor'tion·ist
ex'tra
ex·tract'
ex·tract'a·ble
or ·i·ble
ex·trac'tion
ex·trac'tor
ex'tra·cur·ric'u·
lar
ex'tra·dit'a·ble
ex'tra·dite'
·dit'ed ·dit'ing
ex·tra·di'tion
ex'tra·le'gal
ex'tra·mar'i·tal
ex'tra·mu'ral
ex·tra'ne·ous
ex·traor'di·
nar'i·ly
ex·traor'di·
nar'y
ex·trap'o·late'
·lat'ed ·lat'ing
ex'tra·sen'so·ry
ex'tra·ter'ri·
to'ri·al
ex·trav'a·gance
ex·trav'a·gant
ex·trav'a·gan'za
ex'tra·ve·hic'u·lar
ex·treme'
ex·treme'ly
ex·trem'ism
ex·trem'ist
ex·trem'i·ty
ex'tri·cate'
·cat'ed ·cat'ing
ex·tri·ca'tion
ex·trin'sic
ex·trin'si·cal·ly
ex 'ro·ver'sion
ex'tr ·vert'
ex·trude'
·trud'ed
·trud'ing
ex·tru'sion
ex·u'ber·ance
ex·u'ber·ant
ex'u·da'tion
ex·ude'
·ud'ed ·ud'ing
ex·ult'
ex·ult'ant
ex·ul·ta'tion
ex'urb'
ex·ur'ban·ite'
ex·ur'bi·a

eye
eyed eye'ing
or ey'ing
eye'ball'
eye'brow'
eye'-catch'er
eye'cup'
eye'ful'
eye'glass'
eye'hole'
eye'lash'
eye'let
(hole; SEE islet)
eye'lid'
eye liner
eye'-o'pen·er
eye'piece'
eye shadow
eye'shot'
eye'sight'
eye'sore'
eye'strain'
eye'tooth'
eye'wash'
eye'wink'
eye'wit'ness

F

fa'ble
·bled ·bling
fab'ric
fab'ri·cate'
·cat'ed ·cat'ing
fab'ri·ca'tion
fab'ri·ca'tor
Fab'ri·koid'
fab'u·lous
fa·çade' or ·cade'
face
faced fac'ing
face'plate'
face'-sav'ing
fac'et
fa·ce'tious
fa'cial
fac'ile
fa·cil'i·tate'
·tat'ed ·tat'ing
fa·cil·i·ta'tion
fa·cil'i·ty
·ties
fac·sim'i·le
·led ·ie·ing
fac'tion
fac'tious
fac·ti'tious
(artificial; SEE
fictitious)
fac'tor
fac·to'ri·al
fac'to·ry
·ries
fac·to'tum
fac'tu·al
fac'tu·al·ly

fac'ul·ty
·ties
fad'dish
fad'dism
fade
fad'ed fad'ing
fade'-in'
fade'-out'
fag
fagged
fag'ging
fag'ot·ing
Fahr'en·heit'
fail'-safe'
fail'ure
faint
(weak; SEE feint)
faint'heart'ed
fair'ground'
fair'-haired'
fair'ly
fair'-mind'ed
fair'-spo'ken
fair'-trade'
fair'way'
fair'-weath'er
fair'y
·ies
fair'y·land'
faith'ful
faith'ful·ly
faith'less
fake
faked fak'ing
fak'er
(fraud)
fa·kir'
(Moslem beggar)
fal'cate
fal'con
fal'con·ry
fall
fell fall'en
fall'ing
fal·la'cious
fal'la·cy
·cies
fal'li·bil'i·ty
fal'li·ble
fal'li·bly
fall'ing-out'
fall'off'
fall'out'
fal'low
false
fals'er fals'est
false'heart'ed
false'hood'
fal·set'to
fal'si·fi·ca'tion
fal'si·fi'er
fal'si·fy'
·fied' ·fy'ing
fal'si·ty
·ties
fal'ter
fa·mil'ial
fa·mil'iar

fa·mil'i·ar'i·ty
·ties
fa·mil'iar·i·
za'tion
fa·mil'iar·ize'
·ized' ·iz'ing
fam'i·ly
·lies
fam'ine
fam'ish
fa'mous
fan
fanned fan'ning
fa·nat'ic
fa·nat'i·cal·ly
fa·nat'i·cism
fan'ci·ful
fan'cy
·cies
·ci·er ·ci·est
·cied ·cy·ing
fan'cy-free'
fan'cy·work'
fan'fare'
fan'light'
fan'tail'
fan·ta'si·a
fan'ta·size'
·sized' ·siz'ing
fan·tas'tic
fan·tas'ti·cal·ly
fan'ta·sy
·sies
far
far'ther
far'thest
far'ad
far'a·day'
far'a·way'
farce
farced farc'ing
far'ci·cal
far'ci·cal·ly
fare
fared far'ing
fare'well'
far'fetched'
far'-flung'
fa·ri'na
far'i·na'ceous
farm'hand'
farm'house'
farm'stead'
farm'yard'
far'o
far'-off'
far'-out'
far'-reach'ing
far'row
far'see'ing
far'sight'ed
far'ther
far'thing
fas'ces
fas'ci·cle
fas'ci·nate'
·nat'ed ·nat'ing

fas'ci·na'tion
fas'ci·na'tor
fas'cism
fas'cist
fash'ion
fash'ion·a·ble
fash'ion·a·bly
fast'back'
fas'ten
fas'ten·er
fas'ten·ing
fas·tid'i·ous
fat
fat'ter fat'test
fat'ted fat'ting
fa'tal
fa'tal·ism
fa'tal·ist
fa'tal·is'tic
fa·tal·is'ti·cal·ly
fa·tal'i·ty
·ties
fa'tal·ly
fate'ful
fa'ther·hood'
fa'ther-in-law'
fa'thers-
in-law'
fa'ther·land'
fa'ther·less
fa'ther·li·ness
fa'ther·ly
fath'om
fath'om·a·ble
fath'om·less
fat'i·ga·ble
fa·tigue'
·tigued'
·tigu'ing
fat'-sol'u·ble
fat'ten
fat'ti·ness
fat'ty
·ti·er ·ti·est
fa·tu'i·ty
·ties
fat'u·ous
fat'-wit'ted
fau'cet
fault'find'ing
fault'i·ness
fault'less
fault'y
·i·er ·i·est
faun
(deity; SEE fawn)
fau'na
·nas or ·nae
faux' pas'
faux' pas'
fa'vor·a·ble
fa'vor·a·bly
fa'vored
fa'vor·ite
fa'vor·it·ism
fawn
(deer; act ser-
vilely; SEE faun)

faze
  fazed faz′ing
  (*disturb;* SEE
  phase)
fe′al·ty
fear′ful
fear′ful·ly
fear′less
fear′some
fea·si·bil′i·ty
fea′si·ble
fea′si·bly
feast
feat
  (*deed;* SEE feet)
feath′er·bed′
feath′er·
  bed′ding
feath′er·
  brain′
feath′ered
feath′er·edge′
feath′er·i·ness
feath′er·stitch′
feath′er·weight′
feath′er·y
fea′ture
  ·tured ·tur·ing
fea′ture-length′
feb′ri·fuge′
fe′brile
Feb′ru·ar′y
fe′cal
fe′ces
feck′less
fe′cund
fe′cun·date′
  ·dat′ed ·dat′ing
fe·cun′di·ty
fed′er·al
fed′er·al·ism
fed′er·al·i·
  za′tion
fed′er·al·ize′
  ·ized′ ·iz′ing
fed′er·ate′
  ·at′ed ·at′ing
fed′er·a′tion
fe·do′ra
fee′ble
  ·bler ·blest
fee′ble·mind′ed
feed
  fed feed′ing
feed′back′
feel
  felt feel′ing
fee′-split′ting
feet
  (*pl. of foot;*
  SEE feat)
feign
feint
  (*pretense;* SEE
  faint)
fe·lic′i·tate′
  ·tat′ed ·tat′ing
fe·lic′i·ta′tion

fe·lic′i·tous
fe·lic′i·ty
  ·ties
fe′line
fel′low·ship′
fel′on
fe·lo′ni·ous
fel′o·ny
  ·nies
fe·luc′ca
fe′male
fem′i·nine
fem′i·nin′i·ty
fem′i·nism
fem′i·nize′
  ·nized′ ·niz′ing
femme fa·tale′
  femmes fa·tales′
fence
  fenced fenc′ing
fend′er
fen′es·tra′tion
fen′nel
fer′ment
fer′men·ta′tion
fern
fe·ro′cious
fe·roc′i·ty
fer′ret
fer′ri·age
Fer′ris wheel
fer′rule
  (*metal ring;*
  SEE ferule)
fer′ry
  ·ries
  ·ried ·ry·ing
fer′ry·boat′
fer′tile
fer·til′i·ty
fer′til·iz′a·ble
fer′til·i·za′tion
fer′til·ize′
  ·ized′ ·iz′ing
fer′til·iz′er
fer′ule
  (*stick;* SEE
  ferrule)
fer′vent
fer′vid
fer′vor
fes′cue
fes′tal
fes′ter
fes′ti·val
fes′tive
fes·tiv′i·ty
  ·ties
fes·toon′
fe′tal
fetch′ing
fete *or* fête
  fet′ed *or* fêt′ed
  fet′ing *or* fêt′ing
fe′ti·cide′
fet′id
fet′ish
fet′ish·ism

fet′lock′
fet′ter
fet′tle
fet′tuc·ci′ne
fe′tus
  ·tus·es
feu′dal
feu′dal·ism
feu′dal·is′tic
fe′ver·ish
fez
  fez′zes
fi·an·cé′ *masc.*
fi·an·cée′ *fem.*
fi·as′co
  ·coes *or* ·cos
fi′at
fib
  fibbed fib′bing
fib′ber
fi′ber *or* ·bre
fi′ber·board′
Fi′ber·glas′
fi′bril·la′tion
fi′broid
fi′brous
fib′u·la
  ·lae *or* ·las
fick′le
fic′tion·al·ize′
  ·ized′ ·iz′ing
fic·ti′tious
  (*imaginary;* SEE
  factitious)
fid′dle
  ·dled ·dling
fi·del′i·ty
  ·ties
fidg′et
fidg′et·i·ness
fidg′et·y
fi·du′ci·ar′y
  ·ies
field′er
field′-strip′
field′-test′
field′work′
fiend′ish
fierce
  fierc′er
  fierc′est
fierce′ly
fi′er·i·ness
fi′er·y
  ·i·er ·i·est
fi·es′ta
fif′teen′
fif′ti·eth
fif′ty
  ·ties
fight
  fought
  fight′ing
fig′ment
fig′u·ra′tion
fig′u·ra·tive
fig′ure
  ·ured ·ur·ing

fig′ure·head′
fig′u·rine′
fil′a·ment
fi′lar
fil′bert
file
  filed fil′ing
fi·let′ mi·gnon′
fil′i·al
fil′i·a′tion
fil′i·bus′ter
fil′i·gree′
  ·greed′
  ·gree′ing
fil′ings
Fil′i·pi′no
  ·nos
fil′let
fill′-in′
fill′ing
fil′lip
fil′ly
  ·lies
film′strip′
film′y
  ·i·er ·i·est
fil′ter
  (*strainer;* SEE
  philter)
fil′ter·a·ble
filth′i·ly
filth′i·ness
filth′y
  ·i·er ·i·est
fil′trate
  ·trat·ed ·trat·ing
fin′a·ble
fi·na′gle
  ·gled ·gling
fi·na′le
fi′nal·ist
fi·nal′i·ty
fi′nal·ize′
  ·ized′ ·iz′ing
fi′nal·ly
fi·nance′
  ·nanced′
  ·nanc′ing
fi·nan′cial
fi·nan′cial·ly
fin′an·cier′
find
  found find′ing
find′er
fine
  fin′er fin′est
  fined fin′ing
fine′-cut′
fine′-drawn′
fine′-grained′
fine′ly
fine′ness
fin′er·y
  ·ies
fine′spun′
fi·nesse′
  ·nessed′
  ·ness′ing

fine′-toothed′
fin′ger·board′
fin′gered
fin′ger·nail′
fin′ger·print′
finger tip
fin′i·al
fin′i·cal
fin′ick·i·ness
fin′ick·y
fi′nis
fin′ish
fin′ished
fi′nite
fin′nan had′die
fiord
fir
  (*tree;* SEE fur)
fire
  fired fir′ing
fire′arm′
fire′ball′
fire′boat′
fire′bomb′
fire′box′
fire′brand′
fire′break′
fire′brick′
fire′bug′
fire′clay′
fire′crack′er
fire′-cure′
fire′damp′
fire′dog′
fire′-eat′er
fire escape
fire′fly′
  ·flies′
fire′man
fire′place′
fire′plug′
fire′pow′er
fire′proof′
fire′side′
fire′trap′
fire′wa′ter
fire′wood′
fire′works′
fir′kin
fir′ma·ment
firm′ly
first′born′
first′-class′
first′hand′
first′ly
first′-rate′
firth
fis′cal
fis′cal·ly
fish′bowl′
fish′er·man
fish′er·y
  ·ies
fish′hook′
fish′i·ness
fish′mon′ger
fish′plate′
fish′pond′

fish′tail′
fish′wife′
fish′y
  ·i·er ·i·est
fis′sion
fis′sion·a·ble
fis′sure
  ·sured ·sur·ing
fis′ti·cuffs′
fis′tu·lous
fit
  fit′ted fit′ting
  fit′ter fit′test
fit′ful
fit′ful·ly
fit′ness
five′fold′
fix′ate
  ·at·ed ·at·ing
fix·a′tion
fix′a·tive
fixed
fix′ed·ly
fix′ture
fiz′zle
  ·zled ·zling
fjord
flab′ber·gast′
flab′bi·ness
flab′by
  ·bi·er ·bi·est
flac′cid
flac·cid′i·ty
fla·con′
flag
  flagged
  flag′ging
flag′el·lant
flag′el·late′
  ·lat′ed ·lat′ing
flag′el·la′tion
fla·gel′lum
  ·la *or* ·lums
flag′eo·let′
flag′on
flag′pole′
fla′gran·cy
fla′grant
flag′ship′
flag′stone′
flag′-wav′ing
flail
flair
  (*knack;* SEE flar[e])
flake
  flaked flak′ing
flak′i·ness
flak′y
  ·i·er ·i·est
flam·bé′
flam′beau
  ·beaux *or* ·bea[us]
flam·boy′ance
flam·boy′ant
flame
  flamed flam′in[g]
fla·men′co
  ·cos

flame'out'
flame'proof'
fla·min'go
 ·gos or ·goes
flam'ma·bil'i·ty
flam'ma·ble
flange
 flanged
 flang'ing
flank
flan'nel
flan'nel·ette'
flan'nel-mouthed'
flap
 flapped
 flap'ping
flap'jack'
flap'per
flare
 flared flar'ing
 (blaze; SEE flair)
flare'-up'
flash'back'
flash'bulb'
flash'card'
flash'cube'
flash'i·ly
flash'i·ness
flash'light'
flash'y
 ·i·er ·i·est
flat
 flat'ter flat'test
 flat'ted flat'ting
flat'boat'
flat'car'
flat'fish'
flat'-foot'ed
flat'i'ron
flat'ten
flat'ter
flat'ter·y
flat'u·lent
flat'ware'
flat'work'
flaunt
flau'tist
fla'vor·ful
fla'vor·ing
fla'vor·less
flaw'less
flax'en
flax'seed'
flea'-bit'ten
fledg'ling
flee
 fled flee'ing
fleece
 fleeced fleec'ing
fleec'i·ness
fleec'y
 ·i·er ·i·est
fleet'ing
flesh'-col'ored
flesh'i·ness
flesh'pots'
flesh'y
 ·i·er ·i·est

fleur'-de-lis'
 fleurs'-de-lis'
flex'i·bil'i·ty
flex'i·ble
flex'i·bly
flick'er
flied
 (only in baseball)
fli'er or fly'er
flight'i·ness
flight'less
flight'y
 ·i·er ·i·est
flim'si·ly
flim'si·ness
flim'sy
 ·si·er ·si·est
flinch'ing·ly
fling
 flung fling'ing
flint'lock'
flint'y
 ·i·er ·i·est
flip
 flipped flip'ping
flip'pan·cy
 ·cies
flip'pant
flip'per
flirt·ta'tion
flirt·ta'tious
flit
 flit'ted flit'ting
float'er
float'ing
floc'cu·late'
 ·lat'ed ·lat'ing
floc'cu·lent
floe
 (ice; SEE flow)
flog
 flogged
 flog'ging
flood'gate'
flood'light'
 ·light'ed or ·lit'
 ·light'ing
floor'ing
floor'walk'er
flop
 flopped
 flop'ping
flo'ra
 ·ras or ·rae
flo'ral
flo·res'cence
 (blooming; SEE
 fluorescence)
flo·res'cent
flo'ret
flo'ri·cul'ture
flor'id
Flor'i·da
flo·rid'i·ty
flor'in
flo'rist
floss'y
 ·i·er ·i·est

flo·ta'tion
flo·til'la
flot'sam
flounce
 flounced
 flounc'ing
floun'der
flour'ish
flout
flow
 (glide; SEE floe)
flow'ered
flow'er·i·ness
flow'er·pot'
flow'er·y
 ·i·er ·i·est
flu
 (influenza)
fluc'tu·ate'
 ·at'ed ·at'ing
flue
 (pipe)
flu'en·cy
flu'ent
fluf'fi·ness
fluf'fy
 ·fi·er ·fi·est
flu'id
flu·id'i·ty
flun'ky
 ·kies
flu'o·resce'
 ·resced'
 ·resc'ing
flu'o·res'cence
 (light; SEE
 florescence)
flu'o·res'cent
fluor'i·date'
 ·dat'ed ·dat'ing
fluor'i·da'tion
fluor'i·nate'
 ·nat'ed ·nat'ing
fluor'o·scope'
flu'o·ros'co·py
flur'ry
 ·ries
 ·ried ·ry·ing
flus'ter
flute
 flut'ed flut'ing
flut'ist
flut'ter
flu'vi·al
fly
 flies
 flew flown
 fly'ing
fly'a·ble
fly'a·way'
fly'-by-night'
fly'catch'er
fly'leaf'
 ·leaves
fly'pa'per
fly'speck'
fly'trap'
fly'weight'

fly'wheel'
foam'i·ness
foam'y
 ·i·er ·i·est
fo'cal
fo'cal·ize'
 ·ized' ·iz'ing
fo'cus
 ·cus·es or ·ci
 ·cused or ·cussed
 ·cus·ing or
 ·cus·sing
fod'der
fog
 fogged fog'ging
fog'bound'
fog'gi·ly
fog'gi·ness
fog'gy
 ·gi·er ·gi·est
fog'horn'
fo'gy or fo'gey
 ·gies or ·geys
foi'ble
foist
fold'a·way'
fold'er
fo'li·age
fo'li·ate'
 ·at'ed ·at'ing
fo'li·a'tion
fo'li·o'
 ·os', ·oed' ·o'ing
folk'lore'
folk'way'
fol'li·cle
fol'low·er
fol'low-through'
fol'low-up'
fol'ly
 ·lies
fo·ment'
fo'men·ta'tion
fon'dant
fon'dle
 ·dled ·dling
fond'ness
fon·due'
food'stuff'
fool'har'di·ness
fool'har'dy
fool'ish·ness
fool'proof'
fools'cap'
foot
 feet
foot'age
foot'ball'
foot'bridge'
foot'-can'dle
foot'fall'
foot'hold'
foot'ing
foot'lights'
foot'lock'er
foot'loose'
foot'note'
foot'path'

foot'-pound'
foot'print'
foot'race'
foot'rest'
foot'sore'
foot'step'
foot'stool'
foot'-ton'
foot'wear'
foot'work'
fop'pish
for'age
for'ay
for·bear'
 ·bore' ·borne'
 ·bear'ing
 (abstain; SEE
 forebear)
for·bear'ance
for·bid'
 ·bade' or ·bad'
 ·bid'den
 ·bid'ding
force
 forced forc'ing
force'ful
for'ceps
 ·ceps
for'ci·ble
for'ci·bly
fore'arm'
fore'bear'
 (ancestor; SEE
 forbear)
fore·bode'
 ·bod'ed ·bod'ing
fore'cast'
 ·cast' or ·cast'ed
 ·cast'ing
fore'cas'tle
fore·close'
fore·clo'sure
fore·doom'
fore'fa'ther
fore'fin'ger
fore'foot'
fore·go'
 ·went' ·gone'
 ·go'ing
 (precede; SEE
 forgo)
fore·go'ing
fore'ground'
fore'hand'
fore'hand'ed
fore'head
for'eign
for'eign-born'
for'eign·er
fore'knowl'edge
fore'leg'
fore'lock'
fore'man
fore'most'
fore'named'
fore'noon'
fo·ren'sic
fo·ren'si·cal·ly

fore·or·dain'
fore'paw'
fore'play'
fore'quar'ter
fore'run'ner
fore'sail'
fore·see'
 ·saw' ·seen'
 ·see'ing
fore·see'a·ble
fore·se'er
fore·shad'ow
fore·short'en
fore·show'
 ·showed',
 ·shown' or
 ·showed',
 ·show'ing
fore'sight'
fore'skin'
for'est
fore·stall'
for'est·a'tion
for'est·er
for'est·ry
fore'taste'
fore·tell'
 ·told' ·tell'ing
fore'thought'
for·ev'er
fore·warn'
fore'word'
 (preface; SEE
 forward)
for'feit
for'fei·ture
forge
 forged forg'ing
forg'er
forg'er·y
 ·ies
for·get'
 ·got', ·got'ten
 or ·got',
 ·get'ting
for·get'ful
for·get'-me-not'
for·get'ta·ble
for·giv'a·ble
for·give'
 ·gave' ·giv'en
 ·giv'ing
for·give'ness
for·go' or fore·
 ·went' ·gone'
 ·go'ing
 (do without;
 SEE forego)
forked
fork'lift'
for·lorn'
for'mal
form·al'de·hyde'
for·mal'i·ty
 ·ties
for'mal·i·za'tion
for'mal·ize'
 ·ized' ·iz'ing

for'mal·ly
for'mat
for·ma'tion
form'a·tive
for'mer
For·mi'ca
for'mi·da·ble
for'mi·da·bly
form'less
for'mu·la
·las or ·lae'
for'mu·late'
·lat'ed ·lat'ing
for·mu·la'tion
for'ni·cate'
·cat'ed ·cat'ing
for'ni·ca'tion
for'ni·ca'tor
for·sake'
·sook' ·sak'en
·sak'ing
for·swear'
·swore' ·sworn'
·swear'ing
for·syth'i·a
fort
(fortified place)
forte
(special skill)
forth'com'ing
forth'right'
forth'with'
for'ti·eth
for·ti·fi·ca'tion
for'ti·fi'er
for'ti·fy'
·fied' ·fy'ing
for'ti·tude'
for'tress
for·tu'i·tous
for·tu'i·ty
·ties
for'tu·nate
for'tune
for'tune·tell'er
for'ty
·ties
fo'rum
·rums or ·ra
for'ward
(to the front;
SEE foreword)
fos'sil
fos'ter
foul
(filthy; SEE fowl)
fou·lard'
foul'mouthed'
foun·da'tion
foun'der v.
found'er n.
found'ling
found'ry
·ries
foun'tain
foun'tain·head'
four'·flush'er
four'fold'

four'·foot'ed
Four'·H' club or
4'·H' club
four'·in·hand'
four'·post'er
four'score'
four'some
four'square'
four'·star'
four'teen'
fourth
fourth'·class'
four'·way'
fowl
(bird; SEE foul)
fox'hole'
fox'hound'
fox'i·ly
fox'i·ness
fox'y
·i·er ·i·est
foy'er
fra'cas
frac'tion
frac'tious
frac'ture
·tured ·tur·ing
frag'ile
fra·gil'i·ty
frag'ment
frag·men'tal·ly
frag'men·tar'y
fra'grance·
fra'grant
frail'ty
·ties
frame
framed
fram'ing
frame'·up'
frame'work'
franc
(coin; SEE frank)
fran'chise
·chised ·chis·ing
fran'gi·bil'i·ty
fran'gi·ble
frank
(free; SEE franc)
frank'furt·er
frank'in·cense'
fran'tic
fran'ti·cal·ly
frap·pé'
fra·ter'nal
fra·ter'nal·ly
fra·ter'ni·ty
·ties
frat'er·ni·za'tion
frat'er·nize'
·nized' ·niz'ing
frat'ri·cide'
fraud'u·lence
fraud'u·lent
fraught
freak'ish
freck'le
·led ·ling

free
fre'er fre'est
freed free'ing
free'bie or ·by
·bies
free'born'
freed'man
free'dom
free'·for·all'
free'·form'
free'hand'
free'·lance'
free'load·er
free'man
Free'ma·son
free'·spo'ken
free'·stand'ing
free'stone'
free'think'er
freq'way'
free'wheel'ing
freez'a·ble
freeze
froze froz'en
freez'ing
(become ice; SEE
frieze)
freeze'·dry'
-dried' -dry'ing
freez'er
freight'age
freight'er
French cuff
French doors
French fry
French fries
French toast
fre·net'ic
fre·net'i·cal·ly
fren'zy
·zies
·zied ·zy·ing
fre'quen·cy
·cies
fre'quent
fres'co
·coes or ·cos
fresh'en
fresh'et
fresh'man
fresh'wa'ter
fret
fret'ted
fret'ting
fret'ful
fret'ful·ly
fret'work'
Freud'i·an
fri'a·bil'i·ty
fri'a·ble
fri'ar
fric'as·see'
·seed' ·see'ing
fric'tion
Fri'day
friend'li·ness
friend'ly
·li·er ·li·est

friend'ship
frieze
(in architecture;
SEE freeze)
frig'ate
fright'ened
fright'ful
frig'id
fri·gid'i·ty
frill'y
·i·er ·i·est
fringe
fringed
fring'ing
frip'per·y
·ies
Fris'bee
fri·sé'
frisk'i·ness
frisk'y
·i·er ·i·est
frit'ter
friv·ol'i·ty
·ties
friv'o·lous
friz'zi·ness
frog'man'
frol'ic
·icked ·ick·ing
frol'ick·er
frol'ic·some
front'age
fron'tal
fron·tier'
fron·tiers'man
fron'tis·piece'
front'let
frost'bite'
·bit' ·bit'ten
·bit'ing
frost'i·ly
frost'i·ness
frost'ing
frost'y
·i·er ·i·est
froth'i·ly
froth'i·ness
froth'y
·i·er ·i·est
fro'ward
frown
frow'zi·ness
frow'zy
·zi·er ·zi·est
fro'zen
fruc'ti·fy'
·fied' ·fy'ing
fru'gal
fru·gal'i·ty
fru'gal·ly
fruit'cake'
fruit'ful
fruit'i·ness
fru·i'tion
fruit'less
fruit'wood'
fruit'y
·i·er ·i·est

frump'ish
frus'trate
·trat·ed ·trat·ing
frus·tra'tion
frus'tum
·tums or ·ta
fry
fried fry'ing
fry'er or fri'er
f'·stop'
fuch'sia
fudge
fudged
fudg'ing
fu'el
·eled or ·elled
·el·ing or ·el·ling
fuel cell
fu'gi·tive
fugue
ful'crum
·crums or ·cra
ful·fill' or ·fil'
·filled' ·fill'ing
ful·fill'ment
or ·fil'ment
full'back'
full'·blood'ed
full'·blown'
full'·bod'ied
full'·dress'
full'er's earth
full'·faced'
full'·fash'ioned
full'·fledged'
full'·length'
full'·scale'
full'·time'
full'y
ful'mi·nate'
·nat'ed ·nat'ing
ful'some
fum'ble
·bled ·bling
fume
fumed fum'ing
fu'mi·gant.
fu'mi·gate'
·gat'ed ·gat'ing
fu'mi·ga'tion
fu'mi·ga'tor
func'tion·al
func'tion·al·ly
func'tion·ar'y
·ar'ies
fun'da·men'tal
fun'da·men'tal·
ism
fun'da·men'tal·ly
fund'·rais'er
fu'ner·al
fu·ne're·al
fun'gi·cid'al
fun'gi·cide'
fun'gous adj.
fun'gus n.
·gi or ·gus·es
fu·nic'u·lar

tun'nel
·neled or ·nell
·nel·ing or
·nel·ling
fun'ni·ness
fun'ny
ni·er ·ni·est
ɩ r
ɩ rred fur'ring
nair; SEE fir)
fur·be·low'
fur'bish
fu'ri·ous
fur'long
fur'lough
fur'nace
fur'nish·ings
fur'ni·ture
fu'ror
fur'ri·er
fur'ri·ness
fur'row
fur'r ɪ
·ri·er ·ri·est
fur'ther
fur'ther·ance
fur'ther·more'
fur'ther·most'
fur'thest
fur'tive
fu'ry
·rie
fuse
fused fus'ing
fu'se·lage'
fu'si·bil'i·ty
fu'si·ble
fu'sil·lade'
·lad'ed ·lad'in
fu'sion
fuss'i·ness
fuss'y
·i·er ·i·est
fus'tian
fust'y
·i·er ·i·est
fu'tile
fu'tile·ly
fu·til'i·ty
fu'ture
fu·tu'ri·ty
·ties
fuzz'i·ly
fuzz'i·ness
fuzz'y
·i·er ·i·est

G

gab'ar·dine'
ga'ble
gad'a·bout'
gadg'et
gag
gagged
gag'ging

ge; SEE	gam'ut	gas'tric	gen'er·al·ize'	ger'mi·cide'	gild
e)	gam'y	gas'tro·nome'	·ized' ·iz'ing	ger'mi·nate'	gild'ed or gilt
le	·i·er ·i·est	gas'tro·nom'i·cal	gen'er·al·ly	·nat'ed ·nat'ing	gild'ing
nan'	gan'der	gas·tron'o·my	gen'er·ate'	ger'mi·na'tion	(coat with gold;
ty	Gan'dhi·ism	gate	·at'ed ·at'ing	ger·on·tol'o·gy	SEE guild)
er	ga'nef or ·nof	(door; SEE gait)	gen·er·a'tion	ger'ry·man'der	gilt
ful	gang'land'	gate'way'	gen'er·a·tor	ger'und	(gold; SEE guilt)
ful·ly	gan'gling	gath'er·ing	ge·ner'ic	Ge·stalt'	gilt'-edged'
li·ness	gan'gli·on	gauche	ge·ner'i·cal·ly	ges'tate	gim'bals
ly	·gli·a or ·gli·ons	(lacking grace;	gen·er·os'i·ty	·tat·ed ·tat·ing	gim'crack'
· ·li·est	gang'plank'	SEE gouache)	·ties	ges·ta'tion	gim'let
say'	gan'grene	gau·che·rie'	gen'er·ous	ges·tic'u·late'	gim'mick
' ·say'ing	gan'gre·nous	gaud'i·ly	gen'e·sis	·lat'ed ·lat'ing	gin'ger
of walking;	gang'ster	gaud'i·ness	·ses'	ges·tic'u·la'tion	gin'ger·bread'
gate)	gang'way'	gaud'y	ge·net'ic	ges·tic'u·la'tor	ging'ham
er	gant'let	·i·er ·i·est	ge·net'i·cal·ly	ges'ture	gi·raffe'
·had'	gan'try	gauge	ge'nial	·tured ·tur·ing	gird
x·y	·tries	gauged	ge·ni·al'i·ty	get	gird'ed or girt
int	gap	gaug'ing	ge'nial·ly	got, got or	gird'ing
int·ry	gapped	(measure; SEE	ge'nie	got'ten,	gird'er
on	gap'ping	gage)	gen'i·tal	get'ting	gir'dle
er·y	gape	gauge'a·ble	gen'ius	get'a·way'	·dled ·dling
·y·ing	gaped gap'ing	gaunt	gen'o·cide'	get'-to·geth'er	girl'ish
ey	ga·rage'	gaunt'let	gen'o·type'	gew'gaw	gist
s	·raged' ·rag'ing	gauze	gen're	gey'ser	give
ng	gar'bage	gauz'y	gen·teel'	ghast'li·ness	gave giv'en
·vant'	gar'ble	·i·er ·i·est	gen·teel'ly	ghast'ly	giv'ing
on	·bled ·bling	gav'el	gen'tile	·li·er ·li·est	give'a·way'
op	gar·çon'	gawk'i·ness	gen·til'i·ty	gher'kin	giz'zard
ws	·çons'	gawk'y	gen'tle	ghet'to	gla·cé'
vs·es or ·lows	gar'den·er	·i·er ·i·est	·tler ·tlest	·tos or ·toes	·céed' ·cé'ing
stone'	gar·de'ni·a	gay'ly	gen'tle·man	ghet'to·ize'	gla'cial
re'	Gar·gan'tu·an or	gaze	gen'tle·man·ly	·ized' ·iz'ing	gla'ci·ate'
sh'	gar·gan'tu·an	gazed gaz'ing	gen'tle·wom'an	ghil'lie	·at'ed ·at'ing
loshe'	gar'gle	ga·ze'bo	gent'ly	ghost'li·ness	gla'cier
imph'	·gled ·gling	·bos or ·boes	gen'try	ghost'ly	glad
an'ic	gar'goyle	ga·zelle'	gen'u·flect'	·li·er ·li·est	glad'der
a·nism	gar'ish	ga·zette'	gen'u·ine	ghost'write'	glad'dest
a·ni·za'tion	gar'land	gaz'et·teer'	gen'u·ine·ly	ghost'writ'er	glad'den
a·nize'	gar'lic	gear'box'	ge'nus	ghoul'ish	glad'i·a'tor
ed' ·niz'ing	gar'lick·y	gear'shift'	gen'er·a	gi'ant	glad'i·o'lus or ·la
a·nom'e·ter	gar'ment	gear'wheel'	ge·o·cen'tric	gib'ber·ish	·lus·es or ·li, ·las
bit	gar'ner	Gei'ger	ge·og'ra·pher	gib'bet	glad'some
ble	gar'net	gei'sha	ge·o·graph'i·cal	gib'bon	glair
d ·bling	gar'nish	·sha or ·shas	ge·og'ra·phy	gib·bos'i·ty	(glaze; SEE glare)
k; SEE	gar'nish·ee'	gel	·phies	·ties	glam'or·ize'
bol)	·eed' ·ee'ing	gelled gel'ling	ge·o·log'ic	gib'bous	·ized' ·iz'ing
bler	gar'nish·ment	gel'a·tin or ·tine	ge·o·log'i·cal·ly	gibe	glam'or·ous
bol	gar'ret	ge·lat'i·nize'	ge·ol'o·gist	gibed gib'ing	glam'our or ·or
led or ·bolled	gar'ri·son	·nized' ·niz'ing	ge·ol'o·gy	(taunt; SEE jibe)	glance
·ing or	gar·rote'	ge·lat'i·nous	·gies	gib'let	glanced
·ling	·rot'ed or	geld	ge·o·met'ric	gid'di·ly	glanc'ing
lic; SEE	·rot'ted	geld'ed or gelt	ge·o·met'ri·cal·ly	gid'di·ness	glan'du·lar
ble)	·rot'ing or	geld'ing	ge·om'e·try	gid'dy	glare
brel	·rot'ting	gel'id	·tries	·di·er ·di·est	glared glar'ing
e'cock'	gar·ru'li·ty	ge·lid'i·ty	ge·o·phys'i·cal	gift'ed	(strong light;
e'keep'er	gar'ru·lous	gem'i·nate'	ge·o·phys'i·cist	gift'-wrap'	SEE glair)
es'man·ship'	gar'ter	·nat'ed ·nat'ing	ge·o·phys'ics	·wrapped'	glar'i·ness
in	gas	Gem'i·ni'	ge·o·po·lit'i·cal	·wrap'ping	glar'y
i·ness	gassed	gen'darme	ge·o·pol'i·tics	gig	·i·er ·i·est
ma	gas'sing	gen'der	Geor'gia	gigged gig'ging	glass'ful'
	gas'e·ous	ge·ne·a·log'i·cal	ge·o·stat'ics	gi·gan'tic	·fuls'
	gas'ket	ge·ne·al'o·gy	ge·ot'ro·pism	gi·gan'ti·cal·ly	glass·ine'
	gas'light'	·gies	ge·ra'ni·um	gi·gan'tism	glass'i·ness
	gas·o·line' or	gen'er·al	ger'bil or ·bille	gig'gle	glass'ware'
	·lene'	gen·er·al'i·ty	ger'i·at'rics	·gled ·gling	glass'y
	gas'sy	·ties	ger·mane'	gig'o·lo'	·i·er ·i·est
	·si·er ·si·est	gen·er·al·i·za'tion	ger'mi·cid'al	·los'	glau·co'ma

glaze
  glazed glaz'ing
gla'zier
glean'ings
glee'ful
glee'ful·ly
glib
  glib'ber
  glib'best
glib'ly
glide
  glid'ed glid'ing
glid'er
glim'mer
glimpse
  glimpsed
  glimps'ing
glis·sade'
  ·sad'ed ·sad'ing
glis'ten
glit'ter
glit'ter·y
gloam'ing
gloat
glob'al
globe'-trot'ter
glob'u·lar
glob'ule
glock'en·spiel'
gloom'i·ly
gloom'i·ness
gloom'y
  ·i·er ·i·est
glo'ri·fi·ca'tion
glo'ri·fy'
  ·fied' ·fy'ing
glo'ri·ous
glo'ry
  ·ries
  ·ried ·ry·ing
glos'sa·ry
  ·ries
gloss'i·ness
gloss'y
  ·i·er ·i·est
  ·ies
glot'tal
glove
  gloved glov'ing
glow'er
glow'ing·ly
glow'worm'
glu'cose
glue
  glued glu'ing
glue'y
  glu'i·er
  glu'i·est
glum'ly
glut
  glut'ted
  glut'ting
glu'ten
glu'ten·ous
  (having gluten)
glu'ti·nous
  (gluey)
glut'ton

glut'ton·ous
  (greedy)
glut'ton·y
glyc'er·in or ·ine
gnarled
gnash
gnat
gnaw
  gnawed
  gnaw'ing
gneiss
gnoc'chi
gnome
gno'mic
gno'mon
gnos'tic
gnu
go
  went gone
  go'ing
goad
go'-a·head'
goal'keep'er
goat·ee'
gob'ble
  ·bled ·bling
gob'ble·dy·gook'
go'-be·tween'
gob'let
gob'lin
god'child'
god'daugh'ter
god'dess
god'fa'ther
God'-giv'en
god'li·ness
god'ly
  ·li·er ·li·est
god'moth'er
god'par'ent
god'send'
god'son'
God'speed'
go'-get'ter
gog'gle
  ·gled ·gling
go'-go'
goi'ter or ·tre
gold'en
gold'-filled'
gold'fish'
gold leaf
gold'smith'
golf'er
gon'do·la
gon'do·lier'
gon'or·rhe'a
  or ·rhoe'a
good
  bet'ter best
good'bye' or
  good'-bye'
  ·byes' or -byes'
good'-for-
  noth'ing
good'-heart'ed
good'-hu'mored
good'-look'ing

good'ly
  ·li·er ·li·est
good'-na'tured
good night
good'-sized'
good'-tem'pered
good'y
  ·ies
goo'ey
  goo'i·er goo'i·est
goo'gol
goose
  geese
goose'neck'
goose'-step'
go'pher
gore
  gorged gorg'ing
gorge
  gorged gorg'ing
gor'geous
go·ril'la
  (ape; SEE guerrilla)
gor'i·ness
gor'mand·ize'
  ·ized' ·iz'ing
gor'y
  ·i·er ·i·est
gos'hawk'
gos'ling
gos'pel
gos'sa·mer
gos'sip
got'ten
gouache
  (painting; SEE
  gauche)
gouge
  gouged
  goug'ing
gou'lash
gourd
gour'mand
gour'met
gout
gov'ern·ess
gov'ern·ment
gov'ern·men'tal
gov'er·nor
grab
  grabbed
  grab'bing
grace'ful
grace'ful·ly
grace'less
gra'cious
gra'date
  ·dat·ed ·dat·ing
gra·da'tion
grade
  grad'ed grad'ing
grad'u·al
grad'u·ate'
  ·at'ed ·at'ing
grad·u·a'tion
graf·fi'ti
  (sing. graf·fi'to)
graft'er

gra'ham
grain'i·ness
grain'y
  ·i·er ·i·est
gram'mar
gram·mar'i·an
gram·mat'i·cal
gran'a·ry
  ·ries
grand'aunt'
grand'child'
grand'daugh'ter
gran'deur
grand'fa'ther
gran·dil'o·quent
gran'di·ose'
grand'moth'er
grand'neph'ew
grand'niece'
grand'par'ent
grand'son'
grand'stand'
grand'un'cle
gran'ite
gran'ite·ware'
grant·ee'
grant'-in-aid'
  grants'-in-aid'
grant'or
gran'u·lar
gran'u·late'
  ·lat'ed ·lat'ing
gran'ule
grape'fruit'
grape'vine'
graph'ic
graph'i·cal·ly
graph'ite
graph·ol'o·gy
grap'nel
grap'ple
  ·pled ·pling
grasp'ing
grass'hop'per
grass'y
  ·i·er ·i·est
grate
  grat'ed grat'ing
grate'ful
grate'ful·ly
grat'i·fi·ca'tion
grat'i·fy'
  ·fied' ·fy'ing
gra'tis
grat'i·tude
gra·tu'i·tous
gra·tu'i·ty
  ·ties
grave
  graved, grav'en
  or graved,
  grav'ing
  (carve out)
grave
  graved grav'ing
  (clean the hull)
grave'clothes'

grav'el
  ·eled or ·elled
  ·el·ing or ·el·ling
grav'el·ly
grave'ly
grave'side'
grave'stone'
grave'yard'
grav'i·tate'
  ·tat'ed ·tat'ing
grav'i·ta'tion
grav'i·ty
  ·ties
gra'vy
  ·vies
gray
gray'-head'ed
graze
  grazed graz'ing
grease
  greased
  greas'ing
grease'paint'
greas'i·ness
greas'y
  ·i·er ·i·est
great'-aunt'
great'coat'
great'-grand'child'
great'-grand'par'·
  ent
great'ly
great'-neph'ew
great'ness
great'-niece'
great'-un'cle
greed'i·ly
greed'i·ness
greed'y
  ·i·er ·i·est
Greek'-let'ter
green'back'
green'er·y
green'-eyed'
green'gage'
green'horn'
green'house'
green'room'
green'sward'
greet'ing
gre·gar'i·ous
grem'lin
gre·nade'
gren'a·dier'
gren'a·dine'
grey'hound' or
  gray'·
grid'dle
  ·dled ·dling
grid'dle·cake'
grid'i'ron
grief'-strick'en
griev'ance
grieve
  grieved
  griev'ing
griev'ous
grif'fin

grill
  (broiler grid)
grille
  (open grating)
grill'room'
grim
  grim'mer
  grim'mest
gri·mace'
  ·maced'
  ·mac'ing
grime
  grimed grim'·
grim'i·ly
grim'i·ness
grim'y
  ·i·er ·i·est
grin
  grinned
  grin'ning
grind
  ground
  grind'ing
grind'stone'
grip
  gripped or gri
  grip'ping
  (hold)
gripe
  griped grip'in
  (distress)
grippe
  (influenza)
gris'li·ness
gris'ly
  ·li·er ·li·est
  (horrid)
gris'tle
gris'tly
  (of gristle)
grist'mill'
grit
  grit'ted
  grit'ting
grit'ti·ness
grit'ty
  ·ti·er ·ti·est
griz'zly bear
groan'ing
gro'cer·y
  ·ies
grog'gi·ly
grog'gi·ness
grog'gy
  ·gi·er ·gi·est
groin
grom'met
groom
groove
  grooved
  groov'ing
groov'y
  ·i·er ·i·est
grope
  groped grop'i
gros'grain'
gross'ly
gross'ness

gro·tesque'
gro·tesque'ly
grot'to
·toes or ·tos
grouch'i·ly
grouch'i·ness
grouch'y
·i·er ·i·est
ground'less
grounds'keep'er
ground'speed'
ground'work'
group
grout
grove
grov'el
·eled or ·elled
·el·ing or ·el·ling
grow
grew grown
grow'ing
growl'er
grown'-up'
growth
grub
grubbed
grub'bing
grub'bi·ness
grub'by
·bi·er ·bi·est
grub'stake'
grudge
grudged
grudg'ing
gru'el
gru'el·ing or
gru'el·ling
grue'some
grue'some·ly
gruff'ly
grum'ble
·bled ·bling
grum'bler
grum'bly
grump'i·ness
grump'y
·i·er ·i·est
grun'ion
grunt
Gru·yère'
G'-string'
G'-suit'
guar'an·tee'
·teed' ·tee'ing
guar'an·tor'
guar'an·ty
·ties
·tied ·ty·ing
guard'ed
guard'house'
guard'i·an
guard'rail'
guard'room'
guards'man
gua'va
gu·ber·na·to'ri·al
Guern'sey
·seys

guer·ril'la or gue·
(soldier; SEE
gorilla)
guess'work'
guest
guid'a·ble
guid'ance
guide
guid'ed
guid'ing
guide'book'
guide'line'
guide'post'
guild
(union; SEE gild)
guilds'man
guile'ful
guile'less
guil'lo·tine'
·tined' ·tin'ing
guilt
(blame; SEE gilt)
guilt'i·ly
guilt'i·ness
guilt'y
·i·er ·i·est
guin'ea pig
guise
gui·tar'
gui·tar'ist
gulch
gul'let
gul'li·bil'i·ty
gul'li·ble
gul'li·bly
gul'ly
·lies
gum'drop'
gum'mi·ness
gum'my
·mi·er ·mi·est
gun
gunned
gun'ning
gun'cot'ton
gun'fire'
gung'-ho'
gun'lock'
gun'man
gun'ner·y
gun'ny·sack'
gun'play'
gun'point'
gun'pow'der
gun'run'ning
gun'shot'
gun'-shy'
gun'smith'
gun'stock'
gup'py
·pies
gur'gle
·gled ·gling
gu'ru
gush'er
gush'i·ness
gush'y
·i·er ·i·est

gus'set
gus'ta·to'ry
gus'to
gust'y
·i·er ·i·est
gut
gut'ted
gut'ting
gut'ta-per'cha
gut'ter·snipe'
gut'tur·al
guy
guz'zle
·zled ·zling
guz'zler
gym·na'si·um
·si·ums or ·si·a
gym'nast
gym·nas'tics
gym'no·sperm'
gyn'e·col'o·gist
gyn'e·col'o·gy
gyp
gypped gyp'ping
gyp'sum
Gyp'sy
·sies
gy'rate
·rat·ed ·rat·ing
gy·ra'tion
gy'ro·com'pass
gy'ro·scope'
gy'ro·scop'ic
gy'ro·sta'bi·liz'er

H

ha'be·as cor'pus
hab'er·dash'er·y
·ies
ha·bil'i·tate'
·tat'ed ·tat'ing
hab'it
hab'it·a·ble
hab'i·tat'
hab'i·ta'tion
hab'it-form'ing
ha·bit'u·al
ha·bit'u·ate'
·at'ed ·at'ing
hab'i·tude'
ha·bit'u·é'
ha'ci·en'da
hack'ney
·neys
hack'neyed
hack'saw'
had'dock
hag'gard
hag'gle
·gled ·gling
hai'ku
·ku
hail
(ice; SEE hale)
hail'stone'

hail'storm'
hair'breadth'
hair'cut'
hair'do'
hair'dress'er
hair'i·ness
hair'line'
hair'piece'
hair'-rais'ing
hair'split'ting
hair'spring'
hair'y
·i·er ·i·est
hal'cy·on
hale
haled hal'ing
(healthy; force;
SEE hail)
half
halves
half'back'
half'-baked'
half'-breed'
half'-caste'
half'-cocked'
half'heart'ed
half'-hour'
half'-mast'
half'-moon'
half'tone'
half'track'
half'-truth'
half'way'
half'-wit'ted
hal'i·but
hal'i·to'sis
hal'le·lu'jah
or ·iah
hall'mark'
hal'lowed
Hal'low·een'
hal·lu'ci·nate'
·nat'ed ·nat'ing
hal·lu'ci·na'tion
hal·lu'ci·na·to'ry
hal·lu'ci·no·gen
hall'way'
ha'lo
·los or ·loes
hal'ter
halt'ing·ly
ha·lutz'
ha'lutz·im'
halve
halved halv'ing
hal'yard
ham'burg'er
ham'let
ham'mer
ham'mer·head'
ham'mock
ham'per
ham'ster
ham'string'
hand'bag'
hand'ball'
hand'bar'row
hand'bill'

hand'book'
hand'breadth'
hand'clasp'
hand'cuff'
hand'ful'
·fuls'
hand'gun'
hand'i·cap'
·capped'
·cap'ping
hand'i·craft'
hand'i·ly
hand'i·ness
hand'i·work'
hand'ker·chief
·chiefs
han'dle
·dled ·dling
han'dle·bar'
hand'ler
hand'made'
hand'-me-down'
hand'out'
hand'picked'
hand'rail'
hand'saw'
hand'sel
·seled or ·selled
·sel·ing or ·sel·ling
hand'set'
hand'shake'
hands'-off'
hand'some
hand'spring'
hand'stand'
hand'-to-hand'
hand'-to-mouth'
hand'work'
hand'writ'ing
hand'y
·i·er ·i·est
han'dy·man'
hang
hung hang'ing
(suspend)
hang
hanged hang'ing
(put to death)
hang'ar
(aircraft shed)
hang'dog'
hang'er
(garment holder)
hang'er-on'
hang'ers-on'
hang'man
hang'nail'
hang'o'ver
hang'-up'
hank'er
han'ky-pan'ky
han'som (cab)
Ha'nu·ka'
hap'haz'ard
hap'less
hap'pen
hap'pen·stance'
hap'pi·ly

hap'pi·ness
hap'py
·pi·er ·pi·est
hap'py-go-luck'y
ha'ra-ki'ri
ha·rangue'
·rangued'
·rangu'ing
ha·rangu'er
har·ass'
har'bin·ger
har'bor
hard'back'
hard'-bit'ten
hard'-boiled'
hard'-bound'
hard'-core'
hard'-cov'er
hard'en
hard'fist'ed
hard'goods'
hard'head'ed
hard'heart'ed
har'di·hood'
har'di·ly
har'di·ness
hard'ly
hard'pan'
hard'-shell'
hard'ship'
hard'tack'
hard'top'
hard'ware'
hard'wood'
har'dy
·di·er ·di·est
hare'brained'
hare'lip'
ha'rem
har'le·quin
harm'ful
harm'less
har·mon'ic
har·mon'i·ca
har·mo'ni·ous
har'mo·nize'
·nized' ·niz'ing
har'mo·ny
har'ness
harp'is·
har·poon'
harp'si·chord'
har'py
·pies
har'ri·er
har'row
har'row·ing
har'ry
·ried ·ry·ing
harsh'ness
har'te·beest'
har'um-scar'um
har'vest·er
has'-been'
ha'sen·pfef'fer
hash'ish or ·eesh
has'sle
·sled ·sling

has'sock	head'line'	heav'y-du'ty	hen'na	het'er·o·nym'	high'-strung'
haste	head'long'	heav'y-hand'ed	·naed ·na·ing	het'er·o·sex'u·al	high'-ten'sion
has'ten	head'man	heav'y-heart'ed	hen'ner·y	heu·ris'tic	high'-test'
hast'i·ly	head'mas'ter	heav'y-set'	·ies	heu·ris'ti·cal·ly	high'-toned'
hast'i·ness	head'mis'tress	heav'y·weight'	hen'pecked'	hew	high'way'
hast'y	head'-on'	He·bra'ic	hen'ry	hewed, hewed or	hi'jack'
·i·er ·i·est	head'phone'	He'brew	·rys or ·ries	hewn, hew'ing	hike
hat'band'	head'piece'	heck'le	he·pat'ic	(chop; SEE hue)	hiked hik'ing
hatch'er·y	head'quar'ters	·led ·ling	hep'a·ti'tis	hex'a·gon'	hi·lar'i·ous
·ies	head'rest'	hec'tic	hep'ta·gon'	hex·ag'o·nal	hi·lar'i·ty
hatch'et	head'room'	hec'ti·cal·ly	her'ald	hex'a·he'dron	hill'i·ness
hatch'ing	head'set'	hec'to·graph'	he·ral'dic	·drons or ·dra	hill'ock
hatch'way'	head'stand'	hedge	her'ald·ry	hey'day'	hill'side'
hate	head start	hedged	her·ba'ceous	H'-hour'	hill'y
hat'ed hat'ing	head'stock'	hedg'ing	her'bi·cide'	hi·a'tus	·i·er ·i·est
hate'a·ble	head'strong'	hedge'hop'	her'bi·vore'	·tus·es or ·tus	him·self'
hate'ful	head'wait'er	he'don·ism	her·biv'o·rous	hi·ba'chi	hind
hat'rack'	head'wa'ters	he'do·nis'tic	herds'man	hi'ber·nate'	hind'er,
ha'tred	head'way'	heed'ful	here'a·bout'	·nat'ed ·nat'ing	hind'most' or
hat'ter	head wind	heed'less	here·af'ter	hi'ber·na'tion	hind'er·most'
haugh'ti·ly	head'y	heel	here'by'	hi'ber·na'tor	hin'der
haugh'ti·ness	·i·er ·i·est	(foot part;	he·red'i·tar'y	hi·bis'cus	hin'drance
haugh'ty	heal	SEE heal)	he·red'i·ty	hic'cup or ·cough	hind'sight'
·ti·er ·ti·est	(cure; SEE heel)	heft'y	·ties	·cuped or ·cupped	hinge
haul'age	health'ful	·i·er ·i·est	here·in'	·cup·ing or	hinged hing'ing
haunch	health'i·ly	heif'er	here'in·af'ter	·cup·ping	hin'ter·land'
haunt'ed	health'i·ness	height	here's	hick'o·ry	hip'bone'
haunt'ing	health'y	height'en	her'e·sy	·ries	hip'pie
hau·teur'	·i·er ·i·est	hei'nous	·sies	hide	hip'po·drome'
have	heap	heir	her'e·tic	hid, hid'den or	hip'po·pot'a·mu
had hav'ing	hear	(inheritor; SEE	he·ret'i·cal	hid, hid'ing	·mus·es or ·mi
have'lock	heard hear'ing	air)	here'to·fore'	hide'a·way'	hir'a·ble or hire'
ha'ven	heark'en	heir'ess	here·with'	hide'bound'	hire
have'-not'	hear'say'	heir'loom'	her'it·a·ble	hid'e·ous	hired hir'ing
hav'er·sack'	hearse	hel'i·cal	her'it·age	hide'-out'	hire'ling
hav'oc	heart'ache'	hel'i·cop'ter	her·maph'ro·dite'	hie	hiss'ing
Ha·wai'i	heart'beat'	he'li·o·graph'	her·met'i·cal·ly	hied, hie'ing	his'ta·mine'
Ha·wai'ian	heart'break'	he'li·o·trope'	her'mit	or hy'ing	his·tol'o·gy
hawk	heart'bro'ken	hel'i·port'	her'ni·a	hi'er·ar'chi·cal	his·to'ri·an
hawk'-eyed'	heart'burn'	he'li·um	·as or ·ae'	hi'er·ar'chy	his·tor'i·cal
hawk'ish	heart'en	he'lix	her'ni·ate'	·chies	his·tor'i·cal·ly
haw'ser	heart'felt'	·lix·es or ·li·ces'	·at·ed ·at·ing	hi'er·o·glyph'ic	his'to·ry
hay fever	hearth'stone'	hel'lion	he'ro	hi'-fi'	·ries
hay'field'	heart'i·ly	hel·lo'	·roes	high'ball'	his·tri·on'ic
hay'loft'	heart'i·ness	·los'	he·ro'ic	high'born'	hit
hay'ride'	heart'less	·loed' ·lo'ing	he·ro'i·cal·ly	high'boy'	hit hit'ting
haz'ard	heart'-rend'ing	hel'met	her'o·in	high'bred'	hit'-and-run'
haz'ard·ous	heart'sick'	helms'man	(narcotic)	high'brow'	hitch'hike'
haze	heart'strings'	help'ful	her'o·ine	high'chair'	hith'er·to'
hazed haz'ing	heart'-to-heart'	help'ful·ly	(female hero)	high'-class'	hit'-or-miss'
ha'zel·nut'	heart'warm'ing	help'less	her'o·ism	high'er-up'	hives
ha'zi·ly	heart'y	hel'ter-skel'ter	her'pes	high'fa·lu'tin	hoard
ha'zi·ness	·i·er ·i·est	hem	her'ring·bone'	high'-flown'	(reserve; SEE
ha'zy	heat'ed·ly	hemmed	her·self'	high'-grade'	horde)
·zi·er ·zi·est	heat'er	hem'ming	hes'i·tan·cy	high'hand'ed	hoar'frost'
H'-bomb'	heath	he'ma·tol'o·gy	·cies	high'-keyed'	hoar'i·ness
head'ache'	hea'then	hem'i·sphere'	hes'i·tant	high'land·er	hoarse
head'board'	heath'er	hem'i·spher'i·cal	hes'i·tate'	high'-lev'el	hoar'y
head'cheese'	heat'stroke'	hem'line'	·tat'ed ·tat'ing	high'light'	·i·er ·i·est
head'dress'	heave	he'mo·glo'bin	hes'i·ta'tion	high'ly	hob'ble
head'first'	heaved or hove	he'mo·phil'i·a	het'er·o·dox'	high'-mind'ed	·bled ·bling
head'gear'	heav'ing	hem'or·rhage	het'er·o·dox'y	high'-pitched'	hob'by
head'hunt'er	heav'en·ly	·rhaged	·ies	high'-pow'ered	·bies
head'i·ly	heav'en·ward	·rhag·ing	het'er·o·dyne'	high'-pres'sure	hob'by·horse'
head'i·ness	heav'i·ly	hem'or·rhoid'	·dyned' ·dyn'ing	high'-priced'	hob'gob'lin
head'land	heav'i·ness	hem'stitch'	het'er·o·ge·ne'i·ty	high'-rise'	hob'nail'
head'less	heav'y	hence'forth'	·ties	high'-sound'ing	hob'nob'
head'light'	·i·er ·i·est	hench'man	het'er·o·ge'ne·ous	high'-spir'it·ed	·nobbed' ·nob

ho′bo
·bos *or* ·boes
hock′ey
ho′cus-po′cus
hodge′podge′
hoe
  hoed hoe′ing
hoe′down′
hog′gish
hogs′head′
hog′tie′
  ·tied′, ·ty′ing
  or ·tie′ing
hog′wash′
hoi′ pol·loi′
hoist
hold
  held hold′ing
hold′out′
hold′o′ver
hold′up′
hole
  holed hol′ing
hol′ey
  (*with holes;* SEE
  holy, wholly)
hol′i·day′
ho′li·ly
ho′li·ness
hol′lan·daise′
hol′low
hol′lo·ware′
hol′ly
·lies
hol′ly·hock′
hol′o·caust′
ho·log′ra·phy
hol′stein
hol′ster
ho′ly
  li·er ·li·est
  lies
  (*sacred;* SEE
  holey, wholly)
hom′age
hom′burg
home
  omed hom′ing
home′bod′y
home′bred′
home′com′ing
home′-grown′
home′land′
home′less
home′li·ness
home′ly
  i·er ·li·est
  (*plain;* SEE
  homey)
home′made′
home′mak′er
home′own′er
home′sick′
home′spun′
home′stead′
home′stretch′
home′ward

home′work′
home′y
hom′i·er
hom′i·est
  (*cozy;* SEE
  homely)
home′y·ness
hom′i·ci′dal
hom′i·cide′
hom′i·let′ics
hom′i·ly
  ·lies
hom′i·ny
ho′mo·ge·ne′i·ty
ho′mo·ge′ne·ous
ho·mog′e·nize′
  ·nized′ ·niz′ing
hom′o·graph′
ho·mol′o·gous
hom′o·nym
hom′o·phone′
Ho′mo sa′pi·ens′
ho′mo·sex′u·al
ho′mo·sex′u·
  al′i·ty
hone
  honed hon′ing
hon′est
hon′es·ty
hon′ey
  ·eys, ·eyed *or*
  ·ied, ·ey·ing
hon′ey·bee′
hon′ey·comb′
hon′ey·dew′
hon′ey·moon′
hon′ey·suck′le
hon′or·a·ble
hon′o·ra′ri·um
  ·ri·ums *or* ·ri·a
hon′or·ar′y
hon′or·if′ic
hood′ed
hood′lum
hood′wink′
hoof
hoof′beat′
hook′ah *or* ·a
hook′up′
hook′y
hoo′li·gan
hoop′la
hoot′en·an′ny
  ·nies
hop
  hopped hop′ping
hope
  hoped hop′ing
hope′ful
hope′ful·ly
hope′less
hop′per
horde
  hord′ed hord′ing
  (*crowd;* SEE
  hoard)
hore′hound′
ho·ri′zon

hor′i·zon′tal
hor·mo′nal
hor′mone
hor′net
horn′i·ness
horn′pipe′
horn′y
  ·i·er ·i·est
ho·rol′o·gy
hor′o·scope′
hor·ren′dous
hor′ri·ble
hor′ri·bly
hor′rid
hor′ri·fy′
  ·fied′ ·fy′ing
hor′ror
hors′ d'oeu′vre
  ·vres
horse′back′
horse′fly′
  ·flies′
horse′hair′
horse′hide′
horse′laugh′
horse′man
horse′play′
horse′pow′er
horse′rad′ish
horse′shoe′
  ·shoed′ ·shoe′ing
horse′tail′
horse′whip′
horse′wom′an
hors′i·ness
hors′y
  ·i·er ·i·est
hor′ta·to′ry
hor′ti·cul′ture
hor′ti·cul′tur·ist
ho·san′na
hose
  hosed hos′ing
ho′sier·y
hos′pice
hos′pi·ta·ble
hos′pi·ta·bly
hos′pi·tal
hos′pi·tal′i·ty
  ·ties
hos′pi·tal·i·za′tion
hos′pi·tal·ize′
  ·ized′ ·iz′ing
hos′tage
hos′tel
  (*inn;* SEE hostile)
hos′tel·ry
  ·ries
host′ess
hos′tile
  (*unfriendly;* SEE
  hostel)
hos′tile·ly
hos·til′i·ty
  ·ties
hos′tler
hot
  hot′ter hot′test

hot′bed′
hot′-blood′ed
hot′box′
ho·tel′
ho·tel·ier′
hot′foot′
  ·foots′
hot′head′ed
hot′house′
hot′-tem′pered
hound′ed
hour′glass′
hour′ly
house
  housed hous′ing
house′boat′
house′break′
  ·broke′ ·bro′ken
  ·break′ing
house′clean′ing
house′dress′
house′coat′
house′fly′
  ·flies′
house′ful′
house′hold′
house′keep′er
house′lights′
house′maid′
house′man′
house′moth′er
house organ
house party
house′-rais′ing
house′warm′ing
house′wife′
  ·wives′
house′work′
hous′ing
hov′el
  ·eled *or* ·elled
  ·el·ing *or* ·el·ling
hov′er
how′dah
how·ev′er
how′itz·er
howl′ing
how·so·ev′er
how′-to′
hoy′den
hua·ra′ches
hub′bub′
hub′cap′
huck′le·ber′ry
  ·ries
huck′ster
hud′dle
  ·dled ·dling
hue
  (*color;* SEE hew)
huff′i·ly
huff′i·ness
huff′y
  ·i·er ·i·est
hug
  hugged hug′ging
huge′ness
hulk′ing

hul′la·ba·loo′
hum
  hummed
  hum′ming
hu′man
hu·mane′
hu′man·ism
hu′man·is′tic
hu′man·is′ti·cal·ly
hu·man′i·tar′i·an
hu·man′i·ty
  ·ties
hu′man·ize′
  ·ized′ ·iz′ing
hu′man·kind′
hu′man·ly
hu′man·ness
hu′man·oid′
hum′ble
  ·bler ·blest
  ·bled ·bling
hum′bly
hum′bug′
hum′drum′
hu·mec′tant
hu′mer·us
  ·mer·i′
  (*bone;* SEE
  humorous)
hu′mid
hu·mid′i·fi·ca′tion
hu·mid′i·fi′er
hu·mid′i·fy′
  ·fied′ ·fy′ing
hu·mid′i·ty
hu·mi·dor′
hu·mil′i·ate′
  ·at′ed ·at′ing
hu·mil′i·a′tion
hu·mil′i·ty
hum′ming·bird′
hum′mock
hu′mor
hu′mor·esque′
hu′mor·ist
hu′mor·ous
  (*funny;* SEE
  humerus)
hump′back′
hu′mus
hunch′back′
hun′dred·fold′
hun′dredth
hun′dred·weight′
hun′ger
hun′gri·ly
hun′gri·ness
hun′gry
  ·gri·er ·gri·est
hunt′er
hunt′ress
hunts′man
hur′dle
  ·dled ·dling
  (*barrier;* SEE
  hurtle)
hur′dy-gur′dy
hurl′er

hurl′y-burl′y
hur·rah′
hur′ri·cane′
hur′ried·ly
hur′ry
  ·ried ·ry·ing
hurt
  hurt hurt′ing
hurt′ful
hur′tle
  ·tled ·tling
  (*rush;* SEE hurdle)
hus′band
hus′band·ry
hush′-hush′
husk′i·ly
husk′i·ness
hus′ky
  ·kies
  (*dog*)
husk′y
  ·i·er ·i·est, ·ies
  (*hoarse; robust*)
hus′sy
  ·sies
hus′tle
  ·tled ·tling
hus′tler
hy′a·cinth′
hy′brid
hy′brid·ize′
  ·ized′ ·iz′ing
hy·dran′ge·a
hy′drant
hy′drate
  ·drat·ed ·drat·ing
hy′dra·tor
hy·drau′lic
hy′dro·chlo′ric
hy′dro·dy·nam′ics
hy′dro·e·lec′tric
hy′dro·foil′
hy′dro·gen
hy′dro·gen·ate′
  ·at′ed ·at′ing
hy′dro·gen·a′tion
hy′dro·ki·net′ics
hy·drol′o·gy
hy·drol′y·sis
hy′dro·lyt′ic
hy′dro·me·
  chan′ics
hy·drom′e·ter
hy′dro·naut′
hy′dro·pho′bi·a
hy′dro·plane′
hy′dro·pon′ics
hy′dro·ski′
hy′dro·stat′ics
hy′dro·ther′a·py
hy′drous
hy·e′na
hy′giene
hy′gi·en′ic
hy′gi·en′i·cal·ly
hy′gi·en·ist
hy·grom′e·ter
hy′gro·scope′

hy'men
hy·me·ne'al
hymn
hym'nal
hym·nol'o·gy
hy·per·a·cid'i·ty
hy'per·ac'tive
hy·per'bo·la
(*curve*)
hy·per'bo·le
(*exaggeration*)
hy·per·bol'ic
hy·per·crit'i·cal
(*too critical;* SEE
hypocritical)
hy·per·sen'si·tive
hy·per·son'ic
hy·per·ten'sion
hy·per·ven'ti·
la'tion
hy'phen
hy'phen·ate'
·at'ed ·at'ing
hy'phen·a'tion
hyp·no'sis
·ses
hyp·not'ic
hyp·not'i·cal·ly
hyp'no·tism
hyp'no·tiz'a·ble
hyp'no·tize'
·tized' ·tiz'ing
hy·po·chon'dri·a
hy·po·chon'dri·ac'
hy·po·chon·
dri'a·cal
hy·po·chon·
dri'a·sis
hy·poc'ri·sy
·sies
hyp'o·crite
hyp·o·crit'i·cal
(*deceitful;* SEE
hypercritical)
hy·po·der'mic
hy·pot'e·nuse'
hy·poth'e·cate'
·cat'ed ·cat'ing
hy·poth'e·sis
·ses'
hy·poth'e·size'
·sized' ·siz'ing
hy·po·thet'i·cal
hy·po·thet'i·cal·ly
hys'ter·ec'to·my
·mies
hys·te'ri·a
hys·ter'ic
hys·ter'i·cal
hys·ter'i·cal·ly

I

i·am'bic
ice
iced ic'ing

ice'berg'
ice'bound'
ice'box'
ice'break'er
ice'cap'
ice cream
ice field
ice'house'
ice'man'
ice milk
ich'thy·ol'o·gy
i'ci·cle
i'ci·ly
i'ci·ness
ic'ing
i'con
i·con'ic
i·con'o·clast'
i'cy
i'ci·er i'ci·est
I'da·ho'
i·de'a
i·de'al
i·de'al·ism
i·de'al·ist
i·de·al·is'tic
i·de·al·is'ti·cal·ly
i·de·al·i·za'tion
i·de'al·ize'
·ized' ·iz'ing
i·de'al·ly
i'de·ate'
·at'ed ·at'ing
i·de·a'tion
i·den'ti·cal
i·den'ti·cal·ly
i·den'ti·fi·ca'tion
i·den'ti·fi'er
i·den'ti·fy'
·fied' ·fy'ing
i·den'ti·ty
·ties
id'e·o·gram'
id'e·o·graph'ic
i'de·o·log'i·cal
i'de·o·log'i·cal·ly
i'de·ol'o·gist
i'de·ol'o·gize'
·gized' ·giz'ing
i'de·ol'o·gy
·gies
id'i·o·cy
id'i·om
id'i·o·mat'ic
id'i·o·mat'i·cal·ly
id'i·o·syn'cra·sy
·sies
id'i·o·syn·crat'ic
id'i·ot
id'i·ot'ic
id'i·ot'i·cal·ly
i'dle
i'dler i'dlest
i'dled i'dling
(*not active;* SEE
idol, idyll)
i'dle·ness

i'dler
i'dly
i'dol
(*image worshiped;*
SEE idle, idyll)
i·dol'a·ter
i·dol'a·trous
i·dol'a·try
i'dol·ize'
·ized' ·iz'ing
i'dyll *or* i'dyl
(*pastoral poem;*
SEE idle, idol)
i·dyl'lic
ig'loo
·loos
ig'ne·ous
ig·nit'a·ble
or ·i·ble
ig·nite'
·nit'ed ·nit'ing
ig·ni'tion
ig·no'ble
ig'no·min'i·ous
ig'no·min'y
·ies
ig·no·ra'mus
ig'no·rance
ig'no·rant
ig·nore'
·nored' ·nor'ing
i·gua'na
il'e·um
(*intestine*)
il'i·um
(*bone*)
ill
worse worst
ill'-ad·vised'
ill'-be'ing
ill'-bod'ing
ill'-bred'
ill'-con·sid'ered
ill'-dis·posed'
il·le'gal
il·le·gal'i·ty
·ties
il·le'gal·ly
il·leg·i·bil'i·ty
il·leg'i·ble
il·leg'i·bly
il·le·git'i·ma·cy
·cies
il·le·git'i·mate
il·le·git'i·mate·ly
ill'-fat'ed
ill'-fa'vored
ill'-found'ed
ill'-got'ten
ill'-hu'mored
il·lib'er·al
il·lic'it
(*unlawful;* SEE
elicit)
il·lim'it·a·ble
il·lim'it·a·bly
Il'li·nois'
il·lit'er·a·cy

il·lit'er·ate
il·lit'er·ate·ly
ill'-man'nered
ill'-na'tured
ill'ness
il·log'i·cal
il·log'i·cal·ly
ill'-sort'ed
ill'-spent'
ill'-starred'
ill'-suit'ed
ill'-tem'pered
ill'-timed'
ill'-treat'
il·lu'mi·nate'
·nat'ed ·nat'ing
il·lu'mi·na'tion
il·lu'mi·na'tor
ill'-us'age
ill'-use'
il·lu'sion
(*false idea;* SEE
allusion, elusion)
il·lu'sive
(*deceptive;* SEE
allusive, elusive)
il·lu'so·ri·ly
il·lu'so·ri·ness
il·lu'so·ry
il·lus'trate'
·trat'ed ·trat'ing
il·lus·tra'tion
il·lus'tra·tive
il·lus'tra·tor
il·lus'tri·ous
im'age
·aged ·ag·ing
im'age·ry
·ries
i·mag'i·na·ble
i·mag'i·na·bly
i·mag'i·nar'i·ness
i·mag'i·nar'y
i·mag'i·na'tion
i·mag'i·na·tive
i·mag'ine
·ined ·in·ing
im'ag·ism
im·bal'ance
im'be·cile
im·be·cil'ic
im·be·cil'i·ty
·ties
im·bibe'
·bibed' ·bib'ing
im·bib'er
im'bri·cate'
·cat'ed ·cat'ing
im'bri·ca'tion
im·bro'glio
·glios
im·brue'
·brued' ·bru'ing
im·bue'
·bued' ·bu'ing
im'i·ta·ble
im'i·tate'
·tat'ed ·tat'ing

im'i·ta'tion
im'i·ta'tive
im'i·ta'tor
im·mac'u·late
im'ma·nent
(*inherent;* SEE
imminent)
im·ma·te'ri·al
im·ma·ture'
im·ma·tu'ri·ty
im·meas'ur·a·ble
im·me'di·a·cy
im·me'di·ate
im·me'di·ate·ly
im·me·mo'ri·al
im·mense'
im·mense'ly
im·men'si·ty
im·merge'
·merged'
·merg'ing
(*plunge;* SEE
emerge)
im·mer'gence
im·merse'
·mersed'
·mers'ing
im·mers'i·ble
im·mer'sion
im'mi·grant
im'mi·grate'
·grat'ed ·grat'ing
im'mi·gra'tion
im'mi·nence
im'mi·nent
(*impending;* SEE
eminent,
immanent)
im·mis'ci·ble
im·mit'i·ga·ble
im·mo'bile
im·mo·bil'i·ty
im·mo·bi·li·
za'tion
im·mo'bi·lize'
·lized' ·liz'ing
im·mod'er·ate
im·mod·er·a'tion
im·mod'est
im·mod'es·ty
im·mo·late'
·lat'ed ·lat'ing
im·mo·la'tion
im·mor'al
im·mo·ral'i·ty
·ties
im·mor'tal
im·mor·tal'i·ty
im·mor·tal·i·
za'tion
im·mor'tal·ize'
·ized' ·iz'ing
im·mov'a·bil'i·ty
im·mov'a·ble
im·mune'
im·mu'ni·ty
·ties
im·mu·ni·za'tion

im'mu·nize'
·nized' ·niz'ing
im·mu·nol'o·gy
im·mure'
·mured' ·mur'i
im·mu'ta·bil'i·t
im·mu'ta·ble
im·mu'ta·bly
im·pact'ed
im·pac'tion
im·pair'
im·pale'
·paled' ·pal'in
im·pal·pa·bil'i·
im·pal'pa·ble
im·pan'el
·eled *or* ·elled
·el·ing *or* ·el·l
im·part'
im·part'a·ble
im·par'tial
im·par·ti·al'i·t
im·part'i·ble
im·pas'sa·bil'i·
im·pass'a·ble
(*not passable;*
SEE impassible)
im'passe
im·pas·si·bil'i·
im·pas'si·ble
(*unfeeling;* SE
impassable)
im·pas'sioned
im·pas'sive
im·pas·siv'i·t
im·pa'tience
im·pa'tient
im·peach'
im·peach'a·b
im·pec'ca·bil
im·pec'ca·ble
im·pec'ca·bly
im·pe·cu'ni·
os'i·ty
im·pe·cu'ni·c
im·ped'ance
im·pede'
·ped'ed ·ped
im·ped'i·mer
im·ped'i·mer
im·pel'
·pelled' ·pel
im·pel'lent
im·pel'ler
im·pend'
im·pend'ing
im·pen'e·tra
bil'i·ty
im·pen'e·tra
im·pen'i·ten
im·pen'i·ten
im·per'a·tiv
im·per·cep'
im·per·cep'
im·per'fect
im·per·fec't
im·per'fo·r:
im·pe'ri·al

im·pe'ri·al·ism
im·pe'ri·al·is'tic
im·pe'ri·al·ly
im·per'il
im·pe'ri·ous
im·per'ish·a·ble
im·per'ma·nent
im·per'me·a·ble
im·per·mis'si·ble
im·per'son·al
im·per·son·al'i·ty
im·per'son·al·ize'
im·per'son·ate'
·at'ed ·at'ing
im·per·son·a'tion
im·per'son·a'tor
im·per'ti·nence
im·per'ti·nent
im'per·turb·a·
bil'i·ty
im·per·turb'a·ble
im·per'vi·ous
im'pe·ti'go
im·pet'u·os'i·ty
im·pet'u·ous
im'pe·tus
im·pi'e·ty
·ties
im·pinge'
·pinged' ·ping'ing
im·pinge'ment
im'pi·ous
imp'ish
im·pla'ca·ble
im·plant'
im·plan·ta'tion
im·plau'si·ble
im'ple·ment
im'ple·men'tal
im'ple·men·ta'tion
im'pli·cate'
·cat'ed ·cat'ing
im'pli·ca'tion
im'pli·ca'tive
im·plic'it
im·plode'
·plod'ed ·plod'ing
im·plore'
·plored' ·plor'ing
im·plo'sion
im·ply'
·plied' ·ply'ing
im·po·lite'
im·pol'i·tic
im·pon'der·a·ble
im·port'
im·port'a·ble
im·por'tance
im·por'tant
im·por·ta'tion
im·port'er
im·por'tu·nate
im·por·tune'
·tuned' ·tun'ing
im·por·tu'ni·ty
·ies
im·pose'
·posed' ·pos'ing

im·po·si'tion
im·pos'si·bil'i·ty
·ties
im·pos'si·ble
im'post
im·pos'tor
(deceiver)
im·pos'ture
(deception)
im·po'tence
im'po·tent
im·pound'
im·pov'er·ish
im·prac'ti·ca·
bil'i·ty
im·prac'ti·ca·ble
im·prac'ti·cal
im'pre·cate'
·cat'ed ·cat'ing
im·pre·ca'tion
im·pre·cise'
im·preg'na·bil'i·ty
im·preg'na·ble
im·preg'nate
·nat·ed ·nat·ing
im·preg·na'tion
im·pre·sa'ri·o
·ri·os
im·pre·scrip'ti·ble
im·press'
im·press'i·ble
im·pres'sion
im·pres'sion·a·ble
im·pres'sion·a·bly
im·pres'sion·ism
im·pres'sive
im·pres'sive·ly
im·pri·ma'tur
im·print'
im·pris'on
im·prob'a·ble
im·promp'tu
im·prop'er
im·pro·pri'e·ty
·ties
im·prov'a·ble
im·prove'
·proved' ·prov'ing
im·prove'ment
im·prov'i·dent
im·prov'i·sa'tion
im·pro·vise'
·vised' ·vis'ing
im·pru'dence
im·pru'dent
im·pu'dence
im·pu'dent
im·pugn'
im·pugn'a·ble
im'pulse
im·pul'sion
im·pul'sive
im·pul'sive·ly
im·pu'ni·ty
im·pure'
im·pu'ri·ty
·ties
im·put'a·bil'i·ty

im·put'a·ble
im'pu·ta'tion
im·put'a·tive
im·pute'
·put'ed ·put'ing
in·a·bil'i·ty
in·ac·ces'si·ble
in·ac'cu·ra·cy
·cies
in·ac'cu·rate
in·ac'tion
in·ac'ti·vate'
·vat'ed ·vat'ing
in·ac'ti·va'tion
in·ac'tive
in·ac·tiv'i·ty
in·ad'e·qua·cy
·cies
in·ad'e·quate
in·ad·mis'si·ble
in·ad·vert'ence
in·ad·vert'ent
in·ad·vis'a·bil'i·ty
in·ad·vis'a·ble
in·al'ien·a·ble
in·al'ter·a·ble
in·ane'
in·an'i·mate
in·an'i·ty
·ties
in·ap'pli·ca·ble
in·ap·pre'ci·a·ble
in·ap·proach'a·ble
in·ap·pro'pri·ate
in·ar·tic'u·late
in·ar·tis'tic
in·as·much' as
in·at·ten'tion
in·at·ten'tive
in·au'di·ble
in·au'gu·ral
in·au'gu·rate'
·rat'ed ·rat'ing
in·aus·pi'cious
in'board'
in'born'
in'breed'
·bred' ·breed'ing
in·cal'cu·la·ble
in·cal'cu·la·bly
in·can·des'cence
in·can·des'cent
in·can·ta'tion
in·ca·pa·bil'i·ty
in·ca'pa·ble
in·ca·pac'i·tate'
·tat'ed ·tat'ing
in·ca·pac'i·ta'tion
in·ca·pac'i·ty
in·car'cer·ate'
·at'ed ·at'ing
in·car·cer·a'tion
in·car'nate
·nat·ed ·nat·ing
in·car·na'tion
in·cau'tious
in·cen'di·ar'y
·ies

in'cense
in·cense'
·censed' ·cens'ing
in·cen'tive
in·cep'tion
in·cep'tive
in·cer'ti·tude'
in·ces'sant
in'cest
in·ces'tu·ous
in·cho'ate
in'ci·dence
in'ci·dent
in·ci·den'tal
in·ci·den'tal·ly
in·cin'er·ate'
·at'ed ·at'ing
in·cin·er·a'tion
in·cin'er·a'tor
in·cip'i·ence
in·cip'i·ent
in·cise'
·cised' ·cis'ing
in·ci'sion
in·ci'sive
in·ci'sor
in·cite'
·cit'ed ·cit'ing
in·cit'er
in·ci·vil'i·ty
·ties
in·clem'en·cy
in·clem'ent
in·cli'na·ble
in·cli·na'tion
in·cline'
·clined' ·clin'ing
in·cli·nom'e·ter
in·clude'
·clud'ed
·clud'ing
in·clu'sion
in·clu'sive
in·co·er'ci·ble
in·cog·ni'to
·tos
in·cog'ni·zance
in·cog'ni·zant
in·co·her'ence
in·co·her'ent
in·com·bus'ti·ble
in'come
in'com'ing
in·com·men'su·
ra·ble
in·com·men'su·
rate
in·com·mode'
·mod'ed ·mod'ing
in·com·mo'di·ous
in·com·mu'ni·
ca·ble
in·com·mu'ni·
ca'do
in·com'pa·ra·ble
in·com·pat'i·
bil'i·ty
·ties

in·com·pat'i·ble
in·com'pe·tence
in·com'pe·tent
in·com·plete'
in·com·pre·
hen'si·ble
in·com·press'i·ble
in·com·put'a·ble
in·con·ceiv'a·ble
in·con·clu'sive
in·con·dite'
in·con·form'i·ty
in·con'gru·ent
in·con·gru'i·ty
·ties
in·con'gru·ous
in·con·se·
quen'tial
in·con·sid'er·a·ble
in·con·sid'er·ate
in·con·sid'er·
ate·ly
in·con·sid'er·
a'tion
in·con·sis'ten·cy
·cies
in·con·sis'tent
in·con·sol'a·ble
in·con·spic'u·ous
in·con'stan·cy
in·con'stant
in·con·sum'a·ble
in·con·test'a·ble
in·con'ti·nent
in·con·trol'la·ble
in·con·tro·vert'i·
ble
in·con·ven'ience
in·con·ven'ient
in·con·vert'i·ble
in·co·or'di·nate
in·cor'po·rate'
·rat'ed ·rat'ing
in·cor'po·ra'tion
in·cor'po·ra'tor
in·cor·po're·al
in·cor·rect'
in·cor·ri·gi·bil'i·ty
in·cor'ri·gi·ble
in·cor'ri·gi·bly
in·cor·rupt'
in·cor·rupt'i·ble
in·creas'a·ble
in·crease'
·creased'
·creas'ing
in·creas'ing·ly
in·cred·i·bil'i·ty
in·cred'i·ble
in·cred'i·bly
in·cre·du'li·ty
in·cred'u·lous
in·cre'ment
in·cre·men'tal
in·crim'i·nate'
·nat'ed ·nat'ing
in·crim'i·na'tion
in·crim'i·na·to'ry

in·crust'
in·crus·ta'tion
in'cu·bate'
·bat'ed ·bat'ing
in·cu·ba'tion
in·cu·ba'tor
in·cul'cate
·cat·ed ·cat·ing
in·cul·ca'tion
in·culp'a·ble
in·cul·pa'tion
in·cum'ben·cy
·cies
in·cum'bent
in·cu·nab'u·la
in·cur'
·curred'
·cur'ring
in·cur·a·bil'i·ty
in·cur'a·ble
in·cur'a·bly
in·cu'ri·ous
in·cur'sion
in·debt'ed
in·de'cen·cy
·cies
in·de'cent
in·de·ci'pher·
a·ble
in·de·ci'sion
in·de·ci'sive
in·de·clin'a·ble
in·dec'o·rous
in·de·co'rum
in·deed'
in·de·fat'i·ga·ble
in·de·fat'i·ga·bly
in·de·fea'si·ble
in·de·fect'i·ble
in·de·fen'si·ble
in·def'i·nite
in·del'i·ble
in·del'i·bly
in·del'i·ca·cy
·cies
in·del'i·cate
in·dem'ni·fi·
ca'tion
in·dem'ni·fy'
·fied' ·fy'ing
in·dem'ni·ty
·ties
in·dent'
in·den·ta'tion
in·den'tion
in·den'ture
·tured ·tur·ing
in·de·pend'ence
in·de·pend'ent
in'·depth'
in·de·scrib'a·ble
in·de·scrib'a·bly
in·de·struct'i·ble
in·de·ter'mi·na·
ble
in·de·ter'mi·na·cy
in·de·ter'mi·nate

in·de·ter'mi- na'tion	in·dom'i·ta·bly	in'e·rad'i·ca·ble	in·fer'tile	in·gen'u·ous	in·ju'ri·ous
in'dex	in'door'	in·er'ra·ble	in·fest'	(*frank;* SEE	in'ju·ry
·dex·es *or* ·di·ces'	in'doors'	in·er'rant	in'fi·del	ingenious)	·ries
In'di·an'a	in·dorse'	in·ert'	in'fi·del'i·ty	in·gest'	in·jus'tice
in'di·cate'	·dorsed'	in·er'tia	·ties	in·ges'tion	ink'blot'
·cat'ed ·cat'ing	·dors'ing	in·es·cap'a·ble	in'field'	in·glo'ri·ous	ink'ling
in'di·ca'tion	in·du'bi·ta·ble	in·es·cap'a·bly	in·fil'trate	in'got	ink'y
in·dic'a·tive	in·du'bi·ta·bly	in·es·sen'tial	·trat·ed ·trat·ing	in·grained'	·i·er ·i·est
in'di·ca'tor	in·duce'	in·es'ti·ma·ble	in'fil·tra'tion	in'grate	in'laid'
in·dict'	·duced' ·duc'ing	in·ev'i·ta·bil'i·ty	in'fil·tra'tor	in·gra'ti·ate'	in'land
(*accuse formally;*	in·duce'ment	in·ev'i·ta·ble	in'fi·nite	·at'ed ·at'ing	in'·law'
SEE indite)	in·duct'	in·ev'i·ta·bly	in'fi·nite·ly	in·grat'i·tude'	in'lay'
in·dict'a·ble	in·duct'ance	in·ex·act'	in·fin·i·tes'i·mal	in·gre'di·ent	·laid' ·lay'ing
in·dict'ment	in·duct'ee'	in·ex·cus'a·ble	in·fin'i·tive	in'gress	·lays'
in·dif'fer·ence	in·duc'tile	in·ex·haust'i·ble	in·fin'i·ty	in'·group'	in'let
in·dif'fer·ent	in·duc'tion	in·ex'o·ra·ble	·ties	in'grown'	in'mate'
in'di·gence	in·duc'tive	in·ex·pe'di·ent	in·firm'	in·hab'it	in me·mo'ri·am
in·dig'e·nous	in·duc'tor	in·ex·pen'sive	in·fir'ma·ry	in·hab'it·a·ble	in'most'
in'di·gent	in·dulge'	in·ex·pe'ri·ence	·ries	in·hab'it·ant	in'nards
in·di·gest'i·ble	·dulged'	in·ex'pert	in·fir'mi·ty	in·hal'ant	in'nate'
in'di·ges'tion	·dulg'ing	in·ex'pi·a·ble	·ties	in·ha·la'tion	in'ner·most'
in·dig'nant	in·dul'gence	in·ex'pli·ca·ble	in·flame'	in·hale'	in'ner·spring'
in'dig·na'tion	in·dul'gent	in·ex'pli·ca·bly	·flamed'	·haled' ·hal'ing	in·ner'vate
in·dig'ni·ty	in'du·rate'	in·ex·press'i·ble	·flam'ing	in·hal'er	·vat·ed ·vat·ing
·ties	·rat'ed ·rat'ing	in·ex·press'i·bly	in·flam'ma·ble	in·har·mon'ic	in'ning
in'di·go'	in'du·ra'tion	in·ex·pres'sive	in·flam·ma'tion	in·har·mo'ni·ous	inn'keep'er
in·di·rect'	in·dus'tri·al	in·ex·ten'si·ble	in·flam'ma·to'ry	in·here'	in'no·cence
in'di·rec'tion	in·dus'tri·al·ism	in·ex·tin'guish·a·	in·flate'	·hered' ·her'ing	in'no·cent
in'dis·cern'i·ble	in·dus'tri·al·ist	ble	·flat'ed	in·her'ence	in·noc'u·ous
in'dis·creet'	in·dus'tri·al·i·	in·ex'tri·ca·ble	·flat'ing	in·her'ent	in'no·vate'
(*lacking prudence*)	za'tion	in·ex'tri·ca·bly	in·fla'tion	in·her'it	·vat'ed ·vat'ing
in'dis·crete'	in·dus'tri·al·ize'	in·fal'li·bil'i·ty	in·fla'tion·ar'y	in·her'it·a·ble	in'no·va'tion
(*not separated*)	·ized' ·iz'ing	in·fal'li·ble	in·flect'	in·her'it·ance	in'no·va'tive
in'dis·cre'tion	in·dus'tri·ous	in·fal'li·bly	in·flec'tion	in·her'i·tor	in'no·va'tor
(*indiscreet act*)	in'dus·try	in·fa'mous	in·flex'i·ble	in·hib'it	in·nu·en'do
in'dis·crim'i·nate	·tries	in'fa·my	in·flex'i·bly	in·hi·bi'tion	·does *or* ·dos
in'dis·pen'sa·ble	in·e'bri·ate'	·mies	in·flict'	in·hib'i·tive	in·nu'mer·a·ble
in'dis·pose'	·at'ed ·at'ing	in'fan·cy	in·flic'tion	in·hib'i·tor	in·oc'u·late'
in'dis·po·si'tion	in·e'bri·a'tion	·cies	in'·flight'	in·hos'pi·ta·ble	·lat'ed ·lat'ing
in'dis·pu'ta·ble	in·e·bri'e·ty	in'fant	in'flow'	in·hos·pi·tal'i·ty	in·oc'u·la'tion
in'dis·sol'u·ble	in·ed'i·ble	in·fan'ti·cide'	in'flu·ence	in'·house'	in·of·fen'sive
in'dis·tinct'	in·ed'u·ca·ble	in'fan·tile'	·enced ·enc·ing	in·hu'man	in·op'er·a·tive
in'dis·tinc'tive	in·ef'fa·ble	in'fan·ti·lism	in·flu·en'tial	in·hu·mane'	in·op'er·a·tive
in'dis·tin'guish·	in·ef'fa·bly	in'fan·try	in·flu·en'za	in·hu·man'i·ty	in·op'por·tune'
a·ble	in·ef·face'a·ble	·tries	in'flux'	·ties	in·or'di·nate
in·dite'	in·ef·fec'tive	in'fan·try·man	in'form'	in·im'i·cal	in·or·gan'ic
·dit'ed ·dit'ing	in·ef·fec'tu·al	in·fat'u·ate'	in·for'mal	in·im'i·ta·ble	in'pa'tient
(*write;* SEE indict)	in·ef·fi·ca'cious	·at'ed ·at'ing	in·for·mal'i·ty	in·iq'ui·tous	in'put'
in'di·vid'u·al	in·ef'fi·ca·cy	in·fat'u·a'tion	in·form'ant	in·iq'ui·ty	in'quest
in'di·vid'u·al·ism	in·ef·fi'cien·cy	in·fect'	in·for·ma'tion	·ties	in·qui'e·tude'
in'di·vid'u·al·	in·ef·fi'cient	in·fec'tion	in·form'a·tive	(*wickedness;*	in·quire'
is'tic	in·e·las'tic	in·fec'tious	in·form'er	SEE inequity)	·quired'
in'di·vid'u·al'i·ty	in·e·las'tic'i·ty	in·fec'tive	in·frac'tion	in·i'tial	·quir'ing
in'di·vid'u·al·ize'	in·el'e·gance	in·fec'tor	in·fran'gi·ble	·tialed *or* ·tialled	in'quir·y
·ized' ·iz'ing	in·el'e·gant	in·fe·lic'i·tous	in'fra·red'	·tial·ing *or* ·tial·ling	·ies
in'di·vid'u·al·ly	in·el'i·gi·bil'i·ty	in·fe·lic'i·ty	in·fre'quent	in·i'tial·ly	in·qui·si'tion
in'di·vid'u·ate'	in·el'i·gi·ble	·ties	in·fringe'	in·i'ti·ate'	in·quis'i·tive
·at'ed ·at'ing	in·e·luc'ta·ble	in·fer'	in·fringe'ment	·at'ed ·at'ing	in·quis'i·tor
in'di·vis'i·bil'i·ty	in·e·lud'i·ble	·ferred'	in·fu'ri·ate'	in·i'ti·a·tive	in'road'
in'di·vis'i·ble	in·ept'	·fer'ring	·at'ed ·at'ing	in·i'ti·a'tor	in·sane'
in·doc'tri·nate'	in·ept'i·tude'	in·fer'a·ble	in·fuse'	in·ject'	in·san'i·tar'y
·nat'ed ·nat'ing	in·e·qual'i·ty	in'fer·ence	·fused' ·fus'ing	in·jec'tion	in·san'i·ty
in·doc'tri·na'tion	·ties	in·fer·en'tial	in·fu'sion	in·jec'tor	in·sa'ti·a·ble
in·doc'tri·na'tor	in·eq'ui·ta·ble	in·fe'ri·or	in·gen'ious	in·ju·di'cious	in·scribe'
in'do·lence	in·eq'ui·ty	in·fe'ri·or'i·ty	(*clever;* SEE	in·junc'tion	·scribed'
in'do·lent	·ties	in·fer'nal	ingenuous)	in'jure	·scrib'ing
in·dom'i·ta·ble	(*unfairness;*	in·fer'no	in'gé·nue'	·jured ·jur'ing	in·scrip'tion
	SEE iniquity)	·nos	in·gé·nu'i·ty		in·scru'ta·bil·

in·scru'ta·ble
in'seam'
in'sect
in·sec'ti·cide'
in·se·cure'
in·se·cu'ri·ty
in·sem'i·nate'
·nat·ed ·nat·ing
in·sem'i·na'tion
in·sen'sate
in·sen'si·bil'i·ty
in·sen'si·ble
in·sen'si·tive
n·sen'si·tiv'i·ty
in·sep'a·ra·ble
n·sert'
n·ser'tion
n'·ser'vice
n'side'
n·sid'i·ous
n'sight'
n·sig'ni·a
n·sig·nif'i·cance
n·sig·nif'i·cant
n·sin·cere'
n·sin·cere'ly
n·sin·cer'i·ty
n·sin·u·ate'
·at·ed ·at·ing
·sin·u·a'tion
·sip'id
·si·pid'i·ty
·sist'
·sist'ence
·sist'ent
·so·bri'e·ty
·so·far'
·sole'
·so·lence
·so·lent
·sol'u·ble
·sol'vent
·som'ni·a
·sou'ci·ance
·sou'ci·ant
·spect'
·spec'tion
·spec'tor
·spi·ra'tion
·spire'
·pired' ·spir'ing
·spir'it
·sta·bil'i·ty
·stall' or ·stal'
·talled' ·stall'ing
·stal·la'tion
·stall'ment
·stal'ment
·stance
·stant
·stan·ta'ne·ous
·stan'ter
·state'
·at'ed ·stat'ing
·stead'
·tep'
·sti·gate'
·at'ed ·gat'ing

in'sti·ga'tion
in'sti·ga'tor
in·still' or ·stil'
·stilled' ·still'ing
in'stinct
in·stinc'tive
in'sti·tute'
·tut'ed ·tut'ing
in'sti·tu'tion
in'sti·tu'tion·al·ize'
·ized' ·iz'ing
in·struct'
in·struc'tion
in·struc'tive
in·struc'tor
in'stru·ment
in'stru·men'tal
in'stru·men·tal'i·ty
in'stru·men·ta'tion
in'sub·or'di·nate
in'sub·or'di·na'tion
in'sub·stan'tial
in·suf'fer·a·ble
in·suf·fi'cien·cy
·cies
in·suf·fi'cient
in'su·lar
in'su·late'
·lat'ed ·lat'ing
in'su·la'tion
in'su·la'tor
in'su·lin
in·sult'
in·su'per·a·ble
in·sup·port'a·ble
in·sup·press'i·ble
in·sur'a·bil'i·ty
in·sur'a·ble
in·sur'ance
in·sure'
·sured' ·sur'ing
in·sur'er
in·sur'gence
in·sur'gent
in·sur·mount'a·ble
in·sur·rec'tion
in·tact'
in·tagl'io
·ios
in'take'
in·tan'gi·ble
in'te·ger
in'te·gral
in'te·grate'
·grat'ed ·grat'ing
in'te·gra'tion
in·teg'ri·ty
in·teg'u·ment
in·tel'lect'
in·tel·lec'tu·al
in·tel·lec'tu·al·ize'
·ized' ·iz'ing
in·tel·lec'tu·al·ly

in·tel'li·gence
in·tel'li·gent
in·tel'li·gent'si·a
in·tel'li·gi·bil'i·ty
in·tel'li·gi·ble
in·tel'li·gi·bly
In'tel·sat'
in·tem'per·ance
in·tem'per·ate
in·tend'
in·tend'ant
in·tense'
in·tense'ly
in·ten'si·fi·ca'tion
in·ten'si·fy'
·fied' ·fy'ing
in·ten'si·ty
in·ten'sive
in·tent'
in·ten'tion
in·ten'tion·al
in·ten'tion·al·ly
in·ter'
·terred' ·ter'ring
in·ter·act'
in'ter·ac'tion
in'ter·breed'
·bred' ·breed'ing
in'ter·cede'
·ced'ed ·ced'ing
in'ter·cept'
in'ter·cep'tion
in'ter·cep'tor
in'ter·ces'sion
in'ter·change'
in'ter·change'a·ble
in'ter·com'
in'ter·com·mu'ni·cate'
in'ter·con·nect'
in'ter·course'
in'ter·de·nom'i·na'tion·al
in'ter·de·part'men·tal
in'ter·de·pend'ence
in'ter·dict'
in'ter·dis'ci·pli·nar'y
in'ter·est
in'ter·est·ed
in'ter·faith'
in'ter·fere'
·fered' ·fer'ing
in'ter·fer'ence
in'ter·fer'on
in'ter·im
in·te'ri·or
in'ter·ject'
in'ter·jec'tion
in'ter·lace'
in'ter·leaf'
·leaves'
in'ter·leave'
·leaved'
·leav'ing

in'ter·lin'e·ar
in'ter·lin'ing
in'ter·lock'
in'ter·lo·cu'tion
in'ter·loc'u·tor
in'ter·loc'u·to'ry
in'ter·lope'
·loped' ·lop'ing
in'ter·lop'er
in'ter·lude'
in'ter·mar'riage
in'ter·mar'ry
in'ter·me'di·ar'y
·ar'ies
in'ter·me'di·ate
in·ter'ment
in'ter·mez'zo
·zos or ·zi
in·ter'mi·na·ble
in·ter'min'gle
in'ter·mis'sion
in'ter·mit'tent
in'tern
(doctor)
in·tern'
(detain)
in·ter'nal
in·ter'nal·ize'
·ized' ·iz'ing
in·ter'nal·ly
in'ter·na'tion·al
in·ter'ne·cine
in'tern·ee'
in'tern·ist
in·tern'ment
in'tern·ship'
in'ter·of'fice
in'ter·pen'e·trate'
in'ter·per'son·al
in'ter·phone'
in'ter·plan'e·tar'y
in'ter·play'
in·ter'po·late'
·lat'ed ·lat'ing
in·ter'po·la'tion
in'ter·pose'
in·ter'pret
in·ter'pre·ta'tion
in·ter'pret·er
in'ter·ra'cial
in'ter·re·late'
in'ter·re·la'tion
in'ter·ro·gate'
·gat'ed ·gat'ing
in·ter'ro·ga'tion
in·ter'rog'a·tive
in·ter'rog·a'tor
in·ter'rog'a·to'ry
in'ter·rupt'
in'ter·rup'tion
in'ter·scho·las'tic
in'ter·sect'
in'ter·sec'tion
in'ter·sperse'
·spersed'
·spers'ing

in'ter·sper'sion
in'ter·state'
in'ter·stel'lar
in·ter'stice
·stic·es
in'ter·twine'
in'ter·ur'ban
in'ter·val
in'ter·vene'
·vened' ·ven'ing
in'ter·ven'tion
in'ter·view'
in'ter·view'er
in'ter·weave'
·wove' ·wov'en
·weav'ing
in·tes'tate
in·tes'tin·al
in·tes'tine
in'ti·ma·cy
·cies
in'ti·mate
in'ti·ma'tion
in·tim'i·date'
·dat'ed ·dat'ing
in·tim'i·da'tion
in·tol'er·a·ble
in·tol'er·ance
in·tol'er·ant
in·to·na'tion
in·tone'
in·tox'i·cant
in·tox'i·cate'
·cat'ed ·cat'ing
in·tox'i·ca'tion
in·trac'ta·ble
in'tra·mu'ral
in'tra·mus'cu·lar
in·tran'si·gent
in·tran'si·tive
in'tra·state'
in'tra·u'ter·ine
in'tra·ve'nous
in·trep'id
in'tre·pid'i·ty
in'tri·ca·cy
·cies
in'tri·cate
in·trigue'
·trigued'
·trigu'ing
in·trin'sic
in'tro·duce'
·duced' ·duc'ing
in'tro·duc'tion
in'tro·duc'to·ry
in'tro·spec'tion
in'tro·spec'tive
in'tro·ver'sion
in'tro·vert'
in·trude'
·trud'ed
·trud'ing
in·trud'er
in·tru'sion
in·tru'sive
in·tu·i'tion
in·tu'i·tive

in'un·date'
·dat'ed ·dat'ing
in'un·da'tion
in·ure'
·ured' ·ur'ing
in·vade'
·vad'ed ·vad'ing
in·vad'er
in'va·lid
in·val'id
in·val'i·date'
·dat'ed ·dat'ing
in·val'i·da'tion
in·val'u·a·ble
in·val'u·a·bly
in·var'i·a·ble
in·var'i·a·bly
in·va'sion
in·vec'tive
in·veigh'
in·vei'gle
·gled ·gling
in·vent'
in·ven'tion
in·ven'tive
in·ven'tor
in'ven·to'ry
·ries, ·ried ·ry·ing
in·verse'
in·ver'sion
in·vert'
in·ver'te·brate
in·vert'i·ble
in·vest'
in·ves'ti·gate'
·gat'ed ·gat'ing
in·ves'ti·ga'tion
in·ves'ti·ga'tor
in·ves'ti·ture
in·vest'ment
in·vet'er·ate
in·vi'a·ble
in·vid'i·ous
in·vig'or·ate'
·at'ed ·at'ing
in·vin'ci·bil'i·ty
in·vin'ci·ble
in·vin'ci·bly
in·vi'o·la·ble
in·vi'o·late
in·vis'i·ble
in·vi'ta'tion
in·vite'
·vit'ed ·vit'ing
in'vo·ca'tion
in'voice
·voiced ·voic·ing
in·voke'
·voked' ·vok'ing
in·vol'un·tar'i·ly
in·vol'un·tar'y
in'vo·lute'
in·volve'
·volved'
·volv'ing
in·vul'ner·a·ble
in'ward
i'o·dine'

i'on
i·on·i·za'tion
i'on·ize'
·ized' ·iz'ing
i·on'o·sphere'
i·o'ta
I'o·wa
ip'e·cac'
ip'so fac'to
i·ras'ci·bil'i·ty
i·ras'ci·ble
i·rate'
ire'ful·ly
ir'i·des'cence
ir'i·des'cent
irk'some
i'ron·bound'
i'ron·clad'
i·ron'i·cal
i·ron'i·cal·ly
i'ron·stone'
i'ron·work'
i'ro·ny
·nies
ir·ra'di·ate'
ir·ra'di·a'tion
ir·ra'tion·al
ir·ra'tion·al'i·ty
ir·ra'tion·al·ly
ir·re·claim'a·ble
ir·rec'on·cil'a·ble
ir're·cov'er·a·ble
ir're·deem'a·ble
ir're·duc'i·ble
ir·ref'u·ta·ble
ir·reg'u·lar
ir·reg'u·lar'i·ty
·ties
ir·rel'e·vant
ir·re·li'gious
ir're·me'di·a·ble
ir're·mis'si·ble
ir're·mov'a·ble
ir·rep'a·ra·ble
ir·re·place'a·ble
ir·re·press'i·ble
ir·re·proach'a·ble
ir·re·sist'i·ble
ir·res'o·lute'
ir·re·spec'tive
ir·re·spon'si·ble
ir·re·triev'a·ble
ir·rev'er·ence
ir·rev'er·ent
ir·re·vers'i·ble
ir·rev'o·ca·ble
ir'ri·ga·ble
ir'ri·gate'
·gat'ed ·gat'ing
ir'ri·ga'tion
ir'ri·ta·bil'i·ty
ir'ri·ta·ble
ir'ri·ta·bly
ir'ri·tant
ir'ri·tate'
·tat'ed ·tat'ing
ir'ri·ta'tion
ir·rupt'

ir·rup'tion
i'sin·glass'
is'land
isle
(island; SEE aisle)
is'let
(small island; SEE eyelet)
is'n't
i'so·bar'
i'so·late'
·lat'ed ·lat'ing
i'so·la'tion
i'so·la'tion·ist
i'so·mer
i'so·met'ric
i'so·met'ri·cal·ly
i·sos'ce·les'
i'so·therm'
i'so·tope'
i·so·trop'ic
Is'ra·el
Is·rae'li
is'su·ance
is'sue
·sued ·su·ing
isth'mus
·mus·es or ·mi
i·tal'ic
i·tal'i·cize'
·cized' ·ciz'ing
itch'i·ness
itch'y
·i·er ·i·est
i'tem·ize'
·ized' ·iz'ing
it'er·ate'
·at'ed ·at'ing
it'er·a'tion
i·tin'er·ant
i·tin'er·ar'y
·ies
i·tin'er·ate'
·at'ed ·at'ing
its
(of it)
it's
(it is)
it·self'
I've
i'vied
i'vo·ry
·ries
i'vy
i'vies

J

jab
jabbed jab'bing
jab'ber
ja·bot'
ja'cinth
jack'al
jack'a·napes'
jack'ass'

jack'boot'
jack'et
jack'ham'mer
jack'-in-the-box'
-box'es
jack'knife'
·knives'
·knifed' ·knif'ing
jack'-of-all'-
trades'
jacks'-
jack'-o'-lan'tern
·terns
jack'pot'
jack'screw'
jack'straw'
Jac·quard'
jade
jad'ed jad'ing
jag'ged
jag'uar
jai' a·lai'
jail'bird'
jail'er or ·or
jal'ou·sie'
(door; SEE jealousy)
jam
jammed
jam'ming
jam'ba·lay'a
jam'bo·ree'
jan'gle
·gled ·gling
jan'i·tor
Jan'u·ar'y
·ar'ies
ja·pan'
·panned'
·pan'ning
jar
jarred jar'ring
jar'di·niere'
jar'gon
jas'mine
jas'per
ja'to or JA'TO
jaun'dice
·diced ·dic·ing
jaun'ti·ly
jaun'ti·ness
jaun'ty
·ti·er ·ti·est
jav'e·lin
jaw'bone'
jaw'break'er
Jay'cee'
jay'walk'er
jazz'i·ness
jazz'y
·i·er ·i·est
jeal'ous
jeal'ous·y
·ies
(envy; SEE jalousie)
jeans
jeer'ing·ly

je·june'
jel'li·fy'
·fied' ·fy'ing
jel'ly
·lies, ·lied ·ly·ing
jel'ly·fish'
jel'ly·roll'
jen'ny
·nies
jeop'ard·ize'
·ized' ·iz'ing
jeop'ard·y
je·quir'i·ty
·ties
jer'e·mi'ad
jerk'i·ly
jer'kin
jerk'i·ness
jerk'wa'ter
jerk'y
·i·er ·i·est
(moving fitfully)
jer'ky
(dried beef)
Jer'sey
·seys
(dairy cattle)
jer'sey
·seys
(cloth; shirt)
jest'er
jet
jet'ted jet'ting
jet'-black'
jet'lin'er
jet'port'
jet'-pro·pelled'
jet'sam
jet stream
jet'ti·son
jet'ty
·ties, ·tied ·ty·ing
jew'el
·eled or ·elled
·el·ing or ·el·ling
jew'el·er or ·el·ler
jew'el·ry
Jew'ish
Jew'ry
·ries
jew's'-harp' or jews'-harp'
Jez'e·bel
jib
jibbed jib'bing
jibe
jibed jib'ing
(nautical; agree; SEE gibe)
jig'ger
jig'gle
·gled ·gling
jig'saw'
Jim'-Crow'
jim'my
·mies
·mied ·my·ing

jin'gle
·gled ·gling
jin'go
·goes
jin'go·ism
jin'go·is'ti·cal·ly
jin·ni'
jinn
jin·rik'i·sha
jinx
jit'ney
·neys
jit'ter·y
job
jobbed job'bing
job'ber
jock'ey
·eys
·eyed ·ey·ing
jock'strap'
jo·cose'
jo·cos'i·ty
·ties
joc'u·lar
joc'u·lar'i·ty
joc'und
jo·cun'di·ty
jodh'purs
jog
jogged jog'ging
jog'ger
jog'gle
·gled ·gling
john'ny·cake'
join'er
joint'ly
join'ture
joist
joke
joked jok'ing
jol'li·ness
jol'li·ty
jol'ly
·li·er ·li·est
jon'quil
jos'tle
·tled ·tling
jot
jot'ted jot'ting
jounce
;ounced
jounc'ing
jour'nal
jour'nal·ese'
jour'nal·ism
jour'nal·is'tic
jour'ney
·neys
·neyed ·ney·ing
jour'ney·man
joust
jo'vi·al
jo'vi·al'i·ty
jo'vi·al·ly
jowl
joy'ful
joy'less
joy'ous

ju'bi·lant
ju·bi·la'tion
ju'bi·lee'
Ju·da'i·ca
Ju'da·ism
judge
judged judg'i
judg'ment or judge'
ju'di·ca·to'ry
·ries
ju·di'cial
ju·di'ci·ar'y
·ies
ju·di'cious
ju'do
jug
jugged jug'gin
jug'ger·naut'
jug'gle
·gled ·gling
jug'u·lar
juice
juiced juic'in
juic'er
juic'i·ly
juic'i·ness
juic'y
·i·er ·i·est
ju·jit'su or ju·jut'su
ju'jube
juke'box'
ju'lep
ju·li·enne'
Ju·ly'
·lies'
jum'ble
·bled ·bling
jum'bo
jump'er
jump'i·ness
jump'y
·i·er ·i·est
junc'tion
junc'tu
June
jun'gle
jun'ior
jun·ior'i·ty
ju'ni·per
jun'ket
junk'man'
jun'ta
jun'to
·tos
ju·rid'i·cal
ju·rid'i·cal·ly
ju'ris·dic'tion
ju'ris·pru'den
ju'rist
ju·ris'tic
ju'ror
ju'ry
·ries
ju'ry·man
jus'tice
jus'ti·fi'a·ble

'ti·fi'a·bly
'ti·fi·ca'tion
'ti·fy'
ed' ·fy'ing
t'ly

ıt'ted jut'ting
e
ven·ile
ı'ta·pose'
osed' ·pos'ing
ı'ta·po·si'tion

K

ı·bu'ki
f'fee·klatsch'
i'ser
·lei'do·scope'
·lei'do·scop'ic
l'so·mine'
'mi·ka'ze
n'ga·roo'
an'sas
,'o·lin
'pok
ı·put'
ır'a·kul
ır'at
ı·ra'te
ı'sha
ı'ty·did'
ıtz'en·jam'mer
ıy'ak
ı·zoo'
e·bab'
edge
cedged kedg'ing
cel'haul'
cel'son
cen'ness
cep
cept keep'ing
cep'sake'
eg'ler
e'loid
empt
en'nel
neled or ·nelled
nel·ing or
nel·ling
en·tuck'y
er'a·tin
er'chief
er'mis or ·mess
er'nel
(grain; SEE
colonel)
er'o·sene' or
·sine'
er'sey
seys
etch'up
e'tone
et'tle
et'tle·drum'

key
keys
keyed key'ing
(lock; SEE quay)
key'board'
key club
key'hole'
key'note'
key punch
key'stone'
key'way'
kha'ki
kib'ble
kib·butz'
kib'but·zim'
kib'itz·er
kick'off'
kid'nap
·napped' or
·naped'
·nap'ping or
·nap'ing
kid'nap'per or
kid'nap'er
kid'ney
·neys
kill'er
kill'-joy'
kiln
kil'o·gram'
kil'o·hertz'
·hertz'
kil'o·li·ter
ki·lo'me·ter
kil'o·volt'
kil'o·watt'
kil'o·watt'-hour'
kil'ter
ki·mo'no
·nos
kin'der·gar'ten
kin'der·gart'ner
kind'heart'ed
kin'dle
·dled ·dling
kind'li·ness
kind'ly
·li·er ·li·est
kin'dred
kin'e·mat'ics
kin'e·scope'
ki·ne'sics
kin'es·thet'ic
ki·net'ic
kin'folk'
king'bolt'
king'dom
king'fish'
king'li·ness
king'ly
·li·er ·li·est
king'pin'
king post
king'-size'
kink'i·ness
kink'y
·i·er ·i·est
kin'ship'

kins'man
ki'osk
kis'met
kitch'en
kitch'en·ette'
kitch'en·ware'
kit'ten
kit'ty
·ties
kit'ty-cor'nered
klax'on
Klee'nex
klep'to·ma'ni·ac
klieg light
knack
knack'wurst'
knap'sack'
knave
(rogue; SEE nave)
knav'er·y
knav'ish
knead
(press; SEE need)
knee
kneed knee'ing
knee'cap'
knee'-deep'
knee'-high'
knee'hole'
kneel
knelt or kneeled
kneel'ing
knee'pad'
knell
knick'er·bock'ers
knick'knack'
knife
knives
knifed knif'ing
knife'-edge'
knight
(rank; SEE night)
knight'hood'
knit
knit'ted or knit
knit'ting
knit'ter
knob'by
·bi·er ·bi·est
knock'a·bout'
knock'down'
knock'-kneed'
knock'out'
knoll
knot
knot'ted
knot'ting
knot'hole'
knot'ty
·ti·er ·ti·est
know
knew known
know'ing
know'a·ble
know'-how'
know'-it-all'
knowl'edge
knowl'edge·a·ble

knowl'edge·a·bly
knuck'le
·led ·ling
knurled
ko·a'la
ko'di·ak' bear
kohl'ra'bi
·bies
Ko·ran'
ko'sher
kow'tow'
ku'chen
ku'dos
küm'mel
kum'quat
kwa'shi·or'kor

L

la'bel
·beled or ·belled
·bel·ing or
·bel·ling
la'bi·al
la'bile
la'bor
lab'o·ra·to'ry
·ries
la'bor·er
la·bo'ri·ous
la'bor·sav'ing
lab'y·rinth'
lab'y·rin'thine
lace
laced lac'ing
lac'er·ate'
·at'ed ·at'ing
lac'er·a'tion
lace'work'
lach'ry·mose'
lac'i·ness
lack'a·dai'si·cal
lack'ey
·eys
lack'lus'ter
la·con'ic
la·con'i·cal·ly
lac'quer
la·crosse'
lac'tate
·tat·ed ·tat·ing
lac·ta'tion
lac'te·al
lac'tic
lac'tose
la·cu'na
·nas or ·nae
lac'y
·i·er ·i·est
lad'der
lad'en
lad'ing
la'dle
·dled ·dling
la'dy
·dies

la'dy·bug'
la'dy·fin'ger
la'dy·like'
la'dy·ship'
lag
lagged lag'ging
la'ger
lag'gard
la·gniappe'
la·goon'
lair
(den; SEE layer)
large
larg'er larg'est
large'ly
large'-scale'
lar'gess or ·gesse
lar'i·at
lar'va
·vae or ·vas
la·ryn'ge·al
lar'yn·gi'tis
lar'ynx
lar'ynx·es or
la·ryn'ges
la·sa'gna
las·civ'i·ous
lase
lased las'ing
(emit laser light;
SEE laze)
la'ser
lash'ing
las'si·tude'
las'so
·sos or ·soes
last'-ditch'
Las'tex
last'ing
latch'key'
latch'string'
late
lat'er or lat'ter
lat'est or last
la·teen'
late'ly
la'ten·cy
la'tent
lat'er·al
la'tex
lat'i·ces' or
la'tex·es
lath
(wood strip)
lathe
lathed lath'ing
(machine)
lath'er
lath'ing
lat'i·tude'
lat'ke
·kes
la·trine'
lat'ter-day'
lat'tice
·ticed ·tic·ing
lat'tice·work'
laud'a·ble
laud'a·bly
laud'a·to'ry

laugh'a·ble
laugh'ing·stock'
laugh'ter
laun'der
laun'dress
laun'dro·mat'
laun'dry
 ·dries
laun'dry·man
lau're·ate
lau'rel
la'va
la·va'bo
 ·boes
lav'a·liere'
lav'a·to'ry
 ·ries
lav'en·der
lav'ish
law'-a·bid'ing
law'break'er
law'ful
law'ful·ly
law'giv'er
law'less
law'mak'er
lawn mower
law'suit'
law'yer
lax'a·tive
lax'i·ty
lay
 laid lay'ing
 (put; SEE lie)
lay'er
 (stratum; SEE lair)
lay·ette'
lay'man
lay'off'
lay'out'
lay'o·ver
laze
 lazed laz'ing
 (loaf; SEE lase)
la'zi·ly
la'zi·ness
la'zy
 ·zi·er ·zi·est
leach
 (filter; SEE leech)
lead
 led lead'ing
lead'en
lead'er·ship'
lead'-in'
lead'off'
leaf
 leaves
leaf'let
leaf'y
 ·i·er ·i·est
league
 leagued
 leagu'ing
leagu'er
leak
 (escape; SEE leek)

leak'age
leak'y
 ·i·er ·i·est
lean
 leaned or leant
 lean'ing
lean
 (thin; SEE lien)
lean'ness
lean'-to'
 -tos'
leap
 leaped or leapt
 leap'ing
leap'frog'
 ·frogged'
 ·frog'ging
learn
 learned or learnt
 learn'ing
learn'ed adj.
leas'a·ble
lease
 leased leas'ing
lease'-back'
lease'hold'er
least
leath'er
leath'er·ette'
leath'er·i·ness
leath'er·y
leave
 left leav'ing
 (let stay)
leave
 leaved leav'ing
 (bear leaves)
leav'en·ing
leave'-tak'ing
lech'er·ous
lec'i·thin
lec'tern
lec'ture
 ·tured ·tur·ing
ledge
ledg'er
leech
 (worm; SEE leach)
leek
 (vegetable; SEE leak)
leer'y
 ·i·er ·i·est
lee'ward
lee'way'
left'-hand'ed
left'ist
left'o'ver
left'-wing'er
leg
 legged leg'ging
leg'a·cy
 ·cies
le'gal·ese'
le·gal'i·ty
 ·ties
le'gal·i·za'tion

le'gal·ize'
 ·ized' ·iz'ing
le'gal·ly
leg'a·tee'
le·ga'tion
le·ga'to
leg'end
leg'end·ar'y
leg'er·de·main'
leg'gi·ness
leg'gy
 ·gi·er ·gi·est
leg'i·bil'i·ty
leg'i·ble
leg'i·bly
le'gion
le'gion·naire'
leg'is·late'
 ·lat'ed ·lat'ing
leg'is·la'tion
leg'is·la'tive
leg'is·la'tor
leg'is·la'ture
le·git'i·ma·cy
le·git'i·mate
le·git'i·mize'
 ·mized' ·miz'ing
leg'man'
leg'room'
leg'ume
lei
lei'sure
lei'sure·ly
lem'on·ade'
lend
 lent lend'ing
length'en
length'i·ness
length'wise'
length'y
 ·i·er ·i·est
le'ni·en·cy
le'ni·ent
len'i·tive
len'i·ty
lens
len'til
 (pea; SEE lintel)
leop'ard
le'o·tard'
lep'er
lep're·chaun'
lep'ro·sy
lep'rous
les'bi·an
le'sion
les·see'
less'en
 (make less)
less'er
 (smaller)
les'son
 (instruction)
les'sor
 (one who leases)
let
 let let'ting
let'down'

le'thal
le·thar'gic
le·thar'gi·cal·ly
leth'ar·gize'
 ·gized' ·giz'ing
leth'ar·gy
let'tered
let'ter·head'
let'ter·per'fect
let'ter·press'
let'tuce
let'up'
leu·ke'mi·a
lev'ee
 ·eed ·ee·ing
 (embankment; SEE levy)
lev'el
 ·eled or ·elled
 ·el·ing or ·el·ling
lev'el·head'ed
lev'el·ly
lev'er·age
lev'i·a·ble
lev'i·er
le'vis
lev'i·tate
 ·tat'ed ·tat'ing
lev'i·ta'tion
lev'i·ty
lev'y
 ·ies, ·ied ·y·ing
 (tax; SEE levee)
lewd'ness
lex'i·cog'ra·pher
lex'i·con
li'a·bil'i·ty
 ·ties
li'a·ble
 (likely; SEE libel)
li'ai·son'
li'ar
 (one who tells lies; SEE lyre)
li·ba'tion
li'bel
 ·beled or ·belled
 ·bel·ing or ·bel·ling
 (defame; SEE liable)
li'bel·ous or ·bel·lous
lib'er·al
lib'er·al'i·ty
lib'er·al·ize'
 ·ized' ·iz'ing
lib'er·ate'
 ·at'ed ·at·ing
lib'er·a'tion
lib'er·a'tor
lib'er·tar'i·an
lib'er·tine'
lib'er·ty
 ·ties
li·bid'i·nous
li·bi'do
li·brar'i·an

li'brar'y
 ·ies
li·bret'tist
li·bret'to
 ·tos or ·ti
Lib'ri·um
li'cense
 ·censed ·cens·ing
li·cen'tious
li'chen
lic'it
lic'o·rice
lie
 lay lain ly'ing
 (to rest; SEE lay)
lie
 lied ly'ing
 (tell falsehood; SEE lye)
li'en
 (claim; SEE lean)
lieu
lieu·ten'an·cy
lieu·ten'ant
life
 lives
life belt
life'blood'
life'boat'
life buoy
life'-giv'ing
life'guard'
life'less
life'like'
life'line'
life'long'
life'sav'er
life'-size'
life'time'
life'work'
lift'off'
lig'a·ment
lig'a·ture
 ·tured ·tur·ing
light
 light'ed or lit
 light'ing
light'en
 ·ened ·en·ing
 (make light or less heavy; SEE lightning)
light'face'
light'-fin'gered
light'-foot'ed
light'head'ed
light'heart'ed
light'house'
light'ly
light'-mind'ed
light'ning
 (flash of light; SEE lighten)
light'weight'
light'-year'
lig'ne·ous
lig'nite
lik'a·ble or like'·

like
 liked lik'ing
like'li·hood'
like'ly
like'-mind'ed
lik'en
like'ness
like'wise'
li'lac
Lil'li·pu'tian
lil'y
 ·ies
lil'y-liv'ered
lil'y-white'
limb
 (branch; SEE li
lim'ber
lim'bo
lime
 limed lim'ing
lime'light'
lim'er·ick
lime'stone'
lim'it·a·ble
lim'i·ta'tion
lim'it·ed
limn
 (draw; SEE lim
lim'ou·sine'
lim'pid
limp'ness
lin'age or line
 (number of lir
 SEE lineage)
linch'pin'
Lin'coln
lin'den
line
 lined lin'ing
 (ancestry; SEE linage)
lin'e·al
lin'e·a·ment
 (feature; SEE liniment)
lin'e·ar
line'man
lin'en
lin'er
lines'man
line'up'
lin'ger
lin'ge·rie'
lin'go
 ·goes
lin'gual
lin'guist
lin·guis'tics
lin'i·ment
 (medication; SEE lineament)
lin'ing
link'age
links
 (golf course; SEE lynx)
li·no'le·um

lin'o·type'	live'li·hood'	lodg'er	lo·qua'cious	luck'i·ly	**M**
lin'seed'	live'li·ness	lodg'ment	lo·quac'i·ty	luck'i·ness	
lin'sey-wool'sey	live'long'	loft'i·ly	lor·do'sis	luck'y	ma·ca'bre
lin'tel	live'ly	loft'i·ness	lor·gnette'	·i·er ·i·est	mac·ad'am
(beam; SEE lentil)	·li·er ·li·est	loft'y	lor'ry	lu'cra·tive	mac·ad'am·ize'
li'on·ess	liv'en	·i·er ·i·est	·ries	lu'cre	·ized' ·iz'ing
li'on-heart'ed	liv'er·wurst'	log	lose	lu·cu·bra'tion	mac·a·ro'ni
lip'-read'	liv'er·y	logged log'ging	lost los'ing	lu'di·crous	mac·a·roon'
-read' -read'ing	·ies	log'a·rithm	(mislay; SEE	lug'gage	mac'er·ate'
lip'stick'	live'stock'	loge	loose, loss)	lu·gu'bri·ous	·at'ed ·at'ing
lip'-sync'	liv'id	(theater box;	los'er	luke'warm'	ma·che'te
liq'ue·fac'tion	liz'ard	SEE lodge)	loss	lull'a·by'	Mach'i·a·vel'li·an
liq'ue·fi'a·ble	lla'ma	log'ger·head'	(thing lost; SEE	·bies'	mach'i·nate'
liq'ue·fi'er	(animal; SEE	log'gi·a	loose, lose)	lum'bar	·nat'ed ·nat'ing
liq'ue·fy'	lama)	·gi·as	Lo·thar'i·o'	(of the loins)	mach'i·na'tion
·fied' ·fy'ing	load	log'ic	lo'tion	lum'ber	ma·chine'
li·ques'cent	(burden; SEE lode)	log'i·cal	lot'ter·y	(timber)	·chined'
li·queur'	load'stone'	log'i·cal·ly	·ies	lum'ber·jack'	·chin'ing
liq'uid	loaf	lo·gi'cian	loud'mouthed'	lum'ber·yard'	ma·chin'er·y
liq'ui·date'	loaves	lo·gis'tics	loud'speak'er	lu'men	ma·chin'ist
·dat'ed ·dat'ing	loaf'er	log'o·gram'	Lou·i'si·an'a	·mi·na or ·mens	mack'er·el
liq'ui·da'tion	loam'y	log'o·griph'	lounge	lu'mi·nar'y	mack'i·naw'
liq'ui·da'tor	·i·er ·i·est	log'or·rhe'a	lounged	·ies	mack'in·tosh'
liq'uor	loan	lo'gy	loung'ing	lu'mi·nes'cent	(coat; SEE
isle	(something lent;	·gi·er ·gi·est	louse	lu'mi·nous	McIntosh)
isp'ing·ly	SEE lone)	loin'cloth'	lice	lump'i·ness	mac'ra·mé'
is'some or ·som	loath	loi'ter	lout'ish	lump'y	mac'ro·bi·ot'ics
is'ten	(unwilling)	lol'li·pop' or ·ly·	lou'ver	·i·er ·i·est	mac'ro·cosm
ist'less	loathe	lone	lov'a·ble or	lu'na·cy	ma'cron
it'a·ny	loathed loath'ing	(solitary;	love'·	lu'nar	mac'u·la
·nies	(detest)	SEE loan)	love	lu'na·tic	·lae
'tchi nut	loath'some	lone'li·ness	loved lov'ing	lunch'eon	mad
'ter	lob	lone'ly	love'li·ness	lunge	mad'der
it'er·a·cy	lobbed lob'bing	·li·er ·li·est	love'lorn'	lunged lung'ing	mad'dest
t'er·al	lob'by	lone'some	love'ly	lu'pine	mad'am
(exact; SEE	·bies	long'-dis'tance	·li·er ·li·est	lure	mad'ame
littoral)	·bied ·by·ing	long'-drawn'	lov'ing·kind'ness	lured lur'ing	mes·dames'
t'er·al·ly	lob'by·ist	lon·gev'i·ty	low'boy'	lu'rid	mad'cap'
t'er·ar'y	lobe	long'hand'	low'bred'	lurk'ing	mad'den·ing
t'er·ate	lob'ster	lon'gi·tude'	low'brow'	lus'cious	Ma·deir'a
t'er·a·ture	lo'cal	lon'gi·tu'di·nal	low'-cost'	lush'ness	ma'de·moi·selle'
the'ly	lo·cale'	long'-lived'	low'-down'	lus'ter	made'-to-or'der
th'o·graph'	lo'cal·ism	long'-play'ing	low'er	lust'i·ness	made'-up'
·thog'ra·pher	lo·cal'i·ty	long'-range'	low'er-class'man	lus'trous	mad'house'
·thog'ra·phy	·ties	long'-run'	low'-grade'	lust'y	mad'man'
th'o·sphere'	lo'cal·ize'	long'shore'man	low'-key'	·i·er ·i·est	ma'dras
t'i·ga·ble	·ized' ·iz'ing	long'stand'ing	low'-lev'el	lux·u'ri·ance	mad'ri·gal
t'i·gant	lo'cal·ly	long'-suf'fer·ing	low'li·ness	lux·u'ri·ant	mad'wom·an
t'i·gate'	lo'cate	long'-term'	low'ly	lux·u'ri·ate'	mael'strom
gat'ed ·gat'ing	·cat·ed ·cat·ing	long'-wind'ed	·li·er ·li·est	·at·ed ·at'ing	ma'es·tro
t'i·ga'tion	lo·ca'tion	look'er-on'	low'-mind'ed	lux·u'ri·ous	·tros or ·tri
'mus	lock'er	look'ers-on'	low'-necked'	lux'u·ry	Ma'fi·a or Maf'·
·to·tes	lock'et	look'out'	low'-pitched'	·ries	mag'a·zine'
'ter	lock'out'	loop'hole'	low'-spir'it·ed	ly·ce'um	ma·gen'ta
'ter·bug'	lock'smith'	loose	lox	lye	mag'got
'tle	lo'co·mo'tion	loosed loos'ing	loy'al	(alkaline sub-	mag'ic
t'tler or less or	lo'co·mo'tive	(free; SEE	loy'al·ly	stance; SEE lie)	mag'i·cal·ly
ess'er, lit'tlest	lo'co·weed'	lose, loss)	loy'al·ty	ly'ing-in'	ma·gi'cian
r least	lo'cus	loose'-joint'ed	·ties	lym·phat'ic	mag·is·te'ri·al
'to·ral	·ci	loose'-leaf'	loz'enge	lynch'ing	mag'is·trate'
shore; SEE	lo'cust	loose'ly	lu·au'	lynx	mag·na·nim'i·ty
teral)	lo·cu'tion	loos'en	lu'bri·cant	(animal; SEE links)	mag·nan'i·mous
ur'gi·cal	lode	loose'-tongued'	lu'bri·cate'	ly'on·naise'	mag'nate
ur·gy	(ore; SEE load)	lop	·cat·ed ·cat·ing	lyre	(influential
ies	lode'stone'	lopped lop'ping	lu'bri·ca'tion	(harp; SEE liar)	person)
'a·ble or live'·	lodge	lope	lu'bri·ca'tor	lyr'ic	
e	lodged lodg'ing	loped lop'ing	lu'cid	lyr'i·cal	
ved liv'ing	(house; SEE loge)	lop'sid·ed	lu·cid'i·ty	lyr'i·cist	

mag·ne′sia
mag′net
(iron attracter)
mag·net′ic
mag·net′i·cal·ly
mag′net·ism
mag′net·ize′
·ized′ ·iz′ing
mag·ne′to
·tos
mag·ni·fi·ca′tion
mag·nif′i·cence
mag·nif′i·cent
mag′ni·fi′er
mag′ni·fy′
·fied′ ·fy′ing
mag·nil′o·quent
mag′ni·tude′
mag·no′li·a
mag′num
mag′pie′
ma·ha·ra′jah or
·ra′ja
ma·ha·ra′ni or
·ra′nee
ma·hat′ma
mah′-jongg′
ma·hog′a·ny
maid′en
maid′ser′vant
mail′box′
mail′man′
maim
Maine
main′land′
main′line′
main′ly
main′spring′
main′stream′
main·tain′
main′te·nance
maî′tre d'hô·tel′
maize
(corn; SEE maze)
ma·jes′tic
ma·jes′ti·cal·ly
maj′es·ty
·ties
ma·jol′i·ca
ma′jor
ma′jor-do′mo
·mos
ma·jor′i·ty
·ties
ma·jus′cule
make
made mak′ing
make′-be·lieve′
make′shift′
make′up′
mal′a·dapt′ed
mal′ad·just′ed
mal′ad·min′is·ter
mal′a·droit′
mal′a·dy
·dies
ma·laise′
mal′a·prop·ism

mal′ap·ro·pos′
ma·lar′i·a
mal′con·tent′
mal de mer′
mal′e·dic′tion
mal′e·fac′tion
mal′e·fac′tor
ma·lef′i·cent
male′ness
ma·lev′o·lence
ma·lev′o·lent
mal·fea′sance
mal′for·ma′tion
mal·formed′
mal·func′tion
mal′ice
ma·li′cious
ma·lign′
ma·lig′nan·cy
ma·lig′nant
ma·lig′ni·ty
·ties
ma·lin′ger
ma·lin′ger·er
mall
(promenade; SEE
maul)
mal′lard
mal′le·a·bil′i·ty
mal′le·a·ble
mal′let
malm′sey
mal′nu·tri′tion
mal′oc·clu′sion
mal·o′dor·ous
mal·prac′tice
malt′ose
mal·treat′
mam′mal
mam·ma′li·an
mam′ma·ry
mam′mon
mam′moth
man
men, manned
man′ning
man′a·cle
·cled ·cling
man′age
·aged ·ag·ing
man′age·a·ble
man′age·ment
man′ag·er
man′a·ge′ri·al
ma·ña′na
man′-child′
men′-chil′dren
man·da′mus
man′da·rin
man′date
·dat·ed ·dat·ing
man′da·to′ry
man′di·ble
man′do·lin′
man′drel or ·dril
(metal spindle)
man′drill
(baboon)

man′-eat′er
ma·nège′
(horsemanship;
SEE ménage)
ma·neu′ver
ma·neu′ver·a·ble
man′ful·ly
man′ga·nese′
mange
man′ger
man′gi·ness
man′gle
·gled ·gling
man′go
·goes or ·gos
man′grove
man′gy
·gi·er ·gi·est
man·han′dle
Man·hat′tan
man′hole′
man′hood′
man′-hour′
man′hunt′
ma′ni·a
ma′ni·ac′
ma·ni′a·cal
man′ic
man′i·cot′ti
man′i·cure′
·cured ·cur·ing
man′i·cur′ist
man′i·fest′
man′i·fes·ta′tion
man′i·fes′to
·toes
man′i·fold′
man′i·kin
Ma·ni′la
ma·nip′u·late′
·lat·ed ·lat′ing
ma·nip′u·la′tion
ma·nip′u·la′tive
ma·nip′u·la′tor
man′kind′
man′li·ness
man′ly
·li·er ·li·est
man′-made′
man′na
man′ne·quin
man′ner
(way; SEE manor)
man′ner·ism
man′ner·ly
man′nish
man′-of-war′
men′-of-war′
ma·nom′e·ter
man′or
(residence;
SEE manner)
man′pow′er
man′sard
man′ser′vant
men′ser′vants
man′sion
man′-sized′

man′slaugh′ter
man′teau
·teaus
man′tel
(fireplace fac-
ing; SEE mantle)
man′tel·et
man′tel·piece′
man·til′la
man′tis
·tis·es or ·tes
man′tle
·tled ·tling
(cloak; SEE
mantel)
man′tu·a
man′u·al
man·u·fac′to·ry
·ries
man·u·fac′ture
·tured ·tur·ing
man·u·fac′tur·er
ma·nure′
·nured′ ·nur′ing
man′u·script′
man′y
more most
man′y-sid′ed
map
mapped
map′ping
ma′ple
mar
marred mar′ring
mar′a·bou′
ma·ra′ca
mar′a·schi′no
ma·ras′mus
mar′a·thon′
ma·raud′
mar′ble
·bled ·bling
mar′ble·ize′
·ized′ ·iz′ing
mar′ca·site′
mar·cel′
·celled′ ·cel′ling
March
mar′chion·ess
Mar′di gras′
mare′s′-nest′
mare′s′-tail′
mar′ga·rine
mar′gin
mar′gin·al
mar′gin·al·ly
mar′i·gold′
ma·ri·jua′na or
·hua′na
ma·rim′ba
ma·ri′na
mar′i·nade′
·nad′ed ·nad′ing
mar′i·nate′
·nat′ed ·nat′ing
ma·rine′
mar′i·ner
mar′i·o·nette′

mar′i·tal
(of marriage;
SEE martial)
mar′i·time′
mar′jo·ram
mark′down′
marked
mark′ed·ly
mar′ket·a·bil′i·ty
mar′ket·a·ble
mar′ket·place′
marks′man
mark′up′
mar′lin
(fish)
mar′line
(cord)
mar′line·spike′
mar′ma·lade′
mar′mo·set′
mar′mot
ma·roon′
mar·quee′
mar′quess
mar′que·try
mar′quis
mar·quise′
mar′qui·sette′
mar′riage
mar′riage·a·ble
mar′row
mar′row·bone′
mar′ry
·ried ·ry·ing
Mar·sa′la
mar′shal
·shaled or
·shalled
·shal·ing or
·shal·ling
marsh′mal′low
mar·su′pi·al
mar·su′pi·um
·pi·a
mar′ten
(animal; SEE
martin)
mar′tial
(military; SEE
marital)
Mar′tian
mar′tin
(bird; SEE marten)
mar′ti·net′
mar′tin·gale′
mar·ti′ni
·nis
mar′tyr
mar′tyr·dom
mar′tyr·ize′
·ized′ ·iz′ing
mar′vel
·veled or ·velled
·vel·ing or
·vel·ling
mar′vel·ous
Marx′ism
Mar′y·land

mar′zi·pah
mas·ca′ra
·raed ·ra·ing
mas′con′
mas′cot
mas′cu·line
mas′cu·lin′i·ty
ma′ser
mash′ie
mask
(cover; SEE
masque)
masked
mas′och·ism
mas′och·is′tic
mas′och·is′ti·
cal·ly
ma′son
Ma′son·ite′
ma′son·ry
masque
(masked ball; SEE
mask)
mas′quer·ade′
·ad′ed ·ad′ing
Mas′sa·chu′sett
mas′sa·cre
·cred ·cring
mas·sage′
·saged′ ·sag′ing
mas·seur′
mas·seuse′
mas′sive
mas′ter·ful
mas′ter·ly
mas′ter·mind′
mas′ter·piece′
mas′ter·y
·ies
mast′head′
mas′tic
mas′ti·cate′
·cat′ed ·cat′ing
mas′ti·ca′tion
mas′tiff
mas′to·don′
mas′toid
mas′tur·bate′
·bat′ed ·bat′ing
mas′tur·ba′tion
mat
mat′ted
mat′ting
mat′a·dor′
match′box′
match′less
match′lock′
mate
mat′ed mat′ing
ma·te·las·sé′
ma·te′ri·al
(of matter;
SEE materiel)
ma·te′ri·al·ism
ma·te′ri·al·is′m
ma·te′ri·al·ize′
·ized′ ·iz′ing

ma·te′ri·al·ly
ma·te′ri·el′
  or ·té′ri·el′
  (equipment;
  SEE material)
ma·ter′nal
ma·ter′ni·ty
math′e·mat′i·cal
math′e·ma·ti′cian
math′e·mat′ics
mat′i·nee′
  or ·i·née′
ma′tri·arch′
ma′tri·ar′chal
ma′tri·ar′chy
  ·chies
ma′tri·cide′
ma·tric′u·lant
ma·tric′u·late′
  ·lat′ed ·lat′ing
ma·tric′u·la′tion
mat′ri·mo′ni·al
mat′ri·mo′ny
ma′trix
  ·tri·ces′ or ·trix·es
ma′tron
ma′tron·li·ness
ma′tron·ly
mat′ter
mat′ter-of-fact′
mat′tock
mat′tress
mat′u·rate′
  ·rat′ed ·rat′ing
mat′u·ra′tion
ma·ture′
  ·tured′ ·tur′ing
ma·ture′ly
ma·tu′ri·ty
mat′zo
  ·zot or ·zoth
  or ·zos
maud′lin
maul
  (mallet; injure;
  SEE mall)
maun′der
mau·so·le′um
  ·le′ums or ·le′a
mauve
mav′er·ick
mawk′ish
max·il′la
max′il·lar′y
max′im
max′i·mal
max′i·mize′
  ·mized′ ·miz′ing
max′i·mum
  ·mums or ·ma
May
may′be
May′day′
may′hem
may′on·naise′
may′or
may′or·al·ty
  ·ties

May′pole′
maze
  (labyrinth; SEE
  maize)
maz′el tov′
Mc′In·tosh′
  (apple; SEE
  mackintosh)
mead′ow
mea′ger
meal′time′
meal′y
  ·i·er ·i·est
meal′y-mouthed′
mean v.
  meant mean′ing
mean adj., n.
  (middle; low;
  SEE mien)
me·an′der
mean′ing·ful
mean′ing·less
mean′ness
mean′time′
mean′while′
mea′sles
mea′sly
  ·sli·er ·sli·est
meas′ur·a·bil′i·ty
meas′ur·a·ble
meas′ur·a·bly
meas′ure
  ·ured ·ur·ing
meas′ure·less
meas′ure·ment
meas′ur·er
meat
  (flesh; SEE
  meet, mete)
meat′i·ness
me·a′tus
meat′y
  ·i·er ·i·est
me·chan′ic
me·chan′i·cal
mech′a·ni′cian
me·chan′ics
mech′a·nism
mech′a·ni·za′tion
mech′a·nize′
  ·nized′ ·niz′ing
med′al
  (award;
  SEE meddle)
med′al·ist
me·dal′lion
med′dle
  ·dled ·dling
  (interfere;
  SEE meddle)
med′dler
med′dle·some
me′di·a
  (sing. medium)
me′di·al
me′di·an
me′di·ate′
  ·at′ed ·at′ing

me′di·a′tion
me′di·a′tor
Med′i·caid′
med′i·cal
Med′i·care′
med′i·cate′
  ·cat′ed ·cat′ing
med′i·ca′tion
me·dic′i·nal
med′i·cine
me′di·e′val
  or ·ae′val
me′di·o′cre
me′di·oc′ri·ty
  ·ties
med′i·tate′
  ·tat′ed ·tat′ing
med′i·ta′tion
med′i·ta′tor
Med′i·ter·ra′ne·an
me′di·um
  ·di·ums or ·di·a
med′ley
  ·leys
meer′schaum
meet
  met meet′ing
  (come upon; SEE
  meat, mete)
meg′a·death′
meg′a·hertz′
meg′a·lo·ma′ni·a
meg′a·lop′o·lis
meg′a·phone′
meg′a·ton′
mel′an·cho′li·a
mel′an·chol′ic
mel′an·chol′y
mé′lange′
mel′a·nin
me′lee or mê′lée
mel′io·rate′
  ·rat′ed ·rat′ing
mel′io·ra′tion
mel·lif′lu·ous
mel′low
me·lo′de·on
me·lod′ic
me·lo′di·ous
mel′o·dra′ma
mel′o·dra·mat′ic
mel′o·dy
  ·dies
mel′on
melt′a·ble
mel′ton
.nem′ber·ship′
mem′brane
mem′bra·nous
me·men′to
  ·tos or ·toes
mem′oir
mem′o·ra·bil′i·a
mem′o·ra·ble
mem′o·ra·bly
mem′o·ran′dum
  ·dums or ·da
me·mo′ri·al

me·mo′ri·al·ize′
  ·ized′ ·iz′ing
mem′o·ri·za′tion
mem′o·rize′
  ·rized′ ·riz′ing
mem′o·ry
  ·ries
men′ace
  ·aced ·ac·ing
mé·nage′ or me·
  (household; SEE
  manège)
me·nag′er·ie
men·da′cious
men·dac′i·ty
Men·de′li·an
men′di·cant
me′ni·al
men′in·gi′tis
me·nis′cus
  ·cus·es or ·ci
Men′non·ite′
men′o·pause′
men′ses
men′stru·al
men′stru·ate′
  ·at′ed
  ·at′ing
men′stru·a′tion
men′sur·a·ble
men′su·ra′tion
mens′wear′
men′tal
men·tal′i·ty
men′thol
men′tho·lat′ed
men′tion
men′tor
men′u
  ·us
me·phit′ic
me·pro′ba·inate′
mer′can·tile
mer′can·til·ism
mer′ce·nar′y
  ·nar′ies
mer′cer·ize′
  ·ized′ ·iz′ing
mer′chan·dise′
  ·dised′ ·dis′ing
mer′chan·dis′er
mer′chant
mer′ci·ful
mer′ci·ful·ly
mer′ci·less
mer·cu′ri·al
mer·cu′ro·
  chrome′
mer′cu·ry
mer′cy
  ·cies
mere
mer′est
mere′ly
mer·en′gue
  (dance; SEE
  meringue)
mer′e·tri′cious

merge
  merged merg′ing
merg′er
me·rid′i·an
me·ringue′
  (pie topping;
  SEE merengue)
me·ri′no
  ·nos
mer′it
mer′i·to′ri·ous
mer′maid′
mer′ri·ly
mer′ri·ment
mer′ri·ness
mer′ry
  ·ri·er ·ri·est
mer′ry-an′drew
mer′ry-go-round′
mer′ry·mak′ing
Mer·thi′o·late′
me′sa
mé·sal′li·ance
mes·cal′
mes′ca·line′
mes′dames′
mes·de·moi·selles′
me·shu′ga
mesh′work′
mes′mer·ism
mes′mer·ize′
  ·ized′ ·iz′ing
mes′on
mes′sage
mes′sen·ger
mes·si′ah
mes′sieurs
mess′i·ly
mess′i·ness
mess′y
  ·i·er ·i·est
met′a·bol′ic
me·tab′o·lism
me·tab′o·lize′
  ·lized′ ·liz′ing
met′al
  ·aled or ·alled
  ·al·ing or ·al·ling
  (mineral; SEE
  mettle)
me·tal′lic
met′al·lur′gi·cal
met′al·lur′gist
met′al·lur′gy
met′al·work′
met′a·mor′phic
met′a·mor′phism
met′a·mor′phose
  ·phosed ·phos·ing
met′a·mor′pho·sis
  ·ses
met′a·phor′
met′a·phor′i·cal
met′a·phor′i·
  cal·ly
met′a·phys′i·cal
met′a·phys′ics
met′a·tar′sal

me·tath′e·sis
  ·ses′
mete
  met′ed met′ing
  (allot; SEE meat,
  meet)
me′te·or
me′te·or′ic
me′te·or·ite′
me′te·or·oid′
me′te·or·o·
  log′i·cal
me′te·or·ol′o·gist
me′te·or·ol′o·gy
me′ter
meth′a·done′
meth′ane
meth′a·nol′
meth′e·drine′
meth′od
me·thod′i·cal
me·thod′i·cal·ly
Meth′od·ist
meth′od·ize′
  ·ized′ ·iz′ing
meth′od·ol′o·gy
me·tic′u·lous
mé·tier′
me·ton′y·my
met′ric
met′ri·cal
met′ro·nome′
me·trop′o·lis
met′ro·pol′i·tan
met′tle
  (spirit; SEE metal)
mez′za·nine′
mez′zo-so·pra′no
  ·nos or ·ni
mez′zo·tint′
mi·as′ma
  ·mas or ·ma·ta
mi′ca
Mich′i·gan
mi′cro·bar′
mi′crobe
mi·cro′bic
mi′cro·cop′y
mi′cro·cosm
mi′cro·dot′
mi′cro·fiche′
mi′cro·film′
mi′cro·groove′
mi·cron′e·ter
mi′cro·or′gan·
  ism
mi′cro·phone′
mi′cro·print′
mi′cro·read′er
mi′cro·scope′
mi′cro·scop′ic
mi′cro·scop′i·
  cal·ly
mi′cro·wave′
mid′air′
mid′cult′
mid′day′
mid′dle

mid'dle-aged'
mid'dle-brow'
mid'dle-class'
mid'dle-man'
mid'dle-of-the-
  road'
mid'dle-sized'
mid'dle-weight'
mid'dling
mid'dy
 -dies
midg'et
mid'i'ron
mid'land
mid'night'
mid'point'
mid'riff
mid'ship'man
midst
mid'stream'
mid'sum'mer
mid'term'
mid'-Vic-to'ri-an
mid'way'
mid'week'
Mid'west'
Mid'west'ern-er
mid'wife'
 -wives'
mid'win'ter
mid'year'
mien
 (manner; SEE
 mean)
miffed
might
 (power; SEE mite)
might'i-ly
might'i-ness
might'y
 -i-er -i-est
mi'gnon
mi'graine
mi'grant
mi'grate
 -grat-ed -grat-ing
mi-gra'tion
mi'gra-to'ry
mi-ka'do
 -dos
mi-la'dy
mil'dew'
mild'ly
mile'age
mile'post'
mile'stone'
mi-lieu'
mil'i-tan-cy
mil'i-tant
mil'i-tar'i-ly
mil'i-ta-rism
mil'i-ta-ris'tic
mil'i-ta-ri-za'tion
mil'i-ta-rize'
 -rized' -riz'ing
mil'i-tar'y
mil'i-tate'
 -tat'ed -tat'ing

mi-li'tia
milk'i-ness
milk'maid'
milk'man'
milk'shake'
milk'shed'
milk'sop'
milk toast
 (food; SEE
 milquetoast)
milk'weed'
milk'y
 -i-er -i-est
mill'age
mill'dam'
milled
mil-len'ni-um
 -ni-ums or -ni-a
mill'er
mil'let
mil'liard
mil'li-bar'
mil'li-gram'
mil'li-li'ter
mil'li-me'ter
mil'line'
mil'li-ner
mil'li-ner'y
mill'ing
mil'lion
mil'lion-aire'
mil'lionth
mil'li-pede'
mill'pond'
mill'race'
mill'stone'
mill'stream'
mill wheel
mill'work'
mill'wright'
milque'toast'
 (timid person;
 SEE milk toast)
Mil-wau'kee
mime
mimed mim'ing
mim'e-o-graph'
mim'er
mi-met'ic
mim'ic
 -icked -ick-ing
mim'ick-er
mim'ic-ry
mi-mo'sa
min'a-ret'
min'a-to'ry
mince
minced minc'ing
mince'meat'
mind'ful
mind'less
mind reader
mine
mined min'ing
mine'lay'er
min'er
 (mine worker;
 SEE minor)

min'er-al
min-er-al-i-za'tion
min'er-al-ize'
 -ized' -iz'ing
min-er-al'o-gist
min-er-al'o-gy
mi'ne-stro'ne
min'gle
 -gled -gling
min'i-a-ture
min'i-a-tur'i-
 za'tion
min'i-a-tur-ize'
 -ized' -iz'ing
min'i-bus'
min'i-fi-ca'tion
min'i-fy'
 -fied' -fy'ing
min'im
min'i-mal
min'i-mal-ly
min'i-mize'
 -mized' -miz'ing
min'i-mum
 -mums or -ma
min'ion
 (deputy; SEE
 minyan)
min'i-skirt'
min'is-ter
 (diplomat; clergy-
 man; SEE minster)
min-is-te'ri-al
min'is-trant
min'is-tra'tion
min'is-try
 -tries
min'i-track'
min'i-ver
Min'ne-ap'o-lis
min'ne-sing'er
Min'ne-so'ta
min'now
mi'nor
 (lesser; SEE
 miner)
mi-nor'i-ty
 -ties
min'ster
 (church; SEE
 minister)
min'strel
mint'age
min'u-end'
min'u-et'
mi'nus
mi-nus'cule
min'ute n.
mi-nute' adj.
mi-nute'ly
min'ute-man'
mi-nu'ti-ae'
 (sing. mi-nu'ti-a)
minx
min-yan'
 min'ya-nim'
 (group; SEE
 minion)

mir'a-cle
mi-rac'u-lous
mi-rage'
mire
 mired mir'ing
mir'ror
mirth'ful
mirth'less
mir'y
 -i-er -i-est
mis'ad-ven'ture
mis'ad-vise'
mis-al-li'ance
mis-al'ly'
mis'an-thrope'
mis'an-throp'ic
mis-an'thro-py
mis'ap-pli-ca'tion
mis'ap-ply'
mis'ap-pre-hend'
mis'ap-pre-
 hen'sion
mis'ap-pro'pri-ate'
mis-be-got'ten
mis-be-have'
mis-be-hav'ior
mis-be-lief'
mis-be-lieve'
mis-cal'cu-late'
mis-cal-cu-la'tion
mis-car'riage
mis-car'ry
mis'cast'
mis'ce-ge-na'tion
mis-cel-la'ne-a
mis-cel-la'ne-ous
mis-cel-la'ny
 -nies
mis-chance'
mis'chief
mis'chief-mak'er
mis'chie-vous
mis-ci-bil'i-ty
mis'ci-ble
mis'con-ceive'
mis'con-cep'tion
mis-con'duct
mis'con-
 struc'tion
mis'con-strue'
mis'count'
mis'cre-ant
mis-cue'
mis-date'
mis-deal'
 -dealt' -deal'ing
mis-deed'
mis'de-mean'or
mis'di-rect'
mi'ser
mis'er-a-ble
mis'er-a-bly
mi'ser-ly
mis'er-y
 -ies
mis-es'ti-mate'
mis-fea'sance
mis-file'

mis-fire'
mis'fit'
mis-for'tune
mis-giv'ing
mis-gov'ern
mis-guid'ance
mis-guide'
mis-han'dle
mis'hap
mish'mash'
mis'in-form'
mis'in-for-ma'tion
mis'in-ter'pret
mis-judge'
mis-judg'ment
 or -judge'ment
mis-lay'
 -laid' -lay'ing
mis-lead'
 -led' -lead'ing
mis-man'age
mis-man'age-
 ment
mis-match'
mis-mate'
mis-no'mer
mi-sog'a-mist
mi-sog'a-my
mi-sog'y-nist
mi-sog'y-ny
mis-place'
mis-print'
mis-pri'sion
mis'pro-nounce'
mis'pro-nun'ci-
 a'tion
mis'quo-ta'tion
mis-quote'
mis-read'
 -read' -read'ing
mis'rep-re-sent'
mis'rep-re-sen-
 ta'tion
mis-rule'
Miss
Miss'es
mis'sal
 (book; SEE
 missile, missive)
mis-shape'
mis-shap'en
mis'sile
 (weapon; SEE
 missal, missive)
mis'sion
mis'sion-ar'y
Mis'sis-sip'pi
mis'sive
 (letter; SEE
 missal, missive)
Mis-sour'i
mis-speak'
 -spoke' -spo'ken
 -speak'ing
mis-spell'
 -spelled' or
 -spelt'
 -spell'ing

mis-spend'
 -spent'
 -spend'ing
mis-state'
mis-state'ment
mis-step'
mis-take'
 -took' -tak'en
 -tak'ing
mist'i-ly
mist'i-ness
mis'tle-toe'
mis'tral
mis-treat'ment
mis'tress
mis-tri'al
mis-trust'
mist'y
 -i-er -i-est
mis'un-der-stand
 -stood' -stand'ing
mis-us'age
mis-use'
mis-val'ue
mis-write'
 -wrote' writ'ten
 -writ'ing
mite
 (arachnid; tiny
 thing; SEE might)
mi'ter
mit'i-ga-ble
mit'i-gate'
 -gat'ed -gat'ing
mit'i-ga'tion
mit'i-ga'tor
mi'tral
mitt
mit'ten
mix
 mixed or mixt
mix'ing
mix'er
mix'ture
mix'-up'
miz'zen-mast
mne-mon'ic
moan'ing
moat
 (ditch; SEE mote
mob
 mobbed
 mob'bing
mo'bile
mo-bil'i-ty
mo'bi-li-za'ble
mo'bi-li-za'tion
mo'bi-lize'
 -lized' -liz'ing
mob-oc'ra-cy
 -cies
moc'ca-sin
mo'cha
mock'er-y
 -ies
mock'-he-ro'i
mock'ing-bird
mock'-up'

mod'a·cryl'ic
mod'al
(of a mode)
nod'el
·eled or ·elled
·el·ing or ·el·ling
(copy)
nod'er·ate'
·at'ed ·at'ing
nod'er·ate·ly
nod'er·a'tion
nod'er·a'tor
nod'ern
nod'ern·ism
nod'ern·is'tic
no·der'ni·ty
nod'ern·i·za'tion
nod'ern·ize'
ized' ·iz'ing
nod'ern·ness
nod'est
od'es·ty
od'i·cum
od'i·fi·ca'tion
od'i·fi'er
od'i·fy'
ied' ·fy'ing
od'ish
o·diste'
od'u·lar
od'u·late'
at'ed ·lat'ing
od'u·la'tion
od'u·la'tor
od'ule
·'gul
·'hair
·i'e·ty
·es
·ire
·i·ré'
is'ten
ist'ness
s'ture
is'tur·ize'
ed' ·iz'ing
·'lar
las'ses
d'board'
d'er
d'i·ness
d'ing
d'y
r ·i·est
·e
ec'u·lar
'e·cule'
·'hill'
·'skin'
est'
es·ta'tion
li·fy'
·' ·fy'ing
lusk
y·cod'dle
d ·dling
·en

mo·lyb'de·num
mo'ment
mo'men·tar'i·ly
mo'men·tar'y
mo·men'tous
mo·men'tum
·tums or ·ta
mom'ism
mo·nan'drous
mon'arch
mo·nar'chal
mon'arch·ism
mon'arch·y
·ies
mon'as·ter'y
·ies
mo·nas'tic
mo·nas'ti·cism
mon·au'ral
Mon'day
mon'e·tar'y
mon'e·tize'
·tized' ·tiz'ing
mon'ey
·eys or ·ies
mon'ey·bag'
mon'ey-chang'er
mon'eyed
mon'ey-grub'ber
mon'ey-lend'er
mon'ey-mak'er
mon'ger
Mon'gol·ism
Mon'gol·oid'
mon'goose
·goos·es
mon'grel
mo·ni'tion
mon'i·tor
mon'i·to'ry
·ries
monk
mon'key
·keys
monk's cloth
mon'o·chro·mat'ic
mon'o·chrome'
mon'o·cle
mon'o·coque'
mo·noc'u·lar
mon'o·dra'ma
mo·nog'a·mist
mo·nog'a·mous
mo·nog'a·my
mon'o·gram'
·grammed'
·gram'ming
mon'o·graph'
mo·nog'y·ny
mon'o·lith'
mon'o·logue'
or ·log'
mon'o·logu·ist or
mo·nol'o·gist
mon'o·ma'ni·a
mon'o·met'al·lism
mon'o·nu·cle·o'sis

mon'o·plane'
mo·nop'o·list
mo·nop'o·lis'tic
mo·nop'o·li·za'tion
mo·nop'o·lize'
·lized' ·liz'ing
mo·nop'o·ly
·lies
mon'o·rail'
mon'o·syl·lab'ic
mon'o·syl'la·ble
mon'o·the'ism
mon'o·the·is'tic
mon'o·tone'
mo·not'o·nous
mo·not'o·ny
mon'o·type'
mon·ox'ide
Mon'sei·gneur'
Mes'sei·gneurs'
mon·sieur'
mes'sieurs
Mon·si'gnor
mon·soon'
mon'ster
mon·stros'i·ty
·ties
mon'strous
mon·tage'
·taged' ·tag'ing
Mon·tan'a
month'ly
·lies
mon'u·ment
mon'u·men'tal
mood'i·ly
mood'i·ness
mood'y
·i·er ·i·est
moon'beam'
moon'-faced'
moon'light'
moon'light'ing
moon'lit'
moon'port'
moon'rise'
moon'set'
moon'shine'
moon'shot'
moon'stone'
moon'struck'
moor'age
moor'ing
moose
moose
(deer; SEE
mouse, mousse)
moot
(debatable;
SEE mute)
mop
mopped
mop'ping
mope
moped mop'ing
mop'pet
mop'-up'

mo·raine'
mor'al
mo·rale'
mor'al·ist
mor'al·is'tic
mor·al·is'ti·cal·ly
mo·ral'i·ty
mor'al·ize'
·ized' ·iz'ing
mor'al·ly
mo·rass'
mor·a·to'ri·um
·ri·ums or ·ri·a
mor'bid
mor·bid'i·ty
mor'dant
(corrosive)
mor'dent
(musical term)
more·o'ver
mo'res
mor·ga·nat'ic
morgue
mor'i·bund'
mor'i·bun'di·ty
Mor'mon
morn'ing
(part of day;
SEE mourning)
mo·roc'co
mo'ron
mo·ron'ic
mo·rose'
mor'phine
mor·phol'o·gy
mor'sel
mor'tal
mor·tal'i·ty
mor'tal·ly
mor'tar
mor'tar·board'
mort'gage
·gaged ·gag·ing
mort'ga·gee'
mort'ga·gor
mor·ti'cian
mor·ti·fi·ca'tion
mor'ti·fy'
·fied' ·fy'ing
mor'tise
·tised ·tis·ing
mor'tu·ar'y
·ies
mo·sa'ic
·icked ·ick·ing
mosque
mos·qui'to
·toes or ·tos
moss'back'
moss'i·ness
moss'y
·i·er ·i·est
most'ly
mote
(speck; SEE moat)
mo·tel'
moth'ball'
moth'-eat'en

moth'er·hood'
moth'er-in-law'
moth'ers-in-law'
moth'er·land'
moth'er·li·ness
moth'er·ly
moth'er-of-pearl'
moth'proof'
mo·tif'
mo'tile
mo·til'i·ty
mo'tion·less
mo'ti·vate'
·vat'ed ·vat'ing
mo'ti·va'tion
mo'ti·va'tor
mo'tive
mot'ley
mo'tor·bike'
mo'tor·boat'
mo'tor·bus'
mo'tor·cade'
mo'tor·cy'cle
mo'tor·drome'
mo'tor·ist
mo'tor·ize'
·ized' ·iz'ing
mo'tor·man
mot'tle
·tled ·tling
mot'to
·toes or ·tos
mou·lage'
mound
moun'tain
moun'tain·eer'
moun'tain·ous
moun'te·bank'
mourn'ful
mourn'ing
(grieving;
SEE morning)
mouse
mice
moused mous'ing
(rodent; SEE
moose, mousse)
mous'er
mouse'trap'
mous'i·ness
mousse
(food; SEE
moose, mousse)
mousse·line'
de soie'
mous'y
·i·er ·i·est
mouth'ful'
·fuls'
mouth'part'
mouth'piece'
mouth'-to-mouth'
mouth'wash'
mouth'wa'ter·ing
mou'ton'
(fur; SEE mutton)
mov'a·ble
or move'·

mov'a·bly
move
moved mov'ing
move'ment
mov'ie
mov'ie·go'er
mov'i·o'la
mow
mowed, mowed
or mown,
mow'ing
moz·za·rel'la
Mr.
Messrs.
Mrs.
Mmes.
mu'ci·lage
mu'ci·lag'i·nous
muck'rake'
mu'cous adj.
mu'cus n.
mud'der
mud'di·ness
mud'dle
·dled ·dling
mud'dler
mud'dy
·di·er ·di·est
mud'sling'ing
Muen'ster
mu·ez'zin
muf'fin
muf'fle
·fled ·fling
muf'fler
muf'ti
mug
mugged
mug'ging
mug'gi·ness
mug'gy
·gi·er ·gi·est
mug'wump'
muk'luk'
mu·lat'to
·toes
mul'ber'ry
·ries
mulch
mulct
mul'ish
mul'li·ga·taw'ny
mul'lion
mul'ti·col'ored
mul'ti·far'i·ous
mul'ti·form'
mul'ti·lat'er·al
mul'ti·ple
mul'ti·plex'
mul'ti·pli'a·ble
mul'ti·pli·cand'
mul'ti·pli·ca'tion
mul'ti·plic'i·ty
mul'ti·pli'er
mul'ti·ply'
·plied ·ply'ing
mul'ti tude'
mul'ti·tu'di·nous

mul'ti·ver'si·ty
mum'ble
·bled ·bling
mum'bler
mum'mer·y
mum'mi·fy'
·fied' ·fy'ing
mum'my
·mies
munch
mun·dane'
mu·nic'i·pal
mu·nic'i·pal'i·ty
·ties
mu·nic'i·pal·ize'
·ized' ·iz'ing
mu·nif'i·cence
mu·nif'i·cent
mu·ni'tion
mu'ral
mur'der·er
mur'der·ous
murk'i·ly
murk'i·ness
murk'y
·i·er ·i·est
mur'mur
mur'mur·er
mus'ca·dine
mus'ca·tel'
mus'cle
·cled ·cling
(body part;
SEE mussel)
mus'cle-bound'
mus'cu·lar
mus'cu·la'ture
muse
mused mus'ing
mu·sette'
mu·se'um
mush'i·ness
mush'room
mush'y
·i·er ·i·est
mu'sic
mu'si·cal adj.
mu·si·cale' n.
mu·si'cian
mu·si·col'o·gist
mu·si·col'o·gy
mus'kel·lunge'
mus'ket
musk'i·ness
musk'mel'on
musk'rat'
musk'y
·i·er ·i·est
mus'lin
mus'sel
(shellfish;
SEE muscle)
mus·tache'
or mous·
mus'tang
mus'tard
mus'ter
mus'ti·ness

mus'ty
·ti·er ·ti·est
mu·ta·bil'i·ty
mu'ta·ble
mu'tant
mu'tate
·tat·ed ·tat·ing
mu·ta'tion
mute
mut'ed mut'ing
(silent; SEE moot)
mu'ti·late'
·lat'ed ·lat'ing
mu·ti·la'tion
mu'ti·neer'
mu'ti·nous
mu'ti·ny
·nies
·nied ·ny·ing
mut'ter
mut'ton
(food; SEE
mouton)
mu'tu·al
mu'tu·al'i·ty
mu'tu·al·ly
muu'muu
Mu'zak
muz'zle
·zled ·zling
my'e·li'tis
my'e·lo·gram'
my'lar
my'na or ·nah
mus·cis'sus
my·o'pi·a
my·op'ic
myr'i·ad
myr'i·a·pod'
myr'mi·don'
myrrh
myr'tle
my·self'
mys·te'ri·ous
mys'ter·y
·ies
mys'tic
mys'ti·cal
mys'ti·cal·ly
mys'ti·cism
mys'ti·fi·ca'tion
mys'ti·fy'
·fied' ·fy'ing
mys·tique'
myth'i·cal
myth'o·log'i·cal
my·thol'o·gize'
·gized' ·giz'ing
my·thol'o·gy
·gies
myth'os

N

nab
nabbed nab'bing
na·celle'

na'cre
na'cre·ous
na'dir
nag
nagged nag'ging
nail'head'
nain'sook
na·ive' or ·ïve'
na·ive·te' or ·ïve·
na'ked·ness
nam'by-pam'by
·bies
name
named nam'ing
name'a·ble
or nam'·
name'-drop'per
name'less
name'ly
name'plate'
name'sake'
nan·keen' or ·kin'
nap
napped nap'ping
na'palm
na'per·y
naph'tha
naph'tha·lene'
nap'kin
na·po'le·on
nap'per
nar·cis'sism
nar'cis·sist
nar'cis·sis'tic
nar·cis'sus
nar'co·lep'sy
nar·co'sis
nar·cot'ic
nar'co·tism
nar'rate
·rat·ed ·rat·ing
nar·ra'tion
nar'ra·tive
nar'ra·tor
nar'row-mind'ed
nar'whal
na'sal
na·sal'i·ty
na'sal·ize'
·ized' ·iz'ing
nas'cent
nas'ti·ly
nas'ti·ness
na·stur'tium
nas'ty
·ti·er ·ti·est
na'tal
na'tant
na·ta·to'ri·um
·ri·ums or ·ri·a
na'ta·to'ry
na'tion
na'tion·al
na'tion·al·ism
na'tion·al·is'ti·
cal·ly
na'tion·al'i·ty
·ties

na'tion·al·i·za'tion
na'tion·al·ize'
·ized' ·iz'ing
na'tion·al·ly
na'tion·wide'
na'tive
na'tive-born'
na·tiv'i·ty
·ties
nat'ti·ly
nat'ty
·ti·er ·ti·est
nat'u·ral
nat'u·ral·ism
nat'u·ral·ist
nat'u·ral·is'tic
nat'u·ral·i·za'tion
nat'u·ral·ize'
·ized' ·iz'ing
nat'u·ral·ly
na'ture
naug'a·hyde'
naught
naugh'ti·ly
naugh'ti·ness
naugh'ty
·ti·er ·ti·est
nau'se·a
nau'se·ate'
·at'ed ·at'ing
nau'seous
nau'ti·cal
nau'ti·lus
·lus·es or ·li'
na'val
(of a navy)
nave
(part of a church;
SEE knave)
na'vel
(umbilicus)
nav'i·cert
nav'i·ga·ble
nav'i·gate'
·gat'ed ·gat'ing
nav'i·ga'tion
nav'i·ga'tor
na'vy
·vies
nay
(no; SEE nee,
neigh)
Ne·an'der·thal'
near'by'
near'ly
near'sight'ed
neat'ly
neat'ness
neb'bish
Ne·bras'ka
neb'u·la
·lae' or ·las
neb'u·lar
neb'u·los'i·ty
neb'u·lous
nec'es·sar'i·ly
nec'es·sar'y
·ies

ne·ces'si·tate'
·tat'ed ·tat'ing
ne·ces'si·tous
ne·ces'si·ty
·ties
neck'er·chief
neck'lace
neck'line'
neck'piece'
neck'tie'
neck'wear'
ne·crol'o·gy
·gies
nec'ro·man'cy
nec'tar
nec'tar·ine'
nee or née
(born; SEE nay,
neigh)
need
(require; SEE
knead)
need'ful
need'i·ness
nee'dle
·dled ·dling
nee'dle·like'
nee'dle·point'
nee'dler
need'less
nee'dle·work'
need'n't
need'y
·i·er ·i·est
ne'er'-do-well'
ne·far'i·ous
ne·gate'
·gat'ed ·gat'ing
ne·ga'tion
neg'a·tive
neg'a·tiv·ism
neg·lect'
neg·lect'ful
neg'li·gee'
neg'li·gence
neg'li·gent
neg'li·gi·ble
neg'li·gi·bly
ne·go'ti·a·bil'i·ty
ne·go'ti·a·ble
ne·go'ti·ate'
·at'ed ·at'ing
ne·go'ti·a'tion
ne·go'ti·a'tor
Ne'gro
·groes
Ne'groid
neigh
(whinny; SEE
nay, nee)
neigh'bor
neigh'bor·hood'
neigh'bor·li·ness
neigh'bor·ly
nei'ther
(not either;
SEE nether)
nem'a·tode'

nem'e·sis
·ses
ne'o·clas'sic
ne'o·lith'ic
ne·ol'o·gism
ne'o·my'cin
ne'on
ne'o·phyte'
ne'o·plasm
ne'o·prene'
ne·pen'the
neph'ew
ne·phri'tis
nep'o·tism
Nep'tune
nerve
nerved nerv'ing
nerve'-rack'ing
or -wrack'·
nerv'ous
nerv'y
·i·er ·i·est
nes'ci·ent
nes'tle
·tled ·tling
nest'ling
(young bird)
net
net'ted net'ting
neth'er
(lower; SEE
neither)
net'tle
·tled ·tling
net'work'
Neuf'châ·tel'
neu'ral
neu·ral'gia
neu'ras·the'ni·a
neu·ri'tis
neu·ro·log'i·cal
neu·rol'o·gist
neu·rol'o·gy
neu·ro'sis
·ses
neu·rot'ic
neu'ter
neu'tral
neu·tral'i·ty
neu'tral·i·za'tion
neu'tral·ize'
·ized' ·iz'ing
neu'tral·iz'er
neu·tri'no
neu'tron
Ne·vad'a
nev'er·more'
nev'er·the·less'
ne'vus
·vi
new'born'
new'com'er
new'el
new'fan'gled
new'-fash'ione·
New'found·lan·
New Hamp'shi·
New Jer'sey

ew'ly·wed'
New Mex'i·co
ews'boy'
ews'cast'
ews'deal·er
ews'let'ter
ews'man'
ews'pa·per
ew'speak'
ews'print'
ews'reel'
ews'stand'
ews'wor'thy
New York
ext'-door'
ex'us or nex'us
'a·cin
i·ag'a·ra
b'ble
oled ·bling
b'lick
ce
ic'er n:·'est
ce'ly
'ce·ty
ies
che
recess)
ck
notch)
k'el
led or ·elled
l·ing or ·el·ling
k'el·o'de·on
k'name'
'o·tine'
'o·tin'ism
'ti·tate'
at'ed ·tat'ing
ce
'gard·ly
'gling
ht
arkness; SEE
ight)
ht'cap'
nt'club'
nt'dress'
nt'fall'
nt'gown'
nt'in·gale'
nt'long'
nt'ly
nt'mare'
nt'mar'ish
nt'shirt'
nt'time'
il·ism
l·is'tic
'ble
r ·blest
'bly
'bus
or ·bus·es
com·poop'
'fold'
'pins'

nine'teen'
nine'ti·eth
nine'ty
·ties
nin'ny
·nies
ni'non
ninth
nip
nipped nip'ping
nip'per
nip'pi·ness
nip'ple
nip'py
·pi·er ·pi·est
nip'-up'
nir·va'na
ni'sei
·sei or ·seis
nit'-pick'ing
ni'tro·gen
ni'tro·glyc'er·in
or ·er·ine
nit'ty-grit'ty
no·bil'i·ty
no'ble
·bler ·blest
no'ble·man
no'bly
no'bod'y
·ies
noc·tur'nal
noc·tur'nal·ly
noc'turne
noc'u·ous
nod
nod'ded nod'ding
nod'al
node
nod'u·lar
nod'ule
no·el' or ·ël'
nog'gin
no'-hit'ter
noise
noised nois'ing
noise'less
noise'mak·er
nois'i·ly
nois'i·ness
noi'some
nois'y
·i·er ·i·est
no'mad
no·mad'ic
nom' de plume'
noms' de plume'
no'men·cla'ture
nom'i·nal
nom'i·nal·ly
nom'i·nate'
·nat'ed ·nat'ing
nom'i·na'tion
nom'i·na·tive
nom'i·na'tor
nom'i·nee'
non'a·ge·nar'i·an
non'-book'

nonce
non·cha·lance'
non·cha·lant'
non·com'bat·ant
non'com·mit'tal
non com'pos
men'tis
non'con·form'ist
non'co·op'er·a'·
tion
non'de·script'
non·en'ti·ty
·ties
non'es·sen'tial
none'such'
none'the·less'
non'ex·ist'ent
non·fea'sance
non'he'ro
non·nu'cle·ar
no-non'sense
non'pa·reil'
non·par'ti·san
non·plus'
·plused' or
·plussed'
·plus'ing or
·plus'sing
non·prof'it
non·sched'uled
non'sec·tar'i·an
non'sense
non·sen'si·cal
non·sen'si·cal·ly
non' se'qui·tur
non'-sked'
non'skid'
non'stop'
non'sup·port'
non·un'ion
non·vi'o·lence
noo'dle
noon'day'
no one
noon'time'
noose
noosed noos'ing
no'-par'
nor'mal
nor'mal·cy
nor·mal'i·ty
nor'mal·ize'
·ized' ·iz'ing
nor'mal·ly
north'bound'
North Car'o·li'na
North Da·ko'ta
north'east'
north'east'er·ly
north'east'ern
north'er·ly
north'ern
north'ward
north'west'
north'west'er·ly
north'west'ern
nose
nosed nos'ing

nose'bleed'
nose cone
nose'-dive'
·dived' ·div'ing
nose'gay'
nose'piece'
no'-show'
nos·tal'gia
nos·tal'gic
nos'tril
nos'trum
no'ta·ble
no'ta·bly
no'ta·ri·za'tion
no'ta·rize'
·rized' ·riz'ing
no'ta·ry public
no'ta·ries public
or no'ta·ry publics
no·ta'tion
notched
note
not'ed not'ing
note'book'
note'wor'thy
noth'ing·ness
no'tice
·ticed ·tic·ing
no'tice·a·ble
no'tice·a·bly
no'ti·fi'a·ble
no'ti·fi·ca'tion
no'ti·fy'
·fied' ·fy'ing
no'tion
no·to·ri'e·ty
no·to'ri·ous
no'-trump'
not'with·stand'ing
nou'gat
nought
nour'ish·ment
nou·veau riche'
nou·veaux riches'
no'va
·vas or ·vae
nov'el
nov'el·ette'
nov'el·ist
no·vel'la
nov'el·ty
·ties
No·vem'ber
nov'ice
no·vi'ti·ate
now'a·days'
no'where'
no'wise'
nox'ious
noz'zle
nu'ance
nub'bi·ness
nub'by
·bi·er ·bi·est
nu'bile
nu'cle·ar
nu'cle·ate'
·at'ed ·at'ing

nu'cle·on'ics
nu'cle·us
·cle·i' or
·cle·us·es
nude
nudge
nudged nudg'ing
nud'ist
nu'di·ty
nu'ga·to'ry
nug'get
nui'sance
nul'li·fi·ca'tion
nul'li·fy'
·fied' ·fy'ing
num'ber
num'ber·less
numb'ly
numb'ness
nu'mer·a·ble
nu'mer·al
nu'mer·ate'
·at·ed ·at·ing
nu'mer·a'tion
nu'mer·a'tor
nu·mer'i·cal
nu'mer·ol'o·gy
nu'mer·ous
nu·mis·mat'ic
nu·mis'ma·tist
num'skull'
nun'ner·y
·ies
nup'tial
nurse
nursed nurs'ing
nurse'maid'
nurs'er·y
·ies
nur'ture
·tured ·tur·ing
nut'crack'er
nut'gall'
nut'meat'
nut'meg'
nut'pick'
nu'tri·a
nu'tri·ent
nu'tri·ment
nu·tri'tion
nu·tri'tious
nu'tri·tive
nut'shell'
nuz'zle
·zled ·zling
ny'lon
nymph
nym'pho·
ma'ni·ac'

O

oaf'ish
oa'kum
oar
(pole; SEE ore)

oar'lock'
oars'man
o·a'sis
·ses
oath
oat'meal'
ob'bli·ga'to
·tos or ·ti
ob'du·ra·cy
ob'du·rate
o·be'di·ence
o·be'di·ent
o·bei'sance
o·bei'sant
ob'e·lisk'
o·bese'
o·be'si·ty
o·bey'
ob'fus·cate'
·cat'ed ·cat'ing
ob'i·ter dic'tum
ob'i·ter dic'ta
o·bit'u·ar'y
·ies
ob'ject
ob·jec'tion
ob·jec'tion·a·ble
ob·jec'tion·a·bly
ob·jec'tive
ob·jec'tive·ly
ob·jec'tiv'i·ty
ob·jec'tor
ob'jet d'art'
ob'jets d'art'
ob'jur·gate'
·gat'ed ·gat'ing
ob'jur·ga'tion
ob·la'tion
ob'li·gate'
·gat'ed ·gat'ing
ob'li·ga'tion
ob·lig'a·to'ry
o·blige'
o·bliged'
o·blig'ing
ob·lique'
ob·lique'ly
ob·liq'ui·ty
ob·lit'er·ate'
·at'ed ·at'ing
ob·lit'er·a'tion
ob·lit'er·a'tor
ob·liv'i·on
ob·liv'i·ous
ob'long
ob'lo·quy
·quies
ob·nox'ious
o'boe
o'bo·ist
ob·scene'
ob·scen'i·ty
·ties
ob·scure'
·scured' ·scur'ing
ob·scure'ly
ob·scu'ri·ty
·ties

ob'se·quies
ob·se'qui·ous
ob·serv'a·ble
ob·serv'ance
ob·serv'ant
ob·ser·va'tion
ob·serv'a·to'ry
·ries
ob·serve'
·served' ·serv'ing
ob·serv'er
ob·sess'
ob·ses'sion
ob·ses'sive
ob·sid'i·an
ob'so·lesce'
·lesced' ·lesc'ing
ob·so·les'cence
ob·so·les'cent
ob'so·lete'
ob'sta·cle
ob·stet'ric
ob·stet'ri·cal
ob·ste·tri'cian
ob'sti·na·cy
·cies
ob'sti·nate
ob'sti·nate·ly
ob·strep'er·ous
ob·struct'
ob·struc'tion
ob·struc'tion·ist
ob·struc'tive
ob·tain'
ob·trude'
·trud'ed
·trud'ing
ob·tru'sion
ob·tru'sive
ob·tru'sive·ly
ob·tuse'
ob·verse'
ob·vert'
ob'vi·ate'
·at'ed ·at'ing
ob'vi·ous
ob'vi·ous·ly
oc·a·ri'na
oc·ca'sion
oc·ca'sion·al
oc·ca'sion·al·ly
Oc'ci·dent
Oc'ci·den'tal
oc·cip'i·tal
oc·clude'
·clud'ed
·clud'ing
oc·clu'sion
oc·cult'
oc·cul·ta'tion
oc·cult'ism
oc'cu·pan·cy
·cies
oc'cu·pant
oc'cu·pa'tion
oc'cu·pa'tion·al·ly
oc'cu·py'
·pied' ·py'ing

oc·cur'
·curred'
·cur'ring
oc·cur'rence
o'cean
o'cean·go'ing
o'ce·an'ic
o'ce·a·nog'ra·phy
o'ce·an·ol'o·gy
o'ce·lot'
o'cher or o'chre
o'·clock'
oc'ta·gon'
oc·tag'o·nal
oc'ta·he'dron
oc'tane
oc·tan'gu·lar
oc'tave
oc·ta'vo
·vos
oc·tet' or ·tette'
Oc·to'ber
oc'to·ge·nar'i·an
oc'to·pus
·pus·es or ·pi'
or oc·top'o·des'
oc'tu·ple
oc'u·lar
oc'u·list
odd'i·ty
·ties
odd'ly
odds'-on'
o'di·ous
o'di·um
o·dom'e·ter
o'dor
o'dor·if'er·ous
o'dor·ous
Od'ys·sey
of'fal
off'beat'
off'-col'or
of·fend'
of·fense'
of·fen'sive
of'fer
of'fer·ing
of'fer·to'ry
·ries
off'hand'
off'hand'ed·ly
of'fice
of'fice·hold'er
of'fi·cer
of·fi'cial·ese'
of·fi'cial
of·fi'ci·ate'
·at'ed ·at'ing
of·fi'ci·a'tion
of·fi'ci·a'tor
of·fi'cious
off'ing
off'·key'
off'-lim'its
off'-line'
off'print'
off'set'

off'shoot'
off'shore'
off'side'
off'spring'
·spring' or
·springs'
off'stage'
off'-white'
of'ten
of'ten·times'
o'gle
o'gled o'gling
o'gre
o'gre·ish or
o'grish
O·hi'o
ohm'me'ter
oil'cloth'
oil'i·ness
oil'pa'per
oil'skin'
oil'stone'
oil'y
·i·er ·i·est
oint'ment
OK or O.K.
OK's or O.K.'s
OK'd or O.K.'d
OK'ing or O.K.'ing
O'kla·ho'ma
old'-fash'ioned
old'ish
old'-line'
old'ster
old'-tim'er
old'-world'
o'le·o'
o'le·o·mar'ga·
rine or ·rin
ol·fac'tion
ol·fac'to·ry
·ries
ol'i·garch'
ol'i·garch'y
·ies
ol'i·gop'o·ly
·lies
ol'ive
O·lym'pic
o·me'ga
om'e·let or
·lette
o'men
om'i·nous
o·mis'si·ble
o·mis'sion
o·mit'
o·mit'ted
o·mit'ting
om'ni·bus'
om'ni·far'i·ous
om·nip'o·tence
om·nip'o·tent
om'ni·pres'ence
om'ni·pres'ent
om'ni·range'
om·nis'cience
om·nis'cient

om·niv'o·rous
once'-o'ver
on'com'ing
one'ness
on'er·ous
one'self'
one'-sid'ed
one'-time'
one'-track'
one'-up'
-upped'
-up'ping
one'-up'man·ship'
one'-way'
on'go'ing
on'ion·skin'
on'-line'
on'look'er
on'ly
on·o'mat·o·poe'ia
on'rush'
on'set'
on'shore'
on'side'
on'slaught'
o'nus
on'ward
on'yx
oo'long
ooze
oozed ooz'ing
oo'zi·ness
oo'zy
·zi·er ·zi·est
o·pac'i·ty
o'pal
o'pal·es'cent
o·paque'
o'pen-and-shut'
o'pen-end'
o'pen-end'ed
o'pen·er
o'pen-eyed'
o'pen·hand'ed
o'pen·heart'ed
o'pen-hearth'
o'pen·ly
o'pen-mind'ed
o'pen-mouthed'
o'pen·ness
o'pen·work'
op'er·a
op'er·a·ble
op'er·a'te'
·at'ed ·at'ing
op'er·at'ic
op'er·a'tion
op'er·a'tion·al
op'er·a'tion·al·ly
op'er·a'tive
op'er·a'tor
op'er·et'ta
oph'thal·mol'o·
gist
oph'thal·mol'o·gy
oph·thal'mo·
scope'
o'pi·ate

o·pin'ion
o·pin'ion·at'ed
o·pin'ion·a'tive
o'pi·um
o·pos'sum
op·po'nent
op'por·tune'
op'por·tun'ism
op'por·tun'ist
op'por·tu'ni·ty
·ties
op·pos'a·ble
op·pose'
·posed' ·pos'ing
op·pos'er
op'po·site
op'po·si'tion
op·press'
op·pres'sion
op·pres'sive
op·pres'sive·ly
op·pres'sor
op·pro'bri·ous
op·pro'bri·um
op'tic
op'ti·cal
op·ti'cian
op'ti·mal
op'ti·mism
op'ti·mist
op'ti·mis'tic
op'ti·mis'ti·cal·ly
op'ti·mize'
·mized' ·miz'ing
op'ti·mum
·mums or ·ma
op'tion
op'tion·al
op'tion·al·ly
op·tom'e·trist
op·tom'e·try
op'u·lence
op'u·lent
o'pus
op'er·a or
o'pus·es
or'a·cle
(wise person;
SEE auricle)
o·rac'u·lar
o'ral
(of the mouth;
SEE aural)
o'ral·ly
or'ange
or'ange·ade'
or'ange·wood'
o·rang'u·tan'
o·ra'tion
or'a·tor
or'a·tor'i·cal
or'a·to'ri·o'
·os'
or'a·to'ry
·ries
or·bic'u·lar
or'bit
or'chard

or'ches·tra
or·ches'tral
or'ches·trate'
·trat'ed ·trat'ing
or'ches·tra'tion
or'chid
or·dain'
or·deal'
or'der
or'der·li·ness
or'der·ly
·lies
or'di·nal
or'di·nance
(law; SEE
ordnance)
or'di·nar'i·ly
or'di·nar'y
·ies
or'di·nate
or'di·na'tion
ord'nance
(artillery; SEE
ordinance)
or'dure
ore
(mineral; SEE o
o·reg'a·no
Or'e·gon
or'gan
or'gan·dy or ·
or·gan'ic
or·gan'i·cal·ly
or'gan·ism
or'gan·ist
or'gan·iz'a·ble
or'gan·i·za'tion
or'gan·ize'
·ized' ·iz'ing
or'gan·iz'er
or·gan'za
or'gasm
or·gas'mic
or·gi·as'tic
or'gy
·gies
O'ri·ent n.
o'ri·ent' v.
O'ri·en'tal
o'ri·en·tate'
·tat'ed ·tat'in
o'ri·en·ta'tior
or'i·fice
or'i·ga'mi
or'i·gin
o·rig'i·nal
o·rig'i·nal'i·t
o·rig'i·nal·ly
o·rig'i·nate'
·nat'ed ·nat'
o·rig'i·na'tion
o·rig'i·na'tor
o'ri·ole'
or'lon
or'na·ment
or'na·men'ta
or'na·men'ta
or·nate'

or·nate'ly
or·ni·thol'o·gy
o'ro·tund'
or'phan·age
or'thi·con'
or·tho·don'tics
or·tho·don'tist
or·tho·dox'
or·tho·dox'y
·ies
or·thog'ra·phy
or·tho·pe'dics
or·tho·pe'dist
os'cil·late'
·lat'ed ·lat'ing
(*fluctuate;* SEE
osculate)
os'cil·la'tion
os'cil·la'tor
os'cil·lo·scope'
os'cu·late'
·lat'ed ·lat'ing
(*kiss;* SEE
oscillate)
os·mo'sis
os'prey
·preys
os'si·fy'
·fied' ·fy'ing
os·ten'si·ble
os·ten'si·bly
os·ten'sive
os·ten'sive·ly
os·ten·ta'tion
os·ten·ta'tious
os'te·o·path'
os·te·op'a·thy
os'tra·cism
os'tra·cize'
·cized' ·ciz'ing
os'trich
oth'er·di·rect'ed
oth'er·wise'
o'ti·ose'
ot'ter
ot'to·man
·mans
ought
(*be obliged;* SEE
aught)
our·self'
our·selves'
oust'er
out'-and-out'
out'bid'
·bid' ·bid'ding
out'board'
out'bound'
out'break'
out'build'ing
out'burst'
out'cast'
out'class'
out'come'
out'crop'
out'cry'
·cries'
out'dat'ed

out'dis'tance
·tanced ·tanc·ing
out'do'
·did' ·done'
·do'ing
out'door'
out'doors'
out'er·most'
out'er space
out'er·wear
out'face'
out'field'er
out'fit'
out'fit'ter
out'flank'
out'flow'
out'go'
·went' ·gone'
·go'ing
out'go'
·goes'
out'go'ing
out'grow'
·grew' ·grown'
·grow'ing
out'growth'
out'guess'
out'house'
out'ing
out'land'er
out·land'ish
out·last'
out'law'
out'law·ry
·ries
out'lay'
·laid' ·lay'ing
out'let'
out'li'er
out'line'
out'live'
out'look'
out'ly'ing
out'man'
out'ma·neu'ver
out'mod'ed
out'most'
out'num'ber
out'-of-date'
out'-of-doors'
out'-of-pock'et
out'-of-the-way'
out'-of-town'er
out'pa'tient
out'post'
out'pour'ing
out'put'
out'rage'
out·ra'geous
out'rank'
out'reach'
out'ride'
·rode' ·rid'den
·rid'ing
out'rid'er
out'rig'ger
out'right'

out'run'
·ran' ·run'
·run'ning
out'sell'
·sold' ·sell'ing
out·'set'
out'shine'
·shone' ·shin'ing
out'side'
out'sid'er
out'sit'
·sat' ·sit'ting
out'size'
out'skirts'
out'smart'
out'speak'
·spoke' ·spo'ken
·speak'ing
out'spo'ken·ness
out'spread'
·spread'
·spread'ing
out'stand'ing
out'stare'
out'sta'tion
out'stay'
out'stretch'
out'strip'
out'talk'
out'think'
·thought'
·think'ing
out'vote'
out'ward
out'wear'
·wore' ·worn'
·wear'ing
out'weigh'
out'wit'
·wit'ted
·wit'ting
out'work'
o'val
o'val·ly
o·var'i·an
o'va·ry
·ries
o·va'tion
ov'en
o'ver·age
o'ver·all'
o'ver·alls'
o'ver·awe'
·awed' ·aw'ing
o'ver·bal'ance
o'ver·bear'
·bore' ·borne'
·bear'ing
o'ver·bid'
·bid' ·bid'ding
o'ver·bite'
o'ver·blouse'
o'ver·board'
o'ver·cap'i·tal·
ize'
o'ver·cast'
o'ver·charge'
o'ver·coat'

o'ver·come'
·came' ·come'
·com'ing
o'ver·com'pen·
sate'
o'ver·con'fi·dent
o'ver·crowd'ed
o'ver·do'
·did' ·done'
·do'ing
o'ver·dose'
o'ver·draft'
o'ver·draw'
·drew' ·drawn'
·draw'ing
o'ver·dress'
o'ver·drive'
o'ver·due'
o'ver·flight'
o'ver·flow'
o'ver·fly'
·flew' ·flown'
·fly'ing
o'ver·gar'ment
o'ver·glaze'
o'ver·grow'
·grew' ·grown'
·grow'ing
o'ver·hand'
o'ver·hang'
·hung'
·hang'ing
o'ver·haul'
o'ver·head'
o'ver·hear'
·heard'
·hear'ing
o'ver·heat'
o'ver·in·dul'
gence
o'ver·is'sue
o'ver·joy'
o'ver·lad'en
o'ver·lap'
o'ver·lay'
·laid' ·lay'ing
o'ver·leap'
o'ver·lie'
·lay' ·lain'
·ly'ing
o'ver·load'
o'ver·look'
o'ver·ly
o'ver·nice'
o'ver·night'
o'ver·pass'
o'ver·pay'
·paid' ·pay'ing
o'ver·pop'u·late'
o'ver·pow'er
o'ver·pro·duce'
o'ver·pro·tect'
o'ver·rate'
o'ver·reach'
o'ver·ride'
·rode' ·rid'den
·rid'ing
o'ver·rule'

o'ver·run'
·ran' ·run'
·run'ning
o'ver·seas'
o'ver·see'
·saw' ·seen'
·see'ing
o'ver·se'er
o'ver·sell'
·sold' ·sell'ing
o'ver·sexed'
o'ver·shad'ow
o'ver·shoe'
o'ver·shoot'
·shot' ·shoot'ing
o'ver·sight'
o'ver·sim'pli·fy'
o'ver·size'
o'ver·skirt'
o'ver·slaugh'
o'ver·sleep'
·slept' ·sleep'ing
o'ver·spend'
·spent' ·spend'ing
o'ver·spread'
o'ver·state'
o'ver·stay'
o'ver·step'
o'ver·stock'
o'ver·strung'
o'ver·stuff'
o'ver·sub·scribe'
o'ver·sup·ply'
o·vert'
o'ver·take'
·took' ·tak'en
·tak'ing
o'ver·tax'
o'ver-the-count'er
o'ver·throw'
·threw' ·thrown'
·throw'ing
o'ver·time'
o'ver·tone'
o'ver·ture
o'ver·use'
o'ver·view'
o'ver·ween'ing
o'ver·weight'
o'ver·whelm'
o'ver·wind'
·wound' ·wind'ing
o'ver·work'
o'ver·write'
·wrote' ·writ'ten
·writ'ing
o'ver·wrought'
o·vip'a·rous
o'void
o'vu·late'
·lat'ed ·lat'ing
o'vu·la'tion
o'vule
o'vum
o'va
owe
owed ow'ing
owl'ish

own'er·ship'
ox
ox'en
ox'blood'
ox'bow'
ox'ford
ox'i·da'tion
ox'i·dize'
·dized' ·diz'ing
ox'tail'
ox'y·gen
ox'y·gen·ate'
·at'ed ·at'ing
ox'y·gen·a'tion
ox'y·mo'ron
·mo'ra
ox'y·tet'ra·cy'·
cline
oys'ter
o'zone

P

pab'lum
pace
paced pac'ing
pace'mak'er
pach'y·derm'
pach'y·san'dra
pac'i·fi'a·ble
pa·cif'ic
pac'i·fi·ca'tion
pac'i·fi'er
pac'i·fism
pac'i·fy'
·fied' ·fy'ing
pack'age
·aged ·ag·ing
pack'et
pack'ing
pack'sad'dle
pack'thread'
pact
pad
pad'ded
pad'ding
pad'dle
·dled ·dling
pad'dock
pad'dy
·dies
(*rice;* SEE patty)
pad'lock'
pa'dre
·dres
pae'an
(*song;* SEE peon)
pa'gan
page
paged pag'ing
pag'eant
pag'eant·ry
·ries
page'boy'
pag'i·nate'
·nat·ed ·nat'ing

pag'i·na'tion
pa·go'da
pail
 (*bucket;* SEE
 pale)
pail'ful'
 ·fuls'
pain
 (*hurt;* SEE pane)
pain'ful
pain'less
pains'tak'ing
paint'brush'
paint'er
pair
 (*two;* SEE pare,
 pear)
pais'ley
pa·ja'mas
pal'ace
pal'an·quin'
pal'at·a·ble
pal'at·a·bly
pal'a·tal
pal'ate
 (*roof of mouth;*
 SEE palette, pallet)
pa·la'tial
pal'a·tine'
pa·lav'er
pale
 paled pal'ing
 (*white;* SEE pail)
pale'face'
pale'ly
pa'le·o·lith'ic
pa'le·on·tol'o·gy
pal'ette
 (*paint board;* SEE
 palate, pallet)
pal'in·drome'
pal'ing
pal'i·sade'
pall
 palled pall'ing
pal·la'di·um
pall'bear'er
pal'let
 (*tool; bed;* SEE
 palate, palette)
pal'li·ate'
 ·at'ed ·at'ing
pal'li·a'tive
pal'lid
pall'-mall'
 (*game;* SEE
 pell-mell)
pal'lor
palm
pal·met'to
 ·tos *or* ·toes
palm'is·try
pal'o·mi'no
 ·nos
pal'pa·ble
pal'pa·bly
pal'pate
 ·pat·ed ·pat·ing

pal'pi·tate'
 ·tat'ed ·tat'ing
pal'pi·ta'tion
pal'sy
 ·sied ·sy·ing
pal'tri·ness
pal'try
 ·tri·er ·tri·est
 (*trifling;*
 SEE poultry)
pam'pas
pam'per
pam'phlet
pam'phlet·eer'
pan
 panned pan'ning
pan'a·ce'a
pa·nache'
Pan'-A·mer'i·can
pan'a·tel'a
pan'cake'
pan'chro·mat'ic
pan'cre·as
pan'cre·at'ic
pan·dem'ic
pan'de·mo'ni·um
pan'der
pan·dow'dy
 ·dies
pane
 (*window;* SEE
 pain)
pan'e·gyr'ic
pan'e·gyr'i·cal
pan'el
 ·eled *or* ·elled
 ·el·ing *or* ·el·ling
pan'el·ist
pan'-fry'
 ·fried' ·fry'ing
pan'han'dle
pan'ic
 ·icked ·ick·ing
pan'ic·al·ly
pan'ick·y
pan'ic-strick'en
panne
pan'nier
pan'o·ply
 ·plies
pan'o·ra'ma
pan'o·ram'ic
pan'o·ram'i·cal·ly
pan'ta·loons'
pant'dress'
pan'the·ism
pan'the·is'tic
pan'the·on'
pan'ther
pant'ies
pan'to·graph
pan'to·mime'
 ·mimed'
 ·mim'ing
pan'to·mim'ic
pan'to·mim'ist
pan'try
 ·tries

pant'suit' *or*
 pants suit
pan'ty hose
pa'pa·cy
 ·cies
pa'pal
pa'paw
pa·pa'ya
pa'per·back'
pa'per·bound'
pa'per·hang'er
pa'per·weight'
pa'per·y
pa'pier-mâ·ché'
pa·poose'
pa·pri'ka
pap'ule
pa·py'rus
 ·ri *or* ·rus·es
par
 parred par'ring
par'a·ble
pa·rab'o·la
par'a·bol'ic
par'a·bol'i·cal·ly
par'a·chute'
 ·chut'ed
 ·chut'ing
par'a·chut'ist
pa·rade'
 ·rad'ed ·rad'ing
par'a·digm
par'a·dise'
par'a·dox'
par'a·dox'i·cal
par'a·dox'i·cal·ly
par'af·fin
par'a·gon'
par'a·graph'
par'a·keet'
par'al·lax'
par'al·lel'
 ·leled' *or* ·lelled'
 ·lel'ing *or*
 ·lel'ling
par'al·lel·ism
par'al·lel'o·gram'
pa·ral'y·sis
par'a·lyt'ic
par'a·lyze'
 ·lyzed' ·lyz'ing
par'a·me'ci·um
 ·ci·a
par'a·med'ic
par'a·med'i·cal
pa·ram'e·ter
 (*math. term;* SEE
 perimeter)
par'a·mount'
par'a·mour'
par'a·noi'a
par'a·noi'ac
par'a·noid'
par'a·pet
par'a·pher·na'li·a
par'a·phrase'
 ·phrased'
 ·phras'ing

par'a·ple'gi·a
par'a·ple'gic
par'a·prax'is
 ·es
par'a·psy·chol'o
 gy
par'a·res'cue
par'a·sail'
par'a·site'
par'a·sit'ic
par'a·sol'
par'a·troops'
par'boil'
par'buck'le
par'cel
 ·celed *or* ·celled
 ·cel·ing *or*
 ·cel·ling
parch'ment
par'don·a·ble
par'don·a·bly
pare
 pared par'ing
 (*trim;* SEE pair,
 pear)
par'e·gor'ic
par'ent
par'ent·age
pa·ren'tal
pa·ren'the·sis
 ·ses'
pa·ren'the·size'
 ·sized' ·siz'ing
par'en·thet'i·cal
par'ent·hood'
pa·re'sis
par'e·ve
par ex'cel·lence'
par·fait'
par·he'li·on
 ·li·a
pa·ri'ah
pa·ri'e·tal
par'i·mu'tu·el
par'ish
pa·rish'ion·er
par'i·ty
 ·ties
par'ka
park'way'
parl'ance
par'lay
 (*bet*)
par'ley
 (*confer*)
par'lia·ment
par'lia·men·
 tar'i·an
par'lia·men'ta·ry
par'lor
pa·ro'chi·al
par'o·dist
par'o·dy
 ·dies
 ·died ·dy·ing
pa·role'
 ·roled' ·rol'ing
pa·rol·ee'

pa·rot'id
par'ox·ysm
par'ox·ys'mal
par·quet'
 ·queted'
 ·quet'ing
par'quet·ry
par'ra·keet'
par'ri·cid'al
par'ri·cide'
par'rot
par'ry
 ·ries
 ·ried ·ry·ing
par'sec'
par'si·mo'ni·ous
par'si·mo'ny
pars'ley
pars'nip
par'son
par'son·age
par·take'
 ·took' ·tak'en
 ·tak'ing
par·terre'
par'the·no·gen'e·
 sis
par'tial
par'ti·al'i·ty
par'tial·ly
par'ti·ble
par·tic'i·pant
par·tic'i·pate'
 ·pat'ed ·pat'ing
par·tic'i·pa'tor
par'ti·cip'i·al
par'ti·ci·ple
par'ti·cle
par'ti·col'ored
par·tic'u·lar
par·tic'u·lar'i·ty
 ·ties
par·tic'u·lar·ize'
 ·ized' ·iz'ing
par·tic'u·lar·ly
par'ti·san
par·ti'tion
part'ner
part'ner·ship'
par'tridge
part'-time'
par·tu'ri·ent
par·tu·ri'tion
par'ty
 ·ties
par've·nu'
 ·nus'
pas'chal
pass'a·ble
pass'a·bly
pas'sage
pas'sage·way'
pass'book'
pas·sé'
passed
 (*pp. of pass;*
 SEE past)

pas'sen·ger
passe'-par·tout'
pass'er-by'
 pass'ers-by'
pas'sion
pas'sion·ate
pas'sion·ate·ly
pas'sive
pas'sive·ly
pas·siv'i·ty
pass'key'
Pass'o'ver
pass'port'
pass'-through'
pass'word'
past
 (*gone by; over;*
 SEE passed)
paste
 past'ed past'ing
paste'board'
pas·tel'
pas'teur·i·za'tion
pas'teur·ize'
 ·ized' ·iz'ing
pas·tille'
pas'time'
past'i·ness
pas'tor
pas'to·ral
pas'tor·ate
pas·tra'mi
pas'try
 tries
pas'ture
 ·tured ·tur·ing
past'y
 ·i·er ·i·est
pat
 pat'ted pat'ting
patch'work'
patch'y
 ·i·er ·i·est
pâ·té' de foie'
 gras'
pa·tel'la
 ·las *or* ·lae
pat'ent
pat'ent·ee'
pa·ter'nal
pa·ter'nal·is'tic
pa·ter'ni·ty
pa·thet'ic
pa·thet'i·cal·ly
path'find'er
path'o·gen'ic
path'o·log'i·cal
pa·thol'o·gy
 ·gies
pa'thos
pa'tience
pa'tient
pat'i·na
pa'ti·o'
 ·os'
pa·tis'se·rie
pat'ois
 ·ois

pa′tri·arch′
pa′tri·ar′chal
pa′tri·ar′chy
 ·chies
pa·tri′cian
pat′ri·cide′
pat′ri·mo′ny
 ·nies
pa′tri·ot
pa·tri·ot′ic
pa′tri·ot′i·cal·ly
pa′tri·ot·ism
pa·trol′
 ·trolled′
 ·trol′ling
pa·trol′man
pa′tron
pa′tron·age
pa′tron·ize′
 ·ized′ ·iz′ing
pat′ro·nym′ic
pat′ter
pat′tern·mak′er
pat′ty
 ·ties
 (cake; SEE paddy)
pau′ci·ty
paunch′i·ness
paunch′y
pau′per
pause
 paused paus′ing
pave
 paved pav′ing
pave′ment
pa·vil′ion
pawn′bro·ker
pawn′shop′
pay
 paid pay′ing
pay′a·ble
pay′check′
pay′day′
pay·ee′
pay′load′
pay′mas′ter
pay′ment
pay′off′
pay′roll′
peace
 (harmony;
 SEE piece)
peace′a·ble
peace′a·bly
peace′ful
peace′ful·ly
peace′mak′er
peace pipe
peace′time′
peach
pea′cock′
peak
 (highest point;
 SEE peek, pique)
peaked
 (pointed)
peak′ed
 (thin and drawn)

peal
 (sound; SEE peel)
pea′nut
pear
 (fruit; SEE pair,
 pare)
pearl
 (gem; SEE purl)
pearl′y
 ·i·er ·i·est
pear′-shaped′
peas′ant
peas′ant·ry
peat moss
peau′ de soie′
peb′ble
 ·bled ·bling
peb′bly
 ·bli·er ·bli·est
pe·can′
pec′ca·dil′lo
 ·loes or ·los
pec′cant
peck
pec′tin
pec′to·ral
pec′u·late′
 ·lat·ed ·lat′ing
pec′u·la′tion
pec′u·la′tor
pe·cul′iar
pe·cu′li·ar′i·ty
 ·ties
pe·cu′ni·ar′i·ly
pe·cu′ni·ar′y
ped′a·gog′ic
ped′a·gogue′
 or ·gog′
ped′a·go′gy
ped′al
 ·aled or ·alled
 ·al·ing or
 ·al·ling
 (foot lever; SEE
 peddle)
ped′ant
pe·dan′tic
pe·dan′ti·cal·ly
ped′ant·ry
 ·ries
ped′dle
 ·dled ·dling
 (sell; SEE pedal)
ped′dler
ped′es·tal
pe·des′tri·an
pe′di·a·tri′cian
pe′di·at′rics
ped′i·cure′
ped′i·gree′
ped′i·greed′
ped′i·ment
pe·dom′e·ter
peek
 (look; SEE
 peak, pique)
peel
 (skin; SEE peal)

peep′hole′
peer
 (equal; look;
 SEE pier)
peer group
peer′less
peeve
 peeved peev′ing
pee′vish
peg
 pegged peg′ging
peg′board′
peign·oir′
pe′jo·ra′tion
pe·jo′ra·tive
Pe′king·ese′
pe′koe
pel′i·can
pel·la′gra
pel′let
pell′-mell′
 (without order;
 SEE pall-mall)
pel·lu′cid
pel′vic
pel′vis
pem′mi·can
pen
 penned or pent
 pen′ning
 (enclose)
pen
 penned pen′ning
 (write with pen)
pe′nal
pe′nal·i·za′tion
pe′nal·ize′
 ·ized′ ·iz′ing
pen′al·ty
 ·ties
pen′ance
pen′chant
pen′cil
 ·ciled or ·cilled
 ·cil·ing or
 ·cil·ling
pend′ant or
 ·ent n.
pend′ent or
 ·ant adj.
pend′ing
pen′du·lous
pen′du·lum
pen′e·tra·bil′i·ty
pen′e·tra·ble
pen′e·tra·bly
pen′e·trate′
 ·trat′ed ·trat′ing
pen′e·tra′tion
pen′e·trom′e·ter
pen′guin
pen′hold′er
pen′i·cil′lin
pen·in′su·la
pen·in′su·lar
pe′nis
 ·nis·es or ·nes
pen′i·tence

pen′i·tent
pen′i·ten′tial
pen′i·ten′tia·ry
 ·ries
pen′knife′
 ·knives′
pen′light′ or ·lite′
pen′man·ship′
pen name
pen′nant
pen′non
Penn′syl·va′ni·a
pen′ny
 ·nies
pen′ny ante
pen′ny·weight′
pen′ny·wise′
pen′ny·worth′
pe′no·log′i·cal
pe·nol′o·gist
pe·nol′o·gy
pen′sion
pen′sion·ar′y
 ·ies
pen′sive
pen′sive·ly
pen′stock′
pen′ta·gon′
pen·tag′o·nal
pen′ta·he′dral
pen′ta·he′dron
 ·drons or ·dra
pen·tam′e·ter
Pen′ta·teuch′
pen·tath′lon
Pen′te·cost′
pent′house′
pen·to′mic
pent′-up′
pe·nu′che or ·chi
pe′nult
pe·nul′ti·mate
pe·num′bra
 ·brae or ·bras
pe·nu′ri·ous
pen′u·ry
pe′on
 (laborer; SEE
 paean)
pe′on·age
pe′o·ny
 ·nies
peo′ple
 ·pled ·pling
pep′lum
 ·lums or ·la
pep′per-and-salt′
pep′per·corn′
pep′per·i·ness
pep′per·mint′
pep′per·o′ni
 ·nis or ·ni
pep′per·y
 ·i·er ·i·est
pep′pi·ly
pep′pi·ness
pep′py
 ·pi·er ·pi·est

pep′sin
pep′tic
per·am′bu·late′
 ·lat′ed ·lat′ing
per·am′bu·la′tion
per·am′bu·la′tor
per an′num
 ·er·cale′
per cap′i·ta
per·ceiv′a·ble
per·ceiv′a·bly
per·ceive′
 ·ceived′ ·ceiv′ing
per·cent′ or
 per cent
per·cent′age
per·cen′tile
per′cept
per·cep′ti·ble
per·cep′ti·bly
per·cep′tion
per·cep′tive
per·cep′tive·ly
per·cep′tu·al
per·chance′
Per′che·ron′
per·cip′i·ent
per′co·late′
 ·lat′ed ·lat′ing
per′co·la′tion
per′co·la′tor
per·cus′sion
per·cus′sive
per di′em
per·di′tion
per·du′ or ·due′
per·dur′a·ble
per′e·gri·nate′
 ·nat′ed ·nat′ing
per′e·gri·na′tion
per·emp′to·ri·ly
per·emp′to·ri·ness
per·emp′to·ry
per·en′ni·al
per′fect
per·fect′i·bil′i·ty
per·fect′i·ble
per·fec′tion
per·fec′tion·ism
per·fec′to
 ·tos
per·fid′i·ous
per′fi·dy
 ·dies
per′fo·rate′
 ·rat′ed ·rat′ing
per′fo·ra′tion
per′fo·ra·tor
per·force′
per·form′
per·form′ance
per·fume′
 ·fumed′ ·fum′ing
per′fume n.
per·fum′er
per·func′to·ri·ly
per·func′to·ry
per′go·la

per·haps′
per′i·gee′
per′i·he′li·on
 ·li·ons or ·li·a
per′il
 ·iled or ·illed
 ·il·ing or ·il·ling
per′il·ous
per′i·lune′
pe·rim′e·ter
 (boundary; SEE
 parameter)
pe′ri·od
pe′ri·od′ic
pe′ri·od′i·cal
pe′ri·od′i·cal·ly
pe′ri·o·dic′i·ty
per′i·pa·tet′ic
pe·riph′er·al
pe·riph′er·y
 ·ies
pe·riph′ra·sis
per′i·phras′tic
pe·rique′
per′i·scope′
per′i·scop′ic
per′ish
per′ish·a·bil′i·ty
per′ish·a·ble
per′i·stal′sis
per′i·style′
per′i·to·ni′tis
per′jure
 ·jured ·jur·ing
per′jur·er
per′ju·ry
 ·ries
perk′i·ness
perk′y
 ·i·er ·i·est
per′ma·frost′
perm′al·loy
per′ma·nence
per′ma·nent
per′me·a·bil′i·ty
per′me·a·ble
per′me·ate′
 ·at′ed ·at′ing
per·me·a′tion
per·mis′si·bil′i·ty
per·mis′si·ble
per·mis′si·bly
per·mis′sion
per·mis′sive
per·mis′sive·ly
per·mit′
 ·mit′ted
 ·mit′ting
per·mut′a·ble
per′mu·ta′tion
per·ni′cious
per·nod′
per′o·rate′
 ·rat′ed ·rat′ing
per′o·ra′tion
per·ox′ide
 ·id·ed ·id·ing
per′pen·dic′u·lar

per′pe·trate′
·trat′ed ·trat′ing
per′pe·tra′tion
per′pe·tra′tor
per·pet′u·al
per·pet′u·al·ly
per·pet′u·ate′
·at′ed ·at′ing
per·pet′u·a′tion
per·pet′u·a′tor
per′pe·tu′i·ty
·ties
per·plex′
per·plexed′
per·plex′ed·ly
per·plex′i·ty
·ties
per′qui·site
(privilege; SEE
prerequisite)
per se
per′se·cute′
·cut′ed ·cut′ing
(harass; SEE
prosecute)
per′se·cu′tion
per′se·cu′tor
per·se·ver′ance
per·se·vere′
·vered′ ·ver′ing
per′si·flage′
per·sim′mon
per·sist′
per·sist′ence
per·sist′ent
per′son
per′son·a·ble
per′son·age
per′son·al
(private; SEE
personnel)
per′son·al′i·ty
·ties
per′son·al·ize′
·ized′ ·iz′ing
per′son·al·ly
per′son·ate′
·at′ed ·at′ing
per′son·a′tion
per′son·a′tor
per·son′i·fi·
ca′tion
per·son′i·fy′
·fied′ ·fy′ing
per′son·nel′
(employees; SEE
personal)
per·spec′tive
(view; SEE
prospective)
per·spi·ca′cious
per·spi·cac′i·ty
per·spi·cu′i·ty
per·spic′u·ous
per·spi·ra′tion
per·spir′a·to′ry
per·spire′
·spired′ ·spir′ing

per·suad′a·ble
per·suade′
·suad′ed
·suad′ing
per·sua′si·bil′i·ty
per·sua′sion
per·sua′sive
per·tain′
per′ti·na′cious
per′ti·nac′i·ty
per′ti·nence
per′ti·nent
pert′ly
per·turb′
per·tur·ba′tion
pe·rus′al
pe·ruse′
·rused′ ·rus′ing
per·vade′
·vad′ed ·vad′ing
per·va′sion
per·va′sive
per·verse′
per·verse′ly
per·ver′sion
per·ver′si·ty
per·vert′
per′vi·ous
Pe′sach
pe′so
·sos
pes′si·mism
pes′si·mist
pes′si·mis′tic
pes′si·mis′ti·
cal·ly
pes′ter
pest′hole′
pes′ti·cide′
pes′ti·lence
pes′ti·lent
pes′ti·len′tial
pes′tle
·tled ·tling
pet
pet′ted pet′ting
pet′al
pet′al·like′
pet′cock′
pe·tite′
pe′tit four′
pe′tits fours′
or pe′tit fours′
pe·ti′tion
pet′it jury
pe·tit′ mal′
pet′it point
pe′tri dish
pet′ri·fac′tion
pet′ri·fy′
·fied′ ·fy′ing
pet′ro·la′tum
pe·tro′le·um
pet′ti·coat′
pet′ti·fog′
·fogged′
·fog′ging
pet′ti·fog′ger

pet′ti·ly
pet′ti·ness
pet′ti·pants′
pet′tish
pet′ty
·ti·er ·ti·est
pet′u·lance
pet′u·lant
pew′ter
pha′e·ton
pha′lanx
·lanx·es or
pha·lan′ges
phal′lic
phal′lus
·li or ·lus·es
phan′tasm
phan′tom
phar′i·sa′ic
phar′i·see′
phar′ma·ceu′ti·cal
phar′ma·cist
phar′ma·col′o·gy
phar′ma·co·pe′ia
phar′ma·cy
·cies
phar′ynx
·ynx·es or
pha·ryn′ges
phase
phased phas′ing
(stage; SEE faze)
phase′-out′
pheas′ant
phe′no·bar′bi·tal′
phe·nom′e·nal
phe·nom′e·nal·ly
phe·nom′e·non′
·na or ·nons′
phi′al
Phil′a·del′phi·a
phi·lan′der·er
phil′an·throp′ic
phi·lan′thro·pist
phi·lan′thro·py
·pies
phil′a·tel′ic
phi·lat′e·list
phi·lat′e·ly
phil′har·mon′ic
Phil′ip·pine′
Phil′is·tine′
phil′o·den′dron
phil′o·log′i·cal
phi·lol′o·gist
phi·lol′o·gy
phi·los′o·pher
phil′o·soph′ic
phil′o·soph′i·
cal·ly
phi·los′o·phize′
·phized′ ·phiz′ing
phi·los′o·phy
·phies
phil′ter
(potion; SEE
filter)
phle·bi′tis

phlegm
phleg·mat′ic
phlox
pho′bi·a
pho′bic
phoe′be
Phoe′nix
phone
phoned phon′ing
pho′neme
pho·net′ic
pho·net′i·cal·ly
pho′ne·ti′cian
phon′ics
pho′ni·ness
pho′no·graph′
pho·nol′o·gy
pho′ny
·ni·er ·ni·est
·nies
phos′phate
phos′pho·
res′cence
phos′pho·res′cent
pho′to·chron′o·
graph
pho′to·cop′i·er
pho′to·cop′y
·ies
·ied ·y·ing
pho′to·e·lec′tric
pho′to·en·grave′
·graved′
·grav′ing
pho′to·flash′
pho′to·flood′
pho′to·gen′ic
pho′to·graph′
pho·tog′ra·pher
pho′to·graph′ic
pho·tog′ra·phy
pho′to·gra·vure′
pho′to·lith′o·
graph
pho′to·li·thog′ra·
phy
pho′to·map′
pho·tom′e·ter
pho′to·met′ric
pho·tom′e·try
pho′to·mon·tage′
pho′to·mu′ral
pho′to·off′set′
pho′to·sen′si·tive
pho′to·stat′
·stat′ed or
·stat′ted
·stat′ing or
·stat′ting
pho′to·stat′ic
pho′to·syn′the·sis
phras′al
phras′al·ly
phrase
phrased
phras′ing

phra′se·ol′o·gy
·gies
phre·net′ic
phre·nol′o·gy
phy·lac′ter·y
·ies
phy′lum
·la
phys′ic
·icked ·ick·ing
phys′i·cal
phys′i·cal·ly
phy·si′cian
phys′i·cist
phys′ics
phys′i·og′no·my
phys′i·og′ra·phy
phys′i·o·log′i·cal
phys′i·ol′o·gy
phys′i·o·ther′a·
pist
phys′i·o·ther′a·py
phy·sique′
pi
pied
pie′ing or pi′ing
(jumble; SEE pie)
pi
(Greek letter;
SEE pie)
pi′a·nis′si·mo′
pi·an′ist
pi·an′o
·os
pi′a·no′la
pi·az′za
pi′ca
pic′a·dor′
pic′a·resque′
pic′a·yune′
Pic′ca·dil′ly
pic′ca·lil′li
pic′co·lo′
·los′
pick′ax′ or ·axe′
pick′er·el
pick′et
pick′le
·led ·ling
pick′pock′et
pick′up′
pic′nic
·nicked
·nick·ing
pic′nick·er
pi′cot
·coted ·cot·ing
pic′to·graph′
pic·to′ri·al
pic·to′ri·al·ly
pic′ture
·tured ·tur·ing
pic′tur·esque′
pid′dle
·dled ·dling
pidg′in English
pie
(food; SEE pi)

pie′bald′
piece
pieced piec′in
(part; SEE peac
pièce de ré·sis
tance′
piece′-dyed′
piece′meal′
piece′work′
pied′mont
pier
(structure; SEE
peer)
pierce
pierced
pierc′ing
pier glass
pi′e·tism
pi′e·ty
·ties
pi′geon
pi′geon·hole′
·holed′ ·hol′in
pi′geon-toed′
pig′gish
pig′gy·back′
pig′head·ed
pig iron
pig′let
pig′ment
pig·men·ta′tic
pi·gno′li·a
pig′pen′
pig′skin′
pig′sty′
·sties′
pig′tail′
pi·laf′ or ·laff
pi·las′ter
pile
piled pil′ing
pi′le·ous
pile′up′
pil′fer
pil′fer·age
pil′grim
pil′grim·age
pil′lage
·laged ·lag·in
pil′lar
pill′box′
pil′lion
pil′lo·ry
·ries
·ried ·ry·ing
pil′low
pil′low·case′
pi′lose
pi′lot
pi′lot·house′
Pil′sener or
Pil′sner
pi·men′to or
·mien′·
·tos
pim′ple
pim′ply
pin′a·fore′

pi·ña'ta
pin'ball'
pince'-nez'
pin'cers
pinch'beck'
pinch'-hit'
-hit' -hit'ting
pin'cush'ion
pine
pined pin'ing
pine'ap'ple
pin'feath'er
ping'-pong'
pin'head'
pin'hole'
pin'ion
pink'eye'
pin'na·cle
·cled ·cling
(acme)
pi'noch'le or
·noc'·
(game)
pin'point'
pin stripe
pin'to
·tos
pint'-size'
pin'up'
pin'wale'
pin'wheel'
pin'worm'
pi'o·neer'
pi'ous
pipe
piped pip'ing
pipe'ful'
·fuls'
pipe'line'
pip'er
pipe'stem'
pi·pette' or ·pet'
pet'ted ·pet'ting
pip'pin
pi'quan·cy
pi'quant
pique
piqued piqu'ing
(offend; SEE
peak, peek)
pi·qué' or ·que'
(fabric)
pi'ra·cy
pi·ra'nha
pi'rate
·rat·ed ·rat·ing
pir'ou·ette'
pir'et'ted ·et'ting
pis·ca'to·ri·al
pis'ci·cul'ture
pis·ta'chi·o'
piss'
pis'til
(part of plant)
pis'tol
·toled or ·tolled
·tol·ing or ·tol·ling
(firearm)

pis'tol-whip'
pis'ton
pit
pit'ted pit'ting
pitch'-black'
pitch'blende'
pitch'-dark'
pitch'er·ful'
·fuls'
pitch'fork'
pitch pipe
pit'e·ous
pit'fall'
pith'i·ness
pith'y
·i·er ·i·est
pit'i·a·ble
pit'i·ful
pit'i·less
pit'tance
Pitts'burgh
pi·tu'i·tar'y
pit'y
·ies, ied ·y·ing
piv'ot
piv'ot·al
pix'ie or ·y
·ies
piz'za
piz·ze·ri'a
piz'zi·ca'to
plac'a·bil'i·ty
plac'a·ble
plac'a·bly
plac'ard
pla'cate
·cat·ed ·cat·ing
place
placed plac'ing
place'ment
pla·cen'ta
·tas or ·tae
plac'er
plac'id
pla·cid'i·ty
plack'et
pla'gia·rism
pla'gia·rize'
·rized' ·riz'ing
pla'gia·ry
·ries
plague
plagued
plagu'ing
plagu'er
plaid
plain
(clear; simple;
SEE plane)
plain'ness
plains'man
plain'song'
plain'-spo'ken
plain'tiff
plain'tive
plain'tive·ly

plait
(pleat; braid;
SEE plate)
plan
planned
plan'ning
plane
planed plan'ing
(level; SEE plain)
plan'et
plan'e·tar'i·um
·i·ums or ·i·a
plan'e·tar'y
plan'e·tes'i·mal
plan'et·oid'
plank'ing
plank'ton
plan'ner
plan'tain
plan'tar
(of the sole)
plan·ta'tion
plant'er
(one that plants)
plan'ti·grade'
plaque
plas'ma
plas'ter
plas'ter·board'
plas'ter·er
plas'tic
plas'ti·cal·ly
plas'ti·cine
plas·tic'i·ty
plas'ti·cize'
·cized' ·ciz'ing
plat
plat'ted
plat'ting
(map)
plate
plat'ed plat'ing
(dish; SEE plait)
pla·teau'
·teaus' or
·teaux'
plate'ful'
·fuls'
plat'en
plat'form'
plat'i·num
plat'i·tude
plat'i·tu'di·nous
pla·ton'ic
pla·ton'i·cal·ly
pla·toon'
plat'ter
plau'dit
plau'si·bil'i·ty
plau'si·ble
plau'si·bly
play'back'
play'bill'
play'boy'
play'-by-play'
play'ful·ly
play'go'er
play'ground'

play'house'
play'mate'
play'-off'
play'pen'
play'room'
play'thing'
play'wright'
pla'za
plea
plead
plead'ed or plead
plead'ing
pleas'ant
pleas'ant·ry
·ries
pleat
ple·be'ian
pleb'i·scite'
plec'trum
·trums or ·tra
pledge
pledged
pledg'ing
pledg'ee'
ple'na·ry
plen'i·po·ten'ti·
ar'y
·ies
plen'i·tude'
plen'te·ous
plen'ti·ful
plen'ti·ful·ly
plen'ty
ple'num
·nums or ·nu
ple'o·nasm
pleth'o·ra
pleu'ral
(of the pleura;
SEE plural)
pleu'ri·sy
Plex'i·glas'
pli'a·bil'i·ty
pli'a·ble
pli'an·cy
pli'ant
pli'ers
plight
plis·sé' or ·se'
plod
plod'ded
plod'ding
plop
plopped
plop'ping
plot
plot'ted
plot'ting
plow'share'
pluck'i·ness
pluck'y
·i·er ·i·est

plug
plugged
plug'ging
plum
(fruit)
plum'age
plumb
(lead weight)
plumb'er
plumb'ing
plume
plumed
plum'ing
plum'met
plu'mose
plump'ness
plun'der
plunge
plunged
plung'ing
plung'er
plu·per'fect
plu'ral
(more than one;
SEE pleural)
plu'ral·ism
plu'ral·is'tic
plu·ral'i·ty
·ties
plu'ral·ize'
·ized' ·iz'ing
plush'i·ness
plush'y
·i·er ·i·est
plu·toc'ra·cy
·cies
plu'to·crat'
plu'to·crat'ic
plu·to'ni·um
plu'vi·al
ply
plies
plied ply'ing
ply'wood'
pneu·mat'ic
pneu·mo'ni·a
poached
poach'er
pock'et·book'
(purse)
pocket book
(small book)
pock'et·ful'
·fuls'
pock'et·knife'
·knives'
pock'et·size'
pock'mark'
po·di'a·trist
po·di'a·try
po'di·um
·di·a or ·di·ums
po'em
po·et'ic
po·et'i·cal·ly
po'et·ry
po·go'ni·a
po'go stick

po·grom'
poign'an·cy
poign'ant
poin·set'ti·a
point'-blank'
point'ed·ly
point'er
point'less
poise
poised pois'ing
poi'son·ous
poke
poked pok'ing
pok'er
pok'i·ness
pok'y
·i·er ·i·est
po'lar
po·lar'i·ty
po'lar·i·za'tion
po'lar·ize'
·ized' ·iz'ing
pole
poled pol'ing
(rod; SEE poll)
pole'ax' or ·axe'
po·lem'ic
po·lem'i·cist
pole'star'
pole'-vault' v.
po·lice'
·liced' ·lic'ing
po·lice'man
po·lice'wom'an
pol'i·clin'ic
(outpatient clinic;
SEE polyclinic)
pol'i·cy
·cies
pol'i·cy·hold'er
po'li·o·my'e·li'tis
pol'ish
po·lite'ly
po·lite'ness
pol'i·tic
·ticked ·tick·ing
po·lit'i·cal
po·lit'i·cal·ly
(in a political
manner)
pol'i·ti'cian
pol'i·tic·ly
(shrewdly)
po·lit'i·co'
·cos'
pol'i·tics
pol'i·ty
·ties
pol'ka
pol'ka dot
poll
(vote; SEE pole)
poll'ee'
pol'len
pol'li·nate'
·nat'ed ·nat'ing
pol'li·na'tion
pol'li·wog'

poll'ster
poll tax
pol·lu'tant
pol·lute'
·lut'ed ·lut'ing
pol·lu'tion
pol'ter·geist'
pol·troon'
pol'y·an'drous
pol'y·an'dry
pol'y·clin'ic
(hospital; SEE
policlinic)
pol'y·es'ter
pol'y·eth'yl·ene'
po·lyg'a·mous
po·lyg'a·my
pol'y·glot'
pol'y·gon'
pol'y·graph'
po·lyg'y·ny
pol'y·mer
pol'y·sty'rene
pol'y·syl·lab'ic
pol'y·syl'la·ble
pol'y·tech'nic
pol'y·the·ism
pol'y·un·sat'u·
rat'ed
pom'ace
(pulp; SEE
pumice)
po·ma'ceous
po·made'
pome'gran'ate
pom'mel
·meled or
·melled
·mel·ing or
·mel·ling
pom'pa·dour'
pom'pa·no'
Pom·pei'i
pom'pon'
pom·pos'i·ty
pom'pous
pon'cho
·chos
pon'der
pon'der·a·ble
pon'der·ous
pon·gee'
pon'iard
pon'tiff
pon·tif'i·cal
pon·tif'i·cate'
·cat'ed ·cat'ing
pon·toon'
po'ny
·nies
po'ny·tail'
poo'dle
pooh'-pooh'
pool'room'
poor'house'
pop
popped pop'ping
pop'corn'

pop'eyed'
pop'lar
(tree; SEE
popular)
pop'lin
pop'o'ver
pop'per
pop'pet
pop'py
·pies
pop·u·lace
(the masses;
SEE populous)
pop'u·lar
(liked by many;
SEE poplar)
pop'u·lar'i·ty
pop'u·lar·i·
za'tion
pop'u·lar·ize'
·ized' ·iz'ing
pop'u·late'
·lat'ed ·lat'ing
pop'u·la'tion
pop'u·lous
(full of people;
SEE populace)
por'ce·lain
por'cu·pine'
pore
pored por'ing
(ponder; tiny
opening; SEE
pour)
pork'er
por'no·graph'ic
por·nog'ra·phy
po·ros'i·ty
po'rous
por'phy·ry
·ries
por'poise
por'ridge
por·rin·ger
port·a·bil'i·ty
port'a·ble
por'tage
·taged ·tag·ing
por'tal
port·cul'lis
por·tend'
por'tent
por·ten'tous
por'ter
por'ter·house'
port·fo'li·o'
·os'
port'hole'
por'ti·co'
·coes' or ·cos'
por·tiere'
por'tion
port'li·ness
port'ly
·li·er ·li·est
port·man'teau
·teaus or ·teaux
por'trait

por'trai·ture
por·tray'
por·tray'al
Por'tu·guese'
por'tu·lac'a
pose
posed pos'ing
posh
po·si'tion
pos'i·tive
pos'i·tive·ly
pos'i·tiv·ism
pos'se
pos·sess'
pos·sessed'
pos·ses'sion
pos·ses'sive
pos·ses'sor
pos·si·bil'i·ty
·ties
pos'si·ble
pos'si·bly
post'age
post'al
post'box'
post card
post'date'
post'er
pos·te'ri·or
pos·ter'i·ty
post'grad'u·ate
post'haste'
post'hu·mous
post'hyp·not'ic
pos·til'ion
post'man
post'mark'
post'mas'ter
post'mis'tress
post'-mor'tem
post·na'tal
post'paid'
post·pon'a·ble
post·pone'
·poned' ·pon'ing
post·pone'ment
post'script'
pos'tu·late'
·lat'ed ·lat'ing
pos·tu·la'tion
pos·tu·la'tor
pos'tur·al
pos'ture
·tured ·tur·ing
post'war'
pot
pot'ted pot'ting
po'ta·ble
po·ta'tion
po·ta'to
·toes
pot'bel'lied
pot'bel'ly
·lies
pot'boil'er
po'ten·cy
po'tent
po'ten·tate'

po·ten'tial
po·ten'ti·al'i·ty
·ties
po·ten'tial·ly
po'tent·ly
poth'er
pot'hold'er
pot'hole'
po'tion
pot'latch'
pot'luck'
pot'pour·ri'
pot'sherd'
pot'shot'
pot'tage
pot'ter·y
·ies
pouch'i·ness
poul'tice
poul'try
(fowls; SEE
paltry)
pounce
pounced
poun'cing
pound'-fool'ish
pour
(flow; SEE pore)
pout
pov'er·ty
pow'der·y
·i·er ·i·est
pow'er·ful
pow'er·ful·ly
pow'er·house'
pow'er·less
pow'wow'
pox
prac'ti·ca·bil'i·ty
prac'ti·ca·ble
prac'ti·ca·bly
prac'ti·cal
prac'ti·cal'i·ty
·ties
prac'ti·cal·ly
prac'tice
·ticed ·tic·ing
prac'tic·er
prac'ti·cum
prac·ti'tion·er
prag·mat'ic
prag·mat'i·cal·ly
prag'ma·tism
prag'ma·tist
prai'rie
praise
praised
prais'ing
praise'wor'thy
pra'line
prance
pranced
pranc'ing
prank'ish
prate
prat'ed
prat'ing

prat'tle
·tled ·tling
pray
(implore; SEE
prey)
pray'er
(one who prays)
prayer
(an entreaty)
preach'er
pre'am'ble
pre'ar·range'
·ranged'
·rang'ing
pre'ar·range'ment
preb'end
pre·can'cel
pre·car'i·ous
pre·cau'tion
pre·cau'tion·ar'y
pre·cede'
·ced'ed ·ced'ing
(come before;
SEE proceed)
prec'e·dence
(priority)
prec'e·dent
(example)
pre'·cen'sor
pre'cept
pre·cep'tor
pre·ces'sion
(a going before;
SEE procession)
pre·ces'sion·al
pre'cinct
pre·ci·os'i·ty
pre'cious
prec'i·pice
pre·cip'i·tate'
·tat'ed ·tat'ing
pre·cip'i·ta'tion
pre·cip'i·tous
pré·cis'
·cis'
(abstract)
pre·cise'
(definite)
pre·cise'ly
pre·ci'sion
pre·clude'
·clud'ed
·clud'ing
pre·clu'sion
pre·co'cious
pre·cog·ni'tion
pre·con·ceive'
pre'con·cep'tion
pre·con'scious
pre·cur'sor
pre·cur'so·ry
pre·da'cious
pre·date'
pred'a·tor
pred'a·to'ry
pre·de·cease'
pred'e·ces'sor
pre·des'ti·na'tion

pre·des'tine
·tined ·tin·ing
pre'de·ter'mine
pred'i·ca·bil'i·ty
pred'i·ca·ble
pre·dic'a·ment
pred'i·cate'
·cat'ed ·cat'ing
pred'i·ca'tion
pre·dict'
pre·dict'a·ble
pre·dic'tion
pre·dic'tive
pre·dic'tor
pre'di·gest'
pre'di·lec'tion
pre'dis·pose'
pre'dis·po·si'tion
pre·dom'i·nant
pre·dom'i·nate'
pre·em'i·nence
pre·em'i·nent
pre·empt'
pre·emp'tion
pre·emp'tive
pre·emp'tor
pre'es·tab'lish
pre·ex·ist'
pre·ex·ist'ence
pre'fab'
pre·fab'ri·cate'
pref'ace
·aced ·ac·ing
pref'a·to'ry
pre·fect
pre'fec·ture
pre·fer'
·ferred' ·fer'ring
pref'er·a·ble
pref'er·a·bly
pref'er·ence
pref'er·en'tial
pre·fer'ment
pre'fig·u·ra'tion
pre·fig'ur·a·tive
pre·fig'ure
pre'fix
pre'flight'
preg'na·ble
preg'nan·cy
·cies
preg'nant
pre·hen'sile
pre'his·tor'ic
pre·judge'
pre·judg'ment or
·judge'·
prej'u·dice
·diced ·dic·ing
prej'u·di'cial
prel'a·cy
prel'ate
pre·lim'i·nar'y
·ies
prel'ude
pre·mar'i·tal
pre'ma·ture'
pre'ma·ture'ly

e·med'i·cal	pre·serv'a·tive	pre'view	pri'or·ess	proc'u·ra'tor	prog·nos'ti·ca'tor
e·med'i·tate'	pre·serve'	pre'vi·ous	pri·or'i·ty	pro·cure'	pro'gram
e·mier'	·served'	pre·vi'sion	·ties	·cured' ·cur'ing	·grammed
hief)	·serv'ing	pre'war'	pri'o·ry	pro·cure'ment	or ·gramed
e·mière'	pre·set'	prey	·ries	prod	·gram·ming
nièred'	pre'-shrunk'	(victim; SEE	prism	prod'ded	or ·gram·ing
nièr'ing	pre·side'	pray)	pris·mat'ic	prod'ding	pro'gram·mat'ic
rst showing)	·sid'ed ·sid'ing	pri'a·pism	pris'on	prod'i·gal	pro'gram·mer
em'ise	pres'i·den·cy	price	pris'on·er	prod'i·gal'i·ty	or ·gram·er
sed ·is·ing	·cies	prid'ed prid'ing	pris'tine	pro·di'gious	prog'ress
e'mi·um	pres'i·dent	price'less	pri'va·cy	prod'i·gy	pro·gres'sion
e'mo·ni'tion	pres'i·dent-e·lect'	prick'le	pri'vate	·gies	pro·gres'sive
e·mon'i·to'ry	pres'i·den'tial	·led ·ling	pri·va·teer'	(genius; SEE	pro·gres'siv·ism
e·na'tal	pre·sid'i·um	prick'li·ness	pri·va'tion	protégé)	pro·hib'it
e·oc'cu·pan·cy	·i·a or ·i·ums	prick'ly	priv'et	pro·duce'	pro'hi·bi'tion
e·oc'cu·pa'tion	pre·sig'ni·fy'	·li·er ·li·est	priv'i·lege	·duced'	pro·hib'i·tive
e·oc'cu·py'	press box	pride	·leged ·leg·ing	·duc'ing	pro·hib'i·to'ry
ied' ·py'ing	press'ing	prid'ed prid'ing	priv'y	pro·duc'er	proj'ect
e'or·dain'	press'man	pri'er	·ies	pro·duc'i·ble	pro·jec'tile
e·pack'age	pres'sure	(one who pries;	prize	prod'uct	pro·jec'tion
e·paid'	·sured ·sur·ing	SEE prior)	prized priz'ing	pro·duc'tion	pro·jec'tive
ep'a·ra'tion	pres'sur·ize'	priest'ess	prize'fight'	pro·duc'tive	pro·jec'tor
e·par'a·tive	·ized' ·iz'ing	priest'hood	prob'a·bil'i·ty	pro·duc'tive·ly	pro·lep'sis
e·par'a·to'ry	press'work'	priest'ly	prob'a·ble	pro'duc·tiv'i·ty	·ses
e·pare'	pres'ti·dig'i·ta'tor	·li·er ·li·est	prob'a·bly	prof'a·na'tion	pro'le·tar'i·an
ared' ·par'ing	pres·tige'	prig'gish	pro'bate	pro·fane'	pro'le·tar'i·at
e·par'ed·ness	pres·ti'gious	prim	·bat·ed ·bat·ing	·faned' ·fan'ing	pro·lif'er·ate'
e·pay'	pre'stressed'	prim'mer	pro·ba'tion	pro·fane'ly	·at'ed ·at'ing
paid' ·pay'ing	pre·sum'a·ble	prim'mest	pro·ba'tion·ar'y	pro·fan'i·ty	pro·lif'ic
e·pay'ment	pre·sume'	pri'ma·cy	pro·ba'tion·er	·ties	pro·lix'
e pon'der·ance	·sumed'	pri'ma don'na	pro·ba'tive	pro·fess'	pro·lix'i·ty
e·pon'der·ant	·sum'ing	pri'ma fa'ci·e'	probe	pro·fessed'	pro·loc'u·tor
e·pon'der·ate'	pre·sump'tion	pri'mal	probed prob'ing	pro·fess'ed·ly	pro'logue
at'ed ·at'ing	pre·sump'tive	pri·ma'ri·ly	prob'i·ty	pro·fes'sion	pro·long'
ep'o·si'tion	pre·sump'tu·ous	pri'ma·ry	prob'lem	pro·fes'sion·al·ly	pro·lon'gate
e'pos·sess'	pre'sup·pose'	·ries	prob·lem·at'ic	pro·fes'sor	·gat·ed ·gat·ing
e'pos·sess'ing	pre'sup·po·si'tion	pri'mate	pro·bos'cis	pro·fes·so'ri·al	pro'lon·ga'tion
e·pos'ter·ous	pre·tend'	prime	·cis·es or ·ci·des'	pro·fes·so'ri·ate	prom'e·nade'
e're·cord'	pre·tend'er	primed prim'ing	pro·ce'dur·al	prof'fer	·nad'ed
e·req'ui·site	pre·tense'	prim'er	pro·ce'dure	pro·fi'cien·cy	·nad'ing
requirement; SEE	pre·ten'sion	pri·me'val	pro·ceed'	pro·fi'cient	prom'i·nence
erquisite)	pre·ten'tious	prim'i·tive	(go on; SEE	pro'file	prom'i·nent
re·rog'a·tive	pre'ter·nat'u·ral	prim'i·tive·ly	precede)	·filed ·fil·ing	prom'is·cu'i·ty
re·sage'	pre'text	prim'i·tiv·ism	pro'ceeds	prof'it	·ties
saged' ·sag'ing	pre·tri'al	pri'mo·gen'i·tor	proc'ess	(gain; SEE	pro·mis'cu·ous
res'by·ter	pret'ti·fy'	pri'mo·gen'i·ture	pro·ces'sion	prophet)	prom'ise
res·by·te'ri·an	·fied' ·fy'ing	pri·mor'di·al	(parade; SEE	prof'it·a·ble	·ised ·is·ing
re'school'	pret'ti·ly	primp	precession)	prof'it·a·bly	prom'is·so'ry
re'sci·ence	pret'ti·ness	prim'rose'	pro·ces'sion·al	prof'i·teer'	prom'on·to'ry
re'sci·ent	pret'ty	prince'ling	pro·ces'sor or	prof'li·ga·cy	·ries
re·scribe'	·ti·er ·ti·est	prince'ly	proc'ess·er	prof'li·gate	pro·mot'a·ble
scribed'	·tied ·ty·ing	·li·er ·li·est	pro·claim'	pro·found'	pro·mote'
scrib'ing	pret'zel	prin'cess	proc'la·ma'tion	pro·fun'di·ty	·mot'ed ·mot'ing
order; SEE	pre·vail'	prin'ci·pal	pro·cliv'i·ty	·ties	pro·mot'er
roscribe)	pre·vail'ing	(chief; SEE	·ties	pro·fuse'	pro·mo'tion
re·scrip'tion	prev'a·lence	principle)	pro·cras'ti·nate'	pro·fuse'ly	prompt'er
re·scrip'tive	prev'a·lent	prin'ci·pal'i·ty	·nat'ed ·nat'ing	pro·fu'sion	promp'ti·tude'
res'ence	pre·var'i·cate'	·ties	pro·cras'ti·na'tion	pro·gen'i·tor	prompt'ly
res'ent	·cat'ed ·cat'ing	prin'ci·pal·ly	pro·cras'ti·na'tor	prog'e·ny	prom'ul·gate'
re·sent'a·ble	pre·var'i·ca'tion	prin'ci·ple	pro'cre·ant	·nies	·gat'ed ·gat'ing
re·sen·ta'tion	pre·var'i·ca'tor	(basic rule; SEE	pro'cre·ate'	prog'na·thous	prom'ul·ga'tion
res'ent-day'	pre·ven'ient	principal)	·at'ed ·at'ing	prog·no'sis	prom'ul·ga'tor
re·sen'ti·ment	pre·vent'	prin'ci·pled	pro'cre·a'tor	·ses	prone
premonition)	pre·vent'a·ble or	print'a·ble	proc·tol'o·gy	prog·nos'tic	pronged
re·sent'ment	·i·ble	print'out'	proc'tor	prog·nos'ti·cate'	pro'noun
presentation)	pre·ven'tion	pri'or	proc'to·scope'	·cat'ed ·cat'ing	pro·nounce'
re·serv'a·ble	pre·ven'tive or	(previous; SEE	pro·cum'bent	prog·nos'ti·	·nounced'
res'er·va'tion	·vent'a·tive	prier)	pro·cur'a·ble	ca'tion	·nounc'ing

pro·nounce'a·ble
pro·nounce'ment
pro·nun'ci·a'tion
proof'read'
·read' ·read'ing
prop'a·gan'da
prop'a·gan'dize
·dized ·diz·ing
prop'a·gate'
·gat'ed ·gat'ing
prop'a·ga'tion
prop'a·ga'tor
pro'pane
pro·pel'
·pelled' ·pel'ling
pro·pel'lant or
·lent
pro·pel'ler
pro·pen'si·ty
·ties
prop'er·ly
prop'er·tied
prop'er·ty
·ties
proph'e·cy n.
·cies
proph'e·sy' v.
·sied' ·sy'ing
proph'et
(predictor; SEE
profit)
pro·phet'ic
pro·phet'i·cal·ly
pro'phy·lac'tic
pro'phy·lax'is
·lax'es
pro·pin'qui·ty
pro·pi'ti·ate'
·at'ed ·at'ing
pro·pi'ti·a'tion
pro·pi'ti·a'tor
pro·pi'ti·a·to'ry
pro·pi'tious
pro·po'nent
pro·por'tion
pro·por'tion·al
pro·por'tion·al·ly
pro·por'tion·ate
pro·por'tion·ate·ly
pro·pos'al
pro·pose'
·posed' ·pos'ing
prop'o·si'tion
pro·pound'
pro·pri'e·tar'y
·ies
pro·pri'e·tor
pro·pri'e·tress
pro·pri'e·ty
·ties
pro·pul'sion
pro·pul'sive
pro ra'ta
pro·rat'a·ble
pro·rate'
·rat'ed ·rat'ing
pro·ro·ga'tion

pro·sa'ic
pro·sa'i·cal·ly
pro·sce'ni·um
·ni·ums or ·ni·a
pro·sciut'to
pro·scribe'
·scribed'
·scrib'ing
(forbid; SEE
prescribe)
pro·scrip'tion
prose
pros'e·cut'a·ble
pros'e·cute'
·cut'ed ·cut'ing
(legal term;
SEE persecute)
pros'e·cu'tion
pros'e·cu'tor
pros'e·lyte'
·lyt'ed ·lyt'ing
pros'e·lyt·ism
pros'e·lyt·ize'
·ized' ·iz'ing
pros'o·dy
·dies
pros'pect
pro·spec'tive
(expected; SEE
perspective)
pros'pec·tor
pro·spec'tus
pros'per
pros·per'i·ty
pros'per·ous
pros'tate
(gland; SEE
prostrate)
pros'the·sis
·the·ses'
pros·thet'ic
pros'ti·tute'
·tut'ed ·tut'ing
pros'ti·tu'tion
pros'trate
·trat·ed ·trat·ing
(prone; SEE
prostate)
pros·tra'tion
pros'y
·i·er ·i·est
pro·tag'o·nist
pro·tect'
pro·tec'tion
pro·tec'tive
pro·tec'tor
pro·tec'tor·ate
pro·té·gé'
(one helped by
another; SEE
prodigy)
pro'tein
pro tem'po·re'
pro·test'
Prot'es·tant
prot'es·ta'tion
pro·test'er or
·tes'tor

pro·thon'o·tar'y
·ies
pro'to·col'
pro'ton
pro'to·plasm
pro'to·typ'al
pro'to·type'
pro'to·zo'an
pro·tract'
pro·tract'ed·ly
pro·tract'i·ble
pro·trac'tile
pro·trac'tion
pro·trac'tor
pro·trude'
·trud'ed
·trud'ing
pro·tru'sile
pro·tru'sion
pro·tru'sive
pro·tu'ber·ance
pro·tu'ber·ant
proud'ly
prov'a·bil'i·ty
prov'a·ble
prov'a·bly
prove
proved, proved
or prov'en,
prov'ing
prov'en·der
prov'erb
pro·ver'bi·al
pro·ver'bi·al·ly
pro·vide'
·vid'ed ·vid'ing
prov'i·dence
prov'i·dent
prov'i·den'tial
pro·vid'er
prov'ince
pro·vin'cial
pro·vin'cial·ism
pro·vin'cial·ly
pro·vi'sion
pro·vi'sion·al
pro·vi'sion·al·ly
pro·vi'so
·sos or ·soes
pro·vi'so·ry
prov'o·ca'tion
pro·voc'a·tive
pro·voc'a·tive·ly
pro·voke'
·voked' ·vok'ing
pro·vo·lo'ne
pro'vost
prow'ess
prowl'er
prox'i·mal
prox'i·mate
prox·im'i·ty
prox'i·mo'
prox'y
·ies
pru'dence
pru'dent
pru·den'tial

pru'dent·ly
prud'er·y
prud'ish
prune
pruned prun'ing
pru'ri·ence
pru'ri·ent
pry
pries,pried pry'ing
psalm'book'
psal'mo·dy
psal'ter·y
·ies
pse·phol'o·gy
pseu'do
pseu'do·nym'
pseu'do·nym'i·ty
pseu·don'y·mous
psit'ta·co'sis
pso·ri'a·sis
psy'che
psy'che·de'li·a
psy'che·del'ic
psy'che·del'i·cal·ly
psy'chi·at'ric
psy'chi·at'ri·cal·ly
psy·chi'a·trist
psy·chi'a·try
psy'chic
psy'chi·cal·ly
psy·cho·a·nal'y·sis
psy'cho·an'a·lyst
psy'cho·an'a·lyt'ic
psy'cho·an'a·lyt'i·cal·ly
psy'cho·an'a·lyze'
·lyzed' ·lyz'ing
psy'cho·dra'ma
psy'cho·dy·nam'ics
psy'cho·gen'ic
psy'cho·log'i·cal
psy·chol'o·gist
psy·chol'o·gize'
·gized' ·giz'ing
psy·chol'o·gy
psy·chom'e·try
psy'cho·neu·ro'sis
·ses
psy'cho·neu·rot'ic
psy'cho·path'ic
psy'cho·path·ol'·o·gy
psy'cho·sex'u·al
psy·cho'sis
·ses
psy'cho·so·mat'ic
psy'cho·ther'a·py
psy·chot'ic
pter'o·dac'tyl
pto'maine
pu'ber·ty
pu·bes'cence
pu'bic

pub'lic
pub'li·ca'tion
pub'li·cist
pub·lic'i·ty
pub'li·cize'
·cized' ·ciz'ing
pub'lic·ly
pub'lish
puck'er
pud'ding
pud'dle
·dled ·dling
pudg'i·ness
pudg'y
·i·er ·i·est
pueb'lo
·los
pu'er·ile
Puer'to Ri'co
puff'i·ness
puff'y
·i·er ·i·est
pu'gil·ism
pug·na'cious
pug·nac'i·ty
pul'chri·tude'
pul'chri·tu'di·nous
pull
pul'let
pul'ley
·leys
pull'out'
pull'o'ver
pul'mo·nar'y
pul'mo'tor
pul'pit
pulp'wood'
pulp'y
·i·er ·i·est
pul'sate
·sat·ed ·sat·ing
pul·sa'tion
pulse
pulsed puls'ing
pul'ver·iz'a·ble
pul'ver·i·za'tion
pul'ver·ize'
·ized' ·iz'ing
pum'ice
(rock; SEE pomace)
pum'mel
·meled or
·melled
·mel·ing or
·mel·ling
pump'er·nick'el
pump'kin
pun
punned
pun'ning
punch card
pun'cheon
punc·til'i·o'
·os'
punc·til'i·ous
punc'tu·al
punc'tu·al'i·ty

punc'tu·al·ly
punc'tu·ate'
·at'ed ·at'ing
punc'tu·a'tion
punc'tu·a'tor
punc'tur·a·ble
punc'ture
·tured ·tur·in
pun'dit
pun'gen·cy
pun'gent
pu'ni·ness
pun'ish
pun'ish·a·ble
pun'ish·men
pu'ni·tive
pun'ster
pu'ny
·ni·er ·ni·est
pu'pil
pup'pet
pup'pet·eer'
pup'py
·pies
pur'chas·a·b
pur'chase
·chased
·chas·ing
pure'bred'
pu·rée'
·réed' ·ré'ing
pure'ly
pur·ga'tion
pur'ga·tive
pur'ga·to'ry
purge
purged purg'
pu'ri·fi·ca'tio
pu'ri·fi'er
pu'ri·fy'
·fied' ·fy'ing
pur'ism
pu'ri·tan
pu·ri·tan'i·ca
pu'ri·ty
purl
(stitch; SEE pe
pur·loin'
pu·ro·my'cin
pur'ple
pur'plish
pur'port'
pur'pose
·posed ·pos·i
pur'pose·ful
pur'pose·ful·
pur'pose·less
pur'pose·ly
purr
purs'er
pur·su'ance
pur·sue'
·sued' ·su'in
pur·suit'
pu'ru·lence
pu'ru·lent
pur·vey'
pur·vey'ance

vey'or	qua·drille'	quea'sy	quiv'er	ra'di·o·gram'	ral'li·er
view	quad·ril'lion	·si·er ·si·est	quix·ot'ic	ra'di·o·graph'	ral'ly
'cart'	quad'ri·ple'gi·a	queen'li·ness	quiz	ra'di·og'ra·phy	·lies
'o'ver	quad'ru·ped'	queen'ly	quiz'zes	ra'di·o·i'so·tope'	·lied ·ly·ing
'-up'	quad'ru·ple	·li·er ·li·est	quizzed	ra'di·ol'o·gist	ram
l·lan'i·mous	·pled ·pling	queen'-size'	quiz'zing	ra'di·ol'o·gy	rammed
sy	quad·ru'plet	queer	quiz'zi·cal	ra'di·o·phone'	ram'ming
r ·si·est	quad·ru'pli·cate'	quell	quoin	ra'di·o·pho'no·	ram'ble
h pus)	·cat'ed ·cat'ing	quench'a·ble	(wedge; corner;	graph'	·bled ·bling
'y	quaff	quer'u·lous	SEE coign, coin)	ra'di·o·pho'to	ram'bler
	quag'mire'	que'ry	quoit	·tos	ram·bunc'tious
)	quail	·ries	quon'dam	ra'di·os'co·py	ram'e·kin or ·quin
tu·lant	quaint'ly	·ried ·ry·ing	Quon'set hut	ra'di·o·sonde'	ram'i·fi·ca'tion
ule	quake	quest	quo'rum	ra'di·o·tel'e·	ram'i·fy'
	quaked	ques'tion	quo'ta	phone'	·fied ·fy'ing
put'ting	quak'ing	ques'tion·a·ble	quot'a·ble	ra'di·o·ther'a·py	ram'jet'
ce; SEE putt)	qual'i·fi·ca'tion	ques'tion·naire'	quo·ta'tion	ra'di·o·ther'my	ramp
a·tive	qual'i·fi'er	queue	quote	rad'ish	ram·page'
re·fac'tion	qual'i·fy'	queued	quot'ed quot'ing	ra'di·um	·paged' ·pag'ing
re·fy'	·fied ·fy·ing	queu'ing	quo'tient	ra'di·us	ram·pa'geous
d' ·fy'ing	qual'i·ta'tive	(line; SEE cue)		·di·i' or ·di·us·es	ramp'ant
res'cence	qual'i·ty	quib'ble		ra'dix	ram'part
res'cent	·ties	·bled ·bling	**R**	ra'di·ces' or	ram'rod'
rid	qualm	quick'en		ra'dix·es	ram'shack'le
	quan'da·ry	quick'-freeze'	rab'bet	ra'don	ranch'er
f term; SEE	·ries	-froze' -froz'en	(cut; SEE rabbit)	raf'fi·a	ran'cid
)	quan'ti·ta'tive	-freez'ing	rab'bi	raf'fle	ran'cor
tee'	quan'ti·ty	quick'sand'	·bis or ·bies	·fled ·fling	ran'cor·ous
t'er	·ties	quick'sil'ver	rab·bin'i·cal	raft'er	ran'dom
lf club)	quan'tum	quick'-tem'pered	rab'bit	rag'a·muf'fin	ran'dom·ize'
'ter	·ta	quick'-wit'ted	(hare; SEE rabbet)	rage	·ized' ·iz'ing
sy oneself)	quar'an·tin'a·ble	quid'nunc'	rab'ble	raged rag'ing	range
'ty	quar'an·tine'	qui·es'cence	·bled ·bling	rag'ged	ranged
ed ·ty·ing	·tined' ·tin'ing	qui·es'cent	rab'id	rag'lan	rang'ing
'zle	quar'rel	qui'et	ra'bies	ra·gout'	rang'i·ness
ed ·zling	·reled or ·relled	(still; SEE quite)	rac·coon'	rag'pick'er	rang'y
'zler	·rel·ing or	qui'e·tude'	race	rag'time'	·i·er ·i·est
'my	·rel·ling	qui·e'tus	raced rac'ing	rag'weed'	ran'kle
ies	quar'rel·some	quill	race'horse'	raid'er	·kled ·kling
lon	quar'ry	quilt'ing	rac'er	rail'ing	ran'sack
or·rhe'a	·ries	quince	race track	rail'ler·y	ran'som
'a·mid	·ried ·ry·ing	qui·nel'la	race'way'	·ies	rap
ram'i·dal	quart	quin·quen'ni·al	ra'cial	rail'road'	rapped rap'ping
e	quar'ter	quin·tes'sence	ra'cial·ly	rail'-split'ter	(strike; SEE wrap)
ret'ic	quar'ter·back'	quin·tet'	rac'i·ly	rail'way'	ra·pa'cious
rex	quar'ter·deck'	or ·tette'	rac'i·ness	rai'ment	ra·pac'i·ty
rog'ra·phy	quar'ter·ly	quin·til'lion	rac'ism	rain	rape
ro·ma'ni·a	·lies	quin·tu'ple	rack'et	(water; SEE	raped rap'ing
ro·ma'ni·ac'	quar'ter·mas'ter	·pled ·pling	rack'et·eer'	reign, rein)	rap'id-fire'
ro·tech'nics	quar'ter·saw'	quin·tu'plet	rack'-rent'	rain'bow'	ra·pid'i·ty
rox'y·lin	·sawed', ·sawed'	quin·tu'pli·cate'	rac'on·teur'	rain check	rap'id·ly
thag'o·ras	or ·sawn',	·cat'ed ·cat'ing	rac'y	rain'coat'	ra'pi·er
thon	·saw'ing	quip	·i·er ·i·est	rain'drop'	rap'ine
	quar·tet' or ·tette'	quipped	ra'dar	rain'fall'	rap'ist
	quar'tile	quip'ping	ra'di·al	rain'i·ness	rap·port'
Q	quar'to	quire	ra'di·ance	rain'proof'	rap·proche'ment
	·tos	(of paper; SEE	ra'di·ant	rain'storm'	rap·scal'lion
ack'er·y	quartz	choir)	ra'di·ate'	rain'y	rap·to'ri·al
es	qua'sar	quirk	·at'ed ·at'ing	·i·er ·i·est	rap'ture
ad'ran'gle	quash	quis'ling	ra'di·a'tion	raise	rap'tur·ous
ad·ran'gu·lar	qua'si	quit	ra'di·a'tor	raised rais'ing	rare
ad'rant	qua'ter·na'ry	quit or quit'ted	rad'i·cal	(lift; SEE raze)	rar'er rar'est
ad'rate	·ries	quit'ting	rad'i·cal·ism	rai'sin	rare'bit
at·ed ·rat·ing	quat'rain	quit'claim'	rad'i·cal·ly	rai'son d'etre'	rar'e·fy'
ad·rat'ic	qua'ver	quite	ra'di·o'	ra'jah or ·ja	·fied' ·fy'ing
ad·ren'ni·al	quay	(fully; SEE quiet)	·os', ·oed' ·o'ing	rake	rare'ly
ad'ri·lat'er·al	(wharf; SEE key)	quit'tance	ra'di·o·ac'tive	raked rak'ing	rar'i·ty
	quea'si·ness	quit'ter		rak'ish	·ties

ras'cal
ras·cal'i·ty
ras'cal·ly
rash'er
rash'ness
rasp'ber'ry
·ries
rasp'i·ness
rasp'ing
rasp'y
·i·er ·i·est
rat
rat'ted rat'ting
rat'a·ble or rate'·
ratch'et
rate
rat'ed rat'ing
rath'er
raths'kel'ler
rat'i·fi·ca'tion
rat'i·fi'er
rat'i·fy'
·fied' ·fy'ing
ra'tio
·tios
ra·ti·o'ci·nate'
·nat'ed ·nat'ing
ra'tion·al
ra'tion·ale'
ra'tion·al·ism
ra'tion·al'i·ty
ra'tion·al·i·za'tion
ra'tion·al·ize'
·ized' ·iz'ing
ra'tion·al·ly
rat'line or ·lin
rat'tail'
rat·tan' or ra·tan'
rat'tle
·tled ·tling
rat'tle·brained'
rat'tler
rat'tle·snake'
rat'tle·trap'
rat'tly
rau'cous
rav'age
·aged ·ag·ing
rave
raved rav'ing
rav'el
·eled or ·elled
·el·ing or ·el·ling
ra'ven
rav'e·nous
ra·vine'
ra'vi·o'li
rav'ish
raw'boned'
raw'hide'
ray'on
raze
razed raz'ing
(demolish; SEE
raise)
ra'zor
ra'zor·back'
reach

re·act'
(respond)
re'-act'
(act again)
re·ac'tion
re·ac'tion·ar'y
·ies
re·ac'ti·vate'
·vat'ed ·vat'ing
re·ac'tive·ly
re·ac'tor
read
read read'ing
read'a·bil'i·ty
read'a·ble
read'i·ly
read'i·ness
re'ad·just'
read'out'
read'y
·i·er ·i·est
·ied ·y·ing
read'y-made'
re·a'gent
re'al
(actual; SEE reel)
re'al·ism
re'al·ist
re'al·is'tic
re'al·is'ti·cal·ly
re·al'i·ty
·ties
(real thing; SEE
realty)
re'al·iz'a·ble
re'al·i·za'tion
re'al·ize'
·ized' ·iz'ing
re'al-life'
re'al·ly
realm
Re'al·tor
re'al·ty
(real estate; SEE
reality)
ream'er
re·an'i·mate'
·mat'ed ·mat'ing
reap'er
re'ap·por'tion
rear guard
re·ar'ma·ment
re'ar·range'
re'ar·range'ment
rear'ward
rea'son·a·ble
rea'son·a·bly
re'as·sur'ance
re'as·sure'
·sured' ·sur'ing
re'bate
·bat·ed ·bat·ing
reb'el n.
re·bel' v.
·belled' ·bel'ling
re·bel'lion
re·bel'lious
re·birth'

re·bound'
re·buff'
(blunt refusal)
re'-buff'
(buff again)
re·buke'
·buked'
·buk'ing
re'bus
re·but'
·but'ted
·but'ting
re·but'tal
re·cal'ci·trant
re·call'
re·cant'
re·cap'
·capped'
·cap'ping
re'ca·pit'u·late'
·lat'ed ·lat'ing
re'ca·pit'u·la'tion
re·cap'pa·ble
re·cap'ture
re·cede'
·ced'ed ·ced'ing
re·ceipt'
re·ceiv'a·ble
re·ceive'
·ceived'
·ceiv'ing
re·ceiv'er·ship'
re·cen'sion
re'cent
re·cep'ta·cle
re·cep'tion
re·cep'tive
re·cep'tor
re'cess
re·ces'sion
re·ces'sive
re·charge'a·ble
re·cher'ché
re·cid'i·vism
rec'i·pe
re·cip'i·ent
re·cip'ro·cal
re·cip'ro·cal·ly
re·cip'ro·cate'
·cat·ed ·cat'ing
re·cip'ro·ca'tion
re·cip'ro·ca'tor
rec'i·proc'i·ty
re·ci'sion
re·cit'al
rec'i·ta'tion
rec'i·ta·tive'
re·cite'
·cit'ed ·cit'ing
reck'less
reck'on·ing
re·claim'
(restore for use)
re'-claim'
(claim back)
rec'la·ma'tion
re·cline'
·clined' ·clin'ing

rec'luse
re·clu'sion
rec'og·ni'tion
rec'og·niz'a·ble
re·cog'ni·zance
rec'og·nize'
·nized' ·niz'ing
re·coil'
(draw back)
re'-coil'
(coil again)
re·coil'less
rec'ol·lect'
(remember)
re'-col·lect'
(collect again)
rec'ol·lec'tion
rec'om·mend'
rec'om·men·
da'tion
re·com'mit'
rec'om·pense'
·pensed'
·pens'ing
rec'on·cil'a·ble
rec'on·cile'
·ciled' ·cil'ing
rec'on·cil'i·a'tion
rec'on·dite'
re·con'di·tion
re·con'nais·sance
re·con·struct'
rec'on·noi'ter
re·con·sid'er
re·con·ver'sion
re·con·vert'
re·cord' v.
rec'ord n.
re·cord'er
re·count'
(narrate)
re'-count'
(count again)
re·coup'
re'course
re·cov'er
(get back)
re'-cov'er
(cover again)
re·cov'er·y
·ies
rec're·ant
rec're·ate'
·at'ed ·at'ing
(refresh)
re'-cre·ate'
·at'ed ·at'ing
(create anew)
rec're·a'tion
re'-cre·a'tion
re·crim'i·nate'
·nat'ed ·nat'ing
re·crim'i·na'tion
re·cruit'
rec'tal
rec'tan'gle
rec·tan'gu·lar
rec'ti·fi'a·ble

rec'ti·fi·ca'tion
rec'ti·fi'er
rec'ti·fy'
·fied' ·fy'ing
rec'ti·lin'e·ar
rec'ti·tude'
rec'tor
rec'to·ry
·ries
rec'tum
·tums or ·ta
re·cum'ben·cy
re·cum'bent
re·cu'per·ate'
·at'ed ·at'ing
re·cu'per·a'tion
re·cur'
·curred'
·cur'ring
re·cur'rence
re·cur'rent
rec'u·sant
re·cy'cle
re·dact'
re·dac'tion
re·dac'tor
red'bait'
red'-blood'ed
red'den
re·deem'a·ble
re·demp'tion
re·de·ploy'
re·de·vel'op·ment
red'-hand'ed
red'head'
red'-hot'
re·di·rect'
re·dis'trict
red'-let'ter
re·do'
·did' ·done'
·do'ing
red'o·lence
red'o·lent
re·dou'ble
re·doubt'
re·doubt'a·ble
re·dound'
red'out'
re·dress'
(remedy)
re'-dress'
(dress again)
re·duce'
·duced' ·duc'ing
re·duc'i·ble
re·duc'tion
re·dun'dan·cy
·cies
re·dun'dant
re·du'pli·cate'
re·du'pli·ca'tion
re·ech'o
reed'i·ness
re·ed'it
re·ed'u·cate'
reed'y
·i·er ·i·est

reek
(emit a smell;
wreak)
reel
(whirl; dance;
spool; SEE re
re'e·lect'
re'e·lec'tion
re'em·bark'
re'em·bod'y
re'em·brace'
re'e·merge'
re'em'pha·si
re'em'pha·si
re'em·ploy'
re'en·act'
re'en·dow'
re'en·gage'
re'en·list'
re·en'ter
re·en'try
re'e·quip'
re'es·tab'lish
re'e·val'u·at
re'ex·am'ine
re'ex·chang
re'ex·hib'it
re'ex·pe'ri·e
re'ex·plain'
re'ex·port'
re·fec'tion
re·fer'
·ferred'
·fer'ring
ref'er·a·ble
·eed' ·ee'in
ref'er·ee'
·eed' ·ee'in
ref'er·ence
ref'er·en'du
·dums or ·d
ref'er·ent
re·fer'ral
re·fill'a·ble
re·fine'
·fined' ·fin'i
re·fine'ment
re·fin'er·y
·ies
re·fit'
re·fla'tion
re·flect'
re·flec'tion
re·flec'tive
re·flec'tor
re'flex
re·flex'ive
re·for'est·a'
re·form'
(make better
re'-form'
(form again
ref'or·ma'ti
re·form'a·to
·ries
re·fract'
re·frac'tion
re·frac'to·r

·e·frain'
·e·fran'gi·ble
·e·fresh'
e·fresh'ment
e·frig'er·ant
·e·frig'er·ate'
·at'ed ·at'ing
·e·frig'er·a'tion
·e·frig'er·a'tor
·ef'uge
·ef'u·gee'
·e·ful'gent
·e·fund'
·e·fur'bish
·e·fus'al
·e·fuse' v.
·fused' ·fus'ing
·ef·use n.
·e·fut'a·ble
·ef'u·ta'tion
·e·fute'
fut'ed ·fut'ing
·e·gain'
·'gal adj.
·e·gale' v.
galed' ·gal'ing
·ga'li·a
·gal'i·ty
·ies
·gard'ing
·gard'less
·gat'ta
·'gen·cy
·cies
·gen'er·ate'
·it'ed ·at'ing
gen'er·a'tion
gen'er·a·tive
gen'er·a'tor
gent
·'i·cide'
gime' or ré·
·'i·men
·'i·ment
·'i·men'tal
·'i·men·ta'tion
·gion·al
·'is·ter
·'is·trant
·'is·trar'
·'is·tra'tion
·'is·try
·ies
·gress
·gres'sion
·gres'sive
·gret'
·et'ted
·et'ting
·ret'ful
·ret'ful·ly
·ret'ta·ble
·ret'ta·bly
·'u·lar
·u·lar'i·ty
·s
·'u·late'
·t'ed ·lat'ing

reg'u·la'tion
reg'u·la'tor
re·ha·bil'i·tate'
·tat'ed ·tat'ing
re·gur'gi·ta'tion
re·ha·bil'i·tate'
·tat'ed ·tat'ing
re·ha·bil'i·ta'tion
re·hears'al
re·hearse'
·hearsed'
·hears'ing
reign
(rule; SEE rain, rein)
re'im·burs'a·ble
re'im·burse'
·bursed'
·burs'ing
rein
(control; SEE rain, reign)
re'in·car'nate
·nat·ed ·nat·ing
re'in·car·na'tion
re'in·cur'
rein'deer
re'in·force'
·forced'
·forc'ing
re'in·force'ment
re·in·state'
·stat'ed
·stat'ing
re·it'er·ate'
·at'ed ·at'ing
re·ject'
re·jec'tion
re·joice'
·joiced' ·joic'ing
re·join'der
re·ju've·nate'
·nat'ed ·nat'ing
re·lapse'
·lapsed'
·laps'ing
re·lat'a·ble
re·late'
·lat'ed ·lat'ing
re·la'tion·ship'
rel'a·tive
rel'a·tive·ly
rel'a·tiv'i·ty
re·lax'
re·lax'ant
re'lax·a'tion
re'lay
·layed ·lay·ing
(send by relay)
re'-lay'
·laid' ·lay'ing
(lay again)
re·lease'
·leased'
·leas'ing
(set free)
re'-lease'
(lease again)

rel'e·gate'
·gat'ed ·gat'ing
rel'e·ga'tion
re·lent'less
rel'e·vance
rel'e·vant
re·li·a·bil'i·ty
re·li'a·ble
re·li'a·bly
re·li'ance
re·li'ant
rel'ic
re·lief'
re·liev'a·ble
re·lieve'
·lieved' ·liev'ing
re·liev'er
re·li'gion
re·li'gious
re·lin'quish
rel'i·quar'y
·ies
rel'ish
re·luc'tance
re·luc'tant
re·ly'
·lied' ·ly'ing
re·main'der
re·make'
·made' ·mak'ing
re·mand'
re·mark'a·ble
re·mark'a·bly
re·me'di·a·ble
re·me'di·al
rem'e·dy
·dies
·died ·dy·ing
re·mem'ber
re·mem'brance
re·mind'er
rem'i·nisce'
·nisced'
·nisc'ing
rem'i·nis'cence
rem'i·nis'cent
rem'i·nis'cer
re·miss'
re·mis'si·ble
re·mis'sion
re·mit'
·mit'ted
·mit'ting
re·mit'ta·ble
re·mit'tance
re·mit'tent
rem'nant
re·mod'el
re·mon'strance
re·mon'strate
·strat·ed
·strat·ing
re'mon·stra'tion
re·mon'stra·tor
re·morse'ful
re·morse'less
re·mote'
re·mote'ly

re·mov'a·ble
re·mov'al
re·move'
·moved'
·mov'ing
re·mu'ner·ate'
·at'ed ·at'ing
re·mu'ner·a'tion
re·mu'ner·a·tive
re·mu'ner·a'tor
ren'ais·sance'
re·nas'cent
rend
rent rend'ing
ren'der
ren'dez·vous'
·vous'
·voused'
·vous'ing
ren·di'tion
ren'e·gade'
re·nege'
·neged' ·neg'ing
re·new'al
ren'net
re·nounce'
·nounced'
·nounc'ing
ren'o·vate'
·vat'ed ·vat'ing
ren'o·va'tion
re·nown'
re·nowned'
rent'al
rent'-free'
re·nun'ci·a'tion
re·or'der
re'or·gan·i·za'tion
re·or'gan·ize'
·ized' ·iz'ing
re·pair'man
rep'a·ra·ble
rep'a·ra'tion
rep·ar·tee'
re·past'
re·pa'tri·ate'
·at'ed ·at'ing
re·pa'tri·a'tion
re·pay'
·paid' ·pay'ing
(pay back)
re'-pay'
·paid' ·pay'ing
(pay again)
re·peal'
re·peat'
re·pel'
·pelled' ·pel'ling
re·pel'lent
re·pent'
re·pent'ance
re·pent'ant
re'per·cus'sion
rep'er·toire'
rep'er·to'ry
·ries
rep'e·ti'tion
(a repeating)

re'-pe·ti'tion
(petition again)
rep'e·ti'tious
re·pet'i·tive
re·phrase'
re·place'
re·place'a·ble
re·place'ment
re·plen'ish
re·plete'
re·ple'tion
re·plev'in
rep'li·ca
re·ply'
·plies'
·plied' ·ply'ing
re·port'ed·ly
re·port'er
re·pose'
·posed' ·pos'ing
(rest)
re'-pose'
(pose again)
re·pos'i·to·ry
·ries
re·pos·sess'
re·pos·ses'sion
rep're·hend'
rep're·hen'si·ble
rep're·hen'sion
rep're·sent'
(stand for)
re'-pre·sent'
(present again)
rep're·sen·ta'tion
rep're·sent'a·tive
re·press'
(restrain)
re'-press'
(press again)
re·pressed'
re·press'i·ble
re·pres'sion
re·prieve'
·prieved'
·priev'ing
rep'ri·mand'
re·print'
re·pris'al
re·proach'
re·proach'ful
rep'ro·bate'
·bat'ed ·bat'ing
re·proc'essed
re'pro·duce'
re'pro·duc'i·ble
re'pro·duc'tion
re'pro·duc'tive
re·proof'
re·prove'
·proved'
·prov'ing
(rebuke)
re'-prove'
(prove again)
rep'tile
rep·til'i·an
re·pub'lic

re·pub'li·can
re·pu'di·ate'
·at'ed ·at'ing
re·pu'di·a'tion
re·pug'nance
re·pug'nant
re·pulse'
·pulsed'
·puls'ing
re·pul'sion
re·pul'sive
rep'u·ta·bil'i·ty
rep'u·ta·ble
rep'u·ta·bly
rep'u·ta'tion
re·pute'
·put'ed ·put'ing
re·quest'
Re'qui·em
re·quire'
·quired'
·quir'ing
re·quire'ment
req'ui·site
req'ui·si'tion
re·quit'al
re·quite'
·quit'ed
·quit'ing
rere'dos
re·route'
re·run'
·ran' ·run'
·run'ning
re·sal'a·ble
re'sale'
re·scind'
re·scind'a·ble
re·scis'sion
res'cu·a·ble
res'cue
·cued ·cu·ing
res'cu·er
re·search'
re·sem'blance
re·sem'ble
·bled ·bling
re·sent'
(feel a hurt)
re'-sent'
(sent again)
re·sent'ful
re·sent'ment
res'er·va'tion
re·serve'
·served'
·serv'ing
(set aside)
re'-serve'
(serve again)
re·serv'ed·ly
re·serv'ist
res'er·voir'
re·set'
·set' ·set'ting
re·ship'ment
re·side'
·sid'ed ·sid'ing

res'i·dence
res'i·den·cy
·cies
res'i·dent
res'i·den'tial
re·sid'u·al
re·sid'u·ar'y
res'i·due'
re·sign'
(give up)
re'-sign'
(sign again)
res'ig·na'tion
re·sil'i·ence
re·sil'i·ent
res'in
res'in·ous
re·sist'
re·sist'ance
re·sist'ant
re·sist'er
(one who resists)
re·sist'i·ble
re·sis'tor
(electrical device)
re·sole'
·soled' ·sol'ing
res'o·lute'
res'o·lu'tion
re·solv'a·ble
re·solve'
·solved'
·solv'ing
(break into parts)
re'-solve'
(solve again)
re·sol'vent
res'o·nance
res'o·nant
res'o·na'tor
re·sort'
(go for help)
re'-sort'
(sort again)
re·sound'
(echo)
re'-sound'
(sound again)
re'source
re·source'ful
re·spect'a·bil'i·ty
re·spect'a·ble
re·spect'ful
re·spect'ful·ly
re·spec'tive
re·spec'tive·ly
res'pi·ra'tion
res'pi·ra·tor
res'pi·ra·to'ry
re·spire'
·spired'
·spir'ing
res'pite
·pit·ed ·pit·ing
re·splend'ence
re·splend'ent
re·spond'
re·spond'ent

re·sponse'
re·spon'si·bil'i·ty
·ties
re·spon'si·ble
re·spon'si·bly
re·spon'sive
re·state'
·stat'ed ·stat'ing
res'tau·rant
res'tau·ra·teur'
rest'ful
res'ti·tu'tion
res'tive
rest'less
res'to·ra'tion
re·stor'a·tive
re·store'
·stored' ·stor'ing
re·strain'
(hold back)
re'-strain'
(strain again)
re·straint'
re·strict'
re·stric'tion
re·stric'tive
rest'room'
re·struc'ture
re·sult'
re·sult'ant
re·sum'a·ble
re·sume' v.
·sumed'
·sum'ing
ré'su·mé' n.
re·sump'tion
re·sur'face
re·sur'gence
re·sur'gent
res'ur·rect'
res'ur·rec'tion
re·sus'ci·tate'
·tat'ed ·tat'ing
re·sus'ci·ta'tion
re·sus'ci·ta·tor
re'tail
re·tain'
re·tain'er
re·take'
·took' ·tak'en
·tak'ing
re·tal'i·ate'
·at'ed ·at'ing
re·tal'i·a'tion
re·tal'i·a·to'ry
re·tard'
re·tard'ant
re·tar'date
re·tar·da'tion
retch
(strain to vomit;
SEE wretch)
re·ten'tion
re·ten'tive
re·ten·tiv'i·ty
re·think'
ret'i·cence
ret'i·cent

re·tic'u·lar
re·tic'u·late'
·lat'ed ·lat'ing
ret'i·cule'
ret'i·na
·nas or ·nae'
ret'i·nue'
re·tire'
·tired' ·tir'ing
re·tir'ee'
re·tire'ment
re·tool'
re·tort'
re·touch'
re·trace'
(go back over)
re'-trace'
(trace again)
re·trace'a·ble
re·tract'
re·tract'a·ble
re·trac'tile
re·trac'tion
re·trac'tor
re'tread' v.
·tread'ed
·tread'ing
re'tread' n.
re·treat'
(go back)
re'-treat'
(treat again)
re·trench'
ret'ri·bu'tion
re·triev'a·ble
re·triev'al
re·trieve'
·trieved'
·triev'ing
re·triev'er
ret'ro·ac'tive
ret'ro·ces'sion
ret'ro·fire'
ret'ro·fit'
ret'ro·grade'
·grad'ed
·grad'ing
ret'ro·gress'
ret'ro·gres'sion
ret'ro·rock'et or
ret'ro-rock'et
ret'ro·spect'
ret'ro·spec'tion
re·turn'
re·turn'ee'
re·un'ion
re'u·nite'
re·us'a·ble
re·use'
rev
revved rev'ving
re·vamp'
re·veal'
re'veil·le
rev'el
·eled or ·elled
·el·ing or ·el·ling
rev'e·la'tion

rev'el·ry
re·venge'
·venged'
·veng'ing
re·venge'ful
re·veng'er
rev'e·nue'
re·ver'ber·ant
re·ver'ber·ate'
·at'ed ·at'ing
re·ver'ber·a'tion
re·ver'ber·a·tor
re·ver'ber·a·to'ry
re·vere'
·vered' ·ver'ing
rev'er·ence
rev'er·end
rev'er·ent
rev'er·en'tial
rev'er·ie
re·ver'sal
re·vers'
·vers'
(part of garment)
re·verse'
·versed'
·vers'ing
(turned backward)
re·vers'i·ble
re·vers'i·bly
re·ver'sion
re·ver'sion·ar'y
re·vert'
re·view'
re·view'al
re·view'er
re·vile'
·viled' ·vil'ing
re·vise'
·vised' ·vis'ing
re·vi'sion
re·vi'so·ry
re·vi'tal·ize'
re·viv'a·ble
re·viv'al
re·vive'
·vived' ·viv'ing
re·viv'i·fy'
rev'o·ca·ble
rev'o·ca·bly
rev'o·ca'tion
re·voke'
·voked' ·vok'ing
re·volt'
re·volt'ing
rev'o·lu'tion
rev'o·lu'tion·ar'y
·ies
rev'o·lu'tion·ize'
·ized' ·iz'ing
re·volv'a·ble
re·volve'
·volved'
·volv'ing
re·volv'er
re·vue' or ·view'
re·vul'sion
re·ward'

re·wind'
·wound'
·wind'ing
re·write'
·wrote' ·writ'ten
·writ'ing
rhap·sod'ic
rhap·sod'i·cal·ly
rhap'so·dize'
·dized' ·diz'ing
rhap'so·dy
·dies
rhe'o·stat'
rhe'sus
rhet'o·ric
rhe·tor'i·cal
rhe·tor'i·cal·ly
rhet'o·ri'cian
rheu·mat'ic
rheu'ma·tism
rheu'ma·toid'
rheum'y
·i·er ·i·est
Rh factor
rhine'stone'
rhi·ni'tis
rhi·noc'er·os
rhi'zome
Rhode Island
rho'do·den'dron
rhom'boid
rhom'bus
·bus·es or ·bi
rhu'barb
rhyme
rhymed
rhym'ing
(verse; SEE rime)
rhythm
rhyth'mic
rhyth'mi·cal·ly
rib
ribbed
rib'bing
rib'ald
rib'ald·ry
rib'bon
ri'bo·fla'vin
rice
riced ric'ing
rich'ness
rick'et·i·ness
rick'ets
rick·ett'si·a
·si·ae' or ·si·as
rick'et·y
rick'ey
rick'rack'
rick'shaw or ·sha
ric'o·chet'
·cheted' or
·chet'ted
·chet'ing or
·chet'ting
ri·cot'ta
rid
rid or rid'ded
rid'ding

rid'a·ble or ride'
rid'dance
rid'dle
·dled ·dling
ride
rode rid'den
rid'ing
rid'er·less
ridge
ridged ridg'ing
ridge'pole'
rid'i·cule'
·culed' ·cul'ing
ri·dic'u·lous
rife
rif'fle
·fled ·fling
(shoal; shuffle)
riff'raff'
ri'fle
·fled ·fling
(gun; plunder)
ri'fle·man
rig
rigged rig'ging
ri'ga·to'ni
rig'ger
(one who rigs;
SEE rigor)
right
(correct; SEE rite
right'-an'gled
right'eous
right'ful·ly
right'-hand'ed
right'ist
rig'id
ri·gid'i·ty
rig'ma·role'
rig'or
(stiffness; SEE
rigger)
rig'or mor'tis
rig'or·ous
rile
riled ril'ing
rim
rimmed
rim'ming
rime
rimed rim'ing
(hoarfrost; rh
SEE rhyme)
ring
rang rung
ring'ing
(sound; SEE
wring)
ring
ringed ring'in
(circle; SEE
wring)
ring'er
ring'lead'er
ring'let
ring'mas'ter
ring'side'
rink

se	ro'bot	room'mate'	rough'shod'	ru'di·ment	ru·ta·ba'ga
ised rins'ing	ro·bust'	room'y	rou·lade'	ru'di·men'ta·ry	ruth'less
it·ous	rock'-and-roll'	·i·er ·i·est	rou·leau'	rue	rye
	rock'-bound'	roos'ter	·leaux' or ·leaus'	rued ru'ing	(grain; SEE wry)
oped rip'ping	rock'er	root beer	rou·lette'	rue'ful	
oar'i·an	rock'et	root'er	round'a·bout'	ruff	
'en	rock'e·teer'	root'less	roun'de·lay'	(collar; SEE rough)	**S**
e'ness	rock'et·ry	root'let	round'house'	ruf'fi·an	
noste' or	rock'i·ness	rope	round'up'	ruf'fle	Sab'bath
ost'	rock·oon'	roped rop'ing	round'worm'	·fled ·fling	sab·bat'i·cal
'per	rock'y	rope'walk'	rouse	rug'ged	sa'ber or ·bre
'ple	·i·er ·i·est	Roque'fort	roused rous'ing	ru'in·a'tion	sa'ble
led ·pling	ro·co'co	ro'sa·ry	roust'a·bout'	ru'in·ous	sa'bot
'saw'	ro'dent	·ries	rout	rule	sab'o·tage'
'tide'	ro'de·o'	ro·sé'	(noisy mob; dig	ruled rul'ing	·taged' ·tag'ing
e	·os'	ro'se·ate	up; defeat)	rul'er	sab'o·teur'
ose ris'en	roe	rose'bud'	route	rum'ble	sac
s'ing	(fish eggs; SEE	rose'bush'	rout'ed rout'ing	·bled ·bling	(pouch; SEE sack)
'er	row)	rose'-col'ored	(course)	ru'mi·nant	sac'cha·rin n.
i·bil'i·ty	roent'gen	ro·se'o·la	rou·tine'	ru'mi·nate'	sac'cha·rine adj.
es	rogue	ro·sette'	rove	·nat'ed ·nat'ing	sac'er·do'tal
i·ble	rogued rogu'ing	rose'wood'	roved rov'ing	ru'mi·na'tor	sa·chet'
k'i·ly	ro'guer·y	Rosh' Ha·sha'na	row n., v.	rum'mage	sack
k'i·ness	·ies	ros'i·ly	(line; use oars;	·maged	(bag; SEE sac)
k'y	ro'guish	ros'in	brawl; SEE roe)	·mag·ing	sack'cloth'
er ·i·est	roil	ros'i·ness	row'boat'	ru'mor	sack'ful'
qué'	(stir up; SEE royal)	ros'ter	row'di·ness	(hearsay; SEE	·fuls'
sole	roist'er·er	ros'trum	row'dy	roomer)	sack'ing
e	roist'er·ous	·trums or ·tra	·dies	rum'ple	sac'ra·ment
eremonial act;	role or rôle	ros'y	·di·er ·di·est	·pled ·pling	sac'ra·men'tal
E right, write)	(actor's part)	·i·er ·i·est	row'dy·ism	run	sa'cred
'u·al	roll	rot	row'el	ran run	sac'ri·fice'
'u·al·is'tic	(revolve)	rot'ted	·eled or ·elled	run'ning	·ficed' ·fic'ing
'u·al·ly	roll'a·way'	rot'ting	·el·ing or ·el·ling	run'a·bout'	sac'ri·fi'cial
val	roll'back'	ro'ta·ry	roy'al	run'a·way'	sac'ri·lege
aled or ·valled	roll call	·ries	(regal; SEE roil)	run'-down'	sac'ri·le'gious
al·ing or	roll'er	ro'tat·a·ble	roy'al·ist	rung	sac'ris·tan
al·ling	rol'lick·ing	ro'tate	roy'al·ly	(crossbar; pp. of	sac'ris·ty
val·ry	roll'-top'	·tat·ed ·tat·ing	roy'al·ty	ring; SEE wrung)	·ties
ies	ro·maine'	ro·ta'tion	·ties	run'-in'	sac'ro·il'i·ac'
e	ro·mance'	ro'ta·tor	rub	run'ner-up'	sac'ro·sanct'
ived, rived or	·manced'	rote	rubbed	run'ners-up'	sa'crum
v'en, riv'ing	·manc'ing	(routine; SEE	rub'bing	run'ni·ness	·cra or ·crums
'er·side'	ro·man'tic	wrote)	rub'ber·ize'	run'ny	sad
'et	ro·man'ti·cal·ly	ro·tis'ser·ie	·ized' ·iz'ing	·ni·er ·ni·est	sad'der sad'dest
'et·er	ro·man'ti·cism	ro'to·gra·vure'	rub'ber·y	run'off'	sad'den
'u·let	ro·man'ti·cize'	ro'tor	rub'bish	run'-on'	sad'dle
ach	·cized' ·ciz'ing	rot'ten	rub'ble	run'way'	·dled ·dling
ad'a·bil'i·ty	ron'deau	ro·tund'	(stone; SEE ruble)	rup'ture	sad'dle·bag'
ad'bed'	·deaux	ro·tun'da	rub'down'	·tured ·tur·ing	sad'dle·cloth'
ad'block'	(poem)	ro·tun'di·ty	ru·bel'la	ru'ral	sad'dler
ad'show'	ron'do	rou·é'	ru'bi·cund'	ru'ral·ly	sad'i·ron
ad'side'	·dos	rouge	ru'ble	ruse	sad'ism
ad'ster	(music)	rouged roug'ing	(money; SEE	rush	sad'ist
ad'way'	rood	rough	rubble)	rus'set	sa·dis'tic
ad'work'	(cross; SEE rude)	(not smooth;	ru'bric	rus'tic	sa·dis'ti·cal·ly
am'er	roof'er	SEE ruff)	ru'by	rus'ti·cal·ly	sa·fa'ri
an	rook	rough'age	·bies	rus'ti·cate'	·ris
ar'ing	rook'er·y	rough'cast'	ruche	·cat·ed ·cat'ing	safe
ast'er	·ies	·cast' ·cast'ing	ruch'ing	rust'i·ness	saf'er saf'est
b	rook'ie	rough'-dry'	ruck'sack'	rus'tle	safe'-con'duct
obbed rob'bing	room'er	·dried' ·dry'ing	rud'der	·tled ·tling	safe'-de·pos'it
ob'ber	(lodger; SEE	rough'en	rud'di·ness	rus'tler	safe'guard'
ob'ber·y	rumor)	rough'-hew'	rud'dy	rust'proof'	safe'keep'ing
ies	room·ette'	·hewed', -hewed'	·di·er ·di·est	rust'y	safe'ty
obe	room'ful'	or -hewn',	rude	·i·er ·i·est	·ties
obed rob'ing	·fuls'	-hew'ing	(crude; SEE rood)	rut	saf'fron
ob'in	room'i·ness	rough'ly	rude'ly	rut'ted rut'ting	

sag	salt'wa'ter	san'guine	sat'u·ra'tion	scalp'er	sce'nic
sagged sag'ging	salt'works'	san'i·tar'i·um	Sat'ur·day	scal'y	scent
sa'ga	·works'	·i·ums or ·i·a	sat'ur·nine'	·i·er ·i·est	(odor; SEE se
sa·ga'cious	salt'y	san'i·tar'y	sat'yr	scam'per	scep'ter
sa·gac'i·ty	·i·er ·i·est	san'i·ta'tion	sat'y·ri'a·sis	scan	sched'ule
sage	sa·lu'bri·ous	san'i·tize'	sauce'pan'	scanned	·uled ·ul·ing
sag'er sag'est	sal'u·tar'y	·tized' ·tiz'ing	sau'cer	scan'ning	sche'ma
sage'brush'	sal·u·ta'tion	san'i·ty	sau'ci·ness	scan'dal	·ma·ta
sag'gy	sa·lu'ta·to'ri·an	San'skrit	sau'cy	scan'dal·ize'	sche·mat'ic
·gi·er ·gi·est	sa·lu'ta·to'ry	sap	·ci·er ·ci·est	·ized' ·iz'ing	sche·mat'i·c.
sa'go	·ries	sapped sap'ping	sau'er·bra'ten	scan'dal·mon'ger	scheme
·gos	sa·lute'	sa'pi·ent	sau'er·kraut'	scan'dal·ous	schemed
sail'boat'	·lut'ed ·lut'ing	sap'ling	sau'na	scan'na·ble	schem'ing
sail'cloth'	sal'vage	sa·pon'i·fy'	saun'ter	scan'ner	scher'zo
sail'er	·vaged ·vag·ing	·fied' ·fy'ing	sau'sage	scan'sion	·zos or ·zi
(boat)	sal'vage·a·ble	sap'phire	sau·té'	scant'i·ly	schism
sail'fish'	sal·va'tion	sap'py	·téed' ·té'ing	scant'i·ness	schis·mat'ic
sail'or	salve	·pi·er ·pi·est	sau·terne'	scant'ling	schiz'oid
(person; hat)	salved salv'ing	sap'suck'er	sav'a·ble or	scant'ness	schiz'o·phre
saint'li·ness	sal'ver	sa·ran'	save'·	scant'y	schiz'o·phre
saint'ly	sal'vo	sar'casm	sav'age	·i·er ·i·est	schnau'zer
·li·er ·li·est	·vos or ·voes	sar·cas'tic	sav'age·ly	scape'goat'	schol'ar·ly
sa'ke	Sa·mar'i·tan	sar·cas'ti·cal·ly	sav'age·ry	scape'grace'	schol'ar·ship
(rice wine)	same'ness	sar·co'ma	sa·van'na	scap'u·la	scho·las'tic
sake	sam'i·sen'	·mas or ·ma·ta	sa·vant'	·lae or ·las	scho·las'ti·ca
(purpose)	sam'o·var'	sar·coph'a·gus	save	scap'u·lar	scho·las'ti·ci
sa·laam'	sam'pan	·a·gi	saved sav'ing	scar	school'boy'
sal'a·ble or	sam'ple	sar·dine'	sav'ior	scarred	school girl'
sale'·	·pled ·pling	sar·don'ic	sa'voir-faire'	scar'ring	school'hous
sa·la'cious	sam'pler	sar·don'i·cal·ly	sa'vor	scar'ab	school'mate
sal'ad	sam'u·rai'	sar'do·nyx	sa'vor·i·ness	scar'a·mouch'	school'room
sal'a·man'der	·rai'	sa'ri	sa'vor·y	scarce'ly	school'teach·
sa·la'mi	san'a·tive	·ris	·i·er ·i·est	scar'ci·ty	school'work
sal'a·ried	sanc'ti·fi·ca'tion	sa·rong'	sa·voy'	·ties	schoon'er
sal'a·ry	sanc'ti·fy'	sar'sa·pa·ril'la	saw	scare	schwa
·ries	·fied' ·fy'ing	sar·to'ri·al	sawed saw'ing	scared scar'ing	sci·at'i·ca
sal·e·ra'tus	sanc'ti·mo'ni·ous	sas'sa·fras'	saw'dust'	scare'crow'	sci'ence
sales'clerk'	sanc'ti·mo'ny	sa·tan'ic	saw'horse'	scarf	sci'en·tif'ic
sales'man	sanc'tion	sa·tan'i·cal·ly	saw'mill'	scarfs or scarves	sci'en·tif'i·c·
sales'man·ship'	sanc'ti·ty	satch'el	saw'-toothed'	(long cloth)	sci'en·tist
sales'peo'ple	sanc'tu·ar'y	sate	saw'yer	scarf	scim'i·tar
sales'per'son	·ies	sat'ed sat'ing	sax'o·phone'	scarfs	scin·til'la
sales'wom'an	sanc'tum	sa·teen'	sax'o·phon'ist	(joint; cut)	scin·til'late'
sa'lient	·tums or ·ta	sat'el·lite'	say	scar'i·fi·ca'tion	·lat'ed ·lat'ir
sa'line	san'dal	sa'tia·ble	said say'ing	scar'i·fy'	scin·til·la'to
sa·lin'i·ty	san'daled or	sa'ti·ate'	says	·fied' ·fy'ing	sci'on
sa·li'va	·dalled	·at'ed ·at'ing	say'-so'	scar'i·ness	scis'sors
sal'i·var'y	san'dal·wood'	sa·ti'a'tion	scab	scar'let	scle·ro'sis
sal'i·vate'	sand'bag'	sa·ti'e·ty	scabbed scab'bing	scarp	scoff
·vat'ed ·vat'ing	sand bar	sat'in	scab'bard	scar'y	scold'ing
sal'low	sand'blast'	sat'in·wood'	scab'bi·ness	·i·er ·i·est	sconce
sal'ly	sand'box'	sat'in·y	scab'by	scat	scone
·lies, ·lied ·ly·ing	san'dhi	sat'ire	·bi·er ·bi·est	scat'ted	scoop'ful'
sal'ma·gun'di	sand'hog'	sa·tir'i·cal	scab'rous	scat'ting	·fuls'
salm'on	sand'i·ness	sat'i·rist	scaf'fold	scathe	scoot'er
sal'mo·nel'la	sand'lot'	sat'i·rize'	scagl·io'la	scathed	scope
·lae or ·la or ·las	sand'man'	·rized' ·riz'ing	scal'a·ble	scath'ing	scorch'ing
sa·lon'	sand'pa'per	sat'is·fac'tion	scal'a·wag'	scat'ter	score
sa·loon'	sand'stone'	sat'is·fac'to·ri·ly	scald	scat'ter·brain'	scored scor'
sa·loon'keep'er	sand'storm'	sat'is·fac'to·ry	scale	scav'enge	score'less
sal'si·fy'	sand'wich	sat'is·fy'	scaled scal'ing	·enged ·eng·ing	scorn'ful
salt'box'	sand'y	·fied' ·fy'ing	scale'less	scav'eng·er	scor'pi·on
salt'cel'lar	·i·er ·i·est	sa·to'ri	sca·lene'	sce·nar'i·o'	scot'-free'
salt'i·ly	sane'ly	sa'trap	scal'i·ness	·os'	scoun'drel
salt·ine'	San'for·ize'	sat'su·ma	scal'lion	sce·nar'ist	scour
salt'i·ness	·ized' ·iz'ing	sat'u·ra·ble	scal'lop	scene	scóurge
salt'pe'ter	sang'-froid'	sat'u·rate'	scal'op·pi'ne	sce'ner·y	scourged
salt'shak'er	san'gui·nar'y	·rat'ed ·rat'ing	scal'pel	·ies	scourg'ing

scout'mas'ter	scu'ba	se·ces'sion	seem'li·ness	self'ish	Se·mit'ic
scowl	scuff	se·clude'	seem'ly	self'less	sem'i·trail'er
scrab'ble	scuf'fle	·clud'ed	·li·er ·li·est	self'-load'ing	sem'i·trop'i·cal
·bled ·bling	·fled ·fling	·clud'ing	seep'age	self'-love'	sem'i·week'ly
scrag'gly	scull	se·clu'sion	seer	self'-made'	sem'i·year'ly
·gli·er ·gli·est	(oar; boat; SEE	se·clu'sive	(prophet; SEE	self'-pit'y	sem'o·li'na
scrag'gy	skull)	sec'ond	sear)	self'-por'trait	sen'ate
·gi·er ·gi·est	scul'ler·y	sec'ond·ar'i·ly	seer'suck'er	self'-pos·sessed'	sen'a·tor
scram'ble	·ies	sec'ond·ar'y	see'saw'	self'-pres'er·va'·	sen'a·to'ri·al
·bled ·bling	sculpt	sec'ond-class'	seethe	tion	send
scrap	sculp'tor	sec'ond-guess'	seethed	self'-reg'u·lat'ing	sent send'ing
scrapped	sculp'tur·al	sec'ond-hand'	seeth'ing	self'-re·li'ance	send'-off'
scrap'ping	sculp'ture	sec'ond-rate'	seg'ment	self'-re·proach'	se·nes'cent
scrap'book'	·tured ·tur·ing	se'cre·cy	seg·men'tal	self'-re·spect'	se'nile
scrape	scum'my	se'cret	seg'men·ta'tion	self'-re·straint'	se·nil'i·ty
scraped	·mi·er ·mi·est	sec're·tar'i·al	seg're·gate'	self'-right'eous	sen'ior
scrap'ing	scup'per·nong'	sec're·tar'i·at	·gat'ed ·gat'ing	self'-ris'ing	sen·ior'i·ty
scrap'er	scur·ril'i·ty	sec're·tar'y	seg're·ga'tion	self'-sac'ri·fice'	sen·sa'tion
scrap'heap'	·ties	·ies	seg're·ga'tion·ist	self'same'	sen·sa'tion·al·ly
scrap'ple	scur'ril·ous	se·crete'	sei'del	self'-sat'is·fied'	sense
scrap'py	scur'ry	·cret'ed ·cret'ing	seis'mic	self'-seal'ing	sensed sens'ing
·pi·er ·pi·est	·ried ·ry·ing	se·cre'tion	seis'mi·cal·ly	self'-serv'ice	sense'less
scratch'i·ness	scur'vy	se'cre·tive	seis'mo·graph'	self'-start'er	sen'si·bil'i·ty
scratch'y	·vi·er ·vi·est	se·cre'to·ry	seis·mog'ra·pher	self'-styled'	·ties
·i·er ·i·est	scut'tle	sect	seis·mol'o·gist	self'-suf·fi'cient	sen'si·ble
scrawl	·tled ·tling	sec·tar'i·an	seis·mol'o·gy	self'-sup·port'	sen'si·bly
scraw'ny	scythe	sec'tion·al	seize	self'-taught'	sen'si·tive
·ni·er ·ni·est	scythed	sec'tion·al·ize'	seized seiz'ing	self'-tor'ture	sen'si·tiv'i·ty
scream'ing	scyth'ing	·ized ·iz'ing	sei'zure	self'-willed'	sen'si·ti·za'tion
screech'y	sea'board'	sec'tor	sel'dom	self'-wind'ing	sen'si·tize'
screen'play'	sea'borne'	sec'u·lar	se·lect'	sell	·tized' ·tiz'ing
screw'driv'er	sea'coast'	sec'u·lar·ize'	se·lect'ee'	sold sell'ing	sen'so·ry
scrib'ble	sea'far'er	·ized' ·iz'ing	se·lec'tion	sell'-off'	sen'su·al
·bled ·bling	sea'far'ing	se·cur'a·ble	se·lec'tive	sell'out'	sen'su·al'i·ty
scrib'bler	sea'food'	se·cure'	se·lec·tiv'i·ty	sel'vage or	sen'su·ous
scribe	sea'go'ing	·cured' ·cur'ing	se·lec'tor	·vedge	sent
scribed scrib'ing	seal'ant	se·cure'ly	self	se·man'tic	(transmitted;
scrim'mage	sea level	se·cu'ri·ty	selves	sem'a·phore'	SEE sent)
·maged ·mag·ing	seal'skin'	·ties	self'-act'ing	·phored	sen'tence
scrimp'i·ness	seam	se·dan'	self'-ad·dressed'	·phor'ing	·tenced ·tenc·ing
scrimp'y	sea'man	se·date'	self'-as·sur'ance	sem'blance	sen·ten'tious
·i·er ·i·est	seam'less	·dat'ed ·dat'ing	self'-as·sured'	se'men	sen'tient
scrip	seam'stress	se·date'ly	self'-cen'tered	sem'i·na	sen'ti·ment
(certificate)	seam'y	se·da'tion	self'-con'fi·dence	se·mes'ter	sen'ti·men'tal
script	·i·er ·i·est	sed'a·tive	self'-con'scious	sem'i·an'nu·al	sen'ti·men··
(manuscript)	sé'ance	sed'en·tar'y	self'-con·tained'	sem'i·au'to·	tal'i·ty
scrip'tur·al	sea'plane'	sed'i·ment	self'-con·trol'	mat'ic	sen'ti·men'tal·
scrof'u·la	sea'port'	sed'i·men'ta·ry	self'-de·fense'	sem'i·cir'cle	ize'
scroll'work'	sear	sed'i·men·ta'tion	self'-dis'ci·pline	sem'i·co'lon	·ized' ·iz'ing
scro'tum	(burn; SEE seer)	se·di'tion	self'-driv'en	sem'i·con·duc'tor	sen'ti·nel
·ta or ·tums	search'light'	se·di'tious	self'-ed'u·cat'ed	sem'i·con'scious	·neled or ·nelled
scrounge	sea'scape'	se·duce'	self'-em·ployed'	sem'i·de·tached'	·nel·ing or
scrounged	sea'shell'	·duced' ·duc'ing	self'-es·teem'	sem'i·fi'nal	·nel·ling
scroung'ing	sea'shore'	se·duc'i·ble	self'-ev'i·dent	sem'i·for'mal	sen'try
scrub	sea'sick'ness	se·duc'tion	self'-ex·plan'a·	sem'i·month'ly	·tries
scrubbed	sea'side'	se·duc'tive	to'ry	sem'i·nal	sep'a·ra·ble
scrub'bing	sea'son	se·du'li·ty	self'-ex·pres'sion	sem'i·nar'	sep'a·rate'
scrub'by	sea'son·a·ble	sed'u·lous	self'-gov'ern·ing	sem'i·nar'y	·rat'ed ·rat'ing
·bi·er ·bi·est	sea'son·al	see	self'-im'age	·ies	sep'a·ra'tion
scrunch	seat belt	saw seen see'ing	self'-im·por'tant	sem'i·of·fi'cial	sep'a·ra·tism
scru'ple	sea'ward	seed'bed'	self'-im·posed'	sem'i·pre'cious	sep'a·ra'tor
·pled ·pling	sea'way'	seed'i·ness	self'-im·prove'·	sem'i·pri'vate	se'pi·a
scru'pu·lous	sea'weed'	seed'ling	ment	sem'i·pro·fes'·	Sep·tem'ber
scru'ta·ble	sea'wor'thy	seed'y	self'-in·duced'	sion·al	sep·tet' or
scru'ti·nize'	se·ba'ceous	·i·er ·i·est	self'-in·dul'gence	sem'i·rig'id	·tette'
·nized' ·niz'ing	se'cant	seek	self'-in·flict'ed	sem'i·skilled'	sep'tic
scru'ti·ny	se·cede'	sought seek'ing	self'-in·ter·est	sem'i·sol'id	sep'tu·a·ge·
	·ced'ed ·ced'ing	seem'ing·ly		Sem'ite	nar'i·an

sep·tu'ple
·pled ·pling
sep'ul·cher
se·pul'chral
se'quel
se'quence
se·quen'tial
se·ques'ter
se'quin
se·quoi'a
se·ra'pe
ser'e·nade'
·nad'ed ·nad'ing
ser'en·dip'i·ty
se·rene'
se·ren'i·ty
serf
(*slave;* SEE surf)
serge
(*fabric;* SEE surge)
ser'geant
se'ri·al
(*in a series;*
SEE cereal)
se'ri·al·ize'
·ized' ·iz'ing
se'ries
·ries
ser'if
se'ri·o·com'ic
se'ri·ous
se'ri·ous·mind'ed
ser'mon
se'rous
ser'pent
ser'pen·tine'
ser·rate'
·rat'ed ·rat'ing
se'rum
·rums or ·ra
ser'vant
serve
served serv'ing
serv'ice
·iced ·ic·ing
serv'ice·a·bil'i·ty
serv'ice·a·ble
serv'ice·a·bly
serv'ice·man'
ser'vi·ette'
ser'vile
ser·vil'i·ty
ser'vi·tor
ser'vi·tude'
ses'a·me'
ses'qui·cen·ten'·
ni·al
ses'sion
(*meeting;* SEE
cession)
set
set set'ting
set'back'
set'-in'
set'off'
set'screw'
set·tee'
set'ter

set'tle
·tled ·tling
set'tle·ment
set'tler
set'-to'
-tos'
sev'en·teen'
sev'enth
sev'en·ti·eth
sev'en·ty
·ties
sev'er
sev'er·al
sev'er·al·ly
sev'er·ance
se·vere'
se·vere'ly
se·ver'i·ty
·ties
sew
sewed, sewn or
sewed, sew'ing
(*stitch;* SEE SOW)
sew'age
sew'er
sew'er·age
sex'a·ge·nar'i·an
sex'i·ly
sex'i·ness
sex'less
sex'tant
sex·tet' or
·tette'
sex'ton
sex·tu'ple
·pled ·pling
sex·tu'plet
sex'u·al
sex'u·al'i·ty
sex'u·al·ly
sex'y
·i·er ·i·est
shab'bi·ly
shab'bi·ness
shab'by
·bi·er ·bi·est
shack'le
·led ·ling
shade
shad'ed
shad'ing
shad'i·ness
shad'ow
shad'ow·y
shad'y
·i·er ·i·est
shaft
shag
shagged
shag'ging
shag'gi·ness
shag'gy
·gi·er ·gi·est
shak'a·ble or
shake'a·ble
shake
shook shak'en
shak'ing

Shake'speare'
Shake·spear'e·an
or ·i·an
shake'-up'
shak'i·ly
shak'i·ness
shak'y
·i·er ·i·est
shal'low
sha·lom'
sham
shammed
sham'ming
sham'ble
·bled ·bling
shame
shamed
sham'ing
shame'faced'
shame'ful
shame'ful·ly
shame'less
sham·poo'
·pooed' ·poo'ing
shang'hai
·haied ·hai·ing
shank
shan'tung'
shan'ty
·ties
shape
shaped shap'ing
shape'less
shape'li·ness
shape'ly
·li·er ·li·est
share
shared shar'ing
share'crop'per
share'hold'er
shark'skin'
sharp'en·er
sharp'-eyed'
sharp'shoot'er
sharp'-sight'ed
sharp'-tongued'
sharp'-wit'ted
shat'ter
shat'ter·proof'
shave
shaved, shaved
or shav'en,
shav'ing
shawl
sheaf
sheaves
shear
sheared, sheared
or shorn,
shear'ing
(*cut;* SEE sheer)
shears
sheath
(*a case; dress*)
sheathe
sheathed
sheath'ing
(*put into a sheath*)

sheave
sheaved
sheav'ing
shed
shed shed'ding
sheen
sheep'ish·ly
sheep'skin'
sheep'walk'
sheer
(*thin; steep;*
SEE shear)
sheet'ing
sheik or sheikh
shelf
shelves
shell
shel·lac' or ·lack'
·lacked'
·lack'ing
shell'fish'
shell'-like'
shell'proof'
shel'ter
shelve
shelved
shelv'ing
she·nan'i·gan
shep'herd
sher'bet
sher'iff
sher'ry
·ries
shib'bo·leth
shield
shift'i·ly
shift'i·ness
shift'less
shift'y
·i·er ·i·est
shil·le'lagh or
shil·la'lah
shil'ly-shal'ly
·lied ·ly·ing
shim
shimmed
shim'ming
shim'mer·y
shim'my
·mies
·mied ·my·ing
shin
shinned
shin'ning
shine
shone or shined
shin'ing
shin'gle
·gled ·gling
shin'i·ness
shin'y
·i·er ·i·est
ship
shipped
ship'ping
ship'board'
ship'mate'
ship'ment

ship'own'er
ship'pa·ble
ship'per
ship'shape'
ship'wreck'
ship'wright'
ship'yard'
shirk'er
shirr'ing
shirt'waist'
shiv·a·ree'
·reed' ·ree'ing
shiv'er
shoal
shock'ing
shock'proof'
shod'di·ly
shod'di·ness
shod'dy
·di·er ·di·est
shoe
shod or shoed,
shod or shoed
or shod'den,
shoe'ing
shoe'horn'
shoe'lace'
shoe'mak'er
sho'er
shoe'shine'
shoe'string'
shoe tree
shoo
shooed shoo'ing
shoot
shot shoot'ing
shop
shopped
shop'ping
shop'keep'er
shop'lift'er
shop'per
shop'talk'
shop'worn'
Shor'an or
shor'-
shore'line'
shore'ward
shor'ing
short'age
short'bread'
short'cake'
short'change'
short'-cir'cuit
short'com'ing
short'cut'
short'en
short'en·ing
short'hand'
short'-hand'ed
short'horn'
short'-lived'
short'-range'
short'sight'ed
short'stop'
short'-tem'pered
short'-term'
short'-waist'ed

short'wave'
short'-wind'ed
shot'gun'
should
shoul'der
should'n't
shov'el
·eled or ·elled
·el·ing or ·el·lin
shov'el·ful'
·fuls'
show
showed, shown
or showed,
show'ing
show'boat'
show'case'
show'down'
show'er
show'i·ly
show'i·ness
show'man
show'off'
show'piece'
show'place'
show'room'
show'y
·i·er ·i·est
shrap'nel
shred
shred'ded or
shred
shred'ding
shrewd
shriek
shrill'ness
shril'ly
shrine
shrink
shrank or shrun
shrunk or
shrunk'en,
shrink'ing
shrink'age
shriv'el
·eled or ·elled
·el·ing or ·el·ling
shroud
shrub'ber·y
shrug
shrugged
shrug'ging
shuck
shud'der
shuf'fle
·fled ·fling
shuf'fle·board'
shun
shunned
shun'ning
shunt
shut
shut shut'ting
shut'down'
shut'-in'
shut'-off'
shut'out'
shut'ter

t'tle
d·tling
t'tle·cock

'er or shi'. ·
'est or shi'est
es
ed shy'ing
·mese'
·lance
i·lant
ling
'bed'
'en
'le
'li·ness
'ly
er ·li·est
'room'
e
'ed sid'ing
e'arm'
e arms
e'board'
e'burns'
e'car'
e'light'
e'line'
e'long'
le're·al
e'sad'dle
e'show'
e'slip'
e'split'ting
e'step' v.
e'stroke'
e'swipe'
e'track'
e'walk'
e'ways'
e'wise'
'ing
dle
led ·dling
ge
en'na
er'ra
es'ta
·ve
eved siev'ing
t'er
h
ht
ght
·iew; SEE
te, site)
ght'less
ght'ly
i·er ·li·est
ght'see'ing
ght'sc'er
gn
signal; SEE sinc)
g'nal
naled or ·nalled
nal·ing or
nal-ling
g'nal·ize'
ized' ·iz'ing

sig'nal·ly
sig'na·to'ry
·ries
sig'na·ture
sign'board'
sig'net
sig·nif'i·cance
sig·nif'i·cant
sig'ri·fi·ca'tion
sig'r i·fy'
·fied' ·fy'ing
sign'post'
si'lage
si'lence
·lenced ·lenc·ing
si'lenc·er
si'lent
si'lex
sil'hou·ette'
·et'ted ·et'ting
sil'i·ca
sil'i·cate
si·li'ceous
sil'i·cone'
sil'i·co'sis
silk'en
silk'i·ness
silk'·screen'
silk'worm'
silk'y
·i·er ·i·est
sil'li·ness
sil'ly
·lies, ·li·er ·li·est
si'lo
·los, ·loed ·lo·ing
sil'ver
sil'ver·fisn'
silver plate
sil'ver·smith'
sil'ver·tongued'
sil'ver·ware'
sil'ver·y
sim'i·an
sim'i·lar
sim'i·lar'i·ty
·ties
sim'i·le'
si·mil'i·tude'
sim'mer
si'mon·pure'
sim'per
sim'ple
·pler ·plest
sim'ple·mind'ed
sim'ple·ton
sim·plic'i·ty
·ties
sim'pli·fi·ca'tion
sim'pli·fi'er
sim'pli·fy'
·fied' ·fy'ing
sim'ply
sim'u·lant
sim'u·late'
·lat'ed ·lat'ing
sim'u·la'tion
sim'u·la'tor

si'mul·cast'
·cast' or ·cast'ed
·cast'ing
si'mul·ta'ne·ous
sin
sinned sin'ning
sin·cere'
·cer'er ·cer'est
sin·cere'ly
sin·cer'i·ty
sine
(ratio; SEE sign)
si'ne·cure'
sin'ew·y
sin'ful
sing
sang sung
sing'ing
singe
singed
singe'ing
sin'gle
·gled ·gling
sin'gle·breast'ed
sin'gle·hand'ed
sin'gle·space'
sin'gle·ton
sin'gly
sing'song'
sin'gu·lar
sin'gu·lar'i·ty
sin'gu·lar·ize'
·ized' ·iz'ing
sin'is·ter
sink
sank or sunk,
sunk sink'ing
sin'ner
sin'u·ous
si'nus
si'nus·i'tis
sip
sipped sip'ping
si'phon
sire
sired sir'ing
si'ren
sir'loin
si·roc'co
·cos
si'sal
sis'ter·hood'
sis'ter-in-law'
sis'ters-in-law'
sis'ter·li·ness
sis'ter·ly
sit
sat sit'ting
si·tar'
sit'·down'
site
(place; SEE sight)
sit'·in'
sit'ter
sit'u·ate'
·at'ed ·at'ing
sit'u·a'tion
sit'·up' or sit'up'

sitz bath
six'fold'
six'pen'ny
six'teenth'
sixth
six'ti·eth
six'ty
·ties
siz'a·ble or
size'·
size
sized siz'ing
siz'zle
·zled ·zling
skate
skat'ed skat'ing
skein
skel'e·ton
skep'tic
skep'ti·cal
skep'ti·cal·ly
skep'ti·cism
sketch'book'
sketch'i·ly
sketch'i·ness
sketch'y
·i·er ·i·est
skew'er
ski
skis or ski
skied ski'ing
skid
skid'ded
skid'ding
ski'er
skil'let
skill'ful
skim
skimmed
skim'ming
skimp'i·ly
skimp'i·ness
skimp'y
·i·er ·i·est
skin
skinned
skin'ning
skin'·deep'
skin'flint'
skin'ni·ness
skin'ny
·ni·er ·ni·est
skip
skipped
skip'ping
ski'plane'
skip'per
skir'mish
skit'tish
skul·dug'ger·y
or skull·
skulk
skull
(head; SEE scull)
skull'cap'
sky
skies
sky'cap'

sky'·dive'
·dived' ·div'ing
sky'·high'
sky'lark'
sky'light'
sky'line'
sky'rock'et
sky'scrap'er
sky'ward
sky'ways'
sky'writ'ing
slack'en
slack'er
slake
slaked slak'ing
sla'lom
slam
slammed
slam'ming
slan'der
slan'der·ous
slang'y
·i·er ·i·est
slant'wise'
slap
slapped
slap'ping
slap'dash'
slap'stick'
slash
slate
slat'ed slat'ing
slat'tern
slaugh'ter
slave
slaved slav'ing
slav'er
slav'er·y
·i·er ·i·est
slav'ish·ly
slay
slew slain
slay'ing
(kill; SEE sleigh)
slea'zi·ness
slea'zy
·zi·er ·zi·est
sled
sled'ded
sled'ding
sledge
sledged
sledg'ing
sleek'ly
sleep
slept sleep'ing
sleep'i·ly
sleep'i·ness
sleep'less
sleep'walk'ing
sleep'y·
·i·er ·i·est
sleet
sleeve'less
sleigh
(snow vehicle;
SEE slay)
sleight
(skill; SEE slight)

slen'der
slen'der·ize'
·ized' ·iz'ing
sleuth
slew or slue
(a lot; SEE slue)
slice
sliced slic'ing
slick'er
slide
slid slid'ing
slide rule
slight
(trail; SEE
sleight)
slim
slim'mer
slim'mest
slimmed
slim'ming
slim'i·ness
slim'ness
slim'y
·i·er ·i·est
sling
slung sling'ing
sling'shot'
slink
slunk slink'ing
slip
slipped slip'ping
slip'cov'er
slip'knot'
slip'·on'
slip'page
slip'per·i·ness
slip'per·y
·i·er ·i·est
slip'shod'
slip'stream'
slip'·up'
slit
slit slit'ting
slith'er
sliv'er
sli'vo·vitz'
slob'ber
sloe
(fruit; SEE slow)
sloe'·eyed'
slog
slogged
slog'ging
slo'gan
sloop
slop
slopped
slop'ping
slope
sloped slop'ing
slop'pi·ly
slop'pi·ness
slop'py
·pi·er ·pi·est
slosh
slot
slot'ted slot'ting
sloth'ful

slouch'y	smog'gy	snif'ter	so'cial·ize'	so·lid'i·fi·ca'tion	so·phis'ti·cate'
·i·er ·i·est	·gi·er ·gi·est	snip	·ized' ·iz'ing	so·lid'i·fy'	·cat'ed ·cat'ing
slough	smok'a·ble or	snipped	so·ci'e·tal	·fied' ·fy'ing	so·phis'ti·ca'tio
slov'en·li·ness	smoke'a·ble	snip'ping	so·ci'e·tal·ly	sol'id-state'	soph'is·try
slov'en·ly	smoke	snipe	so·ci'e·ty	so·lil'o·quize'	·tries
·li·er ·li·est	smoked	sniped snip'ing	·ties	·quized'	soph'o·more'
slow	smok'ing	sniv'el	so'ci·o·cul'tu·ral	·quiz'ing	soph'o·mor'ic
(not fast; SEE	smok'er	·eled or ·elled	so'ci·o·e'co·	so·lil'o·quy	sop'o·rif'ic
sloe)	smoke screen	·el·ing or	nom'ic	·quies	so·pra'no
slow'-wit'ted	smoke'stack'	·el·ling	so'ci·o·gram'	sol'i·taire'	·nos or ·ni
sludge	smok'i·ness	snob'ber·y	so'ci·o·log'i·cal	sol'i·tar'y	sor'cer·er
sludg'y	smok'y	snob'bish	so'ci·ol'o·gist	sol'i·tude'	sor'cer·y
·i·er ·i·est	·i·er ·i·est	snoop'er·scope'	so'ci·ol'o·gy	so'lo	·ies
slue or slew	smol'der	snore	so'ci·o·path'	·los	sor'did
slued or slewed	smooth	snored snor'ing	so'ci·o·po·lit'i·cal	so'lo·ist	sore
slu'ing or	smooth'bore'	snor'kel	sock'et	sol'stice	(painful; SEE
slew'ing	smooth'-faced'	snout	sock'eye'	sol'u·bil'i·ty	soar)
(turn; SEE slew)	smooth'-shav'en	snow'ball'	sod	sol'u·ble	sore'ly
slug	smooth'-spo'ken	snow'-blind'	sod'ded sod'ding	sol'ute	sor'ghum
slugged	smor'gas·bord'	snow'bound'	so·dal'i·ty	so·lu'tion	so·ror'i·ty
slug'ging	smoth'er	snow'drift'	·ties	solv'a·bil'i·ty	·ties
slug'gard	smudge	snow'fall'	sod'den·ness	solv'a·ble	sor'rel
slug'gish	smudged	snow'flake'	sod'om·y	solve	sor'ri·ly
sluice	smudg'ing	snow line	soft'ball'	solved	sor'ri·ness
sluiced sluic'ing	smudg'i·ness	snow'mo·bile'	soft'-boiled'	solv'ing	sor'row
slum	smudg'y	·biled' ·bil'ing	soft'-cov'er	sol'ven·cy	sor'row·ful
slummed	·i·er ·i·est	snow'plow'	soft'ten·er	sol'vent	sor'ry
slum'ming	smug	snow'shoe'	soft'heart'ed	som'ber	·ri·er ·ri·est
slum'ber	smug'ger	·shoed'	soft'-shell'	som·bre'ro	sor'tie
slum'ber·ous	smug'gest	·shoe'ing	soft'-spo'ken	·ros	so'-so'
slump	smug'gle	snow'storm'	soft'ware'	some'bod'y	sou·brette'
slur	·gled ·gling	snow'-white'	sog'gi·ness	some'day'	souf·flé'
slurred	smut'ty	snow'y	sog'gy	some'how'	soul
slur'ring	·ti·er ·ti·est	·i·er ·i·est	·gi·er ·gi·est	some'one'	(spirit; SEE sole)
slush'y	snack bar	snub	soil	som'er·sault'	soul'ful
·i·er ·i·est	snaf'fle	snubbed	soi·ree' or ·rée'	some'thing	soul'-search'in
slut'tish	·fled ·fling	snub'bing	so'journ	some'time'	sound'proof'
sly	sna·fu'	snub'-nosed'	sol'ace	some'times'	soup·çon'
sli'er or sly'er	snag	snuff'ers	·aced ·ac·ing	some'what'	source'book'
sli'est or sly'est	snagged	snuf'fle	so'lar	some'where'	sour'dough'
sly'ly or sli'ly	snag'ging	·fled ·fling	so·lar'i·um	som·nam'bu·late'	sour'ness
smack	snail'-paced'	snug	·lar'i·a	·lat·ed ·lat'ing	sou'sa·phone'
small'-mind'ed	snake	snug'ger	sol'der	som'no·lent	souse
small'pox'	snaked snak'ing	snug'gest	(metal alloy)	so'nar	soused sous'ing
small'-scale'	snak'y	snug'gle	sol'dier	so·na'ta	South Car'o·li'
smart	·i·er ·i·est	·gled ·gling	(man in an army)	sonde	South Da·ko'ta
smash'up'	snap	soak'ers	sole	song'ster	south'east'
smat'ter·ing	snapped	soap'box'	soled sol'ing	son'ic	south'east'er·ly
smear'i·ness	snap'ping	soap'suds'	(bottom surface;	son'-in-law'	south'east'ern
smear'y	snap'drag'on	soap'y	only; SEE soul)	sons'-in-law'	south'east'war
·i·er ·i·est	snap'pish	·i·er ·i·est	sol'e·cism	son'net	south'er·ly
smell	snap'shot'	soar	sole'ly	son'net·eer'	south'ern
smelled or smelt	snare	(fly; SEE sore)	sol'emn	so·nor'i·ty	south'ern·er
smell'ing	snared snar'ing	sob	so·lem'ni·fy'	so·no'rous	south'ern·most'
smell'i·ness	snarl'y	sobbed	·fied' ·fy'ing	soon'er	south'ward
smell'y	·i·er ·i·est	sob'bing	so·lem'ni·ty	soothe	south'west'
·i·er ·i·est	snatch	so'ber-mind'ed	·ties	soothed	south'west'er·ly
smidg'en	sneak'i·ly	so·bri'e·ty	sol'em·nize'	sooth'ing	south'west'ern
smile	sneak'i·ness	so'bri·quet'	·nized' ·niz'ing	sooth'say'er	south'west'war
smiled smil'ing	sneak'y	so'-called'	so'le·noid'	soot'i·ness	sou've·nir'
smirch	·i·er ·i·est	soc'cer	sole'plate'	soot'y	sov'er·eign
smirk	sneer'ing·ly	so·cia·bil'i·ty	so·lic'it	·i·er ·i·est	sov'er·eign·ty
smite	sneeze	so'cia·ble	so·lic'i·ta'tion	sop	·ties
smote, smit'ten	sneezed	so'cia·bly	so·lic'i·tor	sopped	so'vi·et
or smote,	sneez'ing	so'cial	so·lic'i·tous	sop'ping	sow
smit'ing	snick'er	so'cial·ism	so·lic'i·tude'	soph'ism	sowed, sown or
smock'ing	snif'fle	so'cial·ite'	sol'id	soph'ist	sowed, sow'ing
smog	·fled ·fling	so'cial·i·za'tion	sol'i·dar'i·ty	so·phis'ti·cal	(plant; SEE sew)

»y'bean'
»ace
paced spac'ing
»ace'craft'
craft'
»ace'flight'
»ace'man
»ace'port'
»ace'ship'
»ace'suit'
»ace'walk'
»a'cious
»ack'le
led ·ling
»ade
»pad'ed
»pad'ing
»ade'work'
»a·ghet'ti
»an
»panned
»pan'ning
»an'dex
»an'drel
»an'gle
-gled ·gling
»an'iel
»an'sule
»par
»parred
»par'ring
»pare
»pared spar'ing
»pare'ribs'
»par'kle
»kled ·kling
»par'kler
»par'row
»parse'ly
»pasm
»pas·mod'ic
»pas·mod'i·cal·ly
»pas'tic
»pa'tial
»pat'ter
»pat'u·la
»pawn
»pay
»peak
spoke spok'en
speak'ing
»peak'er
pear'head'
pear'mint'
pe'cial
pe'cial·ist
pe'cial·ize'
-ized' ·iz'ing
pe'cial·ly
»pe'cial·ty
·ties
pe'cie
(coin money)
»pe'cies
·cies
(kind)
pec'i·fi'a·ble
»pe·cif'ic

spe·cif'i·cal·ly
spec'i·fi·ca'tion
spec'i·fy'
·fied' ·fy'ing
spec'i·men
spe'cious
speck'le
·led ·ling
spec'ta·cle
spec'ta·cled
spec·tac'u·lar
spec'ta·tor
spec'ter
spec'tral
spec'tro·scope'
spec·tros'co·py
spec'trum
·tra or ·trums
spec'u·late'
·lat'ed ·lat'ing
spec'u·la'tion
spec'u·la'tive
spec'u·la'tor
speech'less
speed
sped or speed'ed
speed'ing
speed'boat'
speed'i·ly
speed'i·ness
speed·om'e·ter
speed'up'
speed'y
·i·er ·i·est
spe'le·ol'o·gy
spell
spelled or spelt
spell'ing
(name the letters)
spell
spelled spell'ing
(work in place of)
spell'bind'
·bound' ·bind'ing
spell'down'
spe·lunk'er
spend
spent spend'ing
spend'thrift'
sper'ma·ce'ti
spew
sphere
spher'i·cal
sphe'roid
sphinx
sphinx'es or
sphin'ges
spice
spiced spic'ing
spic'i·ness
spick'-and-span'
spic'y
·i·er ·i·est
spi'der
spi'er
spig'ot
spike
spiked spik'ing

spill
spilled or spilt
spill'ing
spin
spun spin'ning
spin'ach
spi'nal
spin'dle
·dled ·dling
spin'dly
·dli·er ·dli·est
spin'drift'
spine'less
spin'et
spin'ner
spin'off'
spin'ster
spin'y
·i·er ·i·est
spi'ral
·raled or ·ralled
·ral·ing or
·ral·ling
spir'it·less
spir'it·u·al
spir'it·u·ous
spit
spit'ted
spit'ting
(impale)
spit
spit or spat
spit'ting
(eject saliva)
spite
spit'ed
spit'ing
spite'ful
spit'fire'
spit'tle
spit·toon'
spitz
splash'down'
splat'ter
splay'foot'
·feet'
spleen'ful
splen'did
splen'dor
sple·net'ic
splice
spliced
splic'ing
splin'ter
split
split split'ting
split'-lev'el
split'-up'
splotch
splurge
splurged
splurg'ing
splut'ter
spoil
spoiled or spoilt
spoil'ing
spoil'age
spoil'sport'

spoke
spoked spok'ing
spoke'shave'
spokes'man
spo'li·a'tion
sponge
sponged
spong'ing
sponge'cake'
spon'gi·ness
spon'gy
·gi·er ·gi·est
spon'sor
spon·ta·ne'i·ty
·ties
spon·ta'ne·ous
spoon'er·ism
spoon'-feed'
-fed' -feed'ing
spoon'ful'
-fuls'
spo·rad'ic
sport'ing
spor'tive
sports'man
sports'wear'
spot
spot'ted
spot'ting
spot'-check'
spot'light'
spot'ti·ness
spot'ty
·ti·er ·ti·est
spout'less
sprain
sprawl
spray
spread
spread'ing
sprig
sprigged
sprig'ging
spright'li·ness
spright'ly
·li·er ·li·est
spring
sprang or
sprung, sprung,
spring'ing
spring'board'
spring'i·ness
spring'time'
spring'y
·i·er ·i·est
sprin'kle
·kled ·kling
sprin'kler
sprint'er
spritz
sprock'et
sprout
spruce
spruc'er
spruc'est
spruced
spruc'ing

spry
spri'er or spry'er
spri'est or
spry'est
spry'ly
spry'ness
spume
spumed
spum'ing
spu·mo'ni or ·ne
spur
spurred
spur'ring
spu'ri·ous
spurn
spurt
sput'nik
sput'ter
spu'tum
spy
spies
spied spy'ing
spy'glass'
squab'ble
·bled ·bling
squab'bler
squad'ron
squal'id
squall
squal'or
squan'der
square
squared
squar'ing
square'-rigged'
squar'ish
squash'i·ness
squash'y
·i·er ·i·est
squat
squat'ted
squat'ting
squawk
squeak'i·ly
squeak'y
·i·er ·i·est
squeal'er
squeam'ish
squee'gee
·geed ·gee·ing
squeez'a·ble
squeeze
squeezed
squeez'ing
squelch
squig'gle
·gled ·gling
squint'-eyed'
squire
squired
squir'ing
squirm'y
·i·er ·i·est
squir'rel
squirt
stab
stabbed
stab'bing

sta·bil'i·ty
sta'bi·li·za'tion
sta'bi·lize'
·lized' ·liz'ing
sta'bi·liz'er
sta'ble
·bled ·bling
sta'bly
stac·ca'to
·tos
stack'up'
sta'di·um
·di·a or ·di·ums
staff
staffs or staves
(stick; music)
staffs
(people)
stage
staged
stag'ing
stage'craft'
stage'hand'
stage'-struck'
stag'ger
stag'nan·cy
stag'nant
stag'nate
·nat·ed ·nat·ing
stag·na'tion
stag'y
·i·er ·i·est
staid
(sober; SEE stay)
stain'less
stair'case'
stake
staked
stak'ing
(post; share;
SEE steak)
stake'hold'er
stake'out'
sta·lac'tite
sta·lag'mite
stale
stal'er stal'est
staled stal'ing
stale'mate'
·mat'ed ·mat'ing
stalk'ing-ho·se'
stall
stal'lio·1
stal'wart
stam'i·na
stam'mer
stam·pede'
·ped'ed ·ped'ing
stance
stan'chion
stand
stood stand'ing
stand'ard
stand'ard-bear'er
stand'ard·i·
za'tion
stand'ard·ize'
·ized' ·iz'ing

stand'by'
·bys'
stand·ee'
stand'-in'
stand'off'
stand'pat'
stand'point'
stand'still'
stan'za
staph'y·lo·coc'cus
·coc'ci
sta'ple
·pled ·pling
sta'pler
star
starred
star'ring
star'board
starch'i·ness
starch'y
·i·er ·i·est
star'dom
stare
stared
star'ing
star'gaze'
·gazed' ·gaz'ing
stark'-nak'ed
star'let
star'light'
star'lit'
star'ry
·ri·er ·ri·est
star'-span'gled
start'er
star'tle
·tled ·tling
star·va'tion
starve
starved
starv'ing
starve'ling
stat'a·ble
state
stat'ed stat'ing
State'hood'
state'li·ness
state'ly
·li·er ·li·est
state'ment
state'room'
states'man
state'-wide'
stat'ic
stat'i·cal·ly
sta'tion
sta'tion·ar'y
(not moving)
sta'tion·er
sta'tion·er'y
(writing paper)
sta·tis'tic
sta·tis'ti·cal
sta·tis'ti·cal·ly
stat'is·ti'cian
stat'u·ar'y
·ies

stat'ue
stat'u·esque'
stat'u·ette'
stat'ure
sta'tus
sta'tus quo'
stat'ute
stat'u·to'ry
staunch
stave
staved or stove
stav'ing
stay
stayed stay'ing
(stop; SEE staid)
stead'fast'
stead'i·ly
stead'i·ness
stead'y
·i·er ·i·est
·ied ·y·ing
steak
(meat; SEE stake)
steal
stole stol'en
steal'ing
stealth'i·ly
stealth'y
·i·er ·i·est
steam'boat'
steam'er
steam'roll'er
steam'ship'
steam shovel
steam'y
·i·er ·i·est
steel mill
steel wool
steel'work'er
steel'yard'
stee'ple
stee'ple·chase'
stee'ple·jack'
steer'age·way'
steers'man
stein
stel'lar
stem
stemmed
stem'ming
stem'-wind'ing
sten'cil
·ciled or ·cilled
·cil·ing or
·cil·ling
ste·nog'ra·pher
sten'o·graph'ic
ste·nog'ra·phy
sten'o·type'
sten'o·typ'ist
sten'o·typ'y
sten·to'ri·an
step
stepped
step'ping
step'broth'er
step'child'
·chil'dren

step'daugh'ter
step'-down'
step'fa'ther
step'lad'der
step'moth'er
step'par'ent
steppe
(treeless plain)
stepped'-up'
step'ping·stone'
step'sis'ter
step'son'
step'-up'
ster'e·o'
ster'e·o·phon'ic
ster'e·op'ti·con
ster'e·o·scope'
ster'e·o·scop'ic
ster'e·o·type'
·typed' ·typ'ing
ster'e·o·typ'ic
ster'ile
ste·ril'i·ty
ster'i·li·za'tion
ster'i·lize'
·lized' ·liz'ing
ster'ling
stern'ness
stern'-wheel'er
stet
stet'ted
stet'ting
steth'o·scope'
ste've·dore'
stew'ard
stew'ard·ess
stick
stuck stick'ing
stick'i·ness
stick'le
·led ·ling
stick'ler
stick'pin'
stick-to'-it·ive·
ness
stick'y
·i·er ·i·est
stiff'en
stiff'-necked'
sti'fle
·fled ·fling
stig'ma
·mas or ·ma·ta
stig'ma·tize'
·tized' ·tiz'ing
stile
(steps; SEE style)
sti·let'to
·tos or ·toes
still'born'
still life
still'y
stilt'ed
stim'u·lant
stim'u·late'
·lat'ed ·lat'ing
stim'u·la'tion
stim'u·la'tive

stim'u·lus
·li'
sting
stung sting'ing
stin'gi·ly
stin'gi·ness
stin'gy
·gi·er ·gi·est
stink
stank or stunk,
stunk stink'ing
stint'ing·ly
sti'pend
sti·pen'di·ar'y
·ar'ies
stip'ple
·pled ·pling
stip'u·late'
·lat'ed ·lat'ing
stip'u·la'tion
stip'u·la'tor
stir
stirred stir'ring
stir'rup
stitch
stock·ade'
·ad'ed ·ad'ing
stock'bro'ker
stock'hold'er
stock'i·ness
stock'i·nette' or
·net'
stock'ing
stock'pile'
stock'room'
stock'-still'
stock'y
·i·er ·i·est
stock'yard'
stodg'i·ness
stodg'y
·i·er ·i·est
sto'gie or ·gy
·gies
sto'ic
sto'i·cal
sto'i·cism
stoke
stoked stok'ing
stoke'hole'
stok'er
stole
stol'en
(pp. of steal)
stol'id
stol'len
(sweet bread)
stom'ach
stom'ach·ache'
stone
stoned ston'ing
stone'-blind'
stone'cut'ter
stone'-deaf'
stone'ma'son
stone'ware'
stone'work'
ston'i·ly

ston'y
·i·er ·i·est
stoop
(porch; bend;
SEE stoup)
stop
stopped
stop'ping
stop'cock'
stop'gap'
stop'light'
stop'o'ver
stop'page
stop'per
stop'ple
·pled ·pling
stop'watch'
stor'a·ble
stor'age
store
stored stor'ing
store'house'
store'keep'er
store'room'
storm'bound'
storm door
storm'i·ly
storm'i·ness
storm'y
·i·er ·i·est
sto'ry
·ries
·ried ·ry·ing
sto'ry·tell'er
stoup
(basin; SEE
stoop)
stout'heart'ed
stove'pipe'
stow'a·way'
stra·bis'mus
strad'dle
·dled ·dling
Strad'i·var'i·us
strafe
strafed straf'ing
strag'gle
·gled ·gling
strag'gler
straight
(not bent;
SEE strait)
straight'a·way'
straight'edge'
straight'ened
(made straight;
SEE straitened)
straight'-faced'
straight'for'ward
strain'er
strait
(waterway; SEE
straight)
strait'ened
(limited; SEE
straightened)
strait'jack'et
strait'-laced'

strange
strang'er
strang'est
strange'ly
stran'ger
stran'gle
·gled ·gling
stran'gle·hold'
stran'gu·late'
·lat'ed ·lat'ing
stran'gu·la'tio
strap
strapped
strap'ping
strat'a·gem
stra·te'gic
stra·te'gi·cal·l
strat'e·gist
strat'e·gy
·gies
strat'i·fi·ca'tio
strat'i·fy'
·fied' ·fy'ing
strat'o·sphere
stra'tum
·ta or ·tums
stra'tus
·ti
straw'ber'ry
·ries
stray
streak'i·ness
streak'y
·i·er ·i·est
stream'line'
·lined' ·lin'ing
street'car'
strength'en
stren'u·ous
strep'to·coc'c
strep'to·coc'c
·coc'ci
strep'to·my'c
stretch'er
stretch'i·ness
stretch'y
·i·er ·i·est
streu'sel
strew
strewed, strev
or strewn,
strew'ing
stri'ate
·at·ed ·at·ing
stri·a'tion
strict'ly
stric'ture
stride
strode strid'd
strid'ing
stri'dent
strid'u·late'
·lat'ed ·lat'ing
strife
strike
struck, struck
strick'en,
strik'ing

ke'break'er	stu'di·o'	sub·due'	sub·stan'tial·ly	suf·fice'	sun
ng	·os'	·dued' ·du'ing	sub·stan'ti·ate'	·ficed' ·fic'ing	sunned sun'ning
ung	stu'di·ous	sub'gum'	·at'ed ·at'ing	suf·fi'cien·cy	sun bath
ing'ing	stud'y	sub'ject	sub·stan'ti·a'tion	suf·fi'cient	sun'bathe'
n'gen·cy	·ies, ·ied ·y·ing	sub·jec'tive	sub·stan·ti'val	suf'fix	·bathed' ·bath'ing
es	stuff'i·ness	sub'jec·tiv'i·ty	sub·stan·tive	suf·fo·cate'	sun'bath'er
n'gent	stuff'y	sub·join'der	sub'sta'tion	·cat'ed ·cat'ing	sun'beam'
ng'halt'	·i·er ·i·est	sub'ju·gate'	sub'sti·tut'a·ble	suf·fo·ca'tion	sun'burn'
ng'i·ness	stul'ti·fy'	·gat'ed ·gat'ing	sub'sti·tute'	suf'frage	sun'burst'
ng'y	·fied' ·fy'ing	sub'ju·ga'tion	·tut'ed ·tut'ing	suf'fra·gette'	sun'-cured'
er ·i·est	stum'ble	sub'ju·ga'tor	sub'sti·tu'tion	suf'fra·gist	sun'dae
p	·bled ·bling	sub·junc'tive	sub·stra'tum	suf·fuse'	Sun'day
ipped	stun	sub'lease'	·ta or ·tums	·fused' ·fus'ing	sun'di·al
ip'ping	stunned	sub·let'	sub·struc'tur·al	suf·fu'sion	sun'down'
pe	stun'ning	·let' ·let'ting	sub'struc'ture	sug'ar	sun'-dried'
iped	stu'pe·fac'tion	sub'li·mate'	sub'ter·fuge'	sug'ar·coat'	sun'dries
ip'ing	stu'pe·fy'	·mat'ed ·mat·ing	sub'ter·ra'ne·an	sug'ar-cured'	sun'dry
p'ling	·fied' ·fy'ing	sub·li·ma'tion	sub'ti'tle	sug'ar·plum'	sun'glass'es
p'tease'	stu·pen'dous	sub·lime'	sub'tle	sug'ar·y	sunk'en
ve	stu'pid	·limed' ·lim'ing	·tler ·tlest	sug·gest'	sun'lamp'
ove or strived,	stu·pid'i·ty	sub·lim'i·nal	sub'tle·ty	sug·gest'i·ble	sun'light'
iv'en or	·ties	sub·lim'i·ty	·ties	sug·ges'tion	sun'lit'
ived, striv'ing	stu'por	sub·mar'gin·al	sub'tly	sug·ges'tive	sun'ni·ness
be	stur'di·ly	sub·ma·rine'	sub·tract'	su'i·ci'dal	sun'ny
ke	stur'di·ness	sub·merge'	sub·trac'tion	su'i·cide'	·ni·er ·ni·est
oked	stur'dy	sub·mer'gence	sub·tra·hend'	suit	sun'proof'
ok'ing	·di·er ·di·est	sub·mer'gi·ble	sub·trop'i·cal	(set; SEE suite)	sun'rise'
oll'er	stur'geon	sub·merse'	sub'urb	suit'a·bil'i·ty	sun'set'
ong'-arm'	stut'ter	·mersed'	sub·ur'ban	suit'a·ble	sun'shade'
ng'box'	stut'ter·er	;mers'ing	sub·ur'ban·ite'	suit'a·bly	sun'shine'
ng'hold'	sty	sub·mers'i·ble	sub·ur'bi·a	suit'case'	sun'spot'
ng'-mind'ed	sties	sub·mer'sion	sub·ver'sion	suite	sun'stroke'
ng'-willed'	stied sty'ing	sub·mis'sion	sub·ver'sive	(rooms; furniture;	sun'tan'
on'ti·um	(pig pen)	sub·mis'sive	sub·vert'	SEE suit, sweet)	sun'-tanned'
op	sty or stye	sub·mit'	sub'way'	suit'or	sup
opped	sties	·mit'ted	suc·ceed'	su'ki·ya'ki	supped sup'ping
op'ping	(eyelid swelling)	·mit'ting	suc·cess'	sul'fa	su·perb'
uc'tur·al	style	sub·nor'mal	suc·cess'ful	sul'fur	su'per·car'go
uc'ture	styled styl'ing	sub'nor·mal'i·ty	suc·cess'ful·ly	sulk'y	·goes or ·gos
red ·tur·ing	(mode; SEE stile)	sub·or'di·nate'	suc·ces'sion	·i·er ·i·est	su'per·charge'
u'del	style'book'	·nat'ed ·nat'ing	suc·ces'sive	sul'len	su'per·cil'i·ous
ug'gle	styl'ish	sub·or·di·na'tion	suc·ces'sor	sul'ly	su'per·e'go
led ·gling	styl'ist	sub'or·na'tion	suc·cinct'	·lied ·ly·ing	su'per·fi'cial
um	sty·lis'tic	sub'plot'	suc'cor	sul'tan	su'per·fi'ci·al'i·ty
ummed	styl'i·za'tion	sub·poe'na	(help; SEE sucker)	sul·tan'a	·ties
um'ming	styl'ize	·naed ·na·ing	suc'co·tash'	sul'tri·ness	su'per·fi'cial·ly
t	·ized ·iz·ing	sub ro'sa	suc'cu·lence	sul'try	su'per·fine'
ut'ted	sty'lus	sub·scribe'	suc'cu·lent	·tri·er ·tri·est	su'per·flu'i·ty
ut'ting	·lus·es or ·li	·scribed'	suc·cumb'	sum	·ties
ych'nine	sty'mie	·scrib'ing	suck'er	summed	su·per'flu·ous
b	·mied ·mie·ing	sub'script	(one that sucks;	sum'ming	su'per·het'er·
ubbed	styp'tic	sub·scrip'tion	SEE succor)	su'mac	o·dyne'
ib'bing	sty'rene	sub'se·quent	suck'le	sum·mar'i·ly	su'per·hu'man
b'ble	Sty'ro·foam'	sub·ser'vi·ent	·led ·ling	sum'ma·rize'	su'per·im·pose'
b'bly	su'a·ble	sub·side'	su'crose	·rized ·riz'ing	su'per·in·duce'
i·er ·bli·est	sua'sion	·sid'ed ·sid'ing	suc'tion	sum'ma·ry	su'per·in·tend'ent
b'born	suave	sub·sid'i·ar'y	sud'den·ly	·ries	su·pe'ri·or
b'by	suave'ly	·ies	sud'den·ness	(brief account)	su·pe'ri·or'i·ty
i·er ·bi·est	suav'i·ty	sub'si·di·za'tion	su'dor·if'ic	sum·ma'tion	su·per'la·tive
c'co	sub'as·sem'bly	sub'si·dize'	suds'y	sum'mer·time'	su'per·man'
oes or ·cos	sub'base'ment	·dized' ·diz'ing	·i·er ·i·est	sum'mer·y	su'per·mar'ket
oed ·co·ing	sub'com·mit'tee	sub'si·dy	sue	(like summer)	su'per·nat'u·ral
d	sub·con'scious	·dies	sued su'ing	sum'mit	su'per·nu'mer·
ud'ded	sub·con'tract	sub·sist'ence	suede or suède	sum'mon	ar'y
ud'ding	sub'cul'ture	sub'soil'	su'et	sum'mons	·ar'ies
d'book'	sub'cu·ta'ne·ous	sub'stance	suf'fer	·mons·es	su'per·scribe'
d'dent	sub·di·vide'	sub·stand'ard	suf'fer·ance	sump'tu·ar'y	su'per·script'
d'horse'	sub·di·vi'sion	sub·stan'tial	suf'fer·ing	sump'tu·ous	su'per·scrip'tion

su'per·sede'
·sed'ed ·sed'ing
su'per·se'dure
su'per·sen'si·tive
su'per·ses'sion
su'per·son'ic
su'per·sti'tion
su'per·sti'tious
su'per·struc'ture
su'per·vene'
·vened'
·ven'ing
su'per·ven'tion
su'per·vise'
·vised' ·vis'ing
su'per·vi'sion
su'per·vi'sor
su'per·vi'so·ry
su·pine'
sup'per
sup·plant'
sup'ple
sup'ple·ly
sup'ple·ment
sup'ple·men'tal
sup'ple·men'ta·ry
sup'ple·men·
ta'tion
sup'pli·ant
sup'pli·cant
sup'pli·cate'
·cat'ed ·cat'ing
sup'pli·ca'tion
sup·pli'er
sup·ply'
·plied' ·ply'ing
·plies'
sup·port'
sup·port'ive
sup·pose'
·posed' ·pos'ing
sup·pos'ed·ly
sup·po·si'tion
sup·pos'i·to'ry
·ries
sup·press'
sup·press'i·ble
sup·pres'sion
sup·pres'sor
sup'pu·rate'
·rat'ed ·rat'ing
sup'pu·ra'tion
su·prem'a·cist
su·prem'a·cy
su·preme'ly
sur'charge
sur'cin'gle
sure
sur'er sur'est
sure'-foot'ed
sure'ly
sur'e·ty
·ties
surf
(waves; SEE serf)
sur'face
·faced ·fac·ing
surf'board'

surf'boat'
surf'-cast'
sur'feit
surf'er
surge
surged surg'ing
(sudden rush;
SEE serge)
sur'geon
sur'ger·y
·ies
sur'gi·cal
sur'gi·cal·ly
sur'li·ness
sur'ly
·li·er ·li·est
sur·mise'
·mised' ·mis'ing
sur·mount'
sur'name'
·named'
·nam'ing
sur·pass'
sur'plice
(cloak)
sur'plus
(excess)
sur·prise'
·prised' ·pris'ing
sur·pris'ing·ly
sur·re'al
sur·re'al·ism
sur·ren'der
sur'rep·ti'tious
sur'rey
·reys
sur'ro·gate'
·gat'ed ·gat'ing
sur·round'
sur'tax'
sur·veil'lance
sur'vey
·veys
sur·vey'or
sur·viv'a·ble
sur·viv'al
sur·vive'
·vived' ·viv'ing
sur·vi'vor
sus·cep'ti·bil'i·ty
sus·cep'ti·ble
sus·pect'
sus·pend'
sus·pense'
sus·pen'sion
sus·pen'so·ry
sus·pi'cion
sus·pi'cious
sus·tain'
sus·tain'a·ble
sus'te·nance
sut·tee'
su'ture
·tured ·tur·ing
svelte
swab
swabbed
swab'bing

swad'dle
·dled ·dling
swag'ger
swal'low
swal'low-tailed'
swa'mi
·mis
swamp'y
·i·er ·i·est
swan's'-down'
swap
swapped
swap'ping
sward
(turf; SEE sword)
swarm
swarth'y
·i·er ·i·est
swash'buck'ler
swas'ti·ka
swat
swat'ted
swat'ting
swath n.
(strip)
swathe v., n.
swathed
swath'ing
(bandage)
sway'backed'
swear
swore
sworn
swear'ing
swear'word'
sweat
sweat or
sweat'ed,
sweat'ing
sweat'band'
sweat'er
sweat shirt
sweat'shop'
sweat'y
·i·er ·i·est
sweep
swept sweep'ing
sweep'stakes'
·stakes'
sweet
(like sugar;
SEE suite)
sweet'bread'
sweet corn
sweet'en·er
sweet'heart'
sweet'meat'
swell
swelled, swelled
or swol'len,
swell'ing
swel'ter
swept'back'
swerve
swerved
swerv'ing
swift'ness
swill

swim
swam swum
swim'ming
swim'ming·ly
swim'suit'
swin'dle
·dled ·dling
swing
swung
swing'ing
swing'by'
swin'ish
swipe
swiped
swip'ing
swirl
switch'board'
switch'man
swiv'el
·eled or ·elled
·el·ing or ·el·ling
swol'len
sword
(weapon; SEE
sward)
sword'fish'
sword'play'
swords'man
syb'a·rite'
syc'a·more'
syc'o·phant
syc'o·phan'tic
syl·lab'ic
syl·lab'i·fi·ca'tion
syl·lab'i·fy'
·fied' ·fy'ing
syl'la·ble
syl'la·bus
·bus·es or ·bi'
syl'lo·gism
sylph
syl'van
sym·bi·ot'ic
sym'bol
(mark; SEE
cymbal)
sym·bol'ic
sym'bol·ism
sym'bol·is'tic
sym'bol·ize'
·ized' ·iz'ing
sym·met'ri·cal
sym'me·try
·tries
sym'pa·thet'ic
sym'pa·thet'i·
cal·ly
sym'pa·thize'
·thized' ·thiz'ing
sym'pa·thy
·thies
sym·phon'ic
sym'pho·ny
·nies
sym·po'si·um
·ums or ·a
symp'tom
symp'to·mat'ic

syn'a·gogue'
syn'chro·mesh'
syn'chro·nism
syn'chro·ni·
za'tion
syn'chro·nize'
·nized' ·niz'ing
syn'chro·nous
syn'chro·tron'
syn'co·pate'
·pat'ed ·pat'ing
syn'co·pa'tion
syn'co·pe
syn'cre·tize'
·tized' ·tiz'ing
syn'di·cal·ism
syn'di·cate'
·cat'ed ·cat'ing
syn'drome
syn·ec'do·che
syn·e·col'o·gy
syn'er·gism
syn'od
syn·od'i·cal
syn'o·nym
syn·on'y·mous
syn·on'y·my
·mies
syn·op'sis
·ses
syn·op'size
·sized ·siz·ing
syn·op'tic
syn·tac'tic
syn·tac'ti·cal·ly
syn'tax
syn'the·sis
·ses'
syn'the·size'
·sized' ·siz'ing
syn·thet'ic
syn·thet'i·cal·ly
syph'i·lis
syph'i·lit'ic
sy·ringe'
·ringed' ·ring'ing
syr'up
sys'tem
sys'tem·at'ic
sys'tem·at'i·
cal·ly
sys'tem·a·tize'
·tized' ·tiz'ing
sys'tem'ic

T

tab'ard
tab'by
·bies
tab'er·nac'le
ta'ble
·bled ·bling
tab'leau
·leaux or ·leaus
ta'ble·cloth'

ta'ble d'hôte
ta'ble-hop'
ta'ble·land'
ta'ble·spoon
·fuls
tab'let
ta'ble·ware'
tab'loid
ta·boo' or ·b
·boos' or ·b
·booed' or ·
·boo'ing or
·bu'ing
ta'bor or ·bo
tab'o·ret
tab'u·lar
tab'u·late'
·lat'ed ·lat'in
tab'u·la'tion
tab'u·la'tor
ta·chis'to·sc
ta·chom'e·te
tac'it
tac'i·turn'
tac'i·tur'ni·t
tack'i·ness
tack'le
·led ·ling
tack'y
·i·er ·i·est
tact'ful
tact'ful·ly
tac'ti·cal
tac·ti'cian
tac'tics
tac'tile
tact'less
tac'tu·al
tad'pole'
taf'fe·ta
taf'fy
tag
tagged tag'g
tail'gate'
·gat'ed ·gat'i
tail'less
tail'light'
tai'lor
tai'lor-made
tail'piece'
tail'race'
tail'spin'
tail wind
taint'ed
tak'a·ble or t
take
took tak'en
tak'ing
take'off'
take'out'
take'o'ver
talc
tal'cum
tale'bear'er
tal'ent·ed
ta'les·man
(juryman)
tale'tell'er

s·man	ta'pir	taw'dry	tech·ni'cian	tell'er	tense'ly
ans	(animal; SEE	·dri·er ·dri·est	tech'ni·col'or	tell'tale'	tense'ness
ood luck charm)	taper)	taw'ny	tech·nique'	tel'pher or ·fer	ten'sile
'a·tive	tap'pet	·ni·er ·ni·est	tech·noc'ra·cy	Tel'star'	ten·sil'i·ty
'y	tap'room'	tax'a·bil'i·ty	tech·nog'ra·phy	te·mer'i·ty	ten'sion
low	tap'root'	tax'a·ble	tech·no·log'i·cal	tem'per	ten'ta·cle
ly	tar	tax·a'tion	tech·nol'o·gy	tem'per·a	ten'ta·tive
es, ·lied ·ly·ing	tarred tar'ring	tax'·de·duct'i·ble	te'di·ous	tem'per·a·ment	ten'ta·tive·ly
'mud	tar'an·tel'la	tax'·ex·empt'	te'di·um	tem'per·a·	ten'ter
on	ta·ran'tu·la	tax'i	tee	men'tal	ten'ter·hook'
1'a·ble or	tar·boosh'	·is, ·ied	teed tee'ing	tem'per·ance	tenth
me'·	tar'di·ness	·i·ing or ·y·ing	teem	tem'per·ate	ten·u'i·ty
na'le	tar'dy	tax'i·cab'	(abound; SEE	tem'per·a·ture	ten'u·ous
1'bour	·di·er ·di·est	tax'i·der'mist	team)	tem'pered	ten'ure
1'bou·rine'	tare	tax'i·der'my	teen'·age'	tem'pest	(time held;
1e	tared tar'ing	tax'i·me'ter	teen'·ag'er	tem·pes'tu·ous	SEE tenor)
med tam'ing	(weight deduction;	tax'i·way'	tee'ter-tot'ter	tem'plate or ·plet	ten·u'ri·al
1'-o'-shan'ter	SEE tear)	tax·on'o·my	teethe	tem'ple	te'pee or tee'·
1p'er n.	tar'get	tax'pay'er	teethed teeth'ing	tem'po	tep'id
1'per v.	tar'iff	tea bag	tee·to'tal·er	·pos or ·pi	te·pid'i·ty
1'per·er	tar'nish	teach	tee·to'tal·ism	tem'po·ral	te·qui'la
1'pi·on	ta'ro	taught teach'ing	Tef'lon	tem'po·rar'i·ly	ter'cen·te'nar·y
1'pon	·ros	teach'a·ble	teg'u·ment	tem'po·rar'i·ness	·ies
	(plant)	teach'er	tel·au'to·graph'	tem'po·rar'y	ter'gi·ver·sate'
1'ner tan'nest	tar'ot	teach'·in'	tel'e·cast'	tem'po·rize'	·sat'ed ·sat'ing
1ned tan'ning	(playing cards)	tea'cup'	·cast' or ·cast'ed	·rized' ·riz'ing	ter'gi·ver·sa'tor
'dem	tar·pau'lin	tea'cup·ful'	·cast'ing	temp·ta'tion	ter'ma·gant
1'ge·lo'	tar'pon	·fuls'	tel'e·com·mu'·	tempt'er	ter'mi·na·ble
os'	tar'ra·gon'	teak	ni·ca'tion	tempt'ing	ter'mi·na·bly
1'gent	tar'ry	tea'ket'tle	tel'e·course'	tempt'ress	ter'mi·nal
1·gen'tial	·ried ·ry·ing	team	tel'e·gen'ic	tem'pus fu'git	ter'mi·nate'
1·ge·rine'	tar'tan	(group; SEE teem)	tel'e·gram'	ten'a·ble	·nat'ed ·nat'ing
1'gi·ble	tar'tar	team'mate'	tel'e·graph'	te·na'cious	ter'mi·na'tion
1'gi·bly	tar'tar sauce	team'ster	te·leg'ra·pher	te·nac'i·ty	ter'mi·nol'o·gy
1'gle	tart'ly	team'work'	te·leg'ra·phy	ten'an·cy	ter'mi·nus
led ·gling	task force	tea'pot'	tel'e·graph'ic	·cies	·ni' or ·nus·es
1'go	task'mas'ter	tear	te·le·ki·ne'sis	ten'ant	ter'mite
1os	tas'sel	tore torn	tel'e·me'ter	ten'ant·a·ble	ter'na·ry
ng'y	·seled or ·selled	tear'ing	te'le·o·log'i·cal	ten'ant·ry	terp'si·cho·re'an
·er ·i·est	·sel·ing or	(rip; SEE tare)	te·le·ol'o·gy	·ries	ter'race
1k'age	·sel·ling	tear	tel'e·path'ic	tend'en·cy	·raced ·rac·ing
1k'ard	taste	teared tear'ing	te·lep'a·thy	·cies	ter'ra cot'ta
1k'er	tast'ed tast'ing	(eye fluid;	tel'e·phone'	ten'der	ter'ra fir'ma
1k'ful	taste'ful	SEE tier)	·phoned'	(soft; offer)	ter·rain'
uls	taste'ful·ly	tear'drop'	·phon'ing	tend'er	Ter'ra·my'cin
1'ner·y	taste'less	tear'ful	tel'e·phon'ic	(one who tends)	ter'ra·pin
1es	tast'er	tear gas	te·leph'o·ny	ten'der·foot'	ter·rar'i·um
1'nic	tast'i·ness	tear'i·ness	tel'e·pho'to	·foots' or ·feet'	·i·ums or ·i·a
1'nin	tast'y	tea'room'	tel'e·pho'to·graph'	ten'der·heart'ed	ter·raz'zo
1'ta·lize'	·i·er ·i·est	tear'y	tel'e·pho·tog'ra·	ten'der·ize'	ter·res'tri·al
ized' ·liz'ing	tat'ter·de·mal'ion	·i·er ·i·est	phy	·ized' ·iz'ing	ter'ri·ble
1'ta·mount'	tat'tered	tease	tel'e·play'	ten'der·iz'er	ter'ri·bly
1'trum	tat'ter·sall'	teased teas'ing	tel'e·prompt'er	ten'der·loin'	ter'ri·er
1p	tat'tle	tea'sel	tel'e·ran'	ten'don	ter·rif'ic
1pped	·tled ·tling	·seled or ·selled	tel'e·scope'	ten'dril	ter·rif'i·cal·ly
1p'ping	tat'tle·tale'	·sel·ing or	·scoped' ·scop'ing	ten'e·ment	ter'ri·fy'
1pe	tat·too'	·sel·ling	tel'e·scop'ic	ten'et	·fied' ·fy'ing
1pe deck	·toos'	tea'spoon·ful'	tel'e·thon'	ten'fold'	ter'ri·to'ri·al
1'per	·tooed' ·too'ing	·fuls'	Tel'e·type'	Ten'nes·see'	ter'ri·to·ri·al'i·ty
candle; decrease;	taught	teat	·typed' ·typ'ing	ten'nis	ter'ri·to·ry
EE tapir)	(trained; SEE taut)	tea'·ta·ble	tel'e·type'writ'er	ten'on	·ries
1pe'·re·cord'	taunt	tea'tast'er	tel'e·view'er	ten'or	ter'ror
1pe recorder	taupe	tea'time'	tel'e·vise'	(tendency; singer)	ter'ror·ism
1p'es·try	taut	tech'nic	·vised' ·vis'ing	SEE tenure)	ter'ror·ist
tries	(tight; SEE taught)	tech'ni·cal	tel'e·vi'sion	ten'pins'	ter'ror·is'tic
1pe'worm'	tau·tol'o·gy	tech·ni·cal'i·ty	tell	tense	ter'ror·i·za'tion
1p'i·o'ca	·gies	·ties	told tell'ing	tens'er tens'est	ter'ror·ize'
	tav'ern	tech'ni·cal·ly	tell'a·ble	tensed tens'ing	·ized' ·iz'ing

ter'ry	the'o·log'i·cal	thief *n.*	three'-way'	thwart	time'card'
terse	the·ol'o·gy	thieves	three'-wheel'er	thyme	time clock
ters'er ters'est	·gies	thieve *v.*	thren'o·dy	(*herb;* SEE time)	time'-con·su
terse'ness	the'o·rem	thieved thiev'ing	·dies	thy'mus	time'-hon'or
ter'ti·ar'y	the'o·ret'i·cal	thiev'er·y	thresh'er	thy'roid	time'keep'er
tes'sel·late'	the'o·ret'i·cal·ly	·ies	thresh'old	ti·ar'a	time'less
·lat'ed ·lat'ing	the'o·re·ti'cian	thiev'ish·ly	threw	tib'i·a	time'li·ness
tes'sel·la'tion	the'o·rize'	thigh'bone'	(*pt. of throw;*	tic	time'ly
test'a·ble	·rized' ·riz'ing	thim'ble·ful'	SEE through)	(*muscle spasm*)	·li·er ·li·est
tes'ta·ment	the'o·ry	·fuls'	thrice	tick	time'out'
tes'ta·men'ta·ry	·ries	thin	thrift'i·ly	(*click; insect*)	time'piece'
tes'tate	the·os'o·phy	thin'ner	thrift'i·ness	tick'er tape	tim'er
tes'ta·tor	·phies	thin'nest	thrift'y	tick'et	time'sav'ing
tes'ti·cle	ther'a·peu'tic	thinned	·i·er ·i·est	tick'ing	time'ta'ble
tes'ti·fi'er	ther'a·pist	thin'ning	thrill'er	tick'le	time'-test'ed
tes'ti·fy'	ther'a·py	thing	thrive	·led ·ling	time'worn'
·fied' ·fy'ing	·pies	think	thrived or throve,	tick'ler	time zone
tes'ti·ly	there	thought	thrived or	tick'lish	ti·mid'i·ty
tes'ti·mo'ni·al	(*at that place;*	think'ing	thriv'en,	tick'-tack-toe'	tim'id·ly
tes'ti·mo'ny	SEE their, they're)	thin'-skinned'	thriv'ing	tick'y tack'y	tim'or·ous
·nies	there'a·bouts'	third'-class'	throat'y	tid'al	tim'o·thy
tes'ti·ness	there·af'ter	third'-rate'	·i·er ·i·est	tid'bit'	tim'pa·ni
tes'ty	there·at'	thirst'i·ly	throb	tide'land'	tim'pa·nist
·ti·er ·ti·est	there·by'	thirst'i·ness	throbbed	tide'mark'	tin
tet'a·nus	there·for'	thirst'y	throb'bing	tide'wa·ter	tinned tin'ni
tête'-à-tête'	(*for it*)	·i·er ·i·est	throe	ti'di·ly	tinc'ture
teth'er	there'fore'	thir'teenth'	(*pang;* SEE throw)	ti'di·ness	·tured ·tur·in
tet'ra·cy'cline	(*for that reason*)	thir'ti·eth	throm·bo'sis	ti'dings	tin'der·box'
tet'ra·he'dron	there·in'	thir'ty	throne	ti'dy	tin'foil'
·drons or ·dra	there'in·aft'er	·ties	throned	·di·er ·di·est	tinge
te·tral'o·gy	there·in'to	this	thron'ing	·died ·dy·ing	tinged, tinge
·gies ·	there's	these	throng	tie	or ting'ing
Tex'as	(*there is;* SEE	this'tle·down'	throt'tle	tied ty'ing	tin'gle
text'book'	theirs)	thith'er·to'	·tled ·tling	tie'back'	·gled ·gling
tex'tile	there'to·fore'	thole	through	tie'-dye'	tin'gly
tex'tu·al	there'up·on'	thong	(*from end to end*	·dyed' ·dye'ing	·gli·er ·gli·es
tex'tur·al	there·with'	tho·rac'ic	*of;* SEE threw)	tie'-in'	ti'ni·ness
tex'ture	ther'mal	tho'rax	through·out'	tie'pin'	tin'ker
than *conj., prep.*	therm'i·on'ics	·rax·es or ·ra·ces	throw	tier	tin'ker·er
thank'ful	ther'mo·dy·	tho'ri·um	threw thrown	(*row;* SEE tear)	tin'kle
thank'less	nam'ics	thorn'y	throw'ing	ti'er	·kled ·kling
thanks'giv'ing	ther'mo·e·lec'·	·i·er ·i·est	(*hurl;* SEE throe)	(*one that ties;*	tin'ni·ness
that	tric'i·ty	thor'ough	throw'a·way'	SEE tire)	tin·ni'tus
those	ther·mom'e·ter	thor'ough·bred'	throw'back'	tie tack	tin'ny
thatch	ther'mo·nu'cle·ar	thor'ough·fare'	thrum	tie'-up'	·ni·er ·ni·est
thaw	ther'mo·pile'	thor'ough·go'ing	thrummed	ti'ger	tin'-plate'
the·a'ter or ·tre	ther'mo·plas'tic	though	thrum'ming	ti'ger's eye	·plat'ed ·pla
the·at'ri·cal	ther'mos	thought	thrust	tight'en	tin'sel
theft	ther'mo·stat'	thought'ful·ly	thrust thrust'ing	tight'fist'ed	·seled or ·sel
their	ther'mo·stat'i·	thought'ful·ness	thud	tight'fit'ting	·sel·ing or
(*poss. form of*	cal·ly	thought'less	thud'ded	tight'knit'	·sel·ling
they; SEE there,	the·sau'rus	thou'sand·fold'	thud'ding	tight'-lipped'	tin'smith'
they're)	·ri or ·rus·es	thrall'dom	thumb'nail'	tight'rope'	tin'tin·nab'u·
theirs	the'sis	thrash	thumb'screw'	ti'gress	la'tion
(*belonging to*	·ses	thread'bare'	thumb'stall'	tile	tin'type'
them; SEE there's)	they'd	thread'i·ness	thumb'tack'	tiled til'ing	tin'ware'
the'ism	they'll	thread'y	thump	till'a·ble	ti'ny
the·is'tic	they're	·i·er ·i·est	thun'der·bolt'	tilt'-top'	·ni·er ·ni·est
the·mat'ic	(*they are;* SEE	threat'en	thun'der·cloud'	tim'bale	tip
theme	their, there)	3'-D'	thun'der·head'	tim'ber	tipped tip'pir
them·selves'	they've	three'-deck'er	thun'der·ous	(*wood*)	tip'-off'
then	thi'a·mine'	three'-di·men'·	thun'der·show'er	tim'ber·line'	tip'pet
(*at that time*)	thick'en·ing	sion·al	thun'der·squall'	tim'bre	tip'ple
thence'forth'	thick'et	three'fold'	thun'der·storm'	(*quality of sound*)	·pled ·pling
the·oc'ra·cy	thick'ness	three'-ply'	thun'der·struck'	time	tip'sy
·cies	thick'set'	three'-quar'ter	Thurs'day	timed tim'ing	·si·er ·si·est
the·od'o·lite'	thick'-skinned'	three'score'	thus	(*duration;*	tip'toe'
the'o·lo'gian	thick'-wit'ted	three'some	thwack	SEE thyme)	·toed' ·toe'ir

'top'	tol'er·ance	top'i·cal	touch'down'	trade name	trans·fer'
·ade	tol'er·ant	top'knot'	tou·ché'	trades'man	·ferred'
e	tol'er·ate'	top'less	touch'hole'	trades'peo'ple	·fer'ring
'ed tir'ing	·at'ed ·at'ing	top'-lev'el	touch'i·ly	trade wind	trans·fer'a·ble
.eary; rubber	tol'er·a'tion	top'most'	touch'i·ness	tra·di'tion	or ·fer'ra·ble
.op; SEE tier)	tol'er·a'tor	top'-notch'	touch'stone'	tra·di'tion·al	trans·fer'al
ed'ly	toll'booth'	to·pog'ra·pher	touch'-type'	tra·duce'	or ·fer'ral
e'less	toll bridge	top'o·graph'i·cal	touch'-typ'ist	·duced' ·duc'ing	trans·fer·ee'
e'some	toll call	to·pog'ra·phy	touch'y	traf'fic	trans·fer'ence
'sue	toll'gate'	(surface features;	·i·er ·i·est	·ficked ·fick·ing	trans·fer'rer
:an	toll'keep'er	SEE typography)	tough'en	traf'fick·er	trans·fig·u·ra'tion
he	toll road	top'ple	tough'-mind'ed	tra·ge'di·an	trans·fig'ure
.hed tith'ing	tom'a·hawk'	·pled ·pling	tou·pee'	tra·ge'di·enne'	trans·fix'
.ian	to·ma'to	top'sail	tour' de force'	trag'e·dy	trans·form'
'il-late'	·toes	top'-se'cret	tours' de force'	·dies	trans·for·ma'tion
.at'ed ·lat'ing	tom'boy'	top'soil'	tour'ism	trag'ic	trans·form'er
'il-la'tion	tomb'stone'	top'sy-tur'vy	tour'ist	trag'i·cal·ly	trans·fuse'
.tle	tom'cat'	toque	tour'ma·line	trag'i·com'e·dy	trans·fus'i·ble
.led ·tling	tom'fool'er·y	to'rah or ·ra	tour'na·ment	·dies	·dies
.le-hold'er	to·mor'row	torch'bear'er	tour'ney	trag'i·com'ic	trans·fu'sion
'mouse'	tom'-tom'	torch·ier' or	·neys	trail'blaz'er	trans·gress'
.nice'	ton	·iere'	tour'ni·quet	trail'er	trans·gres'sion
'ter	(weight; SEE tun)	torch'light'	tou'sle	train·ee'	trans·gres'sor
'u·lar	ton'al	tor'e·a·dor'	·sled ·sling	train'man	tran'sient
ad'stool'	to·nal'i·ty	tor'ment	tow'age	trait	tran·sis'tor
ad'y	·ties	tor·men'tor	to·ward'	trai'tor	tran·sis'tor·ize'
es, ·ied ·y·ing	tone	tor·na'do	tow'boat'	trai'tor·ous	·ized' ·iz'ing
ad'y·ism	toned ton'ing	·does or ·dos	tow'el	trai'tress	trans'it
'-and-fro'	tone'-deaf'	tor·pe'do	·eled or ·elled	tra·jec'to·ry	tran·si'tion
.ast'mas'ter	tongs	·does	·el·ing or ·el·ling	·ries	tran·si'tion·al·ly
·bac'co	tongue	tor'pid	tow'er·ing	tram'mel	tran'si·tive
:os	tongued	tor·pid'i·ty	tow'head'	·meled or ·melled	tran'si·to'ry
.bac'co·nist	tongu'ing	tor'por	tow'line'	·mel·ing or	trans·lat'a·ble
·bog'gan	tongue'-lash'ing	torque	town'ship	·mel·ling	trans·late'
.c·ca'ta	tongue'-tie'	tor'rent	towns'peo'ple	tram'ple	·lat'ed ·lat'ing
.c'sin	-tied' -ty'ing	tor·ren'tial	tow'path'	·pled ·pling	trans·la'tion
.alarm; SEE toxin)	ton'ic	tor'rid	tow'rope'	tram'po·line'	trans·la'tor
·day'	to·night'	tor·rid'i·ty	tox·e'mi·a	trance	trans·lit'er·ate'
.d'dle	ton'nage	tor'sion	tox'ic	tranced	·at'ed ·at'ing
.dled ·dling	ton·neau'	tor'so	tox'i·cant	tranc'ing	trans·lit'er·a'tion
.d'dler	·neaus' or	·sos or ·si	tox·i·col'o·gy	tran'quil	trans·lu'cence
.d'dy	·neaux'	tort	tox'in	·quil·er or ·quil·ler	trans·lu'cent
.dies	ton'sil	(wrongful act)	(poison; SEE	·quil·est or	trans·mi'grate
·do'	ton'sil·lec'to·my	torte	tocsin)	·quil·lest	·grat·ed ·grat·ing
.e	·mies	(cake)	trace	tran'quil·ize'	trans·mi·gra'tion
.oed toe'ing	ton'sil·li'tis	tor·til'la	traced trac'ing	or ·quil·lize'	trans·mis'si·ble
.e'-dance'	ton·so'ri·al	tor'toise	trace'a·ble	·ized' or ·lized'	trans·mis'sion
.danced'	ton'sure	tor·to'ni	trac'er	·iz'ing or ·liz'ing	trans·mit'
.danc'ing	·sured ·sur·ing	tor'tu·ous	trac'er·y	tran'quil·iz'er or	·mit'ted
.e'hold'	ton'tine	(winding)	·ies	·quil·liz'er	·mit'ting
.e'-in'	tool'mak'er	tor'ture	tra'che·a	tran·quil'li·ty or	trans·mit'tal
.e'less	tooth	·tured ·tur·ing	·ae' or ·as	·quil'i·ty	trans·mit'tance
.e'nail'	teeth	tor'tur·ous	tra·cho'ma	tran'quil·ly	trans·mit'ter
.f'fee or ·fy	tooth'ache'	(agonizing)	track	trans·act'	trans·mut'a·ble
.'ga	tooth'brush'	toss'up'	(trace)	trans·ac'tion	trans'mu·ta'tion
.gas or ·gae	tooth'paste'	to'tal	tract	trans·ac'tor	trans·mute'
.·geth'er	tooth'pick'	·taled or ·talled	(land; leaflet)	trans'at·lan'tic	·mut'ed
.og'gle	tooth'some	·tal·ing or	trac'ta·ble	trans·ceiv'er	·mut'ing
.gled ·gling	top	·tal·ling	trac'tile	tran·scend'	trans·o·ce·an'ic
.oi'let	topped top'ping	to·tal'i·tar'i·an	trac'tion	tran·scend'ent	trans'som
.oi'let·ry	to'paz	to·tal'i·ty	trac'tor	tran'scen·den'tal	trans·son'ic
.·ries	top'coat'	to'tal·i·za'tor	trad'a·ble or	trans·con·ti·	trans·pa·cif'ic
.oil'some	top'-drawer'	to'tal·ly	trade'a·ble	nen'tal	trans·par'en·cy
.oil'worn'	top'-dress'ing	tote	trade	tran·scribe'	·cies
.o'ken	top'-flight'	tot'ed tot'ing	trad'ed trad'ing	·scribed' ·scrib'ing	trans·par'ent
.ole	top'-heav'y	to'tem	trade'-in'	tran'script'	tran·spire'
.ol'er·a·ble	to'pi·ar'y	tot'ter	trade'-last'	tran·scrip'tion	·spired' ·spir'ing
.ol'er·a·bly	top'ic	touch'back'	trade'mark'	tran'sept	trans·plant'
					tran·spon'der

trans·port'
trans·por·ta'tion
trans·pos'a·ble
trans·pose'
·posed' ·pos'ing
trans·po·si'tion
trans·sex'u·al
trans·ship'
·shipped'
·ship'ping
tran'stage'
tran·sub·stan'ti·ate'
trans·val'ue
trans·ver'sal
trans·verse'
trans·verse'ly
trans·ves'tite
trap
trapped trap'ping
trap'door'
tra·peze'
tra·pe'zi·um
trap'e·zoid'
trap'per
trap'pings
trap'shoot'ing
trash'i·ness
trash'y
·i·er ·i·est
trau'ma
·mas or ·ma·ta
trau·mat'ic
trau·mat'i·cal·ly
trav'ail
(hard work)
trav'el
·eled or ·elled
·el·ing or ·el·ling
(journey)
trav'el·er or
·el·ler
trav'e·logue' or
·log'
trav·ers'a·ble
trav·ers'al
trav·erse'
·ersed' ·ers'ing
trav'er·tine'
trav'es·ty
·ties
·tied ·ty·ing
trawl'er
tray
(holder; SEE trey)
treach'er·ous
treach'er·y
·ies
trea'cle
tread
trod, trod'den or
trod, tread'ing
trea'dle
·dled ·dling
tread'mill'
trea'son
trea'son·ous

treas'ure
·ured ·ur·ing
treas'ur·er
treas'ure-trove'
treas'ur·y
·ies
treat'a·ble
trea'tise
treat'ment
trea'ty
·ties
tre'ble
·bled ·bling
tree
treed
tree'ing
tree'nail'
tree'top'
tre'foil
treil'lage
trek
trekked
trek'king
trel'lis
trem'ble
·bled ·bling
tre·men'dous
trem'o·lo'
·los'
trem'or
trem'u·lous
trench'ant
trench mouth
trend
trep·i·da'tion
tres'pass
tress'es
tres'tle
tres'tle·work'
trey
(a three; SEE tray)
tri'a·ble
tri'ad
tri'al
tri·an'gle
tri·an'gu·lar
tri·an'gu·late'
·lat'ed ·lat'ing
tri·an'gu·la'tion
trib'al
trib'al·ism
tribes'man
trib·u·la'tion
tri·bu'nal
trib'une
trib'u·tar'y
·ies
trib'ute
tri·cen·ten'ni·al
tri'ceps
·cep·ses or ·ceps
tri·chi'na
·nae
trich·i·no'sis
tri·chot'o·my
tri'chro·mat'ic
trick'er·y

trick'i·ly
trick'i·ness
trick'le
·led ·ling
trick'ster
trick'y
·i·er ·i·est
tri·col'or
tri'cot
tri'cy·cle
tri·di·men'sion·al
tri·en'ni·al
tri·en'ni·um
·ums or ·a
tri'er
tri'fle
·fled ·fling
tri·fo'cal
trig'ger
trig'o·no·met'ric
trig'o·nom'e·try
tri·lat'er·al
tri·lin'gual
tril'lion
tril'li·um
tril'o·gy
·gies
trim
trimmed
trim'ming
trim'mer
trim'mest
tri·mes'ter
tri·month'ly
trin'i·ty
·ties
trin'ket
tri·no'mi·al
tri'o
·os
trip
tripped trip'ping
tri·par'tite
trip'ham'mer
tri'ple
·pled ·pling
tri'ple-space'
tri'plet
trip'li·cate'
·cat'ed ·cat'ing
tri'ply
tri'pod
trip'per
trip'tych
tri·sect'
triste
tris·tesse'
trite
trit'er trit'est
trite'ly
trit'u·rate'
·rat'ed ·rat'ing
tri'umph
tri·um'phal
tri·um'phant
tri·um'vi·rate
triv'et
triv'i·a

triv'i·al
triv·i·al'i·ty
·ties
triv'i·al·ly
tri·week'ly
·lies
tro'che
(lozenge)
tro'chee
(poetic meter)
trod'den
trof'fer
trog'lo·dyte'
troll
trol'ley
·leys
·leyed ·ley·ing
trol'lop
trom·bone'
trom·bon'ist
troop
(of soldiers;
SEE troupe)
troop'ship'
tro'phy
·phies
trop'ic
trop'i·cal
tro'pism
trop'o·sphere'
trot
trot'ted trot'ting
trot'ter
trou·ba·dour'
trou'ble
·bled ·bling
trou'ble·mak'er
trou'ble·shoot'er
trou'ble·some
trough
trounce
trounced
trounc'ing
troupe
trouped
troup'ing
(of actors;
SEE troop)
troup'er
trou'sers
trous'seau
·seaux or ·seaus
trout
trow'el
·eled or ·elled
·el·ing or ·el·ling
tru'an·cy
·cies
tru'ant
truce
truck farm
truck'le
·led ·ling
truc'u·lence
truc'u·lent
trudge
trudged
trudg'ing

true
tru'er tru'est
trued tru'ing
or true'ing
true'-blue'
true'-life'
true'love'
truf'fle
tru'ism
tru'ly
trump
trumped'-up'
trump'er·y
·ies
trum'pet
trum'pet·er
trun'cate
·cat·ed ·cat·ing
trun·ca'tion
trun'cheon
trun'dle
·dled ·dling
trunk line
trun'nion
truss
trus·tee'
·teed' ·tee'ing
(manager; SEE
trusty)
trus·tee'ship'
trust'ful
trust'ful·ly
trust'i·ness
trust'wor'thy
trust'y
·ies, ·i·er ·i·est
(relied upon;
SEE trustee)
truth'ful
truth'ful·ly
truth'ful·ness
try
tries
tried try'ing
try'out'
tryst
tset'se fly
T'-shirt'
tsim'mes
tsor'is
T square
tsu·na'mi
tub
tubbed tub'bing
tu'ba
·bas or ·bae
tub'ba·ble
tub'bi·ness
tub'by
·bi·er ·bi·est
tube
tubed tub'ing
tu'ber
tu·ber'cle
tu·ber'cu·lar
tu·ber'cu·lin
tu·ber'cu·lo'sis
tu·ber'cu·lous

tube'rose'
(plant)
tu'ber·ous
(having tubers)
tu'bu·lar
tuck'er
Tu'dor
Tues'day
tuft'ed
tug
tugged tug'gin
tug'boat'
tu·i'tion
tu·la·re'mi·a
tu'lip
tulle
tum'ble
·bled ·bling
tum'ble-down'
tum'bler
tum'ble·weed'
tum'brel
tu'me·fy'
·fied' ·fy'ing
tu·mes'cence
tu·mes'cent
tu'mid
tu'mor
tu'mor·ous
tu'mult
tu·mul'tu·ous
tun
tunned tun'nin
(cask; SEE ton)
tun'a·ble
or tune'-
tun'dra
tune
tuned tun'ing
tune'ful
tune'less
tun'er
tune'up' or
tune'-up'
tung'sten
tu'nic
tun'nel
·neled or ·nelle
·nel·ing or
·nel·ling
tu'pe·lo'
·los'
tur'ban
(headdress)
tur'bid
tur'bine
(engine)
tur'bo·jet'
tur'bo·prop'
tur'bu·lence
tur'bu·lent
tu·reen'
turf
tur'gid
tur'key
tur'mer·ic
tur'moil
turn'a·bout'

rn'a·round'
rn'buck'le
rn'coat'
rn'down'
r'nip
rn'key'
keys'
rn'off'
rn'out'
rn'o·ver
rn'pike'
rn'stile'
rn'ta·ble
r'pen·tine'
r'pi·tude'
r'quoise
r'ret
r'tle
r'tle·dove'
r'tle·neck'
s'sle
sled ·sling
r'te·lage
r'te·lar'y
r'tor
r·to'ri·al
rt'ti-frut'ti
r'tu
rx·e'do
·dos
V
TVs or TV's
wang
weak
weed
weed'y
·i·er ·i·est
weeze
tweezed
tweez'ing
weez'ers
welfth
welve'fold'
wen'ti·eth
wen'ty
·ties
wen'ty·fold'
wice'-told'
wid'dle
·dled ·dling
wi'light'
wi'lit
will
wine
twined twin'ing
win'-en'gined
winge
twinged
twing'ing
wi'-night'
win'kle
·kled ·kling
wirl'er
twitch
twit'ter
two'-by-four'
two'-edged'

two'-faced'
two'-fist'ed
two'fold'
two'-hand'ed
two'-leg'ged
two'-piece'
two'-ply'
two'-sid'ed
two'some
two'-way'
ty·coon'
tym·pan'ic
typ'a·ble or type'·
typ'al
type
typed typ'ing
type'bar'
type'cast'
·cast' ·cast'ing
(in acting)
type'-cast'
·cast' ·cast'ing
(in printing)
type'script'
type'set'
·set' ·set'ting
type'set'ter
type'write'
·wrote' ·writ'ten
·writ'ing
type'writ'er
ty'phoid
ty·phoon'
ty'phus
typ'i·cal
typ'i·cal·ly
typ'i·fy'
·fied' ·fy'ing
typ'ist
ty·pog'ra·pher
ty'po·graph'i·cal
ty·pog'ra·phy
(setting of type;
SEE topography)
ty·pol'o·gy
ty·ran'ni·cal
tyr'an·nize'
·nized' ·niz'ing
tyr'an·nous
tyr'an·ny
·nies
ty'rant
ty'ro
·ros
ty'ro·thri'cin

U

u·biq'ui·tous
u·biq'ui·ty
ud'der
(milk gland;
SEE utter)
u·fol'o·gist
ug'li
(fruit)

ug'li·ness
ug'ly
·li·er ·li·est
u'kase
u'ku·le'le
ul'cer
ul'cer·ate'
·at'ed ·at'ing
ul'cer·ous
ul'ster
ul·te'ri·or
ul'ti·mate
ul'ti·mate·ly
ul'ti·ma'tum
·tums or ·ta
ul'tra
ul'tra·con·serv'·
a·tive
ul'tra·ism
ul'tra·ma·rine'
ul'tra·mi'cro·
scope'
ul'tra·mod'ern
ul'tra·na'tion·al·
ism
ul'tra·son'ic
ul'tra·sound'
ul'tra·vi'o·let
ul'u·late'
·lat'ed ·lat'ing
um'ber
um·bil'i·cal
um·bil'i·cus
·ci'
um'bra
·brae or ·bras
um'brage
um·bra'geous
um·brel'la
u'mi·ak' or ·ack'
um'laut
um'pire
·pired ·pir·ing
un·a'ble
un·a'bridged'
un·ac·count'a·ble
un·ac·count'ed-
for'
un·ac·cus'tomed
un·af·fect'ed
un'-A·mer'i·can
u'na·nim'i·ty
u·nan'i·mous
un·apt'
un·armed'
un·as·sum'ing
un·at·tached'
un·a·void'a·ble
un·a·ware'
un·a·wares'
un·bal'anced
un·bear'a·ble
un·beat'a·ble
un·be·com'ing
un·be·known'
un·be·lief'
un·be·liev'a·ble
un·be·liev'er

un·bend'
·bent' or ·bend'ed,
·bend'ing
un·bi'ased or
·assed
un·bid'den
un·bolt'ed
un·bos'om
un·bound'ed
un·bri'dled
un·bro'ken
un·buck'le
un·but'ton
un·called'-for'
un·can'ni·ly
un·can'ni·ness
un·can'ny
un·cared'-for'
un·cer·e·mo'ni·
ous
un·cer'tain
un·cer'tain·ty
·ties
un·char'i·ta·ble
un·chris'tian
un'ci·al
un·civ'il
un·civ'i·lized'
un·clad'
un·class'i·fied
un'cle
un·clothe'
·clothed' or
·clad', ·cloth'ing
un·com'fort·a·ble
un·com'pro·
mis'ing
un·con·cerned'
un'con·di'tion·al
un·con'scion·a·
ble
un·con'scious
un'con·sti·
tu'tion·al
un·cou'ple
un·couth'
unc'tion
unc'tu·ous
un·daunt'ed
un·de·cid'ed
un·de·ni'a·ble
un'der·age
un'der·age
un'der·brush'
un'der·buy'
·bought' ·buy'ing
un'der·car'riage
un'der·class'man
un'der·clothes'
un'der·coat'
un'der·cov'er
un'der·cur'rent
un'der·cut'
un'der·de·vel'·
oped
un'der·do'
·did' ·done'
·do'ing

un·der·dog'
un'der·em·ployed'
un'der·es'ti·mate'
un'der·fired'
un'der·foot'
un'der·gar'ment
un'der·glaze'
un'der·go'
·went' ·gone'
·go'ing
un'der·grad'u·ate
un'der·ground'
un'der·growth'
un'der·hand'
un'der·hand'ed
un'der·hung'
un'der·lay'
·laid' ·lay'ing
un'der·lie'
·lay' ·lain'
·ly'ing
un'der·line'
un'der·ling
un'der·lin'ing
un'der·mine'
un'der·neath'
un'der·nour'ish
un'der·pants'
un'der·part'
un'der·pass'
un'der·pay'
·paid' ·pay'ing
un'der·pin'ning
un'der·play'
un'der·priv'i·
leged
un'der·proof'
un'der·rate'
un'der·score'
un'der·sea'
un'der·sec're·
tar'y
·ies
un'der·sell'
·sold' ·sell'ing
un'der·sexed'
un'der·shirt'
un'der·shot'
un'der·side'
un'der·signed'
un'der·sized'
un'der·staffed'
un'der·stand'
·stood' ·stand'ing
un'der·stand'a·
ble
un'der·stand'a·bly
un'der·state'ment
un'der·stud'y
·ies, ·ied ·y·ing
un'der·take'
·took' ·tak'en
·tak'ing
un'der·tak'ing
un'der·tone'
un'der·tow'
un'der·val'ue
un'der·wa'ter

un'der·wear'
un'der·weight'
un'der·world'
un'der·write'
·wrote' ·writ'ten
·writ'ing
un·do'
·did' ·done'
·do'ing
un·doubt'ed·ly
un·dress'
un·due'
un'du·lant
un'du·late'
·lat'ed ·lat'ing
un·du'ly
un·dy'ing
un·earned'
un·earth'
un·eas'y
un·em·ploy'a·ble
un·e'qualed
or ·qualled
un·e·quiv'o·cal·ly
un·err'ing
un·es·sen'tial
un·e'ven·ness
un·e·vent'ful·ly
un·ex·cep'tion·
a·ble
un·ex·cep'tion·al
un·ex·pect'ed
un·faith'ful
un·fa·mil'iar
un·feel'ing
un·feigned'
un·for·get'ta·ble
un·for·tu'nate
un·found'ed
un·freeze'
·froze' ·froz'en
·freez'ing
un·frock'
un·furl'
un·gain'ly
un·god'ly
un'guent
un'gu·late
un·hand'
un·heard'-of'
un·hoped'-for'
un·horse'
·horsed'
·hors'ing
u'ni·cam'er·al
u'ni·cel'lu·lar
u'ni·corn'
u'ni·cy'cle
u'ni·fi'a·ble
u'ni·fi·ca'tion
u'ni·fi'er
u'ni·form'
u'ni·form'i·ty
u'ni·fy'
·fied' ·fy'ing
u'ni·lat'er·al
un·im·peach'a·ble
un·in·hib'it·ed

un·in·tel′li·gi·ble
un′ion
un′ion·ize′
·ized′ ·iz′ing
u·nique′
u′ni·son
u′nit
U′ni·tar′i·an
u·nite′
·nit′ed ·nit′ing
u′nit·ize′
·ized′ ·iz′ing
u′ni·ty
·ties
u′ni·ver′sal
u′ni·ver·sal′i·ty
u′ni·ver′sal·ly
u′ni·verse′
u′ni·ver′si·ty
·ties
un·kempt′
un·known′
un·lade′
·lad′ed, ·lad′ed
or ·lad′en,
·lad′ing
un·law′ful
un·less′
un·let′tered
un·like′li·hood′
un·like′ly
un·lim′it·ed
un·list′ed
un·looked′-for′
un·loose′
·loosed′ ·loos′ing
un·loos′en
un·luck′y
un·make′
·made′ ·mak′ing
un·man′
·manned′
·man′ning
un·men′tion·a·ble
un·mer′ci·ful
un′mis·tak′a·ble
un·mit′i·gat′ed
un·nat′u·ral
un·nec′es·sar′y
un·nerve′
·nerved′
·nerv′ing
un·num′bered
un·oc′cu·pied′
un·or′gan·ized′
un·paid′-for′
un·par′al·leled′
un·pleas′ant
un·prec′e·dent′ed
un·prej′u·diced
un·prin′ci·pled
un·qual′i·fied
un·ques′tion·a·
bly
un′quote′
un·rav′el
·eled or ·elled
·el·ing or ·el·ling

un′re·al·is′tic
un·rea′son·a·ble
un′re·gen′er·ate
un·rest′
un·rul′i·ness
un·rul′y
·i·er ·i·est
un·said′
un·sa′vor·i·ness
un·sa′vor·y
un·scathed′
un·scru′pu·lous
un·seat′
un·seem′ly
un·shod′
un·sight′li·ness
un·sight′ly
un·speak′a·ble
un·stead′y
un·strung′
un·sung′
un·tan′gle
·gled ·gling
un·ten′a·ble
un·think′a·ble
un·thought′-of′
un·ti′dy
un·tie′
·tied′ ·ty′ing or
·tie′ing
un·til′
un·time′ly
un·told′
un·touch′a·ble
un·to′ward
un·truth′ful
un·tu′tored
un·u′su·al
un·veil′ing
un·want′ed
(not wanted;
SEE unwonted)
un·war′y
un·whole′some
un·wield′i·ness
un·wield′y
un·wit′ting·ly
un·wont′ed
(not usual;
SEE unwanted)
un·wor′thy
un·writ′ten
un·zip′
up′-and-com′ing
up′-and-down′
up′beat′
up·braid′
up·bring′ing
up′coun′try
up·date′
up·end′
up′grade′
up·heav′al
up′hill′
up·hold′
·held′ ·hold′ing
up·hol′ster
up·hol′ster·er

up·hol′ster·y
·ies
up′keep′
up′land
up·lift′
up·on′
up′per-case′
-cased′ -cas′ing
up′per·class′man
up′per·most′
up′right′
up·ris′ing
up′roar′
up·roar′i·ous
up·root′
up·set′
·set′ -set′ting
up′shot′
up′stage′
-staged′
·stag′ing
up′stairs′
up·stand′ing
up′start′
up′state′
up′stream′
up′swept′
up′swing′
up′take′
up′thrust′
up′-tight′ or
up′tight′
up′-to-date′
up′town′
up·turn′
up′ward
u·ra′ni·um
ur′ban
(of the city)
ur·bane′
(socially poised)
ur′ban·ism
ur·ban′i·ty
·ties
ur′ban·i·za′tion
ur′ban·ize′
·ized′ ·iz′ing
ur′chin
u·re′mi·a
u·re′ter
u·re′thra
·thrae or ·thras
urge
urged urg′ing
ur′gen·cy
·cies
ur′gent
u′ri·nal
u′ri·nal′y·sis
·ses′
u′ri·nar′y
u′ri·nate′
·nat′ed ·nat′ing
u′rine
urn
u·ro·log′i·cal
u·rol′o·gy
u·ros′co·py

us′a·ble or use′·
us′age
use
used us′ing
use′ful
use′less
us′er
ush′er
ush′er·ette′
u′su·al
u′su·al·ly
u′su·fruct′
u′su·rer
u·su′ri·ous
u·surp′
u′sur·pa′tion
u′su·ry
·ries
U′tah
u·ten′sil
u′ter·ine
u′ter·us
·ter·i′
u·til′i·tar′i·an
u·til′i·ty
·ties
u′ti·liz′a·ble
u′ti·li·za′tion
u′ti·lize′
·lized′ ·liz′ing
ut′most′
u·to′pi·a
ut′ter
(speak; SEE udder)
ut′ter·ance
U′-turn′
ux·o′ri·ous

V

va′can·cy
·cies
va′cant
va′cate
·cat·ed ·cat·ing
va·ca′tion
vac′ci·nate′
·nat′ed ·nat′ing
vac′ci·na′tion
vac·cine′
vac′il·late′
·lat′ed ·lat′ing
vac′il·la′tion
vac′il·la′tor
va·cu′i·ty
·ties
vac′u·ous
vac′u·um
·ums or ·a
vag′a·bond′
va·gar′y
·ies
va·gi′na
·nas or ·nae
va′gran·cy
·cies
var′i·a·ble
var′i·a·bly
var′i·ance

va′grant
vague
vague′ly
vain
(futile; conceited;
SEE vane, vein)
val′ance
(drapery; SEE
valence)
vale
(valley; SEE veil)
val′e·dic′tion
val′e·dic·to′ri·an
val′e·dic′to·ry
·ries
va′lence
(term in chemis-
try; SEE valance)
val′en·tine′
val′et
val′iant
val′id
val′i·date′
·dat·ed ·dat′ing
val′i·da′tion
va·lid′i·ty
va·lise′
val′ley
·leys
val′or
val′or·i·za′tion
val′u·a·ble
val′u·a′tion
val′ue
·ued ·u·ing
val′ue·less
valve
val′vu·lar
vam′pire
van′dal
van′dal·ism
van′dal·ize′
·ized′ ·iz′ing
Van·dyke′
vane
(blade; SEE
vain, vein)
van′guard′
va·nil′la
van′ish
van′i·ty
·ties
van′quish
van′tage
vap′id
va′por
va′por·i·za′tion
va′por·ize′
·ized′ ·iz′ing
va′por·iz′er
va′por·ous
va·que′ro
·ros

var′i·ant
var′i·a′tion
var′i·col′ored
var′ied
var′i·e·gate′
·gat′ed ·gat′ing
var′i·e·ga′tion
va·ri′e·tal
va·ri′e·ty
·ties
var′i·o′rum
var′i·ous
var′nish
var′si·ty
·ties
var′y
·ied ·y·ing
(change; SEE ve
vas′cu·lar
vas de′fe·rens
vas·e·line′
vas′sal
(a subordinate;
SEE vessel)
vast′ness
vat
vat′ted vat′tin
vat′-dyed′
vaude′ville
vault′ing
vaunt
vec′tor
vec·to′ri·al
V′-E′ Day
veer
veg′e·ta·ble
veg′e·tar′i·an
veg′e·tate′
·tat′ed ·tat′ing
veg′e·ta′tion
veg′e·ta′tive
ve′he·mence
ve′he·ment
ve′hi·cle
ve·hic′u·lar
veil
(screen; SEE val
vein
(blood vessel;
streak; SEE
vain, vane)
Vel′cro
vel′lum
ve·loc′i·pede′
ve·loc′i·ty
·ties
ve·lour′ or ·lo
·lours′
ve·lure′
vel′vet
vel′vet·een′
vel′vet·y
ve′nal
(corrupt; SEE
venial)
ve·nal′i·ty
·ties

ven'dee'
ven·det'ta
ven'dor or
vend'er
ve·neer'
ven'er·a·ble
ven'er·ate'
·at'ed ·at'ing
ven'er·a'tion
ve·ne're·al
ve·ne'tian
venge'ance
venge'ful
ve'ni·al
(pardonable; SEE
venal)
ven'i·son
ven'om·ous
ve'nous
ven'ti·late'
·lat'ed ·lat'ing
ven'ti·la'tion
ven'ti·la'tor
ven'tri·cle
ven·tril'o·quist
ven'ture
·tured ·tur·ing
ven'ture·some
ven'tur·ous
ven'ue
ve·ra'cious
(truthful; SEE
voracious)
ve·rac'i·ty
ve·ran'da or ·dah
ver'bal
ver'bal·i·za'tion
ver'bal·ize'
·ized ·iz'ing
ver'bal·ly
ver·ba'tim
ver·be'na
ver'bi·age
ver·bose'
ver·bos'i·ty
ver'dant
ver'dict
ver'di·gris'
ver'dure
verge
verged verg'ing
ver'i·fi'a·ble
ver'i·fi·ca'tion
ver'i·fy'
·fied' ·fy'ing
ver'i·ly
ver'i·si·mil'i·tude'
ver'i·ta·ble
ver'i·ta·bly
ver'i·ty
·ties
ver·mi·cel'li
ver'mi·cide'
ver·mic'u·lar
ver·mic'u·lite'
ver'mi·form'
ver·mi·fuge'
ver·mil'ion

ver'min
Ver·mont'
ver·mouth'
ver·nac'u·lar
ver'nal
ver'ni·er
ver'sa·tile
ver'sa·tile·ly
ver·sa·til'i·ty
versed
ver'si·fi·ca'tion
ver'si·fy'
·fied' ·fy'ing
ver'sion
ver'sus
ver'te·bra
·brae' or ·bras
ver'te·bral
ver'te·brate
ver'tex
·tex·es or ·ti·ces'
ver'ti·cal
ver·tig'i·nous
ver·tig'o'
verve
ver'y
·i·er ·i·est
(complete; exceed-
ingly; SEE vary)
ves'i·cant
ves'i·cate'
·cat'ed ·cat'ing
ves'i·cle
ves'per
ves'sel
(container; ship;
SEE vassal)
ves'tal
ves'ti·bule
ves'tige
ves·tig'i·al
vest'ment
vest'-pock'et
ves'try
·tries
vet'er·an
vet'er·i·nar'i·an
vet'er·i·nar'y
·ies
ve'to
·toes
·toed ·to·ing
vex·a'tion
vex·a'tious
vi'a·bil'i·ty
vi'a·ble
vi'a·duct'
vi'al
(bottle; SEE
vile, viol)
vi'and
vi'brant
vi'bra·phone'
vi'brate
·brat·ed ·brat·ing
vi·bra'tion
vi·bra'to
·tos

vi'bra·tor
vi'bra·to'ry
vic'ar
vic'ar·age
vi·car'i·al
vi·car'i·ous
vice
(evil conduct;
flaw; SEE vise)
vice'-chair'man
vice'-chan'cel·lor
vice'-con'sul
vice'-pres'i·dent
vice'roy
vi'ce ver'sa
vi'chy·ssoise'
vi·cin'i·ty
·ties
vi'cious
vi·cis'si·tude'
vic'tim
vic'tim·ize'
·ized' ·iz'ing
vic'tor
vic·to'ri·a
vic·to'ri·ous
vic'to·ry
·ries
vi·cu'ña
vid'e·o'
vid'i·con
vie
vied vy'ing
view'point'
vig'il
vig'i·lance
vig'i·lant
vig'i·lan'te
vi·gnette'
vig'or
vig'or·ous
vile
(evil; offensive;
SEE vial, viol)
vile'ly
vil'i·fi·ca'tion
vil'i·fy'
·fied' ·fy'ing
vil'la
vil'lage
vil'lag·er
vil'lain
(scoundrel;
SEE villein)
vil'lain·ous
vil'lain·y
·ies
vil'lein
(serf; SEE
villain)
vin'ai·grette'
vin'ci·ble
vin'di·cate'
·cat'ed ·cat'ing
vin'di·ca'tion
vin'di·ca'tive
vin'di·ca'tor
vin·dic'tive

vin'e·gar
vin'er·y
·ies
vine'yard
vin'i·cul'ture
vi'nous
vin'tage
vint'ner
vi'nyl
vi'ol
(instrument;
SEE vial, vile)
vi·o'la
vi'o·la·ble
vi'o·late'
·lat'ed ·lat'ing
vi'o·la'tion
vi'o·la'tor
vi'o·lence
vi'o·lent
vi'o·let
vi'o·lin'
vi'o·lin'ist
vi'o·lon·cel'lo
·los
VIP or V.I.P.
vi'per
vi·ra'go
·goes or ·gos
vi'ral
vir'gin
vir'gin·al
Vir·gin'ia
vir·gin'i·ty
vir'gule
vir'ile
vi·ril'i·ty
vi·rol'o·gy
vir·tu'
vir'tu·al
vir'tu·al·ly
vir'tue
vir·tu·os'i·ty
vir·tu·o'so
·sos or ·si
vir'tu·ous
vir'u·lence
vir'u·lent
vi'rus
vi'sa
vis'-à-vis'
vis'cer·a
vis'cid
vis·cos'i·ty
vis'count
vis'count·ess
vis'cous
vise
vised vis'ing
(clamp; SEE vice)
vis'i·bil'i·ty
vis'i·ble
vis'i·bly
vi'sion
vi'sion·ar'y
·ies
vis'it

vis'it·ant
vis'it·a'tion
vis'i·tor
vi'sor
vis'ta
vis'u·al
vis'u·al·ize'
·ized' ·iz'ing
vi'ta
·tae
vi'tal
vi·tal'i·ty
·ties
vi'tal·ize'
·ized' ·iz'ing
vi'ta·min
vi'ti·a·ble
vi'ti·ate'
·at'ed ·at'ing
vi'ti·a'tor
vit're·ous
vit'ri·fy'
·fied' ·fy'ing
vit'ri·ol
vit'ri·ol'ic
vi·tu'per·ate'
·at'ed ·at'ing
vi·tu'per·a'tion
vi·va'cious
vi·vac'i·ty
viv'id
viv'i·fy'
·fied' ·fy'ing
vi·vip'a·rous
viv'i·sect'
viv'i·sec'tion
vix'en
V'-J' Day
V'-neck'
vo·cab'u·lar'y
·ies
vo'cal cord
vo'cal·ist
vo'cal·ize'
·ized' ·iz'ing
vo·ca'tion
vo·cif'er·ate'
·at'ed ·at'ing
vo·cif'er·ous
vo'cod'er
vod'ka
vogue
voice'less
voice'print'
void'a·ble
voi·là'
voile
vol'a·tile
vol·a·til'i·ty
vol·can'ic
vol·ca'no
·noes or ·nos
vol'i·tant
vo·li'tion
vol'ley
·leys
·leyed ·ley·ing

vol'ley·ball'
volt'age
vol·ta'ic
vol·tam'e·ter
volt'me'ter
vol'u·bil'i·ty
vol'u·ble
vol'u·bly
vol'ume
vo·lu'mi·nous
vol'un·tar'i·ly
vol'un·tar'y
vol'un·teer'
vo·lup'tu·ar'y
·ies
vo·lup'tu·ous
vo·lute'
vo·lu'tion
vom'it
voo'doo
·doos
vo·ra'cious
(greedy; SEE
veracious)
vo·rac'i·ty
vor'tex
·tex·es or ·ti·ces'
vot'a·ble or vote'
vo'ta·ry
·ries
vote
vot'ed vot'ing
vo'tive
vouch'er
vouch·safe'
·safed' ·saf'ing
vow
vow'el
voy'age
·aged ·ag·ing
voy'ag·er
vo·yeur'
vroom
vul'can·i·za'tion
vul'can·ize'
·ized' ·iz'ing
vul'gar
vul·gar'i·an
vul'gar·ism
vul·gar'i·ty
·ties
vul'gar·ize'
·ized' ·iz'ing
vul'ner·a·bil'i·ty
vul'ner·a·ble
vul'ner·a·bly
vul'ture
vul'tur·ous
vul'va
vy'ing

W

wad
wad'ded
wad'ding

wad'dle
·dled ·dling
wade
wad'ed
wad'ing
wa'fer
waf'fle
waft
wag
wagged
wag'ging
wage
waged wag'ing
wa'ger
wag'ger·y
·ies
wag'gish
wag'gle
·gled ·gling
Wag·ne'ri·an
wag'on·load'
wa·hi'ne
waif
wail
(cry; SEE wale, whale)
wain'scot
·scot·ed or
·scot·ted
·scot·ing or
·scot·ting
wain'wright'
waist'band'
waist'coat
waist'-high'
waist'line'
wait'er
wait'ress
waive
waived waiv'ing
(give up; SEE wave)
waiv'er
(a relinquishing; SEE waver)
wake
woke or waked, waked or wok'·en, wak'ing
wake'ful
wak'en
wale
waled wal'ing
(ridge; SEE wail, whale)
walk
walk'a·way'
walk'ie-talk'ie
walk'-in'
walk'-on'
walk'out'
walk'-through'
walk'-up'
walk'way'
wall'board'
wal'let
wall'eyed'
wall'flow'er

wal'lop·ing
wal'low
wall'pa'per
wall'-to-wall'
wal'nut
wal'rus
waltz
wam'pum
wan
wan'ner
wan'nest
wan'der
(stray; SEE wonder)
wan'der·lust'
wane
waned wan'ing
wan'gle
·gled ·gling
want'ing
wan'ton
(unjustifiable; SEE won ton)
war
warred war'ring
war'ble
·bled ·bling
ward
war'den
ward'robe'
ward'room'
ware'house'
·housed'
·hous'ing
war'fare'
war'head'
war'i·ly
war'i·ness
war'like'
war'lock'
warm'blood'ed
warmed'-o'ver
warm'heart'ed
war'mon'ger
warmth
warm'-up'
warn'ing
warp
war'path'
warped
war'plane'
war'rant
war'ran·ty
·ties
war'ren
war'ri·or
war'ship'
wart
war'time'
war'y
·i·er ·i·est
wash'a·ble
wash'-and-wear'
wash'board'
wash'bowl'
wash'cloth'
washed'-out'
washed'-up'

wash'er
wash'er·wom'an
Wash'ing·ton
wash'out'
wash'room'
wash'stand'
wash'tub'
was'n't
wasp'ish
was'sail
wast'age
waste
wast'ed
wast'ing
waste'bas'ket
waste'ful
waste'land'
waste'pa'per
waste pipe
wast'rel
watch'band'
watch'case'
watch'dog'
watch fire
watch'ful
watch'mak'er
watch'man
watch'tow'er
watch'word'
wa'ter·borne'
wa'ter·col'or
wa'ter-cooled'
water cooler
wa'ter·course'
wa'ter·craft'
wa'ter·cress'
wa'ter·cy'cle
wa'tered
wa'ter·fall'
wa'ter·front'
water glass
water hole
wa'ter·i·ness
wa'ter·less
wa'ter·line'
wa'ter·logged'
wa'ter·mark'
wa'ter·mel'on
water pipe
water power
wa'ter·proof'
wa'ter-re·pel'lent
wa'ter-re·sist'ant
wa'ter·scape'
wa'ter·shed'
wa'ter·side'
wa'ter-ski'
-skied' -ski'ing
wa'ter-ski'er
water skis
wa'ter·soak'
wa'ter·sol'u·ble
wa'ter·spout'
wa'ter·tight'
water tower
wa'ter·way'
water wheel
water wings

wa'ter·works'
wa'ter·worn'
wa'ter·y
watt'age
watt'-hour'
wat'tle
·tled ·tling
watt'me'ter
wave
waved wav'ing
(curving motion; SEE waive)
wave'length'
wav'er
(one that waves; SEE waiver)
wa'ver
(falter; SEE waiver)
wav'i·ness
wav'y
·i·er ·i·est
wax
wax'en
wax'i·ness
wax'work'
wax'y
·i·er ·i·est
way
(route; manner; SEE weigh, whey)
way'bill'
way'far'er
way'far'ing
way'lay'
·laid' ·lay'ing
way'side'
way'ward
weak'en
weak'-kneed'
weak'ling
weak'ly
·li·er ·li·est
weak'-mind'ed
weak'ness
weal
(ridge; welfare; SEE wheal, wheel)
wealth'i·ness
wealth'y
·i·er ·i·est
wean
weap'on
wear
wore worn
wear'ing
wear'a·ble
wea'ri·ly
wea'ri·ness
wea'ri·some
wea'ry
·ri·er ·ri·est
·ried ·ry·ing
wea'sel
weath'er
(atmospheric conditions; SEE whether)

weath'er-beat'en
weath'er-bound'
weath'er·cock'
weath'er·man'
weath'er·proof'
weath'er·strip'
·stripped'
·strip'ping
weather vane
weave
wove, wov'en or
wove, weav'ing
(interlace)
weave
weaved
weav'ing
(move in and out as in traffic)
weav'er
web
webbed
web'bing
web'foot'
·feet'
web'-foot'ed
wed
wed'ded,
wed'ded or
wed, wed'ding
we'd
wedge
wedged
wedg'ing
Wedg'wood'
wed'lock
Wednes'day
wee
we'er we'est
weed'i·ness
week'day'
week'end' or
week'-end'
week'ly
·lies
weep
wept weep'ing
weep'i·ness
weep'y
·i·er ·i·est
wee'vil
weigh
weighed
weigh'ing
(measure weight of; SEE way, whey)
weight'i·ness
weight'less
weight'y
·i·er ·i·est
weir
(dam; SEE we're)
weird
wel'come
·comed ·com·ing
weld'er
wel'fare'
well'-ad·vised'
well'-ap·point'ed

well'-bal'anced
well'-be·haved
well'-be'ing
well'-be·loved'
well'born'
well'-bred'
well'-chos'en
well'-con·tent'
well'-dis·posed
well'do'ing
well'-done'
well'-fa'vored
well'-fed'
well'-found'ed
well'-groomed'
well'-ground'ed
well'-han'dled
well'head'
well'-in·formed
well'-in·ten'·tioned
well'-knit'
well'-known'
well'-made'
well'-man'nered
well'-mean'ing
well'-meant'
well'-nigh'
well'-off'
well'-or·dered
well'-pre·served
well'-read'
well'-round'ed
well'-spo'ken
well'spring'
well'-thought'-of
well'-timed'
well'-to-do'
well'-turned'
well'-wish'er
well'-worn'
we'll
Welsh rabbit
or rarebit
welt'er
welt'er·weight'
we're
(we are; SEE weir)
weren't
were'wolf'
·wolves'
wes'kit
west'er·ly
·lies
west'ern·er
west'ern·ize'
·ized' ·iz'ing
west'-north'west
west'-south'west
West Vir·gin'ia
west'ward
wet
wet'ter wet'test
wet or wet'ted
wet'ting
(moistened; SEE whet)

et'back'
et'ta·ble
hale
whaled whal'ing
(fishlike mammal;
SEE wail, wale)
hale'boat'
hale'bone'
hal'er
harf
wharves or
wharfs
harf'age
harf'in·ger
hat·ev'er
hat'not'
hat'so·ev'er
heal
(pimple; SEE
weal, wheel)
heat
hee'dle
-dled ·dling
heel
(disk for turning;
SEE weal, wheal)
heel'bar'row
heel'base'
heel'chair
heel'house'
heel'wright'
heeze
wheezed
wheez'ing
heez'y
·i·er ·i·est
help
hen
hence
here
herc'a·bouts'
here·as'
here·by'
here'fore'
here·in'
here·of'
here'up·on'
her·ev'er
here·with'
here'with·al
wher'ry
·ries, ·ried ·ry·ing
whet
whet'ted
whet'ting
(sharpen; SEE wet)
wheth'er
(if; SEE weather)
whet'stone'
whey
(thin part of milk;
SEE way, weigh)
which·ev'er
whiff
while
whiled whil'ing
(time; SEE wile)

whim
whim'per
whim'si·cal
whim'sy
·sies
whine
whined whin'ing
(cry; SEE wine)
whin'i·ness
whin'ny
·nies
·nied ·ny·ing
(neigh)
whin'y
·i·er ·i·est
(complaining)
whip
whipped
whip'ping
whip'cord'
whip'lash'
whip'pet
whip'poor·will'
whip'saw'
whip'stitch'
whip'stock'
whir or whirr
whirred
whir'ring
whirl
whirl'pool'
whirl'wind'
whisk broom
whisk'er
whis'key
·keys or ·kies
whis'per
whis'tle
·tled ·tling
whis'tler
whit
(bit; SEE wit)
white
whit'ed whit'ing
white'cap'
white'-col'lar
white'-haired'
white'-hot'
white'-liv'ered
whit'en·er
white'ness
whit'en·ing
white room
white'wall'
white'wash'
whith'er
(where; SEE
wither)
whit'ing
whit'tle
·tled ·tling
whiz or whizz
whizzed
whiz'zing
who·ev'er
whole'heart'ed
whole'sale'
·saled' ·sal'ing

whole'sal'er
whole'some
whole'-wheat'
whol'ly
(completely; SEE
holey, holy)
whom·ev'er
whom'so·ev'er
whoop'ee
whop'per
whore
whorl
who's
(who is; who has)
whose
(poss. of who)
who'so·ev'er
why
wick'ed
wick'er·work'
wick'et
wide'-an'gle
wide'-a·wake'
wide'-eyed'
wid'en
wide'-o'pen
wide'spread'
wid'get
wid'ow
wid'ow·er
width
wield
wield'y
·i·er ·i·est
wie'ner
wife
wives
wife'ly
wig'gle
·gled ·gling
wig'gly
wig'let
wig'wam
wild'cat'
·cat'ted ·cat'ting
wil'de·beest'
wil'der·ness
wild'-eyed'
wild'fire'
wild'life'
wile
wiled wil'ing
(trick; SEE while)
wil'i·ness
will'ful or wil'·
will'ing·ness
will'-o'-the-wisp'
wil'low·y
will'pow'er
wil'ly-nil'ly
wi'ly
·li·er ·li·est
wim'ple
·pled ·pling
win
won win'ning
wince
winced winc'ing

wind
wound wind'ing
wind'blown'
wind'-borne'
wind'break'er
wind'burn'
wind'fall'
wind'i·ness
wind'lass
(winch)
wind'less
(without wind)
wind'mill'
win'dow
win'dow·pane'
win'dow-shop'
wind'row'
wind'shield'
wind'storm'
wind'-swept'
wind'up'
wind'ward
wind'y
·i·er ·i·est
wine
wined win'ing
(drink; SEE whine)
wine cellar
wine'-col'ored
wine'glass'
wine'grow'er
wine press
win'er·y
·ies
Wine'sap'
wine'skin'
wing chair
wing'span'
wing'spread'
win'ner
win'now
win'some
win'ter
win'ter·green'
win'ter·ize'
·ized' ·iz'ing
win'ter·time'
win'try
·tri·er ·tri·est
wipe
wiped wip'ing
wire
wired wir'ing
wire'draw'
·drew' ·drawn'
·draw'ing
wire'hair'
wire'-haired'
wire'less
Wire'pho'to
wire'pull'er
wire'tap'
wire'work'
wir'i·ness
wir'y
·i·er ·i·est
Wis·con'sin
wis'dom

wise
wis'er wis'est
wise'ly
wish'bone'
wish'ful
wisp
wist'ful
wit
(sense; SEE whit)
witch'craft'
witch'er·y
·ies
with·draw'
·drew' ·drawn'
·draw'ing
with·draw'al
with'er
(wilt; SEE whither)
with·hold'
·held' ·hold'ing
with·in'
with·out'
with·stand'
·stood'
·stand'ing
wit'less
wit'ness
wit'ti·cism
wit'ti·ness
wit'ty
·ti·er ·ti·est
wiz'ard
wiz'ard·ry
wiz'ened
wob'ble
·bled ·bling
woe'be·gone'
woe'ful
wolf
wolves
wolf'hound'
wom'an
wom'en
wom'an·hood'
wom'an·kind'
wom'an·li·ness
wom'an·ly
womb
wom'en·folk'
won'der
(marvel; SEE
wander)
won'der·ful
won'der·land'
won'der·work'
won'der-work'er
won'drous
wont
(accustomed)
won't
(will not)
won' ton'
(food; SEE wanton)
wood'carv'ing
wood'chuck'
wood'craft'
wood'cut'
wood'ed

wood'land'
wood'peck'er
wood'pile'
wood pulp
wood'shed'
woods'man
wood'sy
·si·er ·si·est
wood'wind'
wood'work'
wood'y
·i·er ·i·est
woof'er
wool'en
wool'gath'er·ing
wool'grow'er
wool'lies ?
wool'ies
wool'li·ness or
wool'i·ness
wool'ly or
wool'y
·li·er or ·i·er
·li·est or ·i·est
Worces'ter·shire'
word'age
word'book'
word'i·ly
word'i·ness
word'less
word'-of-mouth'
word'play'
word'y
·i·er ·i·est
work
worked or
wrought
work'ing
work'a·ble
work'a·day'
work'bench'
work'book'
work'day'
work'house'
work'ing·man'
work'load'
work'man·like'
work'man·ship'
work'out'
work'room'
work'shop'
work'ta'ble
work'week'
world'li·ness
world'ly
·li·er ·li·est
world'ly-wise'
world'-shak'ing
world'-wea'ry
world'wide'
worm'-eat'en
worm gear
worm'hole'
worm'i·ness
worm wheel
worm'wood'
worm'y
·i·er ·i·est

worn'-out'
wor'ri·er
wor'ri·ment
wor'ri·some
wor'ry
  ·ries
  ·ried ·ry·ing
wor'ry·wart'
worse
wors'en
wor'ship
  ·shiped or
  ·shipped
  ·ship·ing or
  ·ship·ping
wor'ship'er or
  wor'ship'per
wor'ship·ful
worst
wor'sted
wor'thi·ly
wor'thi·ness
worth'less
worth'while'
wor'thy
  ·thi·er ·thi·est
would
would'-be'
wound
wrack
wraith
wran'gle
  ·gled ·gling
wran'gler
wrap
  wrapped or
  wrapt
  wrap'ping
  (cover; SEE rap)
wrap'a·round'
wrap'per
wrath'ful
wreak
  (inflict; SEE reek)

wreath n.
wreathe v.
  wreathed
  wreath'ing
wreck'age
wreck'er
wrench
wres'tle
  ·tled ·tling
wres'tler
wretch
  (miserable
  person; SEE
  retch)
wretch'ed
wrig'gle
  ·gled ·gling
wring
  wrung wring'ing
  (twist; SEE ring)
wrin'kle
  ·kled ·kling
wrin'kly
  ·kli·er ·kli·est
wrist'band'
wrist'let
wrist pin
wrist'watch'
writ
write
  wrote writ'ten
  writ'ing
  (inscribe; SEE
  right, rite)
write'-in'
write'-off'
writ'er
write'-up'
writhe
  writhed
  writh'ing
wrong'do'er
wrong'do'ing
wrong'ful

wrote
  (pt. of write;
  SEE rote)
wrought
wrought'-up'
wrung
  (pt. and pp. of
  wring; SEE rung)
wry
  wried wry'ing
  wri'er wri'est
  (twisted; SEE rye)
wry'ly
Wy·o'ming

X

x
  x-ed or x'd
  x-ing or x'ing
xan'thous
xe'bec
xen'o·pho'bi·a
xe·rog'ra·phy
xe·roph'i·lous
Xe'rox
Xmas
X'-ray' or
  X ray
xy'lo·phone
xy'lo·phon'ist

Y

yacht
yachts'man
Yan'kee

yard'age
yard'arm'
yard'mas'ter
yard'stick'
yarn'-dyed'
yawl
yawn
yea
year'book'
year'ling
year'long'
year'ly
yearn
year'-round'
yeast
yel'low
yelp
yen
  yenned yen'ning
yeo'man
yes
  yessed yes'sing
ye·shi'va
yes'ter·day
yes'ter·year'
yet
yew
  (tree; SEE ewe)
Yid'dish
yield
yip'pie
yo'del
  ·deled or ·delled
  ·del·ing or
  ·del·ling
yo'del·er or
  yo'del·ler
yo'ga
yo'gi
  ·gis
yo'gurt
yoke
  yoked yok'ing
  (harness)

yolk
  (of an egg)
Yom Kip'pur
yon'der
you'd
you'll
young'ster
your
  (poss. of you)
you're
  (you are)
yours
your·self'
  ·selves'
youth'ful
you've
yowl
yo'-yo'
yule log
yule'tide'

Z

zai'ba·tsu'
  ·tsu'
za'ni·ness
za'ny
  ·nies, ·ni·er
  ·ni·est
zeal
zeal'ot
zeal'ous
ze'bra
ze'brass'
ze'bu
Zeit'geist'
Zen
ze'nith
ze'o·lite'

ze'o·lit'ic
zeph'yr
zep'pe·lin
ze'ro
  ·ros or ·roes
  ·roed ·ro·ing
zest'ful·ly
zest'ful·ness
zig'zag'
  ·zagged'
  ·zag'ging
zinc
  zincked or zin
  zinck'ing or
  zinc'ing
zin'ni·a
Zi'on·ism
zip
  zipped zip'ping
  ZIP code
zip'per
zir'con
zith'er
zo'di·ac'
zo·di'a·cal
zom'bie
zon'al
zone
  zoned zon'ing
zoo
zo'o·ge·og'ra·p
zo'o·log'i·cal
zo·ol'o·gist
zo·ol'o·gy
zoom lens
zoy'si·a
zuc·chet'to
  ·tos
zuc·chi'ni
  ·ni or ·nis
zwie'back
zy'gote
zy·mol'o·gy
zy'mur·gy

Index

(PAGE REFERENCES TO ILLUSTRATIONS ARE ITALICIZED)

A

Abbreviations: 53, 63, 66, 67, 68, 81, 116, 122, 134–135, 154, 160, 203, 335. List of: 359–379

Accommodations: 15, 95, 186, 187, 192, 193, 195, 197–198, 199, 201. *See also* Reservations

Accounting records: 191, 215, 216, 219, 229–235

Accuracy: 15, 40, 109, 115, 174, 225–226, 277. Of figures: 40, 222, 226

Added pages: 79–80, 103, 105, 108, 159

Address: Envelope: 80, 134, 136, *137*, 138, 142, 145, 338, 409–414. Letter, inside: *57–62*, 64–67, *64–65*, *74*, 338. Return: 131, 136, 141, 142, 143, 145, 148, 150, 153, 159. Social uses: 203, 205. Street: 66, 117–118, 136, 145, 178. Telegrams: 155–158, *156*, 169. *See also* ZIP code

Address, form of: 67, 409–414

Adjective: 289, 293, 303, 309–310, 315, 319. Comparison: 309. Proper: 338

Advancement of secretary: 14, 18

Adverb: 289, 310, 314, 315, 319. Comparison: 310. Conjunctive: 312, 331, 337

Advertising secretary: 14

Affidavit: 241, 274

Affixes: 333, 341–342. Of names: 126, 160

Agenda: 273

Agents: Corporation: 247–250, 282. Secretarial: 17. Theatrical: 15, 207. Travel: 15, 199–200

Air travel. *See* Transportation, air; Travel

Alignment of paper (typing): 47–48

Alphabetizing: 123–128. *See also* Filing

Ambiguity in writing: 87, 238, 287–288, 293, 298. *See also* Writing style

American Management Association: 4

Annotations: 131

Antecedent (grammar): 294, 295, 296, 298–300

Apostrophe: 82, 294, 298, 326–327

Appearance (personal): 202

Application, job: 17

Appointments: 37, 98–100, 131, 173. By phone: 173, 181–182. Traveling: 187, 190–191, 200. *See also* Cancellations

Appointment book: 24–26

Appositive (grammar): 298, 316, 323

Appreciation, letters of: 65, 73, 210

Arrangement proceedings: 260

Asterisk: 82

Atlas: 350

Attention line: 74–75, 81

Attitude (personal): 27

Authorship of letters. *See* Letters, written by secretary

Automation: 14, 18, 163–164

B

Bank deposit: 215–216, *216*, 219, 220, 222, 224, 234, 249

Bank reconciliation: 222–223. Reconciliation statement: *223*, 223–225

Bank statement: 216, 219–222, *221*, 223–225

Bankruptcy: 244, 260–262